The Culture of Judicial Independence

The Culture of Judicial Independence

Conceptual Foundations and Practical Challenges

Edited by

Shimon Shetreet
Christopher Forsyth

MARTINUS NIJHOFF PUBLISHERS

LEIDEN • BOSTON
2012

This book is printed on acid-free paper.

Library of Congress Cataloging-in-Publication Data

The culture of judicial independence : conceptual foundations and practical challenges / edited by Shimon Shetreet, Christopher Forsyth.
p. cm.
Includes index.
ISBN 978-90-04-18833-4 (hardback : alk. paper)
1. Judicial independence--Congresses. I. Shetreet, Shimon. II. Forsyth, C. F.

K3367.C85 2011
347'.012--dc22

2011011393

ISBN 978 90 04 18833 4

PRINTED BY AD DRUK BV - ZEIST, THE NETHERLANDS

CONTENTS

Part IV – Judicial Appointment, Judicial Conduct and Judicial Accountability

Part V – Country Studies of Judicial Independence

TABLE OF CASES

TABLE OF LEGISLATION

Constitutional Provisions

Statutes

Rules

Treaties, Conventions and Other International Instruments

International Documents Under the Auspices of Governmental and Private Associations

PREFACE

This volume is a natural academic continuation of the volume co-edited by this author and Chief Justice Deschenes, *Judicial Independence: The Contemporary Debate* (1985) published by the same publishers.

The focus of this volume is the culture of judicial independence, the conceptual foundations of judicial independence and accountability and the practical challenges to judicial independence.

The creation of a culture of judicial independence is of central significance both for national domestic legal systems, as well as for the international courts and tribunals. The main aims of this volume are to analyze the development of a culture of judicial independence in comparative perspectives, to offer an examination of the conceptual foundations of the principle of judicial independence, and to discuss in detail the practical challenges facing judiciaries in different jurisdictions.

The judiciary must be both independent and impartial – both requirements are necessary for fair adjudication. Both conditions are necessary in order to avoid the opposing risks of infirmity and tyranny. The risk of infirmity exists when the judiciary is dependent on other branches of government or exposed to outside pressures. The risk of tyranny is associated with a biased judiciary and a lack of judicial accountability.

Judicial independence is critical for the proper functioning of civil society. Without impartial and independent dispute resolution, there is no substantive protection of human rights, no true economic security or free market, and no good government or civil order. The rule of law requires judicial independence as a precondition.

Judicial independence is of central importance, not just in regard to human rights, constitutionality and the rule of law, but also in regard to globalization and free and efficient economic activity and international trade and investments. The legitimate expectation of fair and independent adjudication is one of the reasons for investment in a global economy.

The issues of judicial independence have undergone dynamic development in both the national and international spheres. In the last five years, a group of distinguished experts from many countries – The US, Canada, The UK, Israel, Australia, Belgium, Poland, Malaysia, India, Italy, China, Brazil, Austria, Liechtenstein and others – joined forces in an international project on judicial independence. In the course of this project, the experts studied conceptual and theoretical aspects of judicial independence in national and international levels. In addition, the group of experts developed detailed standards of judicial independence, dealing with different aspects of this matter applicable to both national and international judges.

The principal initiators of this volume, the undersigned, Professor Shimon Shetreet, and Professor Christopher Forsyth believe that the study of judicial independence is significant for all jurisdictions, in that contemporary, detailed debate is required. This is due to the absence of a modern, thorough revision of standards for both national and international judges. In order for standards to remain relevant and in order to assure that they continue to serve as active and useful guidelines for the substantive protection of human rights and a healthy economic state, it is critical that they be contemporary, up to date, and fully responsive to the dynamic needs of the economic and political realities.

This volume offers analysis insights and opinions from academics, judges and practitioners across jurisdictions – both national and international – on the subject of judicial independence, providing both an in-depth and a broad analysis of this important subject.

The volume is based on the papers presented at the six conferences held in the framework of The International Project on Judicial Independence of which the undersigned is the General Coordinator, cosponsored by the Hebrew University of Jerusalem faculty of law and the Centre of Public Law of the University of Cambridge, UK.

The seven conferences in this project were held as follows

1) Jerusalem, 26–27 June, 2007. Chaired by Prof. Shimon Shetreet and Prof. James Crawford
2) Vaduz, 30 November – 1 December, 2007. Co-chaired by HE Markus Buechel and Prof. Shimon Shetreet
3) Jerusalem, 18–20 March, 2008. Co-chaired by Prof. Christopher Forsyth and Prof. Shimon Shetreet
4) Krakow, 25–26 November, 2008. Co-chaired by Prof. Fryderyk Zoll and Prof. Shimon Shetreet
5) Cambridge, 14–16 August, 2009. Co-chaired by Prof. Christopher Forsyth and Prof. Shimon Shetreet
6) Salt Lake City 1–3 October 2010. Co-chaired by Prof. Wayne MacCormack, Dean Hiram Chodosh, and Prof. Shimon Shetreet
7) Vienna 20–22 May 2011. Co-chaired by Prof. Walter Rechberger and Prof. Shimon Shetreet

Shimon Shetreet
Mt Scopus, Jerusalem

May 2011

ACKNOWLEDGEMENTS

This project on judicial independence has been supported by numerous funds, foundations, academic institutions, and distinguished scholars. We are first and foremost indebted to the distinguished scholars who have taken part in the project, in the drafting of the Mount Scopus Standards on Judicial Independence, and in the seven international conferences on judicial independence in Jerusalem (2007 and 2008), Vaduz (2007), Krakow (2008), Cambridge (2009), Salt Lake City (2010) and Vienna (2011). We deeply appreciate the academic contributions by the scholars who take part in this volume.

This project has been conceived during Professor Shetreet's appointment as the Herbert Smith Visiting Professor at the Faculty of Law at the University of Cambridge and as Senior Academic Visitor at Clare College. He would like to express his personal thanks for the privilege of these appointments and the opportunities they offered and he is grateful to the colleagues who helped in developing and realizing the idea Christopher Forsyth, Neil Andrews, James Crawford and David Feldman.

The University of Cambridge, Centre of Public Law, and the Hebrew University, Harry and Michael Sacher Institute of Comparative Law co-sponsored the international project on judicial independence and we are grateful to them for their support. Special thanks are due to the Sacher Family Trust which supported the project all along.

We wish to express our deep thanks to Mr. Daniel Jacobson and the Jacobson Foundation at the Hebrew University for the support granted to this project. We also want to thank the Mizock Chair and the Faculty of Law at the Hebrew University, and the holder of the Chair, Professor Alon Harel for their support.

We wish to express our deep gratitude to the universities and the hosts of the conferences on judicial independence. We wish to thank HE Markus Buechel for hosting the Vaduz conference in December of 2007. We wish to express our thanks to the Jagellonjan Univerisity and the co-Chair of the Conference Profesor Fryderyk Zoll for the Novermber 2008 conference. We are deeply indebted to Professor Christopher Forsyth and the University of Cambridge for hosting the fifth conference in August 2009. We wish to express our thanks to Dean Hiram Chodosh and Professor Wayne MacCormack of the College of Law of the University of Utah for hosting the sixth conference in Salt Lake City in October of 2010. Thanks are due to the Hebrew University for hosting the conferences in Jerusalem in 2007 and 2008.

Thanks are extended to Professor Walter Rechberger of the University of Vienna who hosted the seventh international conference on judicial independence in May of 2011. Support for the project was also given by Old Dominion University in Virginia in the USA for the preparation of the manuscript. Thanks are also due to Viktorija Jakimovska for sterling work in giving research assistance, and to Ronen Avner for his invaluable help in the preparation of the manuscript.

Shimon Shetreet Christopher Forsyth

LIST OF CONTRIBUTORS

Neil Andrews Professor of Civil Justice and Private Law, University of Cambridge, Member of the teaching staff since 1983; Fellow of Clare College, Cambridge; Bencher of Middle Temple, 2007; Member of the American Law Institute since 2000; Council Member of the International Association of Procedural Law.

Sir **Louis Blom-Cooper** QC was called to the Bar by the Middle Temple in July 1952, and was made a Bencher of the Inn in 1978. He took silk in 1970, and was a Deputy High Court Judge from 1992 to 1996, as well as a Judge of Appeal in the Court of Appeal of Jersey and of Guernsey from 1989 to 1996. Publications include *Final Appeal: A Study of the House of Lords in its Judicial Capacity* (1972), co-authored with Gavin Drewry, *The Court of Appeal* (2007), with Gavin Drewry and Charles Blake.

Michael Bohlander had been a member of the German judiciary since 1991 before joining Durham Law School in 2004. From 1999 until 2001 he served as the Senior Legal Officer of a Trial Chamber of the ICTY. He has trained judges and prosecutors from several countries, including the Iraqi High Tribunal which tried Saddam Hussein. He is the Visiting Chair in Criminal Law at the Rijksuniversiteit Groningen Centre for Law and Governance.

Markus Buechel is a senior advocate in the principality of Liechtenstein. He was elected to the Liechtenstein Government as Minister of Finance in 1999 and subsequently as the country's Minister of Foreign Affairs in 1992. He was then voted Prime Minister of the Principality of Liechtenstein in a general election during 1993. Since his retirement from public office he is active as a senior advocate. HE Mr Buechel hosted in Vadouz the second International Conference of judicial Independence December 2007.

Daniela Cavallini is assistant professor at Bologna University (www.dsp.unibo.it) and lawyer. She participated in different comparative research projects on recruitment and career of judges and prosecutors and wrote several publications on judicial discipline.

Hiram E. Chodosh is the Dean and Professor of Law at the University of Utah S.J. Quinney College of Law. A former Fulbright Scholar in India, he has advised the UNDP, the World Bank, the IMF, the U.S. State Department, and many courts, ministries, and commissions in the Middle East and Asia.

Anton Cooray is Associate Dean of Law at City University of Hong Kong. He specializes in comparative public law and is the editor of Asia Pacific Law Review, the first Asia based law journal to be indexed in SSCI.

Irwin Cotler is a Canadian Member of Parliament and the former Minister of Justice and Attorney General of Canada. He is a Professor of Law (Emeritus) at McGill University.

James Crawford LLD, FBA, SC is Whewell Professor of International Law, University of Cambridge and a Fellow of Jesus College, Cambridge. He previously held chairs at Adelaide and Sydney. He is a Senior Counsel (NSW) and a member of the English bar, practicing from Matrix Chambers. He was the first Australian member of the United Nations International Law Commission and was responsible for the ILC's work on the International Criminal Court (1994) and for the second reading of the ILC Articles on State Responsibility (2001). In addition to scholarly work on statehood, collective rights, investment law and international responsibility, he has appeared frequently before the International Court of Justice and other international tribunals, and is engaged as expert, counsel and arbitrator in international arbitration.

Cyrus Das LLB(Hons) Ph.D is a senior legal practitioner at the Malaysian Bar and an Adjunct Professor of Law. His specialties are administrative and constitutional law. He was President of the Malaysian Bar Council and is presently Honorary Life President of the Commonwealth Lawyers Association.

Chandra R. de Silva is Professor of History and Special Assistant to the Provost at Old Dominion University, Virginia, USA. He has written extensively on contemporary education, ethnicity and politics in Sri Lanka. Until 2010 he served as Dean of the College of Arts and Letters at Old Dominion University.

David Feldman QC honoris causa, DCL, MA (Oxford), FBA is the Rouse Ball Professor of English Law in the University of Cambridge, a Fellow of Downing College, Cambridge, and the President of the Society of Legal Scholars for 2010–11. From 2000 to 2004 he was the first Legal Adviser to the Parliamentary Joint Select Committee on Human Rights, and from 2002 to 2010 a Judge (and Vice-President 2006–09) of the Constitutional Court of Bosnia and Herzegovina. His writing is mainly in the fields of constitutional law, comparative public law, civil liberties and human rights, administrative law, criminal procedure, and remedies.

Christopher Forsyth is Professor of Public and Private International Law in the University of Cambridge and Extraordinary Professor of Law in the University of Stellenbosch. From 1997 to 2010 he was Director or Assistant Director of the Centre for Public Law. He is the author with the late Sir William Wade QC of *Administrative Law* (10th ed, OUP 2009) a standard work on the subject recognised as authoritative by courts throughout the common law world. He has written many books and articles in learned journals on all aspects of public law and private international law. His PhD thesis was published as *"In Danger for their Talents: A study of the Appellate Division of the Supreme Court of South Africa from 1950"* (Juta & Co,1985). He has advised several governments on thorny issues of administrative and constitutional law. He is a practicing barrister, a Bencher of the Inner Temple, and sits as a Recorder in the Crown Court in England.

Stephen Goldstein got his B.A. at the University of Pennsylvania, 1959 (Phi Beta Kappa). J.D., University of Pennsylvania 1962, summa cum laude (first in class). Admitted to the Bar in Pennsylvania U.S.A. 1962. Practicing lawyer in Philadelphia, Pennsylvania, 1962–1964. Law Clerk to Justice Arthur Goldberg, United States Supreme Court, 1964–1965. Has been a professor of Law in The University of Pennsylvania. Edward S. Silver Professor of Procedural Law, The Hebrew University of Jerusalem, 1976. Dean of the Hebrew University faculty of Law, 1987–1990. Director, The Harry Sacher Institute of Legislative Research and Comparative Law, 1984–1987. Chairman of the Editorial Board of the Israel Law Review, 1979–1984. Chairman, The United States-Israel Educational Foundation (Fulbright Commission), 1988–1999. Legal Counsel, The American Association of University Professors, 1971–1974. Prof. Goldstein has held visiting positions in numerous universities, including: The University of California, Berkeley, Trinity College, Cambridge University, Tulane University, University of Hong Kong, Kellogg College, University of Oxford, and Chuo University – Tokyo. Member, the Executive Committee of the International Association of Procedural Law. Member, The International Academy of Comparative Law. Member, The American Law Institute; International Adviser to the American Law Institute Project on Transnational Civil Procedure; Judge, Israel Adhesion Contracts Tribunal; Member, Israel Government Council for the Supervision of Experimentation on Animals; Member, Editorial Board of the Israel Law Review. Research interests include fundamental issues in comparative procedural law and dispute resolution structures and mechanisms; reform of procedural law and dispute resolution mechanisms from a comparative perspective; class actions and derivative actions. Prof. Goldstein passed away in 2009.

Ada Pellegrini Grinover
Full professor of procedural law at the University of São Paulo (Brasil),
Doctor "Honoris causa" by the University of Milano (Italy),
Vice-President of International Association of Procedural Law,
Vice-President of Ibero-American Institute of Procedural Law,
Honorary President of Brazilian Institute of Procedural Law,
Author of 24 scientific books and many articles published in Brazil and abroad

Carlo Guarnieri is professor at the University of Bologna, where he teaches Comparative Judicial Systems. Together with P. Pederzoli he is the author of *The Power of Judges. A Comparative Study of Courts and Democracy* (Oxford 2002).

Justice Tassaduq Hussain Jillani is a Judge of the Pakistani Supreme Court.. The Hague Conference has appointed him as the Co-chair of the Working Party on Mediation in Family International Law. The Working Party comprises of Judges and Academics from Europe, United States, Latin America, India and Asia.

Hoong Phun ("H.P.") Lee holds the Sir John Latham Chair of Law at Monash University. Professor Lee's publications include *Constitutional Conflicts in Contemporary Malaysia* (Oxford University Press, 1995) and *The Australian Judiciary* (Cambridge University Press, 2001) (co-author).

Wayne McCormack B.A. Stanford University, J.D. University of Texas. Is E. W. Thode Professor of Law at the University of Utah. He has written widely in constitutional law and international criminal law with emphasis on counter-terrorism.

Joe McIntyre is currently a PhD Candidate at the University of Cambridge, where he is examining the nature of the judicial function. He has previously worked as a Principal Research Officer for the South Australian Parliament, and as legal officer for the South Australian Solicitor-General's and Crown Solicitor's Offices. His practice has principally focused on Australian constitutional law, and involved numerous Supreme Court and High Court appearances.

Daniela Piana is associate professor at the University of Bologna, where she teaches Politics and Institutions of the EU. She is the author of several articles on courts and politics. She has recently published *Judicial Accountabilities in New Europe* (London 2010).

Walter Rechberger born in 1945, is Full Professor (Ordinarius) of Law at the Vienna University School of Law and head of the Department of Civil Procedure (Institut für Zivilverfahrensrecht). He is member of the Council of the International Association of Procedural Law and holds the degree of an honorary doctor of the University of Pècs, Hungary.

Eliezer Rivlin is the Deputy Chief Justice of the Supreme Court of Israel; Director at the Israeli Institute of Extended Studies for Judges; Vice President of the International Organization of Judicial Training; Visiting professor at the University of Florida – School of Law (since 2006);
Author of books and articles in the fields of tort law and constitutional law.

Maimon Schwarzschild is Professor of Law at the University of San Diego, and Affiliated Professor at the University of Haifa. He has recently been Visiting Professor at the University of Paris (Sorbonne) and at the Hebrew University in Jerusalem. He is an English barrister and an American lawyer; he is an associate member of Landmark Chambers, London.

Yuval Shany holds the Hersch Lauterpacht chair in Public International Law at the Law Faculty of the Hebrew University of Jeursalem. Shany is a graduate of Hebrew University (LL.B.), New York University (LL.M.) and London University (Ph.D). He is one of the directors of the Project on International Courts and Tribunals.

Avrom Sherr was appointed as the Woolf Professor of Legal Education at the Institute of Advanced Legal Studies in 1995. He has been Director of the Institute since October 2004. He currently serves as Chair of the Advisory Board of The UK Centre for Legal Education and the Advisory Panel for the Office of the Independent Adjudicator for Higher Education. Professor Sherr is the author of many reports, articles, chapters and papers on legal services, the legal profession, legal education, legal ethics and human rights as well as monographs including: *"Client Care for Lawyers"*, *"Advocacy"* and *"Freedom of Protest, Public Order and the Law"*.

Shimon Shetreet holds the Greenblatt chair of Public and International Law at the Hebrew University of Jerusalem, Israel and is past chairman of the Sacher Institute of Legislative Research and Comparative Law. He is a graduate of the Hebrew University of Jerusalem (LL.B, LL.M) and the University of Chicago (M.C.L, D.C.L). He was a member of the Chief Justice Landau Commission on the Israeli Court System, 1980, and a Judge on the Standard Contract Court (1981–88). He is the author and editor of a number of books, including *Judges on Trial* (1976), *Judicial Independence: The Contemporary Debate* (1985),

"*The Role of Courts in Society*" (1988), *National Security and Free Speech* (1991), *Pioneers in Tears: Anthology on North African Jewry* (1991), *Justice in Israel* (1994), *Women in Law* (1998), *The Good Land between Power and Religion* (1998), *Law and Social Pluralism* (2002) and *On Adjudication* (2004). His book *Judges on Trial: A Study of the Appointment and the Accountability of the English Judiciary(1976)* was relied upon by the House of Lords in the *Pinochet* Case in January 1999 and by the courts in many other countries. Forthcoming Books: *Judges on Trial* 2nd ed. (2012, with Dr. Sopie Turenne), *Uniform Civil Code for India* (2012, with Hiram Chodosh) and *The Executive Branch* (Hebrew, 2012). He served as General Coordinator, International Bar association Project for Minimum Standards of Judicial Independence 1980–1982. In recent years prof. Shetreet together with prof. Christopher Forsyth was the head of the international project on judicial independence which held seven international conferences. Prof. Shetreet has held high public offices. Between 1988 and 1996 he served as Member of the Knesset, the Israeli Parliament. He was a cabinet minister in the Rabin Government. In December 2011 prof. Shetreet was awarded the International Jurists Award 2010 together with Lord Judge Chief Justice of England and Wales.

Marcel Storme is the director of Institute Procedural and European Law. He has graduated from Ghent University in 1952 and received advanced degrees from the University of Paris and London School of Economics. He has published many books, including *Burden of Proof, General Principles of Law*, and numerous articles. Marcel Storme was the president of the working group, which for the first time made proposals for the approximation of procedural laws in the European Union (1993).

Sophie Turenne, M.A. (Cantab.), Ph.D. (Paris II Panthéon-Assas), is Neil Allam/Clifford Chance Lecturer at the Faculty of Law, University of Cambridge. She is a Fellow of Murray Edwards College, Cambridge.

K. K. Venugopal Senior Advocate, Supreme Court of India. (equivalent to Q.C. in England). Served in high legal positions in India including Additional Solicitor General of India, 1979–80, Vice-President, Bar Association of India, President, Supreme Court Bar Association of India, 1990–91, 1994–95 and 1999–2000. Received numerous Awards and Honors Including: "Padma Bhushan" Award on the occasion of the Republic Day, 2002, Honoris Causa Degree of Doctor of Laws (LL.D.) by Utkal University, Orissa, 2010, "Grand Cross" award and medal from the Bar Association of Bagota, Columbia, Global Award 2003 from the Chief Minister of Kerala, and the Eswara Iyer

"Distinguished Lawyer Award" from the Kerala Bar Federation. Served in International leading roles including President, SAARCLAW (The International Association of Lawyers of the SAARC Countries), 1995–97, President, Union Internationale des Avocats 1996–97. Was Editor-in-Chief of the Third and Fourth Editions of the Book *Justice Bachawat's: Law of Arbitration & Conciliation*. Delivered numerous public lectures in India and overseas.

Fryderyk Zoll Professor at the Jagiellonian University in Cracow. Mercator Professor at the University of Osnabrück (from 1.10.2010). Member of the International Academy of Comparative Law. Member of the Acquis Group on the Existing EC Contract Law. Director of the Centre for the Foreign Law Programs at the Jagiellonian University. Head of the Curriculum Team for the National School of Judiciary and Prosecutors in Poland.

CHAPTER ONE

GENERAL INTRODUCTION

This volume is divided into seven parts: Part I, The Significance of the Independence of the Judiciary; Part II, The Judiciary and the Other Branches of Government; Part III, Judicial Independence in International Law and National Law; Part IV, Judicial Appointment, Judicial Conduct and Judicial Accountability; Part V, Country Studies of Judicial Independence; Part VI, International Standards in the Making; and Part VII, Text of the International Standards of Judicial Independence.

Part I; The Significance of the Independence of the Judiciary

Part I focuses on the significance of the independence of the judiciary. This part contains an analysis of the main issues revolving judicial independence. It discusses the importance of judicial independence and how it projects upon the law system around it. The main issues discussed, are issues regarding judicial independence and the rule of law; judicial independence and judicial activism; the importance of judicial independence in creating an efficient and reliable Judiciary and issues regarding the securing of Judicial Independence. This part contains chapters by: Prof. Shimon Shetreet, Prof. Christopher Forsyth, Prof. Marcel Storme, and Prof. Neil Andrews.

This volume begins with chapter 2 by Shimon Shetreet, *Creating a Culture of Judicial Independence: The Practical Challenge and the Conceptual and Constitutional Infrastructure*. The chapter outlines the necessary elements of the culture of judicial independence and defines the concept of judicial independence and sets the stage for the book. Judicial independence is one of the fundamental values which lie at the foundations of most judicial systems. These values include: procedural fairness, efficiency, accessibility, public confidence in the courts, judicial independence, and the value of constitutionality, in the sense of the constitutional protection of the judiciary. Each of these values allows the courts to fulfill their main function, which is the resolution of disputes. It is a part of the governmental culture of the country, affected by the relationship between the branches of the government, and is one of the fundamental values of a proper administration of justice. It is not an individual concept, which can exist in any political climate; therefore, the state must create a culture of judicial independence and establish it on several levels, and in a long and gradual process. Domestic law is influenced by the international law and international standards in the process of creating the culture of judicial independence.

The domestic law and the culture of judicial independence play a role in every part of the judicial system. The institutional level regulates the matters relative to status of the judges and jurisdiction of the courts, the constitutional level anchors in the constitution the institutional aspects. The legislative level regulates in detail the constitutional principles, while the adjudicative level provides for interpretation and additional elements in all the levels. The Ethical traditions and Code of Conduct covers the judge's official and non-official spheres of activities, and shields the judge's substantive independence from dependencies, associations, and even less intensive involvements which might cast doubts on judicial neutrality.

The culture of judicial independence can only exist in a system which is based on the principle of separation of powers. Even once achieved, the continuation of judicial independence is not a matter of course. It is constantly subject to challenges, sometimes by other branches of government, and at other times as the result of different developments.

Another aspect of judicial independence is the internal independence of the judiciary, the independence of a judge from his judicial superiors and colleagues. Another element of judicial independence is substantive independence, which refers to the neutrality of mind of the judge, to that judge's impartiality and total freedom from irrelevant pressures in judicial decision making.

While dealing with judicial independence, a common dillema is the principle of democratic accountability. Democratic accountability demands that a country selects the model of constitutional adjudication that complements its method of judicial appointments.

The controversy regarding the scope of judicial review has an impact on the public confidence in the justice system. The court cannot exercise its power in total detachment from the social and public discourse. In order to continue to faithfully execute its role in society, the court must demarcate in very finely tuned manner this demarcation lines between the Supreme Court and the other branches.

Chapter 3 by Prof. Christopher Forsyth the co-editor of this volume: *The Failure of Institutions: The South African Judicial Service Commission and the Hlophe Saga,* analyses incidents that raise doubts about the integrity of some parts of the South African judiciary. The Judicial Services Commission, which has an unenviable role as the authority which must find that a judge has been guilty of "gross misconduct" before that judge may be removed from office, has been failing in this task. This is of profound and disconcerting consequence for the South African judiciary as a whole and constitutional government in that country. This chapter does not offer any remedy for the state of affairs, but it does point to the possibility that the judiciary itself will, in its own interests and the interests of the polity as a whole, insist upon the JSC adopting proper standards and disciplining errant judges.

Some such unattractive incidents are, perhaps, inevitable in any judiciary and, particularly so, in a judiciary that has undergone the sort of "transformation" the South African judiciary has undergone since the political changes of the early 1990s. However, the almost wholly peaceful transformation of South Africa from an oppressive state in which the majority of the population was excluded from political power on racial grounds into a constitutional order with a constitution that is considered by some the most progressive in the world was an astonishing, almost miraculous, event in world history. Notwithstanding the current difficulties it is still much better than many expected or dared to believe possible. The Hlophe Affair is investigated in detail in this chapter and poses a real challenge to the Judiciary and the political leadership of South Africa.

Chapter 4 by Prof. Marcel Storme on the *Independence of the Judiciary,* seeks to demystify and place into its proper perspective the notion of independence, and also to point to the many ways in which the courts' work is burdened with "*bondages*".

Independence is not an end in itself, but a means of safeguarding a fundamental value, that of the impartiality of the judge. The essence of judicial activity resides in that it is exercised by an impartial and neutral third party. The courts' independence towards the legislature and the executive are self-evident propositions, although they are not invariably respected in practice. Independence must be established with the impartiality of the judge towards public opinion in general, towards himself, towards the parties, and towards their lawyers and acquire a degree of insulation from the press and the rest of the media.

However, due to the burden of "*bondages*", those elements against which the judge is incapable of adopting a position of independence, this independence can be problematic. The link with the prescribed rules, Laws Constitutions and Treaties, is difficult to break. Societal rules, the account of a case given by the parties, the issue of time pressure and judicial accountability all conspire to prevent the realization of judicial independence in its ideal form.

Chapter 5 is the last chapter in the first part. Chapter 5, by Neil Andrews, *A Fresh Start: The Four Pillars of Civil Justice,* examines the essential pillars of Civil Justice. According to Andrews they are: access to legal advice and dispute-resolution systems, equality and fairness between the parties, a focused and speedy process, and adjudicators of integrity. The theoretical background and precedents for these concepts are illustrated in comparative perspective. Andrews lists the elements of ensuring fairness and effectiveness of the judicial process which lie at the foundation of the justice system.

Part II; The Judiciary and the Other Branches of Government

Part II discusses the relationship between an independent judiciary and the executive branch; accountability of judges and the judiciary; the Executive role in the administration of justice. This part will also examine the relationship between an independent judiciary and the legislature; the role of the legislature in creating independent judiciary; securing judicial independence by legislation as compared with a tradition of judicial independence.

This part contains chapters by: Prof. Carlo Guarnieri and Prof. Daniela Piana, the late Prof. Stephen Goldstein, Dato' Dr. Cyrus Das, Prof. Hiram Chodosh, Prof. Wayne McCormack, and Prof. Maimon Schwarzschild.

Chapter 6 by Prof. Carlo Guarnieri and Prof. Daniela Piana, on *Judicial Independence and the Rule of Law: Exploring the European Experience,* offers the comparative empirical analyses of the European Experience with Judicial Independence and the Rule of Law. To be considered legitimate by the parties to the case the judge is expected to adjudicate impartially, according to the rules of the legal system without expectation of benefits or fear of reprisals in order to perform his or her functions effectively. Therefore, judicial independence is a relationship and its main points of reference are the parties: in order to be impartial, the judge must be independent from them. A judge who depends on one of the parties cannot be – and appear to be – impartial. Judicial independence implies a clear political dimension if and when a judge comes to adjudicate a case in which politics is involved: e.g. when the government – or someone politically powerful – is a party. From this point of view the internal dimension of judicial independence can become significant only if it impinges on external independence: for instance, in the case of politically influenced higher ranking judges harassing lower ranks if they decide against powerful political actors.

In Chapter 7 by the Late Prof. Stephen Goldstein, *The Rule of Law vs. the Rule of Judges: a Brandeisian Solution,* Prof. Goldstein analyzed the contributions of Justice Louis D. Brandeis to the debate over the role of judicial activism. In particular, the questions about Brandeis' judicial heritage's place on the ideological spectrum, and where specifically he fits in the context of Israeli judicial personalities. The author concludes that his heritage is largely conservative from the American perspective and his judicial philosophy is based on self-control and restraint as contrasted with judicial activism. This was due to his strongly entrenched belief about the function of the judiciary in a democratic society, on his modesty about the wisdom of judges and on his opposition to the concentration of power, including in the judges. For Brandeis the most important thing judges do is "not to do."

Chapter 8, by Dato' Dr. Cyrus Das, *The Threats to Judicial Independence: Experiences from the Commonwealth,* the author examines the experiences of the British Commonwealth nations with threats to Judicial Independence and that concept's dialectic with constitutionalism. The instances of the threats to judicial independence, in the political evolvement of the new democracies, provide the best illustration of the ever present tension in these countries between constitutionalism and judicial independence. Several key topics are examined with respect to this topic which range from the direct interference with judges due to harassment or removal, circulars and directives to judges, the politics of judicial promotions, and inappropriate consultations, propositions or suggestions to judges. While this is not meant to be an exhaustive list of the ways in which judicial independence can be imperiled, these are all relevant and serve as prerequisites to the proper functioning of the rule of law and are illustrated as such in the case studies presented.

Chapter 9, by Prof. Hiram Chodosh, is on *Corruption and Judicial Independence*. Dean Chodosh analyses the topic of corruption or economic interference and its relation to Judicial Independence. This is distinct from political interference that is the focus of the majority of the literature and reforms on the topic of judicial independence. This analysis suffers from the problems with defining what constitutes economic corruption and how to enact laws that will preserve judicial independence from its effects. Corruption can have a multitude of tangible negative effects on judicial independence, but perhaps most serious is the role it can play in undermining the trust of the public in ostensibly democratic institutions. Combating corruption is particularly challenging as it can simultaneously work to undermine the institutions meant to combat its effects in the first place. Corruption must be defined to be understood and there are a variety of viewpoints on this topic, including political, economic, and cultural and ethical. Once it is understood, then sound policy can be constructed to combat its effects and preserve judicial independence.

Chapter 10, by Prof. Wayne McCormack, *Judicial Independence in the Face of Violence,* examines the dialectic between the role of violence and the rule of law. That is to say that no justice system can operate effectively in the midst of chaos but chaos cannot be forestalled effectively without a functioning justice system. In particular it examines the growth and maintenance of the rule of law in a military or criminally chaotic context. If people do not feel safe and protected, there is little the judiciary can do to build a functioning society.

The international community must press aggressively for local protection of judges, as judges are greatly at risk and their safety is a critical component in realization of the Rule of Law, which is in turn a critical component in achieving a healthy and productive society.

The last chapter of part II, Chapter 11, by Prof. Maimon Schwarzschild, analyses the concept of judicial independence with a more critical analysis. *Judicial Independence and Judicial Hubris* is widely, and rightly, said to be a cornerstone of liberal government, of good government, and of the rule of law. However, judicial independence is not unequivocally a good thing. Good ideas are often bent or distorted on behalf of dubious interests. Judicial independence is surely good and even crucial to the morality of law, but judicial independence in another sense might actually imply judicial over-reaching and abuse of authority: an indefensible sort of independence. That sort of independence is liable in the long run to undermine or to destroy judicial independence in the good sense. This is true in theory and in practice as is seen in developed countries attitudes towards a dubious sort of judicial independence. Further, international legal institutions, and enthusiasm for international norms, may be especially susceptible to fostering the bad sort of judicial independence. If judges around the world overstep their authority, and if the judiciary is seen to be a partisan force in the political and cultural disputes of the era, then democratic public opinion is liable to ensure that there will be less judicial independence, not more.

Part III; Judicial Independence in International Law and National Law

Judicial independence has a central place not only in national law, but also in international law. The norms and standards of judicial independence in each one sphere affects the norms and standards of the other. It discusses the impact of these spheres have one upon the other. This part analyses the development of judicial independence in international law, and the role of judicial independence in the resolution of international disputes. This part of the book contains chapters by: Professor James Crawford and Joe McIntyre; Professor David Feldman; Professor Walter Rechberger; H.E Adv. Markus Buechel; Professor Yuval Shany; and Prof. Michael Bohlander.

The first chapter of part III by Prof. James Crawford and Joe McIntyre, *The Independence and Impartiality of the 'International Judiciary'*, focuses on the standards of judicial independence as applied to the international judiciary. International law now has its own institutions, increasingly interacting with the domestic laws of States. Their emergence calls for an examination of the standards and principles that govern and constrain their operation. In particular, the question arises as to the extent to which, standards international law set for other legal systems apply to its own institutions. This chapter will focus on one emblematic example of this issue, namely the applicability and content of the principles of judicial independence and impartiality to the 'international judiciary'.

Chapter 13, by Professor David Feldman, is on *The Independence of International Judges in National Courts: Lessons from Bosnia Herzegovina.* This chapter analyses the lessons for judicial independence from the experiences of international judges in Bosnia and Herzegovina in the tribunals that followed the conflict. International judges in this context are subject to novel pressures. These derive from their sources of authority in international law, and the particular context of a fractured society, as in this case, recovering from war and genocide. This case showed the utility for judicial independence of introducing the international judges who were able to overcome national concerns, mediate national interests, and protect the integrity of the court. If a legal system is to negotiate a course between the many threats, then all parties concerned have to be aware of a very important point. Judges, other national authorities and international agencies all need to be clear about the institutions, groups or individuals from which and purposes for which judges need to be independent, and conscious of how their activities, undertaken with the best of intentions, can impinge on each other's independence. This is illustrated by the experiences in Bosnia and Herzegovina.

Chapter 14, by Professor Walter Rechberger is on *The Impact of the ECHR Jurisprudence on the Austrian Practice in the Field of Judicial Independence.* The chapter examines the relationship between Austria and the European Court of Human Rights and Fundamental Freedoms (ECHR) and the implications of this relationship for that country's judicial independence. Austria was the first state to incorporate the ECHR fully into its constitutional legal order. This means that the rights laid down in the convention have the same relevance as the original catalogue of fundamental rights in the Austrian Federal Constitution and the Basic Law of the State on the General Rights of Citizens. Therefore legislation has to observe and give effect to the rights and freedoms of the ECHR and additionally all courts and administrative authorities are obliged to apply the ECHR in all proceedings before them, which means that they have to interpret the law in a manner which does not infringe the rights laid down in the ECHR.

Chapter 15, by H.E Adv. Markus Buechel on *The Independence of International Arbitrators*, deals with the topic of International Arbitrators and their independence. There is a general principle that an arbitrator must act and must be seen to act fairly between the parties, and the arbitrator must be and remain impartial and independent. The independence of an arbitrator is an essential feature of judicial independence, despite the fact that most arbitrators are intimately involved in their field of arbitration and the outcomes they produce. Long-standing norms that no one should be a judge in his own cause and that justice should be seen to be done apply equally to international arbitration in order to temper this fact.

Chapter 16 by Professor Yuval Shany, *Judicial Independence as an Indicator of International Court Effectiveness: A Goal-Based Approach*, offers a significant contribution to the debate on the relationship between judicial independence by applying to it a model for international judicial effectiveness developed elsewhere. He disputes some scholars who argue that there is no evidence that independent international courts are more effective that dependent ones. Professor Shany argues that the proper questions that should be discussed are not whether judicial independence is conducive to international court effectiveness, but rather more nuanced ones such as which international courts are better served by judicial independence, what level of judicial independence should courts strive toward, and what image of independence should they seek to project.

The last chapter in Part III, Chapter 17, is a chapter by Prof. Michael Bohlander, *Separation of Powers and the International Judiciary – A Vision of Institutional Judicial Independence in International Law*. The chapter analyses the separation of powers and the international judiciary and lays out a vision of judicial independence's place in international law. This is in contrast to the primary focus on domestic judicial independence and is of growing importance due to the increasing numbers of international criminal tribunals. Not all the courts have proper judicial discipline regimes or even a code of conduct and this imperils their independent credentials. Many of the checks and balances upon the judiciary that ensure its independence in domestic matters are lacking or absent at the international level. It is demonstrated that mechanisms to ensure international courts' independence must be enacted and implemented in order to have a healthy and functioning system.

Part IV; Judicial Appointment, Judicial Conduct and Judicial Accountability

Part IV examines a number of central issues. Judicial appointments have a central effect on the creating or limiting of the independence of the judiciary. This Part discusses the place of the executive and the legislature in the appointment of judges; tenure of judges, and its effect on judicial independence. This part also deals with grounds and procedures of Judicial removal and discipline, which are significant in creating or limiting the independence of the judiciary. The chapters in this part discuss models of removal and discipline for dealing with misconduct of judges. Other issues analyzed in this part include: the creation of formal and informal standards of conduct for the judiciary, and the impact of these standards upon the creation of a culture of judicial independence. This part contains chapters by: The Hon. Prof. Irwin Cotler, M.P, Prof. Dr. hab. Fryderyk Zoll, Justice Eliezer Rivlin, Dr. Daniela Cavallini, Prof. Sir Louis Blom-Cooper, QC, and Prof. Anton Cooray.

Chapter 18, by Prof. Irwin Cotler, *The Supreme Court of Canada Appointment Process: Chronology, Context and Reform,* offers a very meaningful report by the former Minister of Justice of Canada on the process of selection of judges of the supreme court of Canada. The chapter takes the case of Canada's Supreme Court appointment process and looks at the process of its reform. As the Supreme Court is the pinnacle of the court system, the process of appointing its judges is one of critical importance. The shift in Canada from a Parliamentary to a constitutional democracy necessitated some reforms to the existing system in order for the Court to fill a new role. This chapter examines in detail the process by which justices are appointed to the court under the present system.

Chapter 19, by Prof. Dr. hab. Fryderyk Zoll, *The System of Judicial Appointment in Poland – A Question of the Legitimacy of the Judicial Power* examines the system of judicial appointments in Poland. It analyzes the measures taken in support of judicial independence and those features particular to Poland which undermine it, during the appointment process and after the appointment has taken place. The increase of the judicial power in the process of implementing the law would require more democratic legitimacy, but it needs to be counter – balanced by the need to keep the system immune from the direct influence of politics. The chapter illustrates the struggles between independence, legitimacy, and accountability.

In Chapter 20, Deputy Chief Justice of Israel Justice Eliezer Rivlin analyzes the relationship between the *Courts and the Media*. The increasing intensive media coverage of court cases, judicial decisions and legal proceedings presents a challenge to judges and requires careful attention. Justice Rivlin also offers a detailed record of the rules approved by the Israeli judiciary on the procedure and the manner for responses by courts and individual judges to media reports and inquiries. The Israeli practice served as a basis for section six of the Mt. Scopus Standards on Judicial Independence dealing with the media and the Judiciary.

Chapter 21, by Dr. Daniela Cavallini, *Independence and Judicial Discipline: the Italian Code of Judicial Conduct,* examines the Italian Code of Judicial Conduct and how judicial discipline administered under the code affects Italy's Judicial Independence. Disciplinary rules in general can contribute to guaranteeing judicial independence. It helps to avoid disciplining judges for vague, discretionary reasons and without judges knowing *ex ante* what is considered a violation and the penalties they can incur. This will avoid cases where punishment is disproportionately administered. The chapter examines Italy's reform experience and concludes that judicial independence can be best guaranteed through firm and all-encompassing rules, precise sanctions and compulsory disciplinary action. However there is still a place for discretionary powers which cannot be completely excluded from judicial discipline.

Chapter 22 is a chapter by Prof. Sir Louis Blom-Cooper, QC, *The Age of Judicial Responsibility: the Retirement and Resignation of Appellate Court Judges.* It examines the topic of the retirement and resignation of appellate court judges and how this impacts judicial independence. For appellate judges appointment for life, with regular medical check-ups and the functioning of personal resignation, is to be preferred over enforced retirement at a designated age. Impartiality, or perceived impartiality, is enhanced by the existence of the highest quality of judicial output. An effective system of appellate justice calls for a blend of wisdom, experience, diversity and demonstrable merit. The evidence of high quality judicial service at an advanced age is strikingly in favour of appointment for life. Inflexible and arbitrary age limits for appellate court judges exclude capable and competent individuals from contributing to their full potential.

The last chapter in part IV is Chapter 23, by Prof. Anton Cooray, *Standards of Judicial Behaviour and the Impact of Codes of Conduct.* This chapter examines the effect that Codes of Conduct have had on standards of judicial behaviour. Courts must enjoy a privileged position with special protections and immunities, so that they can disburse justice evenly between the citizenry and the government. In order to maintain its independence, the judiciary must be above criticism. Suspicion of partiality, incompetence or abuse of power invites attempts to reign in judicial independence. It is only when the judiciary is, in fact and in appearance, independent and immune from political control that it will be able to gain public confidence and trust. To this end, constitutional principles and conventional practices have evolved to ensure that a special sphere is demarcated for the judiciary. It is the judges' responsibility to demonstrate that they are fair and competent, in both action and the perception of their actions. Judicial codes fulfill this role and have an important place in providing standards for judges to adhere to.

Part V; Country Studies of Judicial Independence

Part V analyzes a number of central aspects of judicial independence in a number of jurisdictions including, UK, Australia, Pakistan, Brazil, Italy, Sri Lanka. Part V contains chapters by Prof. Neil Andrews, Prof. Chandra de Silva, Prof. Hoong Phun (H.P.) Lee, Prof. Avrom Sherr, Dr. Sophie Turenne, Justice Tassaduq Hussain Jillani, Prof. Ada Pellegrini Grinover and Senior Advocate K. K. Venugopal.

Chapter 24, by Prof. Neil Andrews, *Judicial Independence: The British Experience* lays out the British experience with judicial independence and how the British judiciary came to be separate from Parliament, the Executive, other powerful people, party politics, governmental exigency, corporate greed and private interest. This independence has been guaranteed by statute and tradition and is supported by the government and the public. Provided his proposed conduct is consistent with the law and sound judicial practice, a judge in Britain is entitled and bound to act according to his perception of what is just. The support given to the judicial enterprise by these organisations is crucial to the maintenance of judicial independence.

Chapter 25, by Prof. Chandra de Silva, is on *A Recent Challenge to Judicial Independence in Sri Lanka: The Issue of the Constitutional Challenge* examines the experience of Sri Lanka and the challenges that judicial independence has endured there. The British colonial legacy left Sri Lanka with a strong judiciary in the British tradition. However, with the extension of state activity well beyond the maintenance of law and order and the subordination of the bureaucracy to political control there arose among some politicians a tendency towards a desire to curb the independence and power of the judiciary. The exercise of judicial review over legislation in Sri Lanka came under assault and was justified on the basis of popular sovereignty. There was ostensible recognition that such interference with judicial independence was harmful and measures were introduced in an attempt to foster independence in Sri Lanka. However, it is clear that the intention was not to end the politicization of appointments but to ensure that influence in making such appointments should be shared among political groups rather than remain the exclusive privilege of the governing group. To ensure judicial independence, it is important to specifically require the executive to refrain from any act of omission or commission that directly or indirectly interferes with or frustrates the personal, substantive or collective independence of the judiciary, and as yet this has not been achieved in Sri Lanka.

Chapter 26, by Prof. Hoong Phun (H.P.) Lee, *Challenges of Judicial Independence–An Australian Perspective* analyses the Australian experience with judicial independence. While largely federal in nature, the Australian state and federal judicial systems remain relatively integrated. The public feels that such independence is not under any real threat and its legitimacy is fully accepted. Australian courts are seen as highly independent and impartial bodies. The judiciary can ultimately resort to doctrinal weapons to thwart any attempts by the executive to undermine or erode their standing as independent entities. Australian courts render themselves accountable through the operation of the 'open court' principle, the obligation to give reasons for decisions, the application of the apprehension of bias rule and the exercise of oversight by the superior courts over the inferior courts. In Australia, judicial independence is a fundamental value which is viewed by the general populace as a vital aspect of a democratic polity.

Chapter 27, by Prof. Avrom Sherr, *Shrinking Legal Aid, Unrepresented Litigants and Judicial Independence* examines how the role of the judiciary changes when the judge enters the arena in order to balance the position between conflicting parties. It investigates how judicial independence may suffer when one litigant is unrepresented. As a result of reductions in public funding the number of unrepresented litigants is likely to increase further. The chapter considers in some detail how the role and independence of the judge may be affected in such circumstances of inequality of arms. Knowing and acknowledging the effects on judicial independence are an important first step in maintaining judicial approach and status. Developing better means to handle the difficulties as the numbers of unrepresented litigants grows, is the next stage in development.

Chapter 28, by Dr. Sophie Turenne, *The Northern Irish Judiciary in Times of Crisis: The Diplock Courts,* analyses the example of the Diplock Courts in Northern Ireland from the time of the troubles. Northern Irish terrorists were prosecuted as ordinary criminals and tried in criminal courts rather than military tribunals. This led to a two-tiered criminal justice system of trial by jury or single judge adjudicated trials, the latter being known as Diplock Courts which were responsible for seeing the vast majority of terrorism cases. While such arrangements are often used by authoritarian regimes for undemocratic ends, the aim in creating these courts in this example was to ensure some degree of judicial independence in order to guarantee compliance with the minimum requirements of the rights to a fair trial. The judges were able to uphold a certain set of common law principles during the emergency period and did not abdicate their independence. They had a limited ability to safeguard individual rights but did on occasion go against the will of the political regime. When there are grounds to suppose that juries could not be effectively protected from intimidation, as was the case in Northern Ireland in terrorist trials, then courts in the Diplock model can be a workable response to civil disorder and terrorism.

Chapter 29, by Justice Tassaduq Hussain Jillani, *The Challenge of Judicial Independence and the Experience of Pakistan,* examines the experience of Pakistan with judicial independence, from its emergence from colonialism through political instability and martial law to the present day. It is shown that Pakistan struggled through many societal, governmental and political obstacles and has begun to realize the promise of judicial independence. The analysis is done with special attention to historical perspectives.

Chapter 30, by Prof. Ada Pellegrini Grinover, *The Relevance for Brazil of International Standards of Judicial Independence* analyses the topic of judicial independence from the perspective of Brazil which has a blended system of common law and civil law. It examines the powers of Brazilian judges and shows that there is a perception of the judiciary as the protector of individual freedoms, and that impartiality and independence are necessary to guarantee this freedom. The Brazilian Constitution assures the Judiciary of the prerogative of self-governing by applying normative and administrative action of self-organization and self-regulation and provides them tenure. The Brazilian Constitution is in line with international standards of judicial independence.

Chapter 31, by Chandra R. de Silva, *The Role of Law in Developing Countries,* examines the role of law in developing countries. In developing countries there is a greater distance between legal systems and society than exist in developed countries, there is, however, a greater burden on the systems in developing countries. This is critical because legal systems play an important formative role in developing countries in a way that is not as critical in developed countries. In developed countries there are many arenas for dispute settlement, but in developing counties there are many political and personal reasons for bringing cases to court. People in developing countries use these institutions as a means of bringing issues to public attention. Law fashions society and regulates conduct through penalties for violations. It influences conduct by demarcating what is socially acceptable and this is particularly important for developing countries.

Chapter 32, by Senior Advocate K. K. Venugopal, *The Supreme Court and Supremacy of the Judiciary in India* analyzes the Indian Supreme Court and judiciary. In India, it has not been uncommon for a completely independent judiciary to be looked at with suspicion by the executive, the fear being that the courts may set themselves up above the law or as a third house of parliament. Judicial restraint and statesmanship are necessary to prevent breaching the principles of separation of powers by the judiciary. However, it is difficult for the Indian Judiciary to remain silent when the promises of social justice made by the Constitution are nor fully implemented. Thus there is tension between the promise of what the judiciary could accomplish and how they are constrained by the political realities of Indian society and government.

Part VI; International Standards in the Making

Part VI focuses on the International Standards of judicial independence. Part VI contains chapter 33: *The Mt. Scopus International Standards of Judicial Independence: The Innovative Concepts and the Formulation of a Consensus in a Legal Culture of Diversity,* by the under-signed Shimon Shetreet. This chapter offers a detailed analysis of the Mt. Scopus International Standards of Judicial Independence with a focus on the central issues. These issues include: institutional independence of the judiciary, internal judicial independence of the judge *vis-a-vis* superiors and colleagues, the requirement of a pre-determined plan for case assignments. Other issues also included in the analyses in this chapter are: The principle of fair reflection of society by the judiciary, and the definition of the main function of courts in society, the resolution of disputes.

Part VII; Text of the Standards of Judicial Independence

Part VII, contains the text of the International Standards of Judicial Independence. This part includes 9 international standards as follows: *Mount Scopus International Standards of Judicial Independence* (2008), *Draft Standards of the Mt. Scopus standards of Judicial Independence* (2007), IBA *Code of Minimum Standards of Judicial Independence* (1982), *UN Basic Principles on the Independence of the Judiciary* (1985), *Commonwealth (Latimer House) Principles on the Three Branches of Government (2003), Tokyo Principles of the Independence of the Judiciary in the LAWASIA region* (1982), *Universal Declaration on the Independence of Justice* (Montreal 1983), *Bangalore Principles of Judicial Independence* (2002) and the *Kiev Recommendations on Judicial Independence* (2010).

PART I

THE SIGNIFICANCE OF THE INDEPENDENCE OF THE JUDICIARY

CHAPTER TWO

CREATING A CULTURE OF JUDICIAL INDEPENDENCE: THE PRACTICAL CHALLENGE AND THE CONCEPTUAL AND CONSTITUTIONAL INFRASTRUCTURE

*Shimon Shetreet**

I. Introduction

This chapter analyses the conceptual foundations of judicial independence, and the necessary elements for maintaining a culture of judicial independence. Judicial independence is a significant component of governmental culture in every country. It is shaped by the relations between the branches of government, and is one of the basic values which lie at the foundation of the administration of justice. Judicial independence must be supported by the political climate and social consensus. The political leadership and the professional and legal elite must work together to develop a culture of judicial independence along several very significant guidelines and levels. They must do this in a long and gradual process. This chapter offers a detailed analysis of the foundations and a comprehensive examination of the levels of the culture of judicial independence, and the central issues which the legal and professional elite and the political leadership should consider in the process of building a culture of judicial independence.

* LL.B., LL.M., (Hebrew University) M.C.L. D.C.L (Chicago), holds the Greenblatt chair of public and international law at the Hebrew University of Jerusalem, Israel and is past chairman of the Sacher Institute of Legislative Research and Comparative Law. He was a member of the Chief Justice Landau Commission on the Israeli Court System, 1980, and a Judge on the Standard Contract Court (1981–88). He is the author and editor of a number of books, including Judges on Trial (1976), Judicial Independence: The Contemporary Debate (1985), "The Role of Courts in Society" (1988), National Security and Free Speech (1991), Pioneers in Tears: Anthology on North African Jewry (1991), Justice in Israel (1994), Women in Law (1998), The Good Land between Power and Religion (1998), Law and Social Pluralism (2002) and On Adjudication (2004). His book Judges on Trial: A Study of the Appointment and the Accountability of the English Judiciary(1976) was relied upon by the House of Lords in the Pinochet Case in January 1999 and by the courts in many other countries. He served as General Coordinator, International Bar association Project for Minimum Standards of Judicial Independence 1980–1982. In recent years Prof. Shetreet together with Prof. Chris Forsyth was the head of the international project on judicial independence which held seven international conferences. Prof. Shetreet has held high public offices. Between 1988 and 1996 he served as Member of the Knesset, the Israeli Parliament. He was a cabinet minister in the Rabin Government.

The culture of judicial independence is created by five important and essential aspects: creating institutional structures, establishing constitutional infrastructure, introducing legislative provisions and constitutional safeguards, creating adjudicative arrangements and jurisprudence, and maintaining ethical traditions and a code of judicial conduct. The institutional structures regulate the matters relative to the status of the judges and the jurisdiction of the courts. The constitutional infrastructure embodies in the constitution the main provisions of the protection of the judiciary. The legislative provisions offer detailed regulations of the basic constitutional principles. The courts add to the constitutional infrastructure and the legislative provisions complimentary interpretations and jurisprudence on different aspects of the conduct of judges and the operation of courts. The ethical traditions and code of judicial conduct cover the judge's official and non-official spheres of activities, and shield the judge's substantive independence from dependencies, associations, and even less intensive involvements which might cast doubts on judicial neutrality.

International law plays a significant role in creating the culture of judicial independence in domestic law. In this chapter the case of England is presented in order to illustrate the impact of international law on national law as well as to illustrate the earlier impact of the English law and constitutional principles of judicial independence on the U.S. Constitution and other legal cultures in developing judicial independence. I have elsewhere classified this process as the normative cycle of international and national law in the area of judicial independence.[1] International law influences domestic law by virtue of international human rights treaties which provide for principles of fair procedures and for the right to be tried before an impartial and independent tribunal. In addition to international treaties, there are international standards which non-governmental and academic study groups have developed. One such recent project is the Mt. Scopus International Standards of Judicial Independence ("Mt. Scopus Standards").[2]

The principle of judicial independence is one of the fundamental values of the administration of justice. These values include procedural fairness, efficiency, accessibility and public confidence in the courts. In addition, there is a requirement that the fundamental values, including judicial independence should be protected by constitutional provisions, not only by legislative

---

[1] Shetreet, "The Normative Cycle of Shaping Judicial Independence in Domestic and International Law: The Mutual Impact of National and International Jurisprudence and Contemporary Practical and Conceptual Challenges" (2009) 10 Chicago J. of International Law 275–332 (hereinafter: Shetreet's Normative Cycle).

[2] Mt. Scopus International Standards of Judicial Independence (Mar 19, 2008), see Appendix I of this volume (hereinafter: Mt. Scopus Standards).

provisions. This chapter will examine the conceptual foundations of the principle of judicial independence, and will analyse the necessary essential elements of a culture of judicial independence. In addition to the concept of judicial independence, this chapter will analyse the principle of democratic accountability and the proper relations between the Judiciary, the Executive and the Legislature.

The culture of judicial independence can only exist in a system which is based on the doctrine of separation of powers. After it is established, the contituation of judicial independence is not a matter of course. It is constantly subject to challenges, sometimes by other branches of government, and at other times as a result of different types of internal circumstances. In the course of the analysis of the relations between the Judiciary and other branches of government, a number of topics will be examined in this chapter, including retroactive reversal of judicial decisions by legislation, or the introduction of delegated legislation by the Exucitve in matters pending before the court. Attention will be also paid to the analysis of the preferred model of the proper relationship between the judiciary and the other branches of the government. This chapter will also analyse the issue of the role of courts in society, and the proper boundaries of judicial functions. The chapter offers a classification of judicial activism which includes: constitutional activism that relates to judicial activism in judicial review of parliamentary legislation and the promotion of human rights and civil rights. Judicial activism is exercised in other areas of law, including activism in administrative law, private law and criminal law.

The analysis in this chapter demonstrates the need to develop principles for fine tuning of judicial role in society. This process of fine tuning should demarcate the proper boundaries between the judiciary and the other branches of government. Important tools for this process are the doctrine of justiciabitly and the right of standing. A complimentary test for fine tuning of the judicial function is the test of substantial disruption of the proper boundaries between judicial functions and functions of the other branches of the government. The Judiciary must not interfere in a matter, when such judicial intervention will bring about such a substantial disruption of relations between the branches of government.

II. Creating Culture of Judicial Independence in Domestic Law Perspectives

The culture of judicial independence in every jurisdiction is based on a number of levels: the institutional level, which regulates the matters relative to status of the judges and jurisdiction of the courts, the constitutional level which embodies in a constitution the institutional aspects and ensures that the independence of the judiciary shall not be adversely affected by legislation or by Executive action. An additional level is the legislative level, which regulates in detail the constitutional principles, and lastly – the adjudicative level, which is the jurisprudence of the courts, which provides for interpretation and additional elements in all the levels. From the review of court decisions on the matter of judicial independence, it is possible to observe the rules and elements that each country is forging in order to create culture of judicial independence and maintain this culture.

Those who are responsible for formulating and creating the culture of judicial independence are the political leaders, who are responsible also for preserving the culture after it is shaped, and the judges, whose role is expressed in adjudication, in court decisions, and also in laying down appropriate ethical rules and in playing a role in the judicial selection and judicial appointments. Sometimes, judges are also involved in court administration and also assist in the creation of the constitutional infrastructure and the constitutional framework for the judiciary.

The culture of judicial independence in each jurisdiction must facilitate and ensure judicial independence in the substantive adjudication both in public and constitutional law, as well as in the private law in all its aspects and branches. In addition, the culture of judicial independence must ensure institutional and administrative functioning of the judiciary as an institution as well as the substantive and administrative functioning of the individual judge.

In the ensuing discussion it is proposed to analyse the various arrangements that jurisdictions normally provide for the purpose of creating a culture of judicial independence. These arrangements will illustrate the various models that countries have used to ensure the creation and the maintenance of the culture of judicial independence.

The process of building a culture of judicial independence is long and gradual. This process may make significant changes in the judicial branch and might demand changes and cooperation of the other branches of government. The development of self-judicial governance in the United States Federal Judiciary is a good example for such a gradual process for building a culture of judicial independence.[3] It took one hundred and forty years for the

[3] For a detailed description of this process, see: Markus Zimmer, "Judicial Independence in Central and East Europe: The Institutional Context" (2006–2007) 14 Tulsa. J. Comp. & Int'l L 53–87, at pp. 62–69.

United States Federal Judiciary to undergo a process of a gradual change from being under total control of the Executive to attaining the stage of self-judicial governance system.

In the beginning of the process, the administration of the federal judiciary and the courts was governed by the Department of Treasury.[4] Later, in 1849, governance over the judicial branch was entrusted to the Department of the Interior.[5] In the next stage, in 1870, governance was transferred to the Department of Justice.[6] Seventy years later, in 1939, responsibility for the administration of courts and judges was transferred from the Executive to the Judicial branch.[7] A few years later, in 1948, the Judicial Conference of the United States was established.[8]

The process of building self-judicial governance has to be gradual, as it requires a long process of education, both on the professional level and the political level. Self-judicial governance means control of the Judiciary over the judicial system. This control includes budgeting, financial managing, managing human resources and managing of a large system. It also includes the professional management, such as managing case assignment, engaging in rulemaking of the procedures of the courts and enforcing these procedural rules. Likewise, judicial self-governance includes the development and the enforcement of judicial ethics and a code of conduct. In order for the Judiciary to engage in self-governance, it should have a wide diversity of abilities. Administrative abilities are required for managing the system of justice. Self governance also requires the judiciary to act in coordination with the other branches of government. In addition to these abilities, self-judicial governance requires a Judiciary which has financial qualifications. Another area of responsibility in the administration of courts is the security and safety.

In countries where dramatic changes in the system of government or in the economic system were introduced, it is very important to develop a culture of judicial independence to help the society and the branches of government to adopt to the new constitutional system of government or to the new economic system which is based on the free market. This was the situation in Poland, when it changed from a communist system of government, to a constitutional democratic system of government.[9] The proper functioning of government

[4] See: Act of Mar. 3, 1849, ch. 98, 9 Stat. 395 (1849)
[5] *ibid.*
[6] *See:* Act of June 22, 1870, ch. 150, 16 Stat. 162 (1870).
[7] See: Act of Aug. 7, 1939, ch. 501, 53 Stat. 1223 (1939).
[8] See: 28 U.S.C. §331 (2000).
[9] For a detailed analysis of the subject of Poland, See: Tomaz Wardynski & Magdalena Niziotek (eds.), *Independence of the Judiciary and Legal Profession as Foundations of the Rule of the Law: Contemporary Challenges* (LexisNexis 2009, English version begins at pp. 310).

branches and the development of a culture of Rule of Law in societies which are at the transition period of post-communism, depends very much on the ability to create an independent judiciary, which is assisted by the independent legal profession.[10] Similarly, the courts and the legal profession play a very important role in the first formative years of independent countries in developing areas of the world.[11] A similar situation was seen in China which moved to a free market economy.[12]

Part of the culture of judicial independence in all countries is the maintaining of traditions and rules that ensure independence of the legal profession, and independence of the prosecutors.[13]

1. *Institutional Structures*

Institutional structures ensuring judicial independence must be provided in a number of aspects regarding the relations of the Judiciary and the Legislature and the Executive. Debate in the legislature on judges and on the judiciary are legitimate and are even required as part of the legislative function of supervising and controlling the other branches of government including the administration of justice. Some of the debates concern the legitimate interest in the protection of judicial independence and the proper functioning of the courts. Other legislative debates on the judiciary in most jurisdictions are critical of the judiciary, and generally deal with legal matters which are at the centre of public controversies. Normally, in most jurisdictions there is no statutory provision prohibiting the debate of pending cases in courts, but there are self-rules in parliaments which restrain parliamentary debates on pending cases. My own view is that there is no justification for preventing public debates in parliament on pending cases, if such a debate does not adversely affect the right of the parties to the litigation. The proper model is to formulate a rule that will

---

[10] See: Stawceki, "Independence of the Legal Professions and the Rule of Law in Post-Communist Society", *in ibid.*

[11] See: Henderson, "Halfway Home and a Long Way to Go: China's Rule of Law Evolution and the Global Road to Judicial Independence, Judicial Impartiality, and Judicial Integrity", *in* Randall Peerenboom (ed), *Judicial Independence in China: Lessons for Global Rule of Law Promotion* (Cambridge University Press, 2010); De-Silva, "The Role of Law in Society in Developing Countries", Chapter 31 of this volume. For an analysis of the difficulties in creating proper standards of judicial conduct and proper relationships between the judiciary and the political leadership, see: Forsyth, "The Failure of Institutions: The South African Judicial Service Commission and the Hlophe Saga", chapter 3 of this volume.

[12] For a detailed analysis of the case of China, see: Judicial Independence In China, *ibid.*

[13] See: Independence of the Judiciary and Legal Profession, note 10 above; Also see: Shetreet, "Independence and Responsibility of Judges and Lawyers", General Report to the 1991 International Congress of the World Association on Procedural Law in Role and Organisation of Judges and Lawyers in Contemporary Societies, *Papers of the IXth Conference of World Association on Procedural Law*, pp. 119–186 (Coimbra-Lisboa 1991).

balance between the conflicting interests. One is the principle of separation of powers, and the other is legislative sovereignty and the importance of public debates on matters of vital public importance. There are also parliamentary internal rules excluding the debate on a specific judge. However these rules have not prevented in fact parliamentary criticism of specific judges.[14] The proper view on parliamentary or legislative criticism of specific judges is that the Legislature should be permitted to engage in criticism subject to proper style and good taste. Legislative criticism is desirable and is a proper exercise of the principle of democratic accountability of the judiciary.

Judicial independence is maintained by proper methods of judicial selection and appointments, as well as careful regulations of the procedure and grounds for judicial discipline and removal. Likewise, a careful and secure provision for the age of retirement is a necessary constitutional requirement. According to the Mt. Scopus Standards of Judicial Independence it is proper for the Executive and the Legislature to take part in the judicial selection process.[15] These international standards require special concern for meritorial considerations and respect for judicial independence. However, they do not exclude participation in this process by the Legislative and Executive branches. The standards regulate the conditions for discipline and removal of judges and their retirement age.[16] From time to time, legislatures in some jurisdictions have interfered in

---

[14] For English examples see: Shetreet, *Judges on Trial: A Study on the Appointment and Accountability of the English Judiciary* (North Holland 1976), pp. 162–178. For Israeli example, see criticism on the Eichmann trial decisions while the case was still pending in: Shetreet, *Culture of Judicial Independence in Israel: Substantive and Institutional Aspects of the Judiciary in Historical Perspectives* (2009) 10 Law and Business 525 (Hebrew. hereinafter: Shetreet, Law and Business).

[15] Mt. Scopus Standards of Judicial Independence provide that:

> 2.4 Judicial appointments and promotions by the Executive are not inconsistent with judicial independence as long as they are in accordance with Principles 4, And regarding the legislator role.
> 2.14 The principle of democratic accountability should be respected and therefore it is legitimate for the legislature to play a role in judicial appointments and central administration of justice provided that due consideration is given to the principle of judicial independence.

[16] Mt. Scopus Standards of Judicial Independence provide that:

> 4.3 Judicial appointments should generally be for life, subject to removal for cause and compulsory retirement at an age fixed by law at the date of appointment. And
> 4.3.1 Retirement age shall not be reduced for existing judges.
> 4.2 a) The principle of democratic accountability should be respected and therefore it is legitimate for the Executive and the Legislature to play a role in judicial appointments provided that due consideration is given to the principle of Judicial Independence.
> b) The recent trend of establishing judicial selection boards or commissions in which members or representatives of the Legislature, the Executive, the Judiciary and the legal profession take part, should be viewed favourably, provided that a proper balance

judicial independence by changing the tenure or retirement age of judges. For example, in 1973, judicial tenure in Uruguay was abolished.[17] In Bangladesh retirement age was changed to bring about the end of term of service of two specific judges.[18] This is the reason why the International Standards of Judicial Independence regulate specifically the retirement age.[19]

Another example comes from Ecuador, where on April 24, 2007, all nine judges of Ecuador's Constitutional Court were removed following an unpopular ruling. The removal was executed by a congressional vote lacking any legal basis. According to Ecuadorian law, the Constitutional Court's judges are removable only by impeachment. Still, this was the third time in three years that judges were removed by Congress.[20] Another example is the case in Russia regarding the president of the Constitutional Court, which we shall refer as the Zorkin-Yeltsin affair. After the collapse of the Soviet Union, the constitutional court was led by Chief Justice Valery Zorkin in several cases involving the transition of rule from the Soviet to the post-Soviet era. These cases were controversial, and included both an invalidation of one of President Yeltsin's decrees and a finding that Yeltsin's actions were unconstitutional. In response to these and other decisions, Yeltsin shut down the constutional court for several years. When it reopened, Valery Zorkin remained with the court. However, the court's perspective was notably different after its reopening: it began to regularly agree with government actions.[21] An important aspect of building a culture of judicial independence refers to the composition of the judiciary. The selection of judges must respect the principle of reflective judiciary.[22]

---

is maintained in the composition of such boards or commissions of each of the branches of government.

[17] See Shetreet, *Judicial Independence: New Conceptual Dimensions and Contemporary Challenges*, in Shimon Shetreet and Jules Deschênes (eds.), *Judicial Independence: The Contemporary Debate* 591, at pp. 607 (Martinus Nijhoff 1985. Hereinafter: Shetreet, The Contemporary Debate).

[18] See Shetreet, Judicial Independence, *ibid.*

[19] §4.3 of Mt. Scopus Standards.

[20] Human Rights Watch, *Ecuador: Removal of Judges Undermines Judicial Independence* (May 10, 2007), available online at: http://www.hrw.org/en/news/2007/05/10/ecuador-removal-judges-undermines-judicial-independence. (Visited Oct 23, 2010).

[21] Tushnet, *Leadership in Constitutional Courts*, Conference Materials, Krakow (Mar 2008).

[22] See Justice Dobbs, *The Judge and the Defendant: Demographics and Diversity in the Criminal Justice System*, New Developments in Criminal Justice Lecture at King's College London (April 24, 2008), available at: http://www.google.com/url?sa=t&source=web&cd=1&ved=0CBIQFjAA&url=http%3A%2F%2Fwww.crimeandjustice.org.uk%2Fopus619%2FDobbs_speech_24_April_2008.doc&rct=j&q=The%20Judge%20and%20the%20Defendant%3A%20Demographics%20and%20Diversity%20in%20the%20Criminal%20Justice%20System&ei=tDXDTM_JN4nKswbSzpzYCA&usg=AFQjCNFBTse5YDmgqrVq36-QMDjEMERK4A: "By being reflective of society, the courts are given legitimacy. Members of society are more likely to respect and trust courts whose judges include people like themselves. It increases accountability and thus public confidence."; See also the Mt. Scopus Standards:

Personal judicial independence is secured by the provision of appropriate and adequate remuneration protected from undue interference by the Executive or by the Legislature, not related to previously established standards. This does not mean that judicial salaries cannot be affected by general economic measures which are applied to the whole country in situations of austerity.[23] This issue was a centre of controversy in 1931 in England when the judges argued that they should not be included in the measures requiring the reduction of the salaries of all public servants.[24] The judges were right that they were not included in the term "persons in His Majesty's service". However, in terms of general approach, judges should not be excepted from general economic measures applied to all the sectors of the public service.

One of the central issues in which conflict arises between the judicial branch and the Executive branch is the responsibility for the courts' administration. In this matter, a number of central points have to be noted. An important principle is that the Executive should not have control of judicial functions or matters regarding the judicial process, such as case assignment, scheduling of trials, judges' vacations and determination of salaries of specific judges. Whereas the Executive cannot have control of matters of court level, it may have control of the central level and powers over court administration. This includes budgeting, housing of courts and alike. The Executive controls at the central level of court administration and judicial matters, must be exercised with utmost care for judicial independence, to avoid adverse effects on matters that relate directly to judges and judicial affairs.[25]

> 2.15: The process and standards of judicial selection shall give due consideration to the principle of fair reflection by the judiciary of the society in all its aspects.
> 2.15.1: Taking into consideration the principle of fair reflection by the judiciary of the society in all its aspects, in the selection of judges, there shall be no discrimination on the grounds of race, colour, gender, language, religion, national or social origin, property, birth or status, subject however to citizenship requirements.
> For a discussion on surveys of social background of judges in England see: The Judiciary: The Report of a Justice Sub-Committee on the Judiciary (1972), based on an unpublished Master's dissertation by Jenny Brock.

[23] Mt. Scopus Standards of Judicial Independence provide that:

> 2.22: Judicial salaries, pensions, and benefits cannot be decreased during judges' service except as a coherent part of an overall public economic measure.

[24] Shetreet *Judges on Trial*, note 14 above, at pp. 67.

[25] Mt. Scopus Standards of Judicial Independence provide that:

> 2.12 Judicial matters are exclusively within the responsibility of the Judiciary, both in central judicial administration and in court level judicial administration.

Also see: Shetreet, "Judicial Independence: New Conceptual Dimensions and Contemporary Challenges", note 17 above, at pp. 611–612.

There have been cases in a number of jurisdictions of members of the Executive interfering in judicial proceedings. This could happen in the form of public statements violently criticizing a decision of a judge. Such was the case in the Canadian 1976 judges' affair.[26] Critical statements by the Executive of judicial decisions is frequent and widespread in many jurisdictions and the proper response is a proper service of the courts that will provide a timely and detailed response by the relevant judicial officer to the criticism of the Executive or public officer.

Judges must be separated from the Legislature and the Executive and cannot assume legislative or executive functions. However, from time to time, judges are asked to assist in functions that have strong association with the Executive. Such a practice is the appointment of judges to head committees for the study of the revision of legislation. More frequently, judges are required to head public inquiries into issues of vital importance. The principle of separation of powers requires the total detachment between the Judiciary and the Executive. A judge, who is engaged in an executive function, is subject to the Executive in performing this function. Although this situation is temporary, it is inconsistent with the judicial function, which requires total independence and impartiality of the judge in adjudicating disputes between the citizen and the Executive branch. Even though in fact the judge is qualified to distinguish between his executive function and his judicial function, the appearance of independence and impartiality may be affected in the eyes of the public. This may adversely affect public confidence in the independence and impartiality of the judiciary.

The judges may not serve in legislative or Executive functions. Specifically they should not be ministers of the government, nor can they be members of the Legislature or municipal councils, and they should not hold positions in political parties.[27]

---

[26] See the statement of minister Ullet which stated that the decision of the Canadian judge was stupid, and the consequence of this statement. Willet had to quit due to public pressure. See: Russel, *The Judiciary in Canada – The Third Branch of Government* (McGraw-Hill Ryerson 1987), pp. 78–81. There were a number of cases in Israel where there was an attempt to influence the judges in highly publicized cases, for reports see the cases of: *Shalit* (HCJ 58/68 *Shalit v. Minister for Interior Affairs*, 23(2) PD 477, 505), *Abuhazeira* (CrA. 5/82 *Abuhazeira v. State of Israel*, 36(1) PD 247), *The Jewish underground* (HCJ 144/50 *Scheib v. Minister of Defence*, 5 PD 399), *the medical center in Hertzelia* (HCJ 256/88 *Medinvest Medical Center-Herzliya Ltd. v. The Director-General of the Ministry of Health*, 44(1) PD 19). See also: Shimon Shetreet, *Justice in Israel: A Study of the Israeli Judiciary* (Martinus Nijhoff 1994), chapters 6, 8 and 21.

[27] Mt. Scopus Standards of Judicial Independence provide that:

> 7.1 Judges may not serve in Executive or Legislative functions, including as:
> 7.1.1 Ministers of the government; or as
> 7.1.2 Members of the Legislature or of municipal councils.
> 7.2 Judges shall not hold positions in political parties.

The exclusion of judges from assuming Executive functions or legislative functions, does not apply only to official appointments as Ministers or MPs, but also to judges assuming special tasks on behalf of the state or temporary positions which are associated with the Legislative or the Executive.

The involvement of Justice Aharon Barak in Israel, in the peace negotiations conducted by Prime Minister Begin in Camp David in 1978 where the Israeli-Egyptian peace agreement was forged was criticized as improper involvement of a judge in an Executive function.[28]

Another example from earlier period in the United Kingdom is Lord Reading, who was Lord Chief Justice of England, and during his term of office took part in a delegation to raise funds in the United States in 1918. Likewise, while serving as Lord Chief Justice he served as British ambassador to the United States.[29] This would be unthinkable in modern practice.

The exception is when the law expressly provides that a judge may exercise a certain extra judicial function such as serving as members or presiding over commissions of inquiry. This is a very widespread practice in many jurisdictions.[30]

The principle of separation of the judiciary from the other branches of government requires that there should be post-judicial restrictions after a judge retires or resigns from the bench. There should be a cooling-off period before the judge could assume legislative or Executive function. Equally, it is desirable that there should be a cooling-off period between the end of service in a legislative or Executive function before assuming a judicial office. This cooling-off period should not be too long, but should serve the purpose of separating of the branches in the eyes of the public.[31] This rule should be a customary rule and not rigid statutory restriction. The restrictions on judges do not only apply to association of judges with the Executive or the Legislature. Judges are also excluded from engaging in business or in remunerative business.[32]

---

[28] Shetreet, "Judge on a Political Mission", Haaretz 25.10.78 (Hebrew).

[29] Shetreet *Judges on Trial*, note 14 above, at pp. 351–352.

[30] For British examples see: Lord Hutton inquiry of Dr. David Kelly's death, available at: http://www.the-hutton-inquiry.org.uk/content/rulings.htm (Visited: Oct 23, 2010), and see also Justice Jackson Review of Civil Litigation Costs, available at: http://www.judiciary.gov.uk/NR/rdonlyres/8EB9F3F3-9C4A-4139-8A93-56F09672EB6A/0/jacksonfinalreport140110.pdf (Visited: Oct 23, 2010). For Israeli examples see: Justice Shamgar (1st) inquiry on the massacre in the Patriarchs Tomb, Justice Shamgar (2nd) inquiry on the assassination of prime-minister Rabin, Justice Cohen inquiry on the kidnapping of Yemenite children, and Justice Or inquiry on the October 2000 clashes.

[31] A judge, other than a temporary or part-time judge, may not practice law. See also: Shetreet "Who Will Judge – Reflections on the Process and Standards of Judicial Selections" 61 Aust. L. J. (1987) 766.

[32] Mt. Scopus Standards of Judicial Independence provide that:

2. *Constitutional Infrastructure*

In a country where a culture of judicial independence exists, there is a formal constitutional framework and legislative framework which protects the position of the judiciary. This framework regulates central principles which relate to the operation of the courts and the conduct of judges and embodies them in a constitution. This aims to regulate the position of the judges and their independence. The scope of the details of this arrangement in each jurisdiction is different; however, there are a number of matters which are normally regulated in the constitution. These include the qualification of judges, the process of their appointment, the rules of discipline and such additional matters which are necessary to secure their independence.

In order to achieve this purpose it is important to lay down the principles of judicial independence in the constitution. This provision ensures and enhances the independence of the judiciary.[33]

The American Founding Fathers adhered to the doctrine of separation of powers in the US Constitution. They adopted the doctrine of checks and balances, based on the concept that no function of one branch of government should be exercised by another branch and that each branch should function as a check on any improper use of power by the other branches.

The Founding Fathers wished to ensure judicial independence. The Declaration of Independence charged George III with making "Judges dependent on his Will alone, for the tenure of their offices, and the amount and payment of their salaries."[34] The foundations of judicial independence are laid out in Article III of the US Constitution, which states that "[t]he Judges, both of the supreme and inferior Courts, shall hold their Offices during good Behaviour, and shall, at stated Times, receive for their Services a Compensation which shall not be diminished during their Continuance in Office."[35]

This is a very classic illustration of the embodiment of the independence of the judiciary in a formal constitution. This is not always the case. A number of countries provide judicial independence in the legislative level rather than the constitutional level which is not the desirable position. By judicial interpretation

---

7.4 A judge should refrain from business activities **and should avoid from engaging in** other **remunerative activity**, that can affect the exercise of judicial functions or the image of the judge, except in respect of that judge's personal investments, ownership of property, the business activities or ownership of property of family members**, or** that judge's **teaching at a university or a college.**

[33] For the Israeli section see section 2 of the Basic Law: The Judiciary, which provides that there is no authority on the judge except the authority of the law. See Shetreet, On Adjudication: Justice on Trial, chapter 8, p.208 (Yediot Aharonot, Hemed 2004) hereinafter Shetreet, On Adjudication.)

[34] United States Declaration of Independence (1776).

[35] US Const., art. III.

the courts accord to this legislative provisions semi-constitutional status as is the case in Israel.[36]

3. *Legislative Provisions and Constitutional Safeguards*

It must be recognized that certain matters should be regulated in the constitution whereas others may be regulated by ordinary legislation. When a matter is regulated in ordinary legislation, the legislature can introduce an amendment by simple majority. In contrast, the protection granted by the constitution is modifiable only by a constitutional amendment. An example of the importance of regulating substantive issues in the constitution occurred during the controversy over New Deal legislation, US President Franklin Roosevelt attempted to pack the court—increasing the number of judges—which he could do by ordinary legislation.[37]

In addition to general constitutional protections of judicial independence, a more detailed constitutional protection should include six fundamental substantive principles.[38]

In England, the very important step to provide judicial independence was made in 1701, in the Act of Settlement. For centuries, the king was an absolute monarch and thus the source of all governmental and political power. Judges were an integral part of the Royal administration. There was an obscure distinction between judicial and administrative duties.[39] The king enjoyed the cooperation of the judiciary, which was widely accepted. The sovereign did not seek to use judges as instruments in political struggles.[40] In that period, it was obvious that judges were not independent.

The issue in the struggle between Parliament and the Crown was security of tenure. However, it was not until the Act of Settlement in 1701 that an important measure of security was finally guaranteed.[41]

The Act of Settlement provided for judges to be appointed during good behaviour (*quam diu se benegesserint*) and for their salaries to be ascertained

---

[36] See: Shetreet, Law and Business, note 14 above, at pp. 547

[37] Carson and Kleinerman, "A Switch in Time Saves Nine: Institutions, Strategic Actors, and FDR's Court-Packing Plan" (2002) 113 Pub Choice 301; Nelson, "The President and the Court: Reinterpreting the Court-Packing Episode of 1937" (1988) 103 Pol Sci Q 267; Caldeira, "Public Opinion and The US Supreme Court: FDR's Court-Packing Plan" (1987) 81 Am Pol Sci Rev 1139. For cases dealing with issues of judicial independence in the United States, see: *United States v Will*, 449 US 200 (1980); *Chandler v. Judicial Council*, 398 U.S. 74 (1970).

[38] See section IV of this article.

[39] Shetreet, *Judges on Trial*, note 14 above, at pp. 2.

[40] *Ibid.* See also Sir William Searle Holdsworth, *A History of English Law* (Sweet & Maxwell, 2d ed., 1937) at pp. 347.

[41] Act for the Further Limitation of the Crown, 12 & 13, Will 3, ch 2, 10 Statutes at Large at 360.

and established, but upon the address of both Houses of Parliament it may be lawful to remove them. Judicial tenure was still not yet completely secured. It took the initiative of George III in 1760 to help secure the term of judicial office beyond the lifetime of the monarch so that neither the King nor Parliament would be capable of attaining their particular political objectives or ambitions by exercising control over the decisions of the judiciary. The King could no longer dismiss every judge at his pleasure, nor could Parliament attain its own ends by an equally preemptory and almost as effective withdrawal of livelihood.[42]

The modern formula evolved from the consolidation of the Act of Settlement and the said 1760 Act. Section 12(1) of the Supreme Court of Judicature (Consolidation) Act of 1925, which is the modern formulation of the historical development, stated: "All the judges of the High Court and of the Court of Appeal, with the exception of the Lord Chancellor, shall hold their offices during good behaviour, subject to a power of removal by His Majesty on an address to His Majesty by both Houses of Parliament."[43]

Yet, the situation in 1760 was in need of further change, because the system relied on litigants' fees for judicial remuneration, which left the system open to abuse and misconduct. The salary became substantial, and a prohibition against supplementing it was added only at a later stage. In this way, "[t]he additional sources of income were eliminated in a very long gradual evolution extending over three centuries."[44]

An important development affecting judicial independence was the fundamental reform of the Courts Act of 1971,[45] introduced on the recommendations of the Beeching Commission Report.[46] The Courts Act eliminated centuries of local control over courts, established a new class of judges, called circuit judges, set up an administrative hierarchy across the country, and made court personnel a part of the national civil service. The Act, which restructured the criminal court system in England, has been described as a "radical, even a spectacular reform".[47] However, this reform carried with it mixed blessings for the independence of the judiciary in England. While it promoted judicial independence by reducing the dependence of the criminal justice system on part-time judges, the centralization of judicial administration in England

[42] *Beauregard*, 130 DLR 3d 433.
[43] Act of 1925, 15 & 16 Geo 5, ch. 49 (Eng).
[44] Shetreet, *Judges on Trial*, note 14 above, at pp. 11.
[45] Courts Act 1971, ch 23 (1971) (UK), available online at: http://www.opsi.gov.uk/acts/acts1971/pdf/ukpga_19710023_en.pdf (visited Oct 23, 2010).
[46] Lord Beeching, *Royal Commission on Assizes and Quarter Sessions, 1966–1969*, Cmnd 4153 (HMSO 1969).
[47] Lord Hailsham, 312 Hl Deb 1247 (Nov 19, 1970).

brought increased Executive control and thus posed a challenge to judicial independence.[48] This was to be resolved only three decades later in the Constitutional Reform Act and the additional arrangements regarding the establishment of the Courts Service.

In Israel there is a wide debate on the normative level of the provisions relative to judicial independence in the Basic Law: The Judiciary and in the ordinary legislation.[49] It has been suggested that even when ordinary legislation regulates matters relative to judges and courts, they should be viewed as norms of higher level than ordinary legislation. Thus, it has been argued that judicial independence, being one of the fundamental principles of the system of government enjoys higher normative value, even if it is regulated in regular normative legislation. This approach is supported by recourse to international law and jurisprudence on the subject in various jurisdictions.[50]

4. *Adjudicative Arrangements and Jurisprudence*

Court decisions serve the purpose of bridging the gaps which constitutional provisions or legislative provisions leave unanswered. The jurisprudence of the courts contributes significantly to the creation of the culture of judicial independence. In the following analysis we shall offer a number of examples of how jurisprudence in several countries provided for interpretation of the constitution and of legislation in a way that contributed to the building of culture of judicial independence. This was done with regard to a number of aspects that are necessary and meaningful for building this culture of judicial independence. It is noteworthy that in the 17th century there was a conflict between two schools of thought in the courts in England. The Act of Settlement settled the conflicting approaches, as well as the struggle between the King and the Parliament.[51]

In *Valente v. the Queen,* one of Canada's central cases concerning judicial independence, the Supreme Court of Canada listed three major components

---

[48] Lord Lane, *Judicial Independence and the Increasing Executive Role in Judicial Administration*, *in* Shetreet, The Contemporary Debate, note 17 above, at pp. 525–28

[49] See Basic Law: The Judiciary, and see section 15(c) which regulates the jurisdiction of the high court of justice to adjudicate any matters which it sees necessary to give remedy for the sake of justice and which are not in the jurisdiction of any other court or any other tribunal. See the case of *Herut*, and the case of *The Forum co-existence in the Negev*, see Shetreet, Law and Business, note 14 above, at pp. 25.

[50] See: Barak, *Interpretation in Law – Constitutional interpretation* (Hebrew. Nevo 1993), Vol. 3, pp. 411–435; Shetreet, Law and Business, note 14 above, at pp. 547; Shetreet's Normative Cycle, note 1 above. Also see: Canadian Charter of Rights and Freedoms, Part I of the Constitution Act, 1982, Art.11(d).

[51] See above.

of judicial independence,[52] security of tenure, financial security, and institutional independence. The Court clarified that judicial independence needs to be considered in a dual perspective, objective and subjective. The subjective perspective looks at whether a common person would perceive in any particular situation that judicial independence exists.

One of the most significant components for the preservation of the independence of the judiciary, which the supreme court of Canada emphasized, was the terms of service of the judges. When judicial salaries are subjected to the discretion of the other branches of government which can interfere in the terms of service and salaries, this creates a perception of dependence. However, in a number of countries there was a need to introduce changes in the conditions of service of the judges. As a result, the judiciary was faced with the challenge of adjudicating and resolving this issue. For example, in the Canadian case of *Beauregard v. The Queen*[53] it was ruled that not every change in the condition of the service of the judges is unconstitutional. In certain circumstances a change can be legitimate, for example, when a reduction or freezing of previously approved salary increase is made as a general economic austerity measure. In 1985 this matter was debated in Israel and it was agreed that the possibility of reducing the salaries of judges in the framework of a general austerity measure is acceptable. It is so provided in section 10 of the Basic Law: The Judiciary.[54]

When the issue arose whether the judges can adjudicate the constitutionality of a decrease of judicial salary when they are affected by such a ruling, it was decided in *United States v. Will*[55] that despite of the fact that judges are adjudicating in a matter that relates to their own conditions they should not be disqualified because of the rule of necessity. This is because there is no other forum that could adjudicate this matter.

It is known that legal proceedings continue for long periods of time, due to several reasons, and so there are attempts to increase the efficiency of the system. But too much emphasis on efficiency might affect the quality of the judicial process.[56] In the case of *Chandler*,[57] the United States Courts had to resolve

[52] *Valente v. The Queen*, [1985] 2 S.C.R. 673.

[53] *Beauregard v. The Queen* [1986] 2 S.C.R. 5

[54] See Basic Laws of Israel: The Judiciary §10, available online at: http://www.knesset.gov.il/laws/special/eng/basic8_eng.htm (Visited Oct 23, 2010). See also Shetreet, *Justice in Israel*, note 26 above, at chapter 4.

[55] *United States v. Will*, 449 US 200 (1980).

[56] Shetreet, "Basic Principles of the Reform: Thoughts of the Judicial System Image in the Future Based on the Study of Present Problems" (1999) 8 Mechkarei Mishpat 59 (Hebrew).

[57] *Chandler v. Judicial Council*, note 37 above. For a detailed discussion see: Shetreet, "The Administration of Justice: Practical Problems, Value Conflicts and. Changing Concepts" (1979) 13 University of British Columbia Law Review 52–80.

a conflict between efficiency and judicial independence. The matter arose when the Judicial Conference for the Ninth Circuit ordered that no cases would be assigned to Judge Chandler until he finished his backlog. The United States Supreme Court rejected Chandler's case on the grounds that it was legitimate for the Judicial Conference to regulate the allocation of cases and for efficiency purposes it may order that for a certain period cases should not be assigned to the judge with a backlog. Similar controversies regarding assignment of cases arose in other jurisdictions such as in Germany.[58]

The tension between efficient judicial administration and judicial independence was a matter of concern to Israeli former judge Avigdor Mishali, who said after his retirement from the District Court: "The amount of files is insufferable...Many times you can't dedicate the time that you should, and you – not willingly – do things normally you wouldn't, if you considered the case more calmly...".[59] Isgav Nakdimon, another former Israeli judge, resigned due to the excessive amount of cases a judge has to adjudicate. This situation does not allow him to give the proper consideration for each case.[60]

5. *Ethical Traditions and Code of Judicial Conduct*[61]

In the process of decision-making, judges should be free from irrelevant controls, both overt and covert. Two dimensions of this principle should be recognized. First, there is a significant social interest in attaining actual impartiality and neutrality of the judge. Second, but no less important, there is the appearance of the impartiality and neutrality of the judge. The necessity of maintaining not only impartiality, but also the appearance of impartiality, is mandated by the value of public confidence in the courts and the judges and in the judicial process.[62] From this emanates a theoretical approach, which requires the creation of an envelope of rules which covers the judge and protects the judge's substantive independence. This envelope of rules covers the judge's official and non-official spheres of activities, and shields the judge's substantive independence from dependencies, associations, and

---

[58] Shetreet, The Contemporary Debate, note 17 above.

[59] Cited in Shetreet, On Adjudiciation, note 33 above, at pp. 192. See also M. Agmon Gonen, Judical Independence A Threat From Within, 38 ISR. Law Rev. 120 (2005).

[60] "6 months after being appointed, judge Nakdimon declared: I am not able to fulfill my duties due to the amount of cases I have to adjudicate", Haaretz 30.06.10.

[61] See The Guide to Judicial Conduct, available at http://www.judiciary.gov.uk/publications-and-reports/guidance/guide-to-judicial-conduct (Visited Oct 23, 2010). also see: *Revised Draft of Proposed New Canon to American Bar Association's Model Code of Judicial Conduct* (2005), available at: http://www.abanet.org/media/releases/news060105.html (Visited Oct 23, 2010).

[62] See *Regina v. Bow Street Metropolitan Stipendiary Magistrate and Others, Ex Parte Pinochet Ugarte* (no. 2), [2000] 1 A.C. 119, in which a first judgment was set aside on the ground of bias.

even less intensive involvements which might cast doubt on judicial neutrality.[63]

Thus we find a series of protective rules, some of which restrict judicial conduct, and others which restrict the conduct of others when they relate to judges. For instance, there are restrictive rules of conduct excluding judges from association with the other branches of the government, limiting their business associations, and excluding them from matters of public controversy and matters which might put into question the dignity and the integrity of the judiciary.

> In this context, it is noteworthy that the standards of judicial conduct in civil law countries tend to be very permissive in terms of political activities of judges. This is in sharp contrast to the rather restrictive standards prevailing in common law countries.[64] Similar trends are also seen in relation to the nature of professional associations of judges. In civil law countries judicial associations tend to resemble trade unions, whereas this unionization trend is absent in common law countries.[65]

International standards generally forbid all political activities for judges in office, with the exception of mere membership in a political party. A fairly large number of countries prohibit all forms of political involvement, and allow only a passive party-membership. The compromise is expressed in the Mt. Scopus Standards, reflecting directives from the earlier IBA Standards which states that judges may not hold positions in political parties, except where such practice is supported by a long and democratic tradition.

The international standards provide for guidelines regarding the engagement of a judge in a case where he used to be advisor, defendants' counsel and alike.[66]

---

[63] For an analysis of the rules of judicial conduct in the American context, see J.P. MacKenzie, *The Appearance of Justice* (Charles Scribner's Sons 1974); and, in the English context, see Shetreet, *Judges on Trial*, note 14 above, at pp. 269–377.

[64] Shetreet, "Judicial Independence: New Conceptual Dimensions", note 17 above, at 630–632.

[65] Section 7 of The Mt. Scopus Standards direct that judges may not serve in executive or legislative functions, including serving as ministers of the government, members of the legislature, or in municipal councils. Section 7 also forbids judges from holding positions in political parties, and provides that judges should refrain from remunerative activities as well as other activities that can affect the exercise of judicial functions or the judges' image.

[66] Mt. Scopus Standards of Judicial Independence provide that:

> 18.1 Judges shall not serve in a case in which they have previously served as agent, counsel, advisor, advocate, expert or in any other capacity for one of the parties, or as a member of a national or international court or other dispute settlement body which has considered the subject matter of the dispute or in a case where they had previously commented or expressed an opinion concerning the subject matter in a manner that is likely to affect or may reasonably appear to affect their independence or impartiality.

In such cases the standards provide for disqualification of the judge as well as in a case where there is personal interest of the judge.[67] This norm is a matter of course but it illustrates the importance of the envelope of the rules of conduct and ethical standards which is required for the purpose of keeping impartiality and integrity of the judiciary. This practice is required even if it is not expressed and regulated in the constitution, in legislation or in jurisprudence of any jurisdiction. It must be enforced in any jurisdiction which aims at preserving and maintaining judicial independence and maintaining public confidence in the justice system.

III. The Impact of International Law on National Law

The creation of the culture of judicial independence has been a combined process of national and international developments. One can discern that the process consists of a cycle of normative and a conceptual impact of national law on international law and later, of international law on national law.[68]

The United Kingdom provides a most instructive illustration of this phenomenon. The first phase occurred in England with the original conception of judicial independence in the Act of Settlement in 1701.[69] In the second phase, that was evident when England's concepts regarding judicial independence first were adopted in the domestic laws of many countries, this domestic development crossed national boundaries and impacted the thinking of scholars and political leaders in the transnational level. The international community then embodied the principle of judicial independence into international treaties.

> 19.1 Judges shall not sit in any case involving a party for whom they have served as agent, counsel, advisor, advocate or expert within the previous three years or such other period as the court may establish within its rules; or with whom they have had any other significant professional or personal link within the previous three years or such other period as the court may establish within its rules.

[67] Mt. Scopus Standards of Judicial Independence provide that:

> 20.1 Judges shall not sit in any case in the outcome of which they hold any material personal, professional or financial interest.
> 20.2 Judges shall not sit in any case in the outcome of which other persons or entities closely related to them hold a material, personal, professional or financial interest.
> 20.3 Judges must not accept any undisclosed payment from a party to the proceedings or any payment whatsoever on account of a judge's participation in the proceedings.

[68] For a detailed discussion, see: Shetreet's Normative Cycle, note 1 above, at pp. 584.

[69] See generally Shetreet, *Judges on Trial*, note 14 above.

In the third phase, in which we find ourselves today, the international law of judicial independence has impacted the domestic laws of nations with significant and even dramatic results.

The elements of international jurisprudence which are introduced into national laws can be expressed in international treaties that the country joins and incorporates into its own domestic laws.[70] This was the course that England took in the last decades. First the United Kingdom joined the European Convention of Human Rights in the international level by signing and ratifying the treaty. Later it has gone further to actually introducing the European Convention of Human Rights into the British domestic law by virtue of the UK Human Rights Act of 1998.[71]

Elsewhere I analysed the significant impact of the jurisprudence of the European Court of Human Rights ("ECtHR") on the concept of judicial independence in England and Scotland. This process began in the 1990s with the impact in the United Kingdom of cases handed down by the ECtHR before the United Kingdom adopted the Human Rights Act. Later, this process found dramatic expression in the application of the ECHR in the British Human Rights Act, which came into force in 2000.[72]

Whereas the British national law previously impacted the international law of judicial independence, the British Constitutional Reform Act of 2005[73] signalled a shift, with international law now impacting British domestic law. The Constitutional Reform Act dramatically reformed government control over the administration of justice in England and Wales. Importantly, it discontinued the aberrant position of the Lord Chancellor, one of the country's oldest constitutional offices, who was entrusted with a combination of legislative, Executive, and judicial capacities. The Constitutional Reform Act transferred all the judicial functions to the judiciary and entrusted the Lord Chancellor only with what are considered administrative and Executive matters.

Thus, the United Kingdom, where the first phase of judicial independence began over three hundred years ago, illustrates vividly the mutual impact of national and international law and jurisprudence in the area of judicial independence.

One can classify the impact of international law on national law by making reference to a number of sources. The first is the international treaties; others

---

[70] See: Yuval Shany, "How Supreme is the Supreme Law of the Land? Comparative Analysis of the Influence of International Human Rights Treaties upon the Interpretation of Constitutional Text by Domestic Courts" (2006) 31 Brooklyn Journal of International Law 341–404.

[71] Human Rights Act 1998, ch 42 (1998, UK), available at: http://www.opsi.gov.uk/ACTS/acts1998/ukpga_19980042_en_1 (Visited Oct 23, 2010).

[72] Human Rights Act 1998.

are international standards which have been adopted by professional international organizations. In terms of the international treaties we refer to international human rights treaties.

1. *International Human Rights Treaties*

The impact of international law on judicial independence has been influenced by international human rights treaties that contain principles of fair procedure and the right to be tried before an impartial and independent tribunal.[74]

International human rights treaties include sections and articles that deal with judicial independence,[75] and all these provisions have been given interpretation, particularly by the European Court of Human Rights.

---

[73] Constitutional Reform Act 2005, ch 4 (2005, UK), available at: http://www.statutelaw.gov.uk/content.aspx?LegType=Act+(UK+Public+General)&title=constitutional+reform&searchEnacted=0&extentMatchOnly=0&confersPower=0&blanketAmendment=0&sortAlpha=0&TYPE=QS&PageNumber=1&NavFrom=0&activeTextDocId=1974190&parentActi (Visited Oct 23, 2010). For a detailed analysis of the history of this act, see Lord Windlesham, "The Constitutional Reform Act 2005: The Politics of Constitutional Reform" (2006) Pub L 35; Lord Windlesham, "The Constitutional Reform Act 2005: Ministers, Judges and Constitutional Change" (2005) Pub L 806. For accounts of the main players, see Lord Woolf, *The Pursuit of Justice* (Oxford 2008), at pp. 161–74; Lord Phillips, "Constitutional Reform: One Year On", The Judicial Studies Board Annual Lecture (Mar 22, 2007), available at: http://www.judiciary.gov.uk/media/speeches/2007/Judicial+Studies+Board+2007+Lecture (Visited Oct 23, 2010); Lord Woolf, "The Rule of Law and a Change in the Constitution" (2004) 63 Camb. L.J. 317; Tom Bingham, *The Business of Judging: Selected Essays and Speeches* (Oxford 2000), pp. 55–68. All three authors served as Lord Chief Justice in these formative years. Lord Woolf was active in the shaping of the legislation and Lord Phillips succeeded him.

[74] Shetreet's Normative Cycle, note 1 above, at p. 283.

[75] These provisions include Article 10 of the Universal Declaration of Human Rights, General Assembly Res No 217A (III), UN Doc A/810 (1948), which states, "Everyone is entitled in full equality to a fair and public hearing by an independent and impartial tribunal"; Article 6 of the European Convention for the Protection of Human Rights and Fundamental Freedoms, 218 UN Treaty Ser 221 (1950) ("ECHR"), Section 1 of which provides, "In the determination of his civil rights and obligations or of any criminal charge against him, everyone is entitled to a fair and public hearing within a reasonable time by an independent and impartial tribunal established by law"; Article 14 of the International Covenant on Civil and Political Rights, General Assembly Res No 2200 Supp No 16, UN Doc A/6316 (1966) (entered into force Mar 23, 1976), paragraph 1 of which provides, "In the determination of any criminal charge against him, or of his rights and obligations in a suit at law, everyone shall be entitled to a fair and public hearing by a competent, independent and impartial tribunal established by law"; Article 8 of The American Convention on Human Rights (1969), 1114 UN Treaty Ser 123 (1978) ("American Convention"), paragraph 1 of which provides, "Every person has the right to a hearing, with due guarantees and within a reasonable time, by a competent, independent and impartial tribunal, previously established by law"; Article 7 of the African Charter on Human and Peoples' Rights (1981), 21 ILM 58, Section 1 of which provides, "Every individual shall have the right to have his cause heard. This comprises: … (d) the right to be tried within a reasonable time by an impartial court or tribunal"; Article 47 of the Charter of Fundamental Rights of the European Union, 2000 OJ (C 364) 10, which provides, "Everyone whose rights and freedoms guaranteed by the law of the Union are violated has the right to an effective remedy before a tribunal in compliance with the

An example of international jurisprudence influencing domestic laws is *Procola v. Luxembourg*,[76] in which the plaintiffs complained before the ECtHR of an infringement on their right to an independent and impartial tribunal under Article 6, paragraph 1 of the ECHR.[77] The ground for the complaint was that some of the members of the Judicial Committee of Luxembourg who ruled on Procola's application for judicial review had previously given their opinion on the lawfulness of the impugned provisions in their other role as members of the Conseil d'Etat. Their interpretation was that Article 6 is applicable only when the proceedings are decisive for a civil right.

In determining whether Article 6 was violated, the ECtHR ruled that in the context of an institution such as Luxembourg's Conseil d'Etat, the mere fact that certain persons performed both the advisory and the reviewing functions with respect to the same decisions casts doubt on the institution's structural impartiality. Procola had legitimate grounds for fearing that the members of the Judicial Committee would feel bound by the opinion previously issued. That doubt, however slight, was sufficient to vitiate the impartiality of the tribunal in question, thereby breaching Article 6, paragraph 1.

An example in which the US Supreme Court cited international treaties is *Hamdan v. Rumsfeld*.[78] There the Court held that special military commissions established to try non-US service members are not exempt from judicial review.[79] The court considered whether the special military commission set up by the Bush administration to try detainees at Guantanamo Bay violated federal law and whether Congress is permitted to pass legislation preventing accused combatants from being heard by the Supreme Court prior to the military commission. In granting the petition of *habeas corpus*, the court held that constitutional principles are to be applied to military commissions and that courts may enforce articles of the Geneva Convention.[80] Thus, despite the general US distaste for using law from outside its borders, there are examples of the Court referring to international law in making its domestic decisions.

conditions laid down in this Article. Everyone is entitled to a fair and public hearing within a reasonable time by an independent and impartial tribunal previously established by law. Everyone shall have the possibility of being advised, defended and represented. Legal aid shall be made available to those who lack sufficient resources in so far as such aid is necessary to ensure effective access to justice."

[76] *Procola v. Luxembourg*, 326 Eur Ct HR (ser A) (1995).

[77] ECHR, art 6, §1.

[78] *Hamdan v. Rumsfeld*, 548 US 557 (2006).

[79] *Ibid.* at pp. 613–17.

[80] *Ibid.*

Gerald Neuman[81] observed that the decision in *Lawrence v. Texas*[82] provides an illustration of the appropriate use of international law as one of many elements in a complex inquiry into constitutional interpretation.

2. *International Standards*

International standards of judicial independence have made significant contributions to domestic rules, which have been reinforced by international jurisprudence.[83] Some of the most influential international standards were drafted by professional nongovernmental and intergovernmental organizations. One recent example is the *Mt. Scopus International Standards on Judicial Independence* ("*Mt. Scopus Standards*").[84] The development of the *Mt. Scopus Standards* was necessitated by the absence of a modern, thorough revision of standards for both national and international judges.

In this context it is very important to mention a number of models that regulate the relationship between international law and national law, the classic distinction is between the monist and dualist schools, but there are other approaches as well.[85]

IV. The Fundamental Values of the Administration of Justice

The proper administration of justice is dependent upon adherence to certain fundamental values which lie at the foundations of most judicial systems.[86]

[81] Neuman, "The Uses of International Law in Constitutional Interpretation" (2004) 98 The American Journal of International Law 82–90, at pp. 89.

[82] *Lawrence v. Texas*, 539 US 558. The opinion in *Lawrence* cites *King v. Wiseman*, 92 Eng Rep 774, 775 (KB 1718), as well as a decision of the European Court of Human Rights.

[83] See, for example, *Procola*, note 76 above; *McGonnell v. United Kingdom*, 30 Eur HR Rep 289 (2000); *Findlay v. United Kingdom*, 24 Eur HR Rep 221 (1997).

[84] Mt. Scopus Standards, see note 1 above. For other International standards see Part VII of this Volume.

[85] According to the monist school, treaties become the law of the land of ratifying countries, whereas according to the dualist school, a ratified treaty is transformed into the national law only through the implementation of legislation. Vicki Jackson categorizes relationships between international and national law as a resistance, convergent, or engagement model. The resistance model vigorously rejects outside influences on domestic law. The convergent model considers domestic legal systems to be open to outside influences, the crosscurrents of which lead to the general homogenization of legal norms across multiple domestic systems. The middle position, the engagement model, recognizes domestic legal system engagement with transnational legal influences. According to this model, the domestic system is cognizant of, and to some degree accepting of, outside legal influences, but borrows from abroad within the confines of its own constitutional context.

[86] For a detailed discussion see: Shetreet, "Judicial Independence and Accountability: Core Values in Liberal Democracies", *in* H.P. Lee ed., *Comparative Judiciaries* (To be published 2010 by Cambridge University Press).

These values include: procedural fairness, efficiency, accessibility, public confidence in the courts, judicial independence,[87] and the value of constitutionality, in the sense of the constitutional protection of the judiciary. Each of these values allows the courts to fulfil their main function, which is the resolution of disputes.

These fundamental values are interrelated. Sometimes they strengthen one another, being one the result of, or the condition to, the existence or the application of the other while at other times there may be a tension between them. A proper legal system is one which advances each of these values on its own, and achieves a suitable balance between them whenever they conflict with one another.

As to the value of constitutionality, it is expected that the judiciary will be protected by constitutional provisions. Elsewhere I have proposed six principles which lie at the foundation of the constitutional protection of judicial independence. The first principle is the separation between the Judiciary and the Executive, which means judges must not be part of the administrative arm of the Executive branch of the government. The second principle is the prohibition of the diversion of cases from ordinary courts. The third principle is post-decisional independence of the judgment and its respect by the other branches of government. The fourth principle requires that cases be heard by judges according to an internally predetermined plan or schedule prior to commencement of the case. The sixth principle is that changes in the terms of judicial office should not be applied to presently sitting judges unless such changes serve to improve the terms of judicial service.[88]

The value of efficiency requires that the courts must be efficient in terms of time and cost. The courts are the machinery for enforcing laws and regulations. The legal system might have very good laws, but these laws are of little value if the legal system does not provide an accessible, convenient and efficient method for enforcing laws and obtaining redress for violation of rights; hence, the demand for efficient court procedure, for a judicial process which is

[87] For a detailed discussion of the fundamental values of the administration of justice, see Shetreet, "Practical and Value Problems in the Administration of Justice" *in* Shetreet (ed.), *Recent Developments in Israeli Case Law and Legislation, Collection of Lectures Delivered at the Judges' Conference* (Jerusalem: the Harry Sacher Institute 1977), 80; Shetreet, 'The Administration of Justice: Practical Problems, Value Conflicts and Changing Concepts' (1979) 13 *University of British Columbia Law Review* 52; Shetreet, 'The Limits of Expeditious Justice' *in* Justice Howland (ed), *Expeditious Justice* (Canadian Institute for Administration of Justice 1979) 1; Shetreet, "Time Standards of Justice" (1979) 5 *Dalhousie Law Journal* 129; Shetreet, "Adjudication: Challenges of the Presents and Blueprints for the Future" *in Festschrift in Honour of Professor Walter J Habscheid* (W Germany, 1989), Shetreet, On Adjudication, note 33, at Chapter 7. On public confidence in the American Courts see A. Bach, Ordinary Injustice, (Metropolitan Book, Holt, 2009) and B. Friedman, The will of the people (Farrar, Straus and Giroux, 2009).

[88] For detailed analysis, see: Shetreet's Normative Cycle, note 1 above, at p. 290.

not unreasonably slow, and for judicial services which can be obtained at a reasonable cost.[89]

The justice system must be based on the value of procedural fairness and justice. In order to ensure procedural fairness and justice, special procedural rules have been established to govern the method and manner in which disputes are resolved by the courts. An elaborate body of rules governs court procedures which regulate the method of evaluating and weighing the facts and evidence submitted to the courts. The purpose of these rules and laws is to attain justice and to ensure a fair trial by subjecting the conflicting claims to a vigorous and thorough investigation in order to ascertain the truth. These rules include procedural rules and rules of evidence.

Public confidence is another basic value of the justice system. The courts can only perform their function as an institution to resolve disputes in society if they enjoy public confidence. They have recognized the indispensability of this value to the functioning of the legal system, but they can only enjoy such confidence if they are seen as independent and unbiased, and if the process of resolving the dispute is fair, efficient, expedient and accessible. The fundamental principles of the legal system are the 'open court', and the court's duty to state reasons for the decisions at which it has arrived. This significant obligation contributes to the development of logical-analytical methods of thought which lie at the foundations of the legal process, and allows for the review of decisions on appeal and for reliance upon them as precedents. Public confidence in the courts is also enhanced by broad reflection of the judiciary of all social strata, ethnic groups and geographical regions in a given country.

Accessibility of the courts and access to justice is a fundamental value of the justice system. The significance of accessibility is to be found in the opening up of the doors of the courts to the public. The courts have emphasized the great importance of this value. Accessibility includes the provision of judicial services to the public at reasonable cost, provision of the means to go to court for those unable to pay the cost, as well as increasing the awareness of the community so that citizens within the community appreciate that they are entitled to turn to the courts in order to defend their rights.[90]

The principle of judicial independence is the last but not least of the basic values of the justice system. The meaning and content of this principle vary somewhat from one country to another depending upon the system of

---

[89] The demand for efficiency in the administration of justice is equally strong in the criminal and civil spheres.

[90] Article 6(1), as interpreted by the European Court of Human Rights, also ensures the fundamental values of access to justice.

government, local traditions and climate of political opinion, and even in the same country it may carry different meanings in different time periods.

The importance of the principle of an independent judiciary has grown, particularly as a result of the expanding role of the judiciary in society.[91] This increasing judicialisation is in part a result of social developments. Wide ranging primary and secondary legislation has been enacted, and consequently there has been a corresponding expansion in litigation against government services, as well as the development of 'social rights', a typical by-product of the welfare state. In addition, collective procedures, such as the American class action have developed, which have brought about a 'massification' of the law, transforming the traditional two-party litigation into a major multi-party complex litigation.[92]

The increased role of the judiciary in society may be seen as natural and objective, but there are also causes for increased judicialisation that may be viewed as convenience-based processes of judicialisation. This refers to the judicialisation of issues largely for the political convenience of the other branches of government.[93]

Judicial independence requires that judicial accountability be shaped in a very careful way. One of the important points is that incompetence will not be grounds for removal of judges. This is because it may serve as a pretext to removal of judge on undefined ground.[94]

---

[91] See further, Cappelletti, "Who Watches the Watchmen? A Comparative Study on Judicial Responsibility" (1983) 31 *American Journal of Comparative Law* 1, at pp. 7–9. For further discussion on the increasing judicial role in society, see E Vescovi, "La Independencia de la Magistratura en la Evolucion Actual del Derecho" *in* W Habscheid (ed.), *Effectiveness of Judicial Protection and Constitutional Order* (Gieseking 1983) 161, at pp. 169–172. See also Das and Chandra, *Judges and judicial Accountability* (Commonwealth Lawyers Association 2003). For an in-depth discussion of the cultural influences on judicial dispute resolution see: Chase, *Law Cuture and Ritual :Disputing Systems in Cross-Cultural Context* (New York University Press 2005).

[92] For an examination of the massification of the judicial system in criminal cases, see DH Whitbread (ed.), *Mass Production Justice and Constitutional Idea* (Charlottesville Va: Michie Co. 1970) 1. It is worth noting that massification occurs in civil cases as well.

[93] As Sir Ninian Stephen wrote, in 'Judicial Independence – A Fragile Bastion' *in* Shetreet, The Contemporary Debate, note 17 above, at pp. 543:
'Both the legislature and the executive may find it very convenient to shift to the judiciary the task of initiative – taking in [sensitive] areas … Elected bodies may have much to fear if they have to decide such issues for themselves; wise politicians may well prefer to avoid the issue for fear of an electoral backlash.' A similar trend may be observed in Israel, where the relative role of the executive has declined, whereas the judicial role has increased. Two major processes are taking place. First, the realisation of the public that the ordinary bureaucratic and political institutions are failing to solve issues has diverted the public to seek judicial redress where these other institutions have failed. Secondly, the executive has sometimes intentionally shifted questions to the courts in order to secure a judicial resolution of disputes which are economic or political in nature, to avoid having to pay the political price of the decision.

[94] See: Shetreet, Judges on Trial, note 14 above, at pp. 330.

In the transnational jurisprudence Article 6(1) of the European Convention on Human Rights represents the formulation of the core values of the justice system. It refers both to the position of the judge and the tribunal that adjudicates. It also refers to the rights accorded to everyone who stands before the tribunal. Article 6(1) of the Convention provides that: 'In the determination of his civil rights and obligations or of any criminal charge against him, everyone is entitled to a fair and public hearing within a reasonable time by an independent and impartial tribunal established by law.[95]

One of the more recent statements of the requirement of judicial independence was introduced in the new legislation in the United Kingdom section 3 of the *Constitutional Reform Act 2005* which provides that: "The Lord Chancellor, other Ministers of the Crown and all with responsibility for matters relating to the judiciary or otherwise to the administration of justice must uphold the continued independence of the judiciary." It also provides that: "The Lord Chancellor and other Ministers of the Crown must not seek to influence particular judicial decisions through any special access to the judiciary." The Act also imposes a duty on the Executive government to uphold judicial independence. It provides that: "The Lord Chancellor must have regard to (a) the need to defend that independence; (b) the need for the judiciary to have the support necessary to enable them to exercise their functions; (c) the need for the public in regard to matters relating to the judiciary or otherwise to the administration of justice to be properly represented in decisions affecting those matters."

Other scholars selected to define the fundamental values of the justice system in different formulations. This includes Andrews, Storme and Stürner.[96]

---

[95] *Human Rights Act 1998*, s 1(3) Sch 1 incorporates the European Convention on Human Rights into United Kingdom law; Grocz, Beatson and Duffy, *Human Rights: The 1998 Act and the European Convention* (2nd ed, London: Sweet & Maxwell Ltd 2008); Janies, Kay, Bradley, *European Human Rights Law: Text and Materials* (3rd ed, Oxford University Press 2008); Clayton and Tomlinson, *The Law of Human Rights* (2nd ed, Oxford University Press 2008). For example, see *Procola*, 326 Eur Ct HR in which the plaintiffs complained before the ECtHR of an infringement on their right to an independent and impartial tribunal, and *Starrs and Chalmers v. PF Linlithgow*, [2000] JC 208 (Scotland), where the Court ruled that an appointment dependent on the discretion of the minister of executive government renders the judge not independent and violates the ECtHR.

[96] See Andrews, 'Identifying Fundamental Principles of Civil Justice', (Paper delivered at an international conference on judicial independence, Cambridge 2009) 2 and see Andrews, *Principles of Civil Procedure* (London: Sweet & Maxwell 1994) (596 pp text; discussion of pre-CPR system), 96 ALI/UNIDROIT's Principles of Transnational Civil Procedure (Cambridge University Press 2006). See also Andrews, ch. 5 of this volume. The principles were formulated by R Stürner, The Principles of Transnational Civil Procedure, an Introduction to Their Basic Conceptions, 69 Rabels Zeitschrift (Heft 2) 201–54 (Germany: Max Planck Institute, 2005), Storme (ed.), *Approximation of Judiciary Law in the European Union* (Netherlands Kluwer Law International 1994).

V. The Conceptual Foundations of Judicial Independence

In enumerating the theoretical elements of judicial independence a distinction must be made between two aspects of the concept of the independence of the judiciary, the independence of the individual judges and the collective or institutional independence of the judiciary as a body. The independence of the individual judge comprises two essential elements: substantive independence and personal independence. Substantive or decisional independence means that in making judicial decisions and exercising other official duties, individual judges are subject to no other authority but the law. Independence of the judiciary implies that the judge should be removed from financial or business entanglements likely to affect or rather to seem to affect him in the exercise of his judicial functions.

Personal independence means that the judicial terms of office and tenure are adequately secured. It is secured by judicial appointment during good behaviour terminated at retirement age, and by safeguarding judicial remuneration. Thus, Executive control over judges' terms of service, such as extension of term of office, remuneration, pensions, or travel allowance is inconsistent with the concept of judicial independence. Still much less acceptable is any Executive control over case assignment, court scheduling, or moving judges from one court to another, or from one locality to another.

A modern conception of judicial independence must include collective or institutional independence of the judiciary as a whole. The concept of collective independence of the judiciary, which this writer has advocated in recent decades,[97] and which has been accepted by the emerging transnational jurisprudence, has not as yet received adequate scholarly attention. One of the important contributions of the international standards of judicial independence developed by the International Bar Association and in the Montreal Conference was the recognition of this important conceptual component of the principle of judicial independence in modern society.[98]

Another aspect of judicial independence is the internal independence of the judiciary, that is, the independence of a judge from his judicial superiors and colleagues. This also transcends both the substantive and personal independence of the judge vis-à-vis his colleagues and superiors.[99]

---

[97] Shetreet, "The Administration of Justice: Practical Problems, Value Conflicts and Changing Concepts" (1979) 13 *U.B.C.L. Rev.* 52, at 57–62; Shetreet, "The Contemporary Challenges of Judicial Independence", in Shetreet, *Judicial Independence: Jerusalem Conference Papers* (1982), Vol. 1, 63, at pp. 88–95; Shetreet, Justice in Israel, note 26 above, at chapter 15.

[98] Shetreet, Justice in Israel, *ibid.* For the same provisions see also Mt. Scopus Standards §2.3.

[99] *Ibid.* at chapter 16.

Whether and to what extent the judiciary in any country can be viewed as independent will not only depend on the law and constitution of that country, but also on the nature and character of the people who hold the office of judge, on the political structure and social climate, on the traditions prevailing in that country, and on the institutional and constitutional infrastructure of judicial independence.

The concept of judicial independence must recognize realities as well as perceptions. As Chief Justice Howland of the Ontario Supreme Court put it in the Valente case, where the principle of judicial independence was discussed at length, "it is most important that the judiciary be independent and be so perceived by the public. The judges must not have cause to fear that they will be prejudiced by their decisions or that the public would reasonably apprehend this to be the case".[100] The recognition of public perceptions is required by the need to assure public confidence in the courts. It is submitted that the reasonable man test should only be employed in the absence of other, more defined, criteria. The accepted wisdom of human experience coupled with a high commitment to the value of assuring completely neutral judicial dispute resolution can establish a more definitive test, namely, that the existence of Executive controls over judicial terms of service makes the tribunal dependent or not independent. This conclusion can be drawn without recourse to the test of the reasonable man.

The existence of personal controls on judges inevitably casts a cloud of doubt on their independence. For example, court martial judges are military officers, subject to the ordinary personal controls under the military hierarchy and rules, who are personally dependent, and cannot, therefore, try ordinary criminal offences, as distinguished from military offences. According to accepted concepts, their tribunal cannot be considered an independent tribunal.

The importance of substantive adjudication by the judges is evident in various areas, including the resolution of civil disputes, criminal cases, administrative disputes and constitutional controversies. In all these cases judicial review is a significant foundation necessary for effective judicial review and proper adjudication of these cases.[101]

---

[100] *R. V. Valente*, 2 C.C.C. (3d) (1983) 417, at 423.

[101] For a detailed analysis, see: Harlow, "Judicial Review and Administrative Justice", *in* Effective Judicial Review: A Cornerstone of Good Governance 85 (Forsyth, Elliott, Jhaveri, Scully-Hill and Ramsden eds., Oxford: 2010). See also Shetreet, Judicial Independence and Judicial Review of Government action: Necessary Institutional Characteristics and the Appropriate Scope of the Judicial Function, *ibid.* at 187–207. See also: Stack, "The Statutory Fiction of Judicial Review of Administrative Action in the United States", *ibid.* at 317.

Substantive independence encompasses administrative, procedural and substantive aspects of adjudication.[102] It means that in the making of judicial decisions and exercising other official duties, individual judges are subject to no authority other than the law and the commands of that judge's conscience. This aspect of the concept of judicial independence refers to the neutrality of mind of the judge, to that judge's impartiality and total freedom from irrelevant pressures. Adjudicative functions are those official functions for which judges are responsible in the discharge of their official duties. Adjudication is composed of three main aspects: administrative, procedural, and substantive adjudication.[103]

Substantive Independence of the judiciary demands that a judge should be removed from financial or business entanglement likely to affect, or likely to appear to effect, the exercise of judicial functions. It also considers case scheduling and the disposition of procedural motions as just as integral a component of the adjudication function as substantive decision-making, and as such must also be protected against any external interference.[104]

Having made these clarifying observations on the meaning of "independence," let us examine the meaning of the term "judiciary." In recent decades we have witnessed the establishment of numerous administrative tribunals, administrative agencies or regulatory agencies which are often entrusted with both legislative powers to promulgate rules, "delegated legislation," and powers to adjudicate certain matters specifically entrusted to their jurisdiction. The question arises, which of the organs of the state that exercise adjudicative functions, fall within the term "judiciary" and so, according to accepted theory, must be "independent."

Adjudication, which is the function of the judiciary, encompasses administrative and procedural aspects, as well as substantive decision-making.[105] The judiciary could be defined as the organ of government not forming part of the Executive or the Legislature, which is not subject to personal, substantive and collective controls, and which performs the primary function of adjudication. The latter can be exercised by direct resolution of disputes between private parties, between state organs, or between a private party and a state organ.

---

[102] S. Shetreet, *Judicial Responsibility*, in "Israeli Reports to the XIth International Congress of Comparative Law" (S. Goldstein, Editor, 1982) at pp. 88–89.

[103] See S. Shetreet, The Contemporary Debate, note 17 above, at pp. 590–601.

[104] Id. at 598, 630; L. Atkins, *The Shifting Focus of Judicial Reform: From Independence to Capacity*, in EUMAP (Aug 2002), available online at <http://www.eumap.org/journal/features/2002/aug02/indeptocapacity> (visited Nov 20, 2008).

[105] Shetreet, "Judicial Responsibility", *in* Goldstein (ed.) *Israeli Reports to the XIth International Congress of Comparative Law* (1982) 88, at 88–89. Cappelletti generally accepting this thesis, see: cappelletti, note 91 above, at 570–575.

Adjudication could also be by way of review of adjudicative decisions of tribunals outside the ordinary court system.

The proposed definition will exclude military tribunals from the scope of the term "judiciary," as well as the American administrative law judges in the United States, or the officers of administrative tribunals in England, and their equivalents in other countries, including Israel.

However, independence and impartiality must be respected and maintained by administrative judges as well and this must be a central aim for the upcoming years.[106]

VI. The Principle of Democratic Accountability

One of the most important principles in the contemporary debate on the role of the judiciary in society and its relationship with the Executive and the Legislature is the principle of democratic accountability of the judiciary. This principle has strong relevance to the method of judicial appointment and the models of constitutional adjudication of the constitutionality of executive actions and parliamentary and legislative acts.[107]

Section 4.2 of the Mt. Scopus Standards recognizes the importance of legislative and Executive participation in judicial selection. It considers as legitimate such participation.[108] This model of involving the Legislature and the Executive in judges' selection introduces a form of democratic accountability of the judiciary in the selection process in the beginning of their term of office. This resolves the dilemma of judges making value judgments and issuing constitutional rulings without being accountable to the general society.

This brings us to the linkage between the model of constitutional adjudication and the model of judicial selection. Democratic accountability demands

---

[106] See the concluding remarks of this chapter.

[107] For a detailed discussion over the various procedures for appointment of judges, see: Malleson and Russell (eds.), *Appointing Judges in an Age of Judicial Power: Critical Perspectives from Around the World* (Toronto University Press 2006); Melleson and Moules, *The Legal System* (3rd ed., Oxford University Press 2010); Blom-Cooper, Drewry and Dickson (eds.), *The Judicial House of Lords* (Oxford University Press 2009), Chapters 7–8.

[108] Mt. Scopus Standards of Judicial Independence provide that:

> a) The principle of democratic accountability should be respected and therefore it is legitimate for the Executive and the Legislature to play a role in judicial appointments provided that due consideration is given to the principle of Judicial Independence.
> b) The recent trend of establishing judicial selection boards or commissions in which members or representatives of the Legislature, the Executive, the Judiciary and the legal profession take part, should be viewed favourably, provided that a proper balance is maintained in the composition of such boards or commissions of each of the branches of government. Mt. Scopus Standards, §4.2(a), (b).

that a state select the model of constitutional adjudication that compliments its method of judicial appointments. This is in order to ensure that the power of the judiciary to rule on the unconstitutionality of legislation corresponds with that country's form of judicial appointments. In countries where judicial selection models include the participation of Legislative and Executive input into the process, it is justifiable to adopt an adjudicative model that grants the courts a power to rule that statutes are unconstitutional.[109] On the other hand, where the judiciary is appointed on a professional basis only, without democratic input, then the model of giving the final word to the judiciary in deciding the constitutionality of statutes is not appropriate, and other models should be considered. The two alternative models are declaratory model and the override model. The first, declaratory model, as adopted by the UK Human Rights Act, is that constitutional judgments of the court will be declaratory only. In this model the judiciary does not have the power to invalidate a statute, but only the power to declare incompatibility between the law and the constitution. In the United Kingdom case the constitution is the European Convention of Human Rights introduced into the United Kingdom domestic law. The second model for resolving the lack of democratic accountability allows the court to invalidate a statute, but provides for a parliamentary power to override this invalidation. This model exists in Canada. In both models, after the decision of the court, the legislature may either modify a statute to fit the court's constitutional interpretation, or else decline altogether to engage in statutory modification.

An analysis of the models of constitutional adjudication reveals the link between the scope of judicial review and the provision for democratic accountability.[110] It is generally accepted that the principle of constitutionalism requires the limiting of the power of the legislative branch. This idea is widely accepted, in spite of the reservation voiced in this regard. The dilemma relates to the democratic legitimacy of constitutional adjudication, and the nature of the method of constitutional settlement of disputes in each society.[111]

---

[109] See Shetreet, "Models of Constitutional Adjudication A Comparative Analysis" *in* Pellegrini, Grinover and Calmon (eds.), *Papers Presented at the XII Congress of Procedural Law* 769–98 (Forensa 2007), Shetreet, On Adjudication, note 33, chapters 14–15. For the declaratory model in the UK see Aileen Kavanagh, Constitutional Review under the UK Human Rights Act (Cambridge University Press 2009).

[110] See Dotan, "Judicial Review and Accountability: A Comparative Analysis" (2007) 10 Mishpat Umimshal 520–489 (Hebrew).

[111] See, for example: Gavison, "The Constitutional Revolution: Description of Reality or a Self-Fulfilled Prophecy" (1997) 28 Mishpatim 23, at pp. 28–32 (Hebrew); Dotan, "Constitution for Israel? The Constitutional Dialogue after the Constitutional Revolution" (1996) 27 Mishpatim 149; Ackerman, "The Storrs Lectures: Discovering the Constitution (1984) 93 Yale L. J. 1013, at pp. 1030–31, 1045–47; Sunstein "Constitutionalism and Secession" (1991) 58 U. Chi. L. Rev. 633, at pp. 638, 647.

It should be noted that the fact that the judicial branch serves for longer periods is not to be viewed as a deficient element. However, the fact that the judicial branch exercises judicial review over legislative judgments while exercising constitutional adjudication and, yet, is not subject to any accountability is clearly contrary to the doctrine of separation of powers and the principle of constitutionalism. The dilemma is that in constitutional adjudication the judiciary may limit the political branches but the judiciary itself is not democratically accountable.

To resolve this issue, there are a number of possibilities. One strategy is to formulate a constitution in a precise manner, using detailed and specific rules, so that the constitutional guidelines will advise the judges in the exercise of judicial review of the constitutionality of statutes.[112] A second strategy focuses on the method of the selection of judges. The American model insures democratic input into the federal and state procedures of judicial appointments by congressional confirmation of presidential nominations on the federal levels, and by general elections, in some states, and by Executive and Legislative participation in judicial appointments in other states.[113]

The European model, adopted by several countries, including Germany and Italy, attempts to resolve this dilemma of democratic accountability with regard to constitutional adjudication by entrusting the power of judicial review not to the ordinary court system, but rather to constitutional courts. These courts meet requirements of democratic accountability by providing special procedures for the selection of their members in a different process. This view recognizes that constitutional adjudication requires a wider value-oriented approach and also that the European career judiciary in the ordinary court system cannot adequately ensure democratic accountability.[114]

Normally, the process of election of members of the separate constitutional court is done in the National Legislature, and is more political than the appointment in the ordinary system, which is primarily based on judicial career.[115] As mentioned above, section 4.2 of the Mt. Scopus Standards considers as legitimate such participation of the Executive and the Legislature in the appointment on judges.

---

[112] See Craig, *Administrative Law* (3rd ed., Sweet & Maxwell 1994) 3; Stewart, "The Reformation of American Administrative Law" (1975) 88 Harv. L. Rev. 1667, at pp. 1694–95.

[113] See Resnik, "Judicial Selection and Democratic Theory: Demand, Supply, and Life Tenure" (2005) 26 Cardozo L Rev 579, at pp. 593–94.

[114] This is the reason for the criticism regarding the absence of term limitations for federal justices. See: *ibid.* at 615–616; Stras and Scott "Retaining Life Tenure: The Case for a "Golden Parachute"" (2006) 83 Wash. U. L. Q. 1397, at pp. 1426.

[115] Bell, *Judiciaries within Europe: A Comparative Review* (Cambridge 2006).

The democratic accountability of the courts helps ensure the existence of the rule of law and enhances constitutionalism. The underlying principle of the rule of law is provided for in Section 1 of the Mt. Scopus Standards: "The significance of the Independence of the Judiciary [is to] ensure that all people are able to live securely under the rule of law." This brings to realization the principle of democratic accountability and emphasizes that "Judges are the servants, not the masters. … Servants are accountable, so are judges."[116]

There are other models in addition to the introduction of democratic input into the process of judicial appointments. One is to resolve the issue of the lack of accountability and the possible conflict between the branches of government by providing that the court can only declare incompatibility between a parliamentary statute and constitutional provisions, but the parliament (possibly together with the Executive) must decide what to do next. This is the model adopted in the United Kingdom where the basic norm is not a constitutional one but borrowed from the European Convention of Human Rights and adopted into the law.

Another model designed to respond to the lack of accountability in the judiciary is the common law model. The common law model focuses on restricting the scope of judicial review and abstention from rigid constitutions, thus resolving the issue of the lack of judicial accountability by restricting the circumstances under which the judiciary will find itself in a position where it overrides legislative decisions.[117]

Rigid constitutionalism was adopted only in federal common law states such as Canada and Australia, in order to regulate the interrelationship between their federal and provincial units.

---

[116] As said by Canadian judge, Mr. Justice Riddell. See Shetreet, The Contemporary debate, note 17 above, at pp. 593 (referring to *Davis Acetylene Gas Co v. Morrison*, [1915] 34 OLR 155, 23 DLR 871 (Canada)). See also Constitution Act 1982, Schedule B to the Canada Act 1982, ch 11, § 33 (1982) (UK).

[117] Canada's system of constitutional-override allows Parliament to declare that certain types of legislation shall operate notwithstanding their unconstitutionality, on the condition that Parliament makes this declaration expressly, and that such declaration expires after five years. The wording is as follows:

(1) Parliament or the legislature of a province may expressly declare in an Act of Parliament or of the legislature, as the case may be, that the Act or a provision thereof shall operate notwithstanding a provision included in section 2 or sections 7 to 15 of this Charter.

(2) An Act or a provision of an Act in respect of which a declaration made under this section is in effect shall have such operation as it would have but for the provision of this Charter referred to in the declaration.

(3) A declaration made under subsection (1) shall cease to have effect five years after it comes into force or on such earlier date as may be specified in the declaration. Canada Const, § 33.

VII. Relationship of the Judiciary and the Executive and Legislative: The Preferred Model – Partnership and Dialouge

1. *The Principle of Mutual Respect between the Branches of Government*

When we deal with the building of a culture of judicial independence it is important to view it as part of the operating system of government. The culture of judicial independence cannot exist in every governmental climate. It must exist in a system which is based on separation of powers.

Separation of powers in its classical form was developed by Montesquieu based on the English system of government in the 18th century.[118] The doctrine of separation of powers requires a total separation between the three branches of the government: the judiciary, the Legislature and the Executive. The Legislature is the only branch of government which is empowered to create general norms in society and to issue primary legislation. The Executive is responsible for issuing individual orders and enforce the statutes issued by the Legislature. The judiciary is engaged and entrusted with dispute resolution. This separation is the guarantee for freedom. The total separation is a utopia which cannot really be enforced in any system of government.

The organizational separation between the three branches is possible and it is implemented in most modern system of government. However, from the functional point of view it is not possible to implement a separation of power. There is no system which does not empower the Executive to perform semi-adjudicative functions and issue delegated legislation. There are also administrative powers that are given to the judiciary and there are some administrative powers and some semi-adjudicative powers that are given to the Legislature. This deviation from the classic doctrine of separation of powers is warranted because the realities of operating a system of government and without such a deviation it is not possible to have an effective and efficient government.[119] Today, the classical theory of separation of powers is not adopted in its pure form. Nevertheless it is widely accepted that government powers must not be centred in one power and should be divided and subject to control and review by other authorities. This remains a principle that is adopted and practiced. This principle has been expressed in modern times by the American concept of "checks and balances". This concept divides the power between the different

---

118 See Baron de Montesquieu, *The Spirit of the Laws*, (T. Nugent, trans., Hafner 1949).

119 Klinghofer, *Administrative law* (Hebrew, 2nd ed., Akademon 1974) 10. Klein, "On the Legal Definition of the Parliamentary Regime and on the Israeli Parliamentarism" (1973–1974) 5 *Mishpatim* 308, 309–311 and 324–331 (Hebrew).

branches of government but unlike the classical theory, these powers are subjected to checks and balances of the other branches of government.[120]

Even once achieved, the continuation of judicial independence is not a matter of course. It is constantly subject to challenges, sometimes by other branches of government, and at others as the result of internal developments, changing political circumstances, or social and economic pressures. Violations of accepted principles of judicial independence have occurred in countries that represent all forms of government and all geographic regions in the world. Challenges to judicial independence include interference with personal independence through legislation, including legislation abolishing security of tenure, lowering the retirement age, or abolishing certain courts so as to effectively end the service of a judge.[121]

It is now appropriate to give details of some of the points of contact between the different branches of the government, which is between the judiciary and the legislature and the judiciary and the Executive and thereafter we shall give the preferred model of the proper relationship between the judiciary and the other branches of the government.

It is important to note the significant reform in the UK judicial system. Before the Constitutional Reform Act 2005 the Lord Chancellor was entrusted with three important roles: as speaker of the Upper House of Parliament, the House of Lords;[122] as a member of the Executive branch and member of the senior cabinet; and as head of the judiciary. The *Constitutional Reform Act* (2005)[123] established new lines of demarcation between the Lord Chancellor and the Judiciary, transferring all of the Lord Chancellor's judicial functions to the judiciary, and entrusting the Lord Chancellor solely with what is considered conceptually to be administrative and Executive, and not judicial, matters. Thus the Lord Chancellor became a representative of the Executive, and not of both the Executive and the Judiciary. The *Constitutional Reform Act* (2005) laid down a number of other reforms aimed at providing constitutional safeguards protecting the position of the judiciary. This law established the Supreme Court of the United Kingdom, and passed on to it the jurisdiction of the Judicial Committee of the House of Lords. The law also introduced a major reform in the method of judicial appointments, and provides in Sections 3 and 4 that ministers and other holders of office who have responsibility in matters

[120] Rubinstein, *Israel's Constitutional Law* (Hebrew, 3rd ed., Shoken 1990) at 225–226.

[121] Tushnet, note 21 above. See also: Shetreet, The Contemporary Debate, note 17 above, at pp. 607–08.

[122] See: *The Judicial House of Lords, note 107 above*, chapters 4 and 5.

[123] *Constitutional Reform Act* 2005, note 73 above. See also Windelsham, Woolf and Phillips, note 73 above. See also A. Seldon ed., *Blair's Britain*, chapter 6 by P. Norton (The constitution), chapter 14 by M. Beloff (Law and Judiciary), (Cambridge University Press, 2007).

of the administration of justice, promote and enhance the principle of judicial independence.[124]

In 2007, the English judiciary had many concerns which arose in connection with the establishment of the Ministry of Justice. In 2008, the Lord Chief Justice and the Lord Chancellor announced a new partnership with respect to the operation of the Court Service. On matters for which responsibilities have been moved from government ministers to the judiciary, thought has been given regarding how to ensure a measure of accountability consistent with the principles of judicial independence.[125]

Discussing judicial independence from the British perspective, Neil Andrews notes that there has been a long-standing constitutional perception that English judges form a separate arm of the state, and that the principle of 'judicial independence' is also recognised in the European Convention on Human Rights. The *Constitutional Reform Act* provides that the Executive must uphold the continued independence of the judiciary. The new order sees the Lord Chief Justice, as the head of the judiciary, representing the judiciary and holding responsibility for disciplinary matters. In addition, the Ministry of Justice and the Secretary of State for Justice have executive responsibility for the administration of justice in civil and criminal matters, an arrangement which creates the potential for friction between the judiciary and the Executive. The matter is covered by 'the Concordat', a Constitutional undertaking between the government and the judiciary, which sets out the agreements between the Lord Chancellor and the Lord Chief Justice on their new roles.[126]

2. *Post Decisional Independence: Legislative Reversal of Judicial Decisions and Executive Enforcement of Judgments*

One of the objectionable forms of legislative intervention in judicial decisions is the retroactive reversal of judicial decisions by legislation. Retroactive legislation is a violation of a number of constitutional principles. Such legislation in fact turns the legislature into an additional appellate instance above the final court of appeal in a certain jurisdiction. Such legislation also violates the rule

---

124 Malleson, "The Judicial Appointments Commission in England and Wales: New Wine in New Bottles?" *in* Malleson and Russell (eds.), note 107 above; Malleson, "Selecting Judges in the Era of Devolution and Human Rights" *in* Le Sueur (ed.), *Building the UK's New Supreme Court* (Oxford University Press 2004); Malleson, "Promoting Diversity in the Judiciary: Reforming the Judicial Appointments Process" *in* Thomas (ed.), *Discriminating Lawyers* (Cavendish Press 2000).

125 Beatson, "Reforming an Unwritten Constitution", a lecture delivered in Oxford, 16 may 2009, available at: http://www.judiciary.gov.uk/NR/rdonlyres/A1A84E53-E5C9-4007-BB83-6162C8464974/0/justicebeatsonblackstonelecture160509.pdf (Visited Oct 23, 2010).

126 Andrews, *Judicial Independence: The British Experience.* (this volume, chapter 24)

of law which requires that laws shall be applicable only prospectively. This is because the public should know of legislation and should conduct their behaviour based on their notice of the law. Such retroactive legislation also is a violation of the principle of judicial independence in its substantive meaning because it frustrates the enforcement of the decision of the court and in fact turns it into a dead letter.

The Mt. Scopus international Standards of Judicial Independence provide that retroactive legislation is inappropriate.[127] Nevertheless in a number of situations legislative bodies passed retroactive legislation in order to reverse decisions of supreme courts.[128]

In general, retroactive legislation should be viewed negatively and it must be avoided. The very exceptional cases where retroactive legislation could be justified will be when a judgment of a court will invalidate a great number of governmental actions and will reverse a decision according to which the government or the general public acted on for a long time. In such cases even though the law upon which the general public relied on may have been erroneous, it is not in the public interest to invalidate a great number of government actions. Therefore the courts should apply their decisions prospectively as they have done from time to time. If the courts will select to apply the decisions prospectively, it will not cause a conflict between court decisions and retroactive legislation in such cases. In those cases the legislation will only reinstate the legal situation as it had been before the judgment.

Retroactive legislation may be justified when the judiciary exceeded from its role as it is accepted in a particular jurisdiction. In such a situation the legislative branch may, or perhaps should, reinstate the balance between the two branches of the government that was in fact breached by the judiciary in that case. However, in most cases retroactive legislation is not consistent with the accepted restrictions on the Legislative branch that exclude legislation which impacts judicial decisions.

Legislative reversal of judgments of the court exists in established democracies such as England (the state immunity in times of war)[129] and Canada (injunction on nuisance case).[130] An illustration of the issue of legislative

---

[127] Mt. Scopus Standards of Judicial Independence provide that:

3.1 The Legislature shall not pass legislation which reverses specific court decisions.

[128] For Israeli cases of legislative reversals of judicial decisions, see: Shetreet, Justice in Israel, note 26 above, at pp. 413–418.

[129] *Burmah Oil Co (Burma Trading) Ltd v. Lord Advocate* [1965] AC 75, [1964] 2 All ER 348 which was reversed by War Damage Act 1965 (1965 c 18).

[130] *K.V.P. Co. v. McKie,* [1949] S.C.J. No. 37. See also: Shetreet "Judicial Independence: New Conceptual Dimension", note 17 above, at pp. 610–623.

responses to judicial decisions is illustrated in the Canadian case *K.V.P. Co. Ltd. v. McKie* (1949). In McKie, owners of property along the Spanish River in Ontario sued the operator of an upstream pulp and paper mill for pollution of the river's waters. The court ordered an injunction restraining the K.V.P. Company, the defendant, from depositing foreign substances in the Spanish River. The company appealed, the appeal was dismissed, and the case was then appealed to the Supreme Court of Canada. The Lakes and Rivers Improvement Act was amended, altering the situation of the K.V.P. Company. However, despite the amendment, the company's appeal was dismissed, with the Supreme Court holding that the amended act would not enable the Court to give a judgment that was contrary to law at the time of the Court of Appeal decision.[131] In response, retrospective legislation was passed: the KVP Company Limited Act. Section I of the Act read: "Every injunction heretofore granted against the KVP Company Limited (...) restraining the Company from polluting the waters of the Spanish River, is dissolved".[132]

The second case, crucial for British constitutional law, is *Burmah Oil Company v. Lord Advocate*. The case arose out of the destruction of oil fields in Burma by British forces in 1942 in order to prevent the installations from falling into Japanese hands. The appellants claimed that they were entitled to payment of a sum amounting to the amount of damages sustained by them due to the destruction. Although it was admitted that the demolitions were carried out lawfully, it was argued that every act of requisition done for the good of the public should be compensated.[133]

The Legislature reacted and passed the retrospective War Damage Act (1965), which abolished rights to compensation with respect to destruction of property authorised by the Crown during the war. This Act had the effect of reversing the court's judgment and thus undermining judicial independence.[134]

Another phenomenon is the preemption of the enforcement of judicial decisions by actions of the Executive. Judicial independence of the decision continues after the case is decided. Judicial independence requires that the Executive should respect the decisions of the courts and that the Executive shall not use its powers in a way that will preempt the enforcement of a judgment that has been handed down by the courts. Preemptive measures that frustrate the enforcement of a judgment are a violation of the rule of law and of the doctrine

---

131 *K.V.P. Co. Ltd. v. McKie et al.*, (1949).

132 Weinrib, *Tort Law: Cases and Materials* (Emond Montgomery Publication 2009) 40–41. For the Ontario Act, see also *K.V.P. Company Ltd. Act 1950*, S.O. c. 33.

133 *Burmah Oil Company*, note 129 above.

134 *War Damages Act*, note 129 above.

of separation of powers, and are also a violation of the principle of finality of judgments. In general, most jurisdictions do not engage in preemptive actions that frustrate judicial decisions, but there have been cases in a number of jurisdictions and those cases should be avoided.

The post-decisional independence of the judgments of the courts imposes upon the Executive a duty to enforce the courts' decisions, civil or criminal, and refrain from frustrating them by legal or physical actions or omissions. This principle also requires the legislature to refrain from retroactive reversals of specific judicial decisions. The Mt. Scopus Standards of Judicial Independence imposes a duty on the State to provide adequate budgets for the proper execution of the judgments of the courts.[135]

In optimal conditions it is to be expected that judgment should be executed expeditiously. However in reality this expectation is not practical. In the absence of adequate budgets and resources there has been frequently a backlog in the execution of judgments.[136] Not in every case this failure to execute judgment is intentional. One should recognize that there are practical limits for expeditious enforcement of judgments because of lack of resources. However failure to enforce judgments is to be recognized as improper though it cannot be viewed as a violation of judicial independence. There are cases where there is selective enforcement when the Executive decides to enforce certain categories of cases or intentionally decides not to enforce judgments. In such a situation this Executive decision of selective enforcement or failure of enforcement should be viewed as a violation of judicial independence.

3. *Executive Delegated Legislation and Preemptive Actions in Pending Matters before the Courts*

Executive intervention in judicial proceedings is affected generally by the exercise of executive powers. This could take place by way of ministers using their position to influence judicial proceedings. Such interventions prevent the court from independent and impartial adjudication.

In this context one could envisage delegated legislation in matters pending before the court. In these cases one should clarify the nature of the

---

[135] §15.1 of the Mt. Scopus Standards of Judicial Independence provides that:

> 15.1 States, parties and international organisations shall provide adequate resources, including facilities and levels of staffing, to enable courts and the judges to perform their functions effectively.

[136] See: HCJ 309/62 *Bank Hapoel Hamizrahi v. Head of the Execution Office* 16(4) PD 2602, in which the Israeli Supreme Court has refused to give a decree stating the police has to arrest a person, because it was convinced that due to lack of resources, the police will not be able to follow the decree.

delegated legislation which is aimed at regulating the issue that lies at the centre of the dispute between the citizen and the administrative authority. When the delegated legislation will regulate the matter in favour of the citizen, then it is acceptable, but if the delegated legislation is aimed at frustrating the judicial process and regulating the matter in the opposite direction, which supports the position of the Executive, then it is unacceptable. Delegated legislation of the second category which adopts the solution that is advocated by the Executive is inappropriate and violates judicial independence. It is true that prohibiting such delegated legislation limits the legislative powers of the Executive, but such a limitation is necessary for the protection of judicial independence.

It should be noted that the general approach which excludes delegated legislation in pending matters before the court does not mean that the delegated legislation is totally excluded but it is excluded from affecting the specific case pending before the court. Such delegated legislation can apply to other parties who are not party to the case.

The rule that excludes delegated legislation on matters pending before the court should be confined to situations when the litigation was initiated by the citizen without good faith. This is a situation where the petitioner knew that the Executive was going to introduce delegated legislation and nevertheless this petitioner went to court. It is not proper that in such a way, by filing a petition to the court such citizen can tie the hands of the Executive from regulating the matter in delegated legislation. The exception is where it can be shown that the petitioner intended to limit the freedom and the discretion of the Executive. Normally, the Executive should not legislate in such pending matters.

Another form of Executive intervention in judicial adjudication is by preemption of such a decision. The court is limited to deal only with cases that are brought before it and only when its decision is effectively enforceable. Preempting actions by the Executive is possible because the Executive can engage in an action that will frustrate the adjudication.

An important element of judicial independence vis-à-vis the Executive is the duty to refrain from actions which frustrate judicial remedies. In other words, the Executive may not engage in preemptive frustrations of judicial remedies by parties to case. Such action is, for example, when a petitioner who files a legal challenge to his deportation is deported before the case is adjudcated.[137]

[137] Such a case took place in the Dr. Soblen affair. Dr. Soblen was expelled from Israel and by his expulsion the judicial review of his deportation was frustrated. For a detailed discussion see: Shetreet, Justice in Israel, note 26 above, at Chapter 12.

4. *Judicial Role in Society*

The judiciary is entrusted with the function of dispute resolution. In the course of resolving disputes, the courts have to make decisions regarding the interpretation of the laws and the interpretation of previous decisions. In this process the judiciary frequently has to create new norms that will be responsive to new social and economic conditions and that may bridge the gap between the letter and the text of the law and the economic or social realities of the time. One of the very important issues regarding the adjudication by the judiciary is the issue whether the judges have to perform an activist role or should they be engaged in self-restraint.

Judicial activism is important for society because it can provide bridging the gap between the law, the statutes and the changing realities in social, economic and business matters.[138] However, this useful practice of judicial activism has to be exercised carefully in order not to cause an overdraft of the judicial institutional capital that is very dear and scarce.

This author proposes the classification of judicial activism into a number of categories. The categories are constitutional activism, administrative activism, and activism in other areas of the law including private law, commercial law, labour law, criminal law, torts, or procedural law. Constitutional activism, which relates to judicial activism in judicial review of parliamentary legislation and in promoting the protection of human rights and civil rights not necessarily in relation to judicial review of statutes. In addition to constitutional judicial activism there is also judicial activism that is exercised in other areas of law,[139] for example, judicial activism in administrative law which may relate to the exercise of power by political authorities.[140]

---

[138] For the analysis of the attitudes of the English law and judges on issues of bridging the gap between social and economic realities and the law, see: Shetreet, "on assessing the role of courts in society" (1979–1980) 10 Man. L. J. 382., et seq. (Judicial interpretation).

[139] For examples of judicial activism, see: The Judicial House of Lords, note 107 above, part E.

[140] In Israel the judicial activism in the administrative law area found its expression in the limitations of the doctrine of justiciability, in the very flexible approach to the right of standing and in the wide scope of the grounds of judicial review of the administrative decisions on the ground of proportionality and reasonableness. This grounds where used by the courts to invalidate actions by the executive. Gavison, Kremnitzer and Dotan, *judicial activism: cons and pros, the place of the High Court of justice in the Israeli society* (Hebrew. Yediot Aharonot 1999). See also I. Zamir and A. Zysblat, Public Law in Israel (Clarendon Press, Oxford, 1996).

Judicial activism is not limited to constitutional or administrative law activism.[141] It could be found in private and commercial law[142], labour law[143], criminal law,[144] torts,[145] as well as in procedural law.[146]

However, the main controversy on judicial activism is not focusing on judicial activism in criminal law, civil law or procedural law; rather it is focusing on constitutional activism and administrative law activism. Clearly, it is not possible to discuss the relationship between the branches of government without discussing the role of the judiciary in reviewing the actions of the Executive and the judicial review of statutes of the legislature. The idea that limiting the power of the legislative branch may be justified in proper circumstances is widely accepted in most systems of government. This is in spite of the dilemma raised by the constitutional restrictions imposed on the legislative branch in representative democracies.

This dilemma relates to the democratic legitimacy of constitutional adjudication, and the nature of the method of constitutional settlement of disputes in each society.[147] The constitutional power of the judiciary to review discretionary decisions of the democratic, representative legislative branch requires that the exercise of this power by the supervising judicial authority be subject to a set of rules aimed at the prevention of judicial abuse of power.

Based on the previous analysis, there is a need to develop principles for fine tuning the judicial role in society and we will demarcate the proper boundaries

---

[141] For examples of the different kinds of activism in England, see: Shetreet, "On Assessing the Role of Courts in Society", note 138 above. For examples in the different areas of law, see: *The Judicial House of Lords, note 107 above*, chapters 30 (Human Rights), 36 (Family Law), 37 (Land Law), 38 (Commercial Law), 39 (Intellectual Property), and 40 (Tax Law).

[142] In civil law, judicial activism can be found in application of public norms in private law, as happened in the case of *Castenboum* (CA 294/91 *Hevra Kadisha v. Castenboum* 46(2) PD 464) where it was ruled that public norms of dignity will apply in contractual transactions by using the terminology of public policy or the terminology of an oppressive contractual term in standard contract and by defining the organization as a dual nature organization.

[143] Segal and Litur, *Judicial Activism and Passivism, the Test of the High Court of Justice and the National Labor Court* (Hebrew. Nevo 2008) 111–131.

[144] For examples in criminal law see: Gross, "the adversary procedure in criminal law: does it allow judicial activism?" (1993) 17(3) Iyunei Mishpat 867 (Hebrew); Also See: Porat, Erez and Yaakov (eds.) *Judicial Activism* 397 (Tel-Aviv University press 1993). For more examples, see: *The Judicial House of Lords, note 107 above*, chapter 32.

[145] See: *The Judicial House of Lords*, *ibid*, chapter 34.

[146] We are also witnessing judicial activism in the procedural law. The very illustrative example is the case of *Nachmany* (CA 5587/93 *Nachmany v. Nachmany*, and CFH 2401/95 *Nachmany v. Nachmany*, 50(5) PD 661), where it was decided that there can be a further hearing of a case by the Supreme Court, even though the first hearing was before five judges, and even though the letter of the law speaks about further hearing in a case only when the first hearing was before three judges. Also see: Levin, "Judicial Activism in Law of Evidence and Civil Procedure" *in judicial activism*, note 141 above, at pp. 393 (Hebrew). See also, *ibid*, chapter 29.

[147] See note 111 above for examples.

between the Legislature, the Executive and the Judiciary. Two of the important principles are the justiciability and the right of standing.

The duty to finely tune the demarcation of lines and boundaries between the powers of the three branches of government derives from the doctrine of separation of powers. According to this theory, every branch of government should exercise its powers in its own province, and every branch should perform as a check and balance of the other two branches. The expansion of the scope of judicial review without proper limits will exceed the appropriate balance of the judiciary and may disrupt the proper relationship between the branches of government.

There are two different approaches: Legal formalism or judicial restraint, on the one hand, and judicial activism on the other hand. Legal formalism is founded on the desire to view the law as a logical, closed system, detached from particular historical, social and cultural circumstances; the law is comprised of a system of rules, including rules established for the purpose of fact-determination. By applying relevant legal rules to concrete events, a logical outcome is arrived at which is not based on the judge's subjective social policy preferences. Judicial activism, on the other hand, is founded on the notion that the essence of legal life lies in reality rather than logic. The law is a dynamic, developing process, incorporating a synthesis of opposing conceptions and perceptions. Judicial activity involves the making of decisions within a particular social context, and the object of the law is to outline policies which will serve to resolve social conflicts.[148] The perception of the court as a body engaged in resolving disputes on the basis of socio-political norms characterizes the school known as Critical Legal Studies.

Although the two approaches are distinct in theory, in practice it is not always possible to make clear-cut, precise distinctions between "conservative" (restrained) and "liberal" (activist) judges, or between "formalist" and "non-formalist" judges.[149] Indeed, on occasion, a single judge might select one of the two approaches according to the particular circumstances of a case.

The judiciary also plays an important role in crises created by national security events requiring special measures, incidents of terror, and the need to take preventive measures. The situations of tension are created more frequently in

---

[148] For a discussion on the struggle between judicial restraint and judicial activism see: Lahav, "The American Doctrine of Judicial Review: Themes and Variations" (1984) 10 *Iyunei Mishpat* 491 (Hebrew).

[149] For an attempt to categorize see Shetreet, *On* Assessing the Role of Courts in Society, note 138 above, at pp. 364.

multi-cultural, multi-religious societies and in ideologically and religiously divided societies.[150]

5. *Procedural Tools and Substantive Tests for Fine Tuning of Judicial Roles in Society*

In the early years of the State of Israel, judicial supervision played an important role in reviewing Executive decisions which were based on security considerations and which interfered with civil rights. However, this review was based on procedural or jurisdictional defects and did not involve an examination of the substantive decision of the administrative authorities.

In later years, the courts have shown a greater willingness to review substantive decisions of the Executive, as distinct from reviewing decisions on the grounds of procedural or jurisdictional deficiencies. It was thought that judges are not members of the security establishment and they should refrain from interfering in security considerations. Over the years it has been held that security considerations are not unique insofar as judicial review is concerned. Judges are not administrators, yet the principle of separation of powers requires that they review the lawfulness of administrative decisions. In this regard, security considerations do not enjoy a different status".[151]

Several of the Israeli Supreme Court's decisions reveal a tendency to limit governmental authorities in other areas related to the employment of security considerations.[152] Supreme Court jurisprudence, ruling that the scope of judicial review in security matters is basically similar to that in other matters, has had a very important impact on the practice of the security authorities, and on the handling of challenges directed at the validity of security measures and actions.[153]

Sometimes a court's influence is visible in cases settled out of court, or when the requested remedy is given by a governmental authority before or during

---

[150] See Shetreet, "Judicial Independence and Judicial Review of Government Action: Necessary Institutional Characteristics and Appropriate Scope of Judicial Review", *in* Forsyth, Elliott, Jhaveri, Scully-Hill and Ramsden (eds.), *Effective Judicial Review: A Cornerstone of Good Governance* (Oxford University Press, 2010), 187–207.

[151] HCJ 680/88 *Schnitzer v. Chief Military Censor* 42(4) PD 639.

[152] For example, the Court has ruled that if an authority is allowed by law not to reason its decision, yet chooses nevertheless to do so, then those stated reasons are subject to High Court review. HCJ 2/79 *Al-Asad v. Minister of Interior* 34(1) PD 505; HCJ 541/83 *Asli v. Jerusalem District Commissioner* 37(4) PD 837. For recent cases see Shetreet, Law and Business, note 14, at 568–572.

[153] Briksman, "High Court of Justice Petitions on Occupied Territory Matters – Practitional Aspects" (1990) 2 Israel Association of Public Law Journal 13.

judicial proceedings,[154] when the very possibility of lodging a petition brings about a change in the authorities' attitude.[155]

The judiciary has not limited itself to the review of specific administrative actions. More than once, the Israeli Supreme Court has expressed a deep concern regarding the exercise of emergency powers used to regulate general economic matters unrelated to dangers emanating from a state of emergency, and which should instead be regulated by ordinary parliamentary legislation.[156]

Judicial review of discretionary powers in matters of security in Israel has essentially become similar to the review of any other governmental activity. Israeli democracy is very hesitant to rid itself of legal emergency mechanisms instituted to protect state security. However, it can be said that the significance of security considerations is gradually diminishing, whereas considerations relating to the rule of law are being reinforced.[157]

a. *The Test of Substantial Interruption of the Proper boundaries Between Judicial Functions and Functions of the Other Branches of Government*

In 1994, this author expressed the view that the Israeli Supreme Court should engage in the fine tuning of the demarcation lines between the Supreme Court, the Knesset and the cabinet.[158]

Since 1994, the controversy regarding the scope of judicial review of the decisions of the political branches of government and the controversy regarding the role of the Supreme Court and its power to invalidate Knesset legislation just became more intensive than before.[159]

The controversy regarding the scope of judicial review has an impact on public confidence in the justice system in Israel. The court cannot exercise its power in total detachment from the social and public discourse. In order to continue to faithfully execute its role in society, the court must demarcate in a very finely tuned manner the demarcation lines between the Supreme Court and the other branches. The test and the basis for the demarcation lines between

---

[154] *Ibid.*

[155] *Ibid.*

[156] Accordingly, the Court has decided that economic matters, such as the regulation of slaughterhouses or transport of bread to shops, should be regulated by normal legislation, and not by emergency powers granted to Ministers under the Supervision of Commodities Law. Commodities and Services (Control) Law, 1957, S.H. 24; 12 L.S.I. 24.

[157] Shetreet, *Law and Social Pluralism* (LexisNexis 2002) at 265–271.

[158] Shetreet, Justice in Israel, note 26 above, at pp. 519–521.

[159] See the proposed draft law to amend Basic Law: The Judiciary (Amendment Justiciability) 5768/208. See: Sela, "Fridman: 'the Supreme Court is an Institution Without Control'" 14.11.2007, available at: http://www.ynet.co.il/articles/0,7340,L-3471170,00.html (Hebrew. Visited: Oct 23, 2010). See also Shetreet, On Adjudication, note 33, chapters 14–15. Shetreet, Law and Business note 14, pp. 562-582. Shetreet, Resolving the Controversy over the Form and Legitimacy of Constitutional Adjudication in Israel: A Blrepiemt for Redifining the Role the Supreme Court and the Knesset, 77 Tulane Law R. 659 (2003).

the judiciary and the other branches of government should be based on the following idea: when judicial intervention in a certain area will bring about a substantial disruption or imbalance between the judicial branch and another branch of government, the court should redefine the lines between the judiciary and the other branches and should refrain from intervening in this area. It is appropriate that the court and the Legislature will develop, parallel to this test, tools that will prevent substantial disruption or imbalance in the relationship between the branches of government. This is in order to create fine tuning of the lines that divide the powers of the branches of government. In the context of this fine tuning, the court should refrain from interfering with a case which is predominantly political and which lacks significant legal issues.[160]

The task of demarcating carefully the boundaries between the judiciary and the political branches is not less challenging than the task of expanding the scope of judicial review. The challenge is to refrain from unnecessary withdrawal of the judiciary from vital areas that must remain under a judicial supervision. At the same time, the challenge is to refrain from continued judicial intervention in areas where such intervention substantially disrupts the proper relationship between the courts and the political branches. Effective tools that may be used for promoting public purposes while preserving the lines of demarcation are the public debate and public discourse.

The press and pressure groups such as human rights organizations and social organizations exercise supervision of the activities of the administrative and governmental agencies. The proper supervision, and control of the governmental activities by these organisations should be by public criticism and not by judicial review. This criticism can have an impact on public opinion and have a positive impact on desirable social change. The opinion of this author is that the pressure groups, the non-government organizations, the social organizations and the human rights organizations can help introduce changes outside the courts, without disrupting the careful and sensitive balance which should exist between the branches of government, and avoiding the excessive recourse to the courts as an instrument of social change.

b. *Maintaining the Basic Doctrines of Standing and Justicibility*

The controversy over the judicial role in society is commonplace in many jurisdictions. The ensuing discussion of the Israeli scene can serve as a basis for possible solutions in order to moderate the controversies in other jurisdictions as well. As a case study of the delicate balance between the courts and the other branches of government, this author offers a special comment on the Israeli scene regarding judicial role in society. In the course of many years this author

---

160 Shetreet, Law and Business, note 14 above, at pp. 576.

has supported the expansion of the right of standing in petitions to the High Court of Justice. This author has represented in court petitioners in cases where the right of standing was given to petitioners based on a liberal approach to standing.[161] The position of this author is based on the assumption that after a long period of expansion of the scope of judicial review and the granting of extended right of standing and a flexible doctrine of justiciability, there will come a period of fine tuning, which will prevent conflicts between the judiciary and the political branches. The approach was that the fine tuning and the adjustments of the boundaries between the judiciary and the other branches of the government should be done by the courts themselves on the basis of considerations based on the test of substantial interruption of the relations as a qualifaction for judicial intervention, and the test of substantial violation of the rule of law and the test of the adverse impact on parliamentary system of government as a basis for judicial intervension.[162]

Today this author holds the view that there is a need to redefine the role of the Israeli Supreme Court, including the issue of the right of standing. This is because of the very heated controversy which is raging in the Israeli society regarding the position of the Supreme Court and its power to set aside Kenesst legislation by judicial review based on Basic Laws. The need to redefine the role of the Supreme Court is also required due to the strong opposition to the Supreme Court as a result of constitutional and public law activism that it exercises and the unfortunate trend of the continued loss of public support of the Supreme Court in Israeli society.

So long as the court had an ample institutional capital of public confidence, and the public controversies regarding its intervention in matters that were brought to its adjudication based on public petitions, it was justified to use the judicial institutional capital for the purpose of insuring good government, ethics, and rule of law and wider values of society by judicial decisions. After a long period of extending the role of the judiciary in society by the court, the judicial capital was drained in the eyes of the public. It is now time, therefore, to consider limiting the right of standing by legislation only to those who have been affected personally. Limiting of the right of standing is required in the Israeli context, in order to stop the phenomenon of solicited petitions. Because of the fact that deep involvement of the Israeli courts in the political governance of Israel, there is a phenomenon that solicited petitions are generated by circles

[161] HCJ 81/1 *Shiran v. Authority of Broadcasting*, 35(3) PD 365 (1981). In this case, owners of television sets in a petition to the High Court against the Israeli Broadcasting Authority; HCJ 86/852 *Aloni v. Minister of Justice*, 41(2) PD 1 (1987) – in this case ordinary citizens filed a petition against the refusal of the Minister of Justice to surrender an extraditable offender.

[162] Shetreet, Justice in Israel, note 26 above, at pp. 519–521.

from all sectors of political spectrum, sometimes even from within the Executive and public administration. Thus, involving the courts in controversies which are beyond their power to resolve.

Additional justification for limiting the right of standing to persons who were affected personally can be found in the fact that non-governmental organizations and civil society organizations in Israel are now very strong, and are able to attain legislative amendments, changes in Executive policy, and other remedies by lobbying, public and parliamentary campaigns, and the use of investigative press. Therefore, deficiencies and problems that in the past could only be remedied by the courts, through public petitions to the Supreme Court, can now be remedied by alternative means without draining the judicial institutional capital. This capital is essential and vital for the Supreme Court in order to adjudicate the classical judicial controversies of petitioners and other litigants who have personally been affected and for the performance of the classical judicial role in society of dispute resolution in the ordinary cases.

VIII. Concluding Remarks: Two Major Challenges in Upcoming Years

In the upcoming years the culture of judicial independence in the national and transnational levels will face particular challenges in two main areas. One is judicial independence in administrative justice, and the other is maintaining judicial independence in international and supranational justice.

The first area is the independence of administrative tribunals and judges and administrative judges that hear cases in administrative agencies. There is an ongoing debate in the United States on what is referred to in England as "tribunal judiciary" and in the United States as "administrative judges". The issue is to what extent can the existing practice of administrative judges acting within administrative agencies be defined as impartial and independent.[163] It is possible that other jurisdictions will follow the United Kingdom's lead in the form of its legislation provided that judicial independence must be guaranteed to "tribunal judiciary."[164]

---

163 See Lubbers, "The Federal Administrative Judiciary: Establishing an Appropriate System of Performance Evaluation for ALJs" (1993–1994) 7 Admin. L. J. Am. U. 589, at pp. 613–17; Timony, "Performance Evaluation of Federal Administrative Law Judges" (1993–1994) 7 Admin. L. J. Am. U. 629, at p. 641.

164 Tribunals, Courts and Enforcement Act 2007, ch 15 (2007) (UK), available at: http://www.opsi.gov.uk/ACTS/acts2007/ukpga_20070015_en_1 (visited Oct 23, 2010). Section 1 amended the Constitutional Reform Act 2005.

Normally scholars and legislatures focus the attention on the high level judiciary, which is the level most relevant to the rule of law and human rights. However, lower court judges, tribunal judges, and administrative judges, as well as other judicial officers also play an important role in the administration of justice. The study of the independence of the judicial officers engaged in administrative justice is therefore critical. This is because the issue of judicial independence is equally important to the citizen whose matter is adjudicated before one of these levels as it is to the person whose case is heard before a supreme court. It seems that the development of the culture of judicial independence is moving in this direction.[165]

The second area which offers a serious challenge in the upcoming years is the independence of international judges and supranational judges.[166] It should be noted that in addition to national and international judges, there is a third category of judges, that is the supranational judges. The difference between the international and supranational judge is in the procedure of enforcement of the judgment in a specific country. The judgment of an international tribunal (as distinguished from a supranational tribunal) must be enforced in a procedure which is required in each country for the integration of an international norm into the domestic law. This may require legislation in the case of treaties, and in the case of judgment, may require an Executive decision. In the case of judgment by supranational tribunal, on the other hand, it applies directly into the domestic law of the country which is a party to the supranational organisation, such as the European Union. In the European Union, the European Court of justice is a supranational court, and therefore its judgment applies to the European countries immediately, without any requirement of an integration procedure into the domestic law. This, in contrast to the rulings of the European Court of Human Rights, which is an international court, that its judgments require a procedure of enforcement relevant to the integration of an international action that needs to be transformed into the domestic law.

It is to be noted that in several jurisdictions it was suggested that the judgment of the European Court of Justice will not be respected, in case

---

[165] *Suratt v. Attorney-General of Trinidad and Tobago*, [2007] UKPC 55 (UK).

[166] For an analysis of the international and supranational judges issue see: Helfer and Slaughter, "Toward a Theory of Effective Supranational Adjudication"(1997) 107 Yale L. Rev. 273–393. See also: Young, "Toward a Framework Statute for Supranational Adjudication" (2007–2008) 57 Emory L.J. 93, and: Volcansek, "The European court of Justice: Supranational Policy-Making" (1992) 15 West European Politics 109–121. See: Malleson, "Promoting Judicial independence in the international Courts: Lessons from the Caribbean" (2009) 58 International and Comparative Law Quarterly Volume 671–697.

of a contradiction between such a judgment and the constitution of the member state.[167]

This issue of the role of international judges and tribunals, as well as of the supranational judges and tribunals, requires special attention with regard to the terms of their service and the protection of their independence *vis-à-vis* their nominating member states, as well as their reappointment to the international and supranational tribunals after the end of their term of appointment.[168]

---

[167] These suggestions have been proposed in the British House of Lords and the German Bundesverfassungsgericht.

[168] For a detailed analyse of this subject, see: Shany, Sands, Romano and Mackenzie (eds.), *The Manual on International Courts and Tribunals* (Oxford 2009); Shany, *The competing jurisdictions of international courts and tribunals* (Oxford, 2003); Shany, "Squaring the Circle? Independence and Impartiality of Party-Appointed Adjudicators in International Legal Proceedings", Hebrew University International Law Research Paper No. 03-08; Shany and Horovitz, "Judicial Independence in The Hague and Freetown: A Tale of Two Cities" (2008), 21 Leiden Journal of International Law 113–129; Crawford and McIntyre, "The Independence and Impartiality of the 'International Judiciary'", chapter 12 of this volume.

CHAPTER THREE

THE FAILURE OF INSTITUTIONS: THE SOUTH AFRICAN JUDICIAL SERVICE COMMISSION AND THE HLOPHE SAGA

*Christopher Forsyth**

This paper tells the tale of certain incidents that raise doubts about the integrity of some parts of the South African judiciary. Some such unattractive incidents are, perhaps, inevitable in any judiciary and, particularly so, in a judiciary that has undergone the sort of "transformation" the South African judiciary has undergone since the political changes of the early 1990s.

But the test of a constitution is the way in which it deals with such incidents. And here the argument of this paper is that the Judicial Services Commission, which has an unenviable role as the authority which must find that a judge has been guilty of "gross misconduct" before that judge may be removed from office, has been failing in this task. This is of profound and disconcerting consequence for the South African judiciary as a whole and constitutional government in that country.

This paper will not offer any remedy for the state of affairs. That is a matter and a test for the constitutional actors in South Africa. But it does point to the possibility that the judiciary itself will, in its own interests and the interests of the polity as a whole, insist upon the JSC adopting proper standards and disciplining errant judges. In other words that the cavalry may come to the rescue!

Before turning to the detail of this tale it will be well to maintain a sense of perspective. The almost wholly peaceful transformation of South Africa from

---

* Christopher Forsyth is Professor of Public and Private International Law in the University of Cambridge and Extraordinary Professor of Law in the University of Stellenbosch. From 1997 to 2010 he was Director or Assistant Director of the Centre for Public Law. He is the author with the late Sir William Wade QC of Administrative Law (10th ed, OUP 2009) a standard work on the subject recognised as authoritative by courts throughout the common law world. He has written many books and articles in learned journals on all aspects of public law and private international law. His PhD thesis was published as "In Danger for their Talents: A study of the Appellate Division of the Supreme Court of South Africa from 1950" (Juta & Co, 1985). He has advised several governments on thorny issues of administrative and constitutional law. He is a practicing barrister, a Bencher of the Inner Temple, and sits as a Recorder in the Crown Court in England.

an oppressive state in which the majority of the population was excluded from political power on racial grounds into a constitutional order with a constitution that is considered by some the most progressive in the world was an astonishing, almost miraculous, event in world history. Notwithstanding the current difficulties it is all so much better than many, myself included, expected or dared to believe possible.

The process of transformation[1] was inevitably complicated and difficult.[2] As Professor Hugh Corder has remarked:

> [Transformation] is a process which necessitates substantial upheavals of established practices and expectations, in which there is a risk of the loss of what might have been conducive of good governance, in pursuit of systemic renewal and a greater degree of equity and justice. So this is a tale of both good and bad, of confusion and poor management in the face of uncharted territory, and of the constant tensions lingering from the wickedness of the past.[3]

I. The Establishment of the Judicial Services Commission

Prior to the constitutional transformation judicial appointment and judicial discipline was dealt with by the executive authorities. Judges of the Superior Courts certainly had security of tenure in law (and none were ever removed from office).[4] But, although there was no barrier in law to the appointment of judges from persons of colour, this was never done until the dying days of the apartheid.[5] The higher judiciary (and most of the lower judiciary for that matter) were exclusively white. In addition, the higher judiciary was almost exclusively male.

---

[1] I should make it clear that I am dealing here only with the constitutional transformation of South Africa (concentrating on the judiciary). I am not dealing with the process of "transformation" much debated in modern South African politics whereby the inequalities of the past (in distribution of wealth, education, etc) are sought to be remedied.

[2] For an account see R. Spitz and M. Chaskalson, *The Politics of Transition: A Hidden History of South Africa's Negotiated Settlement* (Hart, 2000).

[3] In his essay "Appointment, Discipline and Removal of Judges in South Africa" in H.P. Lee (ed.), *Judiciaries in Comparative Perspective* (CUP 2010, ed H.P. Lee) 2 (hereinafter Corder (page numbers are to the unpublished paper)).

[4] Prior to the establishment of the Union of South Africa in 1910 there was the celebrated dismissal of the Chief Justice of the Transvaal Republic (Sir John Kotze) in by then President of the Republic (Paul Kruger) in a dispute over the judiciary's disputed power to test the validity of legislation made by the Volksraad. For accounts see R. Zimmermann and D. Visser (eds.), *The Southern Cross: Civil Law and Common Law in South Africa* (OUP, 1996), at p. 17 (and sources there referred to). See also L.M. Thompson, "Constitutionalism in the South African Republics" (1954) *Butterworths South African Law Review* 49.

[5] When two judges of Indian extraction were appointed.

The appointment of judges was in the hands of the executive. Technically the appointment was made by the Governor-General in Council and on the establishment of the Republic of South Africa in 1961 by the State President in Council. In practice this would be on the advice of Minister of Justice who, it seems, generally consulted other judges and members of the bar.[6] From time to time this procedure led to controversy most prominently in 1955 when the size of the Appellate Division of the Supreme Court was increased and five new judges (of questionable quality) were appointed overnight and without consultation to the court.[7] (The court was "packed" in this way to ensure the success of the government in its unconstitutional plan to remove the remaining small number of mixed race voters from the voters roll.[8])

With the constitutional transformation a Judicial Services Commission was agreed in the negotiations that lead to the Interim Constitution.[9] (The Interim Constitution applied until the Final Constitution was enacted and certified as complying with the laid down Constitutional Principles by the Constitutional Court.) There was ready agreement that the appointment of High Court judges on the advice of the Judicial Services Commission but the mode of appointment of the Constitutional Court judges was controversial. In part because of the poor record of the existing judiciary in protecting civil liberties the fundamental rights that were to form the centre piece of the new constitution were to be protected by a freshly created largely separate Constitutional Court.

The Judicial Services Commission was very nearly denied any role in the appointment of Constitutional Court judges. The interim government was to be a power sharing government with the National Party (that was demitting power) and the African National Congress (which for the first time was exercising power) ruling together until the final constitution was established. These two parties nearly did a deal to keep the appointment of judges to the Constitutional Court in the hands of the executive (so that the judgeships could be shared between their supporters). The National Party apparently making the surprising judgment that they would be able, notwithstanding their reduced position, to influence Cabinet decisions on appointments.

---

[6] Corder, see note 3 above, at p. 3.

[7] See C. F. Forsyth, *In Danger for their Talents: A study of the Appellate Division of the Supreme Court of South Africa from 1950* (Juta & Co,1985), pp. 21–25 (hereinafter Forsyth).

[8] See, Forsyth, *ibid.*, for an account.

[9] I was the first person to call for such a commission after the political logjam broke (see C.F. Forsyth, "Interpreting a Bill of Rights: the future task of a reformed judiciary?" (1991) 7 SAJHR 1, 20) but I have no reason to believe my call was influential.

ANC doubtless wished to enjoy the executive power its predecessor had enjoyed for generations.[10]

But in the end the JSC was given the task of making recommendations for appointment of Constitutional Court judges. This was a close run thing and the agreement to exclude the JSC between the National Party and the ANC nearly took effect. But the liberal Democratic Party protested, the Chief Justice objected, the Deans of all the law schools objected. From the point of view of the rule of law in South Africa this was a crucial moment in the constitutional transformation. If the judges of the Constitutional Court had been appointed by executive whim the constitutional history of South Africa might have been very different.

Of course the basic constitutional point needs to be made: prior to the constitutional changes in South Africa Parliament was sovereign and the judges had no power of judicial review over primary legislation. But now Parliament would no longer be sovereign and the judges would have the enhanced power of judicial review of statutes with the power to quash statutes that breached the fundamental rights protected in the Constitution. That necessarily implies a fundamental change in the judicial role and that too implies a greater measure of judicial power and a change in the method of appointment. No one could argue now that judges were mere technicians applying established law with no political power. There is thus a case to be made for a more political appointment process to apply to the Constitutional Court in the light of this enhanced power. But a politically appointed Constitutional Court would not have appeared independent or impartial and the legitimacy of the constitution would have been in doubt.

This was a crucial moment in the constitutional transformation. And it seems to me that few apart from the Democratic Party emerge with credit.[11] Fortunately, the Democratic Party (and some others in the negotiations) saw the point and dug in their heels, putting the whole of the negotiations at risk. The other parties reluctantly compromised and the role of the JSC was extended from the appointment of High Court judges to the judges of the Constitutional Court (with special arrangements being made for the Chief Justiceship).

[10] There was a fear within the ANC that the agreement to a judicially enforceable Bill of Rights would prevent the incoming government from implementing the policies that it saw as necessary to address the injustices of the past. See, Forsyth, note 9, 1–4.

[11] Amongst those to be found in favour of the executive appointing the Constitutional Court judges are Arthur Chaskalson (a leading counsel prominent in the fight against apartheid and later Chief Justice) and Nelson Mandela himself. See R. Spitz and M. Chaskalson, see note 2 above, at pp. 201–209.

II. The Composition and Tasks of the JSC

The composition of the JSC is set out in section 178 of the Constitution[12] but it is conveniently summarised by Professor Corder in these words:

> Chaired by the Chief Justice, the JSC consists of representatives of the judiciary and of the advocates' and attorneys' professional bodies, a teacher of law, the Minister of Justice and Constitutional Affairs, ten serving members of Parliament drawn from both Houses, and four members designated by the President as head of the executive, after consultation with the leaders of opposition parties. Thus, of the 23 ordinary members of the JSC, fifteen are selected more for their broadly political views than their standing as lawyers, of whom at least twelve are likely to be loyal in the first instance to the ruling party in Parliament.[13]

It would be wrong to see the JSC as dominated by party politics but it is undeniable that there is a significant political influence in the body. Views will differ on the best composition of a JSC but it is worth noting that the UK equivalent, the Judicial Appointments Commission, has no similar political input.[14] But on the other hand, the executive remains involved in judicial appointments in all sorts of ways across the common law world.

The primary task of the JSC is its role in the appointment of judicial officers.[15] Constitutional Court judges are appointed by the President from a

---

[12] Which reads in part: "178. Judicial Service Commission

1. There is a Judicial Service Commission consisting of
   a. the Chief Justice, who presides at meetings of the Commission;
   b. the President of the Supreme Court of Appeal;
   c. one Judge President designated by the Judges President;
   d. the Cabinet member responsible for the administration of justice, or an alternate designated by that Cabinet member;
   e. two practising advocates nominated from within the advocates' profession to represent the profession as a whole, and appointed by the President;
   f. two practising attorneys nominated from within the attorneys' profession to represent the profession as a whole, and appointed by the President;
   g. one teacher of law designated by teachers of law at South African universities;
   h. six persons designated by the National Assembly from among its members, at least three of whom must be members of opposition parties represented in the Assembly;
   i. four permanent delegates to the National Council of Provinces designated together by the Council with a supporting vote of at least six provinces;
   j. four persons designated by the President as head of the national executive, after consulting the leaders of all the parties in the National Assembly; and
   k. when considering matters relating to a specific High Court, the Judge President of that Court and the Premier of the province concerned, or an alternate designated by each of them."

[13] Corder, see note 3 above, at p. 7 (footnotes omitted).

[14] Constitutional Reform Act 2005, Schedule 12.

[15] The detailed procedures are set out in section 174 of the Constitution.

list drawn up by the JSC in which there are three more names than the number of vacancies. But with the more senior officers (Chief Justice and Deputy Chief Justice, President, and Deputy President of the Supreme Court of Appeal) the President need only consult with the JSC; and in the case of Chief Justice and Deputy Chief Justice there is the further requirement of consultation with the leaders of the parties in the National Assembly. Less elevated judges are appointed simply in the advice of the JSC. The JSC and the President are obliged to consider "the need for the judiciary to reflect broadly the racial and gender composition of South Africa".[16]

In the years since it came into existence the JSC has played a central role in the demographic transformation of the South African judiciary. Again in Professor Corder's words:

> From the almost all-white, all-male Bench in place in early 1994, the current demographic composition of judicial ranks is as follows: 78 African (16 women),16 coloured (four women),18 Indian (eight women), and 91 white (14 women) judges. So, of the 203 judges permanently appointed to the Bench, just over 55% were broadly "black", while only just over 20% were female. In addition, all but one of the Heads of Court are black African men, and this has been the case for several years now.[17]

But our concern in this paper is not primarily with the appointment but with the removal of judges. And here too the JSC has a crucial role. Section 177 of the Constitution provides that:

> A judge may be removed from office only if (a) the Judicial Service Commission finds that the judge suffers from an incapacity, is grossly incompetent or is guilty of gross misconduct; and the National Assembly calls for that judge to be removed, by a resolution adopted with a supporting vote of at least two thirds of its members.[18]

So the upshot of this is that, setting aside questions of incompetence and incapacity, the removal of a judge from his office requires a finding by the Judicial Service Commission of "gross misconduct".[19] When making such a finding the JSC sits without its ten serving members of the National Assembly.[20]

The Constitution does not specify the procedure to be adopted by the Commission in making its finding. On the contrary, it provides that the JSC "may determine its own procedure, but decisions of the Commission must be

---

[16] Section 174(2) of theh Constitution.

[17] Corder, see note 3 above, at p. 12. The statistics result from a personal inquiry by Professor Corder to the Department of Justice.

[18] Section 177 of the Constitution.

[19] *Ibid.*

[20] Section 178(5) of the Constitution.

supported by a majority of its members."[21] But, very clearly, a high degree of procedural protection will be required in its deliberations.

III. Judge President Hlophe

The Hon. Mr Justice Hlophe grew up in rural Natal during the 1960s and 1970s when apartheid was at its height. Although from relatively humble origins his ability and determination soon made itself known. As a black man he was inevitably discriminated against in many ways but he succeeded in obtaining a good education and being admitted to one of South Africa's leading law schools (the University of Natal (now the University of Kwa-Zulu Natal)) in Pietermaritzburg after studying at the equally famous University of Fort Hare.

From the University of Natal he made his way to Cambridge and was awarded both the LLM degree and, in due course, a PhD. His thesis was ironically enough (as will become clear as the discussion proceeds) on "Natural Justice in South Africa".[22] He might easily have sought a career as an academic in the "outside world" but he returned to apartheid South Africa first to the University of Natal as a senior lecturer and then to the University of Transkei as a professor. So he had a successful career as a scholar well underway when the political transformation of South Africa commenced in the early 1990s.

But now the glittering prizes were laid before him. He was a very able, highly qualified legal scholar at precisely the moment in which the South Africa judiciary was about to be transformed. He was very much in demand. He was appointed a Judge of the Cape High Court at the age of 36 in 1995 and was, I believe, the first full time academic appointed direct to the High Court Bench in South Africa. His youth was both a blessing and a curse.

Most judges in South Africa are appointed in their fifties and retire at the statutory retirement age of seventy after a judicial career of only about fifteen years. Mr Justice Hlophe might reasonably have anticipated a judicial career of thirty four years. Plainly many, many opportunities for advancement and promotion would be laid before him. He might reasonably anticipate that he would become in due course one of, if not the, most senior and respected judge in South Africa. But at the same time he was very young and, moreover, his career thus far had been almost entirely in the academic world. So he lacked the experience of day to day practice that a more conventional appointee

---

[21] Section 174(3) of the Constitution.

[22] This thesis was supervised by the present author (who consequently knows Mr Justice Hlophe well) and examined by the late Professor Sir David Williams (Emeritus Vice-chancellor of the University of Cambridge) and Professor Lawrence Baxter of Duke University (and an authority on South African Administrative Law).

would have had. And he, perhaps, lacked the maturity an older man would have had in responding to the challenges he faced.

Barely four years after his first appointment to the bench, however, the judge presidency of the Cape fell vacant.[23] Mr Justice Hlophe was, to be frank, still feeling his way as a puisne judge but making good progress. He should have waited. He could have waited. There would be many other opportunities in the thirty years ahead in which the judge presidency — and even greater offices — would fall vacant and in which he would be the frontrunner. But this was not to be. He grasped the opportunity and was appointed Judge President in 2000.

The task that now faced the judge was a daunting one with heavy administrative responsibilities and an expectation of leadership. Yet there were doubtless colleagues on the bench who were sceptical of his rapid promotion and saw it as being at the expense of their advancement. Many at the bar were similarly sceptical and critical especially when the judge's inexperience showed. This being South Africa the ugly cry of racism was part of the currency of discourse. Doubtless sometimes this was justified but oftentimes it was not. The consequence, of course, was much bitterness with compromise and reconciliation made more difficult.[24]

Anyway there was no doubt that the judge was (and is) a controversial judge president. Wikipedia lists some eleven controversial incidents in the years from 2004 to 2009.[25] Some of these concern politically sensitive or controversial cases which are an inevitable part of a judge's lot; and it is proper that such cases be closely scrutinised but the involvement in such cases (and even the making of errors in deciding such cases) do not in themselves raise doubts about the judge's fitness for office. Others concern the trading of insults between the Judge President and other the judges on the Cape Bench and between the judiciary and the bar. The Judge President was sued (and is still being sued) for defamation by a quondam acting judge, etc. This is all very unattractive but none of these matters led to proceedings before the Judicial Service Commission so we shall say no more about them.

But two matters did lead to such proceedings and on these we now concentrate.

---

[23] The Judge Presidency of a High Court is in effective a mini- Chief Justice with administrative responsibilities (allocating the roll, etc) as well as representative and ceremonial functions.

[24] Hlophe JP in fact made a report to the Minister of Justice on Racism in the Cape Bench and Bar accusing various counsel who were doughty fighters against apartheid of racism (without giving them an opportunity to contradict his views).

[25] http://en.wikipedia.org/wiki/John_Hlophe (visited 16th September 2010). The page is (inevitably) subject to dispute but I noted no obvious inaccuracy in the various controversies listed.

IV. The Oasis Incident[26]

From November 2000 to 2005, Oasis Asset Management[27] made monthly payments to Mr Justice Hlophe amounting in total to R500 000 (a sum of approximately US$ 50,000). These payments were apparently made in respect of service as a trustee of a pension fund. Employment outside his judicial role by a judge required, under the applicable law, the consent of the Minister of Justice[28] and it is clear that no written consent was given. When Mr Justice Hlophe was taxed with the question of whether consent had been obtained, his response was that it had been granted orally by a Minister of Justice, Dullah Omar, who had since died. In fact Mr Omar had died some eighteen months before Mr Justice Hlophe's commenced his employment with Oasis[29] and so was unable to confirm Mr Justice Hlophe's account of consent given orally.[30]

However the fact of these payments only came to light in the context of a defamation action that was brought by Oasis Asset Management against another judge of the Cape High Court, Siraj Desai. We need not concern ourselves with the rights and wrongs of this action other than to note under the relevant legislation the consent of the relevant High Court is required before an action can proceed against a judge.[31] The fact is that while in receipt of payments from Oasis Mr Justice Hlophe granted consent for Oasis to sue Mr Justice Desai. To any lawyer the appearance of bias is palpable, even if the decision to grant consent was fully justified.

When this matter was laid before the JSC in October 2007 a divided Commission decided that there was "insufficient evidence" for any further action to be taken. This is a remarkable decision since the facts seem to be very clear. Even if one accepts that the ante mortem oral permission of the Minister

---

[26] At the same time as it considered these matters outlined in the text the JSC considered two other complaints against Judge Hlophe. These concerned a racist remark had been made to a legal practitioner and that he had disparaged a fellow judge to counsel.

[27] A Cape Town based firm providing financial products for investors.

[28] The relevant statutory provision is Supreme Court Act 59 of 1959, s.11, which reads: "Judge not to hold any other office of profit. No judge of the Supreme Court shall without the consent of the Minister accept, hold or perform any other office of profit or receive in respect of any service any fees, emoluments or other remuneration apart from his salary and any allowances which may be payable to him in his capacity as such a judge."

[29] There remains doubt as to whether Mr Justice Hlophe paid tax on the receipts from this appointment.

[30] I am unaware of any evidence that the Oasis employment was under consideration 18 months before it commenced.

[31] The relevant statutory provision is Supreme Court Act 59 of 1959, s. 25, which reads: " No process to be issued against judge except with consent of court.—(1) Notwithstanding anything to the contrary in any law contained, no summons or subpoena against the Chief Justice, a judge of appeal or any other judge of the Supreme Court shall in any civil action be issued out of any court except with the consent of that court..."

cast the mantle of propriety over the receipt of the Oasis payments post mortem, there remains the question of the grant of leave to Oasis to sue Judge Desai. The fact of that does not seem to be in dispute in any way and there seems to be no justification put forward.

Naturally the decision of the JSC was very controversial and much criticised. And many eminent retired judges and counsel went public with their views stating that Judge Hlophe was not "fit for the bench".[32] But Judge Hlophe had escaped and remained in office. The JSC did, however, state the grant of leave to sue Judge Desai was in the circumstances "a matter warranting adverse comment".[33] So adverse comment was made but no further action was taken.

V. The Constitutional Court Incident

But the career of Mr Justice Hlophe was not to settle down into placidity. The current President of South Africa, Jacob Zuma, is also no stranger to controversy; and his tale and that of Hlophe JP now become for a period intertwined.

Mr Zuma was an ambitious politician but his path to the highest office seemed blocked by allegations of corruption. These were serious allegations for a financial adviser and associate of his, Schabir Shaik,[34] had stood trial and been convicted of fraud and corruption concerning a large arms deal at the time that Mr Zuma was Deputy President of South Africa.[35] The judge in Shaik's trial used words that suggested that there was a corrupt relationship between Shaik and Zuma. Zuma was dismissed as Deputy President by the then President, Thabo Mbeki; and faced the prospect of a trial for corruption.[36]

Although loud in his assertions of innocence and allegations that the prosecution against him was contrived by his political opponents, Mr Zuma seemed reluctant to stand trial. There were several attempts to delay or prevent the trial

---

[32] http://www.iol.co.za/index.php?art_id=vn20071009035449895C346531

[33] http://www.legalbrief.co.za/article.php?story=20071023145931920. The complainant in the racist remark comment had withdrawn the complaint and Judge Hlophe had apologised for the disparagement of a fellow judge to counsel. So neither of these matters were taken further.

[34] http://en.wikipedia.org/wiki/Schabir_Shaik

[35] Shaik was sentenced to some fifteen years imprisonment. He was released on parole in March 2008 after serving two years and four months. This was under the Correctional Services Act, No 111 of 1998, s. 17, which provides for the release on parole of prisoners suffering from a terminal illness "to die a consolatory and dignified death". When last heard of Mr Shaik was seemingly in good health, playing golf, etc.

[36] Indeed it is a puzzle why Zuma did not stand trial with Shaik.

by various interlocutory applications. One of these concerned a challenge to the validity of six search warrants which had been executed against various offices and homes of Mr Zuma and his co-accused (a company called Thint (Pty) Ltd). The warrants were challenged on various grounds including that some of the documents seized might have been subject to legal professional privilege. Anyway, these were in the issues that were argued before the Constitutional Court in March 2008. Judgement was given on the 31st of July 2008 rejecting the appeals against the validity of the warrants.[37]

This was the background against which the storm broke on the 30th May 2008 when the judges of the Constitutional Court issued a press statement in which it was alleged that Judge President Hlophe had attempted improperly to influence two of their number to decide the case then under consideration in a manner favourable to Jacob Zuma.

As Professor Corder puts it:

> The following weeks witnessed a slew of accusation, counter-accusation, rumour, outright denial by Judge Hlophe, calls for his dismissal by political parties and others, and vigorous defence of Judge Hlophe by several commentators…It became known that the two judges whom Judge Hlophe had met and with whom he had discussed the case were Justice Bess Nkabinde and Acting Justice Chris Jafta.….[Delays in making the allegations and the responses to them] led to speculation about the politics of the move within the Court itself and within the broader legal profession, as well as counter-complaints of procedural unfairness, both from Judge Hlophe and increasingly vociferously from his supporters. These exchanges culminated in Judge Hlophe (who had been granted special leave of absence by the Minister of Justice pending the resolution of this matter) submitting a counter-complaint to the JSC, alleging that the Constitutional Court's decision had been politically motivated and threatened the independence of the judiciary.[38]

So this was the position: different judges had complained to the JSC about each other! There was a great fuss in the newspapers and much vociferous comment (much of it ill informed) with allegations of racism and political interference being liberally spread about.[39] But any sympathetic observer of the South Africa judiciary was surely close to despair. And things got worse when Judge Hlophe sought to prevent the JSC's consideration of the Constitutional Court's complaint on the ground that that court should have given him a hearing before it could make a complaint to the JSC. There was also litigation over

[37] *Thint (Pty) Ltd and Zuma v. National Director of Public Prosecutions* (2009) 1 SA 1(CC).

[38] H. Corder, 2008 Annual Survey of South African Law, (hereinafter Corder (Annual Survey)) (in the press).

[39] The allegations about race are particularly inapposite in this context in that all the protagonists were of the same race.

whether the JSC could consider the complaint and counter complaint in open or closed proceedings.

What became clear was that Judge Hlophe had met separately with Acting Constitutional Court Justice Christopher Jafta and Constitutional Court Justice Bess Nkabinde after argument but before decision in the Zuma matter. But what happened then was much disputed. The Constitutional Court's complaint alleged that Judge Hlophe had told Nkabinde he held a "mandate" to make his approach and that Zuma was being persecuted and there was no real case against him: "Judge Jafta confirmed that a similar approach had been made to him" and that Hlophe had told him that he was '...*our last hope*....'"[40] Both Judges stated that they had dealt with the matter firmly and rejected Judge Hlophe's advances. Judge Hlophe made a lengthy response to the Constitutional Court's complaint alleging that the complaint was "trumped up and politically motivated".[41]

Faced with the clashing accounts of the meetings between the judges the Disciplinary Committee of the JSC decided on the 7th July 2008 "that oral hearings were necessary to resolve the disputes of fact".[42] The JSC was it seems keen to get on with resolving the controversy before it could fester further. But it was now delayed for more than one year by the litigation mentioned earlier when Judge Hlophe sought to prevent the JSC proceedings by alleging that the complaint itself infringed his constitutional rights. Eventually the Supreme Court of Appeal found against Judge Hlophe on these issues although expressing no view of the merits of the complaints.[43]

And when the matter returned from the courts to the JSC about a year later the world had changed. Jacob Zuma had become president and had persuaded the Director of Public Prosecutions to drop the corruption charges against him.[44] Furthermore, as we have seen, the President in consultation with the leaders of the opposition parties appointed some four members of the JSC.

---

[40] Corder (Annual Survey) citing Jafta's account.

[41] Corder (Annual Survey) see note 3 above.

[42] Corder (Annual Survey), *ibid.*

[43] I will not burden this text with the detail of Judge Hlophe's application. (For that detail, see Corder (Annual Survey), *ibid.*). It is enough to say that the Supreme Court of Appeal found decisively against him. See *Langa and Others v. Hlophe* [2009] ZASCA 36; [2009] 3 All SA 417 (SCA); 2009 (8) BCLR 823 (SCA). The SCA rejected both the points raised on Judge Hlophe's behalf. First, the appellants, although judges of the CC, were not acting in a judicial capacity as so were not obliged to give Judge Hlophe a hearing before making their complaint to the JSC. Secondly, they were not obliged to keep the fact of the complaint confidential. The judgement of the SCA is, with respect, wholly convincing.

[44] The reason given was that telephone intercepts had revealed that there was a conspiracy between the NDPP and one of the investigators over the timing of the charges against Zuma. It was said this was done to secure a political advantage to Zuma's rival Thabo Mbeki.

The term of office of the four Presidential appointees had come to an end and four new members had been appointed. This may have affected the outcome of the subsequent proceedings.[45]

When the matter came before the JSC on the 28th August 2009 it decided (by a majority) not to proceed with the full hearing of the complaint against Judge Hlophe. The JSC's reasons were, first, while they accepted that Judge Hlophe had said to Jafta and Nkabinde JJ that the *Zuma/Thint* matter had to be decided "properly" they did not find that that the complainant judges had with sufficient consistency said that he had said that the case must be decided in a particular way (ie favourable to Zuma). In fact one of the judges said that Judge Hlophe had never said that the case should be decided in a particular way. This meant that "a hearing would not be necessary as there was no evidence that Hlophe had improperly tried to influence the judges to decide the case one way or another."[46]

The distinction drawn by the JSC between a general injunction to decide "properly" and a specific statement to decide in favour of one party has been aptly described "so absurd as to border on the irrational. It means that if a judge wants to improperly influence [sic] other judges he or she could get away with it as long as he or she never says the magic words: 'Decide the case in favour of X.' He or she could say the case must be decided 'properly', and can argue what a 'proper' decision would be, but this would not, according to the wise people at the JSC, constitute an attempt to influence the judge approached."[47] So while it was not disputed that Judge Hlophe had discussed the pending case with Nkabinde and Jafta JJ, this was not "gross misconduct" but at most "unwise, ill-considered, imprudent, not thought through".[48] No hearing would be held on either complaint.

This unpersuasive decision to take no further action in the Hlophe cases was, inevitably, itself very controversial and disconcerting. Although the JSC received evidence (mostly in written form) from those involved and revealed that evidence to all those involved, there was no cross examination to test whether the Constitutional Court judges' account of their meetings with Hlophe or Hlophe's account was to be preferred.

As Professor Corder remarks in summing up that these incidents have "done considerable harm to the precious level of legitimacy earned by the

---

[45] Contrast Professor Pierre de Vos at http://constitutionallyspeaking.co.za/new-jsc-appointments-bad-news-for-hlophe/.

[46] Professor Pierre de Vos in Constitutionally Speaking at http://constitutionallyspeaking.co.za/a-sad-day-for-our-judiciary-and-the-jsc/.

[47] *Ibid.*

[48] *Ibid.*

post-apartheid judiciary, in particular the CC, as a secure and independent protector of the Constitution and good governance, and because the arguments raised chiefly in support of Hlophe … have plumbed new depths of irrationality, in which racism features prominently."[49]

VI. Conclusions

The tale just told has not yet come to its end. Judge Hlophe has twenty years of his judicial career left. He need not retire until 2030. In the coming years there will be many vacancies on the Constitutional Court and as Chief Justice. It is sobering to note that in the midst of his difficulties with the JSC a "Justice for Hlophe" campaign sprung up to support him generally and his candidature for the soon to be vacant Chief Justiceship or one of the vacant positions on the Constitutional Court.[50] In the event he was not appointed to any of these positions, but is such a campaign to be expected on every similar occasion for the next twenty years?

One expects that the judge does not see it this way but the whole controversy is a personal tragedy. Whether the judge succeeds in securing such advancement or not these incidents will be indelibly connected with his name; and consequently that name will not bring lustre to the judiciary. All this was quite unnecessary: the judge has the talent and had to the opportunity to make the most brilliant career.

But the broader issue is the failure of the JSC to rise to its constitutional role of considering allegations of "gross misconduct" against judges. It is right, of course, that it should be very difficult to dismiss judges. It is right, of course, that the independence of the judiciary is so important that some apparent misconduct and incapacity by judges must needs be tolerated in the wider interest. But it is in the interest of the judiciary and the public that plausible allegations of misconduct are properly investigated. Whatever else might be the position these allegations were not trivial – a high standard of conduct is rightly required of judges — and they should have been investigated. The JSC would have faced the challenge of a proper investigation into the misconduct of a judge at some point (Judge Hlophe was simply the occasion for this challenge). And in the political charged circumstances the JSC was simply not up to the task.

Against this sombre background there are two positive points with which to end.

---

[49] Corder, see note 3 above, at p. 20.
[50] See http://www.justiceforhlophealliance.co.za/.

In the first place the decision of the JSC is being subject to judicial review by a leading NGO, Freedom under Law established, as a not for profit organisation "in order to promote democracy under law and to advance the understanding and respect of the rule of law and the principle of legality".[51] The nub of the case being that the JSC decision to dismiss the complaints was premature and absurd in the circumstances.

The Supreme Court of Appeal has just (31st March 2011) handed down its judgment in this matter; and has quashed the decision of the JSC to dismiss the complaints (see *Freedom Under Law v JSC* [2011] ZASCA 59). An unanimous SCA decided that, in the circumstances, that decision was "irrational". The JSC's response is not known. But at least it can be said that the Supreme Court of Appeal is not a failing institution. Future developments may be awaited with interest.

But perhaps even more positive is a legislative development which addresses the lacuna in the existing law as to the procedure and structure of the JSC when considering the disciplining of judges. As outlined above the MP members of the JSC, but not those appointed by the President, do not participate when considering allegations of judicial misconduct. But now a further and positive legislative step has been taken with the enactment in 2008 of the Judicial Services Commission Amendment Act, 20 of 2008.[52] The important point of this Act (which has not yet been brought into force) is that it establishes a Judicial Conduct Committee which has an entirely judicial membership. The JCC consists of the Chief Justice and Deputy Chief Justice who sit ex officio and four judges (at least two of whom must be woman) designated by the CJ in consultation with the Minister of Justice.

The role of the Judicial Conduct Committee is "to receive, consider and deal with complaints" against judges. The procedures for dealing with the less serious complaints of misconduct by judges need not detain us (they are dealt with by the CJ and a committee member subject to appeal to the JCC). But the most serious allegations of misconduct involving potential removal from officer may lead the JCC to recommend to the Commission the appointment of an investigative Tribunal. The three members of the tribunal are appointed by the Chief Justice. Two are judges and one is not but is selected by the CJ from a list maintained by the JSC of suitable persons appointed to the list by the CJ with the concurrence of the Minister of Justice. The Tribunal follows the procedure

[51] http://www.freedomunderlaw.org/

[52] This measure forms the remnant of a wider measure designed to subject the administration of the courts to the executive that was very controversial and is not for the moment to be enacted. See Corder, note 3 above, at p. 20. The Act amends the Judicial Service Commission Act, 9 of 1994.

of a classic tribunal of inquiry with counsel to the tribunal and rules of procedure, etc. It reports to the Commission which will then make findings and decide what to do (presumably where gross misconduct is found the matter is referred to Parliament for a resolution praying for removal to be put (which as explained above would require a two thirds majority)).

Had this legislation been in force for the Hlophe saga it is difficult to suppose that the JSC would have been able to reach the conclusions that it did. The largely judicial tribunal of inquiry would have subjected the evidence of apparent misconduct to proper assessment and would have reached a justifiable conclusion on it. But under the Constitution the decision to find "gross misconduct" remains that of the JSC, so it would still technically be open to the JSC in the face of a damming report of the Tribunal to refuse to find "gross misconduct". It is also difficult to suppose that under these procedures, if the JCC had recommended a tribunal, that the JSC would have been able to refuse one.

So when this legislation comes into force some important positive steps will have been taken to ensure that the next "Hlophe saga" will be better handled.

CHAPTER FOUR

INDEPENDENCE OF THE JUDICIARY: THE EUROPEAN PERSPECTIVE

*Marcel Storme**

"The way of Justice is a tightrope
where no prince is safe for one instant"
(W.H. Auden, The Sea and the Mirror, II).

Some years ago already, we compiled under the leadership of Shimon Shetreet a document in which an attempt was made to draw up the "*General Standards on the Independence of the Judiciary*"[1]. And again we continued under the same guidance our quest for an independent judiciary.

In this Report, I am seeking not only to demystify and put into its proper perspective the notion of independence, but also to point, on the other hand, to the many ways in which the courts' work is burdened with "*bondages*".

Also, quite apart from the important debate surrounding the independence of the courts, the status of the judiciary presents a number of other aspects, some of which will be clarified below.

I. Independence Revisited

"Judges must be shielded from coercion of any sort particularly from executive control over the performance of their judicial duties"
(Lord Chief Justice Lane)

In the first instance, it must be pointed out that the independence of the courts does not entail that the latter are not accountable to no-one, because if that were the case, their independence would degenerate into irresponsibility.

---

* Marcel Storme is the director of Institute Procedural and European Law. He has graduated from Ghent University in 1952 and received advanced degrees from the University of Paris and London School of Economics. He has published many books, including *Burden of Proof*, *General Principles of Law*, and numerous articles. Marcel Storme was the president of the working group, which for the first time made proposals for the approximation of procedural laws in the European Union (1993).

[1] Shetreet, S., "*L'indépendance et la responsabilité des juges et des avocats*", in: Pessoa Vaz, A.M., Role and Organisation of Judges and Lawyers in Contemporary Societies (1995) Coimbra, p. 113 et seq.

Independence, in other words, is not an end in itself, but an "*instrumental value*"[2], a means of safeguarding a fundamental value, that of the impartiality of the judge, which for centuries has been symbolised by the blindfolded Lady of Justice. The essence of judicial activity resides in that it is exercised by an impartial and neutral third party.

In the explanation given below, I will attempt to draw up a typological classification for this kind of independence, adding a few comments. I would also refer to the abundant literature on the independence of the judiciary[3].

1. Independence towards the three constitutional authorities

The courts' independence towards the legislature and the executive are self-evident propositions, although they are not invariably respected in practice.

Indeed, the courts' dependence of the legislature continues to express itself through laws which are retroactive in their effect, or, worse still, intervene in pending proceedings. Less directly, but no less nefariously, does it come to expression in the budget laws which, throughout the world with the exception of Costa Rica, provide inadequate financial scope for the efficient operation of the courts.

That Parliament is seeking, in a subtle manner, to retain its hold on the judiciary is something which emerges from trend shown by the former to act as a substitute for the courts and to arrogate to itself certain powers of enquiry. Here, the frustration experienced by the Parliaments at no longer being able to control governments is being channelled into controlling the judiciary. The Van Traa Commission in the Netherlands and the Dutroux-commission in Belgium are examples of this.

The dependence of the courts of the executive remains an important consideration in those countries where the appointment of judges remains one of the prerogatives of the executive. However, there is a much more subtle danger in this context, which is that of management development by the

[2] Cappelletti, M., "Who watches the watchmen", in *The Judicial Process in Comparative Perspective* (1989) Oxford, p. 70.

[3] for a historical overview, cf. Picardi, N., "*L'indépendance et la responsabilité des juges et des avocats, Apercu historique*", in Pessoa Vaz, A.M., op. cit. p. 71 et seq.; cf. in particular the excellent comparative study made on the occasion of the Congresses of the International Association of Procedural Law in Würzburg (1983) and in Coimbra (1991) by Schwab, K.H., and Gottwald, P., "*Verfassung und Zivilprozess*", in Habscheid, W., Effektiver Rechtsschutz und verfassungsmäßige Ordnung (1983), Bielefeld, p. 1–89; Vescovi. E., "*La independencia de la magistratura*", ibid., p. 161–214; cf. also Picardi, N. and Shetreet, S., "*Indépendance et responsabilité des juges et des avocats*", in Pessoa Vaz, A.M., Role and organsiation of judges amd lawyers in contemporary societies (1995) Coïmbra, p. 73–144; Roth, G., "*Organisation und soziale Status der Richter*", in: Pessoa Vaz, A.M., op. cit. p. 147–186).

Ministry of Justice. This has nothing to do with our plea for productivity analyses and managerial justice among the judiciary (on this subject, cf. infra).

The real threat is that of making the judiciary an official field service of the Ministry of Justice. It has been proposed that management functions be conferred on the decision-making judges, on which regular reports would need to be submitted to the Minister; the latter could, if a negative verdict was returned on this management, request the Supreme Court to remove the judge in question from his managerial office.

However, there is also the question of the independence of the courts towards the judges as a body, both collectively and individually. Unfortunately, the threat of conformity and corporatism is as real as it ever has been.

Another threat is that of the collegiate attitude within a particular court. The story which concerned the American Supreme Court, and which was published in The Brethren[4] stands, if true, as a frightening example of this attitude.

A man who had been condemned to death had appealed to the Supreme Court, arguing that his verdict had been reached in an improper manner. Judge Blackmun, who was considered to be a member of the conservative camp, had, on behalf of the majority, drawn up a decision stating the reasons why the complaints made were unfounded, or at least could not serve to reverse the verdict. Against this view, Judge Marshall had advanced a dissenting opinion which carried such conviction with some members of the majority that they changed their minds. However, this was still insufficient to obtain a majority for Marshall's viewpoint. In order to obtain that majority, it was necessary that one more judge should change camps. Hopes were pinned on the progressive Judge Brennan. The latter was approached for this purpose by one of his clerks. How-ever, Brennan refused to withdraw his vote from the Blackmun majority verdict. He was alleged to have given the following reason for his refusal: he considered it undesirable to go against Judge Blackmun – who had recently shown signs of moving slightly in a progressive direction – by turning against his opinion, which had been prepared with such care, at a time when a number of more important cases needed to be decided in which it was important to obtain Blackmun's support.

A number of comments should be made in relation to the first type of independence.

(a) The principle of the separation of powers was abandoned some considerable time ago. Therefore it is legitimate to require that the independence of the

---

[4] Woodward and Armstrong, The Brethren.

courts, which is essentially a form of autonomy, should not stand in the way of co-operation between the three fundamental powers.

Here, we are talking of co-operation with the legislature which enabled the Plenary Council of the Supreme Court in the former Soviet Union to have the right to initiate legislation, or which allowed the French Cour de Cassation to make proposals for the improvement of legislation in its annual report.

We are also talking about co-operation with the executive which enables the courts to request information from the administration as is the case with the European Court of Justice[5].

(b) Within the judiciary, collective independence may not degenerate into the autonomy of individual judges, who object to co-operation of any kind in the battle against the slowness and delays in the judicial process.

I am not suggesting that energetic judges should take over the case files of their more indolent colleagues. The latter should be the subject of much more expedient disciplinary action.

However, it is an established and objective fact that certain judges and courts have a heavier workload than others. The latter would then need to be mobilised in order to obtain a fairer distribution of work.

This will also enable the judiciary to make it clear that it is facing up to its responsibility to solve itself the problems of slowness and delays.

2. The judiciary and its members must adopt an independent attitude towards the world of politics. The latter does not make this very easy, since in many countries judges are still being appointed by those in political authority, and the size, appropriation and management of the justice budget is mostly removed from the involvement of the judiciary. All this constitutes a threat to the independence of the judges.

For many years now, I have been teaching my students that a judge must suffer from a Becket-complex, referring to Thomas Becket who, following his appointment as Lord Chancellor by Henry II, informed the latter: "I was your friend, now I am your Lord Chancellor". When I told this story to the Chairman of the Supreme Court of Argentina, of whom it was said that he was a notorious friend of President Menem, he answered tersely: "I have remained President Menem's friend".

---

[5] Article 21 of the Statute of the Court of Justice; cf. Article 138 of the Belgian Judicial Code, which stipulates that, in the course of labour disputes, the Public Prosecutor may request information from the appropriate authority; cf. also on this subject Koopmans, T., "*Judicial activism and procedural law*", in:(1993) European Review of Private Law (ERPL) 67 et seq.; at p. 81.

However, I have also taught my students that it is impossible to be a judge and at the same time man the barricades. The well-known "phénomène Magnaud" is never far away.

3. The last-named point brings me to to a very special – and perhaps the most fundamental – application of the independence principle, to wit, the impartiality of the judge, towards himself, towards the parties, and towards their lawyers.

He must be impartial towards himself, which means that the judge must leave behind his own philosophical, ideological, political and other beliefs when adjudicating a case. If he does not consider himself capable of doing so, he must withdraw from the case. This I could well imagine that a judge, whose child had been killed by a drunken driver, could not be in a position to settle a similar case with the necessary degree of detachment.

He must be impartial towards the parties, a requirement which is imposed by statute in virtually all the systems of court procedure throughout the world. If this does not suffice, reliance can be placed on the impartial judge principle laid down in Article 6 of the ECHR and Article 14 of the International Convention on Civil and Political Rights.

However, he must also be impartial towards the lawyers, especially if these lawyers play an important part in the social system, or if they belong to what Yves Dezalay has called the "marchands de droit qui cumulent la triple fonction de conseiller les auteurs de normes, de plaider les litiges qu'elles suscitent et de commenter les décisions qui les appliquent" ("those salesmen of the law who combine the three functions of consulting the authors of rules, of pleading in the disputes which these provoke, and of commenting the decisions which apply them").

4. Finally, the judge must adopt an attitude of impartiality towards public opinion in general, which requires a kind of so-called "insulation" – particularly from the press and the rest of the media.

Even though the judge must listen to that which is happening in society he is not allowed to give a ruling on the basis of that which public opinion thinks or expects. On the occasion of a recent tragic car collision which happened in the mist of dawn, and in which several people died, one of the lorry drivers responsible was immediately arrested, which was clearly done under the pressure of public opinion, since it was hardly appropriate in the circumstances to claim the need for an inquiry. Recently, I heard an examining judge state that public opinion would not understand if he released X, who was at that moment in custody pending trial. Surely this is wrong.

As far as the communication media are concerned, I remain in favour of a rigid application of the sub judice principle: that which must still be decided judicially may not be made public, let alone commented on or criticised. In this respect, I would refer to that which Wolfram Henckel wrote some time ago: "Die Gerichtsberichterstattung der Medien sollte erkennen dass auch schon der Anschein bewusster oder unbewusster Einflussnahme auf laufende Gerichtsverfahren den Rechtsstaat gefährdet. Der Richter kann sich dagegen nicht wehren. Der Berichterstattung und Kommentierung wächst damit eine hohe Verantwortung zu, die mit dem Abschluss des Verfahrens nicht endet. Das Vertrauen der Bürger zu den Richtern und dem Rechtsstaat wird wesentlich beeinflusst durch die Darstellung und Kommentierung der Urteile in Zeitungen, Rundfunk und Fernsehen. Der im Grundgesetz verbrieften Freiheit und Unabhängigkeit der Presse muss in gleicher Weise wie der Unabhängigkeit der Richter die Verantwortung für die Erhaltung unseres demokratischen und sozialen Rechtstaat zur Seite stehen. Wer diese Freiheit nicht verantwortlich gebraucht, untergräbt die Verfassung und schwächt die Organe, die allein die Freiheit garantieren können" ("When reporting on court cases, the media should recognise that even the semblance of a conscious or subconscious influence on the case pending imperils the rule of law. The judge is unable to defend himself against this. Therefore, those responsible for reporting and commenting on cases have a considerable responsibility which does not end with the conclusion of the proceedings. The confidence placed by the citizen in the courts and in the rule of law is influenced to a considerable extent by the manner in which decisions are presented and commented on in the newspapers, as well as on radio and television. The constitutional values of the freedom and independence of the press must, to the same extent as this is the case with the independence of the courts, be buttressed by the responsibility for the safeguarding of our rule of law as it expresses itself in the democratic and social arenas. Anyone who fails to use this freedom in a responsible manner undermines the Constitution and weakens those organs which are the only ones capable of guaranteeing freedom"[6].

II. The "*Bondages*"

Sometimes authors make reference to "*le mythe de l'indépendance*" (the independence myth)[7]:

---

[6] Richter im demokratischen und sozialen Rechtsstaat, (1987) JZ, 209 et seq., at p. 215
[7] Lallemand, R., in Juger (5/1993), p. 6

> L'indépendance est un mythe. Mais elle est un des mythes constitutifs de la Justice et de la démocratie.
> La revendication de l'indépendance est liée à celle de la séparation des pouvoirs: le juge est indépendant parce que le corps des magistrats l'est par rapport au pouvoir exécutif. Mais cette affirmation, formulée in abstracto, comme principe et comme réalité ne manque pas d'audace.
> Dans un monde dominé par l'interdépendance des hommes et des circonstances, elle est une gageure et un défi.
> Les philosphes, les économistes ou les psychologues trouveront qu'il est plus insensé pour un juge de revendiquer son indépendance qu'à une molécule d'affirmer sa liberté.
> Non seulement cette exigence est irréaliste mais, poussée à l'extrême, elle est dangereuse. Quel risque ne court pas le citoyen livré au jugement d'un homme qui ne se reconnaît aucune dépendance ?
> Car, le voilà, du coup, lié à un être qui prétend échapper aux hiérarchies, aux filiations, à la causalité générale qui conduit le monde.
>
> (Independence is a myth. However, it is one of the myths which contribute towards justice and democracy.
> The justification for the independence of the judge is linked to that given for the separation of powers: the judge is independent because as a body, the judges are independent towards the executive. However, this statement, which is formulated in the abstract sense, is not without audacity either as a principle and as a reality.
> In a world dominated by the interdependence between men and circumstances, it is a challenge and a test.
> Philosophers, economists and psychologists will be of the opinion that there is less sense in a judge proclaiming his independence than there is in a molecule claiming its freedom.
> Not only is this requirement an unrealistic one, but, taken to its ultimate conclusion, it is a dangerous concept. What risk is there not for the citizen who is exposed to the judgment of a man who does not acknowledge any dependence?
> The fate of that citizen is thereby linked to a being who claims to elude all hierarchies, relationships, and the general causation which governs this world).

Naturally the above passage paints a totally distorted picture. Independence is not a myth, but is the reality; however, in the words of a President of the French Cour de Cassation, the judge has "autant de dépendances que d'indépendance" (as many elements of dependence as of independence).

In fact, this is what this topic is all about: all those elements against which the judge is incapable of adopting a position of independence.

1. Laws, Constitutions and Treaties. In spite of the very broad scope for interpretation, to which we have already drawn the attention above, the link with the prescribed rules remains an essential one. Radbruch had already expressed this very well where he wrote: "So ist juristische Interpretation nicht Nachdenken eines Vorgedachten, sondern zu Ende Denken eines Gedachten.

…" ("Thus legal interpretation is not about thinking about a previous idea but about thinking it through to its conclusion…")[8].

2. One aspect which tends to be forgotten is that the judge is bound by the facts which feature in the account given to him by the parties. The judge puts these facts into their proper legal perspective. The account of the facts often has the solution – even the legal solution – woven into its fabric.

3. It is unthinkable for the post-modern judge not to be guided by that which actually occurs in society. He has to "keep his ear to the ground" and follow that which is happening in society; in so doing, he must announce that which is to come, put into words that which is already latent, and, on one solitary occasion, call a halt to developments which he considers to be negative.

4. The judiciary is a public service which must not only operate, but also, and especially operate in time. The sole legal provision to deal with this issue is the well-known Article 6 of the ECHR, which has the "reasonable time" requirement – but nothing more. In the words of President Pierre Drai: "Ignorant ou feignant d'ignorer le "facteur temps", le juge civil ne rend plus que des décisions qui, s'étant trop fait attendre, ne font plus peur ou ne sont plus crédibles" ("In disregarding, or pretending to disregard, the time factor, the civil judge merely makes decisions which, because of their excessive delay, no longer deter and are no longer credible")[9].

We are therefore dealing here with a public service which supplies products – i.e. decisions and judgments – whose delivery deadline has not been determined. This is, moreover, the most important and elevated of public services, that which is required to solve human conflicts, to make legal pronouncements, and to ensure that justice is done. However, the superior nature of this activity does not justify the circumstance that in most cases it is not subject to any time limits.

The quality of the product, to use that terminology again, is, however, open to criticism. Not only are there the many remedies, which serve to give the producer a second opportunity ("opposition", objection by third parties, and, to a certain extent, withdrawal of res judicata) or which transfer to another

[8] "*Arten der Interpretation*", in: Recueil d'Etudes sur les sources du droit en l'honneur de François Gény (1934) Paris, T.II, p. 218.

[9] "*L'exécution des décisions judiciaires et les moyens de pression à la disposition du tribunal*", (1986) RIDC at 512).

product (appeal, review by the Supreme Court, Strasbourg), as well as the liability of the producer himself (both civil and criminal liability, in the shape of secondary action against the judge and the criminal action for refusal to adjudicate). Sometimes even the State, seen as a business, can be held liable for unsatisfactory products supplied by the judicial subsidiary (cf. the Belgian Anca decision, of which more below). However, delivery which is late or out of time is not as yet the subject-matter of sanctioning in the national legal systems.

It will of course, be objected that any comparison with punctual delivery by a business concern is defective because the courts, as a service, can only operate properly where the parties and their counsels have made a timely and complete delivery of the raw materials in the shape of the case file containing the facts, arguments and evidence.

This criticism fails to take into account that any properly functioning business also has firm arrangements with the supplier of raw materials and/or with its subcontractors.

Applied by analogy to the courts, this means that the judge must be able to impose on the parties and on their counsels time limits for the communication of their documents, the provision of evidence, the submission of their pleadings and the presentation of their oral findings, in order to ensure that the case in its entirety is settled within a reasonable period. As long as this is not the case, the acute perception of the time factor by the parties involved in a case will fail to be satisfactorily allayed in our court proceedings.

5. Judges must also be accountable. However, this accountability must be regulated in an efficient and formal manner, in order to avoid a situation whereby the judges are judged by the media, because, as Cappelletti rightly remarked longtime ago, "The worst of all kinds of trials: trial by newspapermen".[10]

I have in the past personally advocated that a productivity study be applied to the courts[11]. However, recent experiences of mine has led me to make another proposal.

Since 1996, I had the privilege to have chaired, in the Netherlands, in Belgium, in Latvia, an audit Committee, which was responsible for examining the quality of legal training at the Faculties of Law, and to draw up a report on its findings for the benefit of those responsible for policymaking in university education.

---

[10] ("Who watches the watchmen? A comparative study on judicial responsibility", Amer. Journ. Comp. Law, Vol 31, 1 et seq., in particular 60).

[11] Mijmeringen van een jurist bij 1984 (1984) Antwerp, p. 109 et seq.

The Commission consisting of some more members, received, prior to each Faculty visit, a so-called "self study", in which the Faculty in question introduced itself, explained its objectives, working methods and programmes, and subjected its strengths and weaknesses to critical appraisal. In the course of the visit, members representing the Faculty at all levels were invited and interviewed. This was followed by a comprehensive report on the current situation. These visits take place every five years.

Similarly, the courts could be visited every five years by a commission consisting of professors, judges, lawyers and representatives of the citizens. A report would be submitted to Parliament.

At least once every year, the president of each tribunal would need to submit a report to the Justice Commission of the Parliament. The citizen should be in a position to learn about the manner in which the public funds – which in most countries amount to puny sums – allocated to the administration of justice are expended.

6. We are also dealing here with a public service organised for the benefit of the citizen, who has a right to a fair trial. This requirement can be analysed more closely by applying four criteria: (a) participation (cf. supra on the subject of the decision-making process), (b) interpersonal respect (the parties and/or their counsels need to be treated with respect), (c) neutrality (cf. supra on the subject of independence) and (d) fairness of outcome[12].

The judge is also subject to this customer-friendly approach, under which the judge is no longer the bogey man, but is rather cast in the role of a parent who listens to the accounts and questions put to him or her by the people. Every party expects to be treated in a decent manner.

That this requirement of fairness of outcome is deeply embedded in the cultural and historical dimension of the anthropological approach towards the law, is apparent from the fact that, in the famous passage which relates to Achilles's shield, Homer makes a reference to judges who are due to solve a dispute, and mischievously adds: "Two golden talents lay amidst, in sight, The prize of him who best adjudged the right"[13]

7. It is of course out of the question that the increasing power of the judges should fail to be accompanied by an increase, not only in their responsibility, but also in their accountability. There is currently general agreement on this

---

[12] Tyler, T., "*Procedure or result ? what do disputants want from legal authorities ?*", in: A Handbook of Dispute Resolution, A.D.R. in action, edited by K.J. Mackie, (1991) London, p. 19 et seq.

[13] Ilias, 18, 508–509

proposition, but there is less consensus on the manner in which this should be achieved and on those who should appraise them on this point. It was Juvenal who had already asked the question: "*Quis custodiet ipsos custodes ?*"[14].

Everybody stands to be judged by the judges: the citizen as well as the authorities, the executive as well as the legislature (the latter proposition can no longer be doubted after the landmark decisions of the European Court of Justice in Francovich and Brasserie de l'Europe). But how can the judges themselves be judged ?

Since everything has already been said on this subject, and that there is insufficient space in this paper to go into this topic in greater detail, I would refer to the available literature on the subject[15].

It is appropriate here to recall the ever valid conclusion drawn by M. Cappeletti, which is that there is only "one main road for modern society to tread – the road of a "responsive" model. This, of course, is a model that avoids the excesses of each of those discussed above. To do so, the responsive model will prevent a corporate insulation of the judiciary, as well as an uncontrolled, irresponsible anarchy of the individual judges, by combining a reasonable degree of legal (civil, disciplinary and penal) responsibility, without, however, either subordinating the judges to the political branches, political parties, or other societal organisations, or exposing them to the vexatious suits of irritated litigants"[16].

This direction has already been in part adopted by a number of countries[17]. It was also followed to a certain extent by the Belgian Hof van Cassatie in the Anca decision of 19 December 1991, according to which the State is liable for the damage which may result from a judicial decision which turned out to be unlawful.

I take the personal view that this last-named principle should be completed by means of recovery liability of the judge, should the latter have committed gross negligence. There are elements of this last-named solution in the systems adopted in France and in Germany[18].

---

[14] Saturne VI, 347-8

[15] (the reader is more particularly referred to two masterpieces on this topic, Cappelletti, M., "Who watches the watchmen", in *The Judicial Process in Comparative Perspective*, op. cit p. 57 et seq; Van Oevelen, A., De overheidsaansprakelijkheid voor het optreden van de rechterlijke macht, Antwerpen, 1987, cf. also Storme, M., "*Wie berecht de onoordeelkundige rechter ?*", in Feestbundel F. Dumon (1983) Brussels, 695 et seq.).

[16] op. cit. p. 112

[17] cf. Cappelletti, supra; cf. also Graziadei, M. and Mattei, U., "*Judicial responsibility in Italy: a new statute*" (1990) Amer. Journ. Comp. Law, 103 et seq.

[18] action récursoire, Rückgriff: Cappelletti, op. cit. p. 87–88, see also: M. Breuer, Staatshaftung für judikatives Unrecht, 2011.

CHAPTER FIVE

A FRESH START: THE FOUR PILLARS OF CIVIL JUSTICE

*Neil Andrews**

I. Introduction

Principles of civil justice have become an important field of comparative study, and constitutional procedural principles have come into prominence (for example, this topic was brilliantly examined from both Israeli and transnational perspectives by our recently departed colleague Stephen Goldstein).[1] In Europe this is partly because Convention States, including the United Kingdom, must comply with the jurisprudence of the Strasbourg court on the procedural guarantees contained in Article 6(1) of the European Convention on Human Rights. A non-binding but stimulating source is the UNIDROIT/American Law Institute's *Principles of Transnational Civil Procedure*- published in 2006.[2] Besides these external influences, there is the internal task of arranging a set of fundamental procedural norms. Such a canon of principles seems indispensable if lawyers are to view procedural justice in a coherent and systematic way, liberated from the fine detail of individual rules. The main suggestion in this chapter will be that the wide array of fundamental and important principles of civil justice can be arranged under four headings, which I have called the four pillars of civil justice.[3] These are:

---

* Professor of Civil Justice and Private Law, University of Cambridge, Member of the teaching staff, Faculty of Law since 1983; Fellow of Clare College, Cambridge; Bencher of Middle Temple, 2007; Member of the American Law Institute since 2000; Council Member of the International Association of Procedural Law.

[1] Stephen Goldstein, "The Influences of Constitutional Principles on Civil Procedure in Israel" (1982) 17 Israel L.R. 467–510; and "Constitutional Norms of Civil Procedure as Reflected in the ALI/UNIDROIT Principles of Transnational Civil Procedure" (*Estudios en Homenage a Hector Fix-Zamudio*); "The Proposed ALI/UNIDROIT Principles and Rules: the Utility of Such A Harmonization Project" (2001–4) VI Uniform L.R. 789–801.

[2] ALI/UNIDROIT's *Principles of Transnational Civil Procedure* (Cambridge 2006).

[3] The author's decision to seek to re-order his 2003 long list of 24 principles (Neil Andrews, *English Civil Procedure* (Oxford 2003) ch.'s 4 to 6) was prompted by Shimon Shetreet during conversation in Cambridge in March 2010, and at a Colloquium in Clare College, May 21, 2010, in honour of Professor Kurt Lipstein. But Shimon Shetreet and I differ on how best to arrange these principles (Professor Shetreet visited in 2010 Clare College, Cambridge, and the Faculty of Law, Cambridge, during his re-election as Herbert Smith Visiting Professor of Law; and in 2010 he was elected to be a Senior Academic Visitor by Clare College, in recognition of his scholarly achievements).

I. Access to Legal Advice and Dispute-Resolution Systems
II. Equality and Fairness between the Parties
III. A Focused and Speedy Process
IV. Adjudicators of Integrity

II. Author's First List of Principles: Principles of Civil Procedure (1994)

Having been given an opportunity in the mid 1980s to teach civil procedure in Cambridge, I wrote *Principles of Civil Procedure* (1994).[4] The eleven principles selected in that text were:[5]

(i) due notice;
(ii) pre-trial disclosure;
(iii) protection against spurious claims and defences;
(iv) justice is not to be evaded;
(v) accelerated justice;
(vi) oral proceedings;
(vii) publicity;
(viii) promoting settlement;
(ix) finality;
(x) the adversarial principle;
(xi) the principle of privity.

Some of these had been highlighted by Sir Jack Jacob in his *The Fabric of English Civil Justice* (1987).[6] In *Principles of Civil Procedure* (1994) I said that these eleven principles "lie within the realm of practical politics". I then mentioned the following three "noble aims", and expressed doubt whether they might ever "be fully attained":[7]

I. access to justice;
II. prevention of undue delay;
III. management of complex litigation.

---

[4] Neil Andrews, *Principles of Civil Procedure* (London 1994) (Sweet & Maxwell, 596 pp. text; discussion of *pre-C.P.R.* system).
[5] *Ibid.*, paras. 2–003 ff.
[6] (London 1987) (Hamlyn Lectures for the year 1986).
[7] Neil Andrews, *Principles of Civil Procedure* (London 1994), para. 2–013.

Later in the 1994 book (chapter 21, where these "persistent", perhaps perennial,[8] problems were more fully analysed), I said:[9] "Accessibility, speed and simplicity are closely related virtues...When the cost increases, the court system is closed off from all but the very poor [an allusion to civil legal aid], the rich and the mad." Lord Justice Jackson's "Civil Litigation Costs Review" (December 2009)[10] has placed the whole topic of costs and funding under scrutiny.

Neither I, in 1994, nor Sir Jack Jacob, in 1987, had thought it necessary to spell out the implied term that civil judges should enjoy judicial independence. But Tony Jolowicz in 1973 had rightly emphasised this principle and observed its close connexion with the question of impartiality:

> Without a judiciary which can and will administer law fairly and fearlessly between the parties, no other guarantee given to the litigants by the law is likely to be of value...The judge must be free from interference by the state itself; he must also be free of interference or influence outside the proceedings from the parties or others; he must also himself be unbiased and personally disinterested in the question at issue in the litigation he has to try.[11]

III. "Woolf Changes" of Principle: C.P.R. (1998)

On 28 March 1994, Lord Mackay LC of Clashfern (Lord Chancellor 1987–97) appointed Lord Woolf to make recommendations concerning civil procedure, with the following aims:[12] (i) *improving access to justice and reducing the cost of litigation* (ii) *reducing the complexity of the rules* (iii) *modernising terminology* (iv) *removing unnecessary distinctions of practice and procedure*. Woolf's interim and final reports appeared in 1995[13] and 1996,[14] and they stimulated a substantial literature.[15] The C.P.R. was enacted in 1998 and took effect on 26 April 1999.

---

[8] Sir Anthony Clarke MR, "The Supercase-Problems and Solutions", 2007 Annual K.P.M.G. Forensic Lecture: available at http://www.judiciary.gov.uk/docs/speeches/kpmg_speech.pdf.

[9] Neil Andrews, *Principles of Civil Procedure* (London 1994), para. 21-001.

[10] Sir Rupert Jackson, *Review of Civil Litigation Costs* (December, 2009: London 2010); on which A.A.S. Zuckerman, "The Jackson Final Report on Costs—Plastering the Cracks to Shore up a Dysfunctional System" (2010) 29 C.J.Q. 263.

[11] J.A. Jolowicz in M. Cappelletti and D. Tallon (eds.), *Fundamental Guarantees of the Parties in Civil Litigation* (Milano 1973), p. 121.

[12] Terms of appointment cited in Lord Woolf, *Access to Justice: Interim Report* (London 1995), introduction.

[13] *Ibid.* It and its successor are available on-line at: http://www.dca.gov.uk/civil/reportfr.htm

[14] *Access to Justice: Final Report* (London 1996).

[15] A.A.S. Zuckerman and R. Cranston (eds.), *The Reform of Civil Procedure: Essays on "Access to Justice"* (Oxford 1995); R. Cranston, *How Law Works: The Machinery and Impact of Civil*

From the perspective of overarching principle, the main features[16] of this exciting fresh start can be summarised as follows. The new C.P.R. system recognised and sought to promote these principles, values, or aims: (1) proportionality, (2) procedural equality, (3) active judicial involvement in a case's progress (4) accelerated access to justice by improved summary procedures, (5) curbing excessive documentary disclosure, (6) greater resort to the disciplinary use of costs orders, (7) curbing appeals, (8) stimulating settlement through costs incentives to accept settlement offers, and (9) judicial encouragement of resort to ADR, notably mediation. These bare points are fleshed out in the following nine sub-paragraphs.

(1) "The Overriding Objective" in C.P.R. Part I gives prominence to the notion of "proportionality" both in the organisation of levels of procedure—small claims, fast-track, or multi-track proceedings[17]—and in the exercise of the court's extensive case-management powers.[18]
(2) Part I also emphasises the requirement of procedural equality.
(3) The principle of party-control was modified.[19] The C.P.R. created a general framework for active involvement of judges in the pre-trial development of moderately or extremely complex litigation. Judges are required to ensure that litigation proceeds with reasonable speed and that the issues are identified and prioritised. At trial (and during its preparation), judges should control the volume of evidence.

Justice (Oxford 2006), ch. 5; Neil Andrews, *English Civil Procedure* (Oxford 2003), ch. 2; Neil Andrews, "A New Civil Procedural Code for England: Party-Control 'Going, Going, Gone'" (2000) 19 C.J.Q. 19–38; S. Flanders, "Case Management: Failure in America? Success in England and Wales?" (1998) 17 C.J.Q. 308; J.A. Jolowicz, "The Woolf Report and the Adversary System" (1996) 15 C.J.Q. 198; M. Zander, "The Government's Plans on Civil Justice" (1998) 61 M.L.R. 383 and "The Woolf Report: Forwards or Backwards for the New Lord Chancellor?" (1997) 16 C.J.Q. 208; A.A.S. Zuckerman, "The Woolf Report on Access to Justice" (1997) 2 ZZPInt 31 ff.

[16] The author's most recent examination of the C.P.R. system is: Neil Andrews, *The Modern Civil Process* (Mohr & Siebeck, Tübingen, Germany 2008) (also considering the rise of ADR); see also N Andrews, The Three Paths of Justice (Springer Publishing, 2011).

[17] Respectively, C.P.R. Parts 27, 28, 29.

[18] C.P.R. 1.4(2); C.P.R. 3.1(2); C.P.R. Parts 26, 28, 29; Neil Andrews, *The Modern Civil Process* (Mohr & Siebeck, Tübingen, Germany 2008) 3.13 ff; Neil Andrews, *English Civil Justice and Remedies: Progress and Challenges: Nagoya Lectures* (Shinzan Sha Publishers, Tokyo 2007), ch. 3; see now the "Admiralty and Commercial Courts Guide" (2009), Section D, at pp. 17–31; and note the anxious discussions engendered by "rogue" "super-cases": the Long Trials Working Party Report December 2007; and a pilot scheme since 2008; for the background, Sir Anthony Clarke MR, "The Supercase-Problems and Solutions", 2007 Annual K.P.M.G. Forensic Lecture: available at http://www.judiciary.gov.uk/docs/speeches/kpmg_speech.pdf.

[19] On the C.P.R. system from the perspective of the traditional principle of party control, Neil Andrews, "A New Civil Procedural Code for England: Party-Control 'Going, Going, Gone'" (2000) 19 C.J.Q. 19–38; Neil Andrews, *English Civil Procedure* (Oxford 2003), paras. 13.12 to 13.41; 14.04 to 14.45; 15.65 to 15.72.

But there are limits to judicial initiative:

(a) parties still select factual witnesses and draw up witness statements;[20]

(b) parties still select party-appointed experts (they can also agree upon selection of a single, joint expert, this "shared" expert being an innovation of the C.P.R. system); judicial permission to use experts is required, but judicial selection of individual experts is avoided, unless the parties reach stalemate in agreeing a single, joint expert;[21]

(c) the Court of Appeal has said that excessive intervention by trial judges during the course of evidence is prohibited because it would be wrong for a judge to "arrogate to himself a quasi-inquisitorial role", this being something which is "entirely at odds with the adversarial system."[22]

(4) Summary disposal of cases is promoted by introduction of a more searching test of "real prospect of success", in C.P.R. Part 24.[23]

(5) "Standard disclosure" was intended to subject documentary discovery to a more focused notion of relevance.

"Standard disclosure"[24] covers documents on which a party will rely; or which adversely affect his case; or adversely affect the opponent's case; or support the opponent's case.

(6) Procedural discipline would be reinforced by a more discretionary approach to costs decisions.[25] The courts could adjust costs awards and so reflect the fact that a victorious party had raised unnecessary issues.

Lord Woolf MR in *AEI Rediffusion Music Ltd v. Phonographic Performance Ltd* (1999), attempting to temper the perceived rigidity of the "winner takes all" approach, said: "too robust an application of the "follow the event principle" encourages litigants to increase the costs of litigation"; and he suggested "if you

---

[20] Neil Andrews, *The Modern Civil Process* (Mohr & Siebeck, Tübingen, Germany 2008), paras. 8.04 ff.

[21] On these aspects of C.P.R. Part 35, Neil Andrews, *ibid.*, ch. 7; D Dwyer, *The Judicial Assessment of Expert Evidence* (Cambridge 2008).

[22] *Southwark LBC v. Maamefowaa Kofiadu* [2006] EWCA Civ 281, at [148].

[23] C.P.R. 24.2: *Swain v. Hillman* [2001] 1 All E.R. 91, 92, C.A.; Neil Andrews, *The Modern Civil Process* (Mohr & Siebeck, Tübingen, Germany 2008), paras. 5.18 ff.

[24] C.P.R. 31.6; Andrews, *op. cit.*, ch. 6, notably, paras. 6.04, 6.22; on the pre-C.P.R. excessive documentary disclosure system, Lord Woolf, *Access to Justice: Interim Report* (London 1995) ch. 21, paras 1–9 (commenting on the "*Peruvian Guano*" test: *Compagnie Financière v. Peruvian Guano Co.* (1882) 11 QBD 55, 63, C.A.); Sir Johan Steyn (later Lord Steyn), preface to Hodge and Malek, *Discovery* (London 1992); R Cranston, "Complex Litigation: the Commercial Court" (2007) 26 C.J.Q. 190, 203.

[25] Neil Andrews, *The Modern Civil Process* (Mohr & Siebeck, Tübingen, Germany 2008), paras. 9.09 ff.

recover all your costs as long as you win, you are encouraged to leave no stone unturned in your effort to do so."[26]

(7) Finality of judgment would be fortified by the requirement that an appellant would require permission to appeal.[27]

Nearly all appeals require the court to give its permission (formerly known as "leave"),[28] in response to the appellant's speedy request to the first instance court (normally within fourteen days;[29] a period which cannot be extended by party agreement).[30] If the lower court refuses permission, a fresh application for permission can be made to the appeal court.

(8) Settlement would be promoted by the capacity of both claimants and defendants to make settlement offers backed by costs sanctions.[31]

In essence: under the English C.P.R. system, Part 36, the claimant's costs risk arises if he does not accept the defendant's settlement offer. In that situation, if the claimant at trial "fails to obtain a judgment more advantageous than a defendant's Part 36 offer", then, "unless [the court] considers it unjust to do so", the claimant must pay the defendant's costs incurred after the date when the claimant should have accepted the settlement offer. The defendant will only be liable for the claimant's costs incurred before that date.

The defendant's costs risk arises if he does not accept the claimant's settlement offer. If "judgment against the defendant is at least as advantageous to the claimant as the proposals contained in a claimant's Part 36 offer", then, "unless [the court] considers it unjust to do so", the defendant will be liable to pay the claimant not just the ordinary measure of costs ("standard" costs) but an aggravated measure (so-called "indemnity costs"), with the further possibility of a high level of interest on those costs.

(9) The courts were charged with the duty to promote resort to ADR,[32] especially mediation, though use of costs orders,[33] and the staying of proceedings.[34]

---

[26] [1999] 1 W.L.R. 1507, 1522–3, C.A.

[27] Neil Andrews, *The Modern Civil Process* (Mohr & Siebeck, Tübingen, Germany 2008), paras. 8.12 ff.

[28] C.P.R. 52.3(1): except decisions affecting a person's liberty.

[29] C.P.R. 52.4(2); appeals out of time will only exceptionally be permitted: *Smith v. Brough* [2005] EWCA 261; [2006] C.P. Rep. 17.

[30] C.P.R. 52.6(1) (2).

[31] Neil Andrews, *The Modern Civil Process* (Mohr & Siebeck, Tübingen, Germany 2008), paras. 10.15 ff.

[32] C.P.R. 1.4(2)(e).

[33] Notably, *Dunnett v. Railtrack plc* [2002] 1 W.L.R. 2434, C.A.; *Halsey v. Milton Keynes General NHA Trust* [2004] 1 W.L.R. 3002, C.A.; *Nigel Witham Ltd v. Smith* [2008] EWHC 12 (T.C.C.), at [36] (J. Sorabji (2008) 27 C.J.Q. 427); on this line of cases, Neil Andrews, *The Modern Civil Process* (Mohr & Siebeck, Tübingen, Germany 2008), paras. 11.40 ff.

[34] C.P.R. 3.1(2)(f); Neil Andrews, *op. cit.*, 11.31.

IV. Article 6(1), European Convention on Human Rights

The Human Rights Act 1998, which took effect in October 2000, rendered the European Convention on Human Rights directly applicable in English courts. Article 6(1) of the Convention states:[35]

> *Right to a Fair Trial*: In the determination of his civil rights and obligations or of any criminal charge against him, everyone is entitled to a fair and public hearing within a reasonable time by an independent and impartial tribunal established by law.

That important codification of fundamental principle consists of the following elements:

(i) The right to "a fair hearing": this is a wide concept embracing:[36]
  the right to be present at an adversarial hearing;
  the right to equality of arms;
  the right to fair presentation of the evidence;
  the right to cross examine opponents" witnesses;
  the right to a reasoned judgment.[37]

(ii) "a public hearing": including the right to a public pronouncement of judgment;[38]
(iii) "a hearing within a reasonable time"; and
(iv) "a hearing before an independent[39] and impartial[40] tribunal established by law".

As for judicial independence, section 3 of the Constitutional Reform Act 2005 states:

> The Lord Chancellor, other Ministers of the Crown and all with responsibility for matters relating to the judiciary or otherwise to the administration of justice must uphold the continued independence of the judiciary. The Lord Chancellor and other Ministers of the Crown must not seek to influence particular judicial decisions through any special access to the judiciary. The Lord Chancellor must have

---

[35] (Cmd 8969); Human Rights Act 1998, s. 1(3), Sch. 1 incorporates the European Convention on Human Rights into UK law; S. Grocz, J. Beatson and P. Duffy, *Human Rights: The 1998 Act and the European Convention* (2nd ed., 2008); M.W. Janies, R.S. Kay, A. Bradley, *European Human Rights Law: Text and Materials* (3rd ed., Oxford 2008); R. Clayton and H. Tomlinson, *The Law of Human Rights* (2nd ed., Oxford 2008).

[36] R. Clayton and H. Tomlinson, *op. cit.*, ch. 11.

[37] Neil Andrews, *English Civil Procedure* (Oxford 2003), paras. 5.39 to 5.68.

[38] *Ibid.*, paras. 4.59 to end of chapter; Strasbourg authorities cited, *ibid.*, 7.21 to 7.79.

[39] *Starrs v. Ruxton* 2000 J.C. 208, 243; 17 November 1999, *The Times* (High Court of Justiciary) *per* Lord Reed; *Millar v. Dickson* [2002] 1 W.L.R. 1615, PC; Neil Andrews, *English Civil Procedure* (Oxford 2003), paras. 4.02 to 4.27 (judicial independence).

[40] *Porter v. Magill* [2002] 2 A.C. 357, H.L.

> regard to (a) the need to defend that independence; (b) the need for the judiciary to have the support necessary to enable them to exercise their functions; (c) the need for the public in regard to matters relating to the judiciary or otherwise to the administration of justice to be properly represented in decisions affecting those matters.

Of great interest is that the Strasbourg court divined an implicit fundamental right of "access to court". Lord Bingham in *Brown v. Stott* (2001) explained:[41]

> Article 6(1) contains no express right of access to justice, but in *Golder v. U.K.* the European Court of Human Rights said that it was "inconceivable" that this provision should give detailed procedural guarantees without protecting access to justice.[42] The court in the *Golder* case conceded that this implied right was not absolute and so admitted limitations.[43]

The Court of Appeal in *English v. Emery Reimbold & Strick Ltd* (2002) noted that Article 6(1) requires a court to provide a reasoned judgment:[44]

> The [European Convention on Human Rights] ... requires that a judgment should contain reasons that are sufficient to demonstrate that the essential issues that have been raised by the parties have been addressed by the domestic court and how those issues have been resolved. It does not seem ... that the Strasbourg jurisprudence goes further and requires a judgment to explain why one contention, or piece of evidence, has been preferred to another.

V. UNIDROIT/ALI Project (2000–2006)

The working group[45] of the UNIDROIT/American Law Institute project[46]—now known as *Principles of Transnational Civil Procedure*- published by

[41] [2003] 1 A.C. 681, 694, P.C.

[42] (1975) 1 E.H.R.R. 524, 536, at [35].

[43] *Ibid.*, at [38].

[44] [2002] EWCA Civ 605; [2002] 1 W.L.R. 2409, C.A., at [12] (adumbrated by *Flannery* v. *Halifax Estate Agencies Ltd* [2000] 1 W.L.R. 377, C.A.; noted J.A. Jolowicz, [2000] C.L.J. 263 (judge must give intelligible reasons for rejecting one side's expert testimony and preferring the other side's; a common law decision which ante-dated commencement of the Human Rights Act on 2 October 2000).

[45] The members of the drafting group were: Neil Andrews, University of Cambridge, UK; Professor Frédérique Ferrand, Lyon, France; Professor Pierre Lalive, formerly University of Geneva, sometime Goodhart Professor Legal Science, Cambridge, in practice as an international commercial arbitrator, Switzerland; Professor Masanori Kawano, Nagoya University, Japan; Mme Justice Aida Kemelmajer de Carlucci, Supreme Court, Mendoza, Argentina; Professor Geoffrey Hazard Jr., now Hastings College of the Law, San Francisco, USA; Professor Ronald Nhlapo, formerly of the Law Commission, South Africa; Professor Dr iur Rolf Stürner, University of Freiburg, Germany, and Judge at the Court of Appeals of the German State Baden-Württemberg, Karlsruhe; the assistant to these discussions was Antonio Gidi (USA and Brazil).

[46] Neil Andrews, "The Modern Procedural Synthesis: the American Law Institute and UNIDROIT's "Principles and Rules of Transnational Civil Procedure" "(2008) 164 *Revista de*

Cambridge University Press in 2006,[47] met first in Rome in 2000. On the table on day one was a fairly detailed document containing Rules of Transnational Civil Procedure, drafted by Geoff Hazard and Michele Taruffo. By the second day of this first meeting, the working group had drawn up a list of principles, and these were elaborated during the working group's meetings 2000 to 2003. The Rules were relegated to an unofficial appendix to the main project.

Rolf Stürner, appointed to be the General Reporter of the UNIDROIT side of this collaborative project, has chronicled the working group's elaboration of these principles.[48] And Neil Andrews suggested that the UNIDROIT/ALI principles range from (1) quasi-constitutional declarations of fundamental procedural guarantees to (2) major guidelines concerning the style and course of procedure to (3) points of important detail.[49]

fundamental procedural guarantees:

judicial competence; judicial independence; judicial impartiality; procedural equality;

due notice or the right to be heard; publicity; reasoned decisions;

prompt and accelerated justice;

professional independence of counsel; right to assistance of counsel; attorney-client privilege ("legal professional privilege");

the privilege against self-incrimination.

leading principles concerning the style and course of procedure:

jurisdiction over parties; venue rules; party initiation of proceedings;

party's definition of scope of proceedings; joinder rules; allocation of burden and nature of standard of proof; pleadings; parties" duty to avoid false pleading and abuse of process;

rights of access to information; judicial initiative in evidential matters; experts;

Processo 109–120 (Brazil) also published in (2009) Tijdschrift voor Civiele Rechtspleging 52–7 (Netherlands).

[47] ALI/UNIDROIT's *Principles of Transnational Civil Procedure* (Cambridge 2006).

[48] Rolf Stürner, "The Principles of Transnational Civil Procedure." (2005) *Rabels Zeitschrift* 201–254.

[49] Neil Andrews "Embracing the Noble Quest for Transnational Procedural Principles" in M. Andenas, N. Andrews, R. Nazzini, (eds.), *The Future of Transnational Commercial Litigation: English Responses to the ALI-UNIDROIT Draft Principles and Rules of Transnational Civil Procedure* (London 2003; re-printed 2006), pp. 23–5 (a collection of essays and comments by British judges and commentators on the draft UNIDROIT/American Law Institute's project).

judicial management of proceedings; sanctions against default and non-compliance; need for proportionality in use of sanctions;

parties" duty to act fairly and to promote efficient and speedy proceedings; parties" duty to co-operate;

parties" right to discontinue or settle proceedings; judicial encouragement of settlement,

right to oral stage of procedure; final hearing before ultimate adjudicators; judicial responsibility for correct application of the law;

basic costs shifting rule; finality of decisions; appeal mechanisms;

effective enforcement; recognition by foreign courts; international judicial co-operation.

points of important detail:

protection of parties lacking capacity; security for costs; expedited forms of communication; non-party submissions; making of judicial "suggestions".

The UNIDROIT/ALI project was not the first attempt at bridging the division between Civilian and Common Law procedures. Marcel Storme (and his team, including Tony Jolowicz) had led the way.[50] But, thus far, the UNIDROIT/ALI project is the most detailed identification of points of common ground.

VI. Author's Second List of Principles: English Civil Procedure (2003)

Having participated in the UNIDROIT/American Law Institute project, and stimulated by the first years of the brave new C.P.R. world, in *English Civil Procedure* (Oxford UP, 2003) I decided to look again at the kaleidoscope of procedural principle because it was obvious that new patterns had emerged. In chapters 4 and 5, I examined the various procedural "guarantees". In chapter 6, entitled "*Leading Procedural Principles*", I examined an array of major requirements, ranging from "Access to Justice" to "Finality". And of course in chapter 7 of the 2003 book it was necessary to examine the British reception of Article 6(1) of the European Convention.

---

[50] M. Storme (ed.), *Approximation of Judiciary Law in the European Union* (Gent 1994).

VII. A Fresh Start: Four Pillars of Civil Justice

I suggest that principles of civil justice can be usefully arranged under four headings, which I call the four pillars of civil justice:

I. Access to Legal Advice and Dispute-Resolution Systems
II. Equality and Fairness between the Parties
III. Focused and Speedy Justice
IV. Adjudicators of Integrity

In greater detail, this is how the various leading and fundamental principles of civil justice can be arranged using this four-fold classification.

I. *ACCESS TO LEGAL ADVICE AND DISPUTE-RESOLUTION SYSTEMS*
Access to Justice
Right to Choose a Lawyer
Confidential Legal Consultation
Protection against Bad or Spurious Claims and Defences
Promoting Settlement and Facilitating Resort to Alternative Forms of Dispute-Resolution, notably Mediation and Arbitration.

II. *EQUALITY AND FAIRNESS BETWEEN THE PARTIES*
Procedural Equality
Disclosure
Accuracy
Fair Play Between Litigants
Procedural Equity

III. *A FOCUSED AND SPEEDY PROCESS*
Judicial Control of the Civil Process to Ensure Focus
Proportionality
Avoidance of Undue Delay
Effectiveness
Finality

IV. *ADJUDICATORS OF INTEGRITY*
Judicial Independence
Judicial Impartiality
Publicity or Open Justice
Judicial Duty to Avoid Surprise: The Principle of Due Notice
Judicial Duty to Give Reasons

VIII. Concluding Remarks

International scholarly discussion thrives on fundamental principle. There are now many studies of comparative civil justice.[51] Students of civil justice will surely make brilliant advances during this dynamic century. They will be standing on the shoulders of Hazard,[52] Jolowicz,[53] Kawano,[54]

[51] In the English language, these include: J.A. Jolowicz, *On Civil Procedure* (Cambridge 2000) (thereafter in chronological order): M. Cappelletti and J. Perillo, *Civil Procedure in Italy* (The Hague 1995); M. Cappelletti (ed.), *International Encyclopaedia of Comparative Law* (The Hague, and Tübingen 1976), volume XVI "Civil Procedure"; J. Langbein, "The German Advantage in Civil Procedure" (1985) 52 Univ. of Chi. L.R. 823–66; M. Damaska, *The Faces of Justice and State Authority: A Comparative Approach to the Legal Process* (New Haven 1986); M. Cappelletti, *The Judicial Process in Comparative Perspective* (Oxford 1989); M. Storme (ed.), *Approximation of Judiciary Law in the EU* (Dordrecht 1994); A.A.S. Zuckerman (ed.), *Civil Justice in Crisis: Comparative Perspectives of Civil Procedure* (Oxford 1999); W. Rechberger and H. Klicka (eds.), *Procedural Law on the Threshold of a New Millenium, XI. World Congress of Procedural Law* (Center for Legal Competence, Vienna 2002); D. Asser et al, "A summary of the interim report on Fundamental Review of the Dutch Law of Civil Procedure" (2003) 8 ZZPInt 329–387; M. Storme (ed.), *Procedural Laws in Europe – Towards Harmonization*, (Maklu, Antwerpen/Apeldoorn 2003); M. Storme and B. Hess (eds.), *Discretionary Power of the Judge: Limits and Control* (Kluwer, Dordrecht 2003); Peter Murray and Rolf Stürner, *German Civil Justice* (Durham, USA 2004); C.H. van Rhee (ed.), *The Law's Delays: Essays on Undue Delay in Civil Litigation* (Antwerp and Oxford 2007); C.H. van Rhee, *European Traditions in Civil Procedure* (Intersentia and Hart, Oxford 2005); N. Trocker and V. Varano (eds.), *The Reforms of Civil Procedure in Comparative Perspective* (Torino 2005); Oscar Chase, Helen Hershkoff, Linda Silberman, Vincenzo Varano, Yasuhei Taniguchi, Adrian Zuckerman, *Civil Procedure in Comparative Context* (Thomson West 2007); A. Pellegrini Grinover and R. Calmon (eds.), *Direito Processual Comparado: XIII World Congress of Procedural Law* (Editora Forense, Rio de Janeiro 2007), pp. 201–42; A. Uzelac and C.H. van Rhee (eds.), *Public and Private Justice* (Antwerp and Oxford 2007); M. Deguchi and M. Storme (eds.), *The Reception and Transmission of Civil Procedural Law in the Global Society* (Maklu, Antwerp 2008). And on "transnational principles", M. Storme (ed.), *Approximation of Judiciary Law in the European Union* (Gent 1994) and ALI/UNIDROIT's *Principles of Transnational Civil Procedure* (Cambridge 2006); on this project, H. Kronke (ed.), special issue of the Uniform Law Review (2002) Vol. VI; M. Andenas, N. Andrews, R. Nazzini (eds.), *The Future of Transnational Commercial Litigation: English Responses to the ALI/UNIDROIT Draft Principles and Rules of Transnational Civil Procedure* (British Institute of Comparative and International Law, London 2006); Rolf Stürner, "The Principles of Transnational Civil Procedure." (2005) *Rabels Zeitschrift*, 201–254.

[52] ALI/UNIDROIT's *Principles of Transnational Civil Procedure* (Cambridge 2006).

[53] J.A. Jolowicz, *On Civil Procedure* (Cambridge 2000).

[54] Nagoya/Freiburg project on "A New Framework for Transnational Business Litigation", a project led by Professor Masanori Kawano; the published works in this series (so far) are: Rolf Stürner and Masanori Kawano (eds.), *Current Topics of International Litigation* (Mohr Siebeck, Tübingen 2009); national studies: Neil Andrews, *English Civil Justice and Remedies: Progress and Challenges: Nagoya Lectures* (Shinzan Sha Publishers, Tokyo 2007); Laura Ervo (ed.), *Civil Justice in Finland* (Jigakusha Publishing, Tokyo 2009); Carlos Eslugues-Mota and Silvia Barona-Vilar (eds.), *Civil Justice in Spain* (Jigakusha Publishing, Tokyo 2009); Miklos Kengyel and Viktoria Harsagi, *Civil Justice in Hungary* (Jigakusha Publishing, Tokyo 2010); Neil Andrews, *Contracts and English Dispute Resolution* (Jigakusha Publishing, Tokyo 2010); Dimitris Maniotis and Spyros Tsantinis, *Civil Justice in Greece* (Jigakusha Publishing, Tokyo 2010); Stephanie Schmidt, *Civil Justice in France* (Jigakusha Publishing, Tokyo 2010); Marco de Cristofaro and Nicolo Trocker (eds.), *Civil Justice in Italy* (Jigakusha Publishing, Tokyo 2010).

Murray,[55] Shetreet,[56] Storme,[57] Stürner,[58] and Taruffo.[59] These celebrated authors have consistently emphasised the need to attend to matters of first principle.

More generally, constitutional and fundamental procedural principles have now come into prominence partly because of the transnational sway of the European Convention on Human Rights and partly because ever aggressive and controlling Government has taught us not to take anything for granted. It is hoped that the author's proposed quartet of four pillars of civil justice will enable jurists to keep in view the deeper and wider dimensions of this subject.

In this chapter my main contention has been that the wide array of fundamental and important principles of civil justice can be arranged under four headings, which I have called the four pillars of civil justice. These are:

I. Access to Legal Advice and Dispute-Resolution Systems
II. Equality and Fairness between the Parties
III. A Focused and Speedy Process
IV. Adjudicators of Integrity.

---

[55] Peter Murray and Rolf Stürner, *German Civil Justice* (Durham, USA 2004).

[56] Mount Scopus International Standards of Judicial Independence.

[57] M. Storme (ed.), *Approximation of Judiciary Law in the European Union* (Gent 1994); see also M. Storme (ed.), *Procedural Laws in Europe – Towards Harmonization*, (Maklu, Antwerpen/Apeldoorn 2003); M. Storme and B Hess (eds.), *Discretionary Power of the Judge: Limits and Control* (Kluwer, Dordrecht 2003).

[58] Peter Murray and Rolf Stürner, *German Civil Justice* (Durham, USA 2004); ALI/UNIDROIT's *Principles of Transnational Civil Procedure* (Cambridge 2006).

[59] ALI/UNIDROIT's *Principles of Transnational Civil Procedure* (Cambridge 2006).

PART II

THE JUDICIARY AND THE OTHER BRANCHES OF GOVERNMENT

CHAPTER SIX

JUDICIAL INDEPENDENCE AND THE RULE OF LAW: EXPLORING THE EUROPEAN EXPERIENCE

*Carlo Guarnieri and Daniela Piana**

The Rule of Law is increasingly considered to be a necessary condition for the development of a market economy and a successful democracy. The creation of a stable institutional setting, the introduction of transparent, well-formulated and predictable legal norms, the establishment of a system of checks and balances restraining the exercise of political power, have all been the preferred target of policies promoted by international organizations. In this context, an independent judicial system has emerged as one of the pillars of the Rule of Law (RoL). Independent judges are considered a fundamental instrument in order to establish and implement a system of impartial and fair rules.

In Europe, this view has been supported especially by the Council of Europe. Since the early 1990's the Council has developed a large array of recommendations and standards concerning judicial organization, court management, judicial training and ethics. Among them, significant is the 1994 Recommendation requiring that "in the decision-making process, judges should be independent and be able to act without any restriction, improper influence, inducements, pressures, threats or interferences, direct or indirect, from any quarter or for any reason."[1]

This attitude finds support in the social sciences. For instance, in a recent significant contribution to the subject Feld and Voigt[2] focus on highest courts and introduce a distinction between de jure and de facto judicial independence (JI). De jure indicators refer only to legal rules concerning the status of

* Carlo Guarnieri is professor at the University of Bologna, where he teaches Comparative Judicial Systems. Together with P. Pederzoli he is the author of *The Power of Judges. A Comparative Study of Courts and Democracy* (Oxford 2002).

Daniela Piana is associate professor at the University of Bologna, where she teaches Politics and Institutions of the EU. She is the author of several articles on courts and politics. She has recently published *Judicial Accountabilities in New Europe* (London 2010).

[1] See *Independence, efficiency and role of the judges*, Recommendation n. 12 (94). The Recommendation is to a large extent influenced by the "Basic Principles on the Independence of the Judiciary" enacted by the United Nations in 1985. Recently, in November 2010, a new Recommendation – (2010) 12 – has reaffirmed and further strengthened this position.

[2] L. Feld and S. Voigt, "Economic Growth and Judicial Independence" (2003) 19 European Journal of Political Economy 497.

judges and their competencies and powers, while de facto indicators try to catch the empirical dimension of JI and deal with both the status of judges and their powers in practice. They find a good relation between de facto JI and economic growth, although also de jure JI seems to influence, maybe with a time lag, de facto JI.[3] Also judicial accountability (JA) – defined as institutional arrangements aiming at assuring that judges decide according to "the letter of the law" – is important, as it is statistically associated to higher income and less corruption.[4] The finding is explained through the consideration that independent judges could behave in an inefficient or corrupt way or apply the law inconsistently. Thus, in order for JI to support the implementation of the RoL, judges should be accountable: they need incentives to decide according to the law. Voigt maintains that JI and JA are not in tension, since JA aims only at having judges behaving according to the law.[5]

I. The Meaning of Judicial Independence

The above-mentioned contributions stress the positive role played by JI. However, some scholars seem to be less sanguine on the virtues of JI. For instance, Russell[6] judges "quite unreal" the attempt at wholly insulating judges from their environment and therefore criticizes the definitions adopted at the international level. According to Martin Shapiro, since no regime "is likely to allow significant political power to be wielded by an isolated judicial corps free of political restraints",[7] JI is always to some extent limited. In fact, the actual content of JI remains, at least to some extent, undecided. Current definitions seem to miss some important distinctions.

Following Russell,[8] the concept of JI should be clarified, first of all, by identifying its main rationale. In order to perform her functions effectively – and therefore be considered legitimate by the parties to the case – the judge is expected to adjudicate impartially, according to the rules of the legal system, *sine spe ac metu,* i.e. without expectation of benefits or fear of reprisals. Therefore, JI is a relationship and its main points of reference are the parties: in order to be impartial, the judge must be independent from them. A judge who

---

[3] B. Hayo and S. Voigt, "Explaining de facto Judicial Independence" (2007) 27 International Review of Law and Economics 269, 286.

[4] S. Voigt, "The economic effect of judicial accountability: cross-country evidence" (2008) 25 European Journal of Law and Economics 95.

[5] But, as any legal philosopher knows, deciding weather a judge has "applied the law" is not a simple matter.

[6] P.H. Russell, "Toward a General Theory of Judicial Independence" in P. H. Russell and D. O'Brien (eds.), *Judicial Independence in the Age of Democracy* (Charlottesville 2001), p. 12.

[7] M. Shapiro, *Courts. A Political and Comparative Analysis* (Chicago 1981), p. 34.

[8] Russell, *op. cit.*, p.9.

depends on one of the parties cannot be – and appear to be – impartial.[9] JI implies a clear political dimension if and when a judge comes to adjudicate a case in which politics is involved: e.g. when the government – or someone politically powerful – is a party. From this point of view the internal[10] dimension of JI can become significant only if it impinges on external independence: for instance, in the case of politically influenced higher ranking judges harassing lower ranks if they decide against powerful political actors.

Therefore, we should distinguish between at least two different meanings of the concept:[11]

- *Institutional* independence, which is usually further distinguished[12] in substantive – i.e. the principle that the judge is subject only to the law – and personal. This latter dimension – an important support to the former – concerns all those safeguards allowing the judge to decide impartially without fearing negative consequences: matters of removal, discipline, career and salary need to be strictly regulated. However, in analyzing institutional JI – and especially the personal dimension – we should also distinguish between:
    a. Formal rules: they are not necessarily applied, as often in non democratic and transitional regime but rarely in consolidated democratic countries, since rule implementation is an element of regime consolidation.
    b. Institutional rules: to the extent that formal rules are implemented, you can infer institutional independence.
    c. Unwritten rules, practices, customs *praeter legem* supportive of JI: they are important, especially in cases of high institutional continuity (*e.g.* UK).
- *Behavioural* independence or "independence on the bench"[13], i.e. the extent to which the judge actually adjudicates impartially. From this point of view institutional JI should be considered a necessary but not sufficient condition: although behavioural independence involves several factors related in a complex way, institutional independence plays without doubt a significant – although not decisive – role in allowing judges to decide impartially.

---

[9] See Shapiro, *op. cit.*, ch. 1.

[10] While external independence refers to the relations between the judiciary and the other branches of government, internal independence focuses on guarantees aimed at protecting individual judges from undue pressures from high ranking judges.

[11] See Russell, *op. cit.*, pp. 6–9.

[12] See S. Shetreet, "Judicial Independence: New Conceptual Dimensions and Contemporary Challenges" in S. Shetreet and J. Deschenes (eds.), *Judicial Independence: The Contemporary Debate* (Dordrecht 1985), pp. 590–681.

[13] D. O'Brien and Y. Ohkoshi, "Stifling Judicial Independence from Within: The Japanese Judiciary" in Russell and O'Brien, *op. cit.*, p. 38.

Of course, in order to fully assess the impact of judicial independence, the wider context in which judges decide must be taken into account. We should consider the extent to which judicial decisions really matter. In fact, if the RoL implies a set of rules guaranteeing basic civil and political rights, it needs a judiciary not only autonomous but also with the power to enforce those rights. This power is influenced by several factors: among them, the structure of the judicial system, the prerogatives of the judge and the role played by public prosecution, which deeply influences the access to criminal justice and therefore the extent to which significant cases can access the judicial system (e.g. cases against political corruption). However, all the specifications made, institutional independence plays a crucial role for the development and implementation of the RoL, since impartial judges are a basic instrument to enforce the law in a fair and effective way.

II. Types of Judicial Independence

As we have seen, some degree of JI seems to be a precondition for the development of the RoL, but also the need of forms of accountability has to be taken into account. It is possible to make accountability and independence compatible, although much depends on the way they are defined. How is the situation in practice? How is JI implemented? And how does it impact on the state of the RoL?

The EU countries provide a good case to improve the analysis and to introduce a testing of the proposition that JI plays a crucial and positive role in the establishment and consolidation of the RoL. They are all democracies (more o less consolidated): the risk of lumping together radically different types of regime is therefore avoided. In addition, there is a lot of useful information on the state of courts' independence in all these countries. Therefore, although the findings of our analysis will be circumscribed to the set of cases considered, the evidence seems to be relatively stronger than in other studies and, on the whole, rather homogeneous. Last, in the EU a strong engagement in favour of the RoL and JI has been under way in recent decades, supported also by the Council of Europe.

Our evaluation of the state of JI in Europe has been carried out, first, by identifying four different types of relationships between courts and politics (Fig. 1), corresponding to increasing levels of institutional independence:

1) *Full politicization:* in this setting politics can exert direct influence on all significant elements of the status of judges: recruitment, career and discipline (including removal). A low level of (especially external) independence is the result, although the actual role of the courts depends

		External Independence	
		–	+
Internal Independence	–	2. Limited Political Influence	3. Hierarchy
	+	1. Full Politicization	4. Self-Government

Fig.1. Types of Judicial Independence

to a large extent on the structure – more or less polycentric – of the political system.

2) *Limited political influence:* in this case politics exert influence only on the top of the judicial hierarchy – e.g. by appointing supreme court judges – while lower ranks are recruited on a technical, non-political basis and are shielded from direct political influence.[14] Here much depends on the level of internal independence: it tends to be low, thus implying a strong influence by politically appointed higher ranks, with the consequence of politics influencing *indirectly* all the corps. On the other hand, we should take into account that organizations made up of career personnel always enjoy some degree of autonomy vis-à-vis the political leadership. Therefore, the overall level of institutional JI can be judged moderate to low (in the case of very low internal JI).
3) *Hierarchy:* political influence here is reduced since all judges enjoy high guarantees of external independence. However, internal independence tends to be low, thanks to the powers over recruitment, career and discipline entrusted to the higher ranks. Highest positions tend to be assigned through a sort of cooptation.
4) *Self-government:* judicial reforms in the second part of the XX century have brought about in some countries a strong increase of JI in both its dimensions. Political influence has been severely restricted and also the role of higher ranks has been narrowed and in some cases completely erased. As a rule, this setting has been achieved through the institution of a Judicial Council in which all ranks are represented. In some case – Italy – the traditional role of the hierarchy has been completely dismantled, achieving in this way the highest degree of institutional independence among EU countries.

[14] A variation can be political influence channelled on the judicial corps through a Judicial Council composed mostly of political appointees. Although Judicial Councils are often considered to be an effective means to bolster JI, much depends on their composition and powers.

III. Judicial Independence and the Rule of Law in the European Union

For each country the most significant elements of institutional independence have been assessed, providing also an overall average evaluation (Tab. 1).[15] It should be emphasized that the evaluation is qualitative. So, the ranking of the countries is ordinal and there is some simplification in summing up the scores of the different properties. However, the average evaluations should provide us with the type of judicial setting to which specific countries are more proximate to. As we can see, the third and fourth types – Hierarchy and Self-government – tend to prevail. Only Sweden, Estonia and Malta seem to display a relatively lower level of institutional independence.

The state of the RoL in Europe has been assessed through the index provided by the World Governance Indicators (WGI) of the World Bank (Tab. 2).[16] The index tries to assess the general state of legality, pointing at an evaluation of the performance of all public institutions involved (and therefore taking into account also institutions other than judicial). The analysis of the data confirms that the relationship between JI and RoL is more complex than it is usually assumed. As Table 3 shows, higher RoL scores do not correspond to higher levels of JI. In fact, countries exhibiting the fourth type of JI – Self-government, the highest – show definitively lower scores. The only generalization that comes out confirmed is that relating judicial reforms to a weak RoL: countries with a weak RoL seem more likely to exhibit a higher level of courts' institutional independence. Reverse causality could be at work here: high independence can be the answer to an initial low level of the RoL. But in order to shed more light on the matter we are going to consider the "Two" Europes in a separate way.

Also in the more consolidated democracies of "Old" Europe[17] JI does not seem to be related to the development of the RoL: countries with the highest level of JI score lower on the RoL index (Tab. 4). If we consider specific countries, two cases seem particularly significant, although for different reasons: Italy and Sweden. Italy is the country in which institutional independence has been strengthened the most in the last 50 years, but so far with disappointing results.[18] On the contrary, Sweden is a country with a lower – and stable – level

[15] We have relied especially on reports on judicial independence by the Open Society Institute and the European Commission for the Efficiency of Justice (CEPEJ) and, in some cases, on interviews with local experts. As a point of reference, also an appraisal of the US is included.

[16] For the way the index is composed see www.govindicators.com. Although sometimes criticized, the index represents so far the most comprehensive effort at assessing the state of the RoL in the countries of the world.

[17] Greece, Portugal and Spain moved to democracy in the mid 1970s. All the remaining countries have enjoyed democracy at least since the end of the Second World War.

[18] See G. Di Federico (ed.), *Recruitment, Professional Evaluation and Career of Judges and Prosecutors in Europe*, (Bologna 2005), pp. 127–158.

Tab.1. Judicial Independence in the EU (2007)

Country	app	career	disc	average
Malta	2	2	1	1,667
Estonia	2	2	3	2,333
Sweden	2	2	3	2,333
Ireland	3	3	3	3,000
Cyprus	3	3	3	3,000
UK	3	3	3	3,000
Germany	3	2	4	3,000
Greece	3	3	3	3,000
Czech R.	3	3	3	3,000
Latvia	3	3	3	3,000
Lithuania	3	3	3	3,000
Austria	3	3	4	3,333
Denmark	3	3	4	3,333
Finland	3	3	4	3,333
France	3	3	4	3,333
Luxembourg	3	3	4	3,333
Spain	4	2	4	3,333
Netherlands	3	4	4	3,667
Poland	4	4	3	3,667
Bulgaria	4	4	3	3,667
Portugal	4	4	4	4,000
Hungary	4	4	4	4,000
Belgium	4	4	4	4,000
Slovenia	4	4	4	4,000
Romania	4	4	4	4,000
Slovak R.	4	4	4	4,000
Italy	4	4	4	4,000
USA	1	1	1	1,000

Countries of Central and East Europe are in bold. We add USA as a reference point.
app: initial recruitment; career: promotions after initial appointment; disc: discipline and removal.

of institutional independence[19] but exhibiting remarkable scores on the WGI index.

The new EU Central and Eastern European countries (CEECs) provide a good opportunity to enlarge and improve the analysis of the impact of judicial

[19] See J. Bell, *Judiciaries within Europe*, (Cambridge 2006), pp. 234–297.

Tab.2. The WGI Rule of Law index

Country	1996	2007
Bulgaria	−0,11	−0,14
Romania	−0,15	−0,17
Poland	0,64	0,28
Slovak R.	0,23	0,35
Italy	0,98	0,43
Lithuania	0,29	0,49
Latvia	0,13	0,57
Greece	0,94	0,65
Hungary	0,84	0,74
Czech R.	0,87	0,77
Slovenia	0,87	0,84
Portugal	1,14	0,95
Cyprus	0,76	0,96
Estonia	0,51	1,00
Spain	1,35	1,12
France	1,47	1,32
Belgium	1,55	1,52
Malta	0,43	1,55
UK	1,83	1,75
Netherlands	1,81	1,76
Ireland	1,71	1,77
Germany	1,79	1,78
Luxembourg	1,61	1,85
Finland	1,90	1,87
Austria	1,91	1,90
Sweden	1,84	1,90
Denmark	1,87	1,95

Countries are ordered according the 2007 RoL score. Those of Central and East Europe are in bold.

Tab.3. Judicial Independence and the Rule of Law in the EU (2007)

Type of Independence	RoL average 2007	N
1. Full politicization		–
2. Limited political influence	1,483	3
3. Hierarchy	1,339	14
4. Self-government	0,656	10
Total	1,102	27

Tab.4. Judicial Independence and the Rule of Law in Old Europe (2007)

Type of Independence	RoL average 2007	N
1. Full politicization		–
2. Limited political influence	1,725	2
3. Hierarchy	1,538	11
4. Self-government	1,165	4
Total	1,472	17

Tab.5. Judicial Independence in New Europe (1997)

Country	app	career	disc	average
Romania	1	1	1	1,000
Bulgaria	1	1	1	1,000
Lithuania	1	2	1	1,333
Estonia	2	2	3	2,333
Slovak R.	3	3	3	3,000
Czech R.	3	3	3	3,000
Latvia	3	3	3	3,000
Poland	4	2	3	3,000
Hungary	4	3	3	3,333
Slovenia	4	4	3	3,667
(DDR)	1	1	1	1,000

reforms on the RoL. They share a common political heritage – late and troubled State-building and a long period of non democratic and communist regime – experienced a democratic transition and have been under a strong pressure, especially by the EU, to conform to RoL prescriptions.

The available data allow us to introduce in a systematic way the diachronic dimension. The survey of the state of judicial reforms in the CEECs has been carried out distinguishing between institutional changes introduced in the first period after the demise of communist regimes (1989–1997) and later (1998–2007): see Tables 1 and 5. Already in 1997, JI had been more or less strengthened in several countries, at least in comparison with the situation in previous communist regimes, exemplified by the DDR. In the following decade (1998–2007), thanks also to the strong pressure exerted by the EU, additional reforms have been implemented, all aiming at strengthening JI. Although with different timing, the transition to democracy in the area has implied a general strengthening of JI.

Tab.6. Judicial Independence and the Rule of Law in New Europe

Type of Independence in 1997	RoL 1996	RoL 2007	N
1. Full politicization	0,010	0,060	3
2. Limited political influence	0,510	1,000	1
3. Hierarchy	0,542	0,542	5
4. Self-government	0,87	0,84	1
Total Average	0,412	0,473	10

With the implementation of reforms we would expect, maybe with some time lag, a general improvement of the WGI index, especially for countries adopting stronger types of JI. Table 6, taking as a point of reference the institutional setting of 1997, shows the evolution of WGI data. The situation does not show a clear relationship, at least so far: RoL index scores have remained more or less stagnant for all types of JI.

Looking to specific countries, some – Estonia, Latvia and, to a lesser degree, Lithuania and Bulgaria – exhibit an improvement in WGI scores. Others – Romania, Slovakia and Slovenia – are more or less stable. On the contrary, the Czech Republic, Hungary and especially Poland show a decline. Although the time span of the analysis can be considered rather short, the data do not seem to agree with mainstream hypotheses about the impact of judicial reforms. Czech Republic, Poland and especially Hungary and Slovenia had the highest level of institutional independence in 1997 and have more or less maintained their WGI scores in the following decade, although we should have expected an improvement.[20] Only in the case of Latvia and – but to a lesser extent – Estonia the improvement in WGI scores can be related to a previous situation of, relative, independence. However, Estonia, the country presently exhibiting the highest WGI scores, had a modest level of independence in 1997 and not much has changed since then.

IV. Some Conclusions

In "Old" Europe judicial reforms aiming at reinforcing judicial independence do not seem to have had a significant impact. The more moderate Hierarchy type performs consistently better than Self-Government. In addition, the few

[20] Actually, Poland exhibits a significant drop in the RoL score.

countries belonging to the Limited Political Influence type – like Sweden – perform even better. It is likely that a sort of reverse causality is at work here, with countries of the Latin area strengthening judicial independence with the goal of improving their situation. In this context the weak impact of judicial reforms in Italy should be emphasized: the country that has most consistently carried out independence reforms.

As we have pointed out, "New" Europe provides a more significant set of cases but, so far, the impact of judicial reforms seems to have been rather modest. In Slovenia, Hungary, Poland and the Czech Republic, where early reforms (1989–97) were more radical, there are no sign of improvement in the WGI index in the later period (1996–2007). On the other hand, the country with the stronger improvement in the WGI index is Estonia, a country with a modest level of independence in 1997.

The analysis carried out in the previous pages – although focused only on one of the potentially significant variable: institutional JI – seems to confirm that the effectiveness of judicial reforms in supporting the development of the RoL should not be overvalued. The reasons can be several. First of all, in the case of transition from non democratic regimes we must take into account the dubious impact of institutional independence. In fact, the relatively deluding performance of countries such Poland and Hungary can be tentatively explained by considering that the increase of institutional independence at the very beginning of the transition contributed to consolidate a judicial personnel to a large extent socialized in the previous regimes. These people remained in office and constituted the "new" judiciary, very likely with negative consequences for the implementation of RoL values.

In general, it seems that reforms strengthening judicial independence are supportive of the RoL but, if carried out beyond a certain level, their positive impact tends to decrease. In other words, while some degree of independence is necessary, it must be balanced with forms of accountability. Data showing the better performance of the Hierarchy type of institutional setting – where accountability is strengthened by the fact that higher ranking judges can check the activity of their colleagues – tend to support this view, pointing at the risks of an excessive level of internal independence. More precisely, in order to have judges supportive of the RoL professionalism is likely to be as important as independence. In fact, identification with the institutional requirements of the judicial role – i.e. impartially adjudicating cases according to the law – is related to the professional qualifications of the judge. This can be the reason why a too high level of – especially internal – independence is dysfunctional, especially when coupled with weak professional checks. Too independent judges – if they become unaccountable – can be captured by powerful external interests and this can happen especially where professional identification is already weak. Sweden seems to provide a good counter-example: Swedish judges, although enjoying a modest level of – especially internal – independence, seem to exhibit a strong professional outlook.[21] Therefore, it seems that in designing and implementing judicial reforms the role of the broader set of organizational constraints judges face should be taken fully into account.

[21] See Bell, *op. cit.*

CHAPTER SEVEN

THE RULE OF LAW VS. THE RULE OF JUDGES: A BRANDEISIAN SOLUTION

*Stephen Goldstein**

I. Introduction

Israel is currently engaged in a heated debate, both in the legal community and in the general public, about judicial activism. The proponents of strong judicial activism see it as a necessary mechanism to protect the "rule of law" while the opponents see the same phenomenon not as protecting the rule of law, which, of course, is not self-executing, but rather as creating the "rule of judges." A similar debate has been going on in the United States for many decades. While the debate in the United States may be no less heated than in Israel, I should note at the outset that even the most extreme judicial activism in the United States has never come close to that in Israel in the last twenty-five years

* Stephen Goldstein got his B.A. at the University of Pennsylvania, 1959 (Phi Beta Kappa). J.D., University of Pennsylvania, 1962, summa cum laude (first in class). Admitted to the Bar in Pennsylvania, U.S.A. 1962. Practicing lawyer in Philadelphia, Pennsylvania, 1962–1964. Law Clerk to Justice Arthur Goldberg, United States Supreme Court, 1964–1965. Has been professor of Law in The University of Pennsylvania. Edward S. Silver Professor of Procedural Law, The Hebrew University of Jerusalem, 1976. Dean of the Hebrew University faculty of Law, 1987–1990. Director, The Harry Sacher Institute of Legislative Research and Comparative Law, 1984–1987. Chairman of the Editorial Board of the Israel Law Review, 1979–1984. Chairman, The United States-Israel Educational Foundation (Fulbright Commission), 1988–1999. Legal Counsel, The American Association of University Professors, 1971–1974. Prof. Goldstein has held visiting positions in numerous universities, including: The University of California, Berkeley, Trinity College, Cambridge University, Tulane University, University of Hong Kong, Kellogg College, University of Oxford, and Chuo University – Tokyo. Member, the Executive Committee of the International Association of Procedural Law. Member, The International Academy of Comparative Law. Member, The American Law Institute; International Adviser to the American Law Institute Project on Transnational Civil Procedure; Judge, Israel Adhesion Contracts Tribunal; Member, Israel Government Council for the Supervision of Experimentation on Animals; Member, Editorial Board of the Israel Law Review. Research interests include fundamental issues in comparative procedural law and dispute resolution structures and mechanisms; reform of procedural law and dispute resolution mechanisms from a comparative perspective; class actions and derivative actions. Prof. Goldstein passed away in 2009.

or so, particularly in terms of judicial intervention in governmental activity not connected with the protection of individual civil liberties.[1]

In this Paper I will discuss the judicial heritage of that most outstanding American-Jewish jurist, Justice Louis D. Brandeis in the context of these debates.

Before getting into the details of this Heritage, I must confront the basic question of whether it is even possible to apply the ideas of Brandeis from the first half of the 20th century in the United States to our much later time and indeed, to another place, such as Israel. Everyone acts on the background of his time and place. This is especially true of Justice Brandeis, as the period of his judicial activity in the United States was during a most unique time. Is it then legitimate to apply what Brandeis did in his time to later times and to other countries?

As to specific issues, such as "how would Brandeis decide questions relating to abortions or affirmative actions?" which engage the United States Supreme Court today, it is not possible to find answers in the Brandeis heritage; it is clear that we cannot find answers to such questions in the ideas that he set forth in his time, and it is a shame even to ask such worthless questions. A fortiori, one should not ask that kind of question as to specific issues which today trouble the any other country's judiciary.

However, that does not mean that there is nothing in the Brandeis judicial heritage that may be relevant to matters that are of interest today in the United States as well as other countries. This relevant heritage does not concern specific issues, but rather general approaches and attitudes in the field of judicial policy. Also in this area of general judicial policy we must be cautious in drawing absolute conclusions from the Brandeisian heritage since also as to his judicial policy Brandeis acted in the context of his time and place. However, as to issues of general judicial policy, I believe we can draw some cautious conclusions from the heritage of Brandeis which are indeed relevant today.

In this line at the end of this presentation, I will go out on a limb and attempt to answer the following two questions:

1. Whether the Brandeis judicial heritage is closer to the position of American justices who are termed "conservatives" or to those termed "liberals" in terms of judicial activism? and

2. Whether, in terms of Israel, the judicial heritage of Brandeis is closer to the extreme judicial activism camp of former Supreme Court President

[1] For an example see: HJC 1031/99 *Kabel v. State of Israel*, IsrSC 56 (3) 640 (2002), in which the Supreme Court has stroke down a law giving retroactive approval to illegal radio station.

Aharon Barak and the present President Dorit Beinish or to the more restrained view represented by former Supreme Court President Landau and Deputy President Alon as well as Minister of Justice Danny Friedman?

Before discussing in detail this heritage I should mention that the discussion in this paper is based on a previous, much longer paper, published in Hebrew in 2004.[2]

II. The Judicial Heritage of Brandies

1. *Judicial Self-Control, Restraint and Modesty*

Brandeis was appointed to the United States Supreme Court in 1916 at age 60 and served until his retirement at age 82. His appointment followed a 38 year career as a very successful private attorney.[3] This career, which I discussed at length in the Hebrew paper mentioned above, itself serves as an ideal model for a private attorney dedicated also to public service activities. During his career as a private attorney, Brandeis developed much of his judicial philosophy which came to the fore in his judicial career.

A cardinal principle of this philosophy resulted from his adamant opposition to the judicial activism of the US Supreme Court during the Lochner[4] era which resulted in the striking down, using the 14th amendment, of state legislation aimed at bettering the lot of the weaker elements in society, in general, and the workers, in particular. This opposition led him to the view that courts should act with restraint and self-control rather than with judicial activism.

And, indeed, judicial restraint was the outstanding characteristic of Brandeis the judge. He, himself, summed it up well in his famous aphorism: "The most important thing we [judges] do is not to do".[5] This "not to do" came to the fore in three areas: (a) insistence on the existence of the necessary preconditions for

---

[2] Stephan Goldstein, "Hamasoret Hamishpatit Shel Louis Brandeis" *Judicial Heritage of Louis Brandeis* (Ed. Alon Gal), (Jerusalem: The Israel Academy of Sciences and Humanities, 2004). (Hebrew)

[3] Levy, David W.; Murphy, Bruce Allen, "Preserving the Progressive Spirit in a Conservative Time: The Joint Reform Efforts of Justice Brandeis and Professor Frankfurter, 1916–1933" (1979–1980), 78 Mich. L. Rev. 1252; also see: P. Strumm, Louis D. Brandeis – Justice for the People (Cambridge: Mass, 1984).

[4] This era received its name from the Lochner case (*Lochner v. New York*, 198 U.S. 45), and lasts from the Seventies of the 19th century until the Thirties of the 20th century.

[5] A. Bickel, *The Least Dangerous Branch* 71 (New York: Bobbs-Merril 1962).

the conduct of judicial litigation; (b) insistence on the principles by which the court is to narrow the scope of its decisions; and (c) narrowing the substantive principles of judicial review.

More than any justice of his generation, Brandeis insisted that there exist the traditional procedural preconditions required to bring judicial actions before the court would entertain the case.[6] These preconditions included the "standing" of the plaintiff, which required that he is complaining of a personal injury to himself; that the matter be "justiciable" – and, of course, not everything is justiciable;[7] that the matter be "ripe" for adjudication (*e.g.*, the rejection of requests for declaratory judgments prior to the birth of a real claim);[8] and the existence of real adversity between the litigants (the refusal to determine a fictitious matter created by the litigants in order to have a judicial determination of a certain matter no matter how convenient this would be for the litigants and how important was the constitutional issue involved).[9] In addition in appeals cases Brandeis refused to consider issues that had not been raised in the lower court.[10]

In brief, in the view of Brandeis, the only function of courts, including supreme courts, is to determine real and actual disputes between litigants. Other so-called purposes, such as preservation of the rule of law and enforcing constitutional norms, if they are achieved at all, can only be achieved as incidental to a court's function of determining real and actual disputes.[11]

Moreover, with Brandeis the procedural preconditions to judicial action were not merely platitudes, but were acted on by him not only when it was convenient for him to do so but also when they prevented Brandeis from reaching what he would have considered to be a desirable result on the merits.[12]

Brandeis applied these procedural preconditions to judicial action both as to regular litigation and to litigation that raised constitutional questions. However, he believed that the insistence on their existence was even more important in constitutional litigation since, in his view, in constitutional litigation it was especially important for courts "not to do."

---

[6] P. Strumm, "Brandeis and the living constitution", *Brandeis and American*, Lexington, KY 1989, pp. 118–132; F. Frankfurter, "Mr. Justice Brandeis and the constitution" Harvard L.Rev 1931 (45), pp. 33, 79–87.

[7] See: *Ashwander v. Tennessee Valley Authorit*, 275 U.S. 288, 341–348 (1936).

[8] See: *California v. Arizona*, 283 U.S. 423, 463–464 (1934).

[9] See Brandeis' memo in: *Atherton Mills v. Johnston*, 259 U.S. 13 (1922), and the discussion over it in Bickel's book, *supra note* 5, pp. 1–20.

[10] See: *Whitney v. California*, 274 U.S. 357, 372, 379–380 (1927).

[11] PA Freund, "Mr. Justice Brandeis: A Centennial Memoir" (1956) Harv. L. Rev, pp 70.

[12] See Brandeis' opinion in Atherton Mills and the discussion in Bickel's book (supra note 9), and also the opinions in *Whitney v. California* (supra note 10) and in Ashwrander v. Tennessee (supra note 7).

This approach of Brandeis to constitutional litigation was set forth most comprehensively in his famous 1936 concurring opinion in *Ashwander*,[13] This opinion remains until today the guiding light to those who believe in judicial restraint in constitutional litigation. In his *Ashwander* opinion Brandeis adopted as the basis for the special self-restraint required of a judge who is asked to declare a law unconstitutional, the following words of Cooley:

> It must be evident to any one that the power to declare a legislative enactment void is one which the judge, conscious of the fallibility of the human judgment, will shrink from exercising in any case where he can conscientiously and with due regard to duty and official oath decline the responsibility.[14]

He then discussed a number of principles pursuant to which the United States Supreme Court "has avoided passing upon a large part of all the constitutional questions pressed upon it for decision". These principles included most of the procedural preconditions to judicial action which I have already discussed as well as other principles which are designed to limit the scope of the court's decision even when the procedural preconditions to judicial action exist.

This second group of principles included:

a. A primary principle that the Court will never pass upon a constitutional issue unless it is absolutely necessary to do so in the determination of a real, earnest and vital controversy between individuals;
b. the Court will not formulate a rule of constitutional law broader than is required by the precise facts to which it is to be applied;
c. "the Court will not pass upon a constitutional question although properly presented by the record, if there is also some other ground upon which the case may be disposed of";
d. "the Court will not pass upon the constitutionality of a statute at the instance of one who has availed himself of its benefits";
e. "when the validity of an act of the Congress is drawn in question, and even if a serious doubt of constitutionality is raised, it is a cardinal principle that this Court will first ascertain whether a construction of the statute is fairly possible by which the question may be avoided".

Brandeis did not invent these principles. Rather, as a cautious common law judge, he carefully based them on US Supreme Court precedents. However, as I have stated, by bringing them together in his lucid presentation in *Ashwander*,

---

[13] *Supra note* 7.

[14] *Ibid*, at page 345; Th. Clooley, *A treatise on the Constitutional Limitations which Rest upon the Legislative Power of the States of the American Union* 8th ed., [1868], p. 332.

Brandeis made a most important contribution to American constitutional law, that of principles of judicial self-control and restraint. No less important, Brandeis applied these principles even when such application prevented him from reaching a result on the merits which he would have found desirable. He did so both before and after his opinion in *Ashwander*.[15]

It is also enlightening to discuss briefly the dissenting opinion of Brandeis in *International News Service (INS)* case,[16] which is not concerned with constitutional issues and thus is not generally included among his most famous opinions. Yet, in my view, it testifies well to Brandeis being a most modest, self-controlled and restrained judge. In this case the Associated Press (AP) complained that the INS had violated its intellectual property rights by copying and disseminating AP "news dispatches" under the INS name. No statute had then recognized an intellectual property right as complained of by the AP and Brandeis dissented strongly from the majority's recognition of such a right without a statutory basis. In his dissenting opinion he argued:

> The creation or recognition by courts of a new private right may work serious injury to the general public, unless the boundaries of the right are definitely established and wisely guarded... Courts are ill-equipped to make the investigations which should precede a determination of the limitations which should be set upon any property right in news, or the circumstances under which news gathered by a private agency should be deemed affected with a public interest. Courts would be powerless to prescribe the detailed regulations essential to full enjoyment of the rights conferred or to introduce the machinery required for enforcement of such regulations. Considerations such as these should lead us to decline to establish a new rule of law in the effort to redress a newly-disclosed wrong, although the propriety of such remedy appears to be clear.[17]

In other words, Brandeis, like the majority, recognized that there had been created a new legal problem which should be solved. However, in his view the governmental organ which should solve the problem was the legislature – not the court. In short, and in Israeli terminology, Brandeis objected to "judicial legislation".

A fortiori he would have opposed most strongly judicial invalidation of governmental actions at the highest level in such matters as the appointment of directors general of ministries, selection of ministers and their retention in office, decisions of the Attorney General not to prosecute or to enter into plea bargains, as well as high-level governmental decisions concerning matters of defense and security, when such invalidations are not based on the enforcement

---

[15] See examples given in *supra note* 12, and also *Carter v. Carter*, 298 U.S. 238 (1936).

[16] *International News Service v. Associated Press*, 248 U.S. 215, 248 (1918).

[17] *Ibid at pp. 262–263 and 267.*

of clear legal restrictions but rather only on their being "unreasonable" in the opinion of the judges.

Another major feature of the Brandeis jurisprudence was his strong opposition to the concentration of power. He was a Jeffersonian in his belief in the value of the diffusion of power. Thus he was a strong proponent of federalism which diffused power among the several States and the Federal Government. I discussed at length his views on federalism in the Hebrew publication mentioned above. A fuller explanation of it here would be beyond the scope of this paper. What is important to us here is that Brandeis's opposition to the concentration of power also included the concentration of power in the courts in general and the US Supreme Court in particular. This view also led him to judicial self-control and restraint.[18]

2. *Restrained, Moderated and Proportional Judicial Activism*

Despite his strong position of judicial restraint Brandeis was not a proponent of complete judicial passivity. Indeed, he demonstrated judicial activism in two areas of civil liberties, governmental invasions of privacy and freedom of expression. Should these lead us to doubt that Brandeis was a model of judicial restraint?

As to the right of privacy, his dissenting opinion in the *Olmstead*[19] case is justly famous for his ringing proclamation of the right of citizens to be "let alone." However, we should remember that the right of privacy held a special place in his heart, ever since he wrote, with Warren, that famous Harvard Law Review article in 1890 which is viewed as the creator of the right.[20] Moreover, *Olmstead* was a single, isolated case and, therefore it is hard to draw conclusions from it as to his general judicial philosophy.[21]

---

[18] See: *New State Ice Co. v. Liebmann*, 285 U.S. 262, 287 (1932); *Pennsylvania Coal Co. v. Mahon*, 260 U.S. 393, 416 (1922); *Yarborough v. Yarborough*, 290 U.S. 202 (1933); *Bradford Electric Light Co. v. Clapper*, 284 U.S. 221 (1933); *John Hancock v. Yates*, 299 U.S. 215, 248 (1918); For a detailed opinion considering federalism, see *Erie Railroad Co. v. Tompkins*, 304 U.S. 64 (1938).

[19] *Olmstead v. United States*, 277 U.S. 438, 471 (1928).

[20] Louis D. Brandeis and S.D. Warren, "The Right to Privacy", Harvard L.Rev. 4 (1890), p. 193.

[21] It should be mentioned that both in his article and in the Olmstead dissent, Brandeis referred to the classical meaning of "privacy", as the right one have to conceal private information about himself and the banning of such information. This "privacy" has no imagination to the later "privacy" as it is found in *Griswold v. Connecticut*, 381 U.S. 479 (1965) – the right to use birth-controls, in *Roe v. Wade*, 410 U.S 152 (1973) – the right to go through abortion. In the later cases, "privacy" means the autonomy one has over her own body, which is violated by the government's interference. I humbly disagree with Urofsky (see: M.I. Urofsky, "To Guide By the

This, however, is not true as to his opinions concerning freedom of expression. Indeed, if we were to look only at his many decisions concerning freedom of expression, Brandeis would not be seen as a model of judicial restraint. Yet his freedom of expression jurisprudence should not be viewed in isolation but on the background of his generally being a proponent of judicial restraint. Both his *Olmstead* opinion and his freedom of expression jurisprudence should be seen as exceptions to his general rule of judicial restraint, exceptions which prove the rule.

In neither his *Olmstead* dissent nor his freedom of expression jurisprudence did Brandeis engage in wide-ranging, sweeping judicial activity aimed at imposing on society his view of the good. Rather he determined specific, concrete civil liberties issues in a moderated and proportional manner.

We should also remember that the freedom of expression involved in the decisions of Brandeis was political expression. Such expression is fundamental to a robust democracy, in which Brandeis strongly believed. Moreover, the multiplicity of speakers produced by freedom of expression fitted precisely the desire of Brandeis for the diffusion of power. The Holmesian "market place of ideas" is exactly the Brandesian vision of diffused power, as compared with the concentration of governmental power that would be produced by the prevention of individual political expression.

Speaking of Holmes, another aspect of Brandeis's freedom of expression decisions should be mentioned: his relationship to Holmes. When the freedom of expression jurisprudence during Brandeis term as justice is referred to, Holmes and Brandeis are almost invariably cited in the same breath in that order, *i.e.*, the name of Holmes preceding that of Brandeis. This is no coincidence. Rather it represents the fact that then, as well as today, Holmes was considered the leader of the two in this field. And, indeed, it is true that almost all the freedom of expression opinions attributed to the duo were written by Holmes.

More importantly, the Holmes-Brandeis freedom of expression opinions were themselves restrained and moderated. We must not associate their freedom of expression opinions with the extreme and exaggerated, almost religious adulation of freedom of expression that has developed in the US Supreme Court in the last 50 years. In my view the Holmes-Brandeis view of freedom of expression is much closer to the more moderate Israeli view that has developed, beginning with the 1953 Kol Ha'am case,[22] than it is to current American freedom of expression doctrine.

Light of Reason': Mr. Justice Brandeis – An Appreciation", *American Jewish History* 81 [1993], pp. 366, 391–392) who thinks it is possible to study from Brandeis' decisions and articles to the contemporary privacy issues.

[22] HCJ 73/53 *Kol Ha'am Co. LTD v. Minister of the Interior*, ISR. SC 7(2) 871 (1953).

We should remember that the famous Holmesian test for when government can prevent or punish speech, the "clear and present danger" test, was promulgated by him in the Shcneck case,[23] in which the Court unanimously upheld the convictions of a number of First World War anti-war agitators for the federal offence of disseminating material to army conscripts encouraging them to resist the conscription.

Moreover, in the age of Holmes and Brandeis, the use of the clear and present danger test by juries and lower court judges generally led to the conviction of dissenters,[24] which convictions were always upheld by a majority of the Supreme Court. Of course, in a number of these cases Holmes and Brandeis dissented on the grounds that the majority had misapplied the test. However, they never disavowed the test.

Finally, we should emphasize that in one of his most quoted opinions concerning the history and importance of freedom of expression, *i.e.*, the dictum in his concurring opinion in *Whitney v. California*,[25] Brandeis actually joined the rest of the Court in upholding the conviction for speech that he apparently felt was constitutionally protected, because the issue had not been raised in the State trial court. Thus, when the crunch came and his principles of judicial self-control and restraint ("not doing") conflicted with judicial protection of freedom of expression, self-control and restraint won out.

From all of the above, it is clear to me that the jurisprudence of Brandeis concerning freedom of expression and the right of privacy show that his jurisprudence was multi-faceted.[26] However, they do not derogate from the conclusion that the guiding principle of his judicial heritage was judicial restraint, self-control and opposition to the centralization of power, including in the judiciary.

III. Conclusions

We have now reached the questions which I presented at the beginning of this paper and I will repeat them:

---

[23] *Schneck v. United States*, 249 U.S. 47 (1919).

[24] See: *Abrams v. United States*, 250 U.S. 216, 624 (1919); *Gitlow v. New York* 268 U.S. 652, 671 (1925). It should be stated that there were a few cases in which Holmes agreed with the majority and Brandeis dissented (see: *Pierce v. United States*, 252 U.S. 239, 253 [1920]; *Schaefer v. United States*, 251 U.S. 466, 482 (1920); *Gilbert v. Minnesota*, 254 U.S. 325, 342 [1920]), but these dissenting opinions had a smaller influence over the American law considering freedom of expression than Holmes' opinions (both his majority and dissenting opinios).

[25] *Supra note* 10.

[26] Louis L. Jaffe, "Was Brandeis an Activist? The Search for Intermediate Premises" (1966–1967) 80 Harv. L. Rev. 986.

1. Whether the Brandeis judicial heritage is closer to the position of American justices who are termed "conservatives" or to those termed "liberals" in terms of judicial activism; and
2. whether, in terms of Israel, the judicial heritage of Brandeis is closer to the extreme judicial activism camp of former Supreme Court President Aharon Barak and current President Dorit Beinish or to the more restrained view represented by former Supreme Court President Landau and Deputy President Elon as well as the Minister of Justice, Daniel Friedman.

First, in relation to the United States, it is clear from what I have set forth that the Brandeis judicial heritage is closer to the approach of conservative justices than to liberals. This is true both as to judicial restraint and to federalism although I am not concentrating on the latter in this paper.

While the conservative justices today do rely on Brandeis opinions quite often, it is not surprising, given the many years that have passed since he left the Supreme Court, that they do not claim to be his followers. In contrast, in the two generations of justices and scholars that followed Brandeis two outstanding "conservatives" did lay express claim to be his followers: Justice Felix Frankfurter[27] and Prof. Alex Bickel.[28] Both of them were very close to Brandeis in his lifetime and viewed him as their teacher and mentor. Frankfurter was his prodigy and professional confidant during Brandeis's entire judicial service. He also was his successor in the "Jewish seat" on the Court.[29] Bickel served as his law clerk and remained close to Brandeis until the former's death.

As I have mentioned, both of them saw themselves as following in the path of Brandeis and both were without a doubt "conservatives". Frankfurter was the outstanding conservative Supreme Court justice from his appointment in 1939 until his retirement in 1962, a period that included the first nine years of the very "liberal" Warren Court. In maintaining his staunch judicial conservatism during his entire judicial tenure, Frankfurter clearly saw himself as following in the footsteps of his mentor, Brandeis. (As an aside, in my view he went even further than Brandeis in adherence to judicial restraint.)

Likewise Alex Bickel was the "conservative" symbol of Yale Law School in the 1960's and thereafter, which fact speaks for itself. The expression which he

---

[27] See: *Of Life and Law and Other Things that Matter: Papers and Addresses of Felix Frankfurter*, 1956–1963, ed. P.B. Kurland (Cambridge: Mass, 1965), 57 Frankfurter, *supra note* 6.

[28] See Bickel, *supra note* 5.

[29] Bruce Allen Murphy, *The Brandeis/Frunkfuter Connection*, (New York: Oxford University Press 1982), pp 473.

coined "passive virtues" can serve well as a summary of the greatness of the heritage of his teacher and mentor, Brandeis.

Having discussed Frankfurter and Bickel, I would have been able to conclude this discussion of the Brandeis judicial heritage in relation to later American jurists, had I not known, from personal knowledge, of another American Supreme Court Justice who saw himself as a follower of Brandeis – Arthur Goldberg, who succeeded Frankfurter in the "Jewish seat" on the Court. In the three short years (1962–1965) that Goldberg served on the Court he was one of the most activist justices of the Warren Court. How could this most activist of justices see himself as continuing the Brandeis heritage?

One possible answer could be that Brandeis was such an admired figure, particularly among Jewish jurists, that Goldberg wanted to see himself as Brandeis's successor even though he knew that his judicial philosophy was very far from that of Brandeis. Indeed, if we were to ignore their very different judicial philosophies, there were many similarities between Goldberg and Brandeis: both of them were sons of Jewish immigrants who by their own efforts became outstanding lawyers; both were very involved in the American labor movement; and, of course, Goldberg occupied the Jewish seat on the Court as the successor to Brandeis via Frankfurter.

However, Goldberg was not satisfied with these similarities but also wanted to find similarities between himself and Brandeis in their judicial philosophies. In these efforts he could have relied upon the Brandeis jurisprudence concerning freedom of expression and the right of privacy. Of course, as I have stated, in my view this Brandeis jurisprudence is not the rule but rather the exception that proves the rule.

But I would like to discuss one other argument that could be used to justify Goldberg's view, if it is correct. I should mention that I have no reason to think that Goldberg believed in this argument and I never heard him mention it.

However, in a private conversion with me some time after the publication of my Hebrew paper, my former colleague as a law clerk to Justice Goldberg and currently an activist Justice of the Supreme Court, Justice Stephen Breyer, did argue it quite forcefully in trying to refute my view of the judicial heritage of Brandeis as I have set it forth in this paper. I can, therefore, now attribute it to Justice Breyer.

In setting forth this argument, I must return to what I said at the beginning of this paper about the great difficulty involved in discussing a person and his heritage divorced from the historic period in which he operated. In terms of Brandeis, this period was the Lochner era. Justice Breyer argued that during this period the primary body that threatened the protection of human rights in the United States was the courts, in general, and the US Supreme Court, in particular. On the other hand, the main force that was attempting to advance human rights was the State legislatures. In this situation if the strategic aim was to further the protection of human rights, the tactical means to achieve it would have been judicial restraint and strengthening the power of the States in the federal system. In contrast, it is argued, when in the 1960's the situation was reversed and the United States Supreme Court became the protector of human rights along with the national government against the opposition of the States, in order to accomplish the strategic aim of protecting human rights it was necessary to change the tactical means 180 degrees: from judicial restraint to judicial activism and from strengthening the position of the States to strengthening that of the national government.

According to this argument, my entire thesis about the judicial heritage of Brandeis is erroneous and void since I have confused his tactical ideas with his strategic ones.

Due to the inherent difficulty which I have emphasized of taking the Brandeis jurisprudence out of its time and place and attempting to apply it to other times and places, it is not possible to dismiss this argument out of hand. Moreover, many judicial activists like Goldberg and Breyer, really want to see the most admired Brandeis as one of them. However, in my view the argument about tactical aims versus strategic goals is not convincing and must ultimately be rejected.

The judicial philosophy of Brandeis – self-control and restraint as contrasted with judicial activism – was for him not just a tactical position but rather his strategic aim in the full meaning of that term. It was based on his strongly entrenched belief about the function of the judiciary in a democratic society, on his modesty about the wisdom of judges and on his opposition to the concentration of power, including in the judges.

This was how Brandeis was understood by the jurists who were the closest to him and tried to continue in his path. In this list we could also add to Justice Frankfurter and Professor Bickel the name of Professor Paul Freund of Harvard Law School who also served as a Brandeis law clerk and saw himself as following in his footsteps.[30]

Moreover, and most importantly, Brandeis himself remained true to himself and refused to compromise his principles of judicial restraint even in cases in which they prevented him from reaching decisions on the merits which would have been desirable for him, as *Whitney v. California*[31] well illustrates.

---

[30] See: P.A. Freund, "Justice Brandeis – A Law Clerck's Remembrance", *American Jewish History* 68 (1978), p. 7.

[31] *Supra note* 10.

Similarly, his view of the American system of federalism and the place of the States in that system was very clearly strategic. It derived from one of the most entrenched of his principles: opposition to the concentration of power.

As to the dispute in Israel as to judicial activism, the summation is easy. Despite all the difficulties involved in applying the judicial heritage of Brandeis not only to another era but also to another place, it is clear to me that Brandeis would be in the judicial restraint camp of jurists like Landau, Alon and Friedman in contrast to the judicial activism camp represented by Barak and Beinish.

For Brandeis the most important thing judges do is "not to do." That statement well sums up the judicial heritage of a judge who practices self-control, is restrained and, above all, modest as to his ability to know the true and the good. Would that all judges were like him.

CHAPTER EIGHT

THE THREATS TO JUDICIAL INDEPENDENCE: EXPERIENCES FROM THE COMMONWEALTH

*Cyrus Das**

I. Introduction

A culture of judicial independence has to go hand in hand with a culture of constitutionalism. As a former Chief Justice of the Malaysian Federal Court observed, all governments publicly endorse the principle of the rule of law but some quietly work to undermine it and it behoves judges to be on guard against the erosion of their independence[1]. The experience of several of the newly emergent nations of the Commonwealth has illustrated this.

The newly established Commonwealth nations of the post-war era provide a good setting to discuss the co-relation between constitutionalism and judicial independence. These new nations, stretching from Asia to the Caribbeans, attained independence from British colonial rule with a written constitution in place. They were called the Whitehall constitutions[2] and had, as their underpinning philosophy, democracy and the rule of law. A cornerstone feature was an independent judiciary empowered to interpret the written constitution, often proclaimed as the supreme law of the land, and to enforce a bill of rights affording fundamental rights to the citizenry.

After half a century or so, the experiences of these countries with an independent judiciary has been varied. Not all have survived with their original constitutions intact. In some cases the collapse of constitutional government, or a military takeover, has removed all vestiges of an independent judiciary. In others, overpowering political events has debilitated judicial independence.

---

* LLB(Hons) Ph.D.; Honorary Life President of Commonwealth Lawyers Association; Former President Bar Council of Malaysia; Adjunct Professor of Law, HELP University College, Malaysia.

[1] Tun Mohd Suffian, quoted by Lord Ackner in "The Erosion of Judicial Independence" (1996) 146 NLJ 1789 at 1791.

[2] These were Constitutions based on the Westminster model drafted by the Colonial Office at Whitehall: see William Dale, "The Making and Remaking of Commonwealth Constitutions" (1993) 42 ICLQ 67. They were in appropriate cases suitably indigenized to cater for local requirements and underwent a domestic approval process to ensure acceptance by the local populace.

A discussion of judicial independence and constitutionalism in various countries may take the conceptual approach or the illustrative approach. When Justice Ruth Bader Ginsburg of the United States Supreme Court was asked to speak on judicial independence[3], she stated that examples work more forcibly on the mind than precepts. It is a good technique to adopt. Judicial independence has become conceptually overladen with ideas moving as it were from a national law level to the international law level and back in a cycle called 'a normative cycle'[4].

The actual instances of the threats to judicial independence, in the political evolvement of the new democracies, provide the best illustration of the ever present tension in these countries between constitutionalism and judicial independence.

II. Direct Interference by the Removal or Harassment of Judges

In many instances, as seen below, the compelling event that led to the executive proceeding against the judiciary was some important case in court that the executive could not afford to lose or where too much was at stake with the outcome of the case.

The judicial crisis of 1988 in Malaysia that saw the dismissal of the Chief Justice (called the Lord President) and two Supreme Court judges was directly related to some decided cases against the government of the day and a pending case involving the election of the then Prime Minister, Dr. Mahathir. It was obvious that in the months leading to the events of mid-1988, Dr. Mahathir was unhappy with the judiciary over certain decisions that had gone against his government[5]. He persistently attacked the judges saying of their interpretative function '... we know exactly what we want to do, but once we do it, it is interpreted in a different way'[6], and of the independence of judges, he said: 'by

---

[3] See Ruth Bader Ginsburgh "Judicial Independence" (1998) 72 ALJ 611.

[4] See Shimon Shetreet, "The Normative Cycle in Shaping Judicial Independence in International Law: The Mutual Impact of National and International Jurisprudence And the Contemporary Practical and Conceptual Challenges" (2009) 10(1). Chicago Journal of International Law 275 et seq.

[5] "Report of the Panel of Eminent Persons To Review the 1988 Judicial Crisis in Malaysia", 20 July 1988, commissioned by the Malaysian Bar, LAWASIA, International Bar Association, Transparency International Malaysia. The Eminent Persons Group comprised of Mr. Justice J.S. Verma (former Chief Justice of India); Mr. Justice Fakhruddin G. Ebrahim (former Judge of the Supreme Court of Pakistan); Dr. Asma Jahangir, UN Special Rapporteur; Tan Sri Abdul Aziz Abdul Rahman, Senior Advocate, Malaysia; Dr. Gordon Hughes, Former President LAWASIA; Dato' WSW Davidson, Senior Advocate Malaysia. Report available on Malaysian Bar website www.malaysianbar.org.my

[6] Ibid p. 8.

possessing qualities termed as 'fiercely independent' these members (the judges) are indirectly involved with opposition politics. And to display that their independence is really 'fierce' they often bend over backwards to award decisions in favour of those challenging the Government'.[7]

These speeches reflected an obvious misunderstanding of the judiciary's role[8], but importantly the Prime Minister was confirmed in his belief that the judiciary was biased against him and his Government. This had direct relevance to a critical case then before the Supreme Court to be presided over by the Lord President, Tun Salleh Abas. It was an appeal over the challenge to the Prime Minister's election as leader of his party by a wafer-thin majority of 43 votes. The trigger event was the scheduling on 23 May by Tun Salleh of the date of the hearing of the appeal in the Supreme Court. As the Eminent Persons Report observed, with this 'Dr. Mahathir's future hung on the balance'[9]. On 27 May Tun Salleh was suspended. He was subsequently charged with a number of charges on a 'throw-all' basis[10], but in substance, the principal charge was of demonstrable bias against the government. On the day of his suspension, his successor, Tun Hamid Omar, as the Acting Lord President cancelled the notice of hearing. The Report observed of this act, '(Tun Hamid Omar) lost no time in taking this step. This fact further confirms the logical inference of malafide'[11].

The tribunal established to try Tun Salleh was chaired by the very person who was the most likely beneficiary of his removal, namely, the Acting Lord President Tun Hamid Omar.[12] The deficiencies in the composition of the tribunal, the unsubstantiated charges and the proceedings itself has been the subject of much legal literature[13]. As one Queen's Counsel reviewing the case observed

[7] Ibid pp. 14–15.

[8] In another speech, the Prime Minister had likened the judiciary to a branch of the government service like the civil service: Ibid p. 12.

[9] Ibid p. 17–18.

[10] As Tun Salleh himself observed 'had my car been parked along a yellow line that would have been thrown in too': see Tun Salleh Abas, "The Role of an Independent Judiciary" (John Foster Galloway Memorial Lecture, Percetakan A-Z Sdn. Bhd. Kuala Lumpur, 1989) pp. 18–19.

[11] Ibid p. 19–20.

[12] Of Tun Hamid chairing the Tribunal, the Eminent Persons Report concluded that this fact alone vitiated the Report of the Tribunal: see Ibid.

[13] Among others, see H.P. Lee, Constitutional Conflicts in Contemporary Malaysia (OUP, KL, 1995) at pp. 53–73; FA Trinidade, "The Removal of Malaysian Judges" (1990) 106 LQR 51; Dr. Visu Sinnadurai, "The 1988 Judiciary Crisis and its Aftermath" in Harding & Lee (Eds) Constitutional Landmarks in Malaysia: The First Fifty Years (1957–2007) (Lexis-Nexis, KL, 2008) at pp. 173 et seq. For a personal account by the Chief Justice himself, see May Day for Justice (Magnus Books, KL 1989).

of the tribunal's report that it was 'among the most despicable documents in legal history'[14].

The second tribunal report leading to the removal of the two supreme court judges, who had sat with other of their brethren, to issue the stop-order on the first tribunal's report, is equally the subject of scathing criticism[15].

It is not necessary for our present purposes to traverse the grounds of the biting criticism that has been made of the two tribunal reports and the injustice done to the removed judges other than to state that twenty years later the Government of the day that succeeded the Government of Prime Minister Mahathir acknowledged the injustice to the concerned judges and monetarily compensated them[16].

The underlying message of this sorry episode in Malaysia was the visible absence of a culture of constitutionalism in the body politic. It enabled an overbearing executive and its prime minister to lean on the judiciary with nary a contrarian voice from the other judges or from any significant political quarter, save for the Bar. It remains a very regretful event in the political and legal history of the country.

Pakistan is another Commonwealth country that has seen direct interference by the executive into the affairs of the judiciary by the removal and harassment of judges. It has had an unfortunate history of periodic military governments. The usual practice of the Chief Martial Law Administrator on assuming control was to revoke the appointment of the judges and re-engage them by invitation only or require all to swear new oaths of allegiance to the military government. For example, General Musharraf on declaring a military emergency in November 2007 suspended the Constitution and promulgated the Oath of Office (Judges) Order 2007 by which all persons holding office as judges of the Supreme Court, the Federal Shariat Court and the High Court were to cease to hold office with immediate effect unless invited to continue in office on taking a new oath prescribed under the said Order. It was observed that 'the obvious reason was for the military ruler to take control of the justice delivery system and demolish the independence of the judiciary'[17].

The absence of a culture of constitutionalism has been a pervasive feature of Pakistan's constitutional history. In substance there was little difference

[14] Geoffrey Robertson QC quoted in Dr. Visu Sinnadurai, op. cit, p. 180.

[15] See H.P. Lee, Trinidade and Visu Sinnadurai, op. cit.

[16] See New Straits Times, November 7, 2008.

[17] See Justice Rasheed A Razvi, "Future of Judicial Activism in Pakistan", (LAWASIA Conference Paper, Lawasia 21st Conference 2008, 29 October 2008, Kuala Lumpur) at p. 4. Conference Paper on file with writer. The Musharraf emergency was declared unconstitutional by the Pakistan Supreme Court on 31 July 2009, and the appointment of the new judges declared invalid: see Malaysian New Sunday Times 2 August 2009 at p. 38.

between the military and civilian administrations in their attitude towards the judiciary. A former Chief Justice of the Pakistan Supreme Court, Justice Sajjad Ali Shah, observed of his personal experience with the civilian governments of Prime Ministers Benazir Bhutto and Nawaz Sharif: 'Both Benazir and Nawaz as prime minister's wanted absolute power by subjugating the judiciary as they always felt insecure'[18].

Invariably the tension between the judiciary and the executive government arose over some critical case that constituted a threat to the government of the prime minister or his/her continuance in office. Chief Justice Sajjad recounts a story of harassment, and of his eventual removal from office, over certain cases in which the civilian government was deeply involved[19].

A controversy had arisen between the Chief Justice and Prime Minister Benazir Bhutto over the latter's political appointments to the judiciary[20]. A writ petition was then filed by a public body called the Al-Jehad Trust challenging the appointment process of the superior court judges (popularly called 'the Judges' case)[21]. It was evident that the Prime Minister did not want the case heard at that time as being politically inopportune and spoke to the Chief Justice to adjourn the case[22]. However the Chief Justice refused to oblige and the hearings proceeded as scheduled in early 1996.

The Chief Justice was categorical in his belief that as a result of his decision to proceed with the case, he was subjected to harassment by the government. He says this: 'It appears that when the Supreme Court declined to adjourn the case, the federal government, and particularly the prime minister, were very annoyed. Subsequent events will show that deliberate revenge was taken … to intimidate the chief justice and teach him a lesson for not falling in line with the wishes of the prime minister'[23]. According to the Chief Justice, shortly thereafter his son-in-law's house and office was raided by the police for alleged corruption as a civil servant. The Chief Justice was convinced that the raid was ordered by Prime Minister Bhutto who was 'reportedly very angry' that the case was allowed to proceed[24].

In the same month a writ petition was filed by a lawyer questioning the validity of the Chief Justice's appointment as it was said that his appointment was made out of turn by superseding some senior judges. The case itself was

[18] Chief Justice (Rtd) Sajjad Ali Shah, Law Courts In a Glass House (OUP, Karachi, 2001) at p. 526.
[19] Ibid Ch. 8.
[20] Ibid p. 228.
[21] *Al-Jehad Trust v. President of Pakistan* PLD 1996 SC 324.
[22] Sajjad Shah, op. cit. p. 240, p. 277.
[23] Ibid p. 241.
[24] Ibid. p. 242.

heard when Prime Minister Nawaz Sharif had taken office in the elections held after the Presidential dismissal of the Bhutto government. As events went the petition against the Chief Justice succeeded[25]. It was said that Prime Minister Sharif was himself unhappy with the Chief Justice because a contempt case against him had been allowed to continue[26]. It confirmed an endemic problem in Pakistan's judicial history of the everpresent tension between the executive and the judiciary caused by critical cases before the courts.

The experiences of Chief Justice Sajjad[27] at the hands of a popularly elected government reflects an appalling lack of respect for the institution of the judiciary and a lack of understanding of its proper role in a democratic set-up.

But the travails of Pakistan's judiciary has always been worst under the military. In October 1999 Prime Minister Shariff was deposed by General Musharraf. It was not long before the General found Chief Justice Iftikhar Chaudhury too activist for his liking especially the practice of entertaining public interest litigation complaints against the military government. The crunch came when a writ petition was filed challenging General Musharraf's election as President on the ground that a man in uniform could not constitutionally contest the elections for the Presidency.

The military emergency and the promulgation of the Judges Oath Order as stated was a direct consequence of this 'inconvenient' case. One of the objectives of the Order was to be rid of 'troublesome' judges including Chief Justice Chaudhury who were seen to be a hindrance to the executive programmes launched by the military government. It is a redeeming feature of Pakistan's civic society that, as events went, a lawyer-sponsored protest led to the restoration to office of the Chief Justice, the holding of popular elections and the eventual downfall of General Musharraf.

Pakistan's military experience has also been the experience of many of the new nations of Africa. The independence of the judiciary and its freedom from

---

[25] Sajjad Ali Shah's appointment was eventually declared unconstitutional. In the words of the official order his appointment was 'de-notified' and he was reverted as a supreme court justice: Ibid pp. 784–790. See judgment reported as *Asad Ali v. Federation of Pakistan* PLD 1998 SC 161. For a critical account of Chief Justice Sajjad's own conduct in delaying the adjudication on the legality of his appointment, see Justice Ajmal Mian, A Judge Speaks Out (OUP, Karachi, 2004) at p. 250. Justice Ajmal Mian became Acting Chief Justice after the interim suspension of Chief Justice Sajjad's appointment pending the hearing of the writ petition. Ch. 12 of the book under "Judicial Crises" displays a divided Pakistan judiciary in the face of critical cases before the courts and the political machinations behind them. It brings to mind the salutary advice of Justice Bhagwati, the former Chief Justice of India, of the importance of the collegium of judges acting in unity: "If the judges are united no executive on earth can bring them down": see PN Bhagwati, "Independence of the Judiciary in a Democracy", Human Rights Solidarity AHRC Newsletter Vol. 7 No. 2 (1997).

[26] Sajjad Ali Shah, op. cit. 478.

[27] Ibid 478.

executive interference has not been universally accepted as an inviolable principle in the military-led countries or the democracies of Africa. In 1977, Professor B.O. Nwabueze, one of Africa's noted constitutional scholars, described it delicately when he said: 'The African politician, uninhibited by the influence of tradition on which respect for the independence of the judiciary is based in Britain, is exposed to far greater temptation to interfere with the judiciary, with judges ... having to decide red-hot political questions ...'[28]. In spite of the strides made in many African countries in strengthening judicial institutions, the culture of constitutionalism is not strongly rooted in the continent[29]. As recently as in April 2009, the President of Gambia found it appropriate to warn his country's judiciary that 'the state will be involved in the operation of the judiciary and the state will interfere in the delivery of justice if it is believed that the courts decisions are against the states' interests'[30].

III. The Politics of Judicial Promotions

Sometime ago Lord Scarman observed with charmed innocence that 'a judge does not come to the bench looking for further promotion, judicial office is itself the apex of a legal career'[31]. In many countries, the opposite is true, with judges pitted against each other, albeit with civilized politeness, for the prize of a coveted promotion, and the executive using the power of promoting judges as a leverage against individual judges or the judiciary itself.

Promotions, especially within the higher judiciary, when left entirely in the hands of the executive is bound to become the subject of abuse and resultantly corrosive of judicial independence. India's experience illustrates that on more than one occasion the government of the day superseded a deserving candidate

---

[28] B.O. Nwabueze, Judicialism in Commonwealth Africa (C. Hurst & Co., London, 1977) at pp. 266–67.

[29] See generally the "Latimer House Guidelines on Relations between the Executive, Legislature and the Judiciary" sponsored inter alia by the Commonwealth Lawyers Association and the Commonwealth Parliamentary Association. The Edinburgh Plan of Action for the Commonwealth of 2008 to implement the Latimer House proposals focuses in particular on Africa. Both documents are available on the website of the Commonwealth Lawyers Association at www.commonwealthlawyers.com

[30] "CMJA News" (Newsletter of the Commonwealth Magistrates and Judges Association) Vol. 25, April 2009 at p. 1.

[31] Quoted in Shimon Shetreet, Judges on Trial (North-Holland Publishing Co., Netherlands, 1976) at p. 78. That Lord Scarman's view is not universally held even within the English judiciary is seen in Lord Justice Kerr's disappointment in failing to be appointed to the House of Lords, equaled only by his failure to obtain the captaincy of his College football team: see Michael Kerr, As Far As I Remember (Oxford & Portland, Oregon, 2006) at pp. 320 et. seq.

who was next in line for appointment as Chief Justice because of displeasure at his rulings in key constitutional cases.

The first was in 1973 when a full bench of the Indian Supreme Court was hearing an important constitutional case involving the amending power of parliament[32]. Chief Justice Sikri was due for retirement the day after delivery of decision. The decision went against the Government of the then Prime Minister, Mrs. Indira Gandhi. The senior most judges, Justices Hegde, Shelat and Grover were joined with the Chief Justice in ruling against the government. One of the junior judges, a Justice Ray, was a dissentient. The case was the third in a trilogy of constitutional cases that had gone against the government.[33] As events went Justice Ray was appointed Chief Justice in supersession over the three judges senior to him.

There was widespread protest from the Bar and civic society over the supersession. Apparently there was hitherto an unbroken convention where the senior most judge of the Supreme Court became the Chief Justice. The Government of Mrs. Gandhi was hard-placed to defend the promotion. It spoke opaquely of the need for a 'committed judiciary', of 'forward-looking judges' and a chief justice 'who represents the philosophy of the government'.[34] The stinging riposte from India's first Attorney General was that it was expected that a chief justice would represent the philosophy of the Constitution and not that of the ruling party.[35] Of the need for forward-looking and not backward-looking judges, the rebuke came from a former Chief Justice who said it will then produce 'looking-forward judges.'[36]

But it was to happen again, with another example of Mrs. Gandhi being unhappy with a constitutional decision of the Supreme Court. It happened shortly after Mrs. Gandhi in June 1975 had declared a phoney emergency throughout India resulting from the loss of her election petition case in the Allahabad High Court, and the nationwide agitation that followed that she demit office. Along with the proclamation of emergency, the right to habeas corpus was suspended by a presidential decree at her bidding.

Many of the High Courts of India declined to recognise the suspension of habeas corpus on the ground it was inimical to the constitutional guarantee

---

[32] *Kesavanandha Bharti v. State of Kerala* AIR 1973 SC 1416.

[33] The other cases were the Bank Nationalisation case (*RC Cooper v. Union of India* AIR 1970 SC 564) and the Privy Purses case (*Mahadava Rao Scindia v. Union of India* AIR 1971 SC 530); see P. Jaganmohan Reddy, The Judiciary I Served (Orient Longman Ltd., Hyderabad, India) at p. 226.

[34] See generally, N.A. Palkhivala (Ed) A Judiciary Made to Measure (M.R. Pai (Pub.) Bombay, June 1973) at pp. 8 et seq.

[35] M.C. Setalvad. Ibid. p. 8.

[36] M. Hidayatullah in Reddy, op. cit. p. 247.

of a right to life and liberty under Article 21 of the Indian Constitution. The question finally came before the Supreme Court for a definitive ruling. The magnitude of the issue at stake was reflected in the exchange between Justice HR Khanna and the Attorney General at the hearing. To the question 'would there be any remedy if a police officer because of his personal enemity killed another man?', came the appalling reply 'there would be no judicial remedy in such a case so long as the emergency lasts … it may shock your conscience, it shocks mine but … no proceedings can be taken in a court of law on that score'.[37]

The Indian Supreme Court in a regretfully pusillanimous decision upheld the suspension of habeas corpus.[38] The sole dissentient was Justice Khanna. He was next in seniority for the post of Chief Justice, India, with the incumbent due for retirement shortly after the decision. Justice Khanna wrote that it was obvious that he would be by-passed because he 'had become in the eyes of the government persona non grata'; invitations to official functions had stopped and at public functions 'my acquaintances would try to avoid me'.[39] In December of that year, Justice Khanna was by-passed and the judge next after him was appointed Chief Justice. Justice Khanna resigned the same day.

These instances reflect the extreme unsatisfactoriness of leaving promotions of the senior judiciary entirely in the hands of the executive. It should be seen that the power in the executive to confer a benefit or reward by way of promotion of judges is wholly inimical to judicial independence. For example, in Malaysia, the junior High Court judges who sat on the second tribunal leading to the dismissal of two of their seniors during the Judicial Crisis of 1988, all saw preferment and attainment of high judicial office later in their careers. It sent a wrong message down the line to all the judges.

IV. Inappropriate Consulations With Judges

The public perception that judges are part of the power structure of society is something that both the executive and the judiciary should be alert to always. In critical cases where governmental decisions are under challenge before the

[37] H.R. Khanna, Neither Roses Nor Thorns (Eastern Book Company, Lucknow, 2003 Rpt) at p. 78.

[38] *ADM Jabalpur v. Shivkant Shukla* AIR 1976 SC 1207. The decision has been subjected to immense criticism as a failing of the Indian Supreme Court at a critical time in the nation's life. See H.M. Seervai, The Emergency, Future Safeguards and the Habeas Corpus Case (Tripathy, Bombay, 1978); T.R. Andhyarujina, "Judicial Backbone During Times of Emergency & Terrorism" (2009) 18(3) The Commonwealth Lawyer 20 et seq.

[39] Khanna, Ibid, at pp. 81–82.

courts, it is a perception that debilitates public confidence in the judiciary. As Lord Devlin once observed famously, a judge who makes the right decision but not appearing to do so may be thrice blessed in heaven but is of no use on earth.[40]

A practice of consultation of the higher judiciary by the executive on constitutional affairs is something that should be discouraged. It happened in Fiji in 2000 leading to a deep divide within the judiciary which persists to today. Sir Thomas Eichelbaum, the retired Chief Justice of New Zealand, who sat on the Fiji Court of Appeal, wrote that after the George Speight civilian coup in 2000, some members of the judiciary were believed to have assisted the new regime with the drafting of laws.[41] The International Bar Association Report on Fiji[42] records of this event that three senior judges 'assisted the military by providing the President with legal advice during the hostage crisis' after the coup. The then Chief Justice was also involved in the drafting of a decree for the military regime relating to the administration of justice. Quite appropriately when one of them later sat on a case dealing with issues relating to the 2000 coup, he was faced with a motion for his recusal.[43]

Chief Justice Eichelbaum writes that the actions of the judges concerned led to a fall-out within the judiciary which was far reaching. The judiciary became divided, between the constitutionalists (i.e. those who eschewed all political involvement) and the others, and that 'the difference continue down to the present time.' In his view the lesson from Fiji is 'the judiciary must never be seen to be taking part in matters that are properly within the realm of politics; even the appearance of straying into forbidden territory is enough to be damaging of judicial independence.'[44]

Australia provides a famous example of questionable consultations at the highest level between the Governor General and the Chief Justice during a constitutional crisis. This arose during the budget crisis in November 1975 leading to the sacking of Prime Minister Whitlam and his government by the Governor General. The Governor General Sir John Kerr had at that time evidently sought and obtained the written advice of the serving Chief Justice Sir Garfield Barwick, as to his proposed course of action, before dismissing the Whitlam Government. The Chief Justice had advised categorically 'If being

[40] Patrick Devlin, The Judge (OUP, 1981) at p. 3.

[41] Sir Thomas Eichelbaum, Interference with Judicial Independence in the Pacific at http.//www.pacliii.org/PJDP/resources/PJC/Interference.

[42] "Dire Straits: A Report on the Rule of Law in Fiji" at pp. 39–40. See http://www.Chanet.org/Human_Rights_Institute/Work-by-regions/Asia-Pacific/Fiji.aspc

[43] *Citizens Constitutional Forum v. The President* (2001) FJHC 28.

[44] Eichelbaum, op. cit.

unable to secure supply, he (Whitlam) refuses to take either course, your Excellency has constitutional authority to withdraw his commission'.[45] Chief Justice Barwick was severely criticized within and without the profession for the propriety of his rendering this advice while still a serving chief justice.[46] The sacking could have been the subject of legal suit and the role of the Chief Justice in tendering advice for his removal would have been acutely embarrassing to the Australian judiciary in that eventuality.

The Eichelbaum observation that any 'straying into the forbidden territory' of politics would damage the judiciary holds true under all circumstances.

V. Inappropriate Propositions or Suggestions to Judges

The danger of judges being compromised in social settings is ever present. Judges and politicians-in-office tend to meet in official functions ever so regularly. An inappropriate suggestion or a hint on a pending case to a judge in that setting is not unknown to a venal politician or one who is oblivious to the niceties of judicial independence.

Justice Reddy of the Indian Supreme Court spoke of a weekend visit to his home by a cabinet minister and his wife during the hearing of the Fundamental Rights case[47] then before the Supreme Court. Ostensibly a social call, it was obviously with the keen knowledge that Justice Reddy could provide the swing vote to a government victory in the court or that without him the government side would be a minority. The hint was more in the nature of good things to come to Justice Reddy if he did the right thing. He was told that 'if he didn't agree he will be losing a great opportunity for a higher post'.[48]

Such blandishments or inappropriate gestures are by no means the preserve of a third world experience. A shocking example comes from the United States. Chief Justice Earl Warren wrote that shortly after the great school desegregation case[49] was heard by the Supreme Court, and reserved for decision, he and his wife received an unexpected invitation to the White House from President Eisenhower for dinner. Present amongst the invitees was the eminent counsel Mr. John W. Davis who had just argued for the States against desegregation. The counsel for the petitioners Mr. Thurgood Marshall (later Justice) was obviously not invited. During dinner the President went to considerable lengths to

---

45 Sir John Kerr, Matters for Judgment (Macmillan, Australia, 1978) at pp. 342–43.
46 David Marr, Barwick (Allen and Unwin, Sydney, 1980) at pp. 284–85.
47 *Kesavananda Bharti v. State of Kerala* AIR 1976 SC 1416.
48 Reddy, op. cit., p. 248.
49 *Brown v. Board of Education* 349 U.S. 294 (1955).

tell the Chief Justice what a great man Mr. Davis was. After dinner at coffee he took the Chief Justice by the arm, and speaking of the southern states in the segregation case said 'these are not bad people, all they are concerned about is to see that their sweet little girls are not required to sit in schools alongside some big overgrown negroes'. After the decision, which was adverse to the government, the relations between the President and the Chief Justice became distinctly cool not going beyond official and polite greetings when they met.[50]

These are illustrations where the admirable judges mentioned did not fall for the blandishments and sweeteners offered to them. The incidents are known only because they had been written about. In the case of Chief Justice Warren it was obviously something that must have shocked him deeply for him to write about the incident some twenty two years after the event. But many such incidents would not be mentioned at all and the crooked judge who succumbed to the sweetener and enjoyed the reward would not be known at all except possibly to a Bar which has a keen and uncanny eye to detect such things.

In the ultimate the judiciary must be its own guardian. In a speech in April 2009 in Hong Kong, the Lord Chief Justice of England Sir Igor Judge warned 'it is the first steps which have to be watched. The first incursion by the executive into impropriety. The first compromise by the judiciary with principle'.[51] He made this observation when narrating the incident relating to a prominent court case in Brussels where the Minister of Justice was forced to resign when the Prime Minister admitted publicly that one of the Minister's officials had contacted the husband of a judge of the Court of Appeal on several occasions during the course of a controversial litigation. As the Chief Justice observed 'if the judge listened to any of these blandishments without reporting it, she had, in my view, failed in her responsibilities'.[52]

VI. Circulars and Directives to Judges

A sharp line has to be drawn between directives to judges on matters relating to the administration of the courts and those that suggest, usually for the sake of uniformity or efficiency, how particular type of legal matters ought

[50] The Memoirs of Chief Justice Earl Warren (Doubleday, New York, 1977) at pp. 291–92. Eisenhower was reported to have said elsewhere that the Warren appointment was one of the mistakes of his Presidency: see Lawrence Tribe, God Save This Honourable Court (Mentor Book, New York, 1985) at p. 61.

[51] The Rt Hon The Lord Judge, "Judicial Independence and Responsibilities". Speech delivered at the 16th Commonwealth Law Conference Hong Kong 9 April 2009. Conference website copy of speech on file with writer.

[52] Ibid.

to be handled. The former is generally acceptable but the latter is suspect especially if it is in any way a fetter on the freedom of decision-making by the judges. It should not matter that the directive is officially called a Practice Note or Practice Direction from a chief justice.

It brings to mind the incident in December 1992 when the former Lord Chancellor of Britain, Lord Mackay wrote to Mr. Justice Wood, the then President of the Employment Appeal Tribunal (EAT) stating that the current practice of conducting oral preliminary hearings in the EAT to determine appealability was contrary to the EAT Rules (Rule 3) that seem to suggest that non-appealability should be handled administratively by notice to the intended appellant. The Lord Chancellor was legitimately concerned about things like delay and backlog of cases. The Lord Chancellor sought an assurance from Justice Wood that Rule 3 'would be applied in full' and added the words: 'if you do not feel you can give me that assurance I must ask you to consider your position'.

Mr. Justice Wood replied appropriately 'I cannot regard compliance with your demand as conducive to justice'. As events went Justice Wood retired shortly thereafter, two years ahead of time, provoking considerable debate in legal circles and the media whether the Lord Chancellor's letter had prompted his premature retirement.

The incident was also the subject of a debate in the legislative branch of the House of Lords where the Lord Chancellor was obliged to defend his letter and clarify that it was never his intention to pressure Justice Woods or to interfere with his judicial independence and that by hindsight he would have used 'better language'[53].

An initial viewpoint from the Lord Chancellor's Department that judicial independence is limited to the actual trial of cases, met with the rebuff from Lord Oliver during the debate and if it was so limited then the directive from the German Ministry of Justice under the Reich Government that judges should not decide cases in favour of Jews or against party members would be good.[54]

Generally it would be legitimate for judges, true to their oath, to reject circulars and directives that curtail independent decision-making. Of course, any suggestion of how judgments should be crafted must also be rejected, including, one would suppose, literary references in them. Lord Atkin was within his rights in refusing the suggestion of Lord Simon, Lord Chancellor, that he

[53] See generally, "Lord Mackay and the Judiciary" (1994) 144 NLJ 527; Dawn Oliver, "The Lord Chancellor's Department and the Judges" 1994 PL 157.

[54] Dawn Oliver, Ibid p. 169.

should drop the literary reference to Lewis Caroll's 'Through the Looking Glass' in his celebrated dissent in *Liversidge v. Andersen*[55] as it may be wounding of his colleagues. Lord Atkin stood his ground reiterating his respect for his colleagues but stating that his sole intention was to 'hit as hard as he could' on questions of liberty.[56] There was of course never any hint from the Lord Chancellor that Lord Atkin should do anything more about his judgment but an important principle was established in this private correspondence between the two eminent judges of the complete independence of the judge in decision-making right down to how he words his judgment.

VII. Concluding Remarks

The areas mentioned in this paper are by no means exhaustive of the possible pitfalls to judicial independence that may exist. There are other critical areas like the punitive transfer of judges or post-retirement offers of plum government appointments to judges, and the like, all of which are errosive of judicial independence. The rule of law is sine que non to constitutionalism and judicial independence. Mr. Justice Khanna of the Indian Supreme Court, who was by-passed for appointment as Chief Justice because of his sturdy independence, spoke at his farewell of the importance of the rule of law to judicial independence, saying: 'there are three prime requisites for the rule of law, they are a strong Bar, an independent judiciary and enlightened public opinion.'[57] None could quarrel with this observation.

[55] (1942) AC 206 at 245.
[56] See Geoffrey Lewis, Lord Atkin (Butterworths, London, 1983) at p. 139.
[57] Khanna, op. cit. p. 86.

CHAPTER NINE

CORRUPTION AND JUDICIAL INDEPENDENCE

*Hiram E. Chodosh**

I. Introduction

Judicial independence research and reform tend to focus on the relationship between the judiciary and the political branches of government. Terms of employment, budgets, and management raise important questions in conceptions of (and commitments to) the principles judicial independence. However, *political* control is not the only source of interference with judicial independence and impartiality.

Economic interference (corruption) poses a parallel threat to judicial independence. Corruption, however, is less frequently the focus of judicial reforms. Sadly, both political and economic interference with impartial judicial decision-making are disturbingly common in many systems. Further, the combination of these two problems poses a formidable challenge because the solutions for one set of problems may undermine solutions for the other. Judicial independence reforms that protect judges from external interference may simultaneously protect judges from strong integrity and accountability controls, which in turn can create opportunities for political interference with judicial impartiality. Accordingly, the question of how to advance judicial independence in a court system that is vulnerable to corruption poses two challenges: first, how to understand the nature of corruption, and second how to work through the formidable dilemma of simultaneously attacking corruption and promoting independence. This chapter explores this dual challenge.

In the following Section II, Part 1 observes the growing awareness of corruption and its negative impacts. Part 2 observes the varied impacts of

* The primary research for this essay was initially funded by the UNDP in Asia and aided by *Global Research through Justice,* a think tank on global justice issues at the University of Utah S.J. Quinney College of Law. The excellent students who worked on the research include: Peter Gessel, Peter Lattin, Virginia Tomova, Brooke Wilkinson, Gabriel White, Richard Roberts, Alexander Pearson, Matthew Kober, Tasha Williams, Mark LaRocco, Justin Atkinson, Jay Porter, Clark Whisenant, and Aurelio David Borgia. The more heavily documented draft of this research and comprehensive, annotated bibliography of sources are available from the author.

corruption. Part 3 explores competing conceptions and definitions of corruption and how the choices can affect the policy and resource focus of anti-corruption interventions. Part 4 explains briefly why corruption and its impacts are difficult to measure. Part 5 identifies the insights and limits of competing theories of the major factors that contribute to corruption. In Section III, Part 1 briefly describes impediments to reform, including the inability to deal with reform tradeoffs or dilemmas. Part 2 then presents alternative conceptual and practical approaches to navigating the dilemmas in anti-corruption and judicial independence reforms. These include breaking down ostensible polarities, recognizing relative benefits and harms and creating conditions for non-threatening communication and engagement. In sum, the purpose of this essay is to advance collective thinking about judicial independence into the realm of anti-corruption, to recognise the tension between political protections and economic controls, and to sketch some modest ways through the hard choices for reformers concerned about both political and economic threats to judicial independence and impartiality.

II. Corruption

1. *Growing Awareness*

Corruption is increasingly seen as a universal problem, deeply embedded in many national legal systems, and also transnational in nature. It is so endemic that it has generated its own special vernacular, such as Code 1,000 in Honduras (a reference to the 1,000 *lempira* note), *mordida* in Mexico, *arreglo* in Phillipines, *baksheesh* in Egypt, *dash* in Kenya, or *pot de vin* in France.

The institutional response to corruption is now nearly as pervasive as the linguistic usage around the world. NGOs like Transparency International, founded in 1993, have increasingly drawn attention to the problem. Development banks (such as the World Bank and Regional Development Banks), aid agencies (USAID), and other international institutions (the International Monetary Fund and the United Nations and its affiliated groups and units) for many years have conditioned aid to developing countries on their commitment to anti-corruption reforms. These national and international governmental and non-governmental organizations simultaneously provide technical assistance to those countries in search of help.

National, transnational, regional, and international law prohibits corruption and requires that countries take affirmative steps to prevent and prosecute it. Chapter II, Article 5, Paragraph 3 of the United Nations Convention against Corruption provides that "Each State Party shall endeavor to establish and promote effective practices aimed at the prevention of corruption."[1] Many national governments have enacted new domestic laws that increasingly reach extraterritorial conduct, (e.g., the Anti-Corrupt Practices Act) and multilateral treaties (e.g., OECD) that seek to restrain actors from arbitraging more permissive national laws and enforcement capacities in weaker regimes within the global economy. This flood of national, transnational, and international legislative activity is world-wide in its ambition for a comprehensive approach to combat corrupt practices in various branches and agencies of government, including customs, tax, and other regulatory and licensing authorities. Multinationals complain that these measures make them less competitive in highly corrupt economies. Overall, the positive effects, however, of these anti-corruption interventions are difficult to observe.

Corruption is perceived as a major impediment to economic development. Although some opinion leaders have minimised the impact of corruption and perceive higher levels of corruption as merely a consequence of an alternative path to development, international norms through the OECD Bribery Convention have penetrated the domestic norms of many countries. Beyond general perceptions, a closer look at national experiences raises doubt about whether generalised perceptions of a particular region, e.g., Asia, as a geographic, cultural, or historical unit of comparison is at all intelligible. For example, Hong Kong and Singapore are commonly viewed as free from the notorious corruption of Bangladesh, Indonesia, or China.

2. *Impacts*

Increasingly, varied constituencies recognise the serious consequences of corruption on class, poverty, commerce, economic development, democracy, equality, health care, education, the environment, other public services, women, indigenous peoples, and cultural identity. Development organizations find that shockingly large portions of loans or grants never reach their intended beneficiaries. Economists have observed (when compared to high taxation) greater impacts of corruption on growth. Investors do not have confidence in corrupt legal systems. Corruption also deteriorates trust in ostensibly democratic institutions. It advantages the powerful over the weak, and creates resentment between the "haves" and "have nots." Gaining access to health care or good schools is frequently conditioned on making additional payments. If polluters can buy their way out of environmental controls, the ecology of clean air and water deteriorates. Anti-drug enforcement, as another prominent

[1] Chapter II, Art. 5, Para. 3, UN Convention against Corruption.

example, is riddled with corruption. The requirement of an illicit payment to facilitate the provision by an official of birth or death certificates increases the cost and blocks access to basic services. Finally, corrupt practices are falsely and harmfully internalised as a cultural attribute of the country in which they have flourished. Officials who practice corruption are themselves literally and figuratively *demoralised.*

Beyond these more general effects, corruption undermines the very institutions (including the judicial and legal system which is) responsible for enforcing anti-corruption norms. In those countries where corruption is profoundly institutionalised, litigants with meritorious claims or defenses cannot rely on the judicial process to produce a correct and effective result and thus have a higher incentive for employing extra-legal means to win cases. Instead of hiring a better lawyer to obtain a meritorious result, litigants have a strong incentive to retain a less ethical one merely as an intermediary for illicit payments to judges. The ease with which the law is undermined significantly weakens the incentives for compliance. Low compliance with the law in turn imposes an additional burden on the judicial system to resolve greater numbers of conflicts arising from violations of public and private rights and obligations. This produces a vicious cycle of low compliance, more disputes, corrupt practices, and inconsistent, if not illegal, outcomes, which in turn reduces further the incentives to comply with the law. The seemingly interactive nature of corruption and low levels of development raise the prospect of a vicious cycle, thus making it difficult to understand precisely how the *effects* of corruption—under or mal-development—may simultaneously contribute underlying *causes* of corruption.

Corruption is also a formidable impediment to other important avenues of judicial reform. Efforts to increase judicial independence may falter when the judiciary cannot be trusted to police itself. Reforms to reduce delay may encounter entrenched economic interests in maintaining backlogs so that officials can extract rents to push cases forward or back along the line. Greater orality of process and publicity of decisions are not in the interest of those who directly benefit from corrupt practices veiled by an opaque legal process. Measures to increase the speed and continuity of trial may threaten the interest of those served by delay and the complexities and unaccountability of discontinuity. The professions may lack the necessary incentives to improve upon existing levels of intellectual and managerial competence when they view corruption as a necessary source of income far beyond what they can earn honestly. Thus, even seemingly unrelated reform initiatives will be forced to address the nearly intractable problem of corruption.

Finally, the seemingly interactive nature of corruption and low levels of development raise the prospect of intercausality (a vicious cycle), thus frustrating understanding of how the effects of corruption (underdevelopment) may simultaneously create contributing causes of corruption.

3. *Competing Conceptions and Definitions*

Even though the vernacular for corruption is rich, awareness is increasingly acute, and the legal strategies are increasingly aggressive, accepted conceptions and definitions of corruption are far from universal. The primary reason for variance in how one grasps phenomena of corruption is easier to appreciate by noting wide array of behavioural patterns may fall under that general rubric. Concerns vary from those worried about the misuse of public office for private gain to private sector kickbacks for coercive commercial behaviour, or from the illegal appropriation of large public funds to the payment of even modest amounts of money to public officials in charge of ministerial decisions. Given the wide array of phenomena, one should not be surprised to observe definitional diversity.

Yet, three specific problems emerge from this understandable condition. First, survey data in particular can be misleading if the troublesome behaviours are not adequately defined. National comparisons can be easily skewed by the tendency to prioritise certain corrupt behaviours over others. For example, some societies distinguish between those payments made to public officials *before* and others *after* their decisions, and may not view the latter as equally problematic. Second, focusing on the nature of a single transaction can take attention away from web-like networks of corrupt behaviour. Webs of illicit transactions and payoffs often include the supervisors or superiors (who often receive a percentage of a bribe as patronage or compensation for looking the other way). When these networks reach into the very system for enforcing anti-corruption laws, reform challenges become even more insuperable. Finally, and more importantly, without a clear conception of corruption, it becomes more difficult to focus limited resources and attention on the *critically* important patterns of behaviour. Low value bribes for obtaining a birth or death certificate may be viewed differently from a large kickback in a state procurement program, and the level of priority for each should influence reform strategy. In order to gain a sufficiently accurate appreciation of the problems to be addressed, it is first necessary to determine the intricacies of the corrupt practices to be evaluated. Both conception and definition of corruption are thus critically open-ended issues to be resolved with care.

The quest for a universal definition applied to diverse roles of the state and society may also produce counterintuitive effects by ignoring the broader normative role of state and society. Whether corruption harms human development is in part a question of whether the formal public policy, rules, regulations, procedures, and processes (undermined by corruption) are really in the public interest. Arguably, in countries where there is less alignment of public authority and public interests, corruption can be seen as a necessary evil, one that advances human development against the negative effects of a repressive state. Black markets may sustain economic development in overly repressive state economies. Corruption may be the only economic solution to an economically stultifying bureaucracy. Beyond distinctions, therefore, the broader normative context can make a critical difference in the optimal approach to corruption.

4. *Methodological Problems of Measurement*

Related to problems of definition, corruption is also difficult to measure. Surveys provide information that would otherwise be difficult, if not impossible, to obtain. Such data indicates how widespread the perception of corruption in judicial process has become. However, the surveys also carry a number of methodological weaknesses. First, those interviewed have little basis for comparison to other national contexts. Second, they are increasingly aware of results of previous or other surveys and have a tendency to internalise those findings. Third, the questions they are asked are either bluntly stated (in order to make them accessible) and thus too imprecise or detailed (in order to maximise accuracy) and thus too technical. Beyond surveys, scholars have begun to develop macro-quantitative frameworks; however, these are in early stages of development for assessing the extent of different kinds of corruption.

Notwithstanding these concerns, perception itself has an impact on corruption. Persons who perceive corruption to be widespread or common are more likely to participate in corrupt practices. Adversaries in litigation, for example, will have a higher incentive to transmit a bribe if each perceives the other as likely to do the same.

Empirical studies of actual cases, which may also be conducted by survey, are hard to evaluate. They tend to focus on big cases, leaving questions about the arguably more common, if not also more significant, petty cases. Some attempt to draw inferences from the number of disciplinary actions that are reported. This is troublesome because the lack of disciplinary action may be indicative of a more serious problem, whereas a greater number of reported actions may reflect a greater commitment to eliminate corrupt practices.

For example, several years ago, a survey of 21 countries in Asia[2] revealed that out of 238 actions, approximately half of the complaints generated

[2] Judge J. Clifford Wallace, "Resolving Judicial Corruption While Preserving Judicial Independence: Comparative Perspectives" 1998, 28 California Western International Law Journal 341 (discussing the diversity of approaches used in Asian judicial systems to discipline judges).

no action. Most of the actions were for incompetence. Only a half dozen involved bribery or corruption. Additionally, two-thirds of the countries involved the Chief Justice in the process, and most of those surveyed were satisfied with current procedures. The author concluded that there is not only one way to fight corruption effectively. Alternatively, his survey may lead to a more negative conclusion, to wit, that there are many ways to fight corruption ineffectively. As Einstein once observed, it is easier to count what does not matter, more difficult to count what does. Aligning measures with qualitative norms also poses a formidable challenge. Furthermore, the absence of statistical support does not in itself prove that common views of corruption are necessarily incorrect. This gap only suggests that such conclusions yearn for empirical support, which is often lacking.

Accordingly, observers should exercise care in questioning the data and correlations of corruption and prosecutions (generating either false positives when prosecutions are many or false negatives when they are few), or correlations of corruption and human development indices (e.g., when exogenous factors may mask the deleterious impact of corruption on growth).

5. *Competing Theories: Explanatory Power and Limits*

In order to gain a solid understanding of these different patterns, it will be necessary to understand the factors that motivate, fail to deter, or allow corrupt practices to flourish with impunity. Academic experts have searched for a concise formula that can grasp these many factors. The leading authorities alternatively take a political perspective by focusing on power and checks on that power, an economic perspective focused on incentives and risks, or an ethical view of right and wrong, translated into legal or institutional prisms of analysis. These primary conceptions require critical evaluation.

a. *Political Theory: Power Corrupts*

Many observers see corruption as a problem of governance and overly centralised political distributions of power. Klitgaard's formula emphasises the exclusive power of the decision-maker, his or her discretion, and the lack of accountability for abuses of this power and discretion: $C= M + D - A$: corruption equals monopoly plus discretion minus accountability. This theory tends to focus on concentrated, unaccountable power as the primary source of corruption. The more power and unbridled discretion officials have in their formal activities, the easier it is for them to extract rents from people who need their approval, service, or assistance.

This understanding of corruption is insightful and generates a series of reform strategies to disperse power, reduce discretion, and increase accountability (through a series of transparency devices and mechanisms). Klitgaard concludes that fighting corruption must go beyond liberal economic policies, enacting better laws, reducing the number and complexity of regulations, and providing more training. He recommends strategies to reduce monopoly power, clarify the scope of discretion, and increase accountability through transparency and other measures.

Comparative studies draw a positive relationship between localization (or decentralization) and a reduction in corruption. However, the impact of decentralization (widely championed) on corruption is difficult to measure and of arguable empirical weight. Some have questioned whether decentralization in some contexts may enhance the conditions for corruption. In sum, it remains unclear whether decentralization of power is always effective in curtailing corruption. Furthermore, the theory does not explain the underlying incentives to engage in corrupt practices, nor does it explain why some officials extort money or solicit or accept bribes while others (under the same political and economic conditions) do not.

b. *Economic Theory: Incentives Control*

Economic theory may stress alternatively the macro- and micro-economic determinants of corruption. As one exemplary exposition, in partial contrast to the *political* focus on power, discretion, and accountability, Susan Rose-Ackerman locates the main determinants of corruption as the level of available benefits, the riskiness of corrupt deals, and the relative bargaining power of briber and bribee. Like much of the academic literature, this approach postulates that corruption is a "crime of calculation not passion," and thus subject to rational justification.

Rose-Ackerman's economic approach focuses on incentives, and this too is a helpful starting point for investigating the nature of corruption and charting a course for reform. In light of poor salaries, working conditions, and resources, officials in many countries have strong incentives to extort money, take bribes, or solicit gifts. The ability to corrupt the very processes responsible for disciplining judicial behaviour sharply decreases the chances of being caught, disciplined, or prosecuted, and the nature of the penalty to be assessed. The relative bargaining power of the official and the people involved (the degree of financial need, resources, competition, etc.) and the limitation of monetary or non-monetary sanctions each affect the level of corrupt practices.

Accordingly, informed by this theory, reforms would focus on improving the incentives for honest, legal behaviour and simultaneously increasing the risks of detection and punishment. Rose-Ackerman's analysis suggests strategies that attempt to lower the available benefits to be achieved from corruption by reducing the costs of alternative legal means, increase the risks of detection and penalty, and reduce the bargaining power of the bribee by dispersing it to broader constituents in the legal process, e.g., a majority in a political process, or peers within the judiciary. Gray and Kaufmann note the importance of insulating civil servants from political interference, revamping incentives that discourage corruption, liberalizing the economy, reforming regulations, developing a free press, and strengthening legal and judicial systems. Kaufman has subsequently emphasised the importance of *ex ante* over *ex poste* incentives.

The economic approach, however illuminating, does not account for every contributing factor, including profound issues of access to power, wealth, and influence, nor does it lead necessarily to effective reforms. Countering the strong incentives to engage in corruption is a formidable task. Threats of violence often determine the individual decision of whether to accept an illicit bribe. The more repressive the approach to anti-corruption (e.g., the death penalty in China), the higher the stakes, and the more likely corruption in the legal enforcement process itself will result. The economic theory does not explain why in the face of greater rewards and lesser risks, some people engage in corrupt practices while others refuse. Incentive explanations do not explain, for example, why a Supreme Court justice would turn down a $200,000 bribe (when he makes only $12,000 per year in an expensive city and the enforcement systems are weak.) Furthermore, the incentives may not apply well in dysfunctional systems. The economic theory lacks fully solid answers for these questions.

c. *Cultural and Ethical Theory: Values–Right and Wrong*

In contrast to an evaluation of power or incentives, a third approach emphasises the normative failure of society or individuals to appreciate the difference between right and wrong. Under this view, corruption is a moral, ethical breach, and the solutions emphasise a reinforcement of the ethical and legal standards of professional behaviour through legislation, codes of ethics, and professionalism training. This approach helps to explain why some might resist the temptations of power or money; however, it does not explain the particular conditions under which the internalization of these norms in behaviour is more likely to occur.

Culture may also provide a rough theory for explaining corruption. Whether a society is frustrated by the wish to achieve material wealth without the opportunity to do so without corrupt practices, whether family ties and relationships supersede other forms of determination, or whether people with less connection to the interventions of public officials, cultural aspects can be critical factors in corrupt practices. However, definitional clarity and evidentiary support remain weak.

Professional ethics training also remains largely ineffective. To the extent law schools teach professionalism, the pedagogy is mainly doctrinal (not behavioural), and the few schools who involve students in simulations of ethical conduct have not developed assessment tools capable of evaluating whether simulated responses are ethical or not (whether by virtue of the process or ethical judgment or the results). Civil service training in a few countries is worthy of study for its effectiveness; however, doubts remain about whether training alone will do much to counter other more powerful social and economic forces.

Under the rubric of culture, political institutions and other structural factors, though of less frequent interest, are also identified as determinants of corrupt practices. Democracy, religion, and other dimensions of society have been correlated with the level of corruption. Large institutional factors, however, though undoubtedly influential, neither wholly explain nor determine the extent of corruption.

d. *A Tri-Focal Synthesis*

Each of the foregoing approaches, therefore, is of great value in providing a framework through which to understand corruption and chart a course of reform. Disbursements of power, attention to incentives, and broad cultural or ethical approaches to norms that frustrate corruption are all important dimensions of the puzzle. Each alone, however, provides an incomplete answer. Observers of corruption and reformers, therefore, must appreciate the limits of each approach and seek to integrate the political delegations of power, the incentives of the actors, and the internalization of ethical norms into a more accurate behavioural theory of corrupt practices.

III. The Anti-Corruption and Judicial Independence Reform Dilemma

1. *General Impediments to Reform*

The competing definitions, uncertain empirics, and competing theories all contribute to the infirmity of reform strategies. If the definitions are too narrow or fail to take into account the misalignment of public and private interests, if the empirics are vague on the nature of the practice to be curtailed, and if the theories are each helpful but limited, then the responsive reform strategies are less likely to be effective. Forces that sustain corruption are more complex and powerful than reformers would like to believe. Even ostensibly effective reforms may be little more than a power struggle over the gains of corrupt practices. Law itself is limited in its impact, and the ambitious internationalization of corruption as a crime or a human rights offense will still require local enforcement, itself vulnerable to corruption. Reforms in one area may move corrupt practices to another. By themselves, political, economic, or ethical theories are helpful though each limited in their grasp.

In this and other areas, reform initiatives generally make two major types of mistakes. First, they tend to lack a strong empirical or theoretical understanding of the forces running contrary to shared objectives often lack a credible theory of institutional or behavioural change. Second, they often fail to advance ways of dealing with common tradeoffs and dilemmas.

First, beyond positive expressions of the aspirational norms of judicial decisionmaking, judicial independence and other reforms are often based on a poor empirical understanding of conditions on the ground. Presumptions may be either rosy in their assumptions that behaviours necessarily follow law or an alteration of macro-institutional structures or unnecessarily harsh and rash, based on nebulous notions of immutable legal culture. Severe resource limitations and the retrenchment of powerful interests in the status quo are two frequently underappreciated impediments to effective reform. Ineffective reforms also often reflect flimsy theories, based on inexplicit aims, poor design choices, and weak theories of institutional or behavioural change. What is to be achieved often requires reading between the lines, models are unwittingly taken from other systems or chosen as the mere negative of the status quo arrangements, and the internalised micro-incentives at the base of behavioural or collective change are often ignored altogether.

Second, and beyond these difficulties, moving forward involves significant tradeoffs, and reformers face a series of seemingly insuperable dilemmas. Dilemmas fall into a few distinct categories: dilemmas in the design of a reform, the method or process of reform, or the social dilemma of tradeoffs between individual and collective interests. How should we deal with these dilemmas? The following discussion outlines a series of available approaches.

2. *Strategies for Navigating Reform Dilemmas*

a. *Ignoring Competing Values*

A first, somewhat crude, and conclusory option is to ignore the dilemma as such. One may dismiss as trivial the competing values that make the preferred option less than fully satisfactory. Disciplinary systems for judges may appear to compromise their independence, especially if they are themselves subject to abuse. Public admonishment, suspension, and removal are powerful sanctions that could be abused to coerce judges to act in a partial way. Judges in systems a that have been subjected to such political interference in the past appear (at least initially) tend to view independence as an absolute value and thus dismiss the value of accountability or overvalue in this view the importance of independence.

b. *Sweetening the Deal with Side-Payments*

A second option is to improve one of the alternatives through incentives or side-payments. In other words, when faced with unsatisfactory choices, one may sweeten one of the alternatives. Let's take, for example, in an expansive country, with many undesirable, remote venues in which judicial personnel are needed. A mandatory transfer system ensures nation-wide coverage of judicial personnel. Mandatory transfers, however, may be subject to abuse of the individual judge's independence. Yet, on the other hand, the rejection of mandatory transfer may mean that some jurisdictions will lack the necessary judicial personnel to operate the justice system. One way to overcome this dilemma is to provide extra incentives (side payments) (e.g., promotions, perquisites, extra housing, and education benefits) to judges willing to undertake hardship assignments.

c. *Tous Les Deux: Pursuing Both Options*

A third option is to attack the *strength* (or dichotomous nature) of the *either/or* statement in the articulation of the dilemma. Dilemmas may be falsely characterised as presenting mutually exclusive choices between alternative X and Y, when *both* may be pursued to achieve the overall objective. Independence measures are not necessarily exclusive of all other accountability measures. Indeed, reformers can mitigate the downside of any one measure by combining it with others, such that independence measures parallel accountability interventions, with one counterbalancing the other.

In many judicial systems, for example, life tenure may be structured to coexist with strong external controls on corruption. Self-appointment may be designed to co-exist with strong and transparent certification standards. Independent control of a judicial calendar may be implemented to coexist with case and event tracking methods that create greater accountability in the handling of that caseload. And so on.

d. *Finding A Third Way*

A fourth option is to attack the *exclusivity* of (or rigidity of the boundaries set by) a strong either/or choice, i.e., the choice of two options, no more. Reformers frequently look for a *third way*. Instead of being forced to choose between these unsatisfactory alternatives or judicial self-appointment or executive appointment, reformers in search of a third way, may view legislative appointment as the best of *three* options (stronger on independence than executive appointment, and stronger on accountability than judicial self-appointment).

e. *Attacking False Polarities*

A fifth strategy is to recognise that the putative polarity in many perceived dilemmas is false. Either/or statements may be more productively phrased as independence or not independence, accountability or not accountability, and so on. Accordingly, independence measures may be contrasted with those that frustrate independence (rather than those that necessarily advance accountability). Stated differently, accountability is not the opposite of independence; anti-independence is. This means, some measures might support both values. For example, a free press simultaneously can establish greater accountability of judicial institutions to society *and* through publicity of the process of judicial determinations cultivate greater public trust, itself a source of independence for the judiciary from the other political branches.

f. *Divide and Conquer: Aggressive Distinctions*

These tools become significantly more precise through a sixth process of aggressive distinctions. This might be called a divide-and-conquer approach. The goal or cluster of features (independence) may be *divided* further (or disaggregated) into different sub-aims or sub-features. The process of disaggregation helps to resolve dilemmas that are conceptualised too generally.

For example, reformers can easily divide and conquer the independence accountability dilemma by making key distinctions. Decisional independence may be distinguished (though not necessarily entirely separated) from administrative independence. Individual independence may be distinguished from collective or corporate independence. The independence to conduct oneself lawfully in the judge's personal life may be distinguished from the independence to commit crimes with impunity. Independence as a shield from political interference (through self-appointment, proscriptions against forced transfers, salary protections, exclusively internal disciplinary authority and power to remove) may be distinguished from independence as a sword to curb political branch excesses (judicial review of a violation of civil rights). This allows us to distinguish different functional forms of potential interference: from administration on the one extreme to the act of adjudication on the other.

g. *Grasping Relativity of Benefits and Harms*

In addition to the foregoing divide and conquer strategy, opportunities arise from rejecting binary conclusions based on an arbitrarily binary assignment of absolute O or 1 values to the chosen approach. One approach is to embrace the *relativity* of goal satisfaction in degrees of benefits and harms in the pursuit of multiple objectives. Measures that advance independence in judicial systems do so in *relative*, not absolute, ways. For example, a life tenure system does not in itself guarantee full, or even sufficient, judicial independence, and an external disciplinary system by itself is no guaranty for establishing full or even partial accountability.

Thus, the net result of any reform measure is an empirical question (about which we know much too little) that (if we knew more) would render answers in quantifiably relative, rather than absolute terms.

h. *Picking the Poison: Making Tough Value Choices*

What if none of the foregoing options is available, and the dilemma is an undeniably strong and inescapable one? Let's suppose that an independence measure necessarily (and to the same degree) frustrates accountability and vice versa. In such cases, an eighth option for dealing with dilemmas is available. The reformer must *choose* between mistakes, harms, or errors that result from each of the two alternatives.

i. *Explicating Evidentiary Thresholds for Reform*

The clear demarcation of these value choices, however, is rare. The relativity of benefits and costs, coupled with the (relative) ignorance of the nature of systemic problems or the precise effects of any particular reform design or method pose an additional evidentiary problem. What's the threshold for making a critical choice?

Should the risk that an oversight commission will become a source of political interference or corruption prevent reformers from moving ahead with design and implementation? With imperfect information about the problems to be addressed and the effects of the reform interventions, reformers and opponents make determinations on the basis of (frequently implicit) answers to these (rarely posed) questions. Greater attention to explicating implicit, relative, evidentiary burdens of proof might help reformers to manage their ignorance of the facts and choose which mistake they would rather make.

j. *Taking Collective Action on the Social Dilemma*

Many anti-corruption reforms fail not because of a lacking consensus about the purported benefits, but rather because individual and collective interests are poorly aligned or even perversely set against one another. Reforms that accentuate a conflict between the interests of the individual (or some group of individuals) and the collective interest pose a social dilemma. A lawyer may have strong feelings about supporting anti-corruption reform, but may still offer a bribe to a policeman to get an official report for the lawyer's case or may still delay a case for as long as possible if the client wishes that result. Criminal prosecutions are unpopular with those charged to conduct them. Political support for reform and sufficient authority and power are thus considered a key factor in anti-corruption interventions. In sum, reform often fails because it is in fact *threatening*.

Short of a commanding theoretical solution, societies need practical strategies for these types of social dilemmas in part because complex, organised systems defy top-down, command-control solutions.[3] Furthermore, non-threatening, open-ended communication about the nature of the social dilemma and the values at stake may do more to advance reform than any particular resolution advanced by a single leader or individual. Because corruption is filled with value judgments, harsh assessments may get in the way of effective approaches to reform. Experimental research shows that (in addition to side payments which are not always available) non-threatening communication may create more cooperative behaviour (by creating conditions for internalization of the social costs). It may be useful to recall that in the paradigmatic case of the prisoners' dilemma, the two detainees were *not* allowed to confer. Without this restriction, a more collaborative, bottom-up process of individual and collective self-assessment and problem solving may help to break down the constraints imposed by social dilemmas in judicial reform. Thus, joint communication and social coalitions may provide a promising avenue for both judicial independence and anti-corruption reformers.

IV. Conclusion

This chapter sought to extend critical thinking about judicial independence into the realm of anti-corruption. Section II posed a series of critical questions about the nature of corruption and the implications of currently available answers. Section III then charted some modest strategies to assist policy-makers and reformers who are confronted with the tension between political protections and economic controls. This is only a starting point for helping decision-makers find fruitful navigational tools for working through one of many formidable dilemmas in judicial reform.

---

[3] *See* Peter Schuck, *The Limits of Law* (Westview Press 2000), p. 445.(noting the tendency of lawmakers to ignore the competing forces of social norms and markets: "Lawmakers are drawn to top-down forms of law such as command-and-control rules, which seem authoritative, clear, rigorous, and relatively easy to enforce.")

CHAPTER TEN

JUDICIAL INDEPENDENCE IN THE FACE OF VIOLENCE

*Wayne McCormack**

In observing the many legal assistance projects around the world, one cannot help but be struck by the dilemma of violence and the Rule of Law. No justice system can operate effectively in the midst of chaos but chaos cannot be forestalled effectively without a functioning justice system.

Consider three places in which the United States and a number of European nations have taken an active military role while trying to assist nascent or renascent judicial systems: Bosnia, Afghanistan, and Iraq. There are many locales in desperate need of stability and human rights, but these three are ones in which the western military and civilian assistance efforts are ongoing.[1] Bosnia in 2010 is maintaining a tentative hold on peace and stability while its judicial structures evolve from a socialist regime into a hybrid of adversarial and inquisitorial models. In contrast, Afghanistan came close to being peaceful and stable but then disintegrated amid numerous factors, one of which was the lack of a credible legal system. And Iraq has a thousand-year history of a stable legal system that has now been torn apart and is struggling to function in the face of ongoing chaos.

It is tempting to conclude that promoting the Rule of Law is fruitless in a society that is plagued by violence and corruption because it is unrealistic to expect people to turn to law when their very lives are at risk on a daily basis. But the military experience in these countries itself demonstrates that it is not realistic to believe an area can be stable and peaceful without a state that has a near-monopoly on the use of force. The U.S. Military's *Rule of Law Handbook* emphasizes the intersection of force and civilian development in what it calls "stability operations."[2] In the now-famous *Counterinsurgency Field Manual* attributed primarily to General David H. Petraeus,[3] there is a blueprint for

---

* Professor McCormack (B.A. Stanford University, J.D. University of Texas) is E. W. Thode Professor of Law at the University of Utah. He has written widely in constitutional law and international criminal law with emphasis on counter-terrorism.

[1] In the interests of disclosure, these three are also the ones with which I have had some personal involvement.

[2] Center for Law and Military Operations (CLAMO), *Rule of Law Handbook*.

[3] This small, powerful volume is a product of a group process but is commonly attributed to General Petraeus because he organized the effort before becoming Commander of Multinational

dealing with uprisings against an occupying force. It emphasizes in many ways the need to empower local leadership to stabilize their own governance. Rule of Law efforts must coincide with programs, whether military or civilian, to control the violence and corruption. In some of these situations, it may be necessary to promote the appearance and rhetoric of the Rule of Law in aspirational terms while recognizing that the society will continue to struggle with violence until changes in the culture of the community address the underlying causes of violence.

The Rule of Law is designed to create stable social conditions conducive to economic and personal development – in other words, a peaceful and healthy society. Conversely, the Rule of Law is not really possible in conditions under which more powerful actors can operate as they wish with impunity. When developed nations attempt to assist emerging nations with reform of their justice systems, or even when nations attempt to come out from under civil strife, there is a significant difficulty. No justice system can operate in the midst of chaos but chaos is difficult to forestall without a functioning justice system. So where do we start?

Violence against judges occasionally merits headlines, as when the drug lords of Colombia were in their heyday. It would be difficult to determine whether the level of violence against judges is greater than that threatening other segments of society, although judges logically are likely to be targeted by those who fear or resent their potential power. It is clear that judges are subject to violence – what is less clear is the extent to which judges are intimidated by the threat of violence, either against themselves or against their society.

Day-to-day life is terrifying enough in some parts of the world, but judges are threatened and killed precisely because of their role in trying to quell the violence. Judges in Afghanistan and Iraq can hardly function at all, let alone with confidence that their rulings will be obeyed and their families remain secure. Their counterparts in more privileged countries such as Europe and the U.S. have been accustomed to making their decisions with little thought of personal safety but with knowledge that they can affect the peace and sanity of their entire society; in recent years there are emerging threats to the safety of judges in those countries as well.

There is often ridicule directed against the traditional, slightly romantic, stereotype of the judge sitting solemnly above the fray and detached from reality. And there is some merit in the stereotype. But professional analysis of the judicial function usually emphasizes the desirability of judges' remaining

---

Forces – Iraq. There are many valuable lessons in that short volume that can be applied to concerns for violence and judging.

in contact with the "real world." The stereotype of judges' remaining above the fray is not really an option in many settings. At the extreme, instances of violence against judges are sufficiently frequent to be more than a little disturbing.

Just in terms of current tensions that threaten the independence of judicial action, consider three of the world's hot spots where the West has an ongoing military role: Afghanistan, Iraq, and Bosnia-Herzegovina.

In Afghanistan, there are two judicial systems, the formal and the informal. The informal system is not really a system but a custom of deference to village elders known as the *jirga*. In most of the Pashto regions of Afghanistan as well as much of neighboring Pakistan, two people with a dispute will turn to a tribal elder who will first attempt to mediate on his own and then convene a jirga to resolve disputed matters. The jirga will hear from both sides and reach decision by consensus (in other words, by pressure on the timid or weak members from the more vocal and strong-willed members).

Reliable estimates say that as many as 80% of all disputes in Afghanistan are resolved through the informal system. Small wonder when a judge in the formal system is viewed as either corrupt or ineffective or both. A judge may have a salary of $60 per month while a minimal standard of living costs $500 and a family can make $600 growing poppies. Do the math and you see how the incentives for corruption are legion. Meanwhile, the jirga is there with a perceived tradition of "fairness" because the elders hear both sides and reach a consensus that is viewed to be in the best interest of the community. (Even when the best interest of the community consists of giving the 55-year-old plaintiff the 9-year-old daughter of the defendant or meting out stoning of an accused adulteress whose "crime" was being married to a man who now wants another woman – but that's another story.)

Indeed, there have not been a great number of incidents of violence against judges in Afghanistan for the simple reason that most disputants would not consider the judges to be much of a threat. The rare criminal defendant who cannot bribe his way out of a criminal charge with the prosecutor merely bribes the judge or makes a veiled reference to his powerful friends and soon finds that he is on his way – or lacking the resources for a bribe or veiled threat finds that he is in jail (often with no assurance of being released at the end of his sentence – but that's another story).

On May 2, 2006, Provincial Judge Sheikh Mohamed was gunned down leaving his mosque after evening prayers. Although a handful of news reports attribute the killing to Taleban gunmen, I have found no follow-up to this story, no information about Judge Mohamed, and no hint of concern on the internet for the cause of judicial independence in Afghanistan from violence.

By contrast, there is much on the web about threats to judicial independence in Afghanistan from low salaries, corruption, poor qualifications of judges (only 20% are said to have any legal education), and the force of Islamic Shari'a in a system that does not rely on stare decisis (thus reinforcing the perception of arbitrariness and unfairness in the system).

In Iraq, violence against lawyers became rather routine by 2007. In April 2007, the UN was reporting that lawyers in Iraq were afraid to take cases involving volatile disputes such as "cases of adultery, honour killings, claims of property, children's custody and divorces." "According to the Iraqi Lawyers Association (ILA), at least 210 lawyers and judges have been killed since the US-led invasion in 2003."[4] In May 2007, Senator Graham served his tour of duty as an Air Force Reservist in Iraq and had this observation about the "rule of law" portion of the "surge."

> The number one target of the insurgency are judges. If you're a judge in Iraq you're an incredibly brave person. Because they just don't try to kill you, they try to kill your family. So General Petraeus tried to build a compound in Baghdad for judges. Took an old army base, reinforced it, put housing on base for judges and their families and created a brand new courtroom [and] a detention facility to hold people in the compound to give the judges confidence that if they did their job they could do it without fear.[5]

The level of violence in the country generally dampened down over the years 2008 and early 2009, but it has not ceased to have its impacts. In June 2008, a city appellate judge in Iraq was gunned down in a drive-by shooting. The Iraqi judiciary has been praised in many quarters for its professionalism and adherence to the rule of law despite the presence in the 2005 Constitution of a requirement that Shari'a be a source of law in the nation. Given that Iraq has a tradition of civil code adjudication and a long history of reasonably stable educational institutions, there are reasons for hope in the future of Iraq that don't exist in Afghanistan.

To dwell on that difference for a moment, Afghanistan has never had a history of strong educational institutions. It has always been a buffer between contending forces, for centuries between Persian and Indian, then between British and Russian, then after World War II between Soviet and capitalist warlords, and now between Islamist extremists and modernizing influences. There has never been an opportunity for development of an educational system. Meanwhile, the country has been torn over the last 30 years by constant warfare. Given the economic and cultural considerations above, the lack of an

---

[4] http://www.irinnews.org/Report.aspx?ReportId=71864
[5] http://www.cbsnews.com/blogs/2007/05/07/couricandco/entry2769338.shtml

educated leadership, and the chaos of violence gripping the country today, it hardly even makes sense to be talking about the rule of law. As Senator Graham said, "One way to kill the insurgency beyond military force is to create a government that is fair to its citizens and the rule of law to me is about 'what you did' not 'who you are.'"

By contrast, Iraq has centuries of strong legal and educational institutions. That gives the reformers a basis on which to build and a tradition that allows the citizenry to take the judiciary seriously. If the Iraqi security forces can preserve the safety of the judges, there is every indication that the Iraqi judiciary can move forward.

A word of caution, however, on this optimism stems from the impact of 25 years of dictatorial rule by Saddam Hussein. Under Saddam, both the judiciary and the educational institutions were slowly turned to the service of the Baathist agenda and his personal power. The difference between this and the same period of time in Afghanistan, however, is that there were many well-educated persons in Iraq who either left or managed to hang on until the rebuilding effort could begin. Unfortunately, there could be a gap of leadership after the current elder statesmen die off and before the newly educated generation comes of age. This gap will be noticeable unless a new generation of Iraqi descendants educated abroad move in to fill it.

Other incidents of violence against judges must highlight the chaos in Colombia. In 1989, an unofficial report from the government estimated that "about 50 judges and 170 judicial employees have been killed since 1982."[6] In 2002, the International Commission of Jurists provided the following description:

> At least 64 judges, lawyers and prosecutors were victims of attacks between February 2000 and November 2001. Intimidation against other judicial officers and witnesses contributed to the widespread impunity enjoyed by a wide variety of criminal offenders. The criminal justice system failed to address adequately such endemic problems as corruption, armed opposition and paramilitary activities, organised crime, drug-trafficking, human rights violations, leading to widespread public distrust of the judiciary.[7]

The volatile Southern Russian republics have seen violence targeted at judges. Two judges of Dagestan were killed in separate shooting incidents in June and July 2010. The deputy chairman of Ingushetia's Supreme Court was killed in a drive-by shooting in 2008 and his successor was killed just 18 months later

[6] "Colombian Judge Slain in Drug Traffic Capital," Los Angeles Times (Oct. 17, 1989).

[7] International Commission of Jurists, "Colombia – Attacks on Justice, 2002" (Aug. 27, 2002).

after dropping her kids off at school. A judge who allegedly led a fight against organized crime in the North Caucasus Republic of Kabardino-Balkaria, was killed along with another police officer in 2008.

In Cambodia in 2003, a judge and a court clerk were killed and another judge was attacked and beaten.

The U.S. has not been immune from violence against judges. Federal judge Joan Lefkow's husband and mother were killed in their home in Chicago in 2005, reputedly by a man who was upset over her ruling against him in a medical malpractice case. Two weeks later, a judge and two court employees in Atlanta were killed by an inmate who took a guard's gun from him.

In response to the Chicago and Atlanta incidents in 2005, Senator John Cornyn, a former state supreme court justice from Texas, said he wondered "whether there may be some connection between the perception in some quarters on some occasions where judges are making political decisions yet are unaccountable to the public, that it builds up and builds up and builds up to the point where some people … engage in violence."[8] He was instantly rebuked by a number of critics, but the perception that American judges overreach into political arenas is certainly widespread.

A more friendly version of this theory is that American judges serve as "lightning rods" because of their consciously designed independence, their inability to shift the blame for their decisions onto the electorate. In this view, the judge in the American system is supposed to make tough political judgments and take the heat for them. That leads to this thought:

> One way to make judges safer would be to limit their authority or independence. But doing so would reduce the benefits of having an independent judiciary, including the benefits that accrue to other public officials when judges take the heat for contentious issues.[9]

There is no shortage of very interesting avenues to explore in the realm of the American version of judicial review, but none of this theorizing can account for the violence in other societies that are much less open and in which the judges take a far less political role.

The nature of the judicial process is such that judges are usually referees in a zero-sum game. By comparison, sports events generate enormous levels of adrenaline and testosterone charged behaviour. The idea of competition easily transforms into statements about personal merit or worth, and the outcomes may affect careers but most often the outcomes are just effects on one

---

[8] "Senator Links Violence, Judges," Houston Chronicle (April 5, 2005).

[9] Matthew Segal, *Violence Against Judges: Why it Occurs and What We Can Learn from it* (Apr. 25, 2005) http://writ.news.findlaw.com/commentary/20050425_segal.html

participant's self -image. Whatever the reasons, violence among both players and fans in sports such as soccer and hockey can erupt into very serious levels.[10] Given the levels of violence in sports events, it may be surprising that there have been so few assaults on soccer or hockey referees. Social controls, such as expectations of peers, as well as personal inhibitions account for a significant level of restraint toward the person in the neutral uniform. And when assaults do occur, the results are rarely fatal.

Similarly, litigation is not a friendly environment. Even in non-adversarial proceedings, the result of dispute resolution is rarely a win-win situation. In the Anglo-American system, it is almost always a zero-sum game – the winner physically takes something away from the loser or keeps what the loser alleges was taken earlier. Again, given the stakes and the emotions generated, it is a tribute to social norms that judges are not physically abused more often.

Of course, once is enough. And in some areas, social controls are not operating to protect judges. Iraq from 2003–08 was a nightmare for judges (as well as for most of the population), Afghanistan's judiciary is virtually nonfunctional, and some countries teeter on the edge, if not over the edge, of anarchy because there is no reliable rule of law.

Even when violence is neither widespread nor fatal, the threat itself is sufficient to impact processes. Judges need to work in public settings, witnesses need to be able to tell their stories without fear, and parties need to have assurance that results will be impartially reached.

When the state loses its perceived monopoly on the use of force, the result is collapse of not just the political system but the entire socioeconomic structure of the country. Therefore, Rule of Law initiatives must begin with assessment of the security potential in a given setting.

What can be done about it? One answer might be that attributed to General Petraeus – lock the judges and their families in a compound and guard them with armed force. This is far from a desirable scenario, but it may be the only solution possible in the short term. It insulates the judges from their social structure, cuts them off from day-to-day understanding of conditions in the community, and produces a heightened perception of elitism among the rest of the community. These are all negative effects on public acceptance of the rule of law.

The other extreme would be telling the judge to live with the threat and hope for the best, maybe with a little bit of weapons training and armed guards

---

[10] See Michael Atkinson & Kevin Young, *Deviance and Social Control in Sport* (2008); Brian Wingate, *Violence at Sports Events* (2008); David W. Rainey & Peter Duggan, *Assaults on Basketball Referees: A Statewide Survey*, 21 J. Sport Behaviour (1998).

thrown in for good measure. But this approach is even less acceptable than the compound approach.

So if neither extreme is acceptable, what is in the middle? In a variety of ways, both of the U.S. military books reinforce the proposition that a productive and peaceful civil society depends on the acceptance by the populace of the Rule of Law. "Political power is the central issue in insurgencies and counterinsurgencies; each side aims to get the people to accept its governance or authority as legitimate."[11] That acceptance requires taking the moral high ground and staying there – while at the same time recognizing that force is often necessary and also recognizing that limitations on the use of force can put your own personnel at risk. Turning the other cheek can be dangerous but sometimes it works.

Granted that we are not often embroiled in genuine counterinsurgency operations, there are some important lessons to be learned from the military's soul searching. First, Rule of Law initiatives, including those directed toward an independent judiciary, cannot be successful without effective control of the countryside. If people do not feel safe and protected, there is little the judiciary can do to build a functioning society. Although civilian government support efforts are essential from the very beginning of a newly emerging nation, they must coincide with a realistic assessment and involvement with the military. Second, a legitimate government is the creature of the local populace. It is not our judiciary but their judiciary which must be supported. Third, a government that is accepted as the sole legitimate governing body will be accessible to the people – this means risk to judges as well as other officials.

If political judgements have been made that western forces (the U.S. in particular) will enter a nation in support of a host government, then the U.S. military leadership now has a blueprint that will include support of Rule of Law activities. But what about the many nations that have not invited the West to assist with the use of force? In those instances, the international community has a greater burden to press aggressively for local protection of judges. Can we make a case that judges deserve protection more than the rest of the populace? Of course not, but we can make the case that the judges are greatly at risk and their safety is a critical component in realization of the Rule of Law, which is in turn a critical component is achieving a healthy and productive society.

[11] *Field Manual* (1–3)

CHAPTER ELEVEN

JUDICIAL INDEPENDENCE AND JUDICIAL HUBRIS

*Maimon Schwarzschild**

Judicial independence is widely, and rightly, said to be a cornerstone of liberal government, of good government, and of the rule of law. It might seem perverse, therefore, to suggest that judicial independence is not unequivocally a good thing. But good ideas – like the phrases or catchwords that describe them – are often bent or distorted in behalf dubious interests. While judicial independence in some senses of the phrase is surely good and even crucial to what Lon Fuller called the (internal) morality of law,[1] judicial independence in another sense might actually imply judicial over-reaching and abuse of authority: an indefensible sort of independence. Predictably enough, that sort of independence is liable in the long run to undermine or to destroy judicial independence in the good sense.

It is not merely in theory that judicial independence is equivocal. There are growing tendencies in many developed countries towards a dubious sort of judicial independence. Moreover, international legal institutions, and enthusiasm for international norms, may be especially susceptible to fostering the bad sort of judicial independence.

I. Judicial Independence and the Changing Ambitions of the Courts

Judicial independence in the good sense implies that judges should be free from improper interference by political authorities; that they should be free from improper pressure by powerful private forces as well, or from mob pressure; and at a bare minimum, that judges should not yield to corruption or bribery or to personal conflicts of interest. Perhaps a little more broadly, judicial independence implies that a judge should be intellectually independent: not a slave to intellectual or social conformity.

---

* Maimon Schwarzschild is Professor of Law at the University of San Diego, and Affiliated Professor at the University of Haifa. He has recently been Visiting Professor at the University of Paris (Sorbonne) and at the Hebrew University in Jerusalem. He is an English barrister and an American lawyer; he is an associate member of Landmark Chambers, London.

[1] Lon L. Fuller, *The Morality of Law*, rev'd ed. (New Haven 1965).

Some aspects of judicial independence might coincide with the sort of independence we expect from executive and legislative officials as well as from judges – or that we might expect from any honest human being. Bribery and corruption, for example, are not evil only when they involve judges.

Yet insofar as adjudication is distinct from politics, judges ought to be independent in some ways that are distinctive. Examples or symbols of such independence include lengthy and secure tenure in office (such as life tenure for federal judges in the United States),[2] and being given elaborate deference in the courtroom and often outside the courtroom.[3] When judges fulfil their proper role – interpreting and applying the law in accordance with the letter and the spirit of the law, faithful to text and precedent as the morality of law requires – then we might want judges to be independent of public or private pressures, to be above the fray, in ways that we don't necessarily want elected officials to be independent of the people who elect them.[4] Judges are expected to be impartial. Officials elected on a partisan basis cannot be non-partisan or in that sense impartial.

But this implies that there can be judicial independence in a bad sense:

- Independence from democratically enacted laws;
- Independence from democratic responsibility: from reasonable public expectations as to the values and the spirit that will inform adjudication, both judicial interpretation of the positive law and "interstitial" judicial lawmaking;
- Independence, in short, from an obligation to interpret and enforce the law rather than the judge's own will, or the will of unrepresentative interests or elites with whom the judge might identify;
- Independence, more briefly still, from the rule of law itself.

There is no clear or uncontroversial boundary, to be sure, between legitimately interpreting the law, which is a judge's proper function, and substituting the

---

[2] US Constitution, Art. III s.1 ("The Judges, both of the supreme and inferior Courts, shall hold their Offices during good Behaviour…").

[3] But *cf.* Richard A. Posner, "The Supreme Court 2004 Term–Foreword: A Political Court"(2005) 119 Harvard LR 32, 77 ("Cocooned in their marble palace, attended by sycophantic staff, and treated with extreme deference wherever they go, Supreme Court Justices are at risk of acquiring exaggerated opinions of their ability and character").

[4] Edmund Burke's classic defence of a representative's independence was that "[y]our representative owes you, not his industry only, but his judgment; and he betrays, instead of serving you, if he sacrifices it to your opinion." But Burke does not suggest that a representative ought to be immune from lobbying by his constituents, whose "wishes ought to have great weight with him; their opinion, high respect". Edmund Burke, "Speech to the Electors of Bristol" in D. Ravitch and A. Thernstrom eds. *The Democracy Reader* 50 (New York 1992).

judge's own will for the law. In a constitutional system like the United States, the idea of judicial review – the power of the courts to strike down legislation held to violate the Constitution – is long established in principle.[5] The idea that judges should do justice under natural law has still older roots. More than a century and a half before American independence, an English court suggested that "when an Act of Parliament is against common right and reason, or repugnant… the common law will controul it, and adjudge such Act to be void".[6] The risk, of course, is that natural law, or the meaning of the Constitution, will be too much in the eye of the judicial beholder. Much of modern constitutional theory in the United States, and increasingly elsewhere in the world, is devoted to the question of judicial review, its proper scope, its proper limits, and its legitimacy. Yet it is widely agreed that however narrow or broad the boundaries of legitimate judicial authority, those boundaries can be exceeded: and that when they are, judges abuse their authority. Criticism of judicial decisions as reflecting the judges' will, not the law, can – and at various times often has – come from any point on the political spectrum.[7]

There are a variety of reasons why judges might push the limits of their authority and presume to act as unelected legislators. There is always the human impulse to maximise one's own power. But there are also ideals – sometimes legitimate, sometimes perverse, likely in many cases a mixture of the two – that may underlie a judicial reach, or over-reach, for power.

One ideal, both in the United States and around the world, has undoubtedly been the role of the United States Supreme Court in the latter half of the twentieth century, which issued far-reaching decisions against racial discrimination

---

[5] The power of judicial review is not explicit in the US Constitution, but it was proclaimed by the decision in *Marbury v. Madison* (1803) 5 US (1 Cranch) 137, and has been traced to earlier currents in American legal thinking. See P. Hamburger, *Law and Judicial Duty* (Cambridge Mass 2008). But after *Marbury*, the US courts very rarely struck down Acts of Congress as unconstitutional during the nineteenth century; judicial review in that era was directed almost exclusively against the states. See J. B. Thayer, "The Origin and Scope of the American Doctrine of Constitutional Law" (1893) 7 Harvard LR 129.

[6] *Dr Bonham's Case* [1610] 8 Co. Rep. 114 (Court of Common Pleas).

[7] See D.E. Bernstein, "*Lochner v. New York*: A Centennial Retrospective" (2006) 85 Washington ULQ 1469, for an account of the vehement Progressive opposition to the conservative pre-New Deal Supreme Court's laissez-faire jurisprudence. In recent decades, American academic commentary was overwhelmingly enthusiastic about ambitious judicial review, whereas criticism of US Supreme Court decisions as legally ill-grounded impositions of judicial preference tended to come from a handful of right-of-centre critics. See e.g. R. Epstein, "Substantive Due Process By Any Other Name: The Abortion Cases" (1973) 1973 Supreme Court Review 159. More recently still, with the appointment of more conservative Justices by Republican Presidents, the academic pendulum has begun to swing against judicial activism. See e.g. C.R. Sunstein, *One Case at a Time: Judicial Minimalism on the Supreme Court* (Cambridge Mass 2001); M. Tushnet, *Taking the Constitution Away from the Courts* (Princeton 1999); D. Kennedy, *A Critique of Adjudication: Fin de Siecle* (Cambridge Mass 1998).

in the mid-twentieth century, and then went on – inspired or misled by the model of those decisions – to hand down decisions on a wide array of public policy questions: police procedure, electoral constituencies, abortion, sexuality, the death penalty, and much more.[8]

There is virtual unanimity today – although there was controversy at the time – that the mid-century Supreme Court acted properly and admirably in striking down racially discriminatory laws as unconstitutional. Racial discrimination, unjust and evil, was pervasive in much of America and almost monolithic in the South. It seemed practically impervious to extra-judicial challenge, despite America's having fought a Civil War to abolish slavery nearly a century earlier. And after all, the post-Civil War constitutional amendments, by their intent and in their language and spirit, were surely at odds with discriminatory government.

Inspired by decisions like *Brown v. Board of Education*, and eager to maintain or increase the prestige and the influence that these decisions won for the courts, it is perhaps understandable that the American judiciary – cheered on by much of the legal profession and the legal academy – should have begun to adjudicate many other controversial questions of public policy. Yet these new questions did not necessarily present so clear a right and a wrong as "Jim Crow" segregation had done. It was less clear in these cases that representative democracy could not cope: that if the courts did not intervene, then nothing would change for the better. And the legal basis for the courts' rulings, in the language, intent, and spirit of the Constitution or of the laws, was often less persuasive than it had been in the decisions striking down racial discrimination.[9]

It is evident that in at least some areas of public policy, the American Supreme Court has become a kind of super-legislature in recent decades, pre-empting the representative branches. As such, the Court's rulings invite comparison with federal court decisions in the early decades of the twentieth century, now widely discredited, in which the judges would read or misread their preference for laissez faire into the Constitution.[10] But whereas the pre-New Deal laissez faire decisions aroused fierce opposition among opinion leaders and in the

[8] The paradigmatic racial desegregation decision was *Brown v. Board of Education* (1954) 347 US 483. Leading decisions on other matters in the years following *Brown* include *Miranda v. Arizona* (1966) 384 US 436 (police procedure); *Baker v. Carr* (1962) 369 US 186 (electoral constituencies); *Roe v. Wade* (1973) 410 US 113 (abortion); *Romer v. Evans* (1996) 517 US 620 (sexuality); *Furman v. Georgia* (1972) 408 US 238 (death penalty).

[9] John Hart Ely, for example, an eminently mainstream scholar, wrote of *Roe v. Wade* that "it is not constitutional law and gives almost no sense of an obligation to try to be". J. H. Ely, "The Wages of Crying Wolf: A Comment on *Roe* v. *Wade*" (1973) 82 Yale LJ 920, 926.

[10] The paradigm laissez faire "substantive due process" decision was *Lochner v. New York* (1905) 198 US 45.

American legal academy, and attracted no admiration or emulation in foreign countries, the more recent transformation of the Court into an oracle of (generally "progressive") policy has been warmly welcomed by influential sympathisers, especially in the legal academy. As such, the role of the court as super-legislature has become increasingly institutionalised.[11]

Partly as a result of the Supreme Court taking on the role of super-legislature, and partly further promoting this tendency, there is the noteworthy fact that the American federal courts do less ordinary judicial work than they used to do. The Supreme Court now hears only cases that it chooses to hear, through purely discretionary writs of *certiorari* – unlike in the past, when there were categories of cases on appeal that the Court was legally obliged to hear.[12] In fact, the Court hears and decides fewer cases altogether than it did in the past.[13] There is considerable evidence that the Justices choose their cases with a strategic eye toward advancing their ideological or policy goals, although the process itself by which the Court chooses its cases is notably non-transparent[14]. The implication is that deciding ordinary lawsuits, cases that are of primary interest only to the parties, is beneath the dignity of today's Justices in their role as lawgivers, if not as prophets.

Lower courts in the United States, and not only in the United States, tend to follow, as much as they can, the model and spirit of the US Supreme Court. Hence, just as the Supreme Court hears and decides fewer cases, so federal circuit and district judges increasingly offload their ordinary adjudicative tasks to law clerks, magistrates, special masters, administrative law judges, arbitrators, mediators, and the like; not to speak of their encouragement of prosecutorial plea bargaining, which radically reduces their dockets of criminal trials.[15]

There are parallel tendencies in other developed countries. In England, for example, High Court judges hear fewer cases as ordinary litigation is

---

[11] See P.D. Carrington & R.C. Cramton, "Judicial Independence in Excess: Reviving the Judicial Duty of the Supreme Court"(2009) 94 Cornell LR 587, documenting the evolution of American courts into superlegislatures and makers of controvertible public policy, and urging that the trend is incompatible with traditional claims for judicial independence.

[12] *Id.*at p. 590, n. 17.

[13] See K.W. Starr, "The Supreme Court and Its Shrinking Docket: The Ghost of William Howard Taft" (2006) 90 Minnesota LR 1363, 1369.

[14] See M.W. Cordray & R. Cordray, "The Philosophy of Certiorari: Jurisprudential Considerations in Supreme Court Case Selection", (2004) 82 Washington ULQ 389.

[15] "Thus, at all levels, the Justices and judges "holding office" under the Constitution are increasingly preoccupied with making political decisions and are diminishingly concerned with the humdrum task of enforcing the preexisting applicable law to disputed facts or with assuring litigants that their interests have been seriously considered by members of an independent judiciary." Carrington & Cramton, *op. cit.* at p. 629.

increasingly channeled to lower courts or to bureaucratic agencies.[16] Appeals in England are increasingly limited, and there has been extensive promotion of "alternate dispute resolution", pre-empting adjudication altogether. A somewhat similar abdication of judicial obligation is discernible in the practice of the European Court of Justice, which issues its decisions ex cathedra: the European Court's procedure forbids individual opinions or dissents, so the ordinary judicial responsibility of an individual judge to state his or her reasoning is thwarted.[17]

II. The International Dimension

International norms, international legal institutions, and activist organisations promoting an international legal agenda have all gained strength and influence in recent decades. As such, international influence might in principle encourage judicial independence in the good sense around the world. This is especially urgent in countries where the rule of law has traditionally been weak or nonexistent. At a minimum, international influence might discourage "telephone justice", as it used to be called in Soviet Russia, and which evidently persists in Russia and undoubtedly in other countries as well: that is, judges taking instructions (over the telephone or otherwise) from government or police authorities about how to decide politically sensitive cases.[18] One may hope that international promotion of judicial independence does actually strengthen the rule of law in this way.

But there is at least the danger, if not the reality, of a growing international legal culture promoting a more dubious sort of judicial independence.

One troubling model is the growing power of judges in European Union countries to make public policy under the banner of European norms and treaties which are often vague and open-ended, and which therefore seem to

[16] See H.M. Kritzer, "Disappearing Trials? A Comparative Perspective" (2004) 1 Journal of Empirical Legal Studies 735. In the early 1990s, before the "Woolf Reforms" took effect, there were some 350,000 civil cases launched each year in the High Court in England. This fell to some 20,000 such cases in the mid-2000s. See Katy Dowell, "Woolf reforms: lawyers continue to wrangle over merits a decade on", The Lawyer 8 June 2009.

[17] Some, but by no means all, domestic courts in civil law countries in Europe also dispense with individually signed judicial opinions and dissents. There, the implicit idea is that the court is straightforwardly applying the civil code, not exercising discretion. This fiction seems considerably less plausible for the European Court of Justice, which is adjudicating a body of law less well-codified than the developed civil codes of Europe's Napoleonic or quasi-Napoleonic legal systems.

[18] See Bill Bowring, "Legal Nihilism in Russia", oD Russia (Open Democracy Russia) 7 July 2009, posted online at http://www.opendemocracy.net/article/email/legal-nihilism-in-russia (viewed 3 September 2010).

invite judicial over-reaching. A euphemism for this is "teleological" adjudication, which means interpreting or pushing, not to say twisting, the law in a particular direction or towards a particular goal. Often, the goal in question is more power for the European Union and its institutions – "deeper union" – at the expense of the democratic institutions of the constituent nation states.[19] This is a goal, in many cases at least, that the public in European countries would not vote for: a goal that the electorates would reject not merely in the heat of passion, but upon sober reflection. It may be especially troubling for the broader judicial culture that this power to use or abuse European norms is not restricted to a handful of specifically European tribunals, but is devolved – in the name of subsidiarity – to ordinary national judges as well. This tends to enlist the judges in the teleological project and vests them with new, broad, and nebulously accountable powers.[20]

The citation of foreign law by American courts, at least in some contexts, is open to similar criticism. If judicial interpretation of the Constitution or of domestic law is guided by the law of other countries, that tends to circumvent domestic democratic processes. Moreover, on many debatable questions, foreign law is liable to differ from country to country. This creates an obvious risk of arbitrary selectivity about which foreign law to cite, or rather, of tendentious selectivity: that the judge will "pick and choose" whichever bits of foreign law suit the result the judge favours, especially where the result might not be straightforwardly justified under duly enacted domestic law.[21]

More broadly, international legal institutions sometimes seem to promote, and even to embody, judicial independence in a dubious rather than in a desirable or defensible sense. Judges appointed to international tribunals from countries ruled by dictatorships, for example, are unlikely to enjoy much judicial independence in the positive sense. Coming from countries with little or no tradition of the rule of law, where the judge has family members who can be

---

[19] "The central organ of the EU legal system is the European Court of Justice… Almost from the outset of the Common Market, the ECJ took an extremely activist approach to the Treaty of Rome, interpreting it as a proto-constitution." J.A. Rabkin, *Law Without Nations?* p. 131 (Princeton 2005).

[20] *Id.* at p. 141: "National judges were systematically wooed by judges of the European Court at conferences and professional gatherings. And national judges learned to appreciate the extra power and status they would gain as enforcers of European law against their own governments."

[21] There is a running debate between Justices Breyer and Scalia about the citation of foreign law in American courts, in particular in cases involving constitutional interpretation. See Stephen Breyer, "Keynote Address" (2003) ASIL Proc. 265; *Lawrence v. Texas* (2003) 539 US 558, 598 (Scalia, J., dissenting); *Atkins v. Virginia* (2002) 536 US 304, 347–48 (Scalia, J., dissenting). See also M.D. Ramsey, "International Materials and Domestic Rights: Reflections on *Atkins* and *Lawrence*" (2004) 98 American Journal of International Law 69.

implicitly or explicitly threatened, where the judge himself or herself might hope to retire or to pursue a later career, where an independent-minded person is in any event unlikely to have reached a professional position from which appointment to an international tribunal would be plausible, the foundations for judicial independence are scarcely promising.

For international jurists, however, there is often a kind of judicial independence in the dubious sense of being unmoored from a developed legal system, and unaccountable to a democratic citizenry. The body of international law, to put it charitably, is less than fully evolved: it embraces uncertain "custom", treaties sometimes drafted broadly, highly arguable "general principles", and so forth. Members of international tribunals are often appointed in a none-too-transparent process of horse trading among governments, international organisations, and sometimes activist pressure groups.[22] There is no global hierarchy of international courts or a responsible body of supervising jurists. Few if any international jurists are known to the public, much less are they politically removable or otherwise answerable to democratic scrutiny.

And there are surely examples of international adjudication which might be charged with over-reaching: decisions that appear to be more political than legal. The International Court of Justice (the "World Court") issues an advisory opinion condemning Israel's security barrier and demanding that it should be dismantled, a judgment that has been criticised for bias both in its procedure and in outcome;[23] in another advisory opinion, the World Court comes close to declaring nuclear deterrence illegal, although such deterrence is a basic and long-standing element in the defence strategy of the major powers;[24] in yet another controversial ruling, the World Court holds that United States actions concerning Sandinista Nicaragua were illegal, prompting the United States to withdraw from the "compulsory jurisdiction" of the Court.[25] International law has also been invoked to justify "universal jurisdiction" over a variety of international crimes, evoking criticism that this has great potential for selective

22 "In practice, the nomination and election of judges to international courts and tribunals are politicized processes, subject to little transparency, and to widely varying... nomination mechanisms at the national level." R. Mackenzie & P. Sands, "International Courts and Tribunals and the Independence of the International Judge" (2003) 44 Harvard Int'l LJ 271, 278.

23 Legal Consequences of the Construction of a Wall in the Occupied Palestinian Territory, Advisory Opinion (ICJ 9 July 2004), 43 ILM 1009 (2004). See Ruth Wedgwood, "The ICJ Advisory Opinion on the Israeli Security Fence and the Limits of Self-Defense" (2005) 99 Am. J. Int'l L. 52 for a detailed account and criticism of the decision.

24 Legality of the Threat of Use of Nuclear Weapons, Advisory Opinion (ICJ 8 July 1996).

25 *Nicaragua v. United States* (ICJ 27 June 1986). The United States took the position that the Court had no jurisdiction in the case and did not participate in the proceedings on the merits. For the United States withdrawal from the Court's "compulsory" jurisdiction, see Dep't State Bulletin No 2096, March 1985 at p. 64, reprinted at 24 ILM 246 (1985).

enforcement and for politicised show trials. A common thread in all these controversies, and in others, is the suggestion that there are growing tendencies towards bias and politicised adjudication under international law, and that there are too few safeguards against these tendencies.

III. Judicial Hubris vs Judicial Independence

When adjudication intrudes, perhaps even when it appears to intrude, excessively on the prerogatives of representative democracy, judicial independence is liable to suffer. Judicial independence sits uneasily with the idea of judges as "teleological" lawgivers or arbiters. After all, the democratic impulse is anti-deferential: it holds lawmakers accountable, often raucously, to the will of the people. Judges are entitled to a unique kind of independence and to special immunities that others do not enjoy, only so long as they act as judges: that is, only so long as they interpret and apply the law in a way that conforms, within somewhat ill-defined limits, to the morality of law.

When judges follow a model of judging which too often exceeds those limits, the claim for judicial independence and deference is less and less plausible. This can be seen, in practical terms, in the greatly increased bitterness and polarisation, and corresponding decrease in deference, in the judicial appointments and confirmation process in the United States in recent decades.[26] There are implications for a wide variety of issues that touch on the judiciary. For example, the proposal that judges in England should be exempt from compulsory retirement at a given age is less plausible if the judges are active in taking public policy decisions and are increasingly seen as political or ideological partisans.[27] Such a proposal would have to reckon with the example of American Supreme Court Justices, who enjoy life tenure, and who are widely seen as timing or manipulating their retirements for political reasons to ensure that their successors will be nominated by an ideologically sympathetic President.

If judges around the world are encouraged – by academic opinion, by the Zeitgeist in the political elites, by international lawyers and pressure groups – to overstep their authority, and especially if the judiciary is seen to be a partisan force in the great political and cultural disputes of the era, then democratic public opinion is liable, sooner or later, to ensure that there will be less judicial independence, not more. That, sadly, will be as it ought to be.

---

[26] See B. Wittes, *Confirmation Wars: Preserving Independent Courts in Angry Times* (Stanford 2006).

[27] *Cf.* Sir L. Blom-Cooper, "The Age of Judicial Responsibility: the Retirement and Resignation of Appellate Court Judges", this volume, page 339.

PART III

JUDICIAL INDEPENDENCE IN INTERNATIONAL LAW AND NATIONAL LAW

CHAPTER TWELVE

THE INDEPENDENCE AND IMPARTIALITY OF THE 'INTERNATIONAL JUDICIARY'

*James Crawford and Joe McIntyre**

I. Introduction and Overview

International law has, at least to the extent that it deals with matters of governmental structure and authority, long been a critical standard for the conduct of States. That is to say, international law sets minimum standards against which to measure the performance of other legal systems. For most of its history, however, international law has been a law applied in the absence of its own institutions. Grotius saw that as its defining characteristic, no less than Hobbes. From this incorporeal position the issue of applicability of these standards to international law itself could not arise.

This is no longer the case. International law now has its own institutions, increasingly interacting with those of States. Their emergence calls for an examination of the standards and principles that govern and constrain their operation. In particular, the question arises as to the extent to which the standards international law sets for other legal systems apply to its own institutions. This chapter will focus on one emblematic example of this issue, namely the applicability and content of the principles of judicial independence and impartiality to the 'international judiciary'.

---

* James Crawford LLD, FBA, SC is Whewell Professor of International Law, University of Cambridge and a Fellow of Jesus College, Cambridge. He previously held chairs at Adelaide and Sydney. He is a Senior Council (NSW) and a member of the English bar, practicing from Matrix Chambers. He was the first Australian member of the United Nations International Law Commission and was responsible for the ILC's work on the International Criminal Court (1994) and for the second reading of the ILC Articles on State Responsibility (2001). In addition to scholarly work on statehood, collective rights, investment law and international responsibility, he has appeared frequently before the International Court of Justice and other international tribunals, and is engaged as expert, counsel and arbitrator in international arbitration.
Joe McIntyre is currently a PhD Candidate at the University of Cambridge, where he is examining the nature of the judicial function. He has previously worked as a Principal Research Officer for the South Australian Parliament, and as legal officer for the South Australian Solicitor-General's and Crown Solicitor's Offices. His practice has principally focused on Australian constitutional law, and involved numerous Supreme Court and High Court appearances.

1. *The 'International Judiciary': Initial Observations*

The emergence of an 'international judiciary' is a relatively recent development.[1] Nonetheless, with the proliferation of international courts and tribunals of the last twenty years (there are now some 200 international judges among the standing, permanent bodies)[2] it appears indisputable that there is a true 'international judiciary'.[3] This forces us to confront directly the question of how closely analogous the international judge is to the domestic or national one, and whether the differences are sufficient to render inapplicable standard principles of judicial independence and impartiality, or at least to require their substantial modification.[4]

There are obvious similarities between international and domestic judges. First, like national judges, international judges are called on to decide particular disputes, of both law and fact, and to do so on the basis that the law is, in some sense and to some degree (a) determinate and (b) constraining. Thus there appears to be a fundamentally common judicial function. Secondly, there appears to be a broadly shared method of applying existing legal norms, whether 'legislative' or 'judicial' in origin, to discrete disputes through a blend of deductive, analogous and inductive reasoning. Thirdly, if the judge is to be effective in resolving the dispute, the parties must have confidence that the resolution was reached though due and independent process and not by the exercise of some hidden influence. Without such confidence the parties will not respect and may be disinclined to comply with the decision. Finally, any long-term confidence in the institutions depends on the perceived integrity of their personnel.

Against these similarities are obvious differences. Firstly, there is no 'institutional sovereign' in the international system, which is, instead, distinguished by its essentially diplomatic processes. The direct enforcement of decisions by operation of executive action is largely, if not entirely, absent in international institutions. Secondly, there are (except for the WTO Appellate Body, which has been conspicuously successful) no systems of appeal and few avenues for review within the international judiciary. Thirdly, and following from this point, there is little formal structural coherence *between* the various international judicial institutions. This is in contrast to domestic judiciaries

[1] Ruth Mackenzie & Philippe Sands, 'International Courts and Tribunals and the Independence of the International Judge,' (2003) 44(1) *Harvard International Law Journal* 271, 271.
[2] Ibid, 273.
[3] Chester Brown, 'The Evolution and Application of Rules Concerning Independence of the 'International Judiciary',' (2003) 2 *The Law and Practice of International Courts and Tribunals* 63, 64.
[4] See generally Mackenzie & Sands, above n1, 275–6 for a preliminary discussion of this issue.

which are more clearly constituted as 'judicial systems'. Fourthly, under international law, jurisdiction is still largely dependent on consent. While this is changing to some degree (in that advance consent by treaty is now more common), the requirement of consent is, like the lack of coercive means of implementation, grounded in the absence of an 'institutional sovereign'.

It is unclear why these differences call for a lower level of judicial integrity, or to what extent they permit or demand different standards of judicial independence and impartiality. This chapter will seek to unpack these standards and ask whether or to what extent the special features of international judicial institutions may justify differential treatment.

In our view, to suggest that principles of judicial independence and impartiality do not apply to international institutions in the same way as they do to domestic institutions[5] is to fundamentally misunderstand judicial independence as a functional and contextually dependent concept. When properly understood, the critical issue is not *whether* the principles of judicial independence and impartiality apply to the international judiciary, but rather *what* those principles demand.

While there are institutional and political differences that may require a different application of these principles, the core concept remains unchanged. The international judiciary must be free to decide disputes only through the legitimate application of the judicial method, free from undue influences. What is 'acceptable' does depend to some degree on the particular context, and the specific character of the international judiciary may permit practices that would be inappropriate in certain domestic contexts. Nonetheless, there is a shared core concept of judicial impartiality underpinning both domestic and international judiciaries.

The international judiciary is threatened by two particular 'weaknesses' that impact upon judicial independence and impartiality. The first concerns the fact that the bulk of international judging is still done by part-time or *ad hoc* judges; the second is concerned with the fragility of international institutions. While these considerations affect international judicial independence, they do not alter the fundamental presumption that the essential international standards apply with equal force to the international judiciary. International courts and tribunals must live by the standards international law itself sets for the judicial process at the national level.

In this chapter we will begin with a discussion of the terms 'judicial independence' and 'impartiality'. This includes some preliminary observations

[5] *Prosecutor v. Tadic*, Decision on the Defence Motion for Interlocutory Appeal on Jurisdiction, IT-94-1, 2 October 1995.

regarding the relationship between judicial independence and impartiality, and the allied notion of accountability. We will then examine the applicability of those principles to the international judiciary.

II. Defining the Scope and Character of Judicial Independence and Impartiality

Much of the difficulty concerning the applicability of standards of judicial independence and impartiality to the international judiciary can be traced to a failure to adequately define the issues. 'Judicial independence', like 'democratic governance' and 'the rule of law', is an idea easy to appeal to yet difficult to define, a concept 'more easily acclaimed than understood.'[6] The term is often employed to cover issues properly beyond its scope, often in an apparent attempt to bolster the credibility of those issues. Alternatively, much discussion focuses on particular threats to judicial independence, with the resultant risk that the discourse becomes either purely descriptive, or reduces judicial independence to an issue of means rather than results.[7]

1. *Identifying the Foundations of Judicial Independence*

Attempts to identify the core of judicial independence often highlight its relational aspects. Thus we can assert that in order to be 'independent' a tribunal must be independent of the executive,[8] the parties[9] and/or the legislature.[10] Such statements do not, however, explain what it means to be independent, or for what ends that 'independence' is valued. This has often led to a misapprehension as to the underpinnings of the concept, particularly given

---

[6] Sir Ninian Stephen, '*Judicial Independence - A Fragile Bastion,*' in Shimon Shetreet and Jules Deschenes (eds), '*Judicial Independence: The Contemporary Debate*,' (1985), 529.

[7] Seibert-Fohr, 'European Comparative Perspectives on the Rule of Law and Independent Courts' (unpublished paper, on file with the authors) 9–10.

[8] See *Beaumartin v. France*, Application No. 35/1993/430/509, 25 October 1994, [38] (a French court which accepted as binding the interpretation given to the provision of a treaty by the Minister of Foreign Affairs could not be considered 'independent' within the meaning of Art 6 of the *European Convention for the Protection of Human Rights and Fundamental Freedoms*, 4 November 1950, 213 UNTS 222, *entered into force* 3 September 1953, as amended (the 'ECHR').)

[9] *Ringeisen v. Austria*, Application No. 2614/65, 16 July 1971, [95] ('independent' means 'independent of the executive and also of the parties').

[10] See *Pabla KY v. Finland*, Application no. 47221/99, 22 June 2004. In *McGonnell v. UK* the European Court of Human Rights stated that it 'considers that any direct involvement in the passage of legislation, or of executive rules, is likely to be sufficient to cast doubt on the judicial impartiality of a person subsequently called on to determine a dispute over whether reasons exist to permit a variation from the wording of the legislation or rules at issue'): *McGonnell v. UK*, Application no. 28488/95, 8 February 2000, [55].

the historical circumstances in which the consciousness of 'judicial independence' arose. This obligation on the judiciary, to render decisions on the basis of law without undue influence by the government or other actors, has been acknowledged in domestic law, though to varying degrees, since at least the end of absolutism.[11] The visible origin of the concept in constitutional battles between governmental institutions has led to a distracting association of the concept with constitutional doctrines such as the separation of powers. For example, the Inter-American Commission for Human Rights sees judicial independence as being derived 'from the classic separation of the three branches of government',[12] a position mirrored by Shetreet, for whom the 'theoretical underpinning of judicial independence is the doctrine of separation of powers.'[13] These positions mistake cause for effect; the separation of powers is a *means* of ensuring judicial independence and not a cause.

Judicial independence does not depend upon any particular political system, though it may flourish more completely in some systems than in others. As Judge Manfred Lachs observed, independence is a personal quality, and depends on character, not on a political system.[14] This failure to appreciate the distinction between the constitutional principle of separation of powers and that of judicial independence may account to some degree for the belief that the international judiciary is not subject to the latter principle.[15]

2. *Declarations on Judicial Independence and Impartiality*

A better theoretical foundation for judicial independence is found in the concept of impartiality, that is, in the lack of inappropriate bias on the part of the judge. This foundation quickly emerges when one examines the way in which judicial independence is defined in the many international instruments and declarations that deal with the issue. One of the earliest of these declarations,

---

[11] Seibert-Fohr, above n7, 2.

[12] Seventh Report on the Situation of Human Rights in Cuba, (1983), OEA/Ser.L/V/II.61, October 1983.

[13] Shimon Shetreet "Judicial Independence in International Law" http://www.courts.gov.bc.ca/1701/1701%20Papers/Shetreet.htm (accessed 18 May 2010); Shimon Shetreet, '*Judicial Independence: New Conceptual Dimensions and Contemporary Challenges,*' in Shetreet & Deschenes, *Judicial Independence*, above n6, 595.

[14] Judge Manfred Lachs, 'A Few Thoughts on the Independence of Judges of the International Court of Justice', (1986–7) 25 *Columbia Journal of Transnational Law* 593, 596.

[15] See the discussion in *Prosecutor v. Tadic*, Decision on the Defence Motion for Interlocutory Appeal on Jurisdiction, IT-94-1, 2 October 1995, [43]. In *Prosecutor v. Delalić* (*Čelebici* case) three of the appellants argued that Judge Odio Benito should have been disqualified because, following her appointment as Vice-President of Costa Rica, she did not possess the necessary judicial independence required by international law. *Prosecutor v. Delalić*, Judgment, No. IT-96-21-A, 20 February 2001.

the Montreal Declaration of 1983, immediately highlights this connection when it declares that:

> Judges individually shall be free, and it shall be their duty, to decide matters before them impartially, in accordance with their assessment of the facts and their understanding of the law without any restrictions, influences, inducements, pressures, threats or interferences, direct or indirect, from any quarter or for any reason.[16]

This language is largely reproduced in the only UN General Assembly resolution on this topic, the *Basic Principles on the Independence of the Judiciary* of 1985, which states that:

> The judiciary shall decide matters before them impartially, on the basis of facts and in accordance with the law, without any restrictions, improper influences, inducements, pressures, threats or interferences, direct or indirect, from any quarter or for any reason[17]

The only international statement directly concerning the international judiciary, *The Burgh House Principles on the Independence of the International Judiciary*, does not explicitly draw this link, stating only that the 'court and the judges shall exercise their function free from direct or indirect interferences or influences by any person or entity.'[18] However, even these terms co-opt the ideas of appropriate neutrality and decision-making freedom referred to in the earlier statements.

The Council of Europe has been particularly prolific in developing standards and statements concerning judicial independence, and from the earliest such declarations have recognised the interaction between independence and impartiality:

[16] *Universal Declaration on the Independence of Justice*, (1983) unanimously adopted at the final plenary session of the First World Conference on the Independence of Justice held at Montreal on 10 June 1983 ('the Montreal Declaration') §2.02. The text of the Montreal Declaration is reproduced in Shetreet & Deschenes, *Judicial Independence*, above n6, 447–461.

[17] United Nations, *Basic Principles on the Independence of the Judiciary*, (1985) Seventh United Nations Congress on the Prevention of Crime and the Treatment of Offenders, Milan, UN Doc. A/CONF.121/22/Rev.1 at 59 (1985); endorsed by General Assembly resolutions 40/32 of 29 November 1985 and 40/146 of 13 December 1985, §2.

[18] ILA Study Group on the Practice and Procedure of International Courts and Tribunals, *The Burgh House Principles On The Independence Of The International Judiciary*, (2005) §1.1. These Principles were drawn up by a study group of the International Law Association, in association with the Project on International Courts and Tribunals. The drafting of these Principles was informed by a preparatory symposium held in Florence, Italy in 2002, the proceedings of which were published in (2003) 2 *The Law and Practice of International Courts and Tribunals* 1–173. See generally Philippe Sands, Campbell McLachlan & Ruth Mackenzie, 'The Burgh House Principles on the Independence of the Judiciary,' (2005) 4 *The Law and Practice of International Courts and Tribunals* 247. The text of the *Principles* is reproduced in this articles on pages 251–260.

> In the decision-making process, judges should be independent and be able to act without any restriction, improper influence, inducements, pressures, threats or interferences, direct or indirect, from any quarter or for any reason. ... Judges should have unfettered freedom to decide cases impartially, in accordance with their conscience and their interpretation of the facts, and in pursuance of the prevailing rules of law.[19]

More nuanced statements have been developed following the creation of the Consultative Council of European Judges (CCJE), which in its first Opinion, in 2001, outlined the underlying rationale for judicial independence, which, it said, 'serves as the guarantee of impartiality.'[20] It expanded on this statement, observing that:

> Judicial independence presupposes total impartiality on the part of judges. When adjudicating between any parties, judges must be impartial, that is free from any connection, inclination or bias, which affects – or may be seen as affecting – their ability to adjudicate independently. In this regard, judicial independence is an elaboration of the fundamental principle that 'no man may be judge in his own cause'. This principle also has significance well beyond that affecting the particular parties... Not merely the parties to any particular dispute, but society as a whole must be able to trust the judiciary. A judge must thus not merely be free in fact from any inappropriate connection, bias or influence, he or she must also appear to a reasonable observer to be free therefrom. Otherwise, confidence in the independence of the judiciary may be undermined.[21]

These observations are mirrored in the third Opinion, in 2003, where the CCJE states that judicial independence is 'inextricably complemented by and the pre-condition of the impartiality of the judge, which is essential to the credibility of the judicial system and the confidence that it should inspire in a democratic society.'[22]

These themes are consistently carried through to the latest Draft Declaration on this issue, which, after observing that judges 'should have unfettered freedom to decide cases impartially, in accordance with the law and their interpretation of the facts'[23], goes on to define the issue in the following terms:

---

[19] Committee of Ministers, Council of Europe, '*On the Independence, Efficiency and Role of Judges*' (1994) Recommendation No R (94) 12, Adopted by the Committee of Ministers on 13 October 1994 at the 518th meeting of the Minister's Deputies, Principle I, s2(d).

[20] Consultative Council of European Judges, Council of Europe, '*On Standards Concerning the Independence of the Judiciary and the Irremovability of Judges*' (2001) CCJE (2001) OP No1, 23 November 2001, §11.

[21] Ibid., §12.

[22] Consultative Council of European Judges, Council of Europe, '*On the Principles and Rules Governing Judges' Professional Conduct, in Particular Ethics, Incompatible Behaviour and Impartiality*' (2002) CCJE (2002) OP No 3, 19 November 2002[16].

[23] Bureau of the European Committee on Legal Co-Operation, Council of Europe, '*Draft Recommendation on Judges: Independence, Efficiency and Responsibilities and its Explanatory Memorandum,*' (2010) CDCJ-BU (2010) 2, 22 January 2010, §5.

> The principle of judicial independence means the independence of each individual judge in the exercise of adjudicating functions. In their decision-making judges should be independent and impartial and able to act without any restriction, improper influences, pressures, threats or interferences, direct or indirect, from any authority, including authorities internal to the judiciary.[24]

These extracts do not seek to exhaust the many Declarations and Statements concerning judicial independence and impartiality, but can be seen as representative.

3. *Defining the Core of Judicial Independence and Impartiality*

What emerges from these statements is the connection between, and interdependence of, judicial independence and impartiality. Judicial independence is concerned with ensuring that the judge is free to perform the obligations imposed by the judicial function in an appropriately impartial manner. This means the judge should be protected from improper influences, pressures, threats or interferences that may threaten his or her impartiality. Such threats or influences risk rendering the judge improperly partial to one of the parties or the position they take. As we discuss below, the specific issues traditionally dealt with under the rubric of 'judicial independence' represent a particular subset of potential threats to the impartiality of the judge. Ultimately, though, it is critical to stress, as Pasquino does, that the '*independence* of the judicial power has always to be understood as an instrument to achieve the goal of *impartiality*'[25]. This in turn requires a neutrality from the judge, an absence of subordination from 'a) the parties to the conflict, b) from any other power interested in a given resolution of the conflict, and as far as possible c) from the bias of passions and partiality of the judge himself or herself.'[26]

This concept of impartiality represents the 'fundamental value in judicial ethics',[27] and, in general terms, means 'the absence of favour, bias or prejudice in the considerations of cases.'[28] Some statements go too far on this issue, seeking to protect the judge from *any* influence for *any* reason.[29] To talk of judicial

[24] Ibid., §21.

[25] Pasquale Pasquino, 'Prolegomena to a Theory of Judicial Power,' (2003) 2 *The Law and Practice of International Courts and Tribunals* 11, 25.

[26] Ibid.

[27] W Bradley Wendel, 'Impartiality in Judicial Ethics: A Jurisprudential Analysis,' (2008) 22 *Notre Dame Journal of Law, Ethics and Public Policy* 305, 305.

[28] Paul Mahoney, 'The International Judiciary: Independence and Accountability,' (2008) 7 *The Law and Practice of International Courts and Tribunals* 313, 340.

[29] See particularly the *Montreal Declaration* (1983), above n16, §2.02; UN *Basic Principles on the Independence of the Judiciary*, (1985), above n17, §2.

impartiality is not, however, to talk of an absolute impartiality,[30] for there are many legitimate influences upon the judge including existing law, judicial training, the facts of the case and the pleadings of the parties. Rather, impartiality requires that the judge is not unacceptably prejudiced by *improper* influences. Impartiality demands that the judge be 'duty-bound to decide cases on their merits, be open to persuasion, and not be influenced by improper considerations.'[31]

Normative demands of impartiality are directed to ensuring that the judge, in performing the obligations of the judicial function, is influenced only by those considerations deemed relevant by the guiding judicial method. Principles of impartiality, and therefore of judicial independence, seek to protect judicial decision-making from any threat or inducement that may improperly pervert the exercise of that judicial function.

4. *A Relative and Functional Concept*

What emerges from this analysis of rationale and character is that the concepts of judicial independence and impartiality are, fundamentally, functional in character.[32] Rather than ultimate objectives, they are means of achieving the objective of ensuring legitimate performance of the judicial function. In consequence, there can be 'no static notion of judicial independence'[33] either in national or international law, at it is rather a 'functional concept which needs to respond to new developments and contemporary questions.'[34] Malleson highlights that any examination of potential threats to judicial independence and impartiality requires a detailed examination of the specific context:

> Thus identifying and analysing the character and source of potential threats to judicial independence requires a highly specific consideration of the particular context in which any one court operates vis-à-vis other governmental bodies.[35]

This contextually rich examination of potential threats is not limited to the governmental context, but applies to any circumstances of the court that may affect judicial decision-making, particularly cultural factors. The ultimate touchstone is the ability of the judge to perform the judicial function according to the relevant judicial method. The ways in which the judge may be

---

30 See William Lucy, 'The Possibility of Impartiality,' (2005) 25(1) *Oxford Journal of Legal Studies* 3, 18.

31 Wendel, above n27, 305.

32 See Seibert-Fohr, above n7, 1, 11.

33 Ibid., 1.

34 Ibid.

35 Kate Malleson, 'Promoting Judicial Independence in the International Courts: Lessons from the Caribbean,' (2009) 58 *International and Comparative Law Quarterly* 671, 671.

improperly influenced in that task, and the acceptability of any potential influence, are (not unsurprisingly) culturally specific.

Thus there can be no absolute 'standard' of independence and impartiality. The question is not whether a given court is or is not independent, but whether in a given context that court has a sufficient degree of independence and impartiality. This position is consistent with the jurisprudence of the European Court of Human Rights which, in examining the independence of tribunals and the separation of powers, has stated that '[t]he question is always whether, in a given case, the requirements of the Convention are met.'[36] For example, there is no absolute prohibition of part-time judges,[37] appointment to short-term positions[38] or the concurrent exercise of non-judicial functions by judges.[39] However, these are all circumstances which may tend to indicate a lack of independence.

The failure to appreciate the functional character of judicial independence and impartiality results in a static notion of independence which 'increasingly isolates the entire judicial branch as such from the other branches of government, regardless of the function exercised.'[40] Further, it promotes a 'check-list' approach whereby independence is assessed by reference to the presence of certain 'key' indicators, irrespective of the underlying functional impartiality. In doing so it risks transforming the issue from one of 'obligations of results' into an issue of 'obligations of means',[41] impoverishing the concept and undermining the judicial function. There are, of course, well recognised behaviours and patterns of conduct that have been found, through experience, to present unacceptable examples of improper influence. There are also well recognised means of protecting against such threats. To an extent it is possible to create a somewhat standardised list of such threats and potential means of avoiding them, but ultimately what matters is a concrete and particularised examination of the actual and perceived threats to judicial impartiality of a given court at a given time.

It has been argued that this dependence on the particular realisation of independence and impartiality to the given context means that, to some extent,

[36] *Pabla KY v. Finland*, Application no. 47221/99, 22 June 2004, [29].

[37] *Wettstein v. Switzerland*, Application No. 33958/96, [41]. In an impartiality case, the Court stated that 'there is no reason to doubt that legislation and practice on the part-time judiciary in general can be framed so as to be compatible with Article 6.'

[38] *Campbell and Fell v. UK*, Application No. 7819/77 and 7878/77, 28 June 1984, [80]. Members of boards held 'office for a term of three years or such lesser period as the Home Secretary may appoint.'

[39] *McGonnell v. UK*, Application no. 28488/95, 8 February 2000, [52].

[40] Seibert-Fohr, above n7, 9–10.

[41] Ibid.

the 'idea of judicial independence is culture specific', and, by implication not amenable to the application of any international standard.[42] This goes too far. Perhaps a better way of stating it is that while there is a core *concept* of judicial independence and impartiality, the particular *conception* or realisation of that concept will depend upon the specific context.

This essentially dynamic character of the content of judicial independence and impartiality has major implications when assessing the applicability of these principles to the international judiciary. Indeed, it alters the very character of the task of assessing the impact of the 'standards' of international law on the international judiciary, for it requires that all such standards have a considerable degree of flexibility in their implementation and application.

5. *Independence, Impartiality and the Accountability of the Judiciary*

This understanding of the functional character and limited scope of the principles of judicial independence and impartiality underlines a basic point. The attainment of an absolutely independent and impartial judiciary *cannot* be the ultimate goal. The concepts of independence and impartiality are concerned with promoting and protecting the ability of the judge to perform the relevant judicial function. However, judging inevitably involves discretion, and no discretionary power, no matter how well-intentioned its holder may be, can be thought of as unlimited and uncontrolled.[43] Judicial independence and impartiality must be properly constrained, as is consistent with the limited functional character of the concepts. This constraint is traditionally dealt with under the rubric of 'judicial accountability'.

Judicial accountability is a necessary counterpoint to judicial independence and impartiality; indeed it is, in many ways, merely the other side of that coin.[44] Put another way, if principles of independence and impartiality are to be effective, there is 'a need for mechanisms to be in place and available to ensure their application – so that those with concerns, including judges themselves, may know how to raise and address such concerns.'[45] Without means of ensuring the principles of independence and impartiality are properly realised and maintained, they will inevitably become hollow and ineffective. A desiccated and ineffective conception of judicial independence and impartiality is no conception at all, for the functional character demands the principles are realised in a manner that actually and actively promotes and protects the performance of the judicial function.

---

[42] Mackenzie & Sands, above n1, 275.
[43] Mahoney, above n28, 320.
[44] Ibid., 348
[45] Sands, McLachlan & Mackenzie, above n18, 250.

Judicial accountability has many facets. In part it entails transparency as to how the judicial process is carried out, how the judges are to conduct themselves and how the courts regulate collectively the conduct of their members.[46] Accountability incorporates ideas such as open proceedings, written judgments, multi-judge panels, professional and academic critique, training and education, as well as more formal mechanisms including appeals and reviews, and judicial discipline. In a system that depends so heavily on the personal integrity of the judge, accountability is also promoted by such diffuse considerations as professional and personal reputation, and the degree of public respect accorded the office.[47]

The position is no different with the international judiciary.[48] Judicial accountability is a functional and flexible concept that, on any particular matter, may legitimately conflict with, and exist in tension with, considerations of independence and impartiality. This is entirely proper given that the point is to ensure the ultimate function is fulfilled, that the judicial function is properly and effectively performed.[49]

6. *The Characterisation of Threats to Judicial Independence and Impartiality*

It follows from this examination that 'judicial independence' should be seen as a subset and particular form of judicial impartiality. It is not necessary to draw a sharp line between the two, as judicial independence blends into and supports judicial impartiality. The different terms may nonetheless remain useful insofar as they allow us to label and identify particular 'species' of threats to judicial impartiality.[50] Without developing a fully formed typology, a rough division can be established between threats to 'impartiality' and threats to 'independence'.[51]

---

[46] Mahoney, above n28, 348.

[47] For the relationship of independence and accountability see Guy Canivet, Mads Andenas & Duncan Fairgrieve (eds), '*Independence, Accountability, and the Judiciary*,' (2006).

[48] For consideration of some of the matters of judicial accountability of the international judiciary generally, see Mahoney, above n28, 339–348.

[49] Ibid., 348.

[50] Much useful work has been devoted to attempting to categorise and characterise different aspects of judicial independence and impartiality, for example in terms of 'internal' and 'external' independence, or substantive, procedural and functional independence. See for example Shimon Shetreet, 'Judicial Independence: New Conceptual Dimensions and Contemporary Challenges,' in Shetreet & Deschenes, *Judicial Independence*, above n6, 595, 598, 637.

[51] For Brown, the distinction can be conceptualised so that 'judges are independent if there is no external source of control or influence which prevents them from acting in an autonomous fashion; and they fulfil their role with impartiality if there is no bias in the disposal of a case': Brown, above n3, 75. Mahoney seeks to distinguish the two notions in the following way: 'the notion of 'independence' refers to the connection between the judge and the administration,

The term 'judicial independence' is generally used to refer to matters of an institutional or structural character, potential threats that may exist in the abstract, independent of the particular dispute, either as to subject matter or parties. These concerns may crystallise with regards to a discrete case, though they are generally considered at the stage of system design. Such threats may arise with regards to the constitution or conduct of the judicial tribunal; executive direction is only the most familiar of these threats. In this sense, judicial independence can be understood as 'essentially relational', that is, as primarily concerned with the 'relationship between the judges and external bodies – the political branches of government, the media, the public or interest groups – as well as the internal relationships between judges within the judicial hierarchy.'[52] Matters concerning the 'impartiality' of the judge are, in contrast, of a discrete and dependent character, arising in the particular case as a result of a real or apparent concurrence of interests between the judge and one of the parties or their position. This partiality may arise as a result of the relationship between the judge and one of the parties, or because an interest or value of the judge may be advanced (or a negative outcome avoided) by a particular outcome. The paradigm case is the judge taking a bribe, though such corruption is fortunately rare in many countries.[53] The more difficult threat to impartiality involves reliance on irrelevant, extra-legal factors as the basis for a judicial decision.[54]

This characterisation of particular threats as raising issues of either independence or impartiality can be useful in analysing and responding to such threats. However, the distinction between them is fluid and the same factual scenarios may give rise to challenges on both of these bases.[55] Thus, for example,

---

whereas the 'impartiality' must exist in relation to the parties to the suit'. … Judicial independence assures that judges are protected from improper influence or interference by outside sources. Independence 'connotes … a status or relationship to others, particularly to the executive branch of government that rests on objective conditions or guarantees'. …This personal responsibility is notably embodied in the requirements of impartiality – that is, the duty on the judge to be free of bias, actual or perceived, in the consideration of cases': Mahoney, above n28, 320–1. Alternatively, the distinction has been expressed as follows: 'the notion of 'independence' refers to the lack of any other connection between the tribunal and other parts of government, whereas the 'impartiality' must exist in relation to the parties to the suit and the case at issue': Pieter van Dijk, Fried van Hoof, Arjen van Rijn and Leo Zwaak, (eds), *Theory and Practice of the European Convention on Human Rights* (4th edn., 2006) 613.

[52] Malleson, above n35, 671; citing Russel p8 in Peter H Russell & David M O'Brien (eds), '*Judicial Independence in the Age of Democracy: Critical Perspectives from Around the World*,' (2001).

[53] Wendel, above n27, 305.

[54] Ibid.

[55] *See* for example *Findlay v. the United Kingdom*, Application No. 22107/93, 25 February 1997, [73]: 'The concepts of independence and objective impartiality are closely linked and the

most of the human rights instruments refer to an 'independent and impartial tribunal'.[56] This interconnection between the terms becomes of particular importance when examining the extent to which international courts and tribunals are governed by these principles of judicial independence and impartiality, particularly where only one or the other term is utilised in a given text.

7. *Conclusions*

We have attempted to develop in this section a more complete articulation of the character, scope and purpose of the principles of judicial independence and impartiality. This articulation becomes critical when we examine whether those principles should be applicable to the international judiciary.

The judicial function represents a particular structured form of dispute resolution performed by disinterested third parties according to a relatively certain and defined judicial method. The ability of the judge to perform this function in a way that can resolve the dispute with finality depends to a large degree on the confidence of the parties that the judge is impartial and constrained by that method. Matters of perception and appearance are correspondingly of central concern to the effective operation of judicial institutions.

The principles of judicial independence and impartiality are directed to ensuring that judges are empowered to exercise their decision-making powers according to the demands and imperatives of the judicial method. To that extent, those principles must be understood as essentially functional concepts. Moreover, these principles are flexible and responsive in their manifestation in any particular context. What is acceptable, legitimate and required for public confidence will depend upon the particular social and cultural demands in which any judiciary is situated. Finally, we have argued that a proper understanding of independence and impartiality requires an appreciation of the limited character of the concepts and their relationship to other derivative functional concepts such as judicial accountability.

Court will consider them together as they relate to the present case.'; *Pabla KY v. Finland*, Application no. 47221/99, 22 June 2004, [28].

[56] The African Charter on Human and Peoples' Rights refers to "impartial courts and tribunals" in the context of fair trial guarantees (Article 7) while the "independence of the Courts" is dealt with in a separate article dealing with the establishment of institutions to safeguard the rights in the Charter (Article 26): *African [Banjul] Charter on Human and Peoples' Rights*, adopted June 27, 1981, OAU Doc. CAB/LEG/67/3 rev. 5, 21 ILM 58 (1982), *entered into force* Oct. 21, 1986 (the 'ACHPR'). This has been interpreted in the following way: 'While Article 7 focuses on the individual's right to be heard, Article 26 speaks of the institutions which are essential to give meaning and content to that right.' *Civil Liberties Organization v. Nigeria*, African Commission on Human and Peoples' Rights, No. 129/94 (1995), [16].

Before we examine the extent to which these principles of judicial independence and impartiality are applicable to the international judiciary, it is necessary to make one final observation regarding the concepts we have developed to this point. These principles are dependent on the underlying function, namely the judicial function.[57] At times this term is given an expansive meaning covering a large range of third-party dispute resolution methods;[58] however for our purposes we adopt a narrower construction, limiting the term to public institutional methods. Principles of 'judicial independence' and 'judicial impartiality' should not been taken to apply automatically and in the same manner to arbitral bodies. There are no doubt analogous considerations concerning the exercise of an arbitral function, but there are also core differences in function. The increased role of party consent and the discrete and largely private character of the proceedings fundamentally affect not only the applicable standards, but the underlying objectives as well, particularly with regards to the diminished importance of public confidence. The judicial function imposes stricter considerations of independence and impartiality than is demanded of arbitral functions. It is this stricter concept of judicial independence and impartiality that we have sought to develop in the preceding section.

III. The Applicability of the Principles of Judicial Independence and Impartiality to the International Judiciary

By constructing an understanding judicial independence in terms of its role as a means of maintaining judicial impartiality we have sought to provide a more refined understanding of the character and scope of both concepts. We now examine the extent to which these principles apply to the international judiciary. In contrast to domestic law, principles of judicial independence and impartiality are relatively unchartered in relation to international courts and tribunals.[59] As a former President of the ICTY has, writing extra-curially, observed:

> Many countries have a long and sophisticated tradition of judicial independence and impartiality. For international criminal tribunals, of course, the subject is relatively new.[60]

---

[57] Shimon Shetreet, 'Judicial Independence: New Conceptual Dimensions and Contemporary Challenges', in Shetreet & Deschenes, *Judicial Independence*, above n6, 594.

[58] See for example the Montreal *Universal Declaration on the Independence of Justice* (1985), above n16, §1.01 where 'judge' is defined to include international judges and arbitrators.

[59] Mackenzie & Sands, above n1, 271.

[60] Theodor Meron, 'Judicial Independence and Impartiality in International Criminal Tribunals,' (2005) 99 *American Journal of International Law* 359, 359.

The issue has been addressed sporadically over the last fifty years,[61] but the previous decade has seen a rapid expansion on the literature addressing this issue.[62] While the independence and impartiality of national judiciaries is seen as a matter of legitimate concern for the international community,[63] there has been a reticence about acknowledging the applicability of the principles to the international judiciary. As Mahoney observes:

> ...international organisations, while devoting great energy to promoting the virtues of judicial independence at a national level, are curiously reticent about going on record to affirm the applicability of the principle in the international sphere, that is to say, in their own sphere of action where they might have to observe constraints that they are keen to foist on national authorities.[64]

This reticence appears to be based on an apprehension that there is something fundamentally different in the character of the international judiciary that warrants a departure from these principles.

1. *Arguments for Differential Application*

One of the strongest statements for a differential application of these principles of judicial independence and impartiality to the international judiciary is found in the decision of the Appeals Chamber of ICTY in *Prosecutor v. Tadic.*[65] In that case, the Court held that the guarantees of a fair trial provided in human rights instruments may not apply to international tribunals in the same way that they apply to domestic courts. In the course of considering whether or not the ICTY was 'established by law',[66] the Appeals Chamber considered the relevance of the separation of powers in the international context:

---

[61] See for example: Thomas M Frank, 'Some Psychological Factors in International Third-Party Decision-Making,' (1967) 19 *Stanford Law Review* 1217; Lachs, above n14, 593.

[62] See for example Meron, above n60; Mackenzie & Sands, above n1; Sylvia de Bertodano, 'Judicial Independence in the International Criminal Court,' (2002) 15 *Leiden Journal of International Law* 409; Gilbert Guillaume, 'Some Thoughts on the Independence of International Judges vis-à-vis States,' (2003) 2 *The Law and Practice of International Courts and Tribunals* 163; Mahoney, above n28; Malleson, above n35; Eric Posner & John Yoo, 'Judicial Independence in International Tribunals,' (2005) 93 *California Law Review* 1.

[63] Mackenzie & Sands, above n1, 276.

[64] Mahoney, above n28, 317.

[65] *Prosecutor v. Tadic*, Decision on the Defence Motion for Interlocutory Appeal on Jurisdiction, IT-94-1, 2 October 1995.

[66] Article 14(1) of the *International Covenant on Civil and Political Rights*, G.A. res. 2200A (XXI), 21 UN GAOR Supp. (No. 16) at 52, U.N. Doc. A/6316 (1966), 999 UNTS 171, *entered into force* 23 March 1976 (the 'ICCPR'); Article 6(1) of the ECHR; Article 8(1) of the *American Convention on Human Rights* (1969) Adopted at the Inter-American Specialized Conference on Human Rights, San José, Costa Rica, 22 November 1969, *entered into force* 18 July 1978: AS Treaty Series No. 36; 1144 UNTS 123; reprinted in *Basic Documents Pertaining to Human Rights in the Inter-American System*, OEA/Ser.L.V/II.82 doc.6 rev.1 at 25 (1992) (the 'ACHR');

> For the reasons outlined below, Appellant has not satisfied this Chamber that the requirements laid down in these three conventions must apply not only in the context of national legal systems but also with respect to proceedings conducted before an international court. This Chamber is, however, satisfied that the principle that a tribunal must be established by law … is a general principle of law imposing an international obligation which only applies to the administration of criminal justice in a municipal setting.[67]

The Appeals Chamber noted that, in relation to the European Convention of Human Rights, the guarantee is 'intended to ensure that the administration of justice is not a matter of executive discretion, but is regulated by laws made by the legislature.'[68] The Court concluded that:

> …the legislative, executive and judicial division of powers which is largely followed in most municipal systems does not apply to the international setting nor, more specifically, to the setting of an international organization such as the United Nations. … Consequently the separation of powers element of the requirement that a tribunal be "established by law" finds no application in an international law setting.[69]

The clear implication is that the principles and standards relating to judicial independence and impartiality as developed for domestic judiciaries should not be taken to apply directly to international judiciaries. In so holding the Chamber appears to have been advocating an exceptionalist approach, finding something in the character of the international judiciary that supports a differential application.

One ground for this diverging character justifying differential treatment is said to be the far greater role politics plays in the international judiciary:

> International justice operates in very different circumstances from domestic forms of justice. In most liberal democracies the courts are independent of politics: the politicians make the law, and the judges interpret it. In the international arena, politics has a far greater role.[70]

The argument runs that, as the international judiciary operates in a context where 'the legal and the political are intimately conjoined' it is not possible to

---

67 *Prosecutor v. Tadic*, Decision on the Defence Motion for Interlocutory Appeal on Jurisdiction, IT-94-1, 2 October 1995, [42].

68 Ibid., [43].

69 Ibid., [43]. Similarly in the *Nicaragua* case the ICJ noted that domestic law concepts of the separation of powers "are not applicable to the relations among international institutions for the settlement of disputes": *Military and Paramilitary Activities in and against Nicaragua (Nicaragua v. United States of America), Merits* [1986] ICJ Reports 14, 433 [92]. Posner and Yoo argue that independent international tribunals are less effective than dependent international tribunals. They attribute this to the lack of political unification in international law: See Posner & Yoo, above n62, 72.

70 de Bertodano, above n62, 409.

entirely divorce the work of international courts from the world of international politics.[71] As the jurisdiction of international courts, the co-operation of the parties during the proceedings and enforcement all depend, to some degree, on State consent, the success of the 'project' of international courts depends on the support of the States. This dependence, the argument goes, when coupled with the heightened interplay between law and politics, makes the 'position of the international judge more uncomfortable.'[72]

It is not clear, though, why these considerations should diminish the procedural regularity and integrity demanded by the principles of judicial independence and impartiality. Indeed, the increased intermingling of politics and law, and the fragility of the institutions, might seem to demand *more* rather than *less* stringent application of these principles. Further, the reasoning in *Tadic* gives undue weight to constitutional principles of separation of powers which, as discussed above, should properly be regarded as separate from issues of judicial independence. The functional character of the principles of independence and impartiality developed here entails a dynamic conception that should be flexible enough to respond to any such divergent conditions.

Though the arguments against the application of the principles appear brittle, a positive conclusion requires more. Given the special context of the international judiciary, and its recent development, it is necessary to trace how these principles came to apply to the international judiciary.

a. *Application as a General Principle of Law: Statements and Declarations*

As has been observed above, the principles of judicial independence and impartiality have a rich heritage in most domestic legal systems. The comparative study of the realisation of these principles has been the subject of much writing.[73] Perhaps more importantly for our purposes, they find expression in a number of 'soft law' instruments. Regional and international statements, declarations and reports on judicial independence and impartiality include:

---

[71] Daniel Terris, Cesare P R Romano & Leigh Swigart, '*The International Judge: An Introduction to the Men and Women Who Decide the World's Cases,*' (2007), pp xxi, 149.

[72] Mahoney, above n28, 317–8.

[73] See for example Shimon Shetreet & Jules Deschenes (eds), '*Judicial Independence: The Contemporary Debate*,' (1985); Peter H Russell & David M O'Brien (eds), '*Judicial Independence in the Age of Democracy: Critical Perspectives from Around the World*,' (2001); András Sajó (ed), '*Judicial Integrity*,' (2004); Guy Canivet, Mads Andenas & Duncan Fairgrieve (eds), '*Independence, Accountability, and the Judiciary*,' (2006).

- The IBA 'New Delhi Standards,' *The International Bar Association Code of Minimum Standards of Judicial Independence* (1982);[74]
- The Montreal Declaration (1983);[75]
- The United Nation's *Basic Principles on the Independence of the Judiciary* (1985);[76]
- The Beijing Statement of Principles of the Independence of the Judiciary in the LAWASIA Region (1997);[77]
- The Recommendation of the Committee of Ministers of the Council of Europe to Member States *On the Independence, Efficiency and Role of Judges* (1994);[78]
- The Council of Europe's European Charter on the Statute for Judges (1998);[79]
- The Council of Europe's Consultative Council of European Judges Opinions No 1(2001),[80] 2(2001)[81] and 3(2002);[82]
- The Bangalore Principles of Judicial Conduct (2002);[83]

---

[74] International Bar Association, '*Minimum Standards of Judicial Independence*' (1982) The Jerusalem Approved Standards as adopted at the 19th IBA Biennial Conference held 22 October 1982, New Delhi. The full text is reproduced in Shetreet & Deschenes, *Judicial Independence*, above n6, Ch32, 388–392. For analysis of these Standards, see the following Chapters of that book: David K Haese, 'The International Bar Association Project on Minimum Standards of Judicial Independence' Ch31, 381; Shimon Shetreet, 'The Emerging Transnational Jurisprudence on Judicial Independence: IBA Standards and Montreal Declaration,' Ch33, 388; Leonard King, 'The IBA Standards on Judicial Independence: An Australian Perspective,' Ch34, 393.

[75] The Montreal *Universal Declaration on the Independence of Justice* (1983), above n16.

[76] United Nations, *Basic Principles on the Independence of the Judiciary*, (1985) above n17.

[77] The *Beijing Statement of Principles of the independence of the Judiciary in the LAWASIA Region*, (1997) Adopted at the 6th Conference of Chief Justices of the Asia Pacific Region, in cooperation with the Judicial Section of LAWASIA, held in Beijing in August 1997, and refined during the 7th Conference of Chief Justices, held in Manila in August 1997.

[78] Committee of Ministers, Council of Europe, '*On the Independence, Efficiency and Role of Judges*' (1994) Recommendation No R (94) 12, Adopted by the Committee of Ministers on 13 October 1994 at the 518th meeting of the Minister's Deputies.

[79] Council of Europe, '*European Charter on the Statute for Judges*' (1998) DAJ/DOC (98) 23,

[80] Consultative Council of European Judges, Council of Europe, '*On Standards Concerning the Independence of the Judiciary and the Irremovability of Judges*' (2001) CCJE (2001) OP No1, 23 November 2001.

[81] Consultative Council of European Judges, Council of Europe, '*On the Funding and Management of Courts with Reference to the Efficiency of the Judiciary and to Article 6 of the European Convention on Human Rights*' (2001) CCJE (2001) Op No 2, 23 November 2001.

[82] Consultative Council of European Judges, Council of Europe, '*On the Principles and Rules Governing Judges' Professional Conduct, in Particular Ethics, Incompatible Behaviour and Impartiality*' (2002) CCJE (2002) OP No 3, 19 November 2002.

[83] The Bangalore Draft Code of Judicial Conduct 2001, were first adopted by the UN Judicial Group on Strengthening Judicial Integrity, before being revised and adopted at the Round Table Meeting of Chief Justices held at the Peace Palace, The Hague, November 25–26, 2002. (UN Doc. E/CN.4/2003/65, Annex).

- The Burgh House Principles on the Independence of the International Judiciary (2005);[84] and
- The Draft Recommendations on Judges: Independence, Efficiency and Responsibility (2010).[85]

These many statements are distinguished by the general consistency with which they deal with the principles of judicial independence and impartiality, albeit with differences of nuance and degree. The only one of these statements to be consciously and explicitly directed to the international judiciary,[86] *The Burgh House Principles on the Independence of the International Judiciary*, expressly recognises that the key aspects of the principles of independence and impartiality are of general application:

'*Considering* the following principles of international law to be of general application:

- to ensure the independence of the judiciary, judges must enjoy independence from the parties to cases before them, their own states of nationality or residence, the host countries in which they serve, and the international organisations under the auspices of which the court or tribunal is established;
- judges must be free from undue influence from any source;
- judges shall decide cases impartially, on the basis of the facts of the case and the applicable law;
- judges shall avoid any conflict of interest, as well as being placed in a situation which might reasonably be perceived as giving rise to any conflict of interests;
- judges shall refrain from impropriety in their judicial and related activities;'[87]

In addition to these many statements and declarations, the right to a fair trial before an 'independent' and 'impartial' tribunal is included in all of the major

---

[84] ILA Study Group on the Practice and Procedure of International Courts and Tribunals, *The Burgh House Principles on the Independence of the International Judiciary* (2005), above n18.

[85] Bureau of the European Committee on Legal Co-Operation, Council of Europe, '*Draft Recommendation on Judges: Independence, Efficiency and Responsibilities and its Explanatory Memorandum,* ' (2010) CDCJ-BU (2010) 2, 22 January 2010.

[86] The proposed principles were intended to apply primarily to standing international courts and tribunals and to full-time judges, though it was envisaged that the principles 'should also be applied as appropriate to judges *ad hoc*, judges *ad litem* and part-time judges, to international arbitral proceedings and to other exercises of international judicial power': *The Burgh House Principles on the Independence of the International Judiciary* (2005), above n18, preamble.

[87] *The Burgh House Principles on the Independence of the International Judiciary* (2005), above n18, preamble.

human rights instruments.[88] In *Gonzalez del Rio v. Peru* the Human Rights Committee recalled that 'the right to be tried by an independent and impartial tribunal is an absolute right that may suffer no exception.'[89]

Based on these texts, the United Nations Special Rapporteur on the Independence of the Judiciary and Lawyers was of the opinion that 'the general practice of providing independent and impartial justice is accepted by States as a matter of law, and therefore, an international custom.'[90] But this optimistic conclusion does not of itself answer the underlying question whether these principles apply as such to the international judiciary, whether the international judiciary is bound by principles of international law clearly applicable to States. For this something more is needed.

b. *Application through Express Reference in Governing Statutes*

To a large degree this further degree of reception is found in the express language used in the governing statutes of international courts and tribunals. This reference takes two forms, namely explicit affirmation of the general principles of judicial independence and impartiality or detailed provisions dealing with particular threats to those principles. Within the first category are the provisions typically contained in the statutes of international tribunals stating that members of the tribunal are independent.[91] For example, Article 2 of the ICJ Statute provides that the Court is composed of a 'body of independent judges'.[92]

---

[88] Compare, for example, Article 14(1) of the ICCPR; Article 6(1) of the ECHR; Articles 7(1) and 26 of the ACHPR; Article 8(1) of the ACHR; Article 10 of the *Universal Declaration on Human Rights*, G.A. res. 217A (III), U.N. Doc A/810 at 71 (1948); and Article 37(d) of the *Convention on the Rights of the Child*, G.A. res. 44/25, annex, 44 U.N. GAOR Supp. (No. 49) at 167, U.N. Doc. A/44/49 (1989), *entered into force* Sept. 2, 1990. In relation to penal law, specifically, see Articles 40.2(b)(iii) and (v).

[89] *Gonzalez del Rio v. Peru*, Communication No. 263/1987, 28 October 1992, [5.2].

[90] Dato' Param Cumaraswamy, *Report of the Special Rapporteur on Independence and impartiality of the judiciary, jurors and assessors and the independence of lawyers*, (1995) UN Doc. E/CN.4/1995/39, [35].

[91] *See* Article 2 of the *Statute of the International Court of Justice*, June 26, 1945, 1155 UNTS 331 (the 'ICJ Statute'); Article 14 of the *Convention for the Settlement of Investment Disputes Between States and Nationals of Other States*, 18 March 1965, 575 UNTS 159 (the 'ICSID Convention'); Article 40(1) of the *Rome Statute of the International Criminal Court*, 17 July 1998, UN Doc. 32A/CONF.183/9, 37 ILM 208 (the 'ICC Statute'); Article 8(2) of the *Understanding on Rules and Procedures Governing the Settlement of Disputes*, 15 April 1994, 1869 UNTS 401 (the 'DSU') and Article 2(1) of the *Statute of the International Tribunal for the Law of the Sea*, Annex VI of the United Nations Convention on the Law of the Sea, 10 December 1982, (the 'ITLOS Statute'). This is not an exhaustive list, and in some cases the principle appears implicit.

[92] In relation to Article 2 of the *Statute of the Permanent Court of International Justice*, December 16, 1920, Resolution passed by the Assembly of the League of Nations, December 13, 1920, (the 'PCIJ Statute'), which is substantively identical to Article 2 of the ICJ Statute, Hudson

The second category of reference is found in the particular provisions of the statutes dealing with matters such as qualification, tenure, institutional relationships and immunities. These provisions, often constituting a significant portion of the statutes, represent a practical embodiment of the principles of judicial independence and impartiality.

In some cases, the constituent instrument explicitly links the requirement of independence to the required qualifications of judges. For example, Article 2 of the ICJ Statute provides that:

> The Court shall be composed of a body of independent judges, elected regardless of their nationality from among persons of high moral character, who possess the qualifications required in their respective countries for appointment to the highest judicial offices, or are jurisconsults of recognized competence in international law.[93]

The relationship is not always made so explicit. Provisions dealing with qualification often import other objectives such as geographic distribution of judges,[94] the need to ensure a 'fair representation of female and male judges',[95] or to be otherwise broadly representative of the relevant membership.[96] Besides issues of *realpolitk* these provisions serve the objectives of the principles of judicial independence and impartiality by promoting a legitimising diversity of views and values to ensure at there is not an institutional bias or partiality towards a particular value-set.

Provisions dealing with the term of office and tenure of judges of international courts and tribunals represent a more obvious manifestation of the

---

noted that: 'The expression 'a body of independent judges' occasioned little debate in the Committee of Jurists, which desired to make the judge, so far as possible, independent of the Governments of which they were nationals. The lack of such independence had been one of the factors which wrecked the Central American Court of Justice." Manley Hudson, *The Permanent Court of International Justice*' (1934), 125.

[93] Article 2 of the ICJ Statute. *See* also Article 14 of the ICSID Convention; Articles 2 and 3 of the ITLOS Statute, Article 36 (3)(a) of the ICC Statute, Article 28(2) of the ICCPR; Article 21(1) of the ECHR; Article 8(1) and 17(3) of the DSU; Article 13 of the *Statute of the Special Court for Sierra Leone*, annexed to Agreement between the UN and the Government of Sierra Leone, 16 January 2002, pursuant to SC Res. 1315 (2000) (the 'SCSL Statute'); Article 13 of the *Statute of the International Criminal Tribunal for the Former Yugoslavia*, 25 May 1993, 32 ILM 1192 (1993) ('ICTY Statute'); and Article 4(1) of the *Statute of the Inter-American Court of Human Rights*, O.A.S. Res. 448 (IX-0/79), January 1, 1980 ('IACHR Statute').

[94] See for example, Article 2(2) and 2(3) of the ITLOS Statute and Article 9 of the ICJ Statute. In some instances this broad objective is taken further to become an explicit prohibition against two members of a tribunal may possessing the same nationality: Article 3(1) of the ICJ Statute, Article 3(1) of the ITLOS Statute, Article 36(7) of the ICC Statute and Article 4(2) of the IACHR Statute.

[95] Article 36(8)(a)(iii) of the ICC Statute.

[96] Thus the WTO DSU states that the Appellate Body membership 'shall be broadly representative of membership in the WTO': Article 17(3) of the DSU.

principles of impartiality and independence. Judges are generally elected or appointed for long terms, often 9 years[97] though shorter (e.g. 4 year) terms are also utilised.[98] The key rationale of such fixed terms is to prevent the judge becoming partial to a particular outcome out of a concern for their personal job security. The shorter the term the more vulnerable the judge becomes to this concern. This rationale also underpins provisions prohibiting the diminution of judicial salaries, allowances and compensation during the judges' term of office.[99]

A related issue arises with reference to provisions granting immunities to international judges for actions taken in fulfilling their judicial role. Such provisions often grant members of the Court diplomatic privileges and immunities,[100] or are phrased in terms of 'such privileges and immunities as are necessary for the fulfilment of its purposes.'[101] Again such provisions are designed to ensure the judges are not inappropriately influenced by concern for their personal and financial safety and security when performing their judicial function.

These provisions, both the general affirmations and specific manifestations, represent clear attempts to ensure that judges in every international court and tribunal are 'independent' and 'impartial'. As Mackenzie and Sands state:

> The statutes and rules of the various tribunals address the issue, at least in general terms, by setting out criteria for qualification as a judge and the requirement of independence and impartiality (such as restrictions on outside activities). In many cases these general formulations are supplemented by more detailed rules

---

[97] Article 13(1) of the ICJ Statute; Article 36(9)(a) of the ICC Statute; Article 5(1) of the ITLOS Statute. In relation to the corresponding provision in the PCIJ Statute, Fachiri noted that: "[t]he judges of the international Court, like those of municipal tribunals, must be independent. They must not hold office at the pleasure of any power or authority whatever. At the same time, in the case of an international Court, provision must be made for periodical renewals of the Bench in order to assure the proper distribution of representation ...the term of nine years, during which each member of the Court enjoys absolute security of tenure, except by unanimous decision of his brethren, is long enough to fulfil the essential conditions of independence and continuity of jurisprudence." Alexander Fachiri, *The Permanent Court of International Justice* (2nd ed, Oxford University Press, 1932), 40–41.

[98] See for example Article 13(3) *bis* of the ICTY Statute and Article 12(5) of the *Statute of the International Criminal Tribunal for Rwanda*, 8 November 1994, 33 ILM 1598 (1994) (the 'ICTR Statute').

[99] Article 32(5) of the ICJ Statute; Article 18(5) of the ITLOS Statute. On issues of judicial remuneration more generally see Dinah Shelton, 'Legal Norms to Promote the Independence and Accountability of International Tribunals,' (2003) 2 *The Law and Practice of International Courts and Tribunals* 27, 39–40.

[100] Article 19 of the ICJ Statute.

[101] Article 48(2) of the ICC Statute. *See* also Agreement on the Privileges and Immunities of the International Criminal Court; Article 10 of the ITLOS Statute; Agreement on the Privileges and Immunities of the International Law of the Sea. More generally see Shelton, above n99, 41–6.

> guiding, for example, when judges ought to recuse themselves. In some cases, international courts have extremely strict rules prohibiting all forms of outside activity as a means of ensuring independence. In other cases, the guidelines are more flexible. Although the formulations and practices vary, the rules demonstrate a general commitment to independence and impartiality. *Prima facie, the concept of judicial independence applies to international judges.*[102]

These provisions take the reception of the principles of judicial independence and impartiality much further than a '*prima facie*' application. As Judge Lachs recognised in his separate opinion in the *Nicaragua (Merits)* case, the demands of these principles are of overriding and fundamental importance:

> Apart from the stipulations of Article 2 of the Court's statue, two requirements are overriding: integrity and independence. A judge – as needs no emphasis – is bound to be impartial, objective, detached and unbiased ... [States] must have the certainty that their jural relationship will be properly defined and that no partiality will result in injustice towards them.[103]

Judge Lachs alludes here to perhaps the strongest grounds justifying the application of the principles of judicial independence and impartiality to the international judiciary, not merely as general principles of international law or as implications in the terms of the governing statutes. Rather the application of these principles can be located and justified as clear and necessary implication in the concept of a 'judge' and in the fundamental character of the judicial function.

c. *As a Necessary Implication of the Judicial Function*

There is a close connection between the concepts of judicial independence and impartiality and the very idea of the judge. In order for the international judiciary to perform its role in a *judicial* manner, it must adhere to the principles of independence and impartiality:

> Judicial independence is indissociable from the very concept of justice. Beginning with the UN *Universal Declaration of Human Rights* (1948) (Article 19), there is an abundance of international instruments proclaiming that there can be no proper judicial process in the absence of the independence of the judiciary.[104]

This position emerges from the European case-law that has comprehensively held that 'an adjudicative body cannot be regarded as a 'court' or 'tribunal' unless it satisfies the requirement of independence, "in particular of the

---

[102] Mackenzie & Sands, above n1, 275 (emphasis added).

[103] *Military and Paramilitary Activities in and against Nicaragua (Nicaragua v. United States of America), Merits,* [1986] ICJ Reports 14, 158 (Separate Opinion of Judge Lachs).

[104] Mahoney, above n28, 316.

executive"[105]'[106] This point has likewise been made by the ICJ itself, when it concluded that, as a *court,* it had to act:

> ...only on the basis of the law, independently of all outside influence or interventions whatsoever, in the exercise of the judicial function entrusted to it alone by the Charter and by its Statute. A court *functioning as a court of law* can act in no other way.[107]

In short, the 'international judiciary, like national judiciaries, cannot effectively perform its functions unless it enjoys the requisite independence and hence trust of those subject to it jurisdiction.'[108] By creating an international judiciary, the States parties necessarily incorporated principles of judicial independence and impartiality.

2. *Conclusions Regarding Applicability*

As customary principles of international law, expressly adopted in the governing statues, and necessarily and inherently adopted as a consequence of the judicial function, the principles of judicial independence and impartiality must be taken to apply equally to international judges and to international judicial bodies as they do to domestic tribunals.

It is true that there are significant distinguishing features of the international judiciary, including the fragility of the institutions, the dependence upon States and their continuing good will, and the elevated role of political considerations. However, far from pointing to the inapplicability of these principles, such considerations highlight the need to immunise international judges against interference.[109] As Mahoney concludes:

> The principles of judicial independence are aimed at preserving judges from undue interference and influence. Since judicial independence is inherent in the very notion of justice, there is no reason why it should not in its essentials, subject to appropriate adaptation, apply to the international judiciary. The heightened dependence of international courts and their relative fragility as institutions make the provision in practice of concrete guarantees of judicial independence all the more needed.[110]

---

[105] See, e.g., amongst many other authorities, *Le Compte, Van Leuven and De Meyere v. Belgium*, 23 June 1981, Series A vol. 43, §55; *Benthem v. Netherlands*, 23 October 1985, Series A vol. 97, §43; *Belilos v. Switzerland*, 28 April 1988, Series A vol. 132, §64.

[106] Mahoney, above n28, 317.

[107] *Legal Consequences for States of the Continued Presence of South Africa in Namibia (South West Africa) notwithstanding Security Council Resolution 276 (1970)* [1971] ICJ Reports 16, 23 [29] (emphasis added).

[108] Guillaume, above n62, 163.

[109] Ibid., 318.

[110] Mahoney, above n28, 346.

Such a process of 'appropriate adaption' is necessary for all conceptions of the principles of judicial independence and impartiality. The more interesting and important issue is not *whether* the concepts of 'independence' and 'impartiality' apply to the international judiciary, but *what* those principles may require in this particular context.

For these reasons, there is no scope for the adoption of an exceptionalist approach, which would, in the long term, undermine the essential project of the international judiciary. While the recent explosion of literature would seem to indicate the novelty of this issue, an examination of the history of judicial independence and impartiality in the international sphere would go back at least to the 1899 Peace Conference.[111] Perhaps one of the most important observations on this issue was that made by the US Secretary of State, Elihu Root, at the 1907 Hague Peace Conference, when he stated:

> There can be no doubt that the principal objection to arbitration rests not upon the unwillingness of nations to submit their controversies to impartial arbitrations, but upon an apprehension that the arbitrators to which they submit may not be impartial. It has long been a very general practice for arbitrators to act, not as judges deciding questions of fact and law upon the record before them under a sense of judicial responsibility, but as negotiators effecting settlements of the questions brought before them in accordance with the traditions and usages and subject to all the considerations and influences which affect diplomatic agents. The two methods are radically different, proceed upon different standards of honourable obligation, and frequently lead to widely differing results. It very frequently happens that a nation which would be very willing to subject its differences to an impartial judicial determination is unwilling to subject them to this kind of diplomatic process.[112]

Institutional methods of preserving peace by settling disputes have been described as a 'great step forward in human progress.'[113] But such bodies cannot fulfil their potential unless they embrace the principles of judicial independence and impartiality. Only by showing itself to be resolutely impartial and independent can the international judiciary ensure its long term viability and usefulness.

---

[111] For a discussion of this history see Brown, above n3, 66–86.

[112] Elihu Root, 'Instructions to the American Delegates to the Hague Peace Conference of 1907', in James Brown Scott (ed), *Instructions to the American Delegates to the Hague Peace Conferences and their Official Reports* (1916) 69, 79; cited by Brown, above n3, 69.

[113] Jerome Frank, *Courts on Trial* (1949) 121.

CHAPTER THIRTEEN

THE INDEPENDENCE OF INTERNATIONAL JUDGES IN NATIONAL COURTS: LESSONS FROM BOSNIA AND HERZEGOVINA

*David Feldman**

I. International Judges in Bosnia and Herzegovina

Judges constant face pressures which may compromise their independence. International judges (taken here to include all judges who work in a jurisdiction with which they have no bond of citizenship, and where they are therefore to some degree outsiders) experience special pressures, especially when sitting in national courts, not least because they are likely to be working in fractured societies struggling to recover from war, invasion, genocide or insurrection.

When sitting in international tribunals, judges derive their authority from international law and owe their first allegiance to it. By contrast, when sitting in a national court they owe their primary loyalty to the national legal order. International law is relevant only so far as the constitution allows it to affect obligations and rights within the state's legal order. Where international agencies with extensive powers derived from international law are heavily involved in running a country, this may give rise to distinctive tensions between international law and national constitutional law and further complicate the idea of judicial independence.

Bosnia and Herzegovina (Bosna i Hercegovina, or BiH) illustrates this. Annex 10 to the General Framework Agreement for Peace in Former Yugoslavia (the Dayton Agreement), which provided the framework for reconstructing the country after the war of 1992–1995, established the High Representative

* David Feldman is the Rouse Ball Professor of English Law in the University of Camrbidge, a Fellow of Downing College, Cambridge, and the President of the Society of Legal Scholars for 2010–11. He was educated at Exeter College, Oxford (DCL, MA), and previously taught at the Universities of Bristol and Birmingham and the Australian National University. From 2000 to 2004 he was the first Legal Adviser to the Parliamentary Joint Select Committee on Human Rights, and from 2002 to 2010 a Judge (and Vice-President 2006–09) of the Constitutional Court of Bosnia and Herzegovina. He has been appointed Queen's Counsel honoris causa, elected a Fellow of the British Academy and a member of the European Group of Public Law, and held visiting positions at the Universities of Melbourne (Miegunyah Distinguished Visiting Fellow, 2006) and Nottingham (Sir J. C. Smith Senior Visiting Scholar, 2010). His writing is mainly in the fields of constitutional law, comparative public law, civil liberties and human rights, administrative law, criminal procedure, and remedies.

(HR) to facilitate the civilian implementation of the Dayton Agreement.[1] The HR is empowered to facilitate the resolution of difficulties by making binding decisions as he judges necessary,[2] and is the final authority in theatre on the interpretation of Annex 10.[3] Thus he can effectively determine the scope of his own powers. In 1997 the Peace Implementation Council (PIC), an advisory body of international diplomats, encouraged the then HR to use the powers more aggressively to build institutions and circumvent political obstacles to the implementation of the peace agreement.[4] This has been recognized in more or less annual resolutions of the UN Security Council made under Chapter VII of the UN Charter.[5] By virtue of Article 103 of the UN Charter, Chapter VII resolutions override inconsistent treaty obligations of states. If the HR uses those powers in ways that interfere with constitutional rights, courts must decide whether their primary loyalty lies to national or supranational law. This dilemma is not peculiar to post-conflict states; the relationship between EU law and national constitutions poses analogous questions.[6]

In BiH, international judges have served in three tribunals. The first was the Human Rights Chamber for BiH, one arm of the Human Rights Commission established under Annex 7 to the Dayton Agreement to adjudicate on alleged violations of human rights during and after the 1992–95 war. It inhabited the grey area between international and national legal orders.[7] Of the Human Rights Chamber's 14 judges, eight were international and six were national. Its status insulated it from the pressures that (as we shall see) have affected the independence of national courts in BiH, including the Constitutional Court. It ceased work in December 2004, when many of its functions passed first to a Chamber within the Constitutional Court of BiH and later to the Court itself.

[1] The HR later took on a second role as the EU's Special Representative for BiH, an increasingly important function now that the EU has taken over responsibility for overseeing progress in the country.

[2] Annex 10 to the Dayton Agreement, Article II.1(d).

[3] *Ibid.*, Article V.

[4] Conclusions of the meeting of the PIC on 9-10 December 1997 in Bonn, Article XI.2.

[5] See most recently UN Security Council Resolution 1948 of 18 November 2010, para. 4.

[6] Crunch cases have included *R.* v. *Secretary of State for Transport (No. 2)* (Case C-213/89) [1991] 1 AC 603, ECJ and HL in the UK, and the decision on ratification of the Lisbon Treaty, BvE 2/08 of 30 June 2009, BvfG, accessible at http://www.bundesverfassungsgericht.de/en/decisions/es20090630_2bve000208en.html, in Germany.

[7] The European Court of Human Rights has treated the Chamber as part of the national legal order of BiH for the purpose of deciding whether applicants to the European Court who had applied to the Chamber had already put their case before an international tribunal and whether those who did not had exhausted domestic remedies, despite many indications that it had an international character. See *Jeličić* v. *Bosnia and Herzegovina*, App. No. 41183/02, admissibility decision of 15 November 2005, accessible at http://www.echr.coe.int/ECHR/EN/Header/Case-Law/HUDOC/HUDOC+database/.

The second context in which international judges operate in BiH is the Court of BiH (sometimes known as the State Court). The HR imposed Laws establishing both the Court and a prosecutorial service that included international prosecutors, to deal with serious criminal cases. Initially, the HR appointed the international judges and prosecutors for renewable periods of two years. The last appointments made by decisions of the HR came at the end of June 2006. As from 26 September 2006 the task of appointing international prosecutors and international judges of the Court of BiH passed to the High Judicial and Prosecutorial Council (HJPC), established under a law imposed by the HR, and including some international members appointed by the HR.[8] When trying cases (including war-crimes trials transferred from the International Criminal Tribunal for former Yugoslavia under Rule 11 *bis* of the ICTY's rules of procedure) international and national judges sit alongside one another. Unfortunately, the Court of BiH has struggled to achieve legitimacy in the eyes of the public, for two reasons.

First, there were persistent rumours and anecdotal evidence that international prosecutors were liable to be influenced by international organisations (particularly the HR who had appointed them) and international diplomats. Stories of political interference gained credibility with the precipitate resignation of the chief international prosecutor late in 2004.

Secondly, there was doubt as to whether international judges appointed by the HR were sufficiently independent to secure a defendant's right to a fair hearing by an independent and impartial tribunal.[9] As the HR involves himself in the working of the State at all levels and in executive and legislative capacities, he can be regarded as a combined executive and legislative authority. There was a risk that the possibility of re-appointment by the HR might make the international judges appear reliant on him, and so more sensitive to his views on individual cases, than traditional principles of judicial independence would tolerate.

This issue eventually came before the Constitutional Court of BiH when a defendant appealed against his conviction by the Court of BiH, which had sat

---

[8] *Agreement between the HR for BiH and BiH on the Establishment of the Registry for Section I for War Crimes and Section II for Organized Crime, Economic Crime and Corruption of the Criminal and Appellate Divisions of the Court of BiH and the Special Department for War Crimes and the Special Department for Organized Crime, Economic Crime and Corruption of the Prosecutor's Office of BiH and Establishment of Transitional Council, which replaces the Agreement on the Establishment of the Registry of 1 December 2004 and Annex to that Agreement*, concluded and entering into force on 26 September 2006 (Official Gazette of BiH, no. 93/06), Article 8.

[9] The Constitution of BiH guarantees a right to a fair hearing within a reasonable time before an independent and impartial tribunal established by law: Art. II.2 and 3/e), and ECHR Article 6.1.

as a panel with two international judges appointed by the HR.[10] After the trial but before the decision of the Constitutional Court, the High Judicial and Prosecutorial Council (HJPC), an independent body (though with international members appointed by the HR) which took over supervision of judges and prosecutors in 2006, had reappointed them. The appellant argued (*inter alia*) that the Court of BiH had not been independent because the international judges had been structurally dependent on the HR.

The Constitutional Court dismissed the appeal. It accepted that the obligation of all state institutions to cooperate with the HR[11] could not be used to determine the scope of people's constitutional rights in national law. Nevertheless, when deciding whether people appointed by the HR were independent it was relevant that the HR had acted on a recommendation of the President of the HJPC, indicating that it had been involved in the selection process, and that the judges were applying international criminal law as well as domestic law, were obliged to give effect to the defendant's constitutional due-process rights, and had subsequently been re-appointed by the HJPC. In those circumstances, the Court was not persuaded that the judges had not been independent merely because they had been appointed by the HR.[12]

This reflects the special complexity of judicial independence in divided societies, particularly where international agencies are active in reconstructing the state. Being independent of ethnic loyalty may be as important as being independent of non-judicial institutions, and being independent of international agencies as important as being independent of national executives and legislatures. When the two international judges were first appointed, was important to have some judges who were not connected to the ethnic or national groups which had been fighting each other. International judges fitted the bill, and at that time only the HR had authority to appoint them to try war-crime cases. Upholding the appeal would have meant that the Constitution and the ECHR made it impossible to appoint for him to do so effectively. Such a decision would have been difficult to justify on humanitarian and political grounds. Whilst the HJPC's involvement could not logically establish that the judges were independent—the HR did not have to accept the recommendation of the President of the HJPC, and the HJPC's subsequent decision to re-appoint the judges could not retrospectively confer independence on them—it was appropriate for the Constitutional Court to treat the HJPC's contributions as

[10] Case No. AP-1785/06, *Appeal of Abdulhadim Maktouf*, decision of 30 and 31 March 2007, available at the website of the Constitutional Court of BiH, http://www.ustavnisud.ba.

[11] This obligation is imposed by Annex 10, Article IV to the Dayton Agreement and Art. II.8 of the Constitution of BiH.

[12] See paras. 41–43 of the Court's Decision.

relevant. As a matter of judicial politics, it made sense to regard them as a counter-weight to indications that the international judges might have been seen as structurally or personally dependent on the HR.

The Constitutional Court of BiH itself is the third tribunal in BiH to have international judges.[13] Three of the Court's nine judges are international judges, appointed by the President of the European Court of Human Rights after consulting the State Presidency. They must not be citizens of BiH or of any of the neighbouring states. The national judges are elected by the legislatures of the two sub-national Entities,[14] four by the Legislative Assembly of the Federation of BiH and two by the National Assembly of Republika Srpska (RS). The Constitution puts the three main demographic groups or 'constituent peoples', Bosniacs (Muslims), Croats (Roman Catholics) and Serbs (Serb Orthodox), in a privileged position.[15] By convention, the Federation's judges have been two Croats and two Bosniacs, while the RS has elected two Serbs.

This arrangement has made it difficult for judges to demonstrate their independence. There is a popular assumption that national judges, whose appointment depends partly on their support in the legislature of one of the Entities and partly on membership of one of the constituent peoples, should represent the interests of their entity or people. For international judges, the challenge has been to show that they are independent of the 'international community'. For some time it was assumed that the international judges would regard themselves as bound to support the initiatives and objectives of international organisations. Croats and Serbs perceived them as giving priority to the policy of the Bosniacs and the 'international community' to extend the power of the State at the expense of the Entities. This impression was heightened by a

---

[13] Constitution, Art. VI.3 pr.

[14] The Dayton Agreement and the Constitution recognized two partly self-governing Entities (the Bosniac-Croat Federation of BiH and the Serb-dominated Republika Srpska) operating below the level of the state; the border between them largely follows the front line of the fighting between their respective armies at the ceasefire in September 1995. Following international arbitration, the strategically crucial area around Brčko became a Special Administrative District, demilitarised and supervised by the international community. In 2009 the existence of the District was finally recognized in the Constitution of BiH through an amendment to Article VI.

[15] For example, Article V of the Constitution requires the State Presidency to consist of a Serb elected by the National Assembly of the RS and a Bosniac and a Croat elected by the Legislative Assembly of the FBiH. The European Court of Human Rights has held this to discriminate against Others contrary to Article 1 of Protocol No. 12 to the ECHR (*Sejdić and Finci* v. *Bosnia and Herzegovina*, Apps. Nos. 27996/06 and 34836/06, judgment of 22 December 2009, GC), whereas the Constitutional Court had been unable to say that Article V was unconstitutional by reason of its discriminatory impact since Article VI.3 pr of the Constitution requires the Court to 'uphold this Constitution', which a majority of the Court held prevented them from disapplying any part of it (Case No. AP-2678/06-2006, CC of BiH, accessible at http://www.ustavnisud.ba/eng/odluke/povuci_pdf.php?pid=67930).

tendency in the first mandate of the Court (1997–2002) for Bosniac and international judges to form a majority in politically controversial cases, outvoting the Croat and Serb judges.[16] Those divisions have become far less entrenched in the post-2002 Court.

Despite having been appointed by an outside authority and not being citizens of the State, the international judges, like the national judges, take an oath to uphold the Constitution, and have the same responsibilities, powers and salaries as national judges. The only differences of status between national and international judges are that only national judges are eligible to be President of the Court,[17] and the state has offered diplomatic status to the international judges when within BiH.

II. Political Misperceptions of the Judicial Function

Maintaining judicial independence requires a delicate balance between competing pressures which judges experience in various ways.

In a national court pressure is most likely to come from national officials, from interested parties to litigation, and from the press. A legislature or government may seek to make judges their partners, for example by suggesting that politicians, civil servants and judges share the same aims and values. This fundamentally misunderstands the role of the judiciary in a state based on the rule of law. Unlike political actors, people acting judicially must not be driven by public opinion when testing the legality or constitutionality of governmental or legislative activity.[18] An important part of their job is to rein in other branches of the state in order to preserve the conditions necessary for maintaining the rule of law. They cannot do that if they have been effectively coopted into partnership by other branches. The legitimacy of their judgments depends on them giving effect to the values of the rule of law, not on democracy or popularity. Without the rule of law, no democracy is possible. As Lord Ashdown, a former HR, has argued, in conflict-riven states like BiH, Afghanistan, Kosovo and Iraq democracy will never take hold until the minimum conditions for the rule of law (security against violent insurgency, fair and effective civil policing, an effective and independent judiciary from which

[16] Classic examples are the four partial decisions in the groundbreaking case No. U-5/98 on compatibility of the Entities' constitutions with the Constitution of BiH, decided respectively on 21 January, 18 February, 1 July and 18 August 2000, accessible at the Court's website, www.ustavnisud.ba/eng/odluke/

[17] Rules of the Constitutional Court of BiH, Art. 87 (a measure which establishes a rule that the Presidency rotates among the constituent peoples every three years).

[18] For English authority to this effect, see *R. v. Secretary of State for the Home Department, ex parte Venables* [1998] AC 407, HL.

corruption is excluded, executive respect for judicial decisions, equality before the law, and the equal subjection of all people and institutions, public and private, to the constitution and to ordinary laws) are in place.[19]

International judges in international tribunals may also be subject to pressures. Those appointed or nominated by their governments may find that governments see 'their' judge partly as a representative of the state, particularly in cases involving that state. In the European Court of Human Rights, where every High Contracting Party to the European Convention on Human Rights nominates a panel of potential judges from which the Parliamentary Assembly of the Council of Europe selects one, and the chosen judge (or an *ad hoc* judge chosen by the state concerned) sits in every case brought against his or her state, the sense of being a representative may be particularly strong, especially in judges from states (such as many former republics of the USSR) which have only a short history of respect for judicial independence in politically sensitive matters. Indeed, judges may regard themselves as representatives, and need no pressure to accept or even seek advice or instructions from the state's government as to how to decide particular cases.

Where (as in the case of the European Court of Human Rights before Protocol 14 to the ECHR came into force on 1 June 2010) judges may be re-elected but need to be re-nominated by the state, a judge's desire to keep open the door to re-election may strengthen the state's influence over 'its' judge. A government which dislikes a judge or thinks him or her too independent can block his or her re-election. This happened when the Communist government in Moldova refused to nominate Judge Tudor Pantîru, the Moldovan judge of the European Court of Human Rights from 1996 to 2001, for re-election. Judge Pantîru is highly principled and independent, and strongly anti-Communist. The Parliamentary Assembly of the Council of Europe, which elects the judges, failed to protect him. He was later forced to leave Moldova and emigrated to Romania.[20]

International organisations as well as governments may seek to influence a judge's decisions to favour its work and aims. This risk is heightened where international organisations exercise executive and legislative power in the state. This is becoming increasingly common during post-conflict reconstruction: the role of the HR in BiH is an example. The powers of these officials

---

[19] Paddy Ashdown, *Swords and Ploughshares: Building Peace in the 21st Century* (London: Orion Books, 2009), pp. 69–90.

[20] In 2002, Judge Pantîru became an international judge of the Constitutional Court of BiH and was, until the UN mandate expired on Kosovan independence, a Judge of the Supreme Court of Kosovo. He has since become a Romanian Member of Parliament, representing the Romanian diaspora.

under UN Security Council Resolutions adopted under Chapter VII of the UN Charter to preserve international peace and security have not been sufficiently constitutionalized. The UN Security Council does not regard itself as subject to any requirement to respect fundamental norms of international law, including human-rights standards, when acting under Chapter VII, and the officials to whom wide powers are granted do not regard themselves as subject to requirements of the rule of law, respect for human rights or independence of the judiciary which they expect of national authorities, or to local constitutional standards.[21] This can lead to collisions between international agencies and judges in national courts concerned to preserve their personal and institutional independence and autonomy.

III. The HR and Judicial Independence in BiH

Relying on their powers under Annex 10 to the Dayton Agreement and UN Security Council Chapter VII resolutions, successive HRs have imposed laws and suspended or dismissed people from public office ('removal decisions') when they were indicted by the International Criminal Tribunal for Former Yugoslavia (ICTY), or when, in his view, they obstructed the civilian implement of the Dayton Agreement. Targets have included judges, police officers, prosecutors, elected members of governmental bodies up to and including the level of the Presidency of BiH, and civil servants have been removed from office summarily, without a hearing or any appeal to or review by an independent tribunal. Decisions have barred people from holding public office in the future without the HR's permission, frozen bank accounts, and ordered seizure of travel documents.[22]

This has generated tension between the HR and the Constitutional Court. In September 2002, when nine new judges were about to be sworn in, the HR annulled the elections of the two judges from the RS on the ground that the RS National Assembly had not complied with the procedural requirements for protecting the vital interests of non-Serb constituent peoples under a Decision

[21] See David Feldman, 'The role of constitutional principles in protecting international peace and security through international, supranational and national legal institutions', in Claudia Geiringer and Dean R. Knight (eds.), *Seeing the World Whole: Essays in Honour of Sir Kenneth Keith* (Wellington, NZ: Victoria University Press, 2008), pp. 17–47.

[22] Removal decisions are accessible on the OHR website: www.ohr.int. They reached a peak in 2004, when Lord Ashdown as HR removed 78 people from office. In 2005 the number fell to three. Only four people have been removed in the last four years. In all, some 217 orders for removal, suspension and banning from office or annulling appointments or elections to offices have been made since January 1998 affecting 218 people including 13 judges.

of the HR of 11 January 2001.[23] This left the Court without any Serb judge, and so lacking legitimacy and unable to decide cases. The Deputy HR for Constitutional and Legal Affairs, H.H. Judge Ian Campbell, visited the Court to try to defuse tension, but the remaining judges regarded the annulment as an attack on the authority and independence of the Court. The HR, Lord Ashdown, then invited the judges of the Court to meet him. He explained his reasons, recognized the Court's difficulty, and predicted that replacement judges would be in place soon. However, eight months passed before the first judge from the RS could be sworn in,[24] and a further five months before the second judge was elected.[25]

The meeting between the HR and the judges helped to avoid a public confrontation, but the fact remained that there had been no constitutional basis for annulling the original election. The HR had deployed his extensive interpretation of his own powers in international law to outflank the Constitution's structural protection for the judge against political pressure. Unsurprisingly, the Court has tended to be suspicious of subsequent initiatives affecting the Court, fearing regular interference in their work without constitutional authority.

In practice, this has not happened. The international judges have from time to time been in touch with their ambassadors in Sarajevo to discuss the needs of the Court in the hope of securing international support for it. International agencies, including the OHR, have visited The Court. Informal contact between the Court and the Office of the HR often occurs at times when the agencies of the 'international community' have been worried about the course of events at the Court. For example, in 2004 the President of the Court, Judge Mato Tadić, was indicted on a charge of corruption.[26] He was eventually acquitted, but there was a question as to whether he should resign, be dismissed, or be suspended during the protracted trial process. Before the Court met to consider the matter, the HR telephoned one of the international judges at the Court to discuss it, but ultimately did not intervene.[27] In the event, the Court neither suspended

[23] *Decision annulling the appointment of two judges from the RS to the BiH Constitutional Court*, Decision of 16 September 2002, accessible at http://www.ohr.int.

[24] Prof. Dr. Simović, one of the two whose appointment the HR had previously annulled. At this point the Court was able to start deciding cases again.

[25] Judge Jovo Rosić, an experienced and distinguished judge, had not been elected the first time. He joined the Court in October 2003. Sadly he died in November 2006, a great loss to the Court, and was replaced by Judge Krstan Simić.

[26] For an account of this episode hostile to both Judge Tadić and the Court, see Matthew Parish, *A Free City in the Balkans: Reconstructing a Divided Society in Bosnia* (London: I. B. Tauris, 2010), pp. 166–9.

[27] The conversation was intercepted by a third party and leaked to a weekly news magazine, which published a story claiming that the judge had advised the HR to do nothing and the HR

nor dismissed Judge Tadić, as the State Prosecutor refused to provide any details of the charge against him, let alone the evidence supporting it. There was therefore nothing that could justify dismissal, and neither the Constitution nor the Rules of the Court then provided for suspending a judge.[28]

On another occasion, the Supervisor for the Special Administrative District of Brčko was concerned that the judicial system in Brčko was being brought to its knees by certain rulings of the Court. She issued an Order prohibiting the implementation of the rulings.[29] A member of the OHR's field office in Brčko met the international judges, who asked the Court to review the cases, and rulings of that sort were subsequently handled differently.

Then in September 2008 the Principal Deputy HR and Brčko Supervisor, Dr. Raffi Gregorian,[30] and the Head of the OHR's Legal Department Mr. Edouard D'Aost, approached international judges with a view to having a general discussion about the situation at the Court. The judges insisted on consulting their national colleagues, who agreed to the internationals judges could foster an understanding of the Court's difficult and delicate position and to invite them to visit the Court. However, by then the enthusiasm on the HR's side had passed, and the meeting never took place.

Other attempts to influence the Court have been more formal. For example, the HJPC has periodically tried to extend its supervisory role over judges to the Constitutional Court, which has even had to resist attempts to observe its deliberations.

Another recurring issue is whether the Court, as a constitutionally established body, is subject to ordinary Laws. This aspect of judicial independence is special to constitutional courts. The Court has argued that constitutional criteria for appointing its judges and their terms of service cannot be changed by Laws but only by constitutional amendment or the Court itself. All judges of the Constitutional Court, together with all judges and prosecutors

---

had followed that advice: *Slobodna Bosna*, 24 March 2005, 'Ashdown kapitulirao pred Ustavnim sudom' (Ashdown backs down before Constitutional Court). See also the letter from the judge and the response from Danka Savić, the journalist: *Slobodna Bosna*, 7 April 2005.

[28] Parish, *op. cit.*, n. 26 above, at pp. 96–7 accepts, perhaps too readily, *Slobodna Bosna*'s dramatic account of relations between the HR and the international judges, and suggests that the international judges saw a Law imposed shortly afterwards by the HR to reduce public-sector salaries insulted the international judges by reducing their salaries to the level of national judges of the Court. This is mistaken: the national and international judges had always had the same salaries.

[29] For an account of this episode from the point of view of the Supervisor and hostile to the Constitutional Court, see Parish, *op. cit.*, n. 26 above, pp. 165–174.

[30] One author closely involved in events has described him as having been at his appointment 'the most powerful international official in Bosnia and Herzegovina, as Schwarz-Schilling's announced departure [from the position of HR] had rendered him a lame duck.' Parish, *op. cit.*, p. 187. By September 2008 the new HR, Miroslav Lajčák, was in post.

in the State, were subject to a Law imposed by a Decision of the HR of 9 December 2005 enacting the Law on Salaries and Other Compensations in Judicial and Prosecutorial Institutions at the Level of BiH in order to improve the economic position of the State by cutting the salaries of public servants by about 15 per cent. Had the Law been a reaction to judicial decisions, or reduced the salary of an individual judge who had not been proved guilty of a disciplinary offence, it would have appeared to be an attempt to influence judicial decision-making. However, a general reduction of public-sector salaries, including those of judges, for economic reasons did not compromise judicial independence, though it might be said to have infringed the separation of powers and the special constitutional status of some institutions.

Nevertheless, the Law was prima facie unconstitutional, because Article IX.2 of the Constitution of BiH prohibits any reduction in the salary of a serving official. However, when members of the State Presidency challenged the Law before the Constitutional Court they did not raise that ground, because completely invalidating the Law would have damaged the state's economy. Instead they argued that the Law breached the Constitution in so far as it put the Constitutional Court on a par with judges of ordinary courts.[31] After long deliberation, the Court accepted that argument, and held the Law ineffective solely in its application to the Constitutional Court, since that was the ground which the applicants had advanced.[32] This avoided serious economic damage, but exempting the Court from financial sacrifices imposed (equally unconstitutionally) on other officials in the general public interest risked making the Court appear narrowly self-interested.

Political arms of the State have no lawful influence over dismissal of Judges of the Court. The Constitution provides that a Judge of the Court is to serve until reaching the age of 70 or, below that age, may resign or be removed for cause by consensus of the other Judges.[33] Of course, this does not mean that a decision to dismiss a Judge will be apolitical, but (leaving aside the possibility of extra-constitutional action by the HR) dismissal of judges is in the hands of the judges themselves. Yet the judges may come under political pressure from international or national agents.

---

[31] The Law was said to violate the commitment to the rule of law in Art. I.2 of the Constitution and the special status of the CC under Art. VI.

[32] Case No. U-6/06, Decision of 29th March 2008, accessible from the Court's website, www.ustavnisud.ba/eng/. Article 32 of the Rules of the Constitutional Court of BiH provides, 'During the decision-making procedure, the Constitutional Court shall examine only those violations that are stated in the request/appeal.' This provision can sometimes put the Court in a difficult position.

[33] Constitution of BiH, Art. VI.1/c).

On the only occasion on which a Judge of the Court has been dismissed by his fellow judges, the reasons included his political connections. A leaked letter from Judge Krstan Simić to the leader of the political party which he had previously represented in the RS National Assembly and Government seemed to show a continuing, undue closeness between them. Judge Simić also made working relations with other Judges exceptionally difficult by claiming at a press conference to have evidence that some of them were corrupt but refusing to produce his evidence to the Court, the State Prosecutor, or the press. After a hearing, his fellow judges unanimously dismissed him for failing to uphold the reputation and dignity of the Court and his own reputation and dignity as a Judge.[34]

Whilst it was possible that the leaking of the letter and complaints against him (some of which were dismissed by the Court) had been motivated by political or personal antagonism, the public interest in the authority and impartiality of the judiciary necessitated his dismissal, especially when it became clear that he could not substantiate but would not withdraw his imputations against colleagues. The Court had to perform its constitutional role of protecting its own independence from political pressure, as well as its reputation and ability to function.

IV. Constitutional Review and International Agencies

The HR's claim that, as an international agency with UN backing and powers derived exclusively from international law, he is not subject to the jurisdiction of national tribunals has given rise to tension with the Court in cases where the HR has intervened with people's legal and constitutional rights. The Court distinguishes between individual, executive decisions such as removing people from office, where the Court accepts that he is not subject to constitutional review,[35] and decisions imposing laws of general application, where that law (but not the HR's decision imposing it), is subject to constitutional review like any other law in the State's legal order.[36]

However, the Court became increasingly concerned about the lack of due process for people deprived of offices or livelihoods,[37] and therefore shifted its

---

[34] Rules of the Constitutional Court of BiH, Arts. 94.2 and 101.1, line 5 and 101.2; see Decision on Dismissal of 8th May 2010.

[35] Case No. U-37/01, decision of 2 November 2001, accessible at www.ustavnisud.ba/eng/

[36] See Case No. U-9/00, Decision of 3 November 2000, accessible at www.ustavnisud.ba/eng/

[37] See *Opinion on the Constitutional Situation in BiH and Powers of the HR* adopted at 62nd plenary session of the Venice Commission (Venice, 11–12 March 2005), accessible at the Venice Commission's website, http://www.venice.coe.int/.

attention from the HR to the state, holding that it owed a positive obligation under the Constitution to take reasonably practicable steps to protect the rights of its citizens against violation by international agencies. As State authorities seemed to have made no effort to intervene with the HR to protect the applicant's due process rights, the Court held that the State had violated the applicant's right to an effective remedy before a national authority under Article 13 of the ECHR.[38]

The Court was careful not to challenge the immunity of the HR, but held that such people retained their constitutional rights and focussed on the responsibility of the State towards its citizens. It was hoped that the decision would encourage the HR, Christian Schwartz-Schilling, and the State Presidency to discuss ways of securing a fair hearing for people threatened with dismissal by the HR. Both were sympathetic to the decision.[39] But Schwartz-Schilling came under intense pressure from American colleagues to reverse his stance, and in March 2007, shortly after the Court's reasons were published, he made an Order.[40] It started promisingly by requiring the State Presidency to 'address to the High Representative, as Chair of the Steering Board of the Peace Implementation Council, all matters raised in [the Court's] Decision that ought to be considered by the international authorities referenced in the said Decision.' However, it went on to threaten that anyone else who sought to develop processes for reviewing decisions of the HR would be regarded as undermining the civilian implementation of the Dayton Agreement (a thinly veiled threat to remove such people from office). The Order also deprived all courts of BiH of jurisdiction over any case in which any doubt might be cast on the effectiveness of any Decision of the HR, and prohibited the initiation of such cases without the HR's consent (which of course would not be given).[41]

At first sight this appears to be a somewhat defensive reaction.[42] However, the process of conducting the case may have had some effect, regardless of the actual decision. It was known that the Court was finding the constitutional

---

[38] Case No. AP-953/05, *Appeal of Milorad Bilbija and another*, decision of 8 July 2006, accessible at the Court's website, http://www.ustavnisud.ba. Rights in the ECHR apply directly in BiH and have priority over all other law: Constitution, Art. II.2.

[39] See Parish, *op. cit.*, n. 26 above, p. 249 at n. 29 for Schwartz-Schilling.

[40] Parish (an inside observer), *op. cit.*, p. 249, n. 29, writes, 'The pressure exerted upon him that would make him sign a decision on 23 March 2007 exactly contrary to the sentiments he had previously expressed, can only be imagined.'

[41] *HR's Order on the Implementation of the Decision of the Constitutional Court of BiH in the Appeal of Milorad Bilbija et al. No. AP-953/05*, of 23 March 2007, accessible on the OHR's website, www.ohr.int.

[42] *Kalinić and Bilbija* v. *Bosnia and Herzegovina*, Apps. Nos. 45541/04 and 16587/07, admissibility decision of 13th May 2008, accessible at the website of the European Court of Human Rights, http://echr.coe.int/echr/en/hudoc.

issue difficult to resolve.[43] The uncertainty had complemented the urgings of international institutions, including the Venice Commission, to review removal decisions, which were thought to have been made by an unfair procedure and, in many cases, on questionable evidence, and Schwarz-Schilling's own inclinations.

It is interesting that, soon after Mr. Bilbija lodged his appeal with the Constitutional Court on 6 April 2005, Lord Ashdown as HR issued his first three decisions lifting bans on named individuals holding public office on 5 May 2005.[44] Between then and 8 July 2006, when the Court decided the *Bilbija* case, Lord Ashdown and his successor as HR, Christian Schwartz-Schilling, made a further 41 decisions lifting bans, and even more significantly made three decisions of general application limiting earlier decisions so as no longer to prevent those subject to them from taking positions in the civil service at all levels (28 November 2005), public enterprises and institutions and other posts funded from the public revenue (4 April 2006), and political parties (7 July 2006), unless the person concerned had been dismissed from office for non-compliance with the International Criminal Tribunal for Former Yugoslavia (ICTY).[45]

This might be coincidence, but it could reflect an effort to forestall the judgment and show that the HR was reviewing bans of his own accord. After the Court's judgment but before its publication, Schwarz-Schilling made six more decisions lifting bans before issuing his Order reacting formally to the

---

[43] Parish, *op. cit.*, n. 26 above, p. 96, draws attention to the long gap between the date of the decision of the Constitutional Court (8 July 2006) and the date when the text of the decision was published (March 2007). On p. 218 at n. 28, says (rightly) that the delay 'is far too long to ascribe to ordinary Balkan incompetence', and goes on to speculate about various more or less far-fetched conspiracy theories. In fact, the Court had formally agreed on the dispositive part of the decision (i.e. the order of the Court) on 8 July 2006, but (as one of the international judges had explained to his Ambassador in Sarajevo in the summer of 2006) had found the constitutional and international law issues extremely complex. The Court accordingly spent a long time deliberating on the reasoning part of the decision, which had to be agreed before publication. Parish also suggests at p. 97 that a cynic might think that the decision was the international judges' 'revenge' for the reduction of their salaries to national levels by the HR in 2005 'it being manifest from the text of the decision that its author was one of the international judges on the Court'. This suggestion is misconceived, both because the national and international judges had always received the same salary (see n. 28 above), and because the final version of the reasoning was a composite to which many judges had contributed.

[44] There had been one previous decision lifting a ban. On 19 July 1999 Carlos Westendorp, then HR, lifted the ban from public office he had imposed on Dragan Čavić when removing him from office as a member of the RS National Assembly on 8 October 1998.

[45] *Decision of 28 November 2005 Limiting the Scope of the Ban from Public Office in the Removal Decisions Issued by the High Representative* (Lord Ashdown); *Decision of 4 April 2006 Further Limiting the Scope of the Ban from Public Office in the Removal Decisions Issued by the High Representative* and *Decision of 7 July 2006 Lifting the Ban from Office within Political Parties in the Removal Decisions Issued by the High Representatives* (Christian Schwartz-Schilling). All are accessible at the HR's website, http://www.ohr.int.

judgment. Thereafter he lifted only two more bans, and his successor Miroslav Lajčák issued none. Since Valentin Inzko became HR in March 2009, he has lifted a further 13 banning orders while making two new removal decisions.[46] However, there is still no procedure which would meet due-process requirements, so work remains to be done.

V. Lessons from BiH

Involving international judges in municipal courts can be useful. In divided societies, where national judges tend to be identified in the public eye with the national group or people to which they belong, the region from which they come, international judges can help to demonstrate the court's subjective and objective independence of state institutions and political parties. They can also mediate between national interests, help to ensure that national tensions do not dominate judicial decision-making and protect the integrity of their court against pressure from international agencies, and provide comparative law expertise during deliberations. On the other hand, they may be perceived as having connections to the 'international community' which themselves call their independence in question.

Deep social divisions make the notion of independence highly complex. It must take account of relationships between different communities, between national authorities, and between international agencies and the state. The independence of judges—both national and international—in such systems must be pursued simultaneously on several different social and political planes, requiring different forms of protection, some of which may require independence in another plane to be compromised.

For example, several of the judges whom Carlos Westendorp as HR suspended from office in 1998 were suspected of having manipulated the law for the advantage of members of their constituent people. Their alleged failings amounted to a lack of independence on the social and national planes. But the HR's method of dealing with it made judges generally feel threatened by the HR himself, another threat to independence originating on the international plane.

If a legal system is to negotiate a course between the many threats, judges, other national authorities and international agencies all need to be clear about the institutions, groups or individuals from which and purposes for which judges need to be independent, and conscious of how their activities, undertaken with the best of intentions, can impinge on each other's independence.

[46] Last checked 25 March 2011. Thus 63 banning orders have been entirely lifted, slightly less than 30% of those made so far, and the impact of the others has been much reduced except in relation to people who were dismissed for non-compliance with the ICTY.

CHAPTER FOURTEEN

THE IMPACT OF THE ECHR JURISPRUDENCE ON THE AUSTRIAN PRACTICE IN THE FIELD OF JUDICIAL INDEPENDENCE

*Walter Rechberger**

I. Introduction

There is increasing acknowledgment that an independent judiciary is a main pillar for a democratic society, because the protection of human rights depends at least partly on a robust, fair, and independent judiciary.[1] This independence can take various forms across different jurisdictions and systems of law.[2] But the same principle always applies, namely the protection of human rights is dependent on the guarantee that judges will be free and will be perceived to be free to make impartial decisions based on the facts and the law in each case, and to exercise their role as protectors of the constitution, without any pressure or interference from other sources, especially the executive.[3]

Domestically, constitutions of many countries stipulate that judges should handle their cases in an independent manner without any interference exercised in their business, either by the other branches of government or by any individual.[4] At the international level there are various international instruments that deal with judicial independence.[5]

---

* Walter H. Rechberger, born in 1945, is Full Professor (Ordinarius) of Law at the Vienna University School of Law and head of the Department of Civil Procedure (Institut für Zivilverfahrensrecht). He is member of the Council of the International Association of Procedural Law and holds the degree of an honorary doctor of the University of Pècs, Hungary.

1 Shetreet, "The normative cycle of shaping judicial independence in domestic and international law: The mutual impact of national and international jurisprudence and contemporary practical and conceptual challenges" (2009) *Chicago Journal of International Law* 275 at 277.

2 Sherif/Brown, "Judicial independence in the Arab World", available online at http://www.pogar.org/ publications/judiciary/sherif/jud-independence.pdf (accessed 30.7.2010), 3.

3 Office of the High Commissioner for Human Rights/International Bar Association, *Human rights in the administration of justice* (2003), p. 113.

4 eg Articles 82–94 of the Austrian Federal Constitution.

5 Universal Declaration of Human Rights; European Convention for the Protection of Human Rights and Fundamental Freedoms; International Covenant on Civil and Political Rights; The American Convention on Human Rights; African Charter on Human and Peoples' Rights; Charter of Fundamental Rights of the European Union; In addition to these legal sources, ethical standards have been adopted by professional associations such as judges', prosecutors' and lawyers' associations.

Under public international law states are obliged to establish a system of government which can assure that international guaranteed rights and freedoms are maintained, which means that they have a duty to erect impartial and independent tribunals to decide over human rights violations.[6] Article 6 of the European Convention for the Protection of Human Rights and Fundamental Freedoms (ECHR) entitles everyone to a fair and public hearing within a reasonable time by an independent and impartial tribunal. Therefore the European Court of Human Rights (ECtHR) and its Commission play a major role to ensure the independence of the judiciary in states which ratified the Convention.

Austria joined the Council of Europe in 1956 as its fifteenth Member State, after it had regained its full sovereignty by the State Treaty of Vienna[7]. Because of the accession to the Council of Europe Austria signed and ratified the ECHR and its first additional Protocol of 1952.[8] After its ratification, the Convention was officially published in the Austrian Federal Law Gazette (BGBl) without any comment on its legal status. Since a major controversy arose very soon afterwards, as to whether the ECHR formed part of constitutional law, the legislator finally clarified the status of the ECHR as constitutional law through an amendment to the Constitution in 1964.[9] Austria was the first state to incorporate the ECHR fully into its constitutional legal order. Therefore the rights laid down in the convention have the same relevance as the original catalogue of fundamental rights in the Austrian Federal Constitution and the Basic Law of the State on the General Rights of Citizens. Therefore legislation has to observe and give effect to the rights and freedoms of the ECHR and additionally all courts and administrative authorities are obliged to apply the ECHR in all proceedings before them, which means that they have to interpret the law in a manner which does not infringe the rights laid down in the ECHR.[10] The fact that Austria was the first state to incorporate the ECHR fully into its constitutional legal order created a high level of awareness within Austrian society concerning the ECHR itself as well as its legal and practical implications. Consequently, a relatively large amount of applications was – and is still – lodged against Austria. Most of the applications so far have concerned the

[6] Office of the High Commissioner for Human Rights/International Bar Association, *Human rights in the administration of justice* at 118.

[7] Staatsvertrag betreffend die Wiederherstellung eines unabhängigen und demokratischen Österreich, BGBl Nr 152/1955.

[8] Konvention zum Schutze der Menschenrechte und Grundfreiheiten, BGBl Nr 210/1958.

[9] According to BVG BGBl Nr 59/1964 the ECHR has constitutional rank in Austria.

[10] Walter/Mayer/Kucsko-Stadlmayer, *Bundesverfassungsrecht,* 10th ed. (2007) para 1333.

Articles 5 and 6, some Articles 3, 8, 10 and 11 as well as Article 1 of the First Protocol.[11]

Hence, the ECHR has also a prominent place in Austrian high court jurisprudence.[12] Especially the Austrian Constitutional Court (VfGH) has displayed almost unreserved readiness to follow the European Commission's and ECtHRs' interpretation of the ECHR.[13] Thus, many areas of Austrian legislation over the years have been influenced by the ECHR and the case law of the Strasbourg institutions. However, government and parliament still remain reluctant to observe and entirely fulfil the obligations specified in the ECHR.

II. Decisions of the ECtHR Concerning Judicial Independence

The ECHR expressly recognises the importance of judicial independence and impartiality. The right to a fair trial in Article 6 para 1 ECHR guarantees everyone an entitlement to have cases heard by an independent and impartial tribunal established by law. The right applies equally to criminal cases and cases concerning civil rights and obligations.

1. *Independent and Impartial*

For a tribunal to be independent, it must function independently of the executive and the legislature and base its decisions on its own free opinion about facts and legal grounds.[14] There must be guarantees to enable the court to function independently.[15] Therefore regard must be had to the manner of appointment of the court's members and their term of office. As far as the latter requirement is concerned, it is not necessary that the judges have been appointed for life, provided that they cannot be discharged at will or on

[11] See Tretter/Liegl/Buchinger/Steinkellner, "Strasbourg Court Jurisprudence and Human Rights in Austria: An overview of Litigation, Implementation and Domestic Reform", available online at http://www.juristras.eliamep.gr/wp-content/uploads/2008/09/austria.pdf (accessed 30.7.2010).

[12] Oberhammer, „Einige vermischte Beobachtungen à propos ‚EMRK und Zivilverfahren'" in Renzikowski (ed), *Die EMRK im Privat-, Straf- und Öffentlichen Recht* (2004) pp. 21–38 at 23.

[13] See for instance VfGH 3.12.2009, B 1008/07; VfGH 2.7.2009, B 559/08.

[14] ECtHR, 27.6.1968, *Case of Neumeister* v. *Austria*, no. 1936/63, para 24; ECtHR, 16.7.1971, *Case of Ringeisen* v. *Austria*, no. 2614/65, para 95.

[15] ECtHR, 2.9.1998, *Case of Lauko and Kadubec* v. *Slovakia*, no. 26138/95, paras 63–65 and 56–58, The administrative authorities who had been entrusted with the prosecution and punishment of minor offences, appeared not to be independent of the executive because of the manner of appointment of the officers of the local and district offices and the lack of guarantees against outside pressures.

improper grounds by the authorities.[16] The absence of a formal recognition of the irremovability of judges during their terms of office does not imply a lack of independence as long as it is recognized in fact and the other necessary guarantees are present.[17] Also there must be safeguards against outside pressure. A tribunal that is otherwise separate from the executive is not independent where it seeks and accepts as binding Foreign Office advice on the meaning of a treaty that it has to apply; in such a case it has surrendered its judicial function to the executive.[18] With regard to other bodies, in *Campbell and Fell* v. *UK* the ECtHR indicated the considerations it takes into account when assessing independence: "In determining whether a body can be considered to be independent – notably of the executive and of the parties to the case – the Court has had regard to the manner of appointment of its members and the duration of their term of office, the existence of guarantees against outside pressures and the question whether the body presents an appearance of independence."[19]

For impartiality it is required that the tribunal is not biased with regard to the decision to be taken, does not allow itself to be influenced by information from outside the court room, by popular feeling, or by any pressure whatsoever, but bases its opinion solely on objective arguments on the ground of what has been put forward at the trial.[20]

Even a semblance of dependence must be avoided. In testing whether a tribunal or judge has been prejudiced, the Court makes a distinction between a subjective and an objective approach to impartiality. The subjective approach refers to the personal impartiality of the members of the tribunal involved. This impartiality is presumed as long as the contrary has not been proved.[21] The objective approach refers to the question of whether the way in which the tribunal is composed and organised, or a certain coincidence or succession of functions of one or more of its members, may give rise to doubt as to the impartiality of the tribunal or that member.[22] If there are justified reasons for such doubt, even if subjectively there is no concrete indication of bias of the person in question, this already amounts to an inadmissible jeopardy of the

[16] Implicitly ECtHR, 16.7.1971, *Case of Ringeisen* v. *Austria*, no. 2614/65.

[17] ECtHR, 28.6.1984, *Case of Campbell and Fell* v. *United Kingdom*, nos. 7819/77, 7878/77, para 80; ECtHR, 26.2.2002, *Case of Morris* v. *United Kingdom*, no. 38784/97, para 68.

[18] ECtHR, 24.11.1994, *Case of Beaumartin* v. *France*, no. 15287/89, para 38.

[19] ECtHR, 28.6.1984, *Case of Campbell and Fell* v. *United Kingdom*, nos. 7819/77, 7878/77, para 78.

[20] Wildhaber, "Judicial Impartiality Under the European Convention on Human Rights", available online at http://www.concourt.am/hr/ccl/vestnik/2.12–2001/wildhaber-eng.htm (accessed 30.7.2010).

[21] ECtHR, 1.10.1982, *Case of Piersack* v. *Belgium*, no. 8692/79, paras 30–32.

[22] ECtHR, 26.2.2002, *Case of Morris* v. *United Kingdom*, no. 38784/97, para 58.

confidence which the court must inspire in a democratic society.[23] The fear that the tribunal or a particular judge lacks impartiality must be such that it can "be held to be objectively justified"; consequently, the standpoint of the accused on this matter, although important, is not decisive.[24]

In the *Sramek Case*, where a member of the court was hierarchically subordinate to one of the parties to the suit, the ECtHR held: "Litigants may entertain a legitimate doubt about his independence. Such a situation seriously affects the confidence which the courts must inspire in a democratic society."[25] However, strictly speaking, the latter aspect no longer refers to the independence, but to the impartiality of the tribunal.

There is a close inter-relation between the guarantees of an independent and impartial tribunal.[26] Accordingly there is a certain degree of interchange between the language of the tests used by the Strasbourg Court concerning independence and impartiality. A tribunal that is not independent of the executive is likely to be in breach of the requirement of impartiality also in cases to which the executive is a party. Likewise, a tribunal member who has links with a private party to the case is likely to be in breach of both requirements. For this reason, the ECtHR commonly considers the two requirements together, using the same reasoning to decide whether the tribunal is independent and impartial.[27] In respect of both requirements, there is a breach not only where there is proof of actual dependence or bias (subjective test), but also where the facts raise a legitimate doubt that the requirement has been met (objective test). These tests can be deduced from Lord Hewart C.J.'s famous maxim that "... it is of fundamental importance that justice should not only be done, but should manifestly and undoubtedly be seen to be done".[28]

The principles established in the ECtHR's case law with regard to the notions of independence and impartiality apply to professional judges as well as to lay judges and jurors.[29] Where a complaint concerns lack of impartiality on the part of the decision-making body, the concept of full jurisdiction demands that the reviewing court not only considers the complaint but also has the

---

[23] ECtHR, 1.10.1982, *Case of Piersack* v. *Belgium*, no. 8692/79, paras 31.

[24] ECtHR, 24.5.1989, *Case of Hauschildt* v. *Denmark*, no. 10486/83, para 48; ECtHR (Grand Chamber), 6.5.2003, *Case of Kleyn and Others* v. *Netherlands*, nos. 39343/98, 39651/98, 43147/98 and 46664/99, para 194.

[25] ECtHR, 22.10.1984, *Case of Sramek* v. *Austria*, no. 8790/79, para 42.

[26] Office of the High Commissioner for Human Rights/International Bar Association, "Human rights in the administration of justice" at p. 119.

[27] See ECtHR, 22.6.1989, *Case of Langborger* v. *Sweden*, no. 11179/84, para 32.

[28] *R.* v. *Sussex Justices, ex parte McCarthy* [1924] 1 K.B. 256 at 259.

[29] Kühne in *Internationaler Kommentar zur Europäischen Menschenrechtskonvention* (April 2009) Art 6 ECHR para 290.

power to quash the impugned decision and either take a new decision or remit the case for a new decision by an impartial body.[30]

Many of the decided cases on the meaning of an independent tribunal concern administrative or disciplinary tribunals, in which context the Strasbourg authorities have not imposed standards as high as might be applied to the ordinary, classic courts of law. This is particularly true of such matters as the duration of office of tribunal members and their protection from outside pressures.

In the *Ringeisen Case* the ECtHR held that the Regional Commission could be regarded as a tribunal as it was independent of the executive and also of the parties. The latter element, however, refers in fact not to the independence but to the impartiality of the court. The ECtHR added that the members of the Regional Commission had been appointed for five years and the proceedings before it did offer the necessary guarantees. A comparable line of reasoning was developed in the *Langborger Case*: "In order to establish whether a body can be considered independent, regard must be had to the manner of appointment of its members and their term of office, to the existence of guarantees against outside pressures and to the question whether the body presents an appearance of independence."[31]

2. *Tribunal Established by Law*

The prescription that the tribunal must be established by law implies the guarantee that the organisation of the judiciary is not left to the discretion of the executive, but is regulated by law. The phrase covers not only the legal basis for the very existence of a tribunal. In the opinion of the Commission the organisation and functioning of the tribunal must also have a legal basis.[32] The ECtHR left the issue undecided in the *Piersack Case*, but in the *Posokhov Case* it held that the requirement also covers the composition of the bench in each case.[33] But the tribunal need not be "a court of law of the classic kind, integrated within the standard judicial machinery of the country".[34]

---

[30] ECtHR (Grand Chamber), 28.5.2002, *Case of Kingsley* v. *United Kingdom*, no. 35605/97, para 58.

[31] ECtHR, 22.6.1989, *Case of Langborger* v. *Sweden*, no. 11179/84, para 32; See ECtHR, 28.9.1995, *Case of Procola* v. *Luxembourg*, no. 14570/89, para 43; ECtHR, 22.11.1995, *Case of Bryan* v. *United Kingdom*, no. 19178/91, para 37; ECtHR, 26.2.2002, *Case of Morris* v. *United Kingdom*, no. 38784/97, para 73.

[32] European Commission, 13.5.1981, *Case of Piersack* v. *Belgium*, Report of the Commission, B.47 (1986) at 23.

[33] ECtHR, 4.6.2003, *Case of Posokhov* v. *Russia*, no. 63486/00, para 39.

[34] ECtHR, 28.6.1984, *Case of Campbell and Fell* v. *United Kingdom*, nos. 7819/77, 7878/77, para 76; ECtHR, 22.10.1984, *Case of Sramek* v. *Austria*, no. 8790/79, para 36; ECtHR, 24.2.1995, *Case of McMichael* v. *United Kingdom*, no. 16424/90, para 80.

For the notion of tribunal it is essential that there exists a power to decide matters "on the basis of rules of law, following proceedings conducted in a prescribed manner",[35] and that the judicial body has "full jurisdiction, including the power to quash in all respects, on questions of fact and law, the challenged decision".[36]

A tribunal was defined in the *Belilos Case* as follows: "... a tribunal is characterized in the substantive sense of the term by its judicial function, that is to say determine matters within its competence on the basis of rules of law and after proceedings conducted in a prescribed manner. It must also satisfy a series of further requirements – independence, in particular of the executive; impartiality; duration of its members' terms of office; guarantees afforded by its procedure – several of which appear in text of Article 6 para 1 itself".[37]

This definition is overly comprehensive, insofar as it contains organisational and procedural elements that, as the Court notes, are included or may be subsumed under other guarantees in Article 6 para 1 ECHR. As to the functional element, an important feature of a tribunal is that it must be competent to take legally binding decisions: the capacity to make recommendations or give advice (even if normally followed) is not enough.[38] A tribunal's decisions must also not be subject to being set aside by a non-judicial body and the government must not be empowered by law not to implement them, even though the power is never exercised. The fact that a body has other functions does not in itself prevent it from being a tribunal when exercising its judicial function.

In the *Schmautzer Case* the Court held that the appeal from the administrative authorities to the Administrative Court did not satisfy the requirements of Article 6 ECHR, since the latter did not have full jurisdiction to review and quash the decision of the administrative body both on questions of fact and of law.[39] There, the Court took into consideration that the Administrative Court was sitting in proceedings that were of criminal nature for the purposes of the Convention.[40]

---

[35] ECtHR, 22.10.1984, *Case of Sramek* v. *Austria*, no. 8790/79, para 36 and the report of 8.12.1982 in this case, at 31.

[36] ECtHR, 21.05.2003, *Case of Västberga Taxi Aktiebolag and Vulic* v. *Sweden*, no. 36985797, para 93; ECtHR, 24.2.994, *Case of Bendenoun* v. *France*, no. 12547/86, para 46; ECtHR, 23.10.1995, *Case of Schmautzer* v. *Austria*, no. 15523/89, para 36.

[37] ECtHR, 29.4.1988, *Case of Belilos* v. *Switzerland*, no. 10328/83, para 64.

[38] ECtHR, 23.10.1985, *Case of Benthem* v. *Netherlands*, no. 8848/80, para 40.

[39] ECtHR, 23.10.1995, *Case of Schmautzer* v. *Austria*, no. 15523/89, para 6; ECtHR, 20.9.2000, *Case of Mauer* v. *Austria*, no. 35401/97, para 16.

[40] ECtHR, 22.11.1995, *Case of Bryan* v. *United Kingdom*, no. 19178/91, paras 34–47; ECtHR, 18.1.2001, *Case of Chapman* v. *United Kingdom*, no. 27238/95, para 124.

III. The Impact of the ECHR on the Austrian Legal System

Article 6 of the ECHR has raised serious problems for Austria; some typical for a continental legal system. The Austrian legal system is characterized by the distinction between private and public law. The separation between judicial and administrative authorities and the division of competences among courts and administrative bodies is based on this distinction. Interpreted in the context of this legal tradition, Article 6 ECHR was initially understood as a guarantee, that courts would decide all matters of civil and penal law. The public law area was thought to be completely unaffected.

To safeguard its administrative penal laws, Austria declared a reservation to the ECHR stating that the provisions of Article 5 of the Convention would be applied so as not to interfere with the measures for the deprivation of liberty prescribes in the laws of Administrative Procedure, BGBl 1950/172, subject to review by the Administrative Court and Constitutional Court as provided for in the Austrian Federal Constitution. The fact that the reservation was declared only with respect to Article 5 ECHR was no doubt due to the fact that criminal charges under Article 6 ECHR were at the time of accession understood as referring only to penal proceedings in court. This was soon perceived to be an error. Therefore both the VfGH and the European Commission of Human Rights extended the reservation to encompass Article 6 ECHR.[41]

For a long time the reservation was applied not only to those administrative penalties already in force when the ECHR was ratified, but also to all subsequent penalties which were similar to the earlier ones or based on them.

However, due to growing criticism from scholars and the ECtHR case law the VfGH gradually extended the scope of the application of Article 6 ECHR.[42] For example in the *Apothekerkammer Case*[43] the VfGH placed disciplinary punishments which are autonomously imposed by professional organisations within the scope of Articles 5 and 6 ECHR.

To escape the problems raised by the case law of the Strasbourg organs and the VfGH concerning the application of Article 6 ECHR for Austrian administrative penal law, an amendment to the Federal Constitution Act of 20 November 1988[44] created a new type of authority; independent administrative tribunals

---

[41] VfGH Slg 5021/1965, Slg 9158/1981; European Commission, 3.3.1983, complaint no. 998/80, 32 *Decisions and Reports* 150.

[42] Nowak, "The Implementation of the European Convention on Human Rights in Austria" in Mikkelsen (ed), *The Implementation in National Law of the European Convention on Human Rights* (1989) 28 at 32.

[43] VfGH Slg 11506/1987.

[44] BGBl 1988/685.

(UVS).[45] These tribunals are to rule on administrative offences though only once the administrative stages of appeal have been exhausted.[46] The members of these tribunals, who are required to have legal training, are to be appointed for at least six years.[47] The reform mainly followed the case law of the ECtHR, specifically the ruling in the *Ringeisen Case*. In *Ringeisen*, the ECtHR held that a tribunal for the purposes of Article 6 ECHR, may include authorities which, based on the criteria set forth in the Austrian Federal Constitution, essentially constitute administrative rather than judicial bodies. Such collegial administrative bodies and their members must, however, be independent from the executive branch. Civil servants may only serve in such administrative organs if they are appointed for a period of at least 3 years and if they are not subject to any instructions from administrative bodies.

The principle innovation of this amendment is that a procedure before an UVS has been interposed between the decision of the highest administrative instance and the Austrian Administrative Court (VwGH). The UVS will not decide cases in first instance, but only after the district administrative authority and the office of the federal state have heard the case.[48] At the same time, however, their decisions are not final. Further appeal to the VwGH against the decision of the UVS will still be possible.[49] The UVS's power of review are not confined to questions of law as is that of the VwGH. In fact, a UVS has the power to quash in all respects, on questions of fact and law, the challenged decision.[50] Along with the creation of these tribunals, a comprehensive amendment of the Code of Administrative Procedure was adopted in 1990. The aim was to organise proceedings before the tribunals in conformity with Articles 5 and 6 ECHR (including full cognition with regard to questions of fact and law, publicity and publication of decisions).

Another great impact on the Austrian legal system had the case-law of the ECtHR concerning civil rights and obligations. This was and probably still is problematic for the Austrian legal system, because the ECtHR interprets the civil law concept of Article 6 in an autonomous and very extensive way.[51] This interpretation contradicts the already stated perception, that the public law area would be left unaffected by the ratification of the ECHR.

---

[45] Wiederin, „VStG-Novelle 1990 und EMRK", *JAP 1990/91* 70 at 70; Walter/Mayer/Kucsko-Stadlmayer, *Bundesverfassungsrecht* para 1530.

[46] Art 129a para 1 Austrian Federal Constitution.

[47] Art 129b Austrian Federal Constitution.

[48] It may be provided by statute that in particular cases the decision of a district administrative authority may be directly challenged before on of the UVS.

[49] Hengstschläger, *Verwaltungsverfahrensrecht*, 3rd ed. (2005) para 530.

[50] Thienel, *Verwaltungsverfahrensrecht*, 4th ed. (2006) 290–294.

[51] Walter/Mayer/Kucsko-Stadlmayer, *Bundesverfassungsrecht* para 1524.

According to the case-law of the Strasbourg Court the guarantees of Article 6 must be met, if the contents of the claim or complaint are of a legal pecuniary nature and refer to an infringement of rights which have legal pecuniary implications.[52] As soon as such a claim or obligation is brought Article 6 ECHR applies, regardless of the competent decision making body. Therefore the ECtHR also applied the Convention in administrative proceedings concerning civil rights and obligations.[53]

Nevertheless, the ECtHRs broad interpretation of the civil rights concept had for a long time no impact on the Austrian legal system. As a rule, any decision of an administrative authority affecting individual rights was ultimately subject to review by the VwGH, which can review decisions only on questions of law. The VfGH considered it beyond any doubt that Austria wished to retain its established and approved system of administration under comprehensive VwGH review without any major changes.

In the *Miltner Case*[54] the VfGH discussed the problems arising from the extensive interpretation of the ECtHR. Taking the ECtHR judgments in the *König, Sporrong and Lönnroth and Benthem Cases* as a basis, the VfGH concluded that according to the ECtHR case law all decision making powers of administrative authorities had to be transferred to tribunals within the meaning of Article 6 ECHR. The Court noted that this would compel Austria to restructure its legal structure and took the view that Austria could neither have intended to accept such consequences when it acceded to the ECHR nor have foreseen that the ECtHR would develop such a broad interpretation of civil rights. In the view of the VfGH the ECtHRs extensive interpretation of the civil rights concept in the Convention is a case of manifest judicial extension of law for which there may be sound reasons, but which imposes obligations on states which they neither intended nor agreed to accept.[55] Also, the VfGH raised the question of whether "the transfer of constitutional law-making to an international organ would not constitute a total revision of the Federal Constitution which requires a plebiscite of the whole federal population". The VfGH thus raised the possibility that the Austrian accession to the

---

[52] ECtHR, 16.7.1971, *Case of Ringeisen* v. *Austria*, no. 2614/65, para 94; ECtHR, 28.9.1995, *Case of Procola* v. *Luxembourg*, no. 14570/89, para 39.

[53] Grabenwarter, *Europäische Menschenrechtskonvention* (2009) p. 288; ECtHR, 23.10.1995, *Case of Gradinger* v. *Austria*, no. 15963/90, paras 42-45.

[54] VfGH Slg 11500/1987.

[55] The VfGH based itself in this connection on the separate opinion of the Austrian judge at the ECtHR, Franz Matscher in the *König Case* (ECtHR, 28.6.1978, *Case of König* v. *Germany*, no. 6232/73).

ECHR was unconstitutional, a situation which could be rectified only through a plebiscite.

Consequently, the Strasbourg and the Constitutional Court have developed different approaches concerning the interpretation of the term civil right and obligation. The Constitutional Court differentiates between the core aspects of civil law, the rights and duties of individuals inter se, and those areas where civil rights are only affected as a consequence, in which the result of the procedure must be decisive for the civil right concerned.[56] The latter includes the cases of public interference in private legal circumstances which refer to the status of the individual with regard to the public. The VfGH therefore developed a twofold concept of civil rights: civil rights in the narrower and broader sense.[57] Civil rights in the narrower sense would be decisions on "rights and obligations of citizens among themselves". According to the VfGH such decisions, without exception ought to be taken by a tribunal. In contrast, for decisions affecting the private legal sphere only in a broader sense review by a court, in other words review by the VwGH would suffice.[58]

In practice these differential approaches to the interpretation of civil rights and obligations, are not nearly as problematic as on first sight, because in the course of time the legislator has extended the jurisdiction of the UVS to many proceedings which could concern civil rights and obligations.[59] Therefore, also proceedings before the Austrian administrative authorities are mainly in accord with the Convention.

Last but not least it has to be mentioned that – besides these statements to the system of administrative tribunals – the Austrian civil procedure corresponds with the guarantees for judicial independence contained in the ECHR. The Austrian federal constitution explicitly provides for the judicial independence. The Federal Constitutional Law stipulates in Article 87 that judges are independent in the exercise of their judicial office. Judges are assigned cases in advance for a certain period stipulated by the law on the organisation of the courts. The removal of a matter allocated to the jurisdiction of a judge is governed by Article 87 para 3 of the Federal Constitutional Law. That provision requires a decree of the judiciary's administrative authorities and provides that this can only be done if the judge is prevented from the discharge of her responsibilities or she is unable to cope with her duties within a reasonable time due

---

56 VfGH 10.3.1988, B874/87.

57 Walter/Mayer/Kucsko-Stadlmayer, *Bundesverfassungsrecht* para 1528.

58 VfGH 13.12.1988, B1450/88.

59 Oberhammer, „EMRK und Zivilverfahren" in Renzikowski (ed) at p. 25.

to the extent of the duties. Nonetheless some suggestions for an internal control of the judicial system (e.g. by a High Judicial Council) following international developments exist, in order to improve the structural independence from the other state powers and strengthen the confidence of the people in the judicial activity.[60]

[60] Reissner, „Richterliche Unabhängigkeit, Tendenzen in Österreich und Europa", *RZ 2003* at pp. 41; Reissner, „Der Rat der Gerichtsbarkeit – ein Mittel zur Sicherung einer unabhängigen Rechtsprechung", *RZ 2004* at pp. 4; Aisthleitner, „Richter – Gerichtsbarkeit; Individuelle Unabhängigkeit – Institutionelle Autonomie", *ZUV 2005* at p. 48.

CHAPTER FIFTEEN

THE INDEPENDENCE OF INTERNATIONAL ARBITRATORS

*HE Markus Buechel**

The Independence of Arbitrators is a general principle in arbitration that an arbitrator must act and must be seen to act fairly between the parties, and the arbitrator must be and remain impartial and independent.[1] The independence of an arbitrator is an essential feature of this judicial process. Arbitrators are often closely involved in the market that appoints them, which arise the issues of them being partial, biased, pre-disposed and being interested in the outcome of the arbitration. The long-standing norms that no one should be a judge in his own cause and that justice should be seen to be done apply equally to international arbitration.

Reliance on arbitration as an institution by the international business community is characterized by three principal advantages, e.g., expedition, inexpensiveness and finality. An international arbitration award is more international than a decision of many national courts. It is viewed as a "medium disempowering national laws to be displaced by alternative legal regimes." This international characterization of arbitration as a separate legal regime presupposes that international arbitration institutions try to meet the expectations of the international business community for independent and neutral tribunals. Otherwise, the confidence of the parties in the arbitration system would be seriously dented.[2]

The principle of independence of arbitrators is laid down by the Arbitration Act, No 11 of 1995.[3] Section 15 (1) of the said Act requires arbitral tribunals to

---

* Markus Buechel is a senior advocate in the principality of Liechtenstein. He was elected to the Liechtenstein Government as Minister of Finance in 1999 and subsequently as the country's Minister of Foreign Affairs in 1992. He was then voted Prime Minister of the Principality of Liechtenstein in a general election during 1993. Since his retirement from public office he is active as a senior advocate. HE Mr Buechel hosted in Vadouz the second International Conference of judicial Independence December 2007.

[1] Doak Bishop & Lucy Reed, "Practical Guidelines for Interviewing, Selecting and Challenging Party-Appointed Arbitrators in International Commercial Arbitration" (1998) 14 ARB. INT'L 395.

[2] For a detailed analysis of the value of public confidence in the system of justice, see: Shetreet, "Judicial Independence and Accountability: Core Values in Liberal Democracies", *in* H.P. lee (ed.) *Comparative Judiciaries* (to be published 2011, Cambridge University Press).

[3] Arbitration Act, No 11 of 1995 (PARLIAMENT OF THE DEMOCRATIC SOCIALIST REPUBLIC OF SRI LANKA).

act in an impartial manner. This requirement is further emphasized by section 15 (2) whereby the arbitral tribunal is required to give all the parties an opportunity of presenting their respective cases. The objective of this provision is to ensure that all parties to the arbitration are treated in a fair and an equal manner.

Given the ethical considerations and the objectives of international arbitration as an international judicial process, to preserve its sanctity in the international domain, a set of rules have been established. These rules now govern the conduct of arbitrators in different institutional and *ad hoc* settings. In accordance with these rules of arbitrations and code of conduct of arbitrators, national laws of major international arbitration avenues set down laws and legal principles which make it imperative that in international arbitration, an arbitrator is independent.

All major international arbitral institutions require arbitrators appointed under the rules of their institutions to be impartial and independent. The International Chamber of Commerce [rule 7.2 deals with disclosure],[4] London Court of International Arbitration [rule 5.3 requires arbitrators to make a declaration][5] and International Centre for Settlement of Investment Disputes [rule 6 relates to the declaration by arbitrators][6] are among the well-known institutes that specifically require arbitrators to be independent and impartial. UNCITRAL arbitration rules require independence and impartiality from arbitrators and article 9 require arbitrators to disclose any facts which may make him or her unsuitable for appointment as an arbitrator.

A clearer example of the nature of independence required has been established by the International Chamber of Commerce (ICC), which requires each arbitrator to declare whether there exists any past or present relationship, direct or indirect, with any of the parties. The requirement applies also to relations with any of their counsel, whether financial, professional, social or other kind and whether the nature of such relationship is such that disclosure is called for considering the arbitrator's independence in the eyes of the parties.[7] Independence is determined by applying both objective and subjective tests, but more of subjective in nature.

---

[4] ICC Rules of Arbitration, The Arbitral Tribunal, article 7, rule 7.2 (1998), available online at: http://www.iccwbo.org/court/arbitration/id4093/index.html#article_7 (Visited: Oct 23, 2010).

[5] LCIA Arbitration Rules, Formation of the Arbitral Tribunal, article 5, rule 5.3(1998), available online at: http://www.lcia.org/Dispute_Resolution_Services/LCIA_Arbitration_Rules .aspx#article5 (Visited: Oct 23, 2010).

[6] ICSID CONVENTION, regulation and rules, Establishment of the Commission, rule 6 (2006), available online at: http://icsid.worldbank.org/ICSID/ICSID/RulesMain.jsp (Visited: Oct 23, 2010).

[7] ICC Rules of Arbitration, note 4 above.

The issue of independence of party-appointed arbitrators has been the subject of a long debate. Most of the debate arose from the American jurisprudence on impartiality of the party-appointed arbitrators.[8]

The root of the debate is that in many instances, party-appointed arbitrators are known to the parties their fees is derived from the party, they may have been briefed by the parties as to the issues and evidence in arbitration and also other issues arise out of *ex parte* communication and then it boils down to the question of whether they are qualified to sit as an arbitrator, or they may be viewed as an advocate for a client.

This debate also involves the query as to the need for a three-member panel with one party having a right to nominate an arbitrator. It is true that the role of a party appointed arbitrator is seen as a balance of power of the parties in the tribunal, but in some types of arbitration, their engagement with their "party" suggests that they are working for the party appointing them. This brings their role as an independent and impartial judge of the dispute into scrutiny. Sometimes, in deliberations, they may press hard for the cause of their appointer to influence the award.

In *Tracomin*,[9] it has been noted that such an arbitrator may act as a channel of communication between the party and the tribunal, or even that the arbitrator may advise the parties on some issues in the proceedings. It is common in some "idiosyncratic types" of arbitrations involving commodity trades, but not other arbitrations.

Moreover, the debate opens up the issue as to the standard required of an arbitrator generally. An examination of the major institutional and the *ad hoc* arbitration rules reveals that the UNCITRAL Rules,[10] ICC Rules,[11] and the LCIA Rules[12] make no separate provisions regarding the standard of independence required of a party appointed arbitrator. Accordingly, it has been noted in the context of ICC that the requirement of independence is a reaffirmation of the European concept that a party-appointed arbitrator should not act as the nominating party's agent or representative, thus embracing a requirement of impartiality. Similar standard has been adopted by the IBA's rules of Ethics for

---

[8] See, for example: Murray L. Smith, "Impartiality of the Party-Appointed Arbitrator" (1990) 6 ARB. INT'L 320; Aldo Berlinguer, "Impartiality and Independence of Arbitrators in International Practice" (1995) 6 AM. REV. INT'L ARB. 339, at pp. 340.

[9] *Tracomin S.A. v. Sudan Oil Seeds Co. Ltd.*, [1983] 1 All E.R. 129, 1983 Com. L.R. 17 (Q.B. Div'l Ct.).

[10] United Nations Commission on International Trade Law, arbitration rules (2010), available online at: http://www.uncitral.org/pdf/english/texts/arbitration/arb-rules-revised/pre-arb-rules-revised.pdf (Visited: Oct 23, 2010).

[11] ICC Rules of Arbitration, note 4 above.

[12] LCIA Arbitration Rules, note 5 above.

International Arbitrators.[13] In England and France, the standard has not been lowered regarding a party-appointed arbitrator.

On the other hand, under the AAA Code of Ethics, the non-neutral party appointed arbitrator is not expected to observe the same standard of conduct as the neutral third arbitrator and that the party appointed arbitrator may be predisposed to the nominating party and the disclosure obligation is not that stringent.[14] However, this difference in the standard has been expressed to be of purely domestic in nature and "is not applied in international commercial arbitration."[15]

This view is subject to be revisited in the light of the US Court of Appeal (11th Circuit) decision in *Sunkist Soft Drinks v. Sunkist Growers*,[16] where the party-appointed arbitrator conferred with the party, its counsel and witnesses and therefore, helped the party to prepare its case. The Court of Appeal held that predisposition by a party-appointed arbitrator is not in itself sufficient to vacate him or any award, unless he does not act in good faith and with integrity and fairness.

This case exemplifies what Martin Hunter and Jan Paulsson calls drawing a line between positive bias and general sympathy towards the appointing party.[17] While the later would be commonplace in modern arbitration, but if the former is reached, the arbitrator could either be disqualified or removed or the award be vacated, depending on the 'degree' of the affinity. This line has not yet been decisively drawn in international arbitrations.

In international contracts it is common to find provision for more than one arbitrator. Often it is desirable to have panels of three arbitrators in such contracts so that each party is able to nominate an arbitrator. However even in international contracts if the amount involved is small then it will be more cost effective to have a sole arbitrator than having a panel of three arbitrators which results in considerable cost. At the time of drafting the arbitration clause legal practitioners cannot envisage the size of the dispute that may arise in the future and therefore it is not easy to decide whether there should be a sole arbitrator or a panel of three arbitrators. In view of this the best would be to have a panel

[13] International Bar Association, Rules of Ethics for International Arbitrators, Available online at: http://www.ibanet.org/Publications/publications_IBA_guides_and_free_materials.aspx (visited: Oct 23, 2010).

[14] American Arbitration Association, Code of Ethics, CANON VII.

[15] Philippe Sands, Ruth Mackenzie, and Yuval Shany, *Manual on International Courts and Tribunals* (Butterworths 1999).

[16] *Sunkist Soft Drinks, Inc. v. Sunkist Growers, Inc.*, 10 F.3d 753 (11th Cir. 1993).

[17] Hunter, M and I. Paulsson, "A Code of Ethics for Arbitrators in International Commercial Arbitration" (1985) 13 Arbitration 153.

of three in international contracts but also to reserve the option of having a sole arbitrator if the dispute turns out to be a relatively minor one.

Equally important is the manner of the selection of the arbitrators. In international arbitrations it is important for at least one of the arbitrators to be familiar with the law of the place of arbitration. If all the arbitrators are unfamiliar with the law of the situs there is the risk of them making an award which may not be recognized by the courts of the country where the arbitration took place and therefore may become unenforceable even in other jurisdictions. Therefore it is recommended that at least one of the arbitrators should be knowledgeable in the law of the situs also the chairman of the panel of three should preferably have experience in the practice of arbitration, and writing awards, etc to facilitate the enforcement of the award.

It is common for constituent instruments to provide that no two members of a tribunal may possess the same nationality. The WTO deals with the issue of national representation differently. Citizens of parties to the dispute are not permitted to serve on a panel, unless the parties agree otherwise.

Parties are expected to nominate independent and impartial arbitrators. If a party nominates an arbitrator who is deemed not to be impartial or independent, the other party has the right to challenge the nomination. Most institutions have a provision which requires the arbitrators to disclose the existence of any circumstances which may cast a doubt on his impartiality or independence. Article 5.3 of the LCIA rules and ICC rules art. 7.2 require such disclosure by the arbitrators.[18]

The Iran United States Claims Tribunal is comprised of three arbitrators appointed by Iran, three arbitrators appointed by the US and three arbitrators appointed by agreement between the six party appointed arbitrators. Each three-member Chamber of the Tribunal consists of one US appointed arbitrator, one Iranian appointed arbitrator and one of the arbitrators appointed by agreement between Iran and the US.

In *Bengston v. Federal Republic of Germany*[19] the Commission noted that: "National judges of judicial bodies of a mixed nature hold a special position inasmuch as any grounds asserted for their disqualifications must have a special weight in order to become effective."

In *Amco Asia Corp. v. Indonesia*[20] the two arbitrators considering a challenge to the third arbitrator held that "no distinction can and should be made, as to

---

[18] ICC Rules of Arbitration, article 7.2, note 4 above; LCIA Arbitration Rules, article 5.3, note 5 above.

[19] *Bengston v. Federal Republic of Germany*, [1959] 28 ILR 549 (Arbitral Comm'n on Property, Rights and Interests in Germany).

[20] *AMCO Asia Corp. v. Indonesia*, [1986] ICSID Case No. ARB/81/1, 25 I.L.M. 1439.

the standard of impartiality, between members of an arbitral tribunal, whatever the method of their appointment."

It is important not only to agree on the initial appointment of the arbitrators but also to provide for the appointment of a substitute arbitrator should a vacancy arise. Often it is provided for vacancies to be filled in the same manner as the original appointment was made. Usually provision will be made for any such appointment but where an arbitrator resigns without the consent of the arbitral tribunal at the instigation of the party that appointed him in a move to delay the arbitration there is rarely any provision found to cater to such a situation. Even most institutes do not provide for such an eventuality but ICSID arbitration rules (11 (2) (a))[21] have made provision whereby in the event of such a resignation the replacement will be made by the appointing authority and not the party who appointed him earlier.

Arbitral institutions have attempted to simplify the problem of having to deal with multi-party arbitrations. LCIA rules (art. 13(1) (c))[22] provide for multi-party arbitrations. The ICC in an attempt to deal with this situation has proposed that the International Court of Arbitration of the ICC should appoint all the arbitrators without parties to a multi-party arbitration making the nominations. In this manner the ICC is trying to avoid the potential problems of international recognition and enforcement of awards.

As to removal from office, evidently this depends on the relevant instrument of the court or tribunal. A member of the ICJ may only be dismissed from the Court by a unanimous decision of the other members of the Court that the member has ceased to fill the "required conditions". A judge of the ECHR may be removed if a two-thirds majority of the other judges decides by that that judge has ceased to fill the required conditions. An ICC judge may be removed by a two-thirds majority of States Parties in the event that the judge has been found to have committed serious misconduct, a serious breach of their duties or is unable to exercise the functions required by the ICC Statute. By contrast, the Prosecutor of the ICC may be removed by an absolute majority of the States Parties. A decision to disqualify an ICSID arbitrator may be taken by the two other arbitrators.

The constituent instruments generally distinguish between the removal of a judge from a tribunal altogether and the ineligibility of a judge to sit in a particular case. In *Prosecutor v. Sessay*[23] Justice Robertson was disqualified from

[21] ICSID CONVENTION, rules (11 (2) (a)), note 6 above.

[22] LCIA Arbitration Rules, rules (art. 13(1) (c)), note 5 above.

[23] The Special Court For Sierra Leone, case 15: *Prosecutor v. Sessay, Kallon and Gbao* (RUF CASE) (2004).

acting in all matters involving Revolutionary United Front (RUF) defendants on the basis of apprehended bias arising from various statements made in his book *Crimes Against Humanity*. The defence initially sought Justice Robertson's permanent removal from the Appeals Chamber in relation to all cases (i.e. not just those involving the RUF).

CHAPTER SIXTEEN

JUDICIAL INDEPENDENCE AS AN INDICATOR OF INTERNATIONAL COURT EFFECTIVENESS: A GOAL-BASED APPROACH

*Yuval Shany**

I. Introduction

In a provocative article that was published in 2005 in the California Law Review, Eric Posner and John Yoo argued that there is no evidence that independent international courts are more effective than dependent ones. In fact, they suggested that the reverse may be true, that is, independent courts could be less effective than their dependent counterparts.[1] According to Posner and Yoo, international courts may fulfill a useful function – providing disputant parties with information about facts or legal norms, which may help them resolve their differences; however, the effectiveness of such courts – which in Posner and Yoo's eyes is measured by usage rates, compliance rates and the overall success of the overarching treaty regime – may be negatively correlated to judicial independence:

> Conventional wisdom holds that independence at the international level, like independence at the domestic level, is the key to the rule of law as well as the success of formalized international dispute resolution. We argue, by contrast, that independent tribunals pose a danger to international cooperation because they can render decisions that conflict with the interests of state parties. Indeed, states will be reluctant to use international tribunals unless they have control over the judges. On our view, independence prevents international tribunals from being effective.[2]

Laurence Helfer and Anne-Marie Slaughter published a response article shortly thereafter, in which they challenged the hypothesis and methodology employed

---

* Hersch Lauterpacht Chair in Public International Law, Faculty of Law, Hebrew University of Jerusalem. The research for this article was undertaken with the support of a European Research Council Starting Grant for Frontier Research and with the help of Ms Sharon Avital. I thank the rest of the members of my research team on the effectiveness of international courts – Mr. Thorbjorn Bjornsson, Mr. Rotem Giladi, Ms. Erin Gray- Goldbarsht, Ms. Sigall Horovitz, Mr. Gilad Noam, Ms. Sivan Shlomo and Ms. Yael Vias – for their useful comments and suggestions.

[1] Eric A. Posner and John C. Yoo, 'Judicial Independence in International Tribunals', 93 *Calif. L. Rev.* (2005) 1, 72.

[2] *Ibid*, at 7.

by Posner and Yoo, as well as their ultimate conclusions.[3] According to Helfer and Slaughter, the most effective international courts are independent ones; thus, Posner and Yoo's theoretical conjectures cannot be reconciled with real empirical data, as well as with states' actual preferences. This is hardly surprising since:

> 1) … agreeing to an independent tribunal signals the depth of a state's commitment to a particular international regime in a way that makes it more likely that it will secure the benefits of that regime; and (2) … independent judges - while certainly less bound by political concerns than their dependent counterparts and more able to base their decisions on legal principle - are hardly "lone rangers." They are influenced by a host of structural, political and discursive constraints that states can manipulate ex ante and ex post, as well as by the pressures of professional and personal socialization within a global judicial community.[4]

My purpose in this chapter is to try and contribute to the debate on the relationship between judicial independence and international court effectiveness, by applying to it a model for international judicial effectiveness I have developed elsewhere.[5] In doing so, I hope to illustrate some of the problems attendant to the "broad brush" positions taken by Posner and Yoo (and, at times, also by Helfer and Slaughter). Consequently, I posit that the proper questions we should be discussing is not whether judicial independence is generally conducive to international court effectiveness (a correlation which Ponser and Yoo fail to prove in a statistically meaningful manner, and Helfer and Slaughter do not explicitly claim);[6] but rather, more nuanced ones, such as: Which international courts are better served by judicial independence? What level of actual independence should courts strive to attain? What image of independence should they seek to project?

Note that this contribution focuses exclusively on the relationship between judicial independence – understood hereby as the protection of the decision-making power of judges and other senior court officials (such as prosecutors and registrars) from control and interference by other actors,[7] and international

---

[3] Laurence H Helfer and Anne-Marie Slaughter, 'Why States Create International Tribunals: A Response to Professors Posner and Yoo', 93 *Calif. L. Rev.* (2005) 899.

[4] *Ibid*, at 955. For a response by Posner and Yoo to these arguments, see Eric A. Posner and John C. Yoo, 'Reply to Helfer and Slaughter', 93 *Calif. L. Rev.* (2005) 957.

[5] See Yuval Shany, 'Assessing the Effectiveness of International Courts: Can the Unquantifiable Be Quantified?' (September 1, 2010). Hebrew University International Law Research Paper No. 03-10. Available at SSRN: http://ssrn.com/abstract=1669954 (an updated version of the article will be published in 2012 in the American Journal of International Law).

[6] See Posner and Yoo, *supra* note 1, at 54.

[7] See e.g., B.J. van Heyst, 'The Netherlands', in *Judicial Independence: The Contemporary Debate* (Shimon Shetreet and Jules Deschênes, eds,. 1985) 420, 241 ("judicial independence means that in deciding cases that come before them, members of the judiciary are free from interference by the executive and legislative powers, political and social pressure groups, litigants and fellow members of the judiciary").

court effectiveness. I will not address the related question of the relationship between international court effectiveness and judicial impartiality – understood hereby as an unjustifiable judicial preference affecting judicial decisions in a manner prejudicial to one or more of the parties to litigation.[8] Still, since the concepts of judicial independence and judicial impartiality are closely related and inter-connected, much of the analysis conducted below could be relevant to a discussion of international court effectiveness centered on judicial impartiality.

II. The Effectiveness Model

A leading definition of organizational effectiveness found in the social sciences literature suggests that an effective organization is one that accomplishes its goals.[9] This approach, often referred to in the literature as the 'rational system' approach, requires the identification of organizational goals at a preliminary stage of the analysis aimed at evaluating the level of organizational effectiveness. In a previous research paper, I have discussed some of the challenges of applying the 'rational system' approach to the study of international courts: the existence of multiple constituencies, the ambiguity and elasticity of judicial goals, and the long-term nature of their impact – to name just a few.[10] As a result, I limited the goal-based analysis I undertook to one set of goal-setters (the mandate providers that create courts and fund and monitor their continued existence – typically states and international organizations); at the same time, I proposed considering alongside goal-attainment other performance indicators developed in the social sciences literature, such as cost-effectiveness (the ratio between resource investment and outcomes) and efficiency (the overall utility of the operation of the court in question, in light of the positive or negative side-effects generated by its operation).[11]

Since the study of international court effectiveness relates not only to performance-evaluation, but also assists in institutional design and in assessing the desirability of structural and procedural reforms, the effectiveness model I

[8] See e.g., Ofer Raban, *Modern Legal Theory and Judicial Impartiality* (2003) 1.

[9] See e.g., Chester I. Barnard, *The Function of the Executive* (1938/1968 reprint) 20; James L. Price, 'The Study of Organizational Effectiveness', (1972) 13 *Sociological Quarterly* 3, 3–7; Amitai Etzioni, *Modern Organizations* (1964), at 8; Jeffrey Pfeffer, *Organizations and Organization Theory* (1982), 41; Raymond F. Zammuto, *Assessing Organizational Effectiveness* (1982), 12.

[10] Shany, *supra* note 5, at text accompanying notes 32–51.

[11] *Ibid*, at text accompanying notes 40–44. Some of these evaluation methods are captured by the 'open systems' approach also used in the study of organizational effectiveness. See e.g., W. R. Scott and G. F. Davis,? *Organizations and Organizing: Rational, Natural, and Open Systems Perspectives?* (2006), 31.

have canvassed does not merely assess the relationship between judicial goals and outcomes; it also strives to understand the operative dynamics within international courts, which facilitate or hinder certain outcomes. Consequently, the effectiveness model identifies three 'operational categories' – judicial structure (or input), process and outcome, and posits that through 'reverse engineering' one may understand the contribution of specific structural or procedural aspects to judicial performance.[12] In the same vein, understanding the relationship between judicial structure, process and outcome, may enable us to use structural and procedural indicators (such as the number of cases submitted to the court, or actual adherence to due process standards) in order to better assess, predict and shape judicial outcomes.

Two immediate implications of the effectiveness model for the debate over the relationship between judicial independence and international court effectiveness are as follows: a) Since the concept of judicial effectiveness is an elusive one, unequivocal conclusions as to whether higher degrees of judicial independence promote or hinder effectiveness should be viewed with some apprehension; b) Since international courts have distinct goals and operate in unique institutional and political settings, the need for judicial independence may vary across legal contexts. In other words, the attainment of different goals by different courts may support, at different points in time, different levels of judicial independence.

1. *Judicial Independence as a Structural Feature*

As described below, the effectiveness model distinguishes between structural, procedural and outcome features in the operation of international courts.[13] The structure of the court represents the total powers or capacities it possesses, which may be employed in order to serve its functions and attain its goals.[14] The court's structure thus reflects its overall potential. By contrast, process features pertain to the manner in which the court's 'assets' are employed – that is, the effort invested by the court in the course of its operation.[15] The combination of structure and process produces outcomes – specific impacts on the court's external environment (e.g., the resolution of a conflict, compliance with a norm, increased cooperation),[16] which can then be assessed and evaluated.

---

[12] Shany, *supra* note 5, text accompanying notes 64–70.
[13] Pamela S. Tolbert and Richard Hall, *Organizations: Structures, Processes and Outcomes* 10th ed., (2009), 17.
[14] Shany, *supra* note 5, at text accompanying note 65.
[15] *Ibid*, at text accompanying note 66.
[16] *Ibid*, at text accompanying note 95.

How could judicial independence fit in such a model? Judicial independence is, first and foremost, a notion and an image (or a myth) generated, in turn, by a series of norms or practices governing or relating to the operation of international courts. For instance, Mackenzie and Sands identify two salient independence-generating or enhancing factors, whose application in the context of international courts raises certain challenges:[17] (a) judicial selection-processes;[18] and (b) possible interference in the work of the court by political organs.[19] Posner and Yoo allude to other independence-related features, such as the fixed terms of judges, their protection from salary decreases and the existence of compulsory jurisdiction (as opposed to *ad hoc* jurisdiction).[20] Slaughter and Helfer have identified yet additional factors, such as willingness to decide against governments,[21] and limits on the employment of judges by the parties.[22] For the sake of completion, one may consider other relevant independence-generating or enhancing factors, such as the court's freedom to determine its internal administration, the confidentiality of its deliberations, the elaboration of judicial service conditions in legally binding instruments, the conferment of diplomatic privileges and immunities upon international judges, and the court's adequate budgeting.[23]

Most, though certainly not all, of the factors listed above are structural in nature and pre-date the court's actual operation (they govern its method of establishment and initial powers conferred thereupon and not the manner in which the court's powers are actually exercised). Specifically, these factors regulate the powers possessed by the court and its judges (or, more frequently, render it more difficult for other actors to restrict such powers or influence their application), and advance an institutional design, which enshrines freedom from outside interference.

For example, robust criteria for judicial selection may limit the ability of states and international organizations to nominate judges whose decisions they would then control; the diplomatic privileges and immunities conferred upon judges limit the ability of the host state, in which the court is seated, to harass and pressurize judges; and the availability of adequate budgets minimizes

[17] Ruth Mackenzie and Philippe Sands, 'International Courts and Tribunals and the Independence of the International Judge', 44 *Harv. J. Int'l L.* (2003) 271.

[18] *Ibid,* at 276–279. For a more recent study on the topic, see Ruth Mackenzie *et al, Selecting International Judges: Principle, Process and Politics* (2010).

[19] Mackenzie and Sands, *supra* note 17, at 283–284.

[20] Posner and Yoo, *supra* note 1, at 7.

[21] Laurence R. Helfer and Anne-Marie Slaughter, 'Toward a Theory of Effective Supranational Adjudication', 107 *Yale L.J.* (1997) 273, 313.

[22] *Ibid,* at 346.

[23] See The Burgh House Principles on the Independence of the International Judiciary (2004), http://www.ucl.ac.uk/laws/cict/docs/burgh_final_21204.pdf.

the risk that the court's financial sponsors would try to interfere in its judicial decisions through explicit or implicit threats of withdrawing financial support if certain outcomes were to be reached. Thus, it looks as if judicial independence constitutes an intangible 'asset' (or, according to Posner and Yoo, an intangible liability) – the capacity to operate without interference, accompanied by a reputation for having such a capacity. Such a reputation may be enhanced or eroded by the court's actual operations (see below).

Understanding key aspects of judicial independence as structural features implies that studying the relationship between judicial independence and international court effectiveness should focus considerable attention on court structures – the formal and informal norms that shield the courts and judges from outside control and interference, and the different resources that the court has at its availability to resist attempts for control and interference. In the same vein, to the extent that judicial independence constitutes a structural feature, attempts to modify the level of independence may warrant a structural reform – i.e., changes in the court's institutional design.

2. *Judicial Independence as a Process Feature*

While most of the independence-creating or enhancing factors listed above relate to the court's structure – i.e., to its capacity to act independently, some of the mentioned factors are more closely related to the process taking place before the court– that is, the actual exercise of the court's powers (or, actual interferences by other actors in judicial procedures). This may be the case, for example, if there are indications of attempts by political bodies to interfere with judicial decisions or influence the allocation of specific judges to specific cases,[24] or if confidentiality of judicial deliberations is actually breached in a manner that causes judges to become more susceptible to outside pressure.[25]

Identifying process factors affecting independence would require a different focus of study than a study concentrating on structural factors – focusing less on legal texts and available resources, and more on observation of actual practices of interaction between the court and other actors. Reform proposals directed at independence-related process features could be made at two levels: changes in actual practices, or modification of the structures that have facilitated, or at least did not prevent the practices in need of reform.

---

[24] See, for instance, the discussion of the possible interference by the WTO General Counsel in the *Amicus Curiae* admissibility procedures in the *Asbestos* litigation before the WTO Appellate Body in Mackenzie and Sands, *supra* note 17, at 284.

[25] For the link between confidentiality of deliberations and judicial independence, see Helfer and Slaughter, *supra* note 21, at 327.

3. *Outcome-Related Factors*

Although judicial independence pertains to the conditions governing the decision-making process, and does not concern the outcomes of this process *per se*, studying the actual outcomes generated by the international court in question may provide us with important insights on judicial independence. Most significantly, the court's record in generating decisions running contrary to the interests of powerful states and other constituencies may be indicative of its independence or lack thereof. Such record of clashes with power would also, most probably, impact the court's independent image. Thus, a 'feedback loop' is created in the course of the court's operation (a chain of operative categories involving structure-process-outcome-structure):[26] For example, indications of actual interference in judicial decision making (a process indicator), or a series of controversial decisions issued by the court deemed as catering to the interest of powerful states (an outcome indicator) may suggest that the court in question is less than fully independent, or that an informal structure of dependency has been created. Consequently, the perceived value of the court's independence 'assets' decrease – a development that may impact its ability to attract new cases or generate compliance (states possessing high levels of control or influence over the court may react differently in this regard from states possessing low levels of control or influence) – and modifies its goal-attainment potential. In the same vein, a solid record of 'speaking law to power' may increase the court's independent image – a development that is likely to affect its goal-attaining capabilities and the quality of its outcomes.

In addition, the relations between the different operative categories comprising the effectiveness model are such that one can evaluate more advanced stages of the operative category-chain in order to better understand the nature and quality of antecedent links in the same chain. Hence, evaluation of outcomes may offer us valuable insights on the quality of process, and evaluation of outcomes and process may serve as indicators for the adequacy of the structures that have been put in place.

III. The Relationship between Judicial Independence and Effectiveness

After presenting the effectiveness model and discussing the role of judicial independence within it, I will now move to offer a number of observations

[26] For a comparable discussion of 'feedback loops' in the operation of international courts, see Alec Stone Sweet, *The Judicial Construction of Europe* (2004) 55.

on the relationship between judicial independence and international court effectiveness. As already noted, the effectiveness model requires a highly nuanced, essentially court-specific assessment of effectiveness – an effort which exceeds the limits of the present contribution. Still, by referring to a number of generic goals of international courts I hope to illustrate some of the ways in which judicial independence may be positively or negatively correlated to effectiveness. In a subsequent section I will use as short case studies two occasions in which the institutional independence of the ICTY and ICTR was put to the test, and attempt to use the typology introduced in previous sections in order to analyze and assess the Tribunals' performance in those instances.

1. *The Goals of International Courts*

My research into international judicial effectiveness posits that most international courts are created in order to advance the following four principal overarching goals (referred to in my work as 'ends' or 'ultimate ends').[27] Such goals provide us, *inter alia,* with a critical angle to assess judicial performance and to establish the contribution of judicial independence towards judicial goal attainment:

a) Promoting compliance with the governing international norms (primary norm-compliance)
b) Resolving and preventing international disputes and problems (dispute resolution or problem-solving)
c) Contributing to the operation of related political institutions and cooperative regimes (regime support)
d) Legitimizing associated international norms and institutions (regime legitimization)

Of course, these ends are formulated in an open-ended manner and are non-exclusive in nature; they can also accommodate a plethora of more specific goals (such as deterrence, norm-internalization, normative development, etc.), and support even more abstract ultimate ends (such as increasing legal security or political integration). Moreover, the ends listed hereby overlap with one another and are often inter-related (e.g., regime legitimization, for instance, promotes norm-compliance and *vice versa.*). As a result, one specific feature of judicial structure or process may simultaneously advance more than one end.

[27] See e.g., Yuval Shany, 'Compliance with Decisions of International Courts as Indicative of their Effectiveness: A Goal-Based Analysis', Selected Papers from ESIL Proceedings, Vol. 3 (forthcoming in 2011) at text accompanying notes 19–20.

At the same time, some ends may be in tension with one another, and specific attributes that promote one end may adversely affect the realization of another (for example, appointing diplomats as judges may detract from the quality of the court's norm interpretation function, but improve the prospects of generating a settlement capable of definitively resolving the dispute in question).[28]

Acknowledging the multi-faceted nature of the goals of international courts should encourage us to take with some degree of skepticism Posner and Yoo's assertion that dependent international courts may be more effective than independent ones. Posner and Yoo may be right in observing that dependent judges may be more closely attuned to the interests of the disputing parties than independent judges, and that, as a result, dependent judges may be better situated to facilitate a judicial settlement which would not be resisted by the parties (Posner and Yoo argue that independent judges may sacrifice the parties' dispute resolution needs in order to advance the normative goals of the broader legal and political regime).[29] Still, the premise they rely on – i.e., that international courts are primarily dispute resolution bodies, is rather dubious. In fact, most international courts operating in the field of economic relations (e.g., the WTO dispute settlement mechanism, the European Court of Justice, and the numerous regional courts in Latin America and Africa) are parts of legal regimes that prioritize the regime needs over the immediate interests of the parties to disputes; in the same vein, international courts operating in the field of human rights and criminal law, are primarily created in order to enhance the enforceability of certain legal norms, reflective of important common values, and their dispute resolution role is thus relatively modest.[30]

When viewed from this perspective, it is plausible to maintain that judicial independence may be positively correlated to the success of the overarching regime in which the court operates. If international regimes succeed to the degree that they are able to create stable normative and institutional environments that prioritize the interests of the regime (which coincide with the long term interests of its members) over the short-term interests of the individual member states,[31] then it is not surprising that States joining such regimes agree

---

[28] See e.g., William A Kerr, 'Trade Dispute Settlement Mechanisms: The NAFTA versus the WTO', in *The WTO and the Regulation of International Trade: Recent Trade Disputes between the European Union and the United States* (Nicholas Perdikis and Robert Read, eds., 2005) 49, 50.

[29] Posner and Yoo, *supra* note 1, at 7. For a discussion, see Yuval Shany, 'No Longer a Weak Department of Power? Reflections on the Emergence of a New International Judiciary', 20 *Eur. J. Int'l L.*(1999) 73, 81.

[30] For a discussion of goal prioritization, see Yuval Shany, 'One Law to Rule Them All: Should International Courts be viewed as Guardians of Procedural Order and Legal Uniformity?', in *Unity or Fragmentation of International Law: the Role of International and National Tribunals* (Andre Nollkaemper and Ole Kristian Fauchald, eds., Forthcoming in 2011).

[31] See e.g., Robert Koehane, 'The Demand for International Regimes', in *International Regimes* (Stephen D. Krasner, ed., 1983) 141, 146.

to surrender absolute control over certain areas subject to international cooperation.[32] In this context, the creation of independent courts arguably plays an important role in the establishment and strengthening of regimes – accepting independent judicial review removes from the purview of state control the interpretation and application of the regime's legal norms; it also constitutes a useful method by which states signal their commitment to the success of the regime.[33] Thus, it is somewhat counter-intuitive to claim that courts operating in regimes, such as the EU or WTO, should remain subject to the control of the very same states that agreed to create a cooperative regime, operating beyond their direct control. In other words, Posner and Yoo miss the mark with regard to regime courts: Since a move away from state control is, to a large extent, the raison d'être of sophisticated international regimes of economic cooperation, loss of control over the regime's judiciary – i.e., judicial independence in litigation involving the interpretation and application of regime norms, must be viewed as consistent with the long-term interests of all members who acceded to the regime and in accordance with their expectations about participation in the regime.

In the same vein, human rights and international criminal courts operate in legal environments where states have agreed to surrender control over the interpretation and application of certain international norms of great moral and political importance. The establishment of international courts to monitor states' human rights records and suppress the perpetration of serious international crimes by their nationals is designed to remove such issues from the traditional purview of state sovereignty and self-judgment to an international realm of supervision and enforcement – a move signaling a high degree of normative commitment.[34] Again, it is difficult to accept that such courts would be better off without a high degree of judicial independence. Put differently, a move to judicial dependency would undercut the practical and symbolic value of removing norms in the field of human rights and criminal law from the purview of state control.

At a higher degree of abstraction, one may posit that international courts created in order to support legal norms and institutions would succeed in their task only if they are able to confer upon them a certain degree of legitimacy.[35]

---

[32] See generally, Michael Barnett and Martha Finnemore, *Rules for the World, International Organizations in Global Politics* (2004).

[33] See e.g., Tom Ginsburg, 'Locking in Democracy: Constitutions, Commitment, and International Law', 38 *N.Y.U. J. Int'l L. & Pol.* (2006) 707, 741; Helfer and Slaughter, *supra* note 3, at 955.

[34] See e.g., Gordon Silberstein, 'Judicial Review', *Encyclopedia of Political Science* (Mark Bevir, ed., 2010) 730, 731.

[35] See e.g., Robert Howse, *The WTO System: Law, Politics and Legitimacy* (2007) 213; Nicholas Wheeler, *Saving Strangers: Humanitarian Intervention in International Society* (2000) 4;

Judicial independence, symbolizing procedural fairness and connoting a professional and unbiased decision-making process, increases the legitimacy of the legal norms that international courts apply, and strengthens the image of institutions they monitor. Furthermore, in order to preserve their own authority – a prerequisite for goal-attainment, international courts need to engage in a process of self-legitimization; and judicial independence plays a role in this respect as well.[36] Only legitimate courts can legitimate regime norms and institutions.[37]

But even with regard to international courts' dispute settlement functions *per se*, Posner and Yoo's position on the redundancy, if not counter-productiveness of judicial independence is not fully convincing. The judicial settlement of international disputes through international arbitration or court adjudication has been developed over the centuries as a reaction to the inability of traditional, diplomatic methods of dispute resolution – processes subject to the parties' ultimate control, to resolve sensitive and volatile international disputes. Courts have therefore been created as part of a conscious decision by disputing parties to surrender control over certain conflicts to a third-party adjudicatory mechanism – a move justified by the perception that the costs associated with the prolongation of the unresolved conflict outweigh the risk of losing in adjudication.[38] In other words, a body of independent judges represents, in suitable cases, an alternative method for dispute resolution to the tried and failed control-based (and interest-driven) dispute settlement approaches. Restricting judicial independence thus appears to undercut, at least to some degree, the very impetus for creating international courts in the first place.

2. *Goal-Attainment and Constrained Independence*

Still, where Posner and Yoo may be right after all is that judgments issued by independent judges in disregard of important interests of the disputing parties might antagonize them and lead to under-utilization of the court and reduced compliance with its judgments. Similarly, the attractiveness of legal regimes in

---

Hans Morgenthau, *Politics Among Nations: the Struggle for Power and Peace,* (7th edition, 1993) 3; Nienke Grossman, Legitimacy and International Adjudicative Bodies, 41 *Geo. Wash. Int'l L. Rev*. (2009) 107, 150 *et seq*.

[36] For a discussion of organizational 'maintenance goals', see Stewart Clegg and David Dunkerley, *Organization, Class and Control* (1980) 316; Russell K Schutt, *Organization in a Changing Environment: Unionization of Welfare Employees* (1986) 24.

[37] See Tom Ginsburg, 'International Judicial Lawmaking', in *International Conflict Resolution* (Stefan Voigt *et al*, eds., 2006) 155, 172 (describing the legitimacy of courts and the regimes in which they operate as 'bundled together').

[38] See Shany, *supra* note 29, at 79.

the eyes of existing and potential parties thereto, as well as other relevant constituencies, may suffer if regime institutions, including regime courts, would be viewed as insensitive to the disputing parties' crucial needs and interests. Ultimately, failure by truly independent judges to accommodate, in full or in part, important state interests may also raise questions of legitimacy – courts will enjoy support and be accepted as authoritative only if their existence is perceived by states to be beneficial, at least in the long run.[39] A chronic gap between judicial outcomes and 'client' preferences, may thus erode the status of the court in the eyes of its constituents, and could undermine its effectiveness: Norms might be less complied with, disputes would not be referred to judicial settlement, and defections from legal regimes might occur. So, if judicial independence may be simultaneously a source of legitimacy in the eyes of some constituencies, and a cause of illegitimacy in the eyes of others, how much judicial independence should an international court actually seek to attain?

The notion of 'constrained independence' advanced by Helfer and Slaughter[40] represents an interesting solution to the conundrum of reconciling independence with certain responsiveness to party needs and interests (or accountability).[41] Preserving a meaningful degree of structural and procedural judicial independence that would enable the court in question to credibly claim a reputation for judicial independence appears to be an important method for maintaining judicial legitimacy. At the same time, a host of subtle signaling devices may be put in place to convey to the court, directly or indirectly, the expectations of its constituents. The court is not obliged, of course, to follow such signals, but under certain conditions would meet strong incentives to accommodate them, at least to some extent. The upshot of this may be that Posner and Yoo are correct in criticizing the usefulness of absolute judicial independence (although it may be necessary to sustain such a myth); at the same time, Helfer and Slaughter appear to be correct in observing that Posner and Yoo's criticism is directed against a 'straw man' – that is, in the real word, no international court or judge is an 'island' completely free from influence and threats of sanction.[42]

The focus of our attention should therefore shift from discussing the existence and desirability of an 'ideal type' of judicial independence – a discussion

---

[39] See Jean-Marc Coicaud, *Legitimacy and Politics: A Contribution to the Study of Political Right and Political Responsibility* (2002) at25. For a comparable notion, see Lauren B. Edelman and Mark C Suchman, 'When the 'Haves' Hold Court: The Internalization of Disputing in Organizational Fields', 33 *Law & Society Review* (1999) 941, 968.

[40] Helfer and Slaughter, *supra* note 3, at 929–930.

[41] For a discussion, see Ronli Sifris, 'Weighing Judicial Independence against Judicial Accountability: Do the Scales of the International Criminal Court Balance?', 8 *Chi.-Kent J. Int'l & Comp. L.* (2008) 88.

[42] Helfer and Slaughter, *supra* note 3, at 929–930.

premised on a monolithic understating of the international judicial function, to a study of the nuts and bolts of the constraints put on international courts in the unique institutional and normative environments in which they operate. In this context, normative questions pertaining to the adequacy of the constraints in place, as well as their implications for judicial effectiveness may arise. The next section, dealing in brief with two case studies relating to the political constraints under which the ICTY and ICTR have operated, exemplifies such a discussion of the relationship between constrained independence and judicial effectiveness.

IV. Constrained Independence in Action: ICTY v. NATO, ICTR v. Rwanda

In her recently published memoire, Carla Del Ponte, the former Chief Prosecutor of the ICTY and ICTR discusses two instances in which proceedings before the two Tribunals encountered strong political resistance, which were deemed by the Office of the Prosecutor too powerful to resist. The first of the two cases pertains to the investigation of NATO leaders and service members for alleged crimes committed during the bombing campaign of Yugoslavia in 1999 (in response to the earlier crimes committed by the Yugoslav forces in Kosovo). Del Ponte's predecessor, Louis Arbour, assigned the various allegations raised against NATO to a special committee entrusted with issuing recommendations on whether to prosecute any of the alleged crimes. The committee's report, which was issued in 2000, recommended not to open any criminal investigations, citing with relation to some incidents lack of evidence of a criminal intent, and with relation to others lack of clarity in the applicable legal standards.[43] A number of commentators have strongly criticized the report for its overly-cautious approach, suggesting that the committee went out of its way to get NATO 'off the hook'.[44]

Del Ponte decided to accept the recommendation and to terminate the investigation into the NATO bombing campaign. In her book, she explains the inevitability of the decision:

> No one in NATO ever pressured me to refrain from investigating the bombing campaign or from undertaking a prosecution based upon it. But I quickly

---

[43] Final Report to the Prosecutor by the Committee Established to Review the NATO Bombing Campaign Against the Federal Republic of Yugoslavia (2000), http://www.icty.org/sid/10052.

[44] See e.g., Timothy W Waters, 'Unexploded Bomb: Voice, Silence, and Consequence at The Hague Tribunals: A Legal and Rhetorical Critique', 35 *N.Y.U. J. Int'l L. & Pol.* (2003) 1015; Andreas Lauresen, 'NATO, the War over Kosovo, and the ICTY Investigation', 17 *Am. U. Int'l L. Rev.* (2002) 765.

> concluded that it was impossible to investigate NATO, because NATO and its member states would not cooperate with us. They would not provide us access to the files and documents. Over and above this, however, I understood that I had collided with the edge of the political universe in which the Tribunal was allowed to function. If I went forward with an investigation of NATO, I would not only fail in this investigative effort, I would render my office incapable of continuing to investigate and prosecute the crimes committed by the local forces during the wars of the 1990s. Security for the Tribunal's work in Bosnia and Herzegovina as well as in Kosovo depended upon NATO. The Tribunal's forensics teams were only able to exhume mass graves because they enjoyed NATO escorts. Arrests of fugitives depended upon NATO-country intelligence as well as NATO ground and air support.[45]

In other words, Del Ponte acknowledged the constrained independence of the ICTY, as determined by its structure (e.g., budget, mandate, and lack of independent enforcement capabilities) and tied it to the Tribunal's effectiveness – i.e., its ability to attain the goal of ending impunity in the Balkans. The Tribunal's existence and its ability to attain the goals for which it was created was only rendered possible by virtue of the support of key states; in particular, the ability of the Office of the Prosecutor to employ its procedures (e.g., exhume graves, gain custody over suspects, etc.) depended on NATO's active support. Thus, the formal independence enjoyed by the ICTY and the Prosecutor,[46] was not backed by a structural configuration of power that would enable the Tribunal to actually operate free of pressure and interference. Under such condition, an attempt by the Prosecutor to break her independence constraints by way of asserting the authority of the Office of the Prosecutor vis-à-vis NATO and 'speaking law to power' would have undercut, not strengthened the Tribunal's goal-attainment prospects – i.e., its effectiveness.

A troubling lesson derived from this incident is that independence in decision-making may contribute to court effectiveness only as long as judicial (or prosecutorial) decisions do not conflict with important interests held by powerful states. Thus, in the NATO case, the legitimacy of Tribunal in the eyes of less powerful constituencies (the states of the Balkan, neutral observers, etc.), which a strong version of judicial independence may have sustained, had to be sacrificed in order to preserve the political support afforded by a more powerful constituency – NATO member states, which was necessary, in turn, for the purpose of attaining the Tribunal's overall goals.

---

[45] Carla Del Ponte, *Madame Prosecutor: Confrontations with Humanity's Worst Criminals and the Culture of Impunity* (2009), 60.

[46] Statute of the International Tribunal for Yugoslavia, art. 16(2), adopted on 25 May 1993 by SC Resolution 827 ("The Prosecutor shall act independently as a separate organ of the International Tribunal. He or she shall not seek or receive instructions from any Government or from any other source").

The second incident described by Del Ponte's memoire pertains to the reaction of the Rwandan authorities to the ICTR's Appeals Chamber's decision of 3 November 1999, dismissing the indictment and ordering the release of Jean Bosco Barayagwiza – one of the suspects in the *Radio Mille Collines* case (a case dealing with incitement to genocide by directors of mass media establishments in Rwanda).[47] The Appeals Chamber based its decision on violations of the due process rights of the accused, which the Prosecution committed – in particular, violating his right to be promptly charged. The reaction of the government of Rwanda to the decision was swift and harsh: it suspended all cooperation with the Tribunal – thus derailing its actual ability to access evidence and witnesses for all pending trials, and effectively cutting the Tribunal's life-line.[48]

Del Ponte had to act quickly: She submitted an extraordinary motion to review the decision to release – a move of dubious procedural regularity, which she justified in the following terms:

> I, too, was disturbed that Barayagwiza would escape justice on this procedural question and not face a full trial. But I was more concerned with the real danger that, because of the Barayagwiza fiasco, the Rwandan government would retaliate against the Rwanda Tribunal itself by permanently refusing to cooperate with its work; this would deal a major setback to the cause of international justice in general[49]

The Appeals Chamber agreed to reopen the case and decided on 31 March 2000 to reverse its previous decision and to restore the proceedings against Barayagwiza.[50] Employing a somewhat strained analysis,[51] the judges held that new facts brought to their attention by the Prosecutor have persuaded them the due process violations suffered by Barayagwiza have been less serious than was originally believed, and did not justify, consequently, a dismissal of the indictment and release.

Tellingly perhaps, the Chamber devoted a few sentences to the issue of judicial independence:

> Before proceeding to consider the Motion for Review, the Chamber notes that during the hearing on 22 February 2000 in Arusha, Prosecutor Ms Carla Del Ponte, made a statement regarding the reaction of the government of Rwanda to

---

[47] *Barayagwiza v. Prosecutor*, case ICTR-97-19, Appeals Chamber Decision of 3 Nov. 1999.

[48] See e.g., Robert Cryer, *Prosecuting International Crimes: Selectivity and the International Criminal Law Regime* (2005) 142.

[49] Del Ponte, *supra* note 45, at 73.

[50] *Prosecutor v. Barayagwiza*, case, ICTR-97-19, Appeals Chamber Decision of 31 March 2000 (Prosecutor's Request for Review or Reconsideration).

[51] Cryer, *supra* note 48, at 142.

> the Decision. She stated that: "The government of Rwanda reacted very seriously in a tough manner to the decision of 3 November 1999." Later, the Attorney General of Rwanda appearing as representative of the Rwandan Government, in his submissions as "amicus curiae' to the Appeals Chamber, openly threatened the non co-operation of the peoples of Rwanda with the Tribunal if faced with an unfavourable Decision by the Appeals Chamber on the Motion for Review. The Appeals Chamber wishes to stress that the Tribunal is an independent body, whose decisions are based solely on justice and law. If its decision in any case should be followed by non-cooperation, that consequence would be a matter for the Security Council.[52]

In other words, the Tribunal was aware of the connection between the outcome of the case and its judicial independence image; but unlike Del Ponte, who openly admitted that the "real danger" was permanent Rwandan lack of cooperation, the judges claimed that this factor played no role in their actual decision. While it may be the case that Rwanda's threats were never openly discussed by the judges in their deliberations,[53] and that the Tribunal's judicial independence structural and procedural features remained intact, the idea of constrained independence revolves around subtle messages and signals, which affect judicial perceptions about the outer limits of judicial legitimacy in the eyes of influential constituencies (in this case, the government of Rwanda). It is incredulous to believe that such considerations did not play a part – consciously or sub-consciously, in the judges ultimate decision to reverse the decision of 3 November 1999.[54]

While one may accuse the Tribunal of hypocrisy, if not outright dishonesty, in denying any impact by Rwanda's threats on the 31 March 2000 decision, this appears to me to be too harsh of a judgment on the Tribunal. The Tribunal attempted to walk a fine line between the hard reality that required it to offer a high degree of responsiveness to Rwanda's expectations, and the need to preserve the myth of absolute judicial independence (which is a structural asset, contributing, in turn, to judicial effectiveness). In this particular context, where legitimacy and effectiveness vectors point in a multiplicity of diametrically opposed directions, striking a fully satisfactory balance may have been impossible, and the truth about such impossibility too painful to bear: Complete transparency about the need to consider 'real world' constraints, would have

---

[52] *Prosecutor v. Barayagwiza,* at para. 34.

[53] Schabas wryly notes that the individual opinions by judges Vohrah and Nieto-Navia that insist on that Rwanda's threat played no part in the judicial deliberation appear to insist too much on this point. William A Schabas, 'International Decision: Barayagwiza V. Prosecutor (Prosecutor's Request for Review or Reconsideration))', 92 *AJIL* (2000) 563, 568.

[54] See e.g., *Ibid*, at 570–571.

arguably harmed the myth of judicial independence and might have eroded the Tribunal legitimacy; a rigid application of an absolute notion of judicial independence would have deprived the Tribunal of Rwanda's crucial cooperation. Under these circumstances, a flexible approach to judicial independence, covered up by a 'white lie', may have represented a reasonable goal-attainment or damage-control strategy.

V. Conclusion

Judicial independence is related to international judicial effectiveness in complicated ways. Courts thrive on legitimacy in the eyes of relevant constituencies, and judicial independence – connoting notions of fairness and justice, and fostering professionalism and trustworthiness – are important elements in generating the signals and symbols that provide courts with the support they need in order to function. Still, the relationship between the independence of international courts – complex institutions with myriad goals – and their effectiveness is not linear in nature. In order to attain their goals – i.e., operate effectively to advance norm compliance, dispute resolution, regime support and legitimating, international courts have to generate self-legitimacy (inter alia, through nurturing a reputation for judicial independence), but at the same time be responsive to the expectation of key constituents. Thus, a structural and procedural framework of constrained independence is perhaps a more adequate framework – both normatively and practically, for discussing the actual choices faced by international courts that a caricature-like choice between absolute judicial dependence and independence.

The practice of the ICTY and ICTR suggests that striking the balance between independence and responsiveness (or accountability) to the needs of the principal stakeholders may be quite difficult in certain cases, where the operation of international courts threatens to clash with the political circumstances that allow their existence. It also suggests that, in the face of strong and irreconcilable pressures, attempts to preserve the myth of judicial independence for self-legitimating reasons may generate at the very same time considerable legitimacy costs (loss of transparency, accusations of dishonesty).

CHAPTER SEVENTEEN

SEPARATION OF POWERS AND THE INTERNATIONAL JUDICIARY – A VISION OF INSTITUTIONAL JUDICIAL INDEPENDENCE IN INTERNATIONAL LAW

*Michael Bohlander**

All men dream but not equally. Those who dream by night in the dusty recesses of their minds wake in the day to find that it was vanity; but the dreamers of the day are dangerous men, for they may act their dream with open eyes to make it possible.
T.E. Lawrence, The Seven Pillars of Wisdom

I. Incubus

The state of the national judiciary and its relationship to the other official state powers, executive and legislature, as well as to the unofficial fourth power, the media, have been the object of many publications, conferences, declarations etc. A lot of detailed analysis has gone into fine-tuning the systems of different domestic jurisdictions within themselves and with regard to, where applicable, regional and/or international human rights standards. National systems in recent years have given more and more space to the discussion of the institutional independence of the judiciary beyond issues pertaining to selection and the individual judges' position. If one turns to the realm of the international judiciary, however, that sort of literature seems to pale in comparison and if existing at all, mostly deals with the – certainly central and highly charged – question of selection and recruitment and how to improve the process by tightening the criteria or de-politicizing the process[1]. Not much

---

* Professor Michael Bohlander had been a member of the German judiciary since 1991 before joining Durham Law School in 2004. From 1999 until 2001 he served as the Senior Legal Officer of a Trial Chamber of the ICTY. He has trained judges and prosecutors from several countries, including the Iraqi High Tribunal which tried Saddam Hussein. He is the Visiting Chair in Criminal Law at the Rijksuniversiteit Groningen Centre for Law and Governance.

[1] The book by K. Malleson/P.H. Russell (eds.), *Appointing Judges in an Age of Judicial Power* (Toronto 2006), for example has only one chapter on international judges; see also more recently R. Mackenzie/K. Malleson/P. Martin/P. Sands, *Selecting International Judges: Principle, Process, and Politics* (Oxford 2010).

by way of detailed criticism has been written about the judges at international tribunals, and more to the point the newly relevant international criminal tribunals. The leading commentaries on the International Criminal Court (ICC) by Triffterer[2] and Schabas[3], for example, more or less repeat and annotate the sequence of events in the development of the existing structures, yet there is hardly a word to be found that would criticise the status quo and regress the path to the primary factors influencing the fundamental choices made by those called upon at the time to shape judicial closure mechanisms for international conflicts and atrocities against internationally protected legal interests, such as serious violations of human rights and humanitarian law. This is not really surprising, because many of those decisions are made in the "dusty recesses" of international conference venues, and the real reasons for those decisions may or may not be made public in the drafts emanating from those so-called "informal sessions", another word for talking turkey. Many deliberations are publicly and officially admitted to be confidential, such as, for example, the minutes of the plenary meetings of the judges at the International Criminal Tribunals for Yugoslavia (ICTY) and Rwanda (ICTR)[4]. What applies to the microcosm of the internal workings of a Tribunal must apply *a minore ad maius* to the macrocosm of the political workings of the international community as well or even more so. No-one should therefore think that the state of affairs in the international judicial sphere is beyond criticism. If anything, it is in a more problematic condition due to the fact that despite of almost two decades of international criminal tribunals and an even longer existence of the major international courts such as the International Court of Justice (ICJ), the European Court of Justice (ECJ), the European Court of Human Rights (ECtHR) etc. there is still no uniform standard of approach to regulating the judiciary at the international or supranational level.

---

[2] O. Triffterer (ed.), *Commentary on the Rome Statute of the International Court*, 2nd ed., (Munich et al 2008), Art. 36 ff.

[3] W. Schabas, *The International Criminal Court – A Commentary on the Rome Statute* (Oxford 2010), Art. 36 ff.

[4] This can lead to the disconcerting result that everyone present, including some legal officers allowed to be present at these meetings, knows what the reasons for and the history of a certain new rule or regulation were because they are listed in the minutes, but that no-one can refer to the reasons or the minutes in any proceedings because of their confidentiality, and so any emerging institutional memory is rendered meaningless, and in any case lost once those who heard the reasons first-hand are gone or when junior staff are called upon to draft decisions etc. for the judges and while doing so come up against a snag in the application of the rule so established: How many misunderstandings may exist because access and reference to those materials is restricted? How much richer could the legal argument before these courts be if access was allowed?

As I have tried to show in previous publications[5], there are serious concerns about nepotism, package-deals, the qualifications of candidates to judicial office and the lack of engagement of the international community with the nitty-gritty of the business at hand, to name but a few. One sometimes hears off-the-record comments from players in the system, mostly from defence counsel but occasionally also from judicial brethren, who are exasperated by what they perceive to be an unacceptable degree of incompetence or nonchalance in the handling of the proceedings. Not all the courts have proper judicial discipline regimes or even a code of conduct. Continuing professional development (CPD), a mainstay of any modern domestic legal system these days, is virtually non-existent.

A major contributing factor to this state of affairs worth further in-depth research could actually be the absence of any meaningful judicial institutional self-government on the international level. The level of potential for direct governmental political influence here is much higher than in the formalised and constitutionally protected internal order of each country, where the Executive may face enforceable domestic checks and balances. These checks are virtually absent on the international plane. Just think about the recruitment process for judges: All international judges were at one time candidates put forward by their governments. Their governments, and more to the point the people making the decisions on behalf of the government, had to be pleased with them in order to put their names forward for election. Maybe the mere fact that they pleased their government's people was a decisive factor in their

[5] Flexible Judges or Flexing the Political Muscle? in L.E. De Groot-van Leeuwen/W. Rombouts (eds) *Separation of Powers in Theory and Practice – An International Perspective* (Nijmegen 2010), p. 123 ff.; Death of an Appellant – The termination of the appellate proceedings in the case of Rasim Delic at the ICTY (2010) Criminal Law Forum 495; No Country for Old Men? - Age limits for judges at international criminal tribunals (2009) 1 Indian Yearbook of International Law and Policy 326; Al-haga ela magles llkadaa b'Almania (The Need for a Judicial Council in Germany: How Germany can learn from Egypt) (2010) Egyptian Court of Cassation Review (Megalat Mahkamat al-Nakd al-Misriya) (forthcoming); Pride and Prejudice or Sense and Sensibility? – A pragmatic proposal for the recruitment of judges at the ICC and other international criminal courts (2009) New Criminal Law Review 529.; together with Mark Findlay, The use of domestic sources as a basis for international criminal law principles (2002) The Global Community, Yearbook of International Law and Jurisprudence 3; The influence of academic research on the jurisprudence of the International Criminal Tribunal for the Former Yugoslavia – A first overview, in (2003) The Global Community: Yearbook of International Law and Jurisprudence 195; The International Criminal Judiciary Problems of Judicial Selection, Independence and Ethics, in M. Bohlander (ed) *International Criminal Justice – A Critical Analysis of Institutions and Procedures* (London 2007), pp. 325 ff. (Turkish translation in Uluslararasi Ceza Yargisi: Yargisal Secim, Bagimsizlik ve Etik Sorunlari (2007) Uluslararasi Suçlar ve Tarih (International Crimes and History) (Issue 3/4) 5); The General Part: Judicial Developments, in M Cherif Bassiouni (ed) *International Criminal Law*, vol. 3 (Leiden 2008), pp. 517 ff.

appointment. A government may have many people who could please it by showing relevant experience, knowledge, intellect, integrity, courage and competence. Yet we all know that these qualities do not necessarily carry any greater weight than other qualities, such as ambition, resourcefulness, networking skills and loyalty, qualities to which those in positions of executive political power may even more easily relate than to the former. People are often also selected for their known allegiances to certain political or ideological programmes or attitudes – this is sometimes called "packing the Court" at the national level where there is a much higher risk of direct interference by the Court, especially if that Court has the power to strike down acts of the Executive or even the Legislature.

In other words, the mere idea of a separation of powers on the international level is a much more tender growth than at domestic level, a sapling that may not even have broken through the soil yet: The Executive selects the people that populate the bodies meant to provide a check[6] on the Executive. In the UN, for example, it is not the parliament-like General Assembly that makes the big and globally binding policy decisions (if we leave budgetary issues aside), it is the purely executive-shaped Security Council, which on top of it all is a club with different degrees and privileges of membership, based now only on historical developments and political as well as military clout. National governments are intrinsically inimical to extraneous checks on their activities – why should anything different apply at the international level? It is striking, yet hardly surprising in this context, that the Mt. Scopus Standards, as many other international declarations on judicial independence, exhort domestic systems to allow for a maximum degree of judicial institutional independence or self-governance, yet lack a similar encouragement for the international judiciary. Any seasoned international politician will tell you that such is the way of things in international relations, and that as long ago as in the times of Rousseau[7] people knew that to be the case. The current situation has led people like Jeremy Rabkin to express a general dissatisfaction with an internationally based approach:

---

[6] Whether they develop a sudden independence from the authorities nominating them, as can be observed in some national Supreme Court judiciaries, is far from certain. That depends to a large extent on security of tenure, re-eligibility, and avenues for promotion by returning to the home government etc.

[7] Rousseau wrote: "As for what is called the law of nations, it is clear that without any real sanction these laws are only illusions that are more tenuous even than the notion of natural law. The latter at least addresses itself to the hearts of individuals, whereas decisions based on the law of nations, having no other guarantee than the utility of the one who submits to them, are respected only as long as those decisions confirm one's own self-interest." – Jean-Jacques Rousseau, The State of War; cited in G.M. Reichberg/H. Syse/E. Begby (eds) *The Ethics of War* (London 2006), pp. 482–83.

> Justice is a serious and often difficult responsibility. It is far too serious to be left to an entity so distracted, so divided, so diffuse as 'the international community.' What hope there is for justice in this world must be a hope that resides, where justice has always been sought in the past: in the governments of sovereign nations. It was possible to forget this fact in the giddy, frivolous atmosphere of the 1990s. What previous generations took for granted, the world of the early 21st Century has now relearned. In a more serious world, the lesson is not likely to be forgotten. It is certainly not likely to be effaced by an international criminal court, promising to do justice for humanity, but equipped only to divert a specialized coterie of legal scholars. Justice is too serious to be left to international bureaucrats.[8]

What to do then? Resign before the inevitable? If international criminal justice is to have any chance to survive and grow, that is not an option[9]. If there are no more people of the calibre of those who initiated the development of international justice, a calibre needed to prevent the Executive from clawing back in the mid to long term the concessions made in that "giddy, frivolous atmosphere" Rabkin talked about, the picture will indeed be bleak. Let us therefore now pretend to be dangerous men and dream with open eyes of a time when the separation of powers will have more meaning in international law than it has today. To that effect, we shall look at some of the Mt. Scopus Standards (MSS) for national judiciaries and see if the insertion of the word "international" instead could lead us to the beginning of a path to proper judicial institutional independence that will doubtlessly take many years to walk.

II. International Judicial Institutional Self-Governance – An Idea Worth Pursuing or an Illusion Doomed to Failure?

This question is obviously a topic that would deserve a PhD on its own, yet in the short space of this chapter we shall merely be speaking of the memories that stand out in our minds from the dreams we had so far and of the visions that they in turn may engender. As far as international judges are concerned, the MSS already recognise the need for ensuring the absence of external meddling with judicial affairs:

> 10. INDEPENDENCE
>
> 10.1 The international courts and the judges shall exercise their functions free from direct or indirect interference or influence by any person or entity.

[8] See J. Rabkin, Global Criminal Justice: An Idea Whose Time Has Passed, (2005) 38 Cornell International Law Journal 753.- I partially disagree with this analysis, as I have set out in my introduction to M. Bohlander (ed.) *Globalization of Criminal Justice* (Farnham 2010), p. xiv.

[9] See, for example, the views expressed by M.C. Bassiouni, Perspectives on International Criminal Justice (2010) 50 Virginia Journal of International Law 269 at 308 ff.

10.2 This freedom of the judges and courts shall apply both to the judicial process in pending cases, including the assignment of cases to particular judges, and to the operation of the court and its registry.
10.3 The court shall be free to determine the conditions for its international administration, including staff recruitment policy, information systems and allocation of budgetary expenditure.
10.4 ....
10.5 All Judges of international courts and tribunals shall adhere to the principle that a judges [sic!] who are nationals of a member state of the organisation establishing the court or tribunal when exercising judicial discretion and function shall engage in fair and independent adjudication of the case and by no means in representation of the member state.

However, MSS 10.1 would appear to be a weak statement given the experiences surrounding, for example, the *Barayagwiza* case[10] at the ICTR and UN Security Council Resolution 1422. We already alluded to the election process where it is usually the States who decide who is put forward for candidature. In some cases we also have pre-screening committees whose composition and democratic legitimacy are open to question[11]. MSS 10.2 and 10.3 are subject to the fact that the purse strings for any court's budget are always held by someone else. There is no direct judicial input in the actual budgeting process, leave alone a right to sufficient assets for a proper exercise of the judicial function, such as found in some national constitutions. MSS 10.5 is addressed to the judges, not the governments nominating them. It is again striking that the word "state" used here does not appear in MSS 10.1: It may not have made much of a difference in substance, but for symbolic reasons the mention of states should have been considered.

The MSS aimed at the national context contain a few rules that might be worth transposing to the international level, such as for example

1.1. An independent and impartial judiciary is an institution of the highest value in every society and an essential pillar of liberty and the rule of law.

This could be adapted by deleting "in every society" and inserting "international" before judiciary, and we would have the recognition of the *institution* of an independent international judiciary, not merely of individual judicial

[10] *Prosecutor v. Jean-Bosco Barayagwiza*, No. ICTR-97-19-AR72, Decision on Prosecutor's Request for Review or Reconsideration, of 31 March, 2000.
[11] See, for example, with regard to the international judges for the Lebanese Tribunal, the interview with Nicola Michel at www.globalpolicy.org/intljustice/tribunals/lebanon/2007/0612nicolamichel.htm: "As to the international ones, the member states will submit proposals after we open the way for nominations. All these applications have to be subject to the advice of the selection committee which will present its recommendations to the U.N. Secretary-General."

independence as in MSS 10.1. This should directly be followed up by an adapted version of

> 1.2. The Judiciary as a whole shall be independent.
> 1.3. The Judiciary as a whole shall enjoy collective independence and autonomy vis-à-vis the Executive[,]

where again the word "international" would be inserted before the word "judiciary" and "Executive" replaced by "national governments and executive bodies of international organisations". Nationally-oriented MSS 2.4. to 2.26 could be similarly adapted through the introduction of a permanent General Council of the International Judiciary (GCIJ) which would have direct authority over all international judges – and maybe even prosecutors – of any court using international judges: Any State wishing to support a certain court, be it international, hybrid or national with an international element, would have to sign up to the GCIJ's authority and ideally any Statute of such a court should contain the words:

> The recruitment and terms of service of the international judges of this Court shall be under the authority of the General Council of the International Judiciary and its laws as amended from time to time.

The position and authority of the GCIJ could be graphically described as set out in figure 1.

The GCIJ could be located within the UN institutional framework, given that almost all states are members of the UN and thus the need for a separate sign-up to the GCIJ's role would be superfluous, and ideally as a further primary organ independent of the Security Council and only subject to the budget powers of the General Assembly, but with the recognised right under the UN Charter to a separate and sufficient budget. The functions of the GCIJ would include:

- Budget administration (salaries, non-staff costs etc.)
- Recruitment and promotion of judges (including elevation to major international courts and to leading positions within those courts, such as presidency and presiding judges, where applicable under a court's statute)

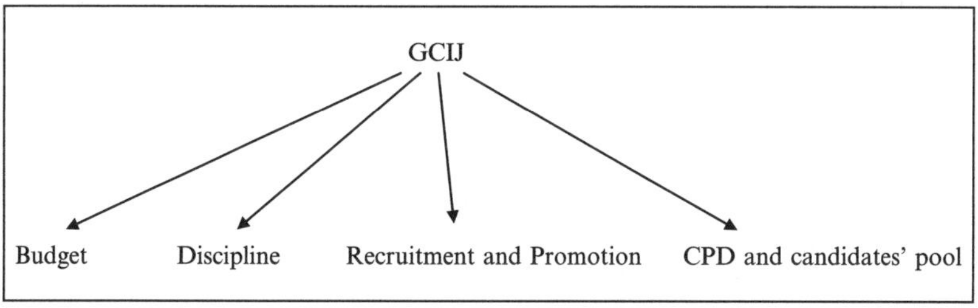

Figure 1: Function of the GCIJ

- Judicial discipline
- CPD and overseeing as well as administering a pool of qualified candidates for new posts[12].

The GCIJ would be staffed by a majority of experienced senior judges and have representatives of the international community as well. There is, of course, the matter of who elects the judicial members and that there will undoubtedly be some political influence in that area; one might think of a mixed system of co-optation from the existing number of international judges and partial election by the General Assembly, but that is more a question of detail. Its President should have the right to seize and address the GA and SC on any matter within its remit and to send delegates to negotiations about courts and tribunals using international judges. It would be difficult for the UN, for example, to oppose this kind of system in principle because it operates it itself in transitional administrations such as the United Nations Mission in Kosovo (UNMIK)[13]. The relevant above-mentioned MSS could thus be adapted into a basic programme mission statement (PMS) for a GCIJ as follows (in a very preliminary draft form):

A General Council of the International Judiciary – programme mission statement

1. There shall be established a General Council of the International Judiciary as a primary organ of the UN (GCIJ) for the purpose of regulating and supervising the service of international judges. The GCIJ shall have exclusive jurisdiction over any and all international judges serving in courts in member states of the UN [unless they are subject to the jurisdiction and equivalent protection of a Judicial Council established for their own region]. The UN shall abstain from entering into any agreement with non-UN member states for or cooperation with a court using international judges unless that court and the parties establishing it have accepted the jurisdiction of the GCIJ as set out in its Statute.
2. An international judge shall be defined as a judge serving, for the time of their service and for any accruing pension entitlements, on the basis of an international agreement or legally binding resolution or a power

[12] See my proposal in Pride and Prejudice or Sense and Sensibility? – A pragmatic proposal for the recruitment of judges at the ICC and other international criminal courts, (2009) New Criminal Law Review 529 at 542.

[13] M. Bohlander, The Legal Framework of the Prosecution and the Courts, in Kai Ambos/Mohamed Othman (eds.) *New Approaches in International Criminal Justice: Kosovo. East Timor, Sierra Leone and Cambodia* (Freiburg i. Br. 2003) pp. 21 ff.

granted to a national administration on the basis of such agreement or resolution, in the judiciary of a fully international court, of a hybrid international court or a court of a country of which he is not a national. The latter shall exclude judges seconded from one country to another on the basis of a purely bilateral agreement for the purpose of administrative support or judges recruited as domestic judges by a country whose laws do not require citizenship in order to serve in its judiciary. National judges nominated by a member state to a hybrid international court under its statute having territorial jurisdiction solely over that state shall be international judges for the purposes of these provisions.

3. The GCIJ shall consist of a President, a Vice-President and an equal number of members drawn from the judiciary and representatives of the international community. The President and Vice-President shall be judges. The judicial members shall be elected by [.....].
4. Judicial appointments, transfers and promotions shall be determined by the GCIJ after hearing the presidency of the court(s) concerned.
5. The GCIJ shall administer the recruitment and training of candidates for international judicial office. It shall establish and administer a pool of qualified candidates and a system of continuing professional development (CPD) in all relevant areas of law and related disciplines required for the proper exercise of judicial office.
6. No court decision shall be reversed other than through the pre-established avenues of appeal. The commutation of any sentence or the exercise of pardon shall require the consent of the GCIJ, after hearing the judges of the court which handed down the decision concerned.
7. No change in the composition of a court may be made that could affect its decision-making. The removal and re-assignment of a judge sitting on a pending case from that case shall only be permitted in exceptional cases for serious cause and shall require the consent of the GCIJ. Provision shall be made ex ante in the law of the relevant courts for the case of the termination of a term of office for any reason such as death, retirement etc. of a judge sitting on a pending case, after consultation with the GCIJ.
8. The discipline and removal from office of judges shall be in the sole jurisdiction of the GCIJ. The GCIJ may receive complaints against judges directly from any interested party. Full judicial accountability and transparency, and due regard for the privacy of the judge concerned shall be the guiding principles of the process. The proceedings shall be conducted in confidentiality with regard to the public, yet with full disclosure of all pertinent correspondence to the parties involved.

The result of the proceedings and the reasons for it shall in all cases be made public.

9. Statutes, rules of procedure and evidence and any other regulations established for or in courts under the jurisdiction of the GCIJ shall require prior consultation with the GCIJ if they can affect matters of judicial terms of service. The GCIJ shall, as far as practicable, be consulted in any process for reform or amendment of existing laws in courts under its jurisdiction not falling under the first sentence above.
10. States shall comply with and enforce decisions of international courts and of the GCIJ.
11. The process and standards of judicial recruitment shall give due consideration to the principle of fair reflection within the judiciary of society in all its aspects. There shall be no discrimination on the grounds of race, colour, gender, language, religion, national or social origin, property, birth or status, or citizenship requirements. Candidates for judicial office shall be individuals of integrity and ability, with high expertise and sufficient practical experience in the field of law they are to be selected for. The selection process shall strive to make integrity and ability, relevant expertise and practical experience the overriding cumulative criteria for recruitment.
12. The GCIJ shall administer its own budget. It shall be the duty of all states accepting the GCIJ's jurisdiction to provide adequate financial resources on a regular basis to allow for the due administration of justice. Judicial salaries and pensions shall be adequate at all times, established by law, and shall be periodically reviewed independently by the GCIJ who shall make the relevant presentations to the bodies providing the funding for its budget.

As can be seen merely from looking at no. 1 of the PMS, the existence of separate international jurisdictions will create obstacles to a unified system. If a Judicial Council exists for as certain region, for example in the EU for the ECJ and the Court of First Instance, or for the Council of Europe for the ECtHR, one might accept that it may be unrealistic to expect the establishing international organisations to yield control to another organisation, but just as easily one might argue that these organisations could conclude a kind of "service agreement" with the GCIJ. Admittedly, the 12 points listed above will never be enacted in a form anywhere near as pure as drafted here and there are almost always reasonable alternatives to any proposal. The important issue, however, is that the idea of an independent judicial council is propagated for all regions of the world.

III. Conclusion

> [...] [A]s the system governing the functioning of the United Nations now stands, the only option available to individuals who wish to have access to an independent tribunal in order to obtain adequate protection of their fundamental rights is to challenge domestic implementing measures before a domestic court. Indeed, the possibility of a successful challenge cannot be entirely unexpected on the Security Council's part, given that it was expressly contemplated by the Analytical Support and Sanctions Monitoring Team of the Sanctions Committee.
>
> Had there been a genuine and effective mechanism of judicial control by an independent tribunal at the level of the United Nations, then this might have released the Community from the obligation to provide for judicial control of implementing measures that apply within the Community legal order. However, no such mechanism currently exists. ... In those circumstances, it must be held that the right to judicial review by an independent tribunal has not been secured at the level of the United Nations. As a consequence, the Community institutions cannot dispense with proper judicial review proceedings when implementing the Security Council resolutions in question within the Community legal order[14].

The Advocate General at the ECJ in the famous *Kadi* proceedings from which these quotes are taken, chastised the situation at the international level with regard to civil liberties and human rights as lacking adequate judicial protection. In other words, there is at present no separation of powers worthy of that name at the apex of the international legal order of the UN, and to a weaker degree in some regional organisations such as the EU, for example. The example of the rise of international criminal justice in recent decades has shown that if there is a will to involve judicial mechanisms in the solution of problems arising out of international affairs, there is a way of establishing such mechanisms, no matter how imperfect and ineffective their deciduous teeth may appear. Judicial independence worth its name in the subordinate international courts cannot be had in the long term unless the idea of institutional judicial independence, as opposed to providing a mere judicial dispute resolution vehicle for the member states of the UN such as the ICJ, starts asserting itself forcefully at the primary root level of the international legal order. There is no middle ground: One either advocates the separation of powers and creates institutions that can bite, or one warns of the "perils of global legalism"[15] and

---

[14] Opinion of Advocate General Poiares Maduro, delivered on 16 January 2008, Case C-402/05 P, *Yassin Abdullah Kadi v. Council of the European Union and Commission of the European Communities* at paras. 38 and 54. See also R. Schütze, On Middle Ground – European Community Law and Public International Law in A.S. Muller/M.A. Loth (eds) *Highest Courts and the Internationalisation of Law* (The Hague 2009), pp. 35 ff.; C. Möllers, *Gewaltengliederung* (Tübingen 2005).

[15] E.A. Posner, *The Perils of Global Legalism* (Chicago 2009).

accepts that the world has not moved on and will not move on from the state of affairs in Rousseau's time. Having a little bit of independence is like having no independence at all, or, as Édouard René Lefèvre de Laboulaye (1811–1883) put it so elegantly in another context surrounding judicial inamovability, a facet of judicial independence: "La suspension temporaire de l'inamovibilité des juges est égal à la suspension temporaire de la virginité."

PART IV

JUDICIAL APPOINTMENT, JUDICIAL CONDUCT AND JUDICIAL ACCOUNTABILITY

CHAPTER EIGHTEEN

THE SUPREME COURT OF CANADA APPOINTMENT PROCESS: CHRONOLOGY, CONTEXT AND REFORM

*Irwin Cotler**

I. Introduction

If asked about my priorities when first appointed Minister of Justice in 2003, I would not have included judicial appointments amongst them; however, I learned to appreciate that this is a critical part of the administration of justice in Canada, if not in any country. This is a legacy issue, and it will live on long after those who have the temporary stewardship of this position are no longer there. If the act of appointing judges is a priority, the process of appointing them is no less so. Indeed, the integrity and fairness of the process is not unrelated to the excellence and independence of the judiciary.

Judicial appointees–and the appointments process–are of crucial importance to our country. The Supreme Court, as the highest appellate court and final arbiter for the resolution of legal disputes is at the pinnacle of our court system, and is both a fundamental pillar of our constitutional democracy and the guardian of the Constitution. It is vested with the responsibility for intervening in the case of a constitutional trespass, either when governments exceed their jurisdiction–in the context of federal-provincial relations–or when they violate rights protected under the *Canadian Charter of Rights and Freedoms*. In other words, our Constitution frames both the distribution of governmental power between the federal government and the provinces –otherwise known as legal federalism or the "powers process"–as well as the limits on the exercise of governmental power, whether federal or provincial–otherwise known as human rights or the "rights process."

The witness testimony before the Parliamentary Standing Committee on Justice and Human Rights[1] examining the judicial appointments process determined that the Supreme Court exercised these responsibilities in an exemplary

* Irwin Cotler is a Canadian Member of Parliament and the former Minister of Justice and Attorney General of Canada. He is a Professor of Law (Emeritus) at McGill University.

[1] Standing Committee on Justice, Human Rights, Public Safety and Emergency Preparedness – 37th Parliament, 3rd Session

fashion and that its excellence resonated beyond Canada's borders. Our highest court is respected across the country and around the world as a model of what a vital, modern, and independent judicial institution should be. For example, representatives of the Québec and Ontario bar testified that the quality of judges on the Supreme Court is "impeccable."[2] Constitutional and legal scholars emphasized in their testimony before the Committee that courts from diverse jurisdictions continually cite rulings from the Canadian Supreme Court. Commentators concurred that it was difficult to discern an "ideological" or "political" predilection in the Court's decision-making.[3] I was always reminded of this when, as Minster of Justice or academic, I went to international scholarly conferences where the Supreme Court of Canada was cited as an international model. One might have asked, therefore, that if the excellence of the Court is not unrelated to the appointments process, why reform an appointments process that has produced such excellent appointees? To use the proverbial vernacular, "if ain't broke, don't fix it."

A confluence of several factors animated the impetus for reform. First, there was the transformative impact of the *Canadian Charter of Rights and Freedoms*, where Canada moved from being a Parliamentary democracy to being a constitutional democracy; where the courts moved from being the arbiters of legal federalism in inter-jurisdictional disputes to being the guarantors of constitutionally protected rights; where individuals and groups were no longer passive bystanders to legal federalism, but were now rights-holders and rights-claimants who could petition government for redress of grievance.

Second, as a corollary, the Supreme Court of Canada assumed a central role in this constitutional revolution, importing into Canadian discourse that which U.S. constitutional scholar Alexander Bickel called the "anti-majoritarian paradox[4]", where unelected, unrepresentative, and unaccountable judges were usurping the decision-making process.

Third, there was the perception of an 'activist Court'[5] propagating "liberal values," which incrementally began to morph into a critique of a Liberal court

---

[2] "La qualité de nos juges à la Cour suprême du Canada est impeccable" Denis Jacques, Lawyer – Barreau du Québec. Testimony before the Standing Committee on Justice, Human Rights, Public Safety and Emergency Preparedness: Thursday, March 25, 2004.

[3] "In fact, however, the six Chrétien appointees are largely indistinguishable on political or ideological grounds from the three current Supreme Court members who were appointed by Mr. Chrétien's predecessor, Brian Mulroney." Patrick Monahan, "Is it Jean Chrétien's court?" The Globe and Mail. Toronto, Ont.: Jun 27, 2003. pg. A.15

[4] Alexander Bickel, *The Least Dangerous Branch: The Supreme Court at the Bar of Politics* (Indianapolis: Bobbs-Merrill, 1962).

[5] "It would be interesting to see if you could devise a process by which the public would better understand the role of the court. It would be wonderful for the court, the public, and everybody. We would stop talking about activism, which in my view is such a bad word. You only use that

propagating Liberal values.[6] Then opposition justice critic Vic Toews reflected this in his words: "this Liberal government has allowed judges to become the most powerful force in setting social policy in Canada. Whether it is by allowing convicted murders to vote or by changing fundamental institutions like marriage, this government has substituted the supremacy of an elected Parliament with unelected judges."[7]

Fourth, the dynamic of judicial decision-making intruding upon, if not overtaking, policy decisions that ought to be made by Parliament also motivated Parliament to inquire into the appointments process underpinning those judicial decisions.

Fifth, the purported politicization of the Supreme Court by a fractious minority Parliament was further exacerbated by allegations in the Gomery Commission hearings that appointees to the Federal Courts (the allegation did not extend to the Supreme Court of Canada) were Liberal appointees, such that the fallout of the Gomery Commission was extended to the judicial appointments process. Finally, there was the perceived anomaly of the executive–effectively the Prime Minister–making appointments to the Supreme Court alone, without any Parliamentary input or accountability. Accordingly, and in light of the foregoing, shortly after my appointment as Justice Minister it became apparent to me that not only was the Supreme Court appointment process in need of reform, but the very constitutional framework which underpinned the process itself had to be explained and understood.

With the foregoing in mind, this article will be organized around five themes. First, I will discuss the chronology of developments that led to the consideration of a reform proposal–the roadmap to reform. Second, I will outline the pre-reform constitutional framework and consultative process, particularly as set forth in my submission to the Parliamentary Committee. Third, I will discuss the Parliamentary Committee's report itself, including the proposal for an interim reform process. Fourth, I will summarize the interim appointments

for people who are supposed to tell Parliament that the legislation is no good, not for people who are reactionaries or activists. The reactionaries are pushing their agenda. Nobody is pushing an agenda, as a matter of fact." Hon. Claire L'Heureux-Dubé, before the Standing Committee on Justice, Human Rights, Public Safety and Emergency Preparedness: Tuesday, March 30, 2004.

[6] "In Canada it doesn't work–that is to say, we know now that with the Supreme Court appointments you can't predict which way the Supreme Court justice will decide by knowing he was appointed by the Liberals, so he'll be on the left, or by the Conservatives, so he'll be on the right. That kind of ideologically driven selection, which is characteristic of the American process, has not been characteristic of the Canadian process at the Supreme Court level."" Denis Jacques, Lawyer – Barreau du Québec. Testimony before the Standing Committee on Justice, Human Rights, Public Safety and Emergency Preparedness: Thursday, March 25, 2004.

[7] HANSARD: 37th PARLIAMENT, 3rd SESSION Monday, February 23, 2004.

process that resulted in the nominations of Justices Abella and Charron. Finally, I will summarize the comprehensive reform proposal that presaged the appointment of Justice Rothstein and now constitutes the basic appointment process to the Supreme Court of Canada.

II. The Road to Reform

On 12 December 2003, Prime Minister Paul Martin's new Liberal government was sworn into office and I was appointed Minister of Justice. That same day, the Prime Minister announced–and it is a dramatic representation of the priority that he attached both to the judicial appointments process and to its democratization–that the government would "specifically consult the Standing Committee on Justice and Human Rights on how best to implement prior review of appointments of Supreme Court of Canada judges"[8] Indeed, in his first discussion with me on that day, the Prime Minister emphasized the importance he ascribed to the reform of the judicial appointments process and the role of Parliament in that reform. On 4 February 2004, the then Liberal government reaffirmed this commitment in its Action Plan for Democratic Reform[9]–again reflecting the importance that the Prime Minister and government attached to the reform of the appointments process.

On 20 February 2004, Justice Arbour announced that she would be leaving the Supreme Court in June 2004 to become the United Nations High Commissioner for Human Rights. The same day, Prime Minister Paul Martin announced that the government would decide on the vacancy, but that MPs would be involved in the selection process. Shortly thereafter, a discussion ensued as to whether there would be an interim appointments process to fill Justice Arbour's vacant seat–what was referred to as a "one-off procedure"–or whether a permanent appointments process would be developed before her departure.

[8] "Parliament will play a greater role in the appointment process. Appointments to certain key positions, including heads of Crown Corporations and agencies, will now be subject to prior Parliamentary review. The government will consult with the appropriate House Committees on how best to proceed on prior review of these appointments, and will specifically consult the Standing Committee on Justice and Human Rights on how best to implement prior review of appointments of Supreme Court of Canada Judges. These committees will also have the opportunity to consider which other appointments could be subject to their review " Press Release – 12 December 2003 entitled: PRIME MINISTER MARTIN ANNOUNCES NEW GOVERNMENT WILL BE GUIDED BY A NEW APPROACH

[9] On February 4, 2004, the Hon. Jacques Saada, PC, MP, Leader of the Government in the House of Commons and Minister responsible for Democratic Reform, tabled Ethics, Responsibility, Accountability: An Action Plan for Democratic Reform in the House.

In a speech before the Québec Chamber of Congress two days later, Prime Minister Paul Martin reiterated yet again the need for a new process of Supreme Court appointments as part of a larger project of democratic reform, saying, "[w]e want to give Parliamentarians the right to review ... appointments to the Supreme Court of Canada"[10] Then, on 19 March 2004, I received a call from then Supreme Court Chief Justice Frank Iacobucci. Justice Iacobucci advised me that he had decided to retire from the Supreme Court for family reasons. As he put it, "Nancy [his wife] has always been there for me all these years, it is time for me to now be there for her and the family and our grandchildren." It was a very moving and emotional conversation with someone who had been a long-time colleague and friend. Later, at his retirement ceremony, I said "[w]e have, the Canadian people, have lost a giant of a Supreme Court judge, a giant of a man."[11]

The unexpected and dramatic announcements from two sitting Supreme Court justices that they were both retiring in June 2004 – coinciding with a decision of the Parliamentary Standing Committee on 23 March 2004 undertake an inquiry into the appointments process itself[12] – accentuated and accelerated the need for establishing a reformed appointments process as soon as possible. These developments also coincided with my projected appearance before the Parliamentary Committee on 30 March 2004.

III. The Pre-Reform Judicial Appointments process: The Constitutional and Consultative Framework as the Contextual Basis for Prospective Reform

The pre-reform appointments process has traditionally been organized around two central considerations. First, respect for the constitutional framework

[10] "In the same spirit of progressive reform, we want to give Parliamentarians the right to review the vast majority of appointments to senior government positions, including appointments to the Supreme Court of Canada. In the past, the process by which the Prime Minister appointed these judges unfolded behind closed doors. We have excellent Supreme Court justices who are recognized the world over. But the way we arrive at these appointments is from a bygone era, and we need to acknowledge this. This has to change. We aren't interested in submitting these appointments to politicized hearings that often make all sorts of noise but don't do much good. What we're interested in, rather, is to put to good use the knowledge and informed opinions of experts and Parliamentarians in order to help the Prime Minister make the best possible decisions." http://www.law-lib.utoronto.ca/conferences/judiciary/chronology.htm

[11] Iacobucci, a 'giant' of a judge, retires; Supreme Court justice known for his civility Canada's legal heavyweights bid fond farewell; Tonda MacCharles. Toronto Star. Toronto, Ont.: Jun 22, 2004. pg. A.16

[12] "You will recall that previously the committee had been looking at the appointment process for all judicial appointments, based on a motion referred to the committee from the House and

governing the appointments process and second, the development of a comprehensive consultative process to give expression to–or to implement–this constitutional responsibility. The constitutional framework anchored in the *Supreme Court Act*[13] vests the constitutional authority for Supreme Court appointments with the Governor in Council–or the cabinet–by way of an Order in Council, such that the executive remains responsible and accountable for the exercise of this important power. Section 5 of the *Act* sets forth the threshold requirement for appointment to the Supreme Court to the effect that any person may be appointed a Justice of the Supreme Court who is or has been a judge of a Superior Court or a barrister or advocate with at least 10 years standing at the bar of a province.[14] Section 6 requires that at least three of the Justices of the Supreme Court must come from Québec.[15] By convention, three Justices are appointed from Ontario, two from the western provinces and one from Atlantic Canada. Justices hold office conditional on good behaviour and can only be removed by the Governor General on address of the Senate and the House of Commons.[16] The mandatory retirement age of Supreme Court Justices is seventy-five.[17]

The consultative process developed to implement this constitutional responsibility and secure the best candidates was never well known – indeed, it may be said to have been relatively unknown. This led some to believe, understandably, that the pre-reform process was both secret and partisan. However, the process was not so much secretive as it was unknown. Accordingly, in the interests of both transparency and accountability, I appeared before the Standing Committee to outline the process for Supreme Court appointments that I following to fill the vacancies on the bench. I did not claim that this consultative process had always been adhered to in every particular by my predecessors, but I indicated that it was the protocol of consultation that I was now engaged in as Minister of Justice. Indeed, the Parliamentary Committee

originally moved by our colleague, Mr. Marceau. Subsequent to that, at the invitation of the Prime Minister, who has spoken publicly on the issue, and following discussion among members, we have agreed to look at this issue in relation to Supreme Court appointments." Derek Lee, Chair, Standing Committee on Justice, Human Rights, Public Safety and Emergency Preparedness Tuesday, March 23, 2004

[13] *Supreme Court Act*, R.S.C. 1985, c. S-26, s. 4(1).

[14] **5.** Any person may be appointed a judge who is or has been a judge of a superior court of a province or a barrister or advocate of at least ten years standing at the bar of a province.

[15] **6.** At least three of the judges shall be appointed from among the judges of the Court of Appeal or of the Superior Court of the Province of Quebec or from among the advocates of that Province.

[16] **9.** (1) Subject to subsection (2), the judges hold office during good behaviour, but are removable by the Governor General on address of the Senate and House of Commons.

[17] 9 (2) A judge shall cease to hold office on attaining the age of seventy-five years.

described my appearance as "the first time that [the appointments process] had been made public. Canadians had their first opportunity to learn who was consulted about Supreme Court appointments and the criteria by which candidates are assessed for their fitness to be a Justice of the Supreme Court."[18]

The first step in the appointments process is a consultative process whereby the Minister identifies prospective candidates from the region where the vacancy originates–be it Ontario, Québec, Atlantic Canada, or the west. The protocol of that consultative process may be described as follows: First, the Minister of Justice identifies potential candidates who may be drawn from judges of the courts in the region–particularly the Courts of Appeal–as well as from senior members of the bar and leading academics in the region. Any interested person may also put a name forward for consideration. Sometimes, names may be identified from previous consultations concerning prior judicial appointments.

In particular, the identification and assessment of potential candidates is based on a broad range of consultations with various individuals. The Minister of Justice specifically consults with the following: the Chief Justice of Canada (and perhaps other members of the Supreme Court of Canada); the Chief Justices of the courts from the province or region with the vacancy; the Attorneys-General of the province or region; at least one senior member of the Canadian Bar Association; and at least one senior member of the law society of the relevant region. The Minister could also consider input from other interested persons, such as academics and organizations who wish to recommend a candidate for consideration. Anyone is free to recommend candidates, and indeed, some choose to do so by way of writing to the Minister of Justice.

The second stage in the appointments process is the assessment and evaluation of potential candidates, with the predominant consideration being merit. The specific criteria for appointment may be classified into three main categories: professional capacity, personal characteristics, and diversity. Professional capacity encompasses not only the highest level of proficiency in the law, but also the following considerations: [Not every candidate must have each of these criteria; rather, they are the composite set of criteria through which evaluation takes place.]

- Superior intellectual ability and analytical and written skills
- Proven ability to listen and to maintain an open mind while hearing all sides of the argument

[18] IMPROVING THE SUPREME COURT OF CANADA APPOINTMENTS PROCESS: REPORT OF THE STANDING COMMITTEE ON JUSTICE, HUMAN RIGHTS, PUBLIC SAFETY AND EMERGENCY PREPAREDNESS, May 2004

- Decisiveness and soundness of judgment
- Capacity to manage and share consistently heavy workload in a collaborative context
- Capacity to manage stress and the pressures of the isolation of the judicial role;
- Strong cooperative interpersonal skills
- Awareness of social context
- Bilingual capacity
- Specific expertise required for the Supreme Court (expertise can be identified by the Court itself or by others)

Under the rubric of personal qualities, the following factors are considered:

- Impeccable personal and professional ethics: honesty, integrity, and forthrightness
- Respect and regard for others: patience, courtesy, tact, humility, impartiality, and tolerance
- Personal sense of responsibility: common sense, punctuality, and reliability

The diversity criterion concerns the extent to which the court's composition adequately reflects the diversity of Canadian society. As well, in reviewing the candidates, the Minister could also consider – where appropriate – jurisprudential profiles prepared by the Department of Justice. These are intended to provide information about the volume of cases written, areas of expertise, the outcome of appeals of the cases, and the degree to which judgments have been followed in lower courts.

Upon completion of the aforementioned assessments and consultations, the Minister would discuss the candidates with the Prime Minister. Note that the Minister may be involved in an ongoing consultation with a range of persons as set forth in the above Protocol. Once a preferred candidate is chosen, the Prime Minister would, in turn, recommend the candidate to cabinet. The appointment then proceeds by way of an Order in Council appointment, as per the *Constitution*.

In my appearance before the Parliamentary Committee, after describing the appointments process as set forth above and sharing with them the protocol of that process, I commented on how the Committee was "engaged in an important review of the role parliamentarians might play in the appointment process. This review may include both a review of the process of appointments and a review of the proposed nominee recommended by the process."[19] In terms of

[19] Testimony before the Standing Committee on Justice, Human Rights, Public Safety and Emergency Preparedness on Tuesday, March 30, 2004

reviewing the appointment process, I urged the Committee to bear in mind the two factors set forth above: the constitutional framework, which vested authority in the executive branch of government; and the consultative process, which had been established to implement the constitutional responsibility through which candidates were identified and evaluated.

I also invited the Parliamentary review Committee to consider the following questions: what is the form that this Parliamentary review might take respecting the vetting of the proposed nominee, and what is the mechanism by which this review might be undertaken, and offered a number of options for consideration. First, the Committee could undertake its review by hearing representations from the Minister of Justice as to why the nominee was chosen. Second, the Committee could engage in a direct interview of the candidate. Third, the review could be conducted by an independent expert representative Committee – sometimes referred to as an 'eminent persons panel' – which would include representatives from Parliament.

There were other issues that I indicated might arise from the modality of review. First, what might be the appropriate composition of the Committee undertaking the review? Second, should the process be confidential or should some of the review be public? In the context of a direct interview with the candidate, what questions might be asked so as not to embarrass the candidate or politicize the process? I then identified for the Parliamentary Committee a number of guiding principles that might assist the Parliamentary review while helping to address some of the above questions. These principles, which underpinned both the Parliamentary review process – and the ultimate comprehensive reform of the appointments process that I subsequently proposed and which will be addressed below – are as follows.

First is the merit principle. The overriding objective of the appointments process, simply put, is to ensure that the best candidates are appointed based on merit. Indeed, a process that would discourage good people from applying is one that is not worth having. Additionally, the Supreme Court bench should, to the extent possible, reflect the diversity of Canadian society. A diverse bench ensures that a plurality of perspectives are brought to bear on the resolution of disputes.

Second, any reforms must preserve both the integrity of the Supreme Court and the administration of justice. The judiciary is an institution vital to the maintenance of the rule of law and the health of our democracy. It must not be politicized, nor should any damage be done to the reputation of its members.

Third, the appointments process must protect and promote judicial independence. The independence of the judiciary is a cornerstone of our legal system, and nothing should be done that might undermine or diminish this principle.

Fourth, the appointments process must be more transparent. The consultation process, which was comprehensive, was simply not known at that time.

Fifth, the appointments process needed to recognize the value of provincial input. While the consultation process did provide for important provincial input through the consultation with appropriate provincial Chief Justices, provincial Attorneys-General, provincial bar association leaders, and other interested provincial bodies that may wish to make recommendations, provincial participation needed to be enhanced and institutionalized.

Sixth, the appointments process needed to factor in the importance of Parliamentary input, as had begun with this Parliamentary review of March 2004. Finally, there was the importance of public input and public participation in the appointments process.

IV. Parliamentary Committee Report and Proposed Interim Reform Process

In May 2004, the Parliamentary Committee published its report titled, "Improving the Supreme Court of Canada Appointments Process."[20] The report reflected a broad Parliamentary consensus on the need for a new Supreme Court of Canada appointments process in order to ensure greater transparency and openness as well as enhanced Parliamentary and public involvement.

The Parliamentary Committee also noted the pace of the Committee's work had been accelerated by the unexpected resignations of Justices Arbour and Iacobucci. Accordingly, the Committee reasoned that, in order to have a full bench of nine Justices for the fall sitting, it would be necessary to appoint two new Justices at some point in the summer of 2004 so as to give the new judges sufficient time to prepare for upcoming cases. It acknowledged that the process for screening and selecting nominees was well underway by the Minister of Justice. Accordingly, the Committee concluded that since there appeared to be insufficient time to put a new long-term process into place, an interim procedure should be established.

The interim process recommended by a majority of the Committee was as follows: the Minister of Justice would appear in a public session to explain the procedure by which the two prospective appointees for the Supreme Court were selected. At a public hearing–and without revealing the contents of any private deliberations–the Minister would explain to parliamentarians and all

[20] *Supra* note 18.

Canadians the process by which candidates were identified and evaluated, the nature of the evaluations conducted, and the qualifications of the candidates. This could involve, for example, an explanation as to what expertise was lost with the departure of Justices Arbour and Iacobucci, and how the new Justices might fill any needs that may have been created. In the course of such a hearing, the Committee expected there would be a greater appreciation of the appointments process, and that a further understanding of the work of the Supreme Court would result. The Committee noted that the establishment of an interim process should not preclude long-term consideration of the Supreme Court of Canada appointments process.

On 23 May 2004, while I was engaged in the consultation process for the identification and evaluation of the two prospective nominees for the Supreme Court of Canada, an election was called, putting all consultations on hold pending the results of the election. The Liberal party was re-elected on 28 June 2004 with a minority government, and I was subsequently reappointed Minister of Justice and resumed my consultations on 19 July 2004. During the next month, I met and consulted with on a number of occasions the Chief Justice of Canada, the Chief Justice of the Ontario Court of Appeal, the Ontario Provincial Attorney-General and other persons designated in the Protocol. On 20 August 2004, I engaged in a series of discussions with the Prime Minister pursuant to which it was determined that the two nominees would be Ontario Court of Appeal Justices Abella and Charron.

V. Interim Process Resulting in Nomination of Justices Abella and Charron

The Interim *Ad Hoc* Committee on the Appointment of Supreme Court Judges[21] was created for the purpose of reviewing the candidacy of the persons recommended for appointment to the Supreme Court of Canada. It was, as noted earlier, a mechanism that had been recommended in the Parliamentary Committee report of May 2004 as a necessary interim measure arising from the vacancies. The *Ad Hoc* Committee was put in place over the course of discussions with the House Leaders of all parties, who agreed that it was an interim body meant to complete a review so that two vacancies on the Supreme Court could be filled before the Supreme Court began its sittings on 4 October 2004. As a result, the review process had to be completed as soon as possible,

[21] REPORT OF THE INTERIM AD HOC COMMITTEE ON THE APPOINTMENT OF SUPREME COURT JUDGES. Online: http://www.justice.gc.ca/en/dept/pub/scc_courtsup/

and preferably no later than the end of August. The Committee recognized that the authority to make Supreme Court appointments was constitutionally vested in the Governor in Council, and that the role of the Committee was purely an advisory one.

The majority of the Committee's members were elected Members of Parliament, consisting of three members of the Liberal Party of Canada, two members of the Conservative Party of Canada, one member of the Bloc Québécois, and one member of the New Democratic Party. In accordance with the written understanding of the political parties, the Committee also included a representative of the Canadian Judicial Council and a representative of the Law Society of Upper Canada. The Committee was subject to special rules of procedure, which were agreed upon by all the parties represented in Parliament. Those parties had also agreed that the hearing of the Committee was to be as open and transparent as possible while ensuring the integrity of the process. The Minister of Justice was to appear before the *ad hoc* committee in order to describe to the Committee the scope and nature of the process used to select the nominees and to present to the Committee the information gathered about the professional qualifications and personal suitability of the nominees, having regard to the criteria as set forth in the Protocol. In particular, the Minister's presentation was to include reference to the consultations he undertook, the written information he reviewed, and the additional personal research he conducted.

Committee members were to have an opportunity to ask questions to the Minister in relation to these issues. No witnesses other than the Minister of Justice were to be called for the interim process. The Committee was to make its views known by way of a written report and provide its advice on the appointment of the proposed nominees by 27 August 2004. Either at that time or as soon as possible thereafter, the Committee could also provide input on the *ad hoc* Committee process itself and its implications for longer term reform, to be considered by the justice Committee in the fall.

My appearance before the *ad hoc* Committee lasted for some two hours. Indeed, as I stated before the Committee, the appearance was, "what one might call a historic occasion. For the first time ever, there is a public hearing and prior Parliamentary review of the nominations to the Supreme Court of Canada."[22] For the benefit of the Committee–and for the benefit of Canadians

[22] SPEAKING NOTES FOR IRWIN COTLER, MINISTER OF JUSTICE AND ATTORNEY GENERAL OF CANADA, ON THE OCCASION OF A PRESENTATION TO THE AD HOC COMMITTEE ON SUPREME COURT OF CANADA APPOINTMENTS AUGUST 25, 2004 OTTAWA http://www.justice.gc.ca/en/news/sp/2004/doc_31212.html

watching the televised hearing–I reviewed the nature of the appointments process: both the constitutional framework in which appointments are made and the nature of the appointments process itself. I added:

> This public hearing – like the prior Parliamentary hearings with its publication of the Protocol of Consultation – marks an important value-added dimension in the interests of increased transparency, Parliamentary participation, improved public awareness and understanding, and a better appreciation of the merits of the individual nominees and the strengths that they bring to the Court.

After describing in detail the process of consultation, the information I reviewed and the qualifications of the candidates, I concluded as follows:

> [W]e can all take pride in this extraordinarily talented group of members of the Ontario Bench and Bar. But decisions have to be taken, recommendations need to be made; and in Justices Rosalie Abella and Louise Charron we have two outstanding jurists whose unique repository of experience and expertise – and remarkable array of professional and personal qualities – not only commend their elevation to the Supreme Court, but promise that profound and enduring contribution to Court and country that will inspire us all.

Following this public session, the Committee proceeded to discuss its report in an *in camera* meeting. It then advised that it was satisfied that the two nominees "are eminently qualified for appointment to the Supreme Court of Canada".

VI. Comprehensive Refom Proposal for the Supreme Court of Canada Appointments Process

On 7 April 2005 I appeared before the then Parliamentary Committee[23] to outline a comprehensive proposal for the Supreme Court of Canada appointments process. The proposal reflected an appreciation of a diversity of views from a broad range of constituencies and perspectives–lawyers, judges, domestic and international academics, parliamentarians, provincial legislators and others. In particular, this proposal was anchored in the deliberations of the Parliamentary Committee and its May 2004 report, in addition to the *ad hoc* committee proceedings of August 2004. Accordingly, the proposal took into account the recommendations of those groups, including those relating to increased transparency and enhanced provincial consultation.

[23] Cotler, Irwin (Minister of Justice and Attorney General of Canada). Testimony before the Standing Committee on Justice, Human Rights, Public Safety and Emergency Preparedness. 38th Parliament, 1st Session. 7 April 2005.

The reform proposal itself created a four-stage process that became the template used to fill the vacancy occasioned by the retirement of Justice Major on 25 December 2005. Justice Rothstein was appointed to the Supreme Court by the new Conservative government on 1 March 2006 effectively using this process. In the first stage of the new process, the Minister of Justice conducts a consultation to identify prospective nominees, similar to the one employed in the Protocol set forth earlier. To ensure that there is a broad base of input into the initial list, the Minister publicly invites the written views of any person or group with respect to meritorious candidates. This engenders a prospective list of five to eight candidates–depending on the province or region–who are then assessed by an Advisory Committee set up for this purpose. Given that some candidates might not wish to have their names considered through this new process, the Minister should seek the prior consent of candidates before putting their names forward.

In the second stage of the process, an Advisory Committee is established each time a vacancy arises. The Advisory Committee itself engages in a consultation and evaluation process, assessing the candidates based on a written mandate from the Minister as well as the established criteria contained in the public protocol. The Advisory Committee is composed of:

- one MP from each recognized party in the House
- one retired judge, nominated by the Canadian Judicial Council
- one member nominated by the provincial Attorneys-General in the region
- one member nominated by the provincial law societies in the region
- two eminent people of recognized stature in the region, nominated by the Minister.[24]

The members are not to be regarded as "representatives" of particular constituencies or points of view. Rather, they bring a diverse set of experiences and perspectives to a common enterprise of assessing candidates for the Supreme Court on the merit-based principle.

The Minister provides a mandate letter to the Advisory Committee, setting out the objectives of the Committee, describing the merit-based criteria, establishing timeframes and providing for a general procedure, particularly in relation to confidentiality. The Minister also meets with the Committee before it begins its work to clarify these issues and to underscore the importance of

[24] *Ibid.*

collegiality and confidentiality in conducting the Advisory Committee's work. The Committee is empowered to seek the consent of the Minister to assess additional candidates that are not on the original list. Before consenting, the Minister once again consults with those whose views he or she sought in relation to the initial list. If the Minister agrees that the new candidate should be assessed, the candidate would, once again, be contacted to ensure he or she is agreeable to having his or her name stand.

The Committee's assessment of the candidates is based on: an appreciation of the relevant experience and expertise of the candidates; a documentary review (CVs, judgments, articles, and so on); as well as consultations with third parties. The Advisory Committee works on a democratic basis, with key committee decisions requiring a consensus or majority vote. Such decisions include who should be consulted, whether an additional candidate should be proposed, and who should be on the short list. This was the approach taken by a majority of the Justice Committee in its May 2004 Report. In my April 2005 proposal I agreed with the Justice Committee–and this also represented the preponderant view of the many consulted–that there should be no in-person interviews. The view expressed was that it was doubtful whether such interviews would elicit relevant information not already available to the Committee through other sources, including the comprehensive consultative and evaluative process. There was also a concern that the potential difficulty in controlling the direction of questioning could distort an assessment on merit-based criteria.

In the matter of confidentiality, it is clear that assessing candidates for the Supreme Court is an extremely important and sensitive responsibility. Accordingly, for the Advisory Committee process to work effectively–indeed, for it to work at all–it is vital that individuals who are consulted by the Advisory Committee be completely candid in their assessments. For the same reason, as recognized by the Parliamentary Committee, it is essential that there be the widest possible scope for discussion within the Advisory Committee. Candid discussions are only possible when the participants can be assured that their views are being held in the strictest of confidence. Robust protections for confidentiality will reassure potential candidates who might otherwise be hesitant about having their names put forward for consideration.

Therefore, confidentiality would be required not only of Advisory Committee members but also of persons being consulted. Given the intense public interest in these appointments, the latter group may present the greater challenge. For these reasons, Committee members as well as those who are consulted are asked to enter into written confidentiality agreements. It is true that there can be no guarantees that these undertakings will never be breached. However, I believed then–and now–that the collegial nature of this process, the stature and reputation of the members of the Advisory Committee, and the national importance of the task will discourage individuals from violating these obligations. A person deciding to undermine such an important process–thereby potentially damaging individuals and the institution of the Court–would face significant public condemnation. This itself acts as a strong deterrent to such mischief-making. It is encouraging that the deliberations that led to the nomination of Justice Rothstein were not attended by any breach of confidentiality.

Once its deliberations are complete, the Advisory Committee provides a confidential short list of three names along with a commentary of the strengths and weaknesses of each candidate to the Minister. In addition, the Committee provides the Minister the full record of consultations and other material on which it relied. If for any reason the Minister felt that the record of consultations was incomplete, the Minister could request that the Advisory Committee conduct further consultations.

In all but the most exceptional circumstances, the candidate will be appointed from the short list. There is a proviso of "exceptional circumstances" that exists as a safety valve. It is principally intended to recognize the legal reality that the ultimate responsibility to make these appointments lies with Cabinet. But it is also there for a practical reason. In implementing this process, the government is taking a bold step forward. It cannot anticipate every possibility or turn of events in the future. At some point, the Advisory Committee process may be significantly undermined by a major breach of confidentiality. In such a case, it would not only be the government's right, but its responsibility, to put a stop to the process and make the appointment in the manner in which it was previously done.

In my view, it would be exceedingly rare for a government to ever make an appointment from outside the short list. I say this for three reasons. First, a government would not want to face the significant public criticism that would arise from an exercise of this power. Second, a decision to appoint from outside the list would seriously undermine the credibility of the appointments process. Third, the exercise of such a power would affect the willingness of prominent Canadians to serve on future advisory Committees. One must also ask why an Advisory Committee member would go through this process if there was a real risk that the government would ignore the Committee's recommendations.

The third stage of the process involves the selection and appointment of a person from the short list recommended by the Advisory Committee. Before the Government fell on 28 November 2005, I had already received the short list, and had made my selection; however, I could but I did not act on it during the election, pending the results.

As it happened, the new government concurred with my recommendation of Justice Rothstein as the nominee for the Supreme Court. Indeed, I was pleased that both the template of this proposal for appointments to the Supreme Court as well as the person who would have been my proposed nominee were adopted by the new government—albeit with certain changes to the composition to the Judicial Advisory Committee, which henceforth comprised:

- one nominee of the provincial Law Society
- one nominee of the provincial branch of the Canadian Bar Association
- one nominee of the Chief Justice of the province
- one nominee of the provincial Attorney General
- one nominee of the law enforcement community
- three nominees of the federal Minister of Justice representing the public
- one ex officio non-voting member: Commissioner for Federal Judicial Affairs or Executive Director, Judicial Appointments[25]

It should be noted that while the newly-elected Conservative Government adopted this overall template, it also added an important dimension – an in-person interview after the nominee was chosen before a specially constituted Parliamentary committee for that purpose. I concurred then with this initiative, proposed by the Conservative government, and believe that the interview with Justice Rothstein only enhanced the process including, in particular, the public understanding of the judicial appointments process and the work of the Supreme Court of Canada.

At the fourth and final stage, after the appointment has been recommended, the original template envisaged that the Minister would appear before the Justice Committee to explain the nomination process and the candidate's personal and professional qualities. This would be similar to my appearance before the *ad hoc* Committee, though in this new proposal, it follows upon the three other considered stages as set forth above. As it now stands, the Conservative government has replaced the appearance by the Minister with the process by which the nominee, rather than the Minister, would appear before the Justice Committee.[26]

The Supreme Court of Canada is a pillar of our constitutional democracy and the guardian of our rights. It deserves an appointments process that is commensurate with its responsibilities and its excellence. During my period as Justice Minister, I had the unprecedented opportunity to not only participate in the appointment of three Supreme Court Justices, but also – in collaboration

---

[25] "Judicial Advisory Committees – Guidelines." *Office of the Commissioner for Federal Judicial Affairs Canada*. Web. 27 May 2010. <http://www.fja-cmf.gc.ca/appointments-nominations/committees-comites/guidelines-lignes-eng.html#Composition>.

[26] Renamed Standing Committee on Justice and Human Rights in the 39th Parliament

with Parliaments of the day, the bench, bar, and academe – to craft and oversee the development of the first-ever comprehensive proposal for, and review of, the Supreme Court appointments process. I trust that the template proposed will achieve its purpose, and with the passage of time be further refined and improved upon.

CHAPTER NINETEEN

THE SYSTEM OF THE JUDICIAL APPOINTMENT IN POLAND A QUESTION OF THE LEGITIMACY OF THE JUDICIAL POWER

*Fryderyk Zoll**

I. The System of the Appointment of the Judges of the General Courts and the Supreme Court in Poland

According to the Polish Constitution the judges of the common courts[1] and the Supreme Court are appointed by the President of the State on request of the National Council of the Judiciary.[2] The National Council of the Judiciary is a body consisting of the representatives of the judiciary itself. These representatives are selected by special assembles, selected by the local assembles of the judges from different circuits and court levels. The President of the Supreme Court and the President of the Superior Administrative Court are members of the Council *ex officio*. In the Council there are also representatives of the Lower and Upper Chamber of the Parliament and of the President of Poland. The Ministry of Justice is also a member of this body. The politicians are, however, a significant minority in this body.[3]

The candidate for the office of the judge must file his or her application to the president of the respective court.[4] The Counsel of the respective court has to evaluate the candidate.[5] The application needs to be presented to the assembly

* Dr hab. Fryderyk Zoll (*1970), Professor at the Jagiellonian University in Cracow. Mercator Professor at the University of Osnabrück (from 1.10.2010). Member of the International Academy of Comparative Law. Member of the Acquis Group on the Existing EC Contract Law. Director of the Centre for the Foreign Law Programs at the Jagiellonian University. Head of the Curriculum Team for the National School of Judiciary and Prosecutors in Poland.

[1] The notion of "common courts" means all courts with the exception of the administrative courts, the Supreme Court and the Constitutional Tribunal.

[2] Art. 179 of the Polish Constitution.

[3] Art. 187 of the Polish Constitution. The members of the Council of Judiciary are: the First President of the Supreme Court, the Ministry of Justice, the President of the Superior Administrative Court, the person appointed by the President of the Republic, 15 members elected from the judges of the Supreme Court, common courts, administrative courts and military courts, four members elected by the Sejm (lower chamber of the Parliament) from its deputies and two senators elected by the Senat (the higher chamber of the Parliament).

[4] Art. 57 § 2 of the Law on the System of Common Courts from 27.07. 2001, Dz. U. (Official Journal) 2001, no. 98, pos. 1070 with sub. amendments.

[5] Art. 57 § 3 of the Law on the System of Common Courts.

general of the judges of the local court. The assembly votes on the candidate.[6] The results of this voting have to be presented to the National Council of the Judiciary, even if the candidate did not get a majority of votes.[7] The voting of the assembly general of the respective court has, at least in the theory, only a consultative power. The National Council of the Judiciary may accept the candidate by the majority voting and present it to the President of Poland,[8] who formally appoints the judge. Exceptionally, the National Council may vote on the candidate who has been presented only by the Ministry of Justice without having the opinion of the respective assembly general of the respective court.[9]

II. The Question of the Delay or Refusal of the Judicial Appointment by the President of the Republic

The practice of the appointment of the judges by the President of Poland was simple. The President was always following the decision of the National Counsel of the Judiciary and the appointment procedure has been driven without delays. When Mr. Lech Kaczyński became President of the country, he has changed this practice, claiming for him a right to review once again the ability of candidates to become a judge or to be promoted. There is not a clear view, whether the President may refuse the candidateship accepted by the National Counsel of the Judiciary.[10] At least a part of the legal doctrine was rather reluctant to support this position.[11] According to this view the new practice of the President has infringed the independence of the judges, mostly in the promotion of the judges applying for a higher position, but also in the case of the first appointments concerning so called "assessors" (the first step of the judicial career – they were appointed by the Ministry of Justice for a definite period of time and after a positive verification they could be promoted to be a judge by the usual procedure of appointment – the Constitutional Court declared the institution of "assessors" non – constitutional[12]). In such cases the judges who already were handling the cases, were waiting for an indefinite period of time for the President's decision. Actually, by the new practice the President got a

[6] Art. 58 § 1 and 2 of the Law on the System of Common Courts.

[7] Art. 58 § 3 of the Law on the System of Common Courts.

[8] Art. 60 of the Law on the System of Common Courts and Art. 2 Section 1 no. 3 of the Law on the National Counsel of the Judiciary from 27.7. 2001, Dz. U. 2001, no. 100, pos. 1082.

[9] Art. 59 of the Law on the System of Common Courts.

[10] So J. Sułkowski, Uprawnienia Prezydenta RP do powoływania sędziów, Przegląd Sejmowy 4/2008, pp. 47 & sub. (in exceptional circumstances).

[11] J. Ciapała, Charakter kompetencji Prezydenta RP. Uwagi w kontekście kompetencji w zakresie powoływania sędziów, Przegląd Sejmowy 4/2008, p. 31 and sub.

[12] Decision of the Polish Constitutional Court from 24.10.2007, SK 7/06.

tool to influence the judicial decisions, which has violated the independence of the judges. The practice of the President was wrong and probably non – constitutional, although the Constitution is quite silent on this issue. The question of the constitutionality of this practice will be probably reviewed in shortly by the Constitutional Court of Poland. One of the candidates, who has been accepted by the Council of Judiciary has been finally rejected by the President and he tries to demand this decision.[13]

The problem of the President has reacted with not acceptable means on the present scheme of the judicial appointments. It does not mean, however, that the system of the judicial appointment in Poland does not raise questions concerning the legitimacy of the judicial power.

III. Access to the Profession in the Hands of the Judiciary

The questionable practice of President Kaczyński uncovers the real problem of the judicial appointment in Poland. The system of the appointment of the judges gives enormous power to the judges themselves. The whole procedure of the appointment is extremely dependent from the consent of the representatives of the judiciary. It is even much more dependent then it is determined by the letter of law. It does not almost happen that a candidate rejected by the general assembly of judges of the respective courts is accepted by the National Council of the Judiciary. The Council is also dominated by the representatives of the judiciary. It is a sort of "cloning system". The judges influence in a decisive way who will be the next judge and who will be promoted. It is quite understandable that this system has been adopted in this shape almost directly after the fall of the communist regime in our country. The creation of the judicial self – government, following to some extend the examples of other legal professions and the system of the professional appointment dominated also by the representatives of the judiciary was aiming to secure the independence of the judges. It was a result of the experience with the abuse of power in the time of communism. The new legal system was supposed to be immune from the possibility to influence it by the world of politics. This system has suffered, however, (although not in comparable dimension) all disadvantages which have been apparent in the other legal profession. The fairness and transparency of the judicial appointment was infringed by some appointment procedure and in some cases not the best candidates have been chosen and appointed. The problem which has been raised by the denial of appointment of

[13] Case SK 8/10.

the judges by the President concerned the question of the legitimacy of the judges, appointed in the frame of such "cloning system". In the system, in which the judicial appointment is mostly an internal affair of the judiciary the question, whether some kind of the democratic legitimacy is missing, has to be raised.

This question has a philosophical dimension, concerning the positioning of the judiciary in the frame of the democratic legal order and the separation of power, but also it touches the practical consequences of the system, in which one branch of the state's power is selected by itself. It creates a structure pretending to protect its own group interests, endangering at least potentially the access to the profession of the best candidates, but who are not familiar to the local members of the judiciary or for some reasons inconvenient to them. On another side there is an essential problem of the securing the system from the political influence of the executive power. It has been proved by our recent experience that this is not only a theoretical problem of Poland. The government of Mr. Kaczyński (the brother of the former President)[14] was trying to put the judiciary stronger under the control of the Ministry of Justice.[15] The existing "cloning system" is surely much more difficult to control then the system in which the politics gets more control over the process of the judicial appointment.[16]

IV. The "Mouths of the Statutes" or the Real Power

An important part of the existing system of the civil law countries is rooted in the ideas of Enlightenment.[17] Part of this process was mistrust towards the judiciary expressed by the idea of limiting its power.[18] The judges restrained by the codes encompassing, at least in the theory, the vast areas of law, should not be at this time subjected to the any judicial interpretation. The judges were supposed to follow the letter of law strictly in their ruling. They were allowed to be only the mouths of the statutes.[19] "Justice" was not supposed to be their

[14] Mr. L. Kaczyński died in the airplane accident on 10.4.2010. in Smoleńsk.

[15] This Law has been declared partially unconstitutional by the Constitutional Court – Decision from 15.1.2009, K 45/07.

[16] The draft of the Constitution proposed by the Party Prawo i Sprawiedliwość (Law and Justice) – the party of J. Kaczyński-contains an entitlement of the President of the Country to remove the judge in case of certain circumstances – see Art. 128 of the draft. See: www.**pis** .org.pl/download.php?g=mmedia&f…**konstytucji**.pdf

[17] See: J.H. Merryman, The Civil Law Tradition, Stanford 1985, p. 27–28; H. P. Glenn, Legal Traditions of the World, Oxford 2000, p. 141; F. Zoll, Jaka szkoła prawa?, Warszawa 2004, p. 39.

[18] J. H. Merryman, The Civil Law Tradition, p. 36.

[19] J. H. Merryman, The Civil Law Tradition, p. 35–36.

responsibility. This system came very quickly to its limits. The codes were full of gapes and much more creative ways of interpretation had to be applied. Some codes expressed directly the idea, that the judge should handle the process of gap filling in the same way as the imaginary legislator would handle it. The new schools of the "jurisprudence" have been created, starting with the Rudolf v. Jhering and his concept of the just law, through the "Interessenjurisprudenz" of Philip Heck, "Wertungsjurisprudenz" of Karl Larenz.[20] The Free Law School of Hermann Kantorowicz was probably not the most influential, but significant symptom of the dramatic change in the perception of the judge's role in a procedure in a continental system.[21] In different civil law countries such a development was differently manifested, in some cases more public in some cases more disguised. The instruments of the more flexible interpretation of the law gave to the judges much more power.[22] This development did not influence, at least in such countries as Poland, the way of the judicial appointment.[23] The internal "cloning system" of the judiciary in the process of appointment ignores the increase of the judicial power within last hundred years. The judges interpreting the law much more freely need to have some more clear democratic legitimacy than deriving only from the circle of judiciary. Finally, it cannot be convincingly explained why the other judges should have a crucial position in determining, who becomes a judge or will be promoted. The process of appointment should secure not only the independence from the influence of the political power but also it should secure a sort of democratic legitimacy for the judicial power.

V. Seeking the Balance Between Legitimacy and Independence

The system of the judicial appointments in Poland needs to be remodeled. There is however not a simple answer for the question, how to gain a sort of democratic legitimacy without endangering the independence of the judiciary. The popular elections of the judges in such a country as Poland cannot be

---

[20] See the presentation of these doctrines by F. Bydlinski, Juristische Methodenlehre und Rechtsbegriff, Wien/New York 1991, p. 109–139.

[21] F. Bydlinski, Juristische Methodenlehre, p. 152–153.

[22] See the analysis of K. Płeszka, Wykładnia rozszerzająca, Warszawa 2010, p. 173–181. M. Zirk – Sadowski describes this process in case of Poland as „a passage from the syllogistic to argumentative – discursive model of the application of law" – M. Zirk-Sadowski, Legal Culture and Epistemological Stressing, in: Biernat/Pałecki/Peczenik/Wong/Zirk-Sadowski, Stressing Legal Decisions, Cracow 2004, p. 96; F. Zoll, Jaka szkoła prawa, p. 41–44.

[23] On the judges in the civil law tradition see: J. H. Merryman, The Civil Law Tradition, p. 34–38.

reasonably considered, because it is not the way to verify the proficiency and the moral standards of the candidate and the candidate cannot really "offer" a political program to the public. The judges of the Constitutional Court are elected by the Parliament,[24] but its results from the specific role of this court, which has to decide about constitutionality of the law and has a function which is sometimes labeled as "negative legislator".[25] This also would not be a proper way of appointment of the regular judges because also the parliament is not the best place for the verification of the qualification of the candidates and in case of promotion it would mean a massive infringement of the independence of the judiciary. The proper solution should be worked out in the frame of the current system. The voting of the general assemblies of the respective courts should be in my opinion abolished. It does not matter whether the future colleagues like or dislike the candidate. The personal configuration of the National Council of the Judiciary should be reconsidered – probably, it needs to be more balance in this body in order to secure a more democratic legitimacy in the process of appointment. Probably, the representatives of the President of the State should have more influence. Maybe also the National Council should be somehow replicated on the regional level, replacing the general assemblies of the courts. The final function of the President in the process of appointment should remain symbolic, since the President would get more power in the National Council.

VI. Debate on the Place of the Profession of Judges in the System of Justice – "Crown of the Legal Professions"

The comparative discussion on the judiciary is sometimes obscured by the used level of generalization. The notion of "judge" in different legal systems does not mean necessarily the same.[26] It is true, that on a very general level all judges have to fulfill a comparable function. The differences which arise from the particular systems influence the subject matter of this debate very strongly. In some systems the judges are on the top of the judicial professions. In other systems there are, despite of their independence, more officials of the system, without more prestige than other members of different legal professions. As I have discussed above the career of the judge starts quite early and usually is not predeceased by having a career as a practicing lawyer. Of course there are quite numerous cases of transfers among different legal professions in all

24 Art. 194, Section 1 of the Polish Constitution.
25 See: K. Płeszka, Wykładnia rozszerzająca, p. 180.
26 J. H. Merryman, The Civil Law Tradition, p. 35.

directions, but it is not a typical path. There were several proposals to change the system into the direction of the judiciary which is seen as the "crown of the legal professions".[27]

According to these ideas to become a judge would require quite long and successful career as a judge. The idea was to immensely elevate (also in matter of remuneration) the position of the judge. It is true, that in our society the judges are not honored by special prestiges. They are respected and there even is a growth of the satisfaction with the functioning of judiciary in the society.[28] However, their position in the society is still not extraordinary high. It is true, that the relatively young age of many judges influences also the phenomenon of the not highest prestige of the judges. Therefore an easy proposal has been formulated: to introduce a minimum age limit for the judges (at least 35 years). All these proposals have overseen that the position of the judges in the legal system is not only a question of the career's path for the judges and the minimum prescribed for age to get an appointment. The position of the judge is the result of the whole concept of the organization of the judiciary and the structure of the procedures. It is quite significant that in Poland there are about 20 judges for 100.000 inhabitants. These are numbers which are much closer to Germany than to England (4 judges), Scandinavian countries (4) or even France (10).[29] This is not an accident. The reason for these numbers is rooted in different duties of the judges in the system. In such procedures, which are in force in Poland, the system was envisaged as being much more protective to the parties. To some extend the procedure can work without lawyers with the hyperactive judge. This is changing already, due to the need of the acceleration of the procedure. Furthermore this active role of the judges becomes a subject of transformation. However, the basis for the system remains the same. Without changing the fundaments of the system it is not possible to achieve a level of the "crown of legal professions" for the judiciary. It is also not inevitably desirable. Even the system which does not elevate the position of the judges over all above all other legal professions may secure sufficient independent judges and allow the proper operation of the justice.

---

[27] See for instance the title of the Conference held by the National Council of Judiciary on the 22. April 2008: The Crown of the Legal Professions – http://prawo.gazetaprawna.pl/artykuly/14748,sedziowie_najlepszy_moment_by_urzad_sedziego_stal_sie_korona_zawodow_prawniczych.html.

[28] These are the quite astonishing results of the surveys conducted by Professor Grażyna Skąpska from Jagiellonian University, which have been presented at the conference on human rights at the University Halle – Wittemberg, April 2010.

[29] European Commission for the Efficiency of Justice (CEPEJ), "European Judicial Systems 2002. See also http://www.dobrowol.org/sprawneisprawiedliwe/judiciary_ilosc_sedziow.pdf.

VII. The School of Judiciary and Prosecutors and the Problem of Independence

Currently the system of the judicial career in Poland is in the process of reorganization. The idea "of the crown of the professions" has been abandoned and replaced by a more realistic model of the professional career. It rises, however, also the questions concerning the selection and legitimacy of the power of the judges. The candidates to the profession have to graduate the School of Judiciary and Prosecutors (with the seat in Cracow).[30] Generally, there is a three and half years program. However, after the first year there is an additional selection.[31] The graduates of the first year, who are not admitted to the further parts of the program, may become clerks to the judges or so called: "referendars" which are magistrates who can adjudicate simple matters. After a certain period of time also these person may be appointed for the position of the judge. The regular way leads, however, through the next 54 months of the school.[32] Then, after additional practice as a clerk, the person should be promoted to the position of a judge. The admission to the school requires to complete an academic legal education and to pass a difficult and competitive exam.[33] The candidates with the best results[34] are admitted in the number determined by the needs of profession. The existence of the school does not change the further details of the system and the formal procedure of appointment, which I have described in this paper. It rises, however, further questions, concerning the legitimacy of the judicial power. In the Polish model the result of the admission exam and of the further qualification after the first year and during the clerkship are decisive for further appointment. It means that the administrative model of the career in the judiciary has become even stronger as it was. In such system there is no space for the "political accountability" in the process of the judicial appointment. At the margin of the question of the independence of the judiciary there is emerging an interesting issue concerning the independence of the School itself. According to the law governing the School the Ministry of Justice has several supervisory competences[35] but the School has also quite far reaching autonomy. In the first year of the operation of the School it was possible to see a tension between the Ministry and the School itself concerning this issue.

---

[30] Law from 23. 1. 2009 on the National School of Judiciary and Prosecutors, Dz. U. 2009, no. 26, Pos. 157. See also www.kssip.gov.pl.
[31] See Art. 25 and Art. 27–29 of the Law on the National School.
[32] Art. 31 Section 1 of the Law on the National School.
[33] See Art. 17 and Art. 22 of the Law on the National School.
[34] Art. 18 of the Law on the National School.
[35] See Art. 13 and 14 of the Law on the National School.

There is no clear answer for the question, how the power over the school should be distributed. If it remains solely in the hands of judiciary it would straighten the "cloning system", if the governmental administration would take control over the School it may infringe the autonomy of the profession. Probably the existing balance of the semi-autonomy of the School is an optimal solution in the existing frame. Finally, there is a common interest in achieving the highest level of education for the profession. Probably the system of the School and the qualification based solemnly on the best educational performance of the candidates is appropriate in a system, in which the judges bears a so huge responsibility for the functioning of the whole system but are also just one of several legal professions.

VIII. Final Remarks

The process of appointment has relevance also from the perspective of the judicial independence. It is true, that probably much more crucial are the guaranties of the independence after the appointment. In Poland, however, the process of promotion replicates the process of the first appointment. It is also true that in such societies like the Polish one, where informal connections within the society play still a role, it is necessary to secure that friends do not select friends or the members of the family. Therefore, the idea that the other judges play a decisive role in the process of appointment is dangerous for the self – confident and independent position of the appointed judge. The increase of the judicial power in the process of implementing the law would require more democratic legitimacy, but it needs to be counter – balanced by the need to keep the system immune from the direct influence of the politics. The latter development and the creation of the School of the Judiciary and Prosecutors may help in establishing a system, in which the appointment to profession depends on the personal achievement of the candidate in the process of education. The access to the third power is then limited by the educational burdens. The process of selection is then deprived of any kind of political influence, but also it limits the "cooptation system" within the judiciary itself. It does not allow securing democratic legitimacy for the judges or at least even the requirement for "accountability". It enhances, however, the chance for the best educated and self-confident judges which is also an important prerequisite of their independence.

CHAPTER TWENTY

COURTS AND THE MEDIA: OPENING NEW DOORS: CURRENT ASPECTS OF COURT – MEDIA INTERACTION IN ISRAEL

*Eliezer Rivlin**

I. Introduction

In Israel, as elsewhere, courts and media are inevitably intertwined. The press, which plays an important role in the current legal landscape, often begins to cover legal proceedings before they officially commence, maintains coverage throughout the process, and continues coverage long after the matter has been legally resolved. As technology has advanced, new forms of media have become prevalent, as is evidenced by the widespread infiltration of the Internet and related technological developments into general journalistic practice. In light of these developments, courts constantly encounter new dilemmas and face new challenges, making it necessary that the judiciary's traditional relationship with the media be rethought in order to accommodate the onslaught of changes that have occurred within recent years.

A redefinition of the ways in which courts and the media relate to one another is required on both sides. As this article will demonstrate, the judiciary has begun to deviate from its long-standing position to avoid all forms of interaction with the media and to restrict itself to the reasoning expressed in its judgments. While a strict policy of remaining uninvolved in the journalistic arena may have rung true in the past, Israeli courts today tend to exert a policy of embracing openness and collaboration with the media, the implications of which are reviewed within the contents of this article. Furthermore, changes have taken place concerning the government's ability to restrict the media's coverage of legal proceedings, and there is good cause to explore the need to make further changes so as to create a better balance between the important role of the media in a democratic society and the special attributes of the judicial process, which sometimes call for restraint on behalf of the media.

* Eliezer Rivlin is the Deputy Chief Justice of the Supreme Court of Israel; Director at the Israeli Institute of Extended Studies for Judges; Vice President of the International Organization of Judicial Training; Visiting professor at the University of Florida – School of Law (since 2006); Author of books and articles in the fields of tort law and constitutional law.

This article focuses on two principal aspects of the judiciary's relationship with the media in Israel. The first aspect seeks to consider the general reorganization of this relationship, focusing particularly on the court system's increased willingness to accommodate electronic media coverage and the use of the Internet as a means of communication. The second aspect seeks to consider recent changes in the Israeli sub judice law. In contemplating these fundamental changes, this article will suggest an approach that will seek to strike a better balance between the need to allow open media coverage of the judicial process and the need to protect the purity of this process and the rights of the parties involved. Both components to the article are closely related and reflect a variety of societal developments, including the recent evolution of the media's ability to cover legal proceedings, and the extent to which the development of an expanding Internet culture has impacted the general population's ability to communicate on a global scale. In order to demonstrate the timeliness of this discussion and to introduce its manifestation in the Israeli context, this article incorporates several examples of the media's coverage of recent legal affairs in Israel.

II. The Accessibility of the Courts to the Media

Since members of the public do not generally frequent the courts in order to attend legal proceedings, the media acts as the public's agent by gathering and publishing information. In doing so, the media publicizes the judicial process while developing and maintaining necessary criticism of the legal authority, which are two crucial and highly valued functions. In the past, however, Israeli courts, have exercised a strict policy of non-involvement. In conjunction with the legal system at large, judges have traditionally refrained from responding to journalistic inquiries regarding legal procedure, judges or the legal system. Conversely, in recent years, partially due to the current communications reality, a new policy has emerged which is meant to enhance the openness and cooperation between the courts and the media.

Both the old and the new approaches stem from the general belief that the public's confidence in the judicial process is an essential component of the Israeli legal system. The older and more restrictive approach stemmed from the notion that the court is a unique actor in the public domain, one that must constantly maintain a position that allows for objective judgment. Such objectivity may be compromised–or, at the very least, appear to be compromised–should judges take too active a role in promoting public discourse. Furthermore, the court's conscious decision not to become embroiled in the media circus and to ignore public and often political debate was a deliberate position instituted in an attempt to protect the dignified status of the judiciary.

The newer approach stems from the same considerations of maintaining public trust in the judicial system. However, the court has shifted its view on how to best go about achieving this goal. As such, courts now tout transparency as the best way to preserve public confidence in the system, allowing easier access to the court's decisions and proceedings. This more open approach is motivated by the realization that, in order to maintain its prominent position within the current social landscape, the court must play a more active role within the media instead of simply relying on its judgments.

Despite the fact that this more open approach is motivated by important concerns, the unique role played by the judiciary within Israeli society must not be forgotten. In considering the boundaries of its relationship with the media, the court has an obligation to ensure that this relationship remains appropriate and that its objectivity is not sacrificed. Thus, in an effort to strike an optimal balance between accessibility and appropriateness, the judiciary has taken two important steps by creating the Courts Spokesperson Office and by examining previous restrictions on the media's ability to cover ongoing legal proceedings.

1. *The Courts Spokesperson Office*

For many years Israeli courts did not employ an official spokesperson due to the traditional view that a judge's voice should be heard via judicial activity alone—since the country's inception, the idea that "[j]udges speak only via their judgment" has appeared to be the official mantra of the Israeli judiciary. However, as time progressed, Israel's legal system recognized the utility of stepping away from this motto and embracing the benefits that could be provided by the use of a spokesperson, and thus began utilizing the services of the Ministry of Justice's official representative. When it became clear that conflicts of interest (for example, concerning various branches of the ministry of justice) made this arrangement untenable, the courts took action and appointed a spokesperson of their own.

In 1999, a judicial committee examined the issue of media publicity and its relationship with the Israeli legal system. In its report, the committee recommended that the judiciary maintain its traditional practice of allowing a judge the ability to speak only through his judgments. Nevertheless, due to changes and developments within the judicial system and the media, the Committee also recommended that the traditional position be substantially overhauled. Accordingly, in subscribing to a new philosophy that demanded tolerance of the media, the Committee deemed publicity to be a public service that the judicial system is obligated to accommodate, recommending that an Office of Professional Publicity be established in order to introduce pre-planned and self-initiated publications (as opposed to passive-responsive ones).

The Committee expressed the opinion that, at times, the judiciary's choice to simply keep quiet would no longer serve in fostering the public's faith in the system; to the contrary, the biased attacks on the judiciary permitted by its policy of non-interventionism served in inflicting serious damage on the legal system's credibility.

Structurally, the Committee made two fundamental recommendations. First, it was determined that a spokesperson should be appointed, the authority of whom would reach the entire Israeli judiciary. Second, the Committee elected to initiate a Justice's Publicity Council, which would allow judges of different courts and ranks to define objectives and directly provide assistance to the appointed spokesperson. Finally, in an effort to promote openness and journalistic freedom, the Committee recommended that an ombudsman for the courts be established, and that both the public and the media be granted access to the Court's Cases Registry.

Today, partly due to the recommendations of the Committee, the Spokesperson's Office provides the media with up-to-date information on the court's activities, including real-time briefings when important or high-profile decisions are rendered. In recent years, courts have also begun to supply the media with summaries of long or complicated decisions of general interest, which have helped journalists to convey judicial analysis to the public with increased accuracy and efficiency. These briefings have had the impact of considerably reducing the general public's misunderstanding of decisions rendered by the courts, a result that is inarguably beneficial to both the media and the Israeli legal system at large. However, the increased use of these briefings has raised several important policy-driven questions. What is the legal status of these briefings, given that they are not official documents of the court? Is it appropriate for the courts to summarize their own judgments, relinquishing important content in light of increased simplicity? Finally, doesn't this new trend imply a devaluation of judicial rhetoric? Interesting as they are, these concerns remain mostly unresolved, and must be considered in order to determine whether this modern practice tends to obfuscate the judiciary's role within society.

There is no question as to the fact that the Spokesperson's Office acts as an important bridge between the media and the judiciary; over the course of the last six months, the Office has issued to the media an average of 1,349 notices per month.[1] Further, the Office now operates its own website, which is used in

[1] In comparison, in 2008 the Spokesperson Office issued an average of 75 notices to the media per month, and received over 400 applications and requests for information by the media per month.

order to disseminate information to parties, attorneys, and the general public. For example, decisions of the Supreme Court and of the District Courts are uploaded daily, enabling the public to review the contents of these opinions quickly and efficiently. The site also offers a wide variety of court-related content to journalists—verdicts, protocols, schedules, statistical data, and electronically encoded pieces of evidence can all be accessed seamlessly.[2]

2. *Opening the Court's Halls to the Media*

The default position of the Israeli judiciary is to allow the public unrestricted access to the courtroom during hearings. This position reflects the principle of holding hearings behind "open doors."[3] Within the Supreme Court, several individual courtrooms are equipped with special booths designed specifically to accommodate journalists and their equipment. However, taking photographs within the courtroom requires the permission of the court,[4] and a journalist who breaches this law may be charged with a felony sentenced by up to six months of imprisonment.[5] When journalists are present at a legal proceeding, a judge will generally allow media crews to photograph the entrance of the parties and the judge into the courtroom. Further, these media crews may also be granted permits allowing them to hold interviews with the parties to the proceeding and the attorneys representing them within the premises of the Court. Although the explicit language of the relevant provision does not speak on whether an actual proceeding may be recorded or broadcasted live, case law has established that a court has the inherent authority to prohibit such behaviour. Historically, Israeli courts have rarely authorized the recording or broadcasting of such proceedings, which has led to the development of a rebuttable *de facto* presumption against electronic publication.

Despite the above-mentioned restrictions, permits have been granted to allow electronic coverage of ceremonies and quasi-judicial proceedings. For example, permission has been granted when journalists have sought to cover proceedings conducted by Public Investigation Committees,[6] or when they

---

[2] For example, in the case of CA 8483/02 Aloniel v. McDonald, IsrSC 54(4) 314, regarding the question of whether a certain advertisement violated a registered trademark, the disputed advertisement was attached as a video file to the electronic version of the verdict.

[3] Section 68(A) of the Courts Law [Consolidated Version], 5744–1984.

[4] According to section 70(B) of the Courts Law, "No man shall photograph at the court hall nor shall publish such a photo unless granted the permission of the court".

[5] Section 70(F) of the Courts Law.

[6] For example: Permission has been given for the filming, recording and broadcasting of the discussions of the Public Investigation Committee on the Massacre in Hebron (headed by Justice Shamgar). A permit was also granted for the electronic coverage of the discussions held by the "Orr Committee" (in this case a media room has been built next to the committee session hall

have sought to publicize the legal process for educational purposes.[7] Furthermore, in a handful of cases that have aroused exceptional public interest and historical significance, permits have been granted, allowing journalists the ability to broadcast legal proceedings conducted within the confines of the courtroom. In the early 1960s, before television broadcasts were used in Israel, the judiciary authorized the radio broadcast of the *Eichmann* trial,[8] in which former Nazi official Adolf Eichmann was tried for war crimes committed during the Holocaust. Additionally, during the late 1980s and early 1990s, permits were granted allowing the live television and radio broadcast of the District Court and Supreme Court proceedings held pursuant to the *Demjanjuk* case,[9] during which Jonn (Ivan) Demjanjuk was also tried (and eventually acquitted) for war crimes allegedly committed during the Holocaust. The authorization to broadcast the events of these cases stemmed from the notion that the results would have significant public and historical importance, a notion which was bolstered by the overwhelming interest of the international community in the results of these proceedings. Finally, in 1996, the judiciary authorized the live broadcast of the judge's entrance to the Tel Aviv District Court for the rendering of the verdict in the case of Yigal Amir, the assassin of the late prime-minister Yitschak Rabin. However, because of a misunderstanding, the broadcasting continued well through the reading of the verdict itself.

Although courts had proven willing to make exceptions under a variety of circumstances, additional pressure was still exerted on the judiciary to completely open its doors to the media. In reaction to this pressure, legislation was presented to the Knesset in 2000, suggesting an amendment to the Courts Law [Consolidated Version], 5744–1984, stipulating that courts would be allowed to prohibit photography, publications, recording and filming within the courtroom only if such a prohibition is necessary to protect a compelling interest.[10] The goal of the bill was to establish a presumption in favor of the electronic coverage of legal proceedings by limiting the discretion of the judiciary.

While deliberations in the Knesset were being conducted, the Committee for the Examination of the Opening of the Israeli Courts to Electronic Media

---

with a window that enabled the filming of the discussions. Generally the summary of the discussions were broadcast on the local news but the main testimonies which were of great public interest were fully broadcast, live on television and radio).

[7] Only certain segments of the proceedings were made available to the public and only after due time has passed.

[8] CrimC 40/61 The State of Israel v. Eichmann, IsrDC 27, 172.

[9] For mention of this permit, see: CrimA 347/88 Demjanjuk v. The State of Israel, decision from 7.11.1988.

[10] The proposed section stated: "The Court is allowed to prohibit the filming or publication of a photograph or the recording only if it so necessary for the protection of one of the purposes enumerated in Section 68(b)".

was appointed, which was led by Justice Dorit Beinisch, who is currently serving as Chief Justice of the Supreme Court of Israel.[11] Following the model of many other states which allow restrictive broadcasting from within the courtroom, the Committee recommended—subject to certain safeguards designed to protect the judicial process and its participants— the adoption of a general policy which would allow limited electronic coverage of legal proceedings. In addition, the Committee saw no need to legislatively codify the recommendation, permitting its boundaries to be determined over time.

In its report, the Committee recommended that this new policy be implemented on an experimental basis only at the Supreme Court while sitting as the High Court of Justice–namely when trying petitions filed against the government. Under this arrangement, the High Court of Justice was to grant requests for electronic coverage only after determining that such coverage serves the interest of the general public and contributes to the knowledge of the public on the work of the courts. Accordingly, the High Court of Justice would have the discretion to prohibit the electronic coverage of legal proceedings or to subject such proceedings to various restrictions. The purpose of these restrictions is to ensure the right of the parties to a fair trial, their right to privacy and dignity, and to preserve the purity of the judicial process. Finally, the Committee recommended that, until further notice, other courts in Israel were to maintain the *status quo* of allowing electronic coverage only under exceptional circumstances.

Following the recommendations of the Beinisch Committee, the Knesset member who had originally initiated the proposed legislative amendment announced that she would restrict the original bill, focusing only on actions taken by the Supreme Court. Accordingly, in 2002, the Knesset was presented with new legislation suggesting the adoption of the recommendations made by the Beinicsh Committee, instituting—subject to limited judicial discretion—the temporary and experimental media coverage of hearings conducted within the Supreme Court[12] The amended bill also stipulated that the Minister of Justice and the Chief Justice of the Supreme Court were to

---

[11] The Report of the Committee for Examining the Opening of Courts in Israel to Electronic Media (2004).

[12] Courts Law (Amendment 36 – Temporary Order) (broadcasting and filming of proceedings in courts) 2002:
Section 70(a): Filming and Recording of Sessions – Temporary Order:
a) Despite Section 70(b) a broadcasting body may film, record or broadcast a public session of the Supreme Court in its capacity as The High Court of Justice, unless the Court decided differently, all in consistency with rules established according to this Section. In this provision "a broadcasting body" is a radio or television body which broadcasts to the public, or to some of the public, and which signed an agreement with the Supreme Court.

jointly formulate rules and guidelines in order to assure appropriate and fair proceedings and to safeguard the dignity of the court and the involved parties. However, the bill was not adopted by the Knesset, and the arrangement codified in section 70(b) of the Courts Law currently remains unchanged.

III. The Sub Judice Rule in the Israeli Legal System

1. *The Democratic Tension over Sub Judice*

The term "sub judice," which literally means "under judgment," refers to the set of legal rules designed to limit the press' ability to publish details about ongoing judicial proceedings so as not to interfere with the right of due process. The specific nature of these limitations varies between different legal systems. In establishing the scope of its sub judice doctrine, a legal system must strike the proper balance between different competing interests and rights: freedom of speech, freedom of the press, and the public's right to obtain information must be considered on the one hand, while judicial purity and the right of due process must be considered on the other. Choosing the appropriate balance is a complex and delicate task, which requires that many considerations be taken into account. A crucial concern is that "a trial by the press," especially in the criminal context, has the potential to harm due process and infringe upon the defendant's right to a fair trial. Another concern considers the public's perception of the legitimacy of the judicial system—on one hand, the public may fear that judges' decisions are impacted by journalistic coverage and that a trial conducted in the atmosphere of a media "circus" is inherently biased, while on the other hand, judicial decisions that are contrary to the tone expressed in the press may go against the public's expectations and thus diminish confidence in the system at large. In all, the balance achieved by a particular legal system between these conflicting considerations often reflects the importance placed by society on rights such as freedom of the press and due process, a phenomenon which is demonstrated by the evolution of the Israeli system's unequivocal shift towards an increasingly pro-media approach.

2. *The Sub Judice Provision in Israeli Law*

Until 2002, the Courts Law included a broad sub judice provision which applied to both civil and criminal proceedings and prohibited any publication

b) The Minister of Justice, with the consent of the President of the Supreme Court, shall establish rules and instructions for the application of this Section, and for assuring due process of the sessions mentioned in sub-section a), fair process and the dignity of the parties and the Court.
c) This Section will apply as of six months after its publication, for the period of two years.

which had the potential of influencing the course of a trial or its outcome.[13] Further, it excluded any publication that reported in good faith an event that occurred within the confines of the courtroom.[14] Case Law in Israel was implemented in order to combat the undeniable possibility that media coverage may have the impact of influencing even members of the bench. Despite the fact that judges are expected to be resilient towards outside influences, the possibility that objectivity will be compromised – even unconsciously – can never be ruled out entirely.[15] Moreover, the previous enactment of the Courts Law reflected the concern that the opinions of parties and witnesses to a trial may also be influenced by unbridled media coverage. As such, it was determined that only a *mens rea* requirement of negligence was necessary in order to implicate the restrictive provisions of the Case Law.[16]

Over time, the general perception of the sub judice doctrine has evolved, and in 2002, a bill was suggested to the Knesset which sought to eliminate the sub judice provision entirely.[17] The rationale underlying the bill asserted that the provision had not been enforced for many years, that the "flow of information" had become unstoppable, and that the ability of a judge to remain professional and impartial was sufficient in safeguarding against concerns about due process. It was also stated that the sub judice provision was used as a means of withholding valuable information from the public. Despite the fact that the amendment to eliminate the sub judice provision in its entirety was not adopted by the Knesset, the proposed legislation brought these fundamental concerns to the forefront, which had the impact of significantly narrowing the scope of the Israeli sub judice doctrine. It should be noted that, as a result of the proposed amendment, the scope of the sub judice law became restricted in two significant ways. First, the rule now applies only to pending criminal proceedings.[18] Second, the requisite *mens rea* necessitates that an offender either have the intent of disturbing the legal process, or that such an impact on the legal process be foreseeable as a probable outcome of the offender's actions.[19]

[13] Section 71(A) of The Courts Law, as it appeared in the Official Gazette: the Book of Laws 5744, 198.

[14] Section 71(B) of The Courts Law, as it appeared in the Official Gazette: the Book of Laws 5744, 198.

[15] CrimA 696/81 Azulai v. The State of Israel, IsrSC 37(2), 565 (1983).

[16] *Id.*

[17] Courts Law Bill (Amendment 32) (Nullification of Limited Publication), 5761–2001, The Official Gazette: Bills, 672.

[18] Indeed the sub judice protection in criminal proceedings was broadened by Section 13 of the Criminal Procedure Law (Suspect Interrogation) 5762–2002, which prohibits the publication of visual or audio documentation of any interrogation conducted by a State Authority without the permission of the court.

[19] Section 71(A) of the Courts Law.

Good faith reports of events occurring within the courtroom remain protected under the modern sub judice doctrine.

The amended law reflects a shift in favor of freedom of expression, and shows that the free flow of information to the public is now viewed as more of a priority than it may have been in the past. Even more, the Attorney General's guidelines on the amendment instruct a policy of minimal indictment—as rarely as the sub judice law was applied *before* the recent legislative change, it appears as though the legislature has moved even further in the direction of a presumption against enforcement.[20] However, despite this policy of limited prosecution, it is important to stress that the legislature made the affirmative choice not to completely eliminate the provision, an option that was well within its power. Thus, in order to better articulate the scope of the amended provision, the Attorney General's guidelines list many of the considerations which should be taken into account in determining whether prosecution is appropriate. Among these guidelines, it is interesting to note that publications attempting to influence witnesses are generally treated with greater severity than are publications attempting to influence judges, which reflects the notion that the professionalism and impartiality attributed to judges serve in effectively insulating them from the potential influence of the media.

In summary, the Israeli legal system allowed certain limitations on free speech for the purpose of guarding the purity of the legal process. The American legal system demonstrated a different approach to the issue of media coverage of legal affairs. As discussed in the next section, American law has assigned greater weight to free speech and to freedom of the press, and includes wide constitutional limitations on the ability to limit media coverage. This is balanced by the existence of several remedies available within the judicial process to a defendant who fears that media coverage may infringe upon his right to a fair and impartial trial.

3. *Treatment of Media Coverage of Legal Proceedings in the American Legal System*

Despite the fact that many nations throughout the world maintain an active sub judice doctrine through which violators may be prosecuted and held in contempt, the American approach is severely constrained by its broad First Amendment protections. The First Amendment, which is also made applicable to State governments via the Fourteenth Amendment, asserts that

[20] Prosecution under Section 71 of the Courts Law also requires the consent of the Attorney General or the Chief Prosecutor themselves.

"Congress shall make no law...abridging the freedom of speech, or of the press."[21] Despite the fact that this constitutional provision must be interpreted in light of the Sixth Amendment, which guarantees criminal defendants the right to jury impartiality and trial fairness,[22] the American approach is unique in that it accords such significant weight to principles of free speech and open justice. Practically speaking, the First Amendment serves in virtually eliminating the government's ability to restrain or sanction members of the media from publicizing the details of a criminal trial.

This can be demonstrated by the ruling in *Bridges v. California*, where a newspaper, associated individuals, and a labor leader were held in contempt by a California state court for composing and publishing editorials critical of the court's ability to properly adjudicate the case. While the sub judice rule originates from the common law concept of contempt-of-court, the Bridges Court made it clear that the constitutionality of the decision given by the California state court must not be examined in light of the English common law. The U.S. Supreme Court therefore applied the "clear and present danger" test outlined in *Schenck v. U.S.*, which determined that speech cannot be suppressed unless "the words are used in such circumstances and are of such a nature as to create a clear and present danger that they will bring about the substantive evils."[23] Pursuant to first amendment adjudication, the *Bridges* Court later developed a working principle which asserted that the substantive evil perpetuated by an utterance must be both extremely imminent and extremely serious in order to be punished.[24] The logic dictated by the *Bridges* opinion was applied three more times between the years of 1946 and 1962,[25] while later opinions applied the "clear and present danger" test to a court's ability to prevent the media from publishing truthful information which was lawfully obtained.[26]

It is interesting to note that legislation relating to legal ethics enforce a quasi-sub judice rule upon lawyers in some states. These rules, however, are extremely narrow, due to constitutional limitations. According to ABA Model Rule 3.6(a), "[a] lawyer who is participating or has participated in the investigation or litigation of a matter shall not make an extrajudicial statement that the lawyer knows or reasonably should know will be disseminated by means of public

[21] U.S. Const. amend. I

[22] U.S. Const. amend. VI

[23] Schenck v. United States, 249 U.S. 47 (1919).

[24] Bridges v. California, 314 U.S. 252, 263 (1941).

[25] Michael Chesterman, *O.J. and the Dingo: How Media Publicity Relating to Criminal Cases Tried by Jury is Dealt With in Australia and America*, 45 Am. J. Comp. L. 109 (1997) (citing Bridges v. California, 314 U.S. 252 (1941); Craig v. Harney, 331 U.S. 367 (1946); Wood v. Georgia, 370 U.S. 375 (1962)).

[26] *Id.* at 126 (citing Cox Broadcasting Co. v. Cohn, 95 S. Ct. 1029 (1975)).

communication and will have a substantial likelihood of materially prejudicing an adjudicative proceeding in the matter."[27] While it is up to each individual state to apply and interpret its embodiment of this Model Rule (or of any other), it has been determined that the drafters of Rule 3.6(a) intended that its language be interpreted in light of the "clear and present danger" test.[28] Thus, the Supreme Court of the United States held that the Rule's "substantial likelihood of material prejudice" test complied with the broad protections of the First Amendment[29] (while rejecting the way that the rule was applied in that specific case).

Generally, American law has taken a different approach to achieving balance between freedom of speech and due process requirements. The main attribute of this approach is to prevent the government's ability to limit the media's freedom on the one hand, while allowing the judicial system to make necessary adjustments to widespread media coverage on the other. One way that the judicial system can adjust to existing media coverage is to grant, under certain circumstances, the requests of a party to have the proceedings conducted in a different venue. The American Constitution asserts that defendants in a criminal trial must be tried in the state and district in which the crime being alleged was committed.[30] However, this venue requirement must be balanced against the defendant's rights to due process and an impartial jury articulated by the Fifth and Sixth Amendments. As such, it has been determined that transfer to a different district pursuant to a defendant's request may be granted in spite of the Constitution's venue prescriptions if it can be shown that extraordinary local prejudice will stand in the way of a fair trial.[31] According to Federal Rule of Criminal Procedure 21, "[u]pon defendant's motion, the court must transfer the proceeding…to another district if the court is satisfied that so great a prejudice against the defendant exists in the transferring district that the defendant cannot obtain a fair and impartial trial here."[32] Given the preventative and anticipatory nature of a request for change of venue, the determination as to whether such a change should be granted is left up to the discretion of the court,[33] which must consider the totality of the circumstances and may make its determination at any time before or during trial. Change of venue seems to be a solution which succeeds in both preserving freedom of speech and in ensuring the impartiality of the judicial process. However, it would not

[27] Model Rules of Prof'l Conduct R. 3.6
[28] Gentile v. State Bar of Nevada, 501 U.S. 1030, 1036 (1991).
[29] *Id.*
[30] *See* U.S. Const. art. III, §2, cl. 3; U.S. Const. amend. XI.
[31] United States v. Skilling, 130 S. Ct. 2896 at 2913 (2010).
[32] Fed. R. Crim. P. 21(a)
[33] United States v. Mitchell, No. 2:08CR125DAK, 2010 U.S. Dist. Lexis 21004, at *6 (D. Utah Mar. 8, 2010).

be a practical solution in the Israeli legal system due to the small geographical size of the country. Media coverage, especially if it is extensive, is almost by nature nation-wide.

Another way that the American legal system can protect a defendant's rights is by vacating a guilty verdict on the constitutional grounds that the right to a fair trial was undermined by prejudice. Proving actual prejudice is very difficult. In order to determine whether actual prejudice exists, the circumstances surrounding the jury, including the selection process and the extent to which the jury was exposed to publicity during trial, must be reviewed. After reviewing the totality of the circumstances, if a reasonable basis exists for the trial judge's determination that the jury could be impartial, then a finding will be made that actual prejudice does not in fact exist.[34] Since trial courts have broad discretion to determine the impact of allegedly prejudicial publicity and to consider juror impartiality upon *voir dire* examination, the standard for proving actual prejudice is not easily satisfied.[35]

While it is generally necessary that the accused be able to provide evidence of actual prejudice in order for a court to determine that a violation of due process has occurred, "at times a procedure employed by the State involves such a probability that prejudice will result that it is deemed inherently lacking in due process."[36] According to the facts of *Sheppard v. Maxwell*, the petitioner was accused of murdering his wife, and was subject to extensive media coverage both prior to and during the nine week trial. The jurors were not sequestered, received constant exposure to the media's coverage while court was not in session, and were allowed to make phone calls during the deliberation period. Further, procedural safeguards such as requests for continuance and change in venue were denied by the trial judge. The Supreme Court determined that "the arrangements made by the judge with the news media caused Sheppard to be deprived of that 'judicial serenity and calm to which [he] was entitled,'"[37] and thus reversed the denial of the petitioner's *habeas* petition. Put differently, in order for a conviction to be overturned pursuant to "a presumption that inflammatory pretrial publicity so permeated the community as to render impossible the seating of an impartial jury, the court must find that the publicity in essence displaced the judicial process, thereby denying the defendant his constitutional right to a fair trial."[38] As a result, despite *Sheppard*,

[34] United States v. Mcveigh, 153 F.3d 1166, 1183 (1998).
[35] United States v. Abello-Silva, 948 F.2d 1168 (1991).
[36] Estes v. Texas, 381 U.S. 532, 542–543 (1965).
[37] Sheppard v. Maxwell, 384 U.S. 333, 355 (1966) (citing Estes, 381 U.S. 532).
[38] McVeigh, 153 F.3d at 1182. (For a more recent analysis, *see* Skilling, 130 S. Ct. 2896, where the Supreme Court focused on several factors in determining whether prejudice should be presumed. The Court considered: (1) media interference with courtroom proceedings; (2) the size

a claim of presumed prejudice must only be granted under rare circumstances,[39] because the bar facing a defendant seeking to prove presumed prejudice is extremely high.[40]

4. *The New Challenges of Extensive Media Coverage, in Light of Recent Legal Affairs in Israel*

As this article demonstrates, a fundamental shift has occurred in the outlook of the Israeli judicial system towards the media; while an attitude of non-involvement has historically been perceived as necessary for maintaining the public's confidence in the judiciary, the modern belief asserts that openness and transparency play an important role in safeguarding the public's confidence. Note that this doctrinal shift, one which has evolved over many years, is reflected in the amendment of Israel's sub judice provision. In this vein, commentators have questioned whether the objective of maintaining public confidence is sufficient to justify an infringement on the right of free speech. However, the analysis regarding the justification of even a limited sub judice provision may be a bit different when considering a circumstance where media coverage could interfere with a defendant's right to a fair trial. Recently, Israel has decided several cases where media coverage has been extensive—so extensive, in fact, that the nature of the coverage could only be called "pseudo-judicial"— that questions have been raised as to the legitimacy of this coverage in light of its impact on the defendants' rights.

Questions pertaining to the sub judice law's boundaries and the legitimacy of the media's ability to cover an ongoing trial were raised pursuant to the coverage of the recent sexual harassment case of a former Minister of Justice. According to the facts of this case, a female soldier filed a complaint against the minister, stating that he had kissed her without consent. After being charged, he resigned from the government and went to trial. While the affair was covered in its entirety, the media paid close attention to the legal proceedings, which were covered in an unprecedented manner. Many journalistic boundaries were crossed: police assessments, testimonies, documents and tapes were leaked to the media and subsequently published. Further, photos of the accused and the alleged victim taken alone together appeared on internet sites and reached an enormous audience, which had the impact of piercing the alleged

---

and characteristics of the community in which the crime occurred; (3) the nature and tone of the media publicity; (4) the amount of time that had elapsed between the crime and the trial; (5) the impact of the crime on the community; and (6) the effect of a co-defendant's well publicized decision to plead guilty).

[39] Abello-Silva, 948 F.2d at 1177.

[40] Stafford v. Saffle, 34 F.3d 1557 (1994).

victim's court-granted anonymity and bringing her to the forefront of the public eye. In response to the general public's thirst for information regarding this particular story, the media endeavored to create what resembled a pseudo-judicial process, publishing articles and opinionated columns "convicting" or "acquitting" the accused, and conducting polls in order to gauge the public's perception of the government's decision to prosecute.

In its verdict, the District Court heavily criticized the media's coverage of the case:

> In our minds, in this case all boundaries were crossed. The term sub-judice declined into a chasm we have never known. The substance of the testimonies was published to the media before witnesses were able to take the stand, and because of that some testimonies were contaminated. We feel that there were attempts, sometimes by hidden messages, and sometimes blatantly to divert the trial. We, the judges, are guided only by our consciences.[41]

Further manifestations of the press's ability to weigh in—sometimes inappropriately so—have appeared in other cases as well. For example, newspapers have asked that witnesses and plaintiffs participate in polygraph tests during the midst of trial, publishing the results of these tests and drawing conclusions as to whether the defendant should be convicted or acquitted. On occasion, newspapers have also introduced evidence that is not admissible in Israeli courts (or in most common-law legal systems). Supreme Court Justice Edmond Levi has expressed great concern over the phenomenon of "trial by the press" and the extent to which such publicity may endanger the right of the accused to a fair trial and a presumption of innocence: "A person may discover he is guilty in the morning, and innocent by night – it all depends on the commentator, the reporter and the daily editor".[42]

In the case of former President of the state, who is currently being tried under charges of rape, the District Court decided that concerns about the privacy of the alleged victims and the purity of the legal process demanded that all testimony was to be given behind closed doors. Moreover, the District Court prohibited the publication of any testimony given at trial,[43] relying on the authority granted to it by section 70(a) of the Courts Law. An appeal of this decision to the Supreme Court was denied,[44] although the Court asserted that deviations from principles seeking to encourage the free flow of information

---

[41] CC (T.A. district) 5461/06.

[42] The dissent was part of a judgment regarding a petition against the prosecution's intention to reach a plea bargain. The petition was denied, but nevertheless a plea bargain was not reached. See: HCJ 5699/07 Jane Doe v. The Attorney General (not reported, 26.2.2008).

[43] Severe Crime Case 1015/09 The State of Israel v. Katzav, decision from 11.10.2009.

[44] CrimApp 8773/09 Yediot Ahronot Ltd. v. The State of Israel (not reported, 20.1.2010).

should be minimal under normal circumstances. The Court also stated that one of the factors influencing the balance between these principles and contradicting ones is the time during which publication is requested (before, during, or after the trial).

IV. Conclusion

Israeli courts have always placed great importance on protecting the media's rights to remain independent and speak freely. In the constitutional arena, freedom of speech was recognized by the High Court of Justice as a "supreme right" in the early case of *Kol Ha'am*[45]–a cornerstone of Israeli constitutional law. Decided in 1953, approximately five years after the founding of the State of Israel, it was here that the Court initially articulated an appropriate balance between freedom of speech and other potentially divergent social interests which were also entitled to protection. In its opinion, the Court decided that freedom of speech may only be limited should it be nearly certain that another protected interest would be substantially and seriously harmed. Further, apart from *Kol Ha'am*, the Court has determined that freedom of speech must be carefully protected in the civil context, and on multiple occasions, Israeli courts have rejected claims of defamation filed against journalists.[46]

Historically, courts have accomplished the goal of preserving freedom of speech and freedom of the press principally through judicial analysis and the narrow interpretation of the sub judice provision. However, courts today have made a strong effort to promote the role of publicity within mainstream society by strengthening their own institutional relationship with the media. In doing so, Israeli courts have adopted a more liberal approach, one that has provided the media with incentives to appropriately publicize the details of legal proceedings. As a result of this concerted effort, the courts have succeeded in strengthening the general public's confidence in the legal process and the judicial system at large.

It is now the belief of the judiciary that the media should have the ability to publicize the implications of all opinions decided by the courts. Therefore, it is in the best interest of the courts to assist the media in accurately conveying the essence of its decisions by making these decisions increasingly accessible. In considering whether the overall impact of these developments is positive, one must make an effort to consider all the principles and values involved,

[45] HCJ 73/53 Kol Ha'am Company v. The Minister of Internal Affairs, IsrSC 7(2), 871.

[46] For example, *see* CA 323/98 Sharon v. Benziman, IsrSC 56(3), 245 (2002); LCrimA 9818/01 Biton v. Sultan, IsrSC 59(6), 554 (2005).

which include public confidence, judicial purity, and the rights of all relevant parties.

Despite the fact that move the Israeli system's liberalization of it's sub judice law has had many positive consequences, it is indisputable that undesirable effects—like the advent of pseudo-judicial coverage—have presented themselves as well. In this vein, it is crucial that courts make a concerted effort to guard both a defendant's right to a fair trial and the purity of the judicial process overall. While it is important that the right to free speech enjoys special protection, other constitutional rights, such as a defendant's right to due process of the law, must not be ignored. In recognizing the need to strike a delicate balance, the Supreme Court has stated that the rule of law, when considered in conjunction with freedom of the press, should always serve in preventing the undesirable outcome of a trial by the media.[47] Indeed, Due Process is more than an abstract concept, for it entails both the right to a fair trial and the presumption of innocence that a criminal defendant is always entitled to receive, rights which must not be threatened by the judiciary's increased tolerance of court-related publicity.

In this context, it is important to distinguish between the effects of the media's coverage of events that occur both before and after a case's conclusion. As stated nearly a century ago, "It is possible very effectually to poison the fountain of justice before it begins to flow. It is not possible to do so when the stream has ceased".[48] In light of the press's growing interest in publicizing the events of pending legal proceedings, it may be necessary for the judiciary to carefully promote the use of the sub judice rule so as to preserve the integrity of the legal process and ensure that the rights of criminal defendants are not infringed upon. At the same time, it is imperative that courts maintain their policy of increased cooperation with the media, which serves the important purpose of allowing the results of crucial legal proceedings to be accurately articulated to the general public. Once a successful balance is achieved—one that is able to adequately consider the right of defendants to due process, the right of the press to freedom of speech, and the interest of the general public in being accurately informed—the media's role will cease to be a contentious issue, and all parties involved will gain substantially from the modern trend towards increased openness and accessibility.

[47] Azulai, IsrSC 37(2).
[48] The King v. Parke [1903] 2 KB 432.

CHAPTER TWENTY ONE

INDEPENDENCE AND JUDICIAL DISCIPLINE: THE ITALIAN CODE OF JUDICIAL CONDUCT

*Daniela Cavallini**

I. The Importance of a Code of Judicial Conduct

In most European Countries judicial discipline is based on generic provisions and misconduct is de facto defined by case law (France, Germany, Austria).[1] However, the concept of fixing standards for judicial conduct is under discussion in many countries and some of them have established more or less detailed binding disciplinary rules, in other words "codes of judicial conduct" (Spain, Italy).[2]

The main reasons for the increasing interest in codes of judicial conduct (hereinafter Codes), and in judicial discipline in general, can be listed as follows: 1) the growing importance of judicial power (in defining the rights of citizens in many significant fields) makes much more evident the need to strengthen the control on judicial conduct, in order to guarantee the "quality" of our judges; 2) judges need specific standards of conduct because of the high degree of authority and discretion their work involves and the need for independence; 3) the provision of disciplinary rules makes it much clearer to judges (and to the general public) what violations they may be called to account for; 4) the provision of detailed rules and sanctions can limit the improper, incorrect use of disciplinary action (e.g. for political reasons); 5) the provision

* Faculty of Political Sciences. Bologna University.

[1] In some countries (Germany), the *status* of judges is governed both by special provisions and by the general law on civil servants, so the duties of judges derive, to a certain extent, from the general duties of the civil servants. See G. Di Federico (ed.), *Recruitment, Professional Evaluation and Career of Judges and Prosecutors in Europe: Austria, France, Germany, Italy, The Netherlands and Spain*, Research Paper, Irsig-Cnr (Bologna 2005), http://www.irsig.cnr.it/pubb_online.html.

[2] Codes of judicial conduct are intended here as disciplinary codes and not as codes of ethics, since ethics consist of moral rules that are not binding for judges and their violation cannot *per se* give rise to disciplinary proceedings. Ethics provide guidelines for judicial conduct, which are not so much compulsory, as suitable or convenient. Codes of ethics simply indicate what behaviour is expected from judges and can be useful for their training, but no sanctions can be imposed in case of violation. Discipline, on the other hand, should rest upon firm and mandatory rules. In Italy, a Code of Ethics was adopted in 1994 by the National Association of Magistrates.

of minimum sanctions applicable in cases of serious violation can improve the effectiveness of disciplinary measures; 6) the conduct of judges – in and beyond their official duties – determines the level of confidence of the general public in the courts.

All these points show that detailed disciplinary rules can contribute to the guaranteeing of judicial independence, from at least two perspectives: avoiding the disciplining of judges for vague, discretionary reasons and without judges knowing *ex ante* what is considered a violation and the penalties they can incur; avoiding cases where serious misconduct (like, for example, lack of impartiality in adjudication) is punished inadequately or not punished at all. If the punishment is not in proportion to the offence, disciplinary control becomes basically vain.

In the following paragraphs I will analyse the reform of judicial discipline that was approved in Italy in 2006 and, in particular, some controversial issues that were considered crucial for the protection of judicial independence, in the transition from the old to the new system.

First, I will briefly explain the aim and the contents of the reform of 2006, then I will focus on four main questions concerning judicial independence that were discussed in detail and finally I will draw some general conclusions.

II. Judicial Discipline in Italy: The Reform of 2006

In Italy, judicial discipline was reformed in 2006, after much debate. Until then it had been based on a vague provision that allowed the Disciplinary Commission of the Superior Council of the Magistracy[3] to decide – using a discretionary evaluation – when and how judicial misconduct should be punished. According to that provision, disciplinary penalties could be imposed on magistrates who "fail to accomplish their duties and conduct themselves, either in or outside the office, in a way that makes them unworthy of the trust and consideration they must enjoy, or when they compromise the prestige of the judiciary".[4]

---

[3] The Disciplinary Commission is a division of the Superior Council of the Magistracy (SCM) in charge of taking disciplinary measures against magistrates (i.e. both judges and prosecutors, as in the Italian system they belong to the same corps). It is composed of 6 members: the Vice-President of SCM, one person chosen by the SCM from among its lay members (i.e. members designated by Parliament) and 4 people chosen by the SCM from among the magistrates (i.e. members elected by the Magistracy). For the *status* of judges and public prosecutors in Italy, see G. Di Federico, "Recruitment, professional evaluation, career and discipline of judges and prosecutors in Italy", in G. Di Federico (ed.), *Recruitment, Professional Evaluation and Career of Judges and Prosecutors in Europe: Austria, France, Germany, Italy, The Netherlands and Spain*, Research Paper, Irsig-Cnr (Bologna 2005), pp. 127–158.

[4] Law 31 May 1941, no. 511, art. 18.

Given that this provision was so general, judicial misconduct had been de facto defined by Disciplinary Commission case law, which had interpreted and applied the above mentioned general provision for more than forty years. Two main types of misconduct could be identified: the violation of duties of office (independence, impartiality, diligence, discretion, efficiency) and any other conduct – in or beyond the course of their duties – which could undermine the prestige of the judiciary, such as, for example, close association with criminals, tax evasion, falling into debt, bribery, *etc.* So, prior to 2006 the Italian system lacked a precise definition of all the cases in which disciplinary measures could be brought.[5]

The main purpose of the reform of 2006 was to reduce discretionary powers in disciplinary proceedings and to improve judicial independence. Three important steps were taken: the introduction of a Code of judicial conduct (i.e. a specific list of disciplinary violations); the provision of minimum sanctions applicable for the most serious violations; the reform of disciplinary proceedings.[6]

The Code consists of 37 disciplinary violations, which are divided into three categories: violations in office (breach of the duties of office, lack of respect towards parties, interference in the activity of a colleague, delays in judicial activities, *etc.*); violations beyond official duties (use of judicial title for personal gain, membership of a political party, close association with criminals, with defendants, *etc.*) and violations as a result of a criminal offence (after conviction for serious crimes or for any crime affecting the magistrate's standing). The Code is the same for judges and public prosecutors.

As regards penalties, misconduct can be punished with: admonition, censure, temporary disqualification from court management functions (up to two years), suspension from judicial functions (up to two years), loss of seniority (up to two years) and, for the most serious cases, expulsion.[7]

There is a particular relationship between sanctions and violations, because for the most serious violations the law sets out minimum sanctions to be applied. This mechanism should limit the power of the Disciplinary Commission when deciding the penalty for the specific case and should improve the effectiveness of the punishment, avoiding instances where the Commission is over-indulgent towards judges, as had occurred in the past, when most proceedings

[5] See G. Oberto, "Judicial ethics in the Italian legal system" (1996) *Rivista di diritto privato* 393.

[6] Law 25 July 2005, no.150; legislative decree 23 February 2006, no. 109.

[7] In case of censure, temporary disqualification, suspension or loss of seniority the judge can also be moved to another court.

ended up in acquittals or admonitions.[8] Now the law states, for example, that censure must be the minimum sanction in case of abuse of office or lack of respect towards parties, witnesses and lawyers. Loss of seniority is the minimum sanction for having close association or business relationships with criminals. Expulsion is the penalty for having obtained loans or favours from a suspect of a crime.

However, this mechanism is mitigated by a general provision stating that no sanction need be inflicted if judge's misconduct is "of low relevance". This is, of course, a controversial point, because it does not seem to be in line with the aim of the reform, which was to limit discretionary powers in disciplinary proceedings.

As far as disciplinary proceedings are concerned, we can briefly say that the structure is similar to that for criminal proceedings. Disciplinary action can be initiated both by the Minister of Justice and the General Prosecutor of the Supreme Court (*Corte di Cassazione*), but for the former it is a discretionary power, whereas for the latter it is compulsory. Investigations are conducted by the General Prosecutor of the Supreme Court who, under certain conditions, can – bypassing the principle of compulsory disciplinary action – dismiss the case without reporting it to the Disciplinary Commission. The hearing is public (with some exceptions).[9] During the course of the disciplinary proceedings, the judge may be suspended from judicial function (and its salary is reduced).

The Disciplinary Commission acts as a court of justice and its decisions can be appealed, on points of law, before the Supreme Court (*Corte di Cassazione*).

III. Some Controversial Issues Regarding Judicial Independence

During the preliminary work on the reform some important questions concerning judicial independence were discussed and led to many subsequent changes in the text of the bill.

[8] Our research shows, for example, that in the period 1995–2002, 251 magistrates were sent before the Disciplinary Commission for repeated delays in performing their functions (they were above all judges who did not lodge their decisions on time). Of these, 55 were punished (34 with admonitions, 13 with censures, 7 with loss of seniority, 1 with expulsion), while 196 were acquitted; D. Cavallini, "La giurisprudenza disciplinare sui ritardi dei magistrati ordinari nell'espletamento delle attività giudiziarie" (2004) *Rivista trimestrale di diritto e procedura civile* 1489–1528.

[9] When it is necessary to guarantee the rights of people not involved in the proceedings or the dignity of judicial function.

Four points can be mentioned here, which were all considered significant for the protection of judicial independence: the exhaustive character of the Code, the protection of judicial independence in adjudication, the limitation of judges' freedom of expression and association, the power of the General Prosecutor of the Supreme Court to dismiss the case.

These points are important because they were also discussed when the new law had already come into force and led to some important modifications.[10]

1. *The Exhaustive Character of the Code*

According to the law, the new Code is supposed to be complete. All possible forms of misconduct are listed in the Code and any other form of behaviour, not mentioned in the list, cannot be punished as a disciplinary violation.

More general provisions such as that which was proposed at the beginning of the reform (the magistrate can be punished for "any other behaviour that can compromise independence and impartiality, even in their appearance"), and also any reference to the "prestige" and "standing" of the magistracy, have been excluded because they are considered in contrast with the notion of the certainty of law and would leave room for discretion.

In the opinion of the people working on the reform, general provisions are not consistent with a Code because they would reduce its effects and do not support judicial independence. So, the need for firm rules was considered much more important than the need for flexibility.[11]

2. *Judicial Independence in Adjudication*

Our Constitution (art. 101) states that "judges are subject only to the law", meaning that the judge, while performing judicial functions, cannot be affected, conditioned, or influenced by any other element, but the law. In other words, the judge must apply the law, act independently in all cases and be free from any outside influence.

As a consequence, judges cannot be disciplined for the way they have applied the law and no control or instructions are possible with regard to adjudication, which is the core of judicial activity and relies on the judge's conscience and free evaluation of the case. This is a way of guaranteeing the judge's independence in adjudication.

---

[10] Law 24 October 2006, no. 269.

[11] Other people believe, on the contrary, that the exhaustive character of the Code is actually a limit of the reform, because it does not allow the list to be adapted to future needs, following cultural and social changes.

Before the reform of 2006, the Disciplinary Commission adopted the following rules: judicial discipline can deal only with a judge's behaviour and not with a judge's decisions, which can be appealed before the superior court. Only in three cases can the substance of judicial decisions be challenged before the Disciplinary Commission: when the judge made a gross, serious mistake in applying the law; when the decision issued is "abnormal"; when the judge used his/her power for personal purposes or other purposes beyond the demands of justice. This was a compromise between the protection of judicial independence in adjudication and the necessity to punish the most serious violations of the law.

As a result of the vagueness of these rules however, some questionable decisions were made. For example, one judge was acquitted in spite of his negligence in the application of the law. He did not realize that an important law had been abolished and he justified his decision by simply saying that the official journal (*Gazzetta Ufficiale*), in which the new law was published, had not been delivered to his office in time.[12] A public prosecutor was acquitted despite the fact that he did not communicate to the judge in charge of the detention of a suspect of a crime factors which might well have led to his release. He was acquitted because no control is possible over the way in which the magistrate has interpreted the law.[13]

The reform of 2006 was an attempt to clarify the situation. On the one hand, it is noted that "activities consisting in the interpretation of the law and evaluation of facts and evidence cannot be disciplined"; on the other hand, specific violations concerning adjudication have been detailed within the Code. So, according to the Code, the judge can be disciplined in cases of: serious violation of the law or misinterpretation of the facts, resulting from ignorance or inexcusable negligence; decisions without motivation; contradictory decisions; decisions adopted without respecting legal provisions or on the basis of a serious mistake or negligence.

The difficulty in defining concepts that until 2006 were left to the free interpretation of the Disciplinary Commission is evident, but the outcome cannot be evaluated as yet. The discussion that led to the Code focused on the problem of the "creative" role of the judge in the interpretation of the law, emphasising that very strict limitations on a judge are not possible in this matter.

---

[12] Disciplinary Commission, 22 July 1997 (proceedings no. 19/97).

[13] Disciplinary Commission, 23 January 1998 (proceedings no. 100-101/97); *Corte di Cassazione*, 22 May 1999, no. 282.

3. *The Limitation of Judges' Freedom of Expression and Association*

In this case the problem was to combine the duties of independence, impartiality and discretion with the basic rights of freedom of expression and association, set out in the Constitution and guaranteed to everybody, including judges.

With respect to freedom of expression, the Superior Council of the Magistracy has on various occasions urged magistrates not to divulge confidential information they come across in the course of their duties and to tread carefully when dealing with the press and other mass media[14] but, despite this, the disclosure of information concerning judicial activities has been quite frequent in the past.

Before the reform of 2006, when deciding on the judge's freedom of expression the Disciplinary Commission used to take into consideration various factors and, in general, the whole situation in which the judge found himself/herself. Importance was given, for instance, to the context (a public meeting, the courtroom, an interview, *etc.*), to the subject and the nature of the information disclosed (political, cultural, judicial; confidential or public information), and also to the citizens' right to be kept informed regarding judicial matters of public interest. Judges were usually allowed to participate in public debates and to express their opinions – both on questions of public interest and on judicial matters – on condition that they spoke in general terms, used moderate tones and did not reveal confidential information. On the other hand, judges were not allowed to disclose the substance of a trial decision before it was officially made public or to make adverse comments regarding the activity of a colleague or a lawyer. In this matter too, the criteria adopted by the Disciplinary Commission could vary a lot, case by case. For example, the disclosure of confidential information (as regards, for example, investigations) was not always disciplined, depending on the specific case and depending on whether it was considered that investigations had been substantially damaged or not.[15] The limitations to judges' freedom of expression were indeed not so strict.

At present, after the reform of 2006, only a few limitations have been set. Judges can be punished if they violate judicial confidentiality, if they make comments on the proceedings they are handling or on the people involved (if they inflict irreparable damage to their rights) and if they divulge information regarding the activity of their office.

---

[14] Regulations 18 April 1990; 19 May 1993 and 01 December 1994.

[15] *Corte di Cassazione*, 9 July 1998, no. 11732 and Disciplinary Commission, 26 November 1999 (proceedings no. 51/97).

The new law focuses above all on violations concerning information on judicial proceedings and activity, whereas no regulation is contemplated on opinions which are outside judicial matters, which seem to remain completely free. The reform does not seem to take account of the importance of regulating judges' freedom of expression in the public arena. This could have adverse effects on the protection of judicial independence, since certain types of conduct, like participating in political debates, expressing political opinions, criticizing public institutions (like the Government, the Prime Minister) or politicians, would seem to be inappropriate for judges, as they are to preserve and demonstrate their impartial role. As we know, judges must not only be impartial, but must also appear as such.

The same principle can also be applied to judges' freedom of association and, in particular, to membership of political parties. The reform is really innovative on this point, since for the first time a judge's membership of political party has been expressly forbidden by law. In the past several similar bills were submitted to Parliament on the matter, but none of them was ever passed.

Before 2006, membership of a political party and participation in political activities were considered inappropriate for judges; notwithstanding, a judge could de facto express his/her political views, take part in an electoral meeting or in a political campaign without sanctions being applied (or serious sanctions). Judges were disciplined only in extreme cases, when it was clear and evident that judicial functions had been substantially influenced by politics.

According to the new law, judges cannot be members or participate in political parties or be involved in economic or financial activities which may affect judicial functions or, in any case, compromise the standing of the magistrate. Moreover, they cannot participate in secret associations or associations whose obligations are not consistent with the performing of judicial functions.

As already pointed out in the past, forbidding membership of political parties is only a formal measure, because a judge can take part in political activities without being member of any party.[16] It seems more important, on the other hand, to limit judges' actual political activities. On this point, the reform states that the participation in political parties is forbidden, but only if "systematic and continuous". This specification – which was introduced later – was considered suitable by the people working on the reform in order to balance independence and freedom of association. Actually, it makes the prohibition rather confused and mitigates de facto its importance.

---

[16] See, for example, G. Di Federico, "Quella commistione tra magistratura e politica molto appetita dai giudici italiani e che il ministro Flick fa finta di voler cancellare" *Il Foglio Quotidiano* (8 April 1997); G. Di Federico, "Magistrati in politica: solo in Italia è una cosa normale" *Il Messaggero* (7 May 2000).

Moreover, it should be noted that in Italy, according to the general provisions on the *status* of magistrate, magistrates can be elected to Parliament and participate in electoral campaigns. Once elected, they are given leave of absence (*fuori ruolo*) for the whole period of their mandate and after having completed their term of office they can return to exercise judicial functions. This provision – which was not modified by the reform – allows a close connection between justice and politics, with adverse effects on judicial independence, and seems to be in contrast with the reform aim to limit judges' political involvement.

4. *The Power of the General Prosecutor of the Supreme Court to Dismiss the Case*

This measure was introduced to counter the obligation for the General Prosecutor of the Supreme Court to initiate disciplinary action. According to the new law, the General Prosecutor must initiate a disciplinary action whenever s/he finds (or is informed of) a possible disciplinary violation. Formally, as a result of compulsory disciplinary action, any complaint coming to the attention of the General Prosecutor must lead to disciplinary proceedings, even if unfounded. In this way, the General Prosecutor is not free to decide whether to initiate disciplinary proceedings or not (as was the case before the reform), since no choice is given to him/her.

The introduction of the compulsory disciplinary action was strongly criticized by magistrates and by the Superior Council of the Magistracy. In their opinion, the number of complaints would increase considerably, with a consequent rise in the number of proceedings going before the Disciplinary Commission, which would prejudice its functioning. As a result of pressure from them, the provision was changed, or rather mitigated, by the introduction of the power of the General Prosecutor to dismiss the case (the Minister however can oppose the dismissal).[17]

This power is intended as a filter to protect judges from unfounded actions, perhaps used as a pretext by the party who lost a case adjudicated by a particular judge, and lastly to protect their independence. At the same time, however, the General Prosecutor has been entrusted with discretionary powers that are crucial for the going on of the proceedings.

[17] The Prosecutor General can dismiss a case when the complaint is unfounded, when the misconduct is not in the Code or it is of low importance and when misconduct does not exist or was not committed by the accused.

IV. Final Remarks

The aim of this article was to point out some controversial issues concerning judicial independence that characterized the discussion and the creation of the new Code of judicial conduct.

The four questions we have analysed show that, according to the aims of the reform, judicial independence can be better guaranteed through firm and all-encompassing rules, precise sanctions and compulsory disciplinary action. They also show, however, that discretionary powers cannot be completely excluded from judicial discipline. Discretionary powers are given to the General Prosecutor to dismiss the case when, for example, judicial misconduct is of low relevance, and also to the Disciplinary Commission in the application and interpretation of the new infringements provided for by the Code, which sometimes appear rather confused.

Taking into account the situation that prevailed before 2006 (the wide discretionary powers of the SCM Disciplinary Commission), I think that the reform should be evaluated in a positive way, above all as regards the introduction of a Code of judicial conduct and the introduction of minimum sanctions applicable for the most serious violations. As already stated, these provisions are intended to reduce discretionary powers in judicial discipline and, consequently, to improve the effectiveness of disciplinary control and the quality of our judges.

The Code, in particular, is an extremely important innovation in our system, because it breaks with a long tradition based on Disciplinary Commission case law. One important point, however, has to be stressed: the Code, in actual fact, stemmed from the Disciplinary Commission case law and reiterates some of the principles and criteria that were adopted before 2006 (*ex facto oritur jus*). Sometimes it is not less confused than the criteria adopted before 2006. The risk of this situation is that the Disciplinary Commission, while interpreting the new Code, could not be able to depart very far from the rules that were applied in the past.

So, I cannot end without saying that, at the moment, the effects of the reform cannot be fully evaluated, because we still do not know the attitude of the SCM Disciplinary Commission. Only by monitoring its future decisions will we be able to understand the real impact of the reform on judicial discipline.

CHAPTER TWENTY TWO

THE AGE OF JUDICIAL RESPONSIBILITY: THE RETIREMENT AND RESIGNATION OF APPELLATE COURT JUDGES

*Sir Louis Blom-Cooper QC**

> Since the populist image of the geriatric judge, out of touch with the real world, is now reflected in the statutory presumption of judicial incompetence at the age of 75 [reduced to 70 for those appointed to the judiciary for the first time after 31 March 1995] this is the last time I shall speak judicially in your Lordships' House. I am happy that the occasion is one when I can agree with your Lordships still in the prime of judicial life who demonstrate so convincingly that common sense and the common law here go hand in hand.
> Lord Bridge of Harwich in *Ruxley Electronics v. Forsyth*[1]

It is axiomatic that a retiring age for judges does not violate the fundamental principle of either their independence or their impartiality, although the existence of a discretionary power on the part of the appointing body to extend the period may give rise to an argument that a conditional extension of office conceivably endangers the independence of the judge. That apart, a fixed limit in judicial office is inviolable. Since the impartiality of a judge, determined by the absence of perceived bias, is dependent on his or her personal and professional attributes, why should those attributes be set aside arbitrarily according to chronological age? In their response to the Government's consultation paper on a Supreme Court for the United Kingdom[2] the Law Lords, although preferring a statutory retirement age of 75 (instead of the existing 70) wrote exhaustively, if not exhaustingly:

> [The attributes to be looked for in a member of the Supreme Court are] integrity, incorruptibility, independence and impartiality; intellect, analytical ability, legal knowledge, relevant experience and the ability to assimilate large quantities of

* Sir Professor Louis Blom-Cooper QC was called to the Bar by the Middle Temple in July 1952, and was made a Bencher of the Inn in 1978. He took silk in 1970, and was a Deputy High Court Judge from 1992 to 1996, as well as a Judge of Appeal in the Court of Appeal of Jersey and of Guernsey from 1989 to 1996. Publications include Final Appeal: A Study of the House of Lords in its Judicial Capacity (1972), co-authored with Gavin Drewry, The Court of Appeal (2007), with Gavin Drewry and Charles Blake.

[1] [1996] 1 AC 344, 354.

[2] Consultation Paper 11/03, July 2003.

> material at short notice; the capacity to formulate legal policy at a high level; open-mindedness, fair-mindedness and single-mindedness; the ability to compose clearly reasoned judgments *without prolixity* [I italicise those two words, given the current disease of judicial verbosity] within a reasonable time; a general knowledge of social conditions and trends; courtesy; common sense; energy and assiduity; decisiveness; and good health…[3]

Apart from the process of ageing, affecting the good health of the judge, these admirable qualities are exhibited in judges of the past who were appointed for life. My thesis is that for appellate judges appointment for life, with regular medical check-ups and the functioning of personal resignation, is to be preferred. The evidence of high quality judicial service at an advanced age is strikingly in favour of appointment for life.

To be parochial for the moment, the greatest judge of post-war Britain was Lord Reid. Appointed in 1948, he sat for 26 years, retiring at the age of 84. He has left us with a legacy of outstanding judgments – he handed down over 500 judgments – which have shaped, and continue to shape our modern law, particularly in the sphere of judicial control over ministers and central and local government. Lord Wilberforce was likewise a distinguished judge and contemporary of Lord Reid, who was appointed to be a judge in 1961 and to the House of Lords in 1964, but retired compulsorily in 1982 after eighteen years as an appellate judge. He lived to the age of 95, at which point he had retained his full mental faculties. He himself expressed the regret that he had just failed (by two years) to gain the judicial freehold. Had he been appointed before 1959, he would have been able to carry on for the rest of his life. The country was deprived of his excellent services for at least 10 (if not more) years.

A more compelling example of the inflexibility of an arbitrary age limit occurred in 2008, when professional gossip in legal circles focused on who would be the first President of the Supreme Court. Under the Constitutional Reform Act 2005 the Senior Law Lord on 1st October 2009 would automatically become the first President. The Senior Law Lord at the time of this legislation was Lord Bingham of Cornhill who reached the retiring age of 75 on 13 October 2008. By universal claim, both within and outwith the legal profession, he was considered to be the ideal first head of the UK Supreme Court, a reform for which he had been a vocal protagonist. Alas, *anno domini* asserted itself. The outstanding talent of a remarkable judge was instantly swept aside.

It is too readily assumed that when age has come upon a judge, his powers (or the full vigour of those powers) are lessened. Any discretion to retire means that when they have lost their discretion, they have not discretion

---

[3] paragraph 30.

enough to retire. One cannot entirely discount this argument, but such potential waning of powers may, and does occur irrespective of any statutory age limit of 70 or 75. But physical ill-health need not dictate resignation. The example of Judge Learned Hand, the judicial colossus of the Second Circuit Court of Appeal is telling. His biographer, Gerald Gunther, noted[4] that at the age of 86, Learned Hand was suffering increasing physical pain and recurrent groundless fears that his mental acuity was waning. Gunther comments: 'The quality of his writings – in judicial opinions, addresses and letters – remained high until the end' which had been effected by his resignation in 1951 at the age of 79 from 'regular active service', although he did continue to participate in many cases on the Second Circuit up until his death at the age of 89. Some of Learned Hand's inspiration to continue judicially beyond three score and ten years was from his idol, Oliver Wendell Holmes. There are recollections of Holmes when that outstanding Supreme Court justice was about ninety. When Holmes considered retiring, he said that he would have a quiet talk with the Great Panjandrum, who would reply, 'Well, Wendell, if that's how you feel, I can arrange it. How about tonight?', to which Holmes (himself notably stoic as a Civil War veteran) would answer, 'Boss, could you as well put that off a fortnight?' (This was a story which Learned Hand repeatedly told in his eighties.)

I give these few examples to illustrate how it is possible, and indeed desirable for a civilised society to nurse the judicial talent of its highest judiciary. And it seems that was the view of our ancestors. Under the Act of Settlement, all judges held office for life. It was thought that their independence could be guaranteed only by their irremovability short of death. At the end of the 19th century, there was a growing opinion that it was in the interests of the public with regard to the due administration of justice that in all appointments of judges an age limit should be fixed for their compulsory retirement. The predictable argument that mental and physical powers begin to dwindle, even deteriorate, with advancing years on the Bench did not arouse any support for ending the lifelong appointment. On 1 March 1898 the MP for Cornwall and Truro, Sir Edwin Lawrence, could find no seconder to a parliamentary motion to fix a time limit for retirement. But by the middle of the 20th century, the die was cast. Judges could no longer be an exception to the general principle that public servants should be compulsorily retired. The trend towards a fixed limit of judgeship was first recommended in 1913 by the St Aldwyn Commission whose report was endorsed in 1936 by the Royal Commission (under the chairmanship of Lord Peel) which suggested that the retiring age for judges of

---

[4] *Learned Hand – The Man and the Judge* (1994) published by Alfred A Knopf Inc, at page 674.

the Queen's Bench Division – they were dealing only with judges of that Division – should be 72. The Peel Commission thought, moreover, that any power to extend was undesirable, since a conditional extension of office might be thought to impinge upon the independence of the judiciary. When Parliament finally got round to legislating in 1959, two issues were considered. First, serious consideration was given to applying different retiring ages for judges of the High Court and for Lords Justices. The Attorney-General, Sir Reginald Manningham-Butler (later Viscount Dilhorne, subsequently a Lord Chancellor and Lord of Appeal in Ordinary) added that 'there have been suggestions that there should be no retiring age for Lords of Appeal'.[5] But the suggestion did not mature into general acceptability, largely because the Bar Council of the day expressed itself in favour of a fixed retiring age of 75 for all members of the higher judiciary. The differential between judges of first instance and those in appellate courts is something I shall develop in a moment.

The second point is that ever since the Act of Settlement (and probably long before) judges have been irremovable. They have had a livelong right to remain in office. In 1959 for the first time in English legal history that irremovability was no longer applicable in its absolutist form. Some MPs asked pertinently whether it was the experience that after reaching the age of 75 judges became so senile as not to be able properly to perform their judicial function. If not, what reason was there for the innovation of the compulsory retiring age? Dr Eric Fletcher, the Labour MP for Islington East, and a prominent practising solicitor in London (and therefore, at that time, a man with no prospect of preferment to the higher judiciary) said that his limited experience of litigation led him to believe that there had been judges on both the High Court and the Court of Appeal 'who were over the age of 75 but were able to discharge their judicial functions at least as well as some younger judges'. And Mr William Ross, MP for Kilmarnock, thought that by insisting on the inflexible rule of retirement at 75 'we may be robbing ourselves of valuable and experienced men who are capable of carrying on for some time'. But the Aristotelian view, that judges of important causes should hold office for life is not a good thing, 'for the mind grows old as well as the body', prevailed. Other than exceptionally, the wear and tear of the office comes with the onset of extreme old age. And as far as I can judge, there has not been in modern times any clamour for the life-long appointment. When the issue of a retiring age was considered in the Judicial Pensions and Retirement Bill in 1993 the sole aim was to introduce consistency throughout the judiciary. At that time some judges had to go

[5] HC Hansard, vol 614, col 246.

before 70, others went at 72 whereas senior judges stayed on till 75. The legislature opted for a general retirement at the age of 70, although strangely there remained the possibility of enabling service to be continued in the public interest, but then only for periods of no more than a year at a time, up to, but not beyond, the judge's 75th birthday. No judge over 75, retired or otherwise, may sit in a judicial capacity. Hence the lament of Lord Bridge of Harwich, cited at the outset of this paper. As one journalist commented, Lord Bridge went off to take a degree in Mathematics at the Open University, having missed out on a university education earlier as a result of wartime service. Critics today want to return to the age limit of 75. Lord Pannick QC, on 25 March 2009, asked in a question in Parliament for such a change, to which the Government replied that it would keep the question under review. Why not now consider restoring the life-long appointment for the judges of the new Supreme Court?

Some basic facts about the age and service of the 112 Law Lords who have sat in the final court of appeal, the Judicial House of Lords from 1876–2009. The mean age of appointment over the period was about 62.[6] The two most recent appointments, in 2009, Lord Kerr of Tonaghmore (61) and Lord Clarke of Stone-cum-Ebony (66) display no sign of earlier preferment to the highest court in the land. Since 1959, it has not been possible for any Law Lord to serve more than 15 years. In fact the average term of service, excluding those currently serving, was just under nine years. Before 1959, there were some notable long-time Law Lords. Lords Reid (October 1948 to January 1975) and Macnaghten (January 1887 to February 1913) served for over 26 years. Both were outstanding jurists, able to deliver a judicial output of significance. Others gave service of likewise quality.[7] The average age of Law Lords on giving up office, for whatever reason, was 71½, although there were wide variations. Five were octogenarians; the youngest were Devlin (58), Robson (59) and Mustill (65). Lord Bowen was only 59 when he died. He was one of only 18 Law Lords who died in office. Notably, it was a relatively common occurrence in early days, but no Law Lord has died in office since Lords Upjohn and

[6] The youngest appointed before the age of 60 were Lords Radcliffe (50), MacDermott (51), Watson (53), Macnaghten (57), Bowen (58), Robertson (54), Sumner (54), Shaw of Dunfermline (58), Parker of Waddington (56), Thankerton (56), Macmillan (57), Reid (58), Denning (58), Devlin (56), Wilberforce (57), Keith of Kinkel (54), Mackay of Clashfern (58), Goff of Chieveley (59), Woolf (59), Hope of Craighead (58), Rodger of Earlsferry (57), [Lady] Hale of Richmond (58).

[7] Lord Atkinson (December 1905 to February 1928) did 22 years; Lord Shaw of Dunfermline (February 1909 to April 1929) over 20 years; Lord Keith of Kinkel (January 1977 to September 1996) just under 20 years. The only runners-up to a 20-year stint were Radcliffe (15 years), Morris of Borth-y-Gest (15 years), Wilberforce (17½ years), Diplock (17 years), Sumner (16 years) and Atkin (16 years).

Donovan (1971) and Diplock (1985). Law Lords appointed after 1876 died at the average age of 72; the comparable figure for the last ten Law Lords to die is 86. Today we all, judges included, live longer and healthier. Of the last 18 Law Lords to retire (otherwise than to take up other judicial office, eg Lord Chancellor or Lord Chief Justice) only two – Lords Lowry (1994) and Bingham (2008) – had effectively reached the statutory retirement age of 75. So much for the argument that a fixed limit has any numerical significance.

None of this indicates a pressing need to avoid the instinctive dislike of an appointment for life for those elevated to the highest court in the land. The public adherence to a retiring age, reflected in the statutory provisions since 1959, is much less about a decline in physical and mental health, and more about a repellence to elderly attitudes. Oliver Wendell Holmes, who was a judge for about 45 years – first in the Supreme Judicial Court of Massachusetts and then for 30 years in the US Supreme Court until his nineties – wrote truly: 'Judges commonly are elderly men, and more likely to hate at sight any analysis to which they are not accustomed, and which disturbs peace of mind, than to fall in love with novelties'. But the wisdom and experience of old age needs only a leavening of those younger judges who both bring contemporary standards to bear on socio-legal problems and are conversant with the concerns of contemporary society. Lord Bingham has written[8] that relatively few of those entitled to serve until 75 chose to retire: 'there has not in practice been a problem of senile judges who should have retired and declined to do so'.

The essence of the problem lies in the functioning of the faculties of judicial personnel. It is the diminution in sight (even blindness need not disqualify a judge) and sound that is crucial to the sound administration of justice in the courtroom. Physical and mental decline is highly variable among people in later life. But impairment of hearing – even in middle age – is a common occurrence; even the minor problem of tinnitus, the sensation of ringing or buzzing in the ears, can be distractive in the listener. Also the tiredness and weariness associated with lengthy periods in court can produce torpor and inattention to witness evidence. These are the prime factors that are engaged in the process of the decision-maker who must hear all the evidence from witnesses and assess its weight. The essential orality of the English legal system calls for adjudication of testimony, given in the witness-box, examined in chief by counsel for one party and cross-examined by the opponent. To put it shortly, there is sound reason why these common afflictions of the human being should lead to compulsory retirement at an age commensurate with

[8] *The Judicial House of Lords 1876–2009*, ed Blom-Cooper, Dickson and Drewry, OUP 2009, chapter 8.

scientific (medical) knowledge of the ageing human condition. But these are afflictions that are infinitely more pertinent to the trial judge than to his appellate counterpart. Most of the work of an appellate judge is reading (often vast amounts of documentary material) and writing judgments. The hearings in the courtroom do require audio-reception, but only from counsel addressing the court. There is no fact-finding, which is the essence of the trial process. The facts of a litigated dispute, as assessed after evaluating the credibility and reliability of witnesses (in addition to documentary material) are already found by the trial judge. The appellate judge may review (or revise) the facts, but that is done by testing the written material. Thus while the ability to hear and see the witnesses is crucial to fact-finding, no such prerequisite applies in appellate proceedings.

In *Baker v. Quantum Clothing Group*,[9] Lord Justice Sedley (against whom there was an unsubstantiated charge of judicial bias) revealed, in a case involving noise-induced deafness in the textile industry, that he did not regard the fact that he himself had mild tinnitus as a disqualifying factor in the proceedings 'any more than if a judge who has back trouble tries a spinal injury case or a judge who is a motorist tries a running down case'. In their joint, supplementary judgment, Lady Justice Smith and Lord Justice Jacob observed:

> We turn to the objection based on the fact that Sedley LJ himself suffers from mild tinnitus and we are accepting for present purposes that this was not disclosed. It too is a point of no substance. It amounts to a contention that no judge with any particular disability should hear a case involving that disability. A judge with poor eyesight or only one eye could not hear a case about an eye injury, a judge in a wheelchair could not hear a case about an injury which made the victim wheelchair bound and so on. And, taken to its logical conclusion, the argument would mean that a disabled judge could not hear a case about disability living allowance, or a woman judge hear a case about sexual discrimination against a woman. The examples multiply.

The judges might have added that some disabilities were even less relevant in the case of an appellate judge.

I. Appointments to Appellate Courts

There is a wealth of difference between the appointment of someone to become a judge for the first time, at whatever level of the judicial hierarchy, and the promotion of a judge up the judicial ladder. The assessment of merit, based on current judicial performance, requires a major input from those who have had

---

[9] 5 June 2009.

just that experience. It is one thing for the Judicial Appointments Commission to deploy the techniques of assessment of those seeking a judicial post and, on the other hand, those seeking promotion. It is always feasible for the non-lawyer to assess the quality of judicial output, through an examination of summings-up to juries in criminal trials or of judgments in civil proceedings; only those who have tasted the output of a trial judge can, however, assess the quality of the judge *qua* judge. The manner in which a judge conducts himself judicially will always be an important factor in assessing merit. There is also the fact that what makes for a good trial judge will not necessarily hold good for the appellate judge. Deciding cases on the basis of fact-finding – always a difficult enough task – is essentially different from that of one appeal court judge, sitting not alone but collegiately, and applying legal rules to finite evidential material.

These considerations lead inevitably to a method of promotional appointments which might materially differ from the way in which first-time judicial appointments are made. If the Judicial Appointments Commission is composed of a majority of higher judicial figures and practising lawyers, the differential is well catered for. Since the Commission contains some lay members, some method will need to be introduced that distinguishes promotional appointments from others. For promotions, the Commission might be limited to making recommendations to the relevant Minister of the Crown, from among a number of suitable candidates. The Minister would then make the choice. For all that, one will need to guard against the possible professional bias within legal circles. Whatever the mode of selection to the Bench adopted by the Commission, any political influence should be scrupulously avoided. As Aaron Barak, former Chief Justice of Israel, pointedly observed, it is one thing for the politicians to be judicially reviewed. It is altogether the opposite: judges should not be politicised. As Professor Harold Laski wrote in 1926,[10] the method by which judges are appointed, 'the kind of men, further, it is customary to choose', questions of constitutionality become a matter of first importance.

Those appointing appellate judges in the future will undoubtedly be alive to the one clear modern influence of political interference in the case of Lord Donaldson of Lymington – a case of double-edged political correctness. As Mr Justice Donaldson, he was appointed by a Conservative administration in 1971 to head the National Industrial Relations Court. His performance greatly displeased the trade unions and the Labour opposition, such that in December 1973 187 Labour MPs moved in Parliament to remove Sir John as president of

[10] Michigan Law Review Vol XXIV, p 529.

the Court for reasons of 'political prejudice and partiality', despite Sir John's justifiable claim that the Industrial Court 'is a court of law ... It is independent of the Government and is in no way concerned with its policies.' The charge was unfair. No vote in Parliament was forthcoming, but the incoming Labour administration made no secret of the fact that Sir John would not be promoted to the Court of Appeal. Nor was he, until the Conservatives returned to power in 1979 when the Lord Chancellor, Lord Hailsham, appointed him to the Court of Appeal. In 1982 Lord Hailsham reported to Mrs Thatcher that a number of judges had expressed the view that Lord Justice Donaldson should not succeed Lord Denning as Master of the Rolls. The Prime Minister is said to have retorted: 'Fortunately, Lord Chancellor, your judges do not appoint the Master of the Rolls. I do.' And she did. Lord Donaldson turned out to be, by common consent of the legal profession, a distinguished Master of the Rolls from 1982 to 1992.

That was an isolated instance of a politicising of the judiciary in modern times. Since the Second World War there has been a distinct absence of any political influence on judicial appointments. The death-knell to any such action that appeared to develop in the 19th and early 20th centuries came in 1948. Lord Reid, a Conservative MP and Lord Advocate in the war-time coalition Government of Winston Churchill, was appointed by Clement Atlee, the Labour Prime Minister. And Lord Reid, over 26 years, was the outstanding Law Lord of the last half of the 20th century. I should observe, contrary to my general proposition for appellate appointees, that Lord Reid was appointed direct from public administration, parliamentary experience and practice at the Scottish Bar.

Impartiality, or perceived impartiality, is enhanced by the existence of the highest quality of judicial output. A system of appellate justice calls for a blend of wisdom, experience, diversity (not just in cultural background, but in age distribution) and demonstrable merit. The final court of appeal should ideally be composed of a sprinkling of octogenarians (nonogenarians might be a step too far) alongside a smattering of 40 and 50 year olds – and every age between – with plenty of time for each appellate judge to reap a rich juristic harvest.

CHAPTER TWENTY THREE

STANDARDS OF JUDICIAL BEHAVIOUR AND THE IMPACT OF CODES OF CONDUCT

*Anton Cooray**

In any civilized society the judiciary must enjoy a high degree of independence in order to be able to fulfil its primary—and one could even contend, only—function, namely to apply the law in the context of dispute resolution.[1] In the common law world, there is no more sacrosanct fundamental principle in the constitutional order of things than the independence of the judiciary. The idea of the independence of the judiciary which is embedded in the doctrine of separation of powers ensures that the judiciary enjoys a special position of autonomy and independence so that it can act freely of any direction or influence emanating from the other two branches of government—the legislature and the executive. Even in non-common law jurisdictions, where there is a more pronounced association between the three branches of government, the recent trend has been to assign to the judiciary a special position of importance.[2] In the common law world, ordinary courts of law are endowed with jurisdiction in both the private and public domains. There are no special courts for public law litigation; citizens and government agencies alike appear as parties before ordinary courts of law.[3] It is for this reason in particular that courts must enjoy a privileged position with special protections and immunities, so that they can hold the scales of justice evenly between the humble citizen and the mighty government.

In order to maintain its independence, the judiciary must be above criticism. Suspicion of partiality, incompetence or abuse of power invites attempts

---

* Professor Anton Cooray is Associate Dean of Law at City University of Hong Kong. He specializes in comparative public law and is the editor of Asia Pacific Law Review, the first Asia based law journal to be indexed in SSCI.

[1] It is not uncommon for the judiciary to be given an advisory jurisdiction or asked to decide on the constitutionality of a proposed parliamentary bill when there is obviously no concrete dispute ripe for resolution.

[2] See, generally, on courts in Europe, Carlo Guarnieri and Patrizia Pederzoli, *The Power of Judges: A Comparative Study of Courts and Democracy* (Oxford 2002).

[3] The British jurist A V Dicey viewed the absence of special courts as an essential feature of the rule of law, in the sense of equality before the courts. See, Jeffrey Jowell, "The Rule of Law Today" in Jeffrey Jowell and Dawn Oliver (eds.), *The Changing Constitution* (6th ed., Oxford 2007), Chapter 1.

to clip its wings. It is only when the judiciary is, in fact and in appearance, independent and immune from political control that it will be able to gain public confidence and trust. To this end, constitutional principles and conventional practices have evolved to ensure that a special sphere is demarcated for the judiciary. These structural arrangements constitute the irreducible minimum requirements to guarantee judicial independence. Building upon them, it is important to cultivate an internal judicial environment which ensures that judicial officers live up to certain accepted norms of behaviour. It is the judges' responsibility to prove that the trust and confidence the public repose in them is not breached in the slightest. It is important not only that judges are independent and fair; they must also appear to be so. A judge may have acted fairly and competently, but if he is perceived to be partial or incompetent, public confidence will be lost.[4]

While it is a constituent part of the State machinery, the judiciary is clearly different from the other two branches of government. The legislature is tasked with policy formulation and law-making, while the executive is tasked with implementing government policies and executing law. The legislature and the executive have to work closely together in policy formulation, law-making and the process of implementing law and policy. What one finds in the modern State is a joint venture rather than a separation between the legislative and executive branches. In contrast, there is a clear demarcation between the legislature and the executive, on the one hand, and the judiciary, on the other. This is in order to ensure that the task of dispute resolution is left in the hands of the judiciary with the ultimate aim of safeguarding community and individual rights. There remains, of course, an inevitable, hazy overlap between the judicial and the legislative/executive spheres, although this does not compromise the autonomy of the judiciary.

It is in this context of judicial-legislative-executive relationships that the effective working of an independent judiciary has to be assessed. On the one hand, there is a compelling constitutional imperative that judges judge and do nothing else. On the other, there is an increasing recognition that the expertise of judges should be put to good use for the public good. There is also a well-recognized need for work of a judicial nature to be entrusted to administrative tribunals and agencies. It is in the context of these competing considerations that an evaluation of judicial independence becomes meaningful. In the complex order of constitutional arrangements, it has always been felt that the judiciary must adopt good practices. Judicial codes of conduct have,

---

[4] It is for this reason that a judge must recuse himself from hearing a case where there is an appearance of bias, even though there is no likelihood of actual bias. See, *R v. Bow Street Magistrate ex p Pinochet Ugarte (No 2)* [2000] 1 A.C. 119 (HL).

therefore, a prominent place in relation to the constitutional perspective of the judiciary's working.

I. Why Should the Judiciary be Independent?

It is axiomatic that justice must be administered impartially and according to law and reason. It is true that it is the responsibility of each judge to act fairly and impartially, but an institutional framework which ensures this has a very important part to play. Thus, to ensure judicial impartiality, rules and practices have evolved which deter outsiders from unduly influencing the judiciary with threats or inducements. If these rules and practices are well observed, the general public can rest assured that courts are no respecters of persons. This is what is mainly meant by "public confidence in the administration of justice". However, this does not necessarily mean that judicial decisions must be generally in keeping with public expectations. Unlike the legislature, which generally reflects majoritarian wishes, judges may sometimes have to take decisions which are unacceptable to the majority or to the government. Acting correctly—but against the majority view of the community—may place the judiciary in a position where it does not have public confidence. If the goal of impartial and fair administration of justice is to be attained, the judiciary must be free to act in disregard of any loss of public confidence that it may cause.[5]

It is in this sense of the insulation of the judiciary that one must view the idea of an independent judiciary. In order to secure this special immunity of the judge, we have developed the offence of contempt of court, the idea of the privilege of judicial proceedings, regulation of Parliamentary debates on judicial conduct and judicial proceedings, and prohibition of attempts to pervert the course of justice. Of course, all these are finely counterbalanced with the need to protect freedom of speech, including the right to criticize, to promote public participation in holding the government—including the judiciary—accountable to people, and to protect legitimate interests of litigants, counsel and the general public.

An important aspect of judicial independence under a constitution founded on a separation of powers relates to the idea that judges must judge and must not do anything else, and that no one other than judges must judge. This idea has been formally expressed as the exclusive vesting of judicial power in the

[5] See, Elizabeth Handsley, "Public Confidence in the Judiciary: A Red Herring for the Separation of Judicial Power" (1998) 20 *Sydney Law Review* 183, at 195: "The purpose of judicial independence is to ensure the rule of law, which means ensuring that judges are willing and able to stand firm against the tide of public opinion. When judges give in to public opinion, we have the rule of 'men', not the rule of 'law' ".

judiciary and has found expression, for example, in Australia and Sri Lanka. In what are called tribunal cases, the Supreme Court of Sri Lanka and the Privy Council demarcated areas where it would be unconstitutional for a tribunal to exercise its statutory powers on the ground that judicial power is exclusively vested in the judiciary. In what are called legislative power cases, the principle was firmly established that the legislature cannot exercise judicial power, for instance by passing a "legislative judgment" or interfering with the discretion of judges in relation to admissibility of evidence or sentencing, for example. These cases clearly upheld the principle that the administration of justice must be left exclusively to ordinary courts of law because there exist special constitutional and statutory safeguards to ensure that courts of law are competent, fair, impartial and free from outside pressure and influence.[6]

The judiciary must be free of influence even from within the judiciary. Pressure on a judge may come from a fellow judge who has an interest in the outcome of a particular case. More seriously, it may come from the senior judicial administration, which may compel or persuade judges to toe an institutional line. This danger is more likely to be present where the judiciary has the power to question the validity of legislation or important administrative regulations. Protection of judges from fellow judges is best secured by unwritten practices which may find their way into codes of conduct.

II. Judging Judges in the Court of Public Opinion

There is an undeniable link between judicial independence and public perception, because it is the confidence that people have in the judiciary as the fair and impartial administrator of justice that lends the judiciary its legitimacy. Perception of judicial fairness is quintessential in the common law tradition because there is no mechanism to hold judges directly accountable to the people. Judges are appointed to their office and not elected by popular vote. Judges do not depend on public support for tenure in office, and it is only in an indirect way—such as through media criticism—that public opinion impacts on judicial behaviour.

At the state level, the United States of America has taken a different approach, and in 39 of its states all or some of the judges are elected and depend on public support for re-election. The idea central to the elective system is that judges are elected for their potential and are re-elected for how they have performed in office. In this way, judges, just like legislators, are directly accountable to the

[6] For a discussion of the historical development of the independence of the judiciary in Sri Lanka, see, M.J.A. Cooray, *Judicial Role under the Constitutions of Ceylon/Sri Lanka: An Historical and Comparative Study* (Colombo, Sri Lanka 1982).

people.[7] There has been and continues to be widespread debate in the United States on the relative merits of the elective and appointive systems. In some states where an elective system is in place, there have been moves to introduce a system of appointment, such as appointment by the State Governor on recommendations made by a selection committee.[8] In some states where judges are appointed to office, there has been criticism that placing judicial appointments in the hands of a selected few would undermine the right of the people to choose their judges.[9] A major problem with electing judges is the actual or perceived partiality of judges towards their sponsors.[10]

The recent decision of the U.S. Supreme Court *Caperton* v. *Massey*,[11] which concerned the impact of election campaign contributions on judges, is a landmark case in relation to the constitutional importance of an independent judiciary. The case concerned the meaning of judicial bias in the context of the "due process clause".[12] In *Caperton* v. *Massey*, the Chief Executive Officer of Massey had contributed, both directly and indirectly, vast amounts of money to the election campaign of Judge Brent Benjamin at a time when Massey was contemplating an appeal against a decision favourable to Caperton. Judge Benjamin was elected to the Supreme Court of West Virginia and, before Massey filed its petition of appeal, Caperton moved to disqualify him. The motion was denied by Judge Benjamin himself. The State Supreme Court Bench, including Judge Benjamin, upheld the appeal and reversed the jury's US$ 50 million award to Caperton. The case went through a rehearing, and more requests were made for Judge Benjamin's recusal, all of which were similarly rejected.

When the matter came before the Supreme Court of the United States, by way of certiorari, the question was whether the due process clause was wide enough to cover the facts of the case. The due process clause is said to

[7] Interestingly, an element of the elective principle is reflected at the federal level, too. Judges of the Federal Courts are appointed after a screening process in the Senate, including a vote—which may sometimes be strictly on party lines—to confirm Presidential nominees.

[8] For example, in Nevada, a ballot initiative has been proposed to move from election to appointment. See, "Proposal to appoint judges seen as hot issue" in *Las Vegas Sun* (7 July 2009); available at: <www.lasvegas.com/news/2009/jul/07/proposal-appoint-judges-seen-hot-issue/>.

[9] For example, in Missouri, where judges are appointed, there was recently a campaign to reintroduce elections for judicial posts. See, Patrick Tuohey, "Electing Judges?" in *The Record Blog* (7 October 2009); available at: <www.missourirecord.com/blog/index.asp?blog=104>.

[10] In June 2006, the *Los Angeles Times* published an investigative report which found that state judges routinely ruled in favour of friends, former clients and business partners and solicited funds from lawyers with cases pending before them. See, Scott Gold, "New Rules Sought for Nevada Judges" in *Los Angeles Times* (3 September 2006); available at: <http://articles.latimes.com/2006/sep/03/nation/na-judges3>.

[11] Argued on 3 March 2009 and decided on 8 June 2009; available at: <http://www.supremecourt.gov/opinions/08pdf/08-22.pdf>.

[12] The "due process clause" has its origins in the Magna Carta. "A fair trial in a fair tribunal is a basic requirement of due process": *In re Murchison* 349 US 133, 136 (1955).

incorporate the common law rule that requires recusal when a judge has "a direct, personal, substantial, pecuniary interest" in a case.[13] Situations where there was no direct, personal, substantial, pecuniary interest but where there would nevertheless be a likelihood of bias or prejudice were left to the states to be regulated by legislation and judicial codes and to be settled at the state level.[14] Over time, the Supreme Court has widened this rather narrow rule of "direct, personal, substantial, pecuniary interest" to cover two additional instances where "the probability of actual bias on the part of the judge or decision-maker is too high to be constitutionally tolerable."[15] These two instances are based on *Tumey* v. *Ohio*,[16] where there was a local tribunal that had a financial interest which was short of a personal or direct interest, and *In re Murchison*,[17] where a judge was held ineligible to try a case of contempt of court because he had in a previous proceeding decided that charges of contempt be brought against the defendants. In *Caperton* v. *Massey*, the Supreme Court by a 5 to 4 decision extended the scope of the due process clause to the context of election campaign funding. This they did by drawing an analogy with the *Tumey* v. *Ohio* and *In re Murchison* cases.

The principal difficulty for the court was the First Amendment right of free speech, which ensures that people are free to participate in election campaigns. This the court did by conceding that probability of bias does not arise every time a litigant or a lawyer makes a contribution and by treating *Caperton* v. *Massey* as an exceptional case.[18] Justice Kennedy, in the majority opinion, emphasized that almost every state had adopted the objective standard stipulated in the American Bar Association's Model Code of Judicial Conduct: "A judge shall avoid impropriety and the appearance of impropriety". Justice Kennedy observed that these codes of conduct "serve to maintain the integrity of the judiciary and the rule of law". Justice Scalia, in his brief dissenting opinion, said that the resort to the due process clause was urged on the need to preserve the public's confidence in the judicial system but observed

[13] See, *Tumey* v. *Ohio* 273 US 510 (1927), where the Supreme Court took a liberal view of judicial bias. See, further, at note 16 below.

[14] See, *Aetna* v. *Lavoie* 475 US 813, 820.

[15] See, *Withrow* v. *Larkin* 421 US 35, 47.

[16] In *Tumey* v. *Ohio* 273 US 510 (1927) the village mayor sat as judge in alcohol possession cases and fines went to the village treasury for village improvement. The Supreme Court considered that his official motive to convict people so as to fill the village treasury was a relevant factor.

[17] *In re Murchison* 349 US 133 (1955).

[18] Massey's CEO had a personal stake in the case, and the funds he had directed to the election of Judge Benjamin were significant and disproportionate. Massey's appeal to the Supreme Court of West Virginia was pending or imminent. The incumbent Supreme Court judge against whom the election campaign was directed was considered to be sympathetic to claimants, whereas Benjamin was expected to toe a different line.

that the decision would have the opposite effect. In a similar vein, Roberts CJ said in his dissenting opinion:

> I believe that opening the door to recusal claims under the Due Process Clause, for an amorphous "probability of bias" will itself bring our judicial system into undeserved disrepute, and diminish the confidence of the American people in the fairness and integrity of their courts.

What is interesting is that both the majority and minority opinions relied on the importance of public confidence in the judiciary as the basis for extending or restricting the reach of the due process clause. The common meeting point for the majority and minority is that they all agreed that much has been done and much remains to be done at state level to ensure judicial independence and integrity. They all recognized the importance of judicial codes of conduct in this context.

III. Indirect Accountability in the Common Law System

The common law system of appointing judges with security of tenure rules out "debts of gratitude" issues that are associated with election of judges, although Justice Scalia suggested during argument in *Caperton* v. *Massey* that an elected judge has no more "debt of gratitude" to his backers than a Supreme Court Judge has to the President who nominated him. It is generally agreed that the judiciary is under constant public scrutiny, especially through the mass media. In this sense, the judiciary is accountable to the people. The question is whether excessive public scrutiny would inhibit judges from doing what is in the best interests of justice.

An interesting story is unfolding in Hong Kong concerning what is generally considered a very lenient sentence imposed on a defendant, the niece of a senior judge. In August 2010, Amina Bokhary was before the Magistrate's Court for the third time since 2002 for assaulting a police officer. She was apparently under the influence of liquor when she committed the offence. The Magistrate put her on probation for one year. There was a public uproar that the sentence was far too lenient and suspicious. There were calls for a review of the decision and, if that failed, an appeal. The Bar Association and the Law Society promptly issued a joint statement saying that, while they recognized the right of the public to voice their views regarding judicial decisions, "any attempt made to bring public pressure on a magistrate or judge to change his mind upon a review of sentence is to be deplored".[19]

---

[19] See, "Pressure on Judges, Magistrates Deplored" in *South China Morning Post* (12 August 2010).

The Department of Justice invited the Magistrate to review the sentence, but he saw no reason to change his mind. The Department of Justice promptly proposed to take the matter on appeal. The rather spontaneous public disquiet about the outcome of the case in the Magistrate's Court led to several newspaper articles dealing with the role of public opinion in relation to judicial administration. A letter to the South China Morning Post rejected the concerns raised by the Law Society and the Bar Association and argued that the public had a legitimate interest in monitoring judicial behaviour.[20] Granville Cross, a former Director of Public Prosecutions, wrote:

> There are sometimes strident demands for the courts to pass severe sentences on particular defendants. An important function of criminal law is to assuage the feelings of those affected by crime, and undue leniency can undermine respect for the system. The courts must therefore provide sound reasons for sentencing decisions, not least because this can help to guide public opinion. Former Chief Justice Ti-Liang Yan once said that although a judge should not insulate himself from public sentiment, "he must not be influenced, let alone be dictated, by them."[21]

Regina Ip, a former civil servant and presently a member of the Legislative Council, viewed the incident as a reflection of the widening inequality between rich and poor. Noting that the defendant received a lenient sentence mainly on the ground that she was suffering from bipolar disorder, Regina Ip pointed out that previously rich defendants had been leniently dealt with on medical evidence of life-threatening illnesses and had gone on to live healthy lives—suggesting that one could "buy" medical opinions.[22] Michael Chugany, well known columnist and broadcaster, wrote about the danger of perceptions of judicial bias toward the well-to-do. He sums up very well the dilemma that courts will be faced with in a situation like this:

> Does the prevailing of justice mean the jailing of Bokhary? If a higher court does jail her, would the people put it down to the fairness of the judicial process? Or would it come across as judicial independence surrendering to public outrage? And what if even the highest court upholds the magistrate's ruling? Would the people accept the outcome, admit they were wrong, put away their anger and say sorry to the magistrate for doubting his fairness? Or would it cast even more doubt on the fairness of the courts, further enraging the people?[23]

---

[20] See, O Oscar Lau, "Public opinion need not be seen as challenge to court's authority" (letter) in *South China Morning Post* (14 August 2010).
[21] See, Granville Cross, "Checks and Balances" in *South China Morning Post* (19 August 2010).
[22] See, Regina Ip, "One Law for the Rich?" in *South China Morning Post* (13 August 2010).
[23] See, Michael Chugany, "Court of Opinion" in *South China Morning Post* (16 August 2010).

The Amina Bokhary situation has to be seen in the context of the Hong Kong judiciary, which has maintained a very high level of popular respect as a competent, fair and independent institution. It may be that, as Regina Yip and Michael Chugany point out, the problem is not so much with deteriorating judicial standards as with evidence of an unequal society. The judiciary is expected to be whiter than white and, in circumstances where there is a genuine concern about the handling of a particular case, respect for the judiciary suffers and suffers irreparably. It is of some significance that in the opinion poll conducted by the Public Opinion Programme of Hong Kong University, the rating for "impartiality of courts", in a survey conducted since 1997, plunged to an all-time low of 6.16 soon after the incident from an all-time high of 7.40 in March 2010.[24]

IV. Courts as an Agency of Government

It is obligatory for a constitution to provide the framework of the judiciary and define the judiciary's relationship with the legislative and executive branches of the government. Because of the constitutional rules and practices that evolved around such rules, it may safely be said that codes of judicial conduct play a part, not so much as rules but as principles which have been extracted from those respected constitutional rules and practices. Having said that, it goes without saying that codes of conduct relating to the judiciary's relationship with the other two branches of the government provide universally accepted minimum standards. The difficulty for codes of conduct in this area is the diversity of constitutional systems and the different socio-political contexts in which they operate. If codes of conduct are to ignore these differences and to impose ideal standards, it will be quite difficult to secure their general acceptance. Some countries confer full judicial review powers on the judiciary, while others may deny or restrict such power of review. Some countries may expect judges only to be involved in what is strictly regarded as judicial work, while others may expect the judiciary to be involved in lawmaking or to render advisory opinions. Some countries may look down on extra judicial work such as manning commissions of inquiry, while others may consider it to be only natural that the government turns to judges for such work.

---

[24] See, "Bokhary Case Sees Confidence in Courts Drop" in *South China Morning Post* (16 August 2010). See the results of this poll at: <http://hkupop.hku.hk/english/popexpress/judiciary/socq56/poll/datatables.html>.

V. Do Codes of Conduct Matter?

Codes of judicial conduct matter because they record consensus on standards that judges are expected to observe as well as protections that have to be accorded to judges and, in general, they lay the foundations for a competent, fair and impartial judiciary. While there has been reluctance in some quarters to prescriptive codes of conduct, *Caperton v. Massey* stands as ample testimony to their importance. Professor Steven Lubet has argued that Judge Benjamin did not pay sufficient attention to the West Virginia Code of Judicial Conduct, which requires a judge to recuse himself if "impartiality might be reasonably questioned". Had he done so, the judge would not have unduly restricted himself to a determination as to whether or not he had an actual interest in the case—a determination which led him to deny the motion of recusal.[25]

Codes of conduct may not be justiciable as legislation, but they are at least of great persuasive authority. By providing evidence of generally accepted standards, they operate in the back of the minds of judges, just like the idea of the rule of law influences legislators.

It is appropriate to end this essay with a direct quotation from the Preamble of the West Virginia Code of Judicial Conduct, which is intended to govern the conduct of judges and to be binding upon them:

> Intrinsic to all sections of this Code are the precepts that judges, individually and collectively, must respect and honor the judicial office as a public trust and strive to enhance and maintain confidence in our legal system. The judge is an arbiter of facts and law for the resolution of disputes and a highly visible symbol of government under the rule of law.
>
> The Code of Judicial Conduct is intended to establish standards for ethical conduct of judges. It consists of broad statements called Canons, specific rules set forth in Sections under each Canon, an Application Canon, Commentary, and a Terminology Section. The text of the Canons, the Sections, and the Terminology is authoritative. The Commentary, by explanation and example, provides guidance with respect to the purpose and meaning of the Canons and Sections. The Commentary is not intended as a statement of additional rules. When the text uses "shall" or "shall not", it is intended to impose binding obligations the violation of which can result in disciplinary action. When "should" or "should not" is used, the text is intended as hortatory and as a statement of what is or is not appropriate conduct but not as a binding rule under which a judge may be disciplined. When "may" is used, it denotes permissible discretion or, depending on the context, it refers to action that is not covered by specific proscriptions.

---

[25] Steven Lubet, "It Takes a Court" (2010) 60:2 *Syracuse Law Review* 221–228. Professor Lubet notes that Judge Benjamin made just one footnote reference to the relevant canon, Canon (3)(E)(1), in all his rulings on recusal motions.

PART V

COUNTRY STUDIES OF JUDICIAL INDEPENDENCE

CHAPTER TWENTY FOUR

JUDICIAL INDEPENDENCE: THE BRITISH EXPERIENCE

*Neil Andrews**

I. Introduction

Recent fundamental legislation seeks to enshrine respect for judicial independence in the United Kingdom,[1] including the "tribunal judiciary".[2] This confirms the long-standing constitutional perception[3] that English judges form a separate arm of the state. It is important that they should neither kowtow to Parliament, nor to the Executive, nor to any princes or other high or powerful persons. Judges must stand above party politics, governmental exigency, corporate greed and private interest.

In the United Kingdom the tradition has been for judges to be selected from among tried-and-tested professional lawyers. In England, for the most part, they have been former advocates (although judges drawn from the solicitor side of the profession include, notably, Lord Collins, F.B.A., LL.D.). Judges tend to be financially secure, because their earnings in practice will have been high. Their long association with the practice of law also ensures that they understand the distinction between law and politics, and between justice and general

* Member of the teaching staff, Faculty of Law, University of Cambridge, since 1983; Fellow of Clare College, Cambridge; Bencher of Middle Temple, 2007; Member of the American Law Institute since 2000; Council Member of the International Association of Procedural Law.

[1] Constitutional Reform Act 2005, s. 3; for a detailed and elegant two-part survey of the 2005 Act's genesis and Parliamentary passage by (Lord) Windlesham, "The Constitutional Reform Act 2005: Ministers, Judges and Constitutional Change" [2005] P.L. 806–823; [2006] P.L. 35–57.

[2] Tribunals, Courts and Enforcement Act 2007, s. 1, amends the 2005 Act by adding that independence should also be guaranteed in favour of the "tribunal judiciary"; for an interesting Privy Council decision in this context, concerning the Equal Opportunities Tribunal in Trinidad and Tobago, see *Suratt* v. *Attorney-General of Trinidad and Tobago* [2007] UKPC 55, in which Lord Bingham dissented; noted I Steele [2008] P.L. 185.

[3] Indeed the jurisprudence of the Privy Council establishes an implied constitutional guarantee: *per* Baroness Hale in *Suratt* v. *Attorney-General of Trinidad and Togago* [2007] UKPC 55, at [38]: "It is implicit in all Constitutions on the Westminster model that the judicial power of the state be exercised by a judiciary whose "independence from all local pressure by Parliament or by the executive" is guaranteed in the manner contemplated by the Constitution in question: see Hinds v. The Queen [1977] A.C. 195, 221, P.C."

public policy.[4] After appointment, High Court judges tend to lead a largely sequestered professional life. On circuit (when attending trial centres away from their home district), they have been accommodated in judges' lodgings.

These traditional arrangements have enabled judges to enjoy the freedom to decide criminal and civil cases "without fear or favour" and, moreover, to be seen by the public to enjoy this security. Certainly, the measured and true administration of law requires strong guarantees of judicial independence. A cordon of security must be provided to the courts when exercising their judicial function (and similarly protection must be afforded to jurors).[5] Improper influence, internal or external, should not be threatened, exerted, or feared. The protected zone must cover all aspects of their judicial role: the results in individual cases; decisions to dissent; the reasons given by judges for their decisions; judges' directions to juries; judicial sentencing decisions, and indeed the entire conduct by judges or public tribunals[6] of the case within the legitimate scope of the relevant procedure.

II. The Demise of an Ancient Office: The 'Intolerable' Constitutional Position of the Lord Chancellor Before 2005

In *McGonnell* v. *UK* (2000) the European Court of Human Rights held that the United Kingdom had infringed the European Convention's guarantee of "judicial independence".[7] This was because the Bailiff of Guernsey had sat in a civil case concerning planning legislation enacted when he was presiding over the legislative chamber on the island. The Strasbourg Court held that such a confusion of legislative and judicial roles is "incompatible with the requisite appearance of independence and impartiality" demanded by Article 6(1).[8]

[4] *Clancy* v. *Caird (No 2)* 2000 S.C. 441; [2000] U.K.H.R.R. 509 (Court of Session, Inner House): at [43] "One of the advantages often claimed for education and professional training and experience in the law is the cultivation of independent habits of thought and judgment."

[5] On the protection of jurors, A.W. Bradley and K. Ewing, *Constitutional and Administrative Law* (14th edn., London 2007), p. 402; Contempt of Court Act 1981, s. 8; Criminal Justice Act 2003, ss. 44 to 46 (powers to conduct criminal cases without a jury in response to the problem of "jury tampering").

[6] Tribunals, Courts and Enforcement Act 2007, s. 1, amends the Constitutional Reform Act 2005 by adding that the independence of the "tribunal judiciary" should also be guaranteed.

[7] (2000) 30 E.H.R.R. 289, E.Ct.H.R.; on which, A Le Sueur, "Access to Justice Rights in the United Kingdom" [2000] 5 E.H.R.L.R. 457, 467, R Cornes, "*McGonnell* v. *UK*, the Lord Chancellor and the Law Lords" [2000] P.L. 166; D Woodhouse, "The Office of Lord Chancellor" (1998) P.L. 617 and "The Office of Lord Chancellor: Time to Abandon the Judicial Role." (2002) 22 LS 128, at pp. 141–3, and, generally, D Woodhouse, *The Office of the Lord Chancellor* (Hart, Oxford 2001).

[8] *McGonnell* case, *ibid.*, at [55]: "Any direct involvement in the passage of legislation or of executive rules is likely to be sufficient to cast doubt on the judicial impartiality of a person

It further held that when a person has presided over a legislative chamber he is precluded from adjudicating in any civil or criminal case requiring interpretation of the relevant enactment.[9]

This European decision raised "human rights" doubts concerning the (pre-2005) Lord Chancellor's capacity to adjudicate in judicial cases. Before the Constitutional Reform Act 2005, on which see below, he had been (i) head of the judiciary, (ii) a member of the Government's Cabinet and the senior minister in charge of a Department of State (the Lord Chancellor's Department, later the Department for Constitutional Affairs), and (iii) the senior member (and hence "Speaker") of the House of Lords' legislative chamber.[10]

In modern times, some Lord Chancellors had sat quite regularly in court.[11] This could produce difficulty if the Government had a direct interest in the relevant case.[12] For this reason, and in the wake of the *McGonnel* case (see above), it was stated during a Parliamentary debate that the Lord Chancellor would not sit in a civil case if the Government had an interest in the case's outcome, whether directly or otherwise.[13]

---

subsequently called to determine a dispute over whether reasons exist to permit a variation from the wording of the legislation or rules at issue…"

[9] *Ibid.*, at [57]; see also *Davidson* v. *Scottish Ministers* (2005) S.C. 7: the House of Lords held that a judge in the Scottish Court of Session was disqualified by virtue of the fact that, in the instant case, he had been required to interpret legislation on which he had advised the House of Lords (in its legislative capacity) when he had been Lord Advocate. Lord Bingham (at [17]) concluded that the fair-minded and informed observer: "would conclude that there was a real possibility that [the judge], sitting judicially, would subconsciously strive to avoid reaching a conclusion which would undermine the very clear assurances he had given to Parliament [as to the effect of the legislation in question]."

[10] For a list of the Law Lords' various roles, R. Cornes, "*McGonnel* v. *UK*, the Lord Chancellor and the Law Lords" (2000) P.L. 166, 174; for comment see also D. Woodhouse, "The office of Lord Chancellor: time to abandon the judicial role–the rest will follow" (2002) 22 LS 128, at pp. 141 ff.

[11] Lord Hailsham sat in House of Lords' appeals for 81 days during his two terms in this office; and Lord Mackay for 60 days. Data disclosed by Lord Irvine LC in HL Deb. 17 February 1999, vol. 597, col. 738; Lord Hailsham was Lord Chancellor from 1970 to 1974 and 1978 to 1988; his notable speeches include: *Hyam* v. *DPP* [1975] A.C. 55, 65, H.L. (although not then LC); *D* v. *N.S.P.C.C.* [1978] A.C. 171, H.L. (public interest immunity and a private investigative body; not then LC); *National Carriers Ltd* v. *Panalpina (Northern) Ltd* [1981] A.C. 675, 684, H.L. (test for frustration of a lease; in his second term as Lord Chancellor).

[12] See the debate on separation of powers, HL Deb. 17 February 1999, vol. 597, cols. 710–739; former Lords Chancellors denied that there was a problem: Lord Hailsham, "The Office of Lord Chancellor and the Separation of Powers" (1989) 8 CJQ 308; Lord Mackay, "The Lord Chancellor in the 1990s" (1991) 44 CLP 241; but for criticism, D Woodhouse "The Office of Lord Chancellor" (1998) P.L. 617; D Oliver "The Lord Chancellor, the Judicial Committee of the Privy Council and Devolution" (1999) P.L. 1; C Munro, *Studies in Constitutional Law* (2nd ed, 1999), 314–7, 328, 331.

[13] Lord Irvine, L.C. in HL Deb. 17 February 1999, vol. 597, col. 736 and HL Deb. 2 March 2000 vol. 610, col. 657 (Lord Goodhart opposed the Lord Chancellor sitting in any adjudication, *ibid.*, vol. 597, col. 729); see also B. Dickson and P Carmichael (eds.) *The House of Lords: Its Parliamentary and Judicial Roles* (London 1998).

But the Constitutional Reform Act 2005 went much further.[14] It stripped out the judicial role from the ancient office of the Lord Chancellor. He has ceased to be a judge. Instead he is merely a representative of the Executive, a Minister of the Crown, in fact a Cabinet member. Furthermore, since the 2005 Act, the Lord Chancellor need not be a lawyer. He can be an outsider, a simple politician. No longer can the judiciary assume, therefore, that "their spokesman" will be "on the top table".[15] And as Professors Bradley and Ewing have said, "the dignity, authority and power of the office of Lord Chancellor have thus been diminished".[16]

Under this new regime, the Lord Chancellor need not be a former practitioner of law, nor even legally qualified. Instead the Prime Minister will now recommend to the Queen that an individual be appointed Lord Chancellor if he "appears…to be qualified" for this office "by experience". Such experience can derive from time spent as a "Minister of the Crown", or as a "member of either House of Parliament", or "as a qualifying practitioner" [that is a practising lawyer in England and Wales, or in Scotland or Northern Ireland], or as a "teacher of law in a university", or finally "other experience that the Prime Minister considers relevant."[17] If the relevant candidate is not already a Member of Parliament, nor already a Peer of the Realm, it will be necessary to confer upon him or her a Peerage. This will render him capable of becoming a Minister of the Crown. He will then be accountable to Parliament, either as a Member of Parliament (within the House of Commons), or as a member of the House of Lords (legislative assembly).

Although the 2005 Act makes "provision for modifying the office of Lord Chancellor" and "the functions of that office" (preamble to the Act), section 1 seeks to remove any sense of constitutional queasiness: "This Act does not adversely affect—(a) the existing constitutional principle of the rule of law, or (b) the Lord Chancellor's existing constitutional role in relation to that principle." The intention is to declare that the torch of the Rule of Law will continue

[14] Anticipating the Constitutional Reform Act 2005, Lord Steyn (now retired as a Lord of Appeal in Ordinary), in his 2002 "All Souls College, Neill Lecture", had criticised the pre-Constitutional Reform Act 2005 position, and the multi-faceted role of the Lord Chancellor. Instead Lord Steyn had proposed: (a) that the Lord Chancellor should cease to sit in cases; (b) the judiciary should not have any "representative" who sits in Cabinet; (c) the head of the judiciary should be the Lord Chief Justice": Lord Steyn, "The Case for a Supreme Court" (2002) 118 L.Q.R. 382; see also Lord Bingham, "The Old Order Changeth" (2006) 122 L.Q.R. 211.

[15] Lord Woolf, *The Pursuit of Justice* (Oxford 2008), p. 165 encapsulating the constitutional sway enjoyed by the old Lord Chancellors, whose union of judicial/Parliamentary/Cabinet roles protected the judiciary from both the Executive and Parliament.

[16] A.W. Bradley and K. Ewing, *Constitutional and Administrative Law* (14th edn., London 2007), p. 407.

[17] Constitutional Reform Act 2005, s. 2.

to be passed from Lord Chancellor to Lord Chancellor: "guardians of an all but sacred flame which animates and enlightens the society in which we live."[18]

III. The Need to Rub Along: Relations Between the Judiciary and the Ministry of Justice

The Constitutional Reform Act 2005 confers upon the Lord Chief Justice immense and pivotal powers. Five strands of responsibility are discernible:[19] (1) he must now act as a conduit for the presentation of its collective "views";[20] including the laying "before Parliament" of "written representations on matter that appear to [the Lord Chief Justice] to be matters of importance relating to the judiciary…";[21] in this context it is important to note the rejuvenated role of "The Judges' Council";[22] (2) he must have custodianship of the judiciary;[23] (3) he must exercise efficient management;[24] (4) he must exercise various disciplinary powers, short of removal from office;[25] (5) furthermore, the Lord Chief Justice will also continue to sit in court in the most important cases, especially selected matters of appeal.

This five-fold multi-tasking is exhausting even to contemplate. The Lord Chief Justice of England must be, in short, a trade-union official, a charismatic General, Chief Executive Officer, Head of Training, and the foremost Judge. Surely even Solomon would turn down this invitation. Although the Ministry of Justice exists in part to support the Judiciary, this new arrangement creates the potential for friction between the Judiciary and the Executive. Therefore it is crucial that there should be harmonious interplay between the Lord Chief Justice and Minister of Justice (and their substantial bodies of civil servants or other colleagues). The matter is covered by "the Concordat", a Constitutional

---

18 Lord Bingham, "The Rule of Law" [2007] C.L.J. 67, 85.

19 Lord Phillips, (former) Lord Chief Justice of England and Wales, The Judicial Studies Board Annual Lecture "Constitutional Reform: One Year On", 22 March 2007 (http://www.judiciary.gov.uk/publications_media/speeches/2007/lcj_220307.htm)

20 Constitutional Reform Act 2005, s. 7(2)(a): "representing the views of the judiciary of England and Wales to Parliament, to the Lord Chancellor and to Ministers of the Crown generally."

21 2005 Act, s. 5(1).

22 Lord Woolf, *The Pursuit of Justice* (Oxford 2008), pp. 186 ff; p. 207; and see, on its formal basis, A.W. Bradley and K. Ewing, *Constitutional and Administrative Law* (14th edn., London 2007), p. 394.

23 Constitutional Reform Act 2005, s. 7(2)(b): "maintenance of appropriate arrangements for the welfare, training and guidance of the judiciary of England and Wales within the resources made available by the Lord Chancellor."

24 2005 Act, s. 7(2)(c): "the maintenance of appropriate arrangements for the deployment of the judiciary of England and Wales and the allocation of work within courts."

25 2005 Act, s. 108.

undertaking between Government and the Judiciary.[26] Already Lord Woolf (the former Lord Chief Justice) has drawn attention to problems raised by conferring on the Minister of Justice control of "resources" (a topic addressed by Lord Phillips in his 2008 address to an Australian audience).[27] In the early period, "the Concordat" has held fast. But one swallow does not make a summer. It is crucial that a cordial relationship should endure, for there is much at stake: the efficiency of court system; the vitality of judicial independence; and reciprocal respect by judges for the legitimate bounds of their role.

IV. Appointment of English Judges

The distinctive (although not unique) feature of the English judiciary is that appointments are made only after a lawyer has gained extensive experience of practice as a solicitor or barrister. In other words, England has no "career judiciary" in the same sense as many Continental systems. But Bell notes that "a typical [English] judge may spend twenty-five years of their professional career involved in judicial work, moving from one post to another, and often gaining promotion."[28] The point, therefore, is that English judges are nearly always appointed at a relatively later stage in their legal careers, having gained extensive experience in practice. Traditionally, High Court judges have been former barristers.[29] The Judicial Appointments Commission[30]

[26] Lord Woolf, *The Pursuit of Justice* (Oxford 2008), p. 169; and Lord Woolf [2004] C.L.J. 317, 324; C. Turpin and A. Tomkins, *British Government and the Constitution* (Cambridge 2007), 118; HL Deb. Vol. 658, col. 1004, 8 March 2004.

[27] http://www.telegraph.co.uk/news/newstopics/lawreports/rozenberg/2076999/Reforming-judge-rewrites-the-rule-book.html#continueF; for earlier remarks on this topic, see Lord Woolf, *The Pursuit of Justice* (Oxford 2008), p. 170; also noting his successor's complaint that "resources" will be a source of strife: Lord Phillips, Lord Chief Justice of England and Wales, The Judicial Studies Board Annual Lecture "Constitutional Reform: One Year On", 22 March 2007 (http://www.judiciary.gov.uk/publications_media/speeches/2007/lcj_220307.htm).

[28] J. Bell, *Judiciaries Within Europe: A Comparative Review* (Cambridge 2006), p. 298.

[29] The highest promotion, thus far, of a former solicitor is Lord Collins, F.B.A., LL.D., a celebrated legal author, and now a member of the Supreme Court; fittingly, the leading English work on private international law has recently been re-named, *Dicey, Morris and Collins on the Conflict of Law* (14th edn., London, 2006); (*per* Bingham L.J. *Re Harrods (Buenos Aires) Ltd.* [1992] Ch. 72, 103, C.A., a "very considerable authority", commenting on Lawrence Collins).

[30] For discussion of judicial appointments in England, and in many other jurisdictions, K. Malleson and P.H. Russell (eds.), *Appointing Judges in an Age of Judicial Power: Critical Perspectives from around the World* (University of Toronto Press 2006); on the position in England, *ibid*., ch. 2, by K. Malleson; see also: http://www.judicialappointments.gov.uk/ ("...It does so on merit, through fair and open competition, from the widest range of eligible candidates"); for details of their background, P Darbishire, "Where do English and Welsh Judges Come From?" [2007] C.L.J. 365; for comparative discussion, J. Bell, *Judiciaries Within Europe: A Comparative Review* (Cambridge 2006), especially pp. 17 ff.

("J.A.C.")[31] now appoints English judges from the ranks of practising solicitors or barristers.[32]

The J.A.C. is required to appoint judges "solely on merit". It must be "satisfied" that "he is of good character".[33] Although "merit" is the foremost criterion, the J.A.C. is required to have "regard to the need to encourage diversity[34] in the range of persons available for selection for appointments".[35] In modern times the convention has been that British judges are appointed without regard to their personal political beliefs, although extreme fascist or communist tendencies would be a bar to appointment (such beliefs or affiliation are certainly bars to appointment to the civil service).

V. The English Pool of Eligible Appointees

John Bell has suggested that the high remuneration and international opportunities enjoyed by cross-border lawyers, both barristers and solicitors, might reduce the attractiveness of appointment to the High Court Bench[36] (on this, see also Andrews).[37] Between 1991 and 2004, on 35 occasions QCs rejected offers of appointment to the Bench.[38] But the new appointments procedure requires an application. Some might fear rejection.[39]

It is crucial that leading practitioners should continue to be attracted to join the Bench. Only a handful of judges in each decade make truly seminal contributions to the law's development, as distinct from routine application or interpretation of settled law, or minor adjustment to doctrine. That said, it must be admitted that the best advocates do not necessarily make the best judges or (if one is to focus on the judicial contribution to law-making) the best judgment writers.

---

[31] Constitutional Reform Act 2005, s. 61, and Sch. 12.

[32] *Ibid.*, ss. 63–107, and Schedule 12; http://www.judiciary.gov.uk/about_judiciary/index.htm; *Judicial Appointments Annual Reports*; C. Turpin and A. Tomkins, *British Government and the Constitution* (Cambridge 2007), pp. 122–3; A.W. Bradley and K. Ewing, *Constitutional and Administrative Law* (14th edn., London 2007), pp. 385–8.

[33] 2005 Act, s. 63(2) and (3).

[34] J. Bell, *Judiciaries Within Europe: A Comparative Review* (Cambridge 2006), pp. 314 ff.

[35] 2005 Act, s. 64.

[36] J. Bell, *op. cit.*, pp. 35, 381.

[37] Neil Andrews, *The Modern Civil Process: Judicial and Alternative Forms of Dispute Resolution in England* (Mohr Siebeck, Tübingen, Germany, 2008), paras. 13-10 ff.

[38] "Departmental Evidence to the Senior Salaries Review Body" (June 2005): *www.dca.gov.uk/judicial/judgepay.pdf* at 16 and at 28.

[39] Sir Derek Oulton, Ph.D., Fellow, Magdalene College, Cambridge; comment to the author.

VI. Remuneration and Dismissal of English Judges[40]

English judges receive their salaries and pensions without Parliamentary special vote.[41] They also enjoy tenure until the specified retirement age (subject to qualifications mentioned in this paragraph). Judges should not be exposed to dismissal or demotion on the ground that their decisions are considered to have been inconsistent with party-political or other extra-legal grounds. Nor should promotion hinge, or be seen to hinge, on such extra-legal criteria.[42] And so, apart from retirement at the specified age, the collapse of their health, or death, judges cease to hold office only if their conduct is flagrantly unprofessional.[43] On the basis of an episode in the 1950s, it appears that a judge's performance can be legitimately criticised as falling short of acceptable standards of competence or contrary to the accepted canon of procedural practice and customs, and that he might even be persuaded to retire or resign.[44]

VII. The United Kingdom Supreme Court

The Supreme Court was established by the Constitutional Reform Act 2005. It is the highest appeal court within the United Kingdom. Its creation achieves

[40] At the Jerusalem conference (March 2008) Professor Keith Uff (University of Birmingham) commented on the arrangements for complaints to be heard concerning English judges or for their discipline.

[41] High Court and Court of Appeal judges are paid out of the Consolidated Fund, Senior Courts Act, s.12(5); the amounts are such "as may be determined by the Lord Chancellor with the concurrence of the Minister for the Civil Service", *ibid.*, s. 2(1); Masters (sitting in the High Court) are paid out of money provided by Parliament, s 89(8), 1981 Act (as determined by the Lord Chancellor with the concurrence of the Treasury), s 89(7A), 1981 Act (as amended by the Constitutional Reform Act 2005, Sch. 3, para. 3(5)); district judges are paid by the Ministry of Justice (as determined by the Lord Chancellor with the concurrence of the Treasury), County Courts Act 1984, s. 6(1) (as amended by the Constitutional Reform Act 2005, Sch. 3, para. 1(1)); Senior Courts Act 1981, s. 12(5), also states that judicial salaries cannot be reduced, see also Administration of Justice Act 1973, s. 9(3).

[42] J. Bell, *Judiciaries Within Europe: A Comparative Review* (Cambridge 2006), pp. 20–3.

[43] Senior Courts Act 1981, ss. 11(3), (3A) (as amended by the Constitutional Reform Act 2005) states: "(3) A person appointed to an office to which this section applies shall hold that office during good behaviour, subject to a power of removal by Her Majesty on an address presented to Her by both Houses of Parliament. (3A) It is for the Lord Chancellor to recommend to Her Majesty the exercise of the power of removal under subsection (3)"; see also Constitutional Reform Act 2005, s. 33, (tenure of Justices of the Supreme Court); 2005 Act, s. 115, (circuit judges and recorders); County Courts Act 1984, s. 11(4); C. Turpin and A. Tomkins, *British Government and the Constitution* (Cambridge 2007), pp. 118–121

[44] For an example of the Lord Chancellor persuading a judge to quit because he had consistently broken one of the ground-rules of adjudication, A.T. Denning, *The Due Process of Law* (London 1980), pp. 58–62 explaining the sequel to *Jones* v. *N.C.B.* [1957] 2 Q.B. 55, C.A.; on this episode, Neil Andrews, *Principles of Civil Procedure* (London 1994), para. 3–012.

a separation of the powers exercised by the judiciary and the upper house of Parliament in the UK. It sat for the first time in October 2009, replacing the Appellate Committee of the House of Lords. The Supreme Court has also assumed the devolution jurisdiction of the Judicial Committee of the Privy Council. The Supreme Court is the highest appellate court for all civil cases within the United Kingdom. It is also the final point of appeal for criminal cases in England, Wales and Northern Ireland. The High Court of Justiciary in Scotland continues to have jurisdiction over criminal cases North of the Border.

The Supreme Court has twelve Justices, including a President, currently Lord Phillips. The first Justices were the Law Lords who made up the Appellate Committee of the House of Lords as at July 2009. The new court's Justices are disqualified from sitting or voting in the Parliamentary debates of the House of Lords. Appointments of Supreme Court Justices are made by the Queen following a series of recommendations: (i) selection by the Judicial Appointments Commission; (ii) approval of this selection by the Lord Chancellor; (iii) adoption of this recommendation by the Prime Minister. The formal qualifications are that the appointee should have "(at any time) held high judicial office for a period of at least 2 years, or been a qualifying practitioner for a period of at least 15 years" (section 25(1), 2005 Act). It is possible, therefore, for a Justice to be selected from the ranks of the Bar or the solicitor profession. In 2009 Jonathan Sumption Q.C., a distinguished Commercial Law barrister, who has sat as a Deputy High Court judge (a part-time function), applied to become a new Justice, even though he has not held full-time judicial office in England. There is no doubt that Sumption has the capacity to adorn this new court, bringing an unusually incisive intellect to the highest chamber (as some influential senior judges had already noted informally). However, in the Autumn of 2009, it became clear that his candidature was opposed by several Court of Appeal judges, who took the view that a candidate should be seen to have made the usual ascent through the *cursus honorum* of the High Court and Court of Appeal. And so Mr Sumption announced his decision to withdraw his application. It is pleasing that his second application was successful in 2011. There is no reason why a Justice of the Supreme Court should have served as a full-time judge elsewhere, and the statutory criteria (cited above) make clear that prior judicial office is not a *sine qua non*. Indeed Baroness Hale, acknowledged in a 2004 journal article, that there is no reason why a Supreme Court Justice in that court should have spent time "in the trenches" as a trial judge,[45] and she advocated selection from a wider base than the Court of Appeal or the

[45] Brenda Hale, "A New Supreme Court for the United Kingdom" (2004) 24 L.S. 36, 41.

High Court, because such appointees might inject a more accessible style of legal reasoning into Supreme Court judgments.[46]

VIII. Concluding Remarks

Institutional arrangements can be installed, and high-sounding declarations made, to promote and safeguard judicial independence. Indeed there is no shortage of national and international instruments declaring the need for such arrangements. The traditional respect shown in Britain towards judicial independence is now enshrined in statute.

However, the day-to-day vitality of judicial independence requires each judge to display courage and integrity. Inappropriate external influence should be resisted. A judge should not be actuated by the fear that his preferred decision, or supporting reasons, might attract ill-informed criticism by the press,[47] or by outside commentators, or prove unpopular within Government[48] or Parliament.[49] Provided his proposed conduct is consistent with the law and sound judicial practice, the judge is entitled and bound to act according to his perception of what is just. He must not become a maverick; but he should not succumb blindly to internal pressures and so become a career functionary; steering a middle course between these extremes is a delicate task.

At times the judiciary, but especially judges sitting alone[50] at first instance, can feel besieged by hostile forces outside the court system. This can happen in ordinary cases, but it is especially likely when High Court judges hear litigation directly affecting the Government, for they stand at the immediate interface of the Executive and the judiciary. In the discharge of their demanding task, judges need institutional and psychological support. Some judges derive fellowship from the Inns of Court system, which also provide a

---

[46] *Ibid.*, at p. 44.

[47] For a summary of the contempt of court rule (Contempt of Court Act 1981, ss. 1 to 4) governing publications "tending to interfere with the course of justice" in "active" criminal or civil matters, A.W. Bradley and K. Ewing, *Constitutional and Administrative Law* (14th edn., London 2007), pp. 396 ff.

[48] As for Ministerial criticism of judges, see material cited concerning recent episodes in C. Turpin and A. Tomkins, *British Government and the Constitution* (Cambridge 2007), p. 123; and in A.W. Bradley and K. Ewing, *ibid.*, (14th edn., London 2007), 390–1.

[49] As for the "long-standing rule" concerning avoidance of Parliamentary criticism, of a judge or of judges in general (in the absence of a substantive motion), A.W. Bradley and K. Ewing, *ibid.*, (14th edn., London 2007), 391 and *Erskine May's Parliamentary Practice* (23rd edn., 2004), pp. 386–7, 438–9.

[50] Lord Woolf, *The Pursuit of Justice* (Oxford 2008), pp. 203–4, "The stresses to which the judiciary are subjected while performing their responsibilities under the glaring scrutiny of the media are often of a different order from those in the past. Judges can need support."

sense of tradition and enjoy connections throughout the Common Law world. The Inns, the Bar, and the Law Society (and their equivalents elsewhere in the United Kingdom) remain fundamental bulwarks against the power of Government, politicians, and the mighty. The support given to the judicial enterprise by these organisations is crucial to the maintenance of judicial independence.

CHAPTER TWENTY FIVE

A RECENT CHALLENGE TO JUDICIAL INDEPENDENCE IN SRI LANKA: THE ISSUE OF THE CONSTITUTIONAL COUNCIL

*Chandra R. de Silva**

I. Background[1]

Although there is no long history of a separate and independent judiciary in Sri Lanka, British colonial rule which ended in 1948, left the country with a strong judiciary immersed in the British tradition of judicial independence.[2] The presence of a high proportion of lawyers trained in British jurisprudence in the legislature in the 1950's and the 1960's helped in fostering respect for judicial independence. However, with the extension of state activity well beyond the maintenance of law and order and the subordination of the bureaucracy to political control there arose among some politicians a tendency towards a desire to curb the independence and power of the judiciary. The exercise of judicial review over legislation in Sri Lanka came under assault and this assault was justified on the basis of popular sovereignty. As a Cabinet Minister explained "We are trying to say that nobody should be higher than the elected representatives of the people; nor should any person not elected by the people have the right to throw out the decisions of the people elected by the people. Why are you saying that a judge once appointed should have the right to say that Parliament is wrong?"[3] In consonance with these ideas, the Constitution of the First Republic of Sri Lanka (1972) decreed that

* Chandra R. de Silva is Professor of History and Special Assistant to the Provost at Old Dominion University. He has written extensively on contemporary education, ethnicity and politics in Sri Lanka.

[1] This is a revised version of a paper presented at the International Conference on Judicial Independence and the Constitutional Position of the Judiciary, Jerusalem, 18th – 20th March, 2008.

[2] See Chandra R. de Silva, 'The Independence of the Judiciary under the Second Republic of Sri Lanka, 1978–1988,' *Ideas for Constitutional Reform,* ed. Chanaka Amaratunga (Colombo: Council for Liberal Democracy, 1989) pp. 481–494, esp. 483–485.

[3] M. J. A. Cooray, *Judicial Role under the Constitutions of Ceylon/Sri Lanka* (Colombo: Lake House, 1982). See also, Lal Wijenayake, *Independence of the Judiciary in Sri Lanka since Independence* (Pannipitiya: Stamford Lake, 2005).

it was the legislature (the National State Assembly) that exercised "...the judicial power of the People through the courts and other institutions created ... by law except in the case of matters relating to its powers and privilege wherein the judicial power of the people may be exercised directly by the National State Assembly according to the law".[4] The Cabinet of Ministers was empowered to appoint all judges and the Minister of Justice could transfer them.[5] Scholars criticized the attenuation of the independence of the judiciary[6] and in 1978 there was an attempt, however flawed, to protect the judiciary in the Constitution of the Second Republic. The highest courts in the country, the Supreme Court and the Court of Appeal, were entrenched in the Constitution.[7] In addition, the appointment, transfer, promotion and disciplinary control of judges in the lower courts were placed in the hands of a Judicial Services Commission (JSC) consisting of the Chief Justice and two other judges of the Supreme Court named to the JSC for five year terms. The independence of the JSC was protected by specifying that these nominated members could be removed only for cause assigned and that salaries paid to members of the Commission cannot be diminished during terms of office.[8]

The Constitution of the Second Republic (1978), however, did have a provision that was inimical to the independence of the judiciary. It stipulated that all Supreme Court and High Court judges holding office shall "cease to hold office".[9] The President subsequently did not reappoint seven Supreme Court

---

[4] *The Constitution of Sri Lanka,*(Colombo: Department of Government Printing, 1972) Section 3.

[5] Lakshman Marasinghe, *The Evolution of Constitutional Governance in Sri Lanka,* (Colombo: Vijitha Yapa, 2007) p. 147.

[6] See Radhika Coomaraswamy, *Sri Lanka: The Crisis of the Anglo-American Constitutional Traditions in a Developing Country,* (New Delhi: Vikas Publications, 1984) and H. L. de Silva, *Sri Lanka. A Nation in Conflict: Threats to Sovereignty, Territorial Integrity Democratic Governance and Peace,* (Boralesgamuwa: Visudunu Prakashakayo, 2008) pp. 405–424.

[7] *The Constitution of the Democratic Socialist Republic of Sri Lanka,* (Colombo: Department of Government Printing, 1978), Article 4. Article 107 (2) of the 1978 constitution also specified that if judges were to be removed through an address of the legislature, the full particulars of the alleged misbehavior or incapacity should be set out. This provision assisted Chief Justice Neville Samarakoon in 1984 when a political party took offense at remarks critical of the government at a school day prize-giving ceremony and unsuccessfully sought to remove him. See William Goodhart, P. N. Bhagwati, and Phineas M. Mojapelo, *Judicial Independence in Sri Lanka: Report of a Mission 14–23 September 1997,* (Geneva: Centre for the Independence of Judges and Lawyers, [1998]) p. 50, R. K. W. Goonesekere, 'Judiciary' *Aspects of 50 years of Law, Justice and Governance in Sri Lanka: A Compilation of Papers Presented at the Conference on Law, Justice and Governance in Sri Lanka,* (Colombo, Law and Society Trust, 2005) pp. 65–66 and de Silva, *op. cit.* p. 491.

[8] *The Constitution of the Democratic Socialist Republic of Sri Lanka,* (Colombo: Department of Government Printing, 1978) Article 112. This system was a return to that provided in the 1946 Ceylon Constitution Order in Council though in that system the third member of the JSC was to be retired Supreme Court judge.

[9] Ibid. Article 163.

judges and five High Court judges because he distrusted their political loyalties.[10] However, it was also realized that this non-reappointment of judges was something that could not be easily repeated,[11] and the position of the judiciary, as a whole, was seen as being better protected than before. The present system of judicial administration and organization is based on the current Constitution, enacted in 1978. The court system comprises the Supreme Court, Court of Appeal, Provincial High Courts, District Courts, Magistrate's Courts and Primary Courts.[12]

II. The Creation of the Constitutional Council

By the 1990's there was recognition that the politicization of all basic governing institutions was harmful. Some measures to inhibit this practice were proposed in drafts for a revised constitution in October 1997 and later in August 2000. The Organization of Professional Associations suggested amending the constitution and establishing a new council to combat politicization. However, the establishment of the Constitutional Council was due more to political calculation than ideology.[13] One of the parties in the governing coalition, the Sri Lanka Muslim Congress, withdrew its support from the government in June 2001. The government, facing the loss of its majority in the legislature, negotiated an agreement with the *Janatha Vimukthi Peramuna* (JVP) which party held 10 seats in the legislature. One of the conditions of the support of the JVP was amending the Constitution to establish a Constitutional Council that would recommend appointments to bodies such as the Judicial Services Commission. It was presumed that this would reduce political interference in those entities. By this time, the government and the opposition had agreed on the need to establish such a body. This is why the 17th Amendment to the Constitution establishing a Constitutional Council was approved with little dissent in October 2001.

In retrospect, it is clear that the intention was not to end the politicization of appointments but to ensure that influence in making such appointments should be shared among political groups rather than remain the exclusive

---

[10] Goodhart *et. al. Judicial Independence in Sri Lanka, op. cit.* p. 51, R. K. W. Goonesekere, *op. cit.* pp. 57–58 and de Silva, *op. cit.* pp. 489–490.

[11] It took the framing of a new constitution to achieve it.

[12] See Appendix 1.

[13] There was recognition that areas of contention between the Judiciary and the Executive were expanding with increased civil conflict. The Sri Lankan judiciary, faced with many writ applications in cases of 'involuntary disappearances,' began to take a more active role in such matters. It also laid down that there needed to be procedural fairness in decision making. For details see R. K. W. Goonesekere, *op. cit.* pp. 73–75.

privilege of the governing group.[14] This is seen in the composition of the Constitutional Council which was to include:

(a) The Prime Minister;
(b) The Speaker;
(c) The Leader of the Opposition in Parliament;
(d) One person appointed by the President for a three year term and eligible for reappointment;
(e) Five persons appointed by the President, on the nomination of both the Prime Minister and the Leader of the Opposition for a three year term (three of them to represent minority interests) who were not eligible for reappointment;
(f) One person nominated by the majority of the Members of Parliament belonging to political parties or independent groups other than the respective political parties or independent groups to which the Prime Minister and the Leader of the Opposition belongs and appointed by the President for a three year term and not eligible for reappointment.

The 17th Amendment listed a number of bodies to which the President of Sri Lanka could not appoint persons without a recommendation of the Constitutional Council. They were the Election Commission, the Public Service Commission, the National Police Commission, the Human Rights Commission of Sri Lanka, the Permanent Commission to Investigate Allegations of Bribery or Corruption, the Finance Commission and the Delimitation Commission.[15] The 17th Amendment also specified that the recommendation of the Constitutional Council was required for the appointment by the President of the following[16]: the Chief Justice and the Judges of the Supreme Court, the President and the Judges of the Court of Appeal, the Members of the Judicial Service Commission other than the Chairman,[17] the Attorney-General, the Auditor-General, the Inspector-General of Police, the Parliamentary Commissioner for Administration (Ombudsman) and the Secretary-General of Parliament. Since the enactment of the 17th Amendment other functions have been assigned to the Constitutional Council.[18]

[14] The 17th Amendment, however, specified that the nominees should be persons of eminence and integrity who have distinguished themselves in public life and who are not members of any political party. (Article 41(A) 4 of the Constitution).
[15] Article 41(B).
[16] Article 41(C).
[17] The Chairman of the Judicial Services Commission is the Chief Justice.
[18] E.g. Recommendations for appointment of three members to the Monetary Board of the Central Bank, five members to the Public Utilities Commission, members of the Welfare Benefits

III. The Executive and the Implementation of the 17th Amendment

The Constitutional Council (CC) was set up in March 2002. However, it soon became clear that the CC, however desirable it was in terms of democratic practices, was not embraced by the Executive. The CC was born of political exigencies, and those exigencies faded when the government majority in the legislature became more secure. The first dispute stemmed from the appointment of the newly created Elections Commission of five members.[19] The 17th Amendment gave Elections Commission the right to conduct elections and referenda and to take over the state radio and TV facilities if they showed bias. In a context where the party controlling the media had used press and television to gain political advantage, the appointment of a chair of the Elections Commission became a contentious issue. The then President, Chandrika Kumaratunga, objected to the person nominated by the CC as chair of the Elections Commission. The CC considered the objections and refused to change its recommendation. The President did not appoint the Elections Commission. A lawsuit filed in the Court of Appeals by a private party[20] led to the judgment that while the President had no discretion once the CC made its recommendations, Article 35(1) of the Constitution gave the President immunity from proceedings instituted or continued against her in any court in respect of anything done or omitted to be done in her official or private capacity, except in limited circumstances constitutionally specified.[21] The Elections Commission was not set up, and when the terms of the five CC members appointed for three year terms expired in March 2005, new members were not appointed. The terms of office of the commissions on Police and Public Service lapsed in late 2005. However, new appointments could not be made because the CC itself was not constituted. This was despite the fact that five nominees were agreed upon by the Prime Minister and the opposition leader and their names were communicated to the President for appointment in late 2005. The President did not make the recommended appointments and the CC has not

---

Board etc. For details see M. C. M. Iqbal, 17th Amendment to the Constitution: A Review of Some Institutions Under It, *Sri Lanka: State of Human Rights 2000,* (Colombo: Law and Society Trust, 2005) pp.104–105. For a discussion on the early operations of the Constitutional Council see, Ruana Rajepakse, *A Guide to Current Constitutional Issues in Sri Lanka,* (Rajagiriya, Citizen's Trust, 2008) pp. 50–58.

[19] Articles 103 and 104 of the Amended Constitution.

[20] See *Public Interest Law Foundation* vs. *the Attorney General and Others*, CA Application No 1396/2003, CA Minutes of 17.12.2003.

[21] See Kishali Pinto-Jayawardena, 'Co-opting the 'Watchdogs': Sombre Thoughts on the Angst of Sri Lanka's 'Civil Society' and the Media, *Article2.org*, Vol. 3 No. 2, February–March, 2006 (Asian Legal Resource Center) http://www.alrc.net/doc/mainfile.php/documents/426/

been reconvened since that time. The government decided in December 2005 that "the arrangements that prevailed prior to the establishment of these Commissions could be resorted to, purely as an interim measure". The responsibilities of the National Police Commission and Public Service Commission were thenceforth taken over by the Inspector General of Police and Secretaries of Ministries or Heads of Departments.[22] It can be argued that the responsibility for the failure to reconstitute the CC was initially due to the inaction of the smaller political parties who did not make a nomination, but it is also true that President Kumaratunga's successor, Mahinda Rajapakse (who took over in February 2006) also did not appoint the five nominees sent to him by his own Prime Minister and the Leader of the Opposition.[23] The two judges of the Supreme Court (who together with the Chief Justice constituted the Judicial Services Commission) resigned with effect from February 2, 2006 from the Judicial Services Commission on grounds of "matters of conscience".[24] President Rajapakse proceeded to make 'acting' appointments to commissions thus avoiding the process prescribed by the 17th Amendment. In the case of the Judicial Services Commission, since the Constitution permits acting appointments only for 14 days, the presumption is that these appointments are being renewed every 14 days. The President also proceeded to appoint two judges to the Court of Appeal, the President of the Court of Appeal and a Supreme Court judge without going to the CC.[25]

Protests came from international bodies such as the European Union, the Commonwealth Human Rights Initiative, Asian Human Right Commission and South Asians for Human Rights. Local opposition came from the major opposition party, the Civil Rights Movement of Sri Lanka, the Center for Policy Alternatives, Transparency International of Sri Lanka and People against Torture. President Rajapakse continued to refuse to constitute the CC partly on the grounds that he wanted a parliamentary select committee to report on the amendment. This committee reported on August 9, 2007 that the council should be able to work with a quorum of six members and suggested that the President's interim appointees to various posts should be dismissed so that the CC could make new appointments.[26] President Rajapakse ignored these

[22] See Statement by the Asian Human Right Commission dated February 14, 2005 (AS-024-2005).

[23] Appointments to the Human Rights Commission lapsed in March 2006 and that ended all appointments approved by the CC

[24] *Daily Mirror*, January 4, 2006. See also Statements by the Asian Human Rights Commission dated 21 February, 2006 (AS-028-2006) and 10 February, 2006 (AS-023-2006).

[25] *Daily Mirror*, June 3, 2006, (Report by Achala Panditha on p. A12).

[26] See Select Committee of Parliament on the 17th Amendment to the Constitution, *Law and Society Review*, 18 (238), 2008, pp. 1–3.

recommendations and continued to make appointments to the judiciary without a CC.

What is even more significant is that when appointments by the President in violation of the 17th Amendment were questioned in the courts, it was ruled that while there was a violation of the Article 41B of the Constitution, the President cannot be sued because Article 35(1) of the Constitution confers immunity against the President from prosecution for all acts of omission or commission while in office except when he assigns himself ministerial functions or in the case of election proceedings against him.[27] The Asian Human Rights Commission (AHRC) commenting on the implications of this decision has pointed out that it enables the President to violate, with impunity, some of the constitutional protections extended to other branches of government including the judiciary. For instance, if "a presidential decree grants a magistrate court, the power of writ jurisdiction, there is nothing that can be done to prevent it by way of an action before a court".[28] As the AHRC points out, "if the appointments to the supreme court, court of appeal and commissions such as public service commission, police commission, and the human rights commission cannot be challenged in a court of law, then, the dismissal of any persons of the supreme court, court of appeal and any of the commissions under the 17th amendment or any other provisions of the constitution" done by the President cannot be challenged either.

This sabotage of the CC had a chilling effect.[29] In fact, in early 2008, the Sri Lankan President transferred the Bribery Commission's Director General Piyasena Ranasinghe from his post, thus confirming the power of the executive to control administrators who resist its will.[30] A 2009 report by the International Crisis Group reported that Chief Justice Sarath N. Silva controlled appointments, promotions, transfers and removals in the lower judiciary, and used those powers to punish those who disagreed with him and to reward others.[31] No inquiry was held on why two Supreme Court judges resigned from the Judicial Services Commission (JSC) citing "matters of conscience". Instead, President Rajapakse, on the recommendation of the then Chief Justice,

---

[27] See Court of Appeal judgment on CA 66/2006.

[28] *The State of Human Rights in Eleven Asian Nations – 2006*, (Hong Kong: Asian Human Rights Commission, 2006) p. 262. The issue is discussed on pp. 257–263 & 301–302.

[29] *Ibid.* p. 263.

[30] David Sabapathy, Opposition Parties Cry 'Cover-up' in Sri Lanka, 22 February, 2008, at http://www.tamileelamnews.com/news/publish/tns_9454.shtml, Tisaranee Gunasekera, Government by Blind Man's Bluff, 24 February, 2008 at http://www.asiantribune.com/?q=node/9731, and Ranjith Jayasundera, President courts impeachment over Constitutional Council at http://www.thesundayleader.lk/20080224/Issues.htm

[31] See *Sri Lanka's Judiciary: Politicized Courts, Compromised Rights*, Asia Report No. 172, 30 June 2009, pp. 14–15 for documentation.

Sarath Silva, nominated two new members to the JSC without input from the CC.[32] As Peter Russell has pointed out, "the danger point in judicial independence may be more in the process of promotion and career advancement than initial appointment".[33] The number of fundamental rights applications filed has declined from 626 in 2004 to 517 in 2005. In 2006 it was less than 400. The number of successful cases is becoming fewer, and the damages granted have fallen substantially.[34] There have been two convictions and five acquittals under the Convention Against Torture Act since it was enacted in 1998. Many cases are delayed and pending.[35]

The erosion of the independence of the judiciary should be viewed in the background of the continuing inability of the judiciary in Sri Lankan courts to prevent abusive detention and torture. The Public Security Ordinance No.25 of 1947 and the Prevention of Terrorism Act (Temporary Provisions) of 1979 have enabled the state to enact 'emergency regulations' that override all laws except the constitution.[36] The Emergency (Miscellaneous Provisions and Powers) Regulations No. 1 of 2005 allow the Ministry of Defence to order the armed forces or police to detain a person up to a year to prevent acts "prejudicial to the national security or the maintenance of public order".[37] It also authorized the use of confessions to the police as evidence. The Prevention of Terrorism Act, originally brought as a temporary measure, was made permanent in 1982 and it is operative even when there is no 'emergency.' It enables detention of persons without trial for up to 18 months though the detained persons need to be produced before a magistrate within 72 hours of the original detention.[38] The Emergency (Prevention and Prohibition of Terrorism and Specified Terrorist Activities) Regulations widened the scope of what was

---

[32] Elaine Chan, Sri Lanka's Constitutional Council, *Law and Society Trust Review*, 18(243), 2008, p. 9.

[33] Peter H. Russell, Towards a General Theory of Judicial Independence, *Judicial Independence in the Age of Democracy: Critical Perspectives from around the World*, ed. Peter H. Russell, and David M. O'Brien (Charlottesville: University Press of Virginia, 2001) pp. 16–17.

[34] *Ibid*. pp. 288–289.

[35] Kishali Pinto-Jayawardena, Subverted justice and the breakdown of the rule of law in Sri Lanka, *Article2.org*, Vol. 6 No. 2 April, 2007 (Asian Legal Resource Center) http://www.article2.org/mainfile.php/0602/277/

[36] See Section 7 of the Public Security Ordinance No.25 of 1947. For the 2005 regulations see *Gazette Extraordinary* No. 1405/5 of 13August, 2005. The Thirteenth Amendment to the Constitution included a provision that a proclamation under this ordinance cannot be challenged in court. Except for a few months, Sri Lanka has been under emergency rule from 1983 to 2001 and from 2005 to 2009.

[37] *Sri Lanka Gazette* No. 563/7, 20 June, 1989. In 2008, this period was extended by a further six months.

[38] The Act also authorizes searches of home without a warrant and makes confession to a judge admissible as evidence.

defined as 'terrorism.'[39] Clearly, these measures were brought in at a time when there was civil war and violence[40] but they remain in force and form part of the background in which the Sri Lankan judicature operates; a background that makes it important to have constitutional restraints on the exercise of power.

In 2008, the pressure on the Sri Lankan President to reconstitute the Constitutional Council became more intense. In February, the minor parties came to a decision on the candidate they wished to nominate and conveyed their wishes to the Speaker.[41] Religious leaders called upon the President to set up the CC.[42] The government has delayed the appointment, first citing a technical difficulty since the nominee of the minor parties is currently on a consultancy under the Secretary General to Parliament who is to be appointed by the CC,[43] and subsequently that it was awaiting the recommendations of a Parliamentary Subcommittee before taking action.[44] The chief opposition whip condemned the government and stated that it was looking for excuses. The opposition explored legal action[45] but found no room for it because the Constitution did not permit the President to be sued while holding office.[46]

However, the pressure on the Sri Lankan President eased in mid-2008 with the armed conflict against the Tamil separatists taking center stage. By May 2009, with the crushing of the separatist forces, President Rajapakse's popularity soared and opposition news outlets faced harassment. Journalists were kidnapped or killed, and the implementation of the 17th Amendment was overshadowed by other controversies. Nevertheless, the government continued to promise to implement the 17th Amendment[47] until the President won

---

[39] See Gazette Extraordinary No. 147/5 of December 6, 2006. For a discussion see Asanga Welikala, *A State of Permanent Crisis: Constitutional Government, Fundamental Rights and States of Emergency in Sri Lanka* (Colombo: Center for Policy Alternatives, 2008) pp. 174–206.

[40] The 2005 regulations were promulgated after the assassination of Foreign Minister Lakshman Kadiragamar and the 2006 regulations after the attempted assassination of Defence Secretary Gotabhaya Rajapakse.

[41] http://www.bbc.co.uk/sinhala/news/story/2008/02/080219_cc_opposition.shtml, BBCSinhala.com, 19 February, 2008. The nominee was S. C. Mayadunne, the former Auditor General.

[42] http://www.bbc.co.uk/sinhala/news/story/2008/02/080222_cc_religious.shtml, BBCSinhala.com, 22 February, 2008. Professor Bellanwila Wimalarathana spoke on behalf of the Religious Conference.

[43] http://www.nation.lk/2008/02/24/mynation.htm

[44] http://www.news.lk/index.php?option=com_content&task=view&id=5072&Itemid=44 See also article by Rohan Edirisinhe, The Continuing Violation of the Seventeenth Amendment: Yet More Unconvincing Excuses, *Groundviews*, March 2008 @ http://www.groundviews.org

[45] http://www.bbc.co.uk/sinhala/news/story/2008/02/080229_cc_unp.shtml

[46] *Sri Lanka's Judiciary: Politicized Courts, Compromised Rights,* Asia Report No. 172, 30 June 2009, p. 10.

[47] 17th Amendment to be implemented after election – Minister Premajayantha, 11 February, 2010, at http://www.news.lk

an overwhelming re-election victory in January 2010, and his supporters won 144 of 225 seats in the legislature in April 2010. After that, the government changed its public stance and on June 12, 2010 the cabinet approved changing the 17th Amendment to allow the President to appoint members of the institutions specified in that amendment.[48] There was continued international criticism of this proposal. The European Union offered to extend the GSP Plus concession for goods exported from Sri Lanka to the EU beyond August 15, 2010 if (among other things) the 'independent and impartial appointments to key public positions is fully safeguarded, including through a Constitutional Council which adequately reflects the interests of all political, ethnic and religious groups and minorities within Sri Lankan society.'[49] On June 25, 2010, Foreign Minister G. L. Peiris announced that Sri Lanka would reject the offer and soon after the EU did not renew the concession on customs dues.[50] On 30 August 2010, the Sri Lankan Cabinet proposed the 18th Amendment to the Constitution. The Amendment was approved by the Supreme Court as a bill requiring a two-third majority in Parliament and received that majority on September 8, 2010. Among other provisions, this law repeals the 17th Amendment and vests the appointment of officials vested in the CC with the President, who is merely obliged to seek the 'observations' of a Parliamentary Council.[51] This gave the Sri Lankan President a virtual free hand in appointing all judges of the Supreme Court (including the Chief Justice), judges of the Court of Appeal and members of the Judicial Services Commission.[52]

IV. Conclusion

It would be incorrect to view every instance of change initiated by the executive or the legislature as a threat to judicial independence. Judicial structures need to be flexible to accommodate change.[53] On the other hand, the independence of the judiciary often depends on actions performed by the executive. It is therefore important to specifically require the executive to

[48] Ranga Jayasuriya, Constitutional amendment disaster at http://www.lakbimanews.lk/special/spe10.htm

[49] See, AHRC-STM-122-2010 June 24, 2010 A Statement by the Asian Human Rights Commission: Sri Lanka: Duty to Protect Rule of Law and Economic Wellbeing

[50] http://www.thehindu.com/news/international/article484110.ece

[51] See http://material.ahrchk.net/srilanka/SL18thAmendment.pdf for the text of the amendment. The Parliamentary Council (PC) is to be made up by the Speaker, the Prime Minister, the Leader of the Opposition, a nominee of the Prime Minister and a nominee of the Leader of the Opposition.

[52] See Schedule II of Article 41A of the proposed amendment. The 18th Amendment also removed the restriction on the President to serve for a maximum of two terms.

[53] AHRC-STM-122-2010, *op. cit.* p.13

refrain from any act of omission or commission that directly or indirectly interferes with or frustrates the personal, substantive or collective independence of the judiciary. The refusal of the Sri Lankan executive to implement the 17th amendment to the Constitution from 2002 onwards had the effect of undermining judicial independence in that country. The 18th Amendment legally empowers the President of Sri Lanka to continue to do so.

V. Appendix: Courts of Law in Sri Lanka

a. THE SUPREME COURT OF SRI LANKA

The Court consists of the Chief Justice and not less than six and not more than ten other judges. The Supreme Court is the highest and final superior court of record and is empowered to exercise jurisdiction on constitutional matters, for the protection of fundamental rights, consultative jurisdiction, final appellate jurisdiction, on petitions relating to election of President, petitions relating to the validity of a referendum; appeals from orders/judgments of the Court of Appeal in other election petitions, and jurisdiction in respect of any breach of the privileges of Parliament. Appeals from judgments, sentences and orders pronounced at a High Court Trial at Bar are sent to the Supreme Court.

b. THE COURT OF APPEAL OF SRI LANKA

The Court of Appeal consists of the President of the Court and not less than six and not more than eleven other judges. The regulations for appointment and removal of judges are identical to those that apply to judges of the Supreme Court. The Court is vested with jurisdiction on appeals from the High Court in the exercise of its appellate or original jurisdiction and from any court of first instance and any tribunal or other institution, sole and exclusive cognizance by way of appeal, revision and restitution and power and authority to inspect and examine records of any court of first instance. It also has jurisdiction to grant and issue writs other than on matters relating to the exercise of the powers of the Elections Commission, to grant and issue writs of *habeas corpus*, jurisdiction to grant Injunctions, and jurisdiction to try election petitions in respect of the election of members of Parliament. Appeals from judgments pronounced at a High Court Trial at Bar proceed direct to the Supreme Court.

c. HIGH COURT OF SRI LANKA

The High Court consists of not less than ten and not more than forty judges. The Constitution provides for the establishment of the Provincial High Courts to which judges are appointed by the Chief Justice from among judges of the High Court of Sri Lanka. Judges of the High Court are appointed by the President on the recommendation of the Judicial Service Commission after consultation with the Attorney General. Judges of the High Court are removable by the President and are subject to disciplinary control by the President on the recommendation of the Judicial Service Commission.

The High Court has original jurisdiction over all prosecutions on indictment (exercised by Provincial High Courts in respect of offences committed within the province); admiralty jurisdiction, commercial jurisdiction, jurisdiction to hear and determine an offences relating to influencing or attempting to influence decisions of the Judicial Service Commission, applications for the return of or access to a child. Appellate jurisdiction of Provincial High Courts include convictions, sentences, orders entered or imposed by Magistrate's Courts and Primary Courts within the province; writ jurisdiction in respect of powers exercised under any law or under any statutes made by the Provincial Council of that province and in respect of any matter on the Provincial Council list and appeals from Labour Tribunals, Agrarian Tribunals and Small Claims Courts.

d. DISTRICT COURTS

District Courts are established for each judicial district in Sri Lanka. There are 54 judicial districts in Sri Lanka. Every District Court is a court of record and is vested with unlimited original jurisdiction in all civil, revenue, trust, insolvency and testamentary matters other than such matters as are assigned to any other court by Law. All Judges of the District Courts are appointed by the Judicial Service Commission which is also vested with the power of dismissal and disciplinary control. Appeals from judgments, decrees and orders of the District Court are to the Court of Appeal.

e. MAGISTRATE'S COURTS

Magistrate's Courts are established for each judicial division in Sri Lanka. There are 74 judicial divisions in Sri Lanka. Every Magistrate's Court is vested with original criminal jurisdiction (other than in respect of offences upon indictment in the High Court), and is ordinarily empowered to impose sentences up to a fine of Rs. 1,500 and/or 2 years rigorous/simple imprisonment unless power is vested in the Magistrate's Court to impose higher penalties by special provision. All Magistrates are appointed by the Judicial Service Commission which is also vested with the power of dismissal and disciplinary control of the Judges. Appeals from convictions, sentences or orders of Magistrate's Courts within a province are to the High Court of the province.

f. PRIMARY COURTS

There are seven Primary Courts and where they do not sit, the Magistrate's Courts exercise the jurisdiction of the Primary Courts. A Primary Court is vested with original civil jurisdiction where the debt, damage, demand or claim does not exceed Rs. 1,500, the enforcement of by-laws of local authorities and matters relating to recovery of revenue of such authorities, exclusive criminal jurisdiction in respect of offences prescribed by the Minister by Regulation and offences in violation of provisions of any Act or subsidiary legislation in respect of which jurisdiction is vested. All judges of the Primary Court are appointed by the Judicial Service Commission which is also vested with the power of dismissal and disciplinary control of the judges.

CHAPTER TWENTY SIX

CHALLENGES OF JUDICIAL INDEPENDENCE — AN AUSTRALIAN PERSPECTIVE

*H.P. Lee**

Under the federal system in Australia the federal parliament and the legislatures of the States are empowered to establish courts. In the case of the Territories, their courts arise from federal enactments. While the distinctions between federal and State courts and between federal and State jurisdiction remain, the Australian judicial systems 'are nevertheless integrated, to an extent'.[1] In the words of Gleeson CJ in *Forge v. Australian Securities and Investments Commission*: 'Australia has an integrated, but not a unitary, court system.'[2] This integration has been brought about as a result of the establishment of the High Court of Australia as the ultimate court of appeal for Australia and by the use of State courts as repositories of federal jurisdiction.[3]

Every day, hundreds of judicial officers across the land quietly go about their judicial role of resolving conflicts between citizen and citizen, citizen and state, State and State, and State and Commonwealth. In Australia, judicial independence is a fundamental value which is viewed by the general populace as a vital aspect of a democratic polity. It is not a convincing assertion in contemporary Australia that the independence of the judicial institution, whether at Commonwealth or State level, is under serious or overt threat. Indeed it is an acceptable proposition to say that the Australian judiciary is held in very high esteem. The judgments and orders of the courts are accepted and enforced as a matter of course.

I. The Underpinnings of Judicial Independence

Judicial independence is secured by constitutional provisions which guarantee judges security of tenure. Section 72 of the Australian Constitution provides

* Professor Hoong Phun ("H.P.") Lee holds the Sir John Latham Chair of Law at Monash University. Professor Lee's publications include Constitutional Conflicts in Contemporary Malaysia (Oxford University Press, 1995) and The Australian Judiciary (Cambridge University Press, 2001) (co-author).

[1] E. Campbell and H.P. Lee, *The Australian Judiciary* (Cambridge and New York 2001), 14.

[2] (2006) 228 CLR 45, at [36].

[3] Above n 1, 14.

for federal judges to hold office until the age of 70 years and also ensures that their remuneration shall not be diminished during their continuance in office. These twin pillars buttressing judicial independence are similarly found in statutory or the constitutional frameworks of the States and the Territories.

Judicial independence is further underpinned by judicial affirmation of a separation of powers in the federal constitutional framework. The framers in designing the constitutional framework provided for the vesting of the different categories of powers through three different chapters of the Constitution. Such a compartmentalisation of executive, legislative and judicial powers in three different organs of government led to the judicial declaration that the principle of separation of powers is embodied in the Constitution.[4]

The current doctrine of separation of judicial power declares that the federal judicial power cannot be invested in a court that does not satisfy the requirements of Chapter III of the Australian Constitution; and that a non-judicial power, other than a power which is ancillary or incidental to the judicial power, cannot be invested in a Chapter III court. In *Lane v. Morrison*,[5] provisions of a federal statute which provided for the establishment of the Australian Military Court (AMC) were declared by the High Court, in a unanimous decision, to be invalid. The AMC was not comprised of judges who were appointed by the Governor-General in Council and with the tenure prescribed by s 72 of the Commonwealth Constitution. The finding of invalidity was based on the Court's view that the AMC was established to exercise the judicial power of the Commonwealth.

The actual operation of the separation of judicial power doctrine has given rise to much controversy and difficulties, particularly in the demarcation between a judicial and a non-judicial function.[6] The complexities in determining whether a power is judicial or non-judicial are compounded by various judicially recognised exceptions and the operation of a 'chameleon' doctrine ('A function may take its character from that of the tribunal in which it is reposed.'[7])

II. Legislative Intrusions into the Judicial Sphere

It is an established doctrine that the Australian States are not subject to a separation of powers doctrine.[8] Chapter III contemplates the exercise of federal

[4] See *New South Wales v. Commonwealth* (1915) 20 CLR 54.
[5] [2009] HCA 29.
[6] For a much quoted or 'classic' definition of 'judicial power' see *Huddart, Parker & Co Pty v. Moorehead* (1909) 8 CLR 330, 357 per Griffith CJ.
[7] *R v. Hegarty; Ex parte City of Salisbury* (1981) 147 CLR 617, 628.
[8] See: *Clyne v. East* (1967) 68 SR (NSW) 385; *Building Construction Employees' and Builders Labourers' Federation of NSW v. Minister for Industrial Relations* (1986) 7 NSWLR 372.

jurisdiction by State courts. Section 71 in Chapter III states that the judicial power of the Commonwealth 'shall be vested in a Federal Supreme Court, to be called the High Court of Australia, and in such other federal courts as the Parliament creates, and in such other courts as it invests with federal jurisdiction'. The State courts are invested by federal legislation with federal jurisdiction. In *Kable v. Director of Public Prosecutions*,[9] the High Court of Australia held that a State legislature is precluded from conferring a function on a State court, 'which substantially impairs its institutional integrity, and which is therefore incompatible with its role as a repository of federal jurisdiction'.[10] This '*Kable* principle' led to the invalidation of the impugned *ad hominem* legislation authorising a State Supreme Court judge to issue a preventative detention order in the case. The High Court was concerned to ensure that the Supreme Court was not perceived to be 'an instrument of executive government policy' and that 'public confidence in the impartial administration of the judicial functions of the Supreme Court' would not be impaired.[11] The majority of the High Court in *Kable* 'considered that the appearance of institutional impartiality of the Supreme Court [of New South Wales] was seriously damaged by a statute which drew it into what was, in substance, a political exercise.'[12] In order for a State court to be capable of exercising federal jurisdiction, it must be and appear to be an 'independent and impartial' tribunal.[13]

In *Gypsy Jokers Motorcycle Club Incorporated v. Commissioner of Police,*[14] the statutory framework enabled the Commissioner of Police in the State of Western Australia to order the removal or modification of a 'fortification' within a fixed period of time. A person to whom such a notice has been issued can apply to the Supreme Court of Western Australia for a review of whether the Commissioner of Police could have reasonably had the relevant belief when issuing the notice. The High Court upheld the validity of s 76(2) of the Corruption and Crime Commission Act 2003 (WA) which provides that the Commissioner of Police may identify any information provided to the court for the purposes of the review as confidential if its disclosure might prejudice the operations of the Commissioner of Police. Furthermore, the section provides that the information so identified is for the court's use only and is not to be disclosed to any other person, whether or not a party to the proceedings, or publicly disclosed in any way.

---

[9] (1996) 189 CLR 51. See Wheeler, 'The *Kable* Doctrine and State Legislative Power Over State Courts' (2005) 20(2) *Australasian Parliamentary Review* 15.

[10] *Fardon v. Attorney-General for the State of Queensland* (2004) 223 CLR 575, at [15] (per Gleeson J).

[11] (1996) 189 CLR 51, at 124.

[12] (2004) 223 CLR 575, at [16].

[13] *Aboriginal Legal Aid Service Inc v. Bradley* (2004) 218 CLR 146, 163, at [29].

[14] (2008) 234 CLR 532.

On appeal to the High Court, Kirby J, the only dissenting judge, construed the impugned provision as involving 'an impermissible legislative direction to the Supreme Court' and imposing in effect 'the decision of an officer of the Executive Government upon the Supreme Court'.[15] However, the majority of the High Court, Gleeson CJ, Gummow, Hayne, Heydon, Kiefel and Crennan JJ, reached a different conclusion regarding the construction of s 76(2). In Gleeson CJ's words, the provision did not empower the Commissioner of Police to 'dictate' to the Supreme Court of Western Australia to accept the Commissioner's decision as to the confidentiality of information.[16]

A similar point as that raised in *Gypsy Jokers* arose in the 2007 case of *K-Generation Pty Ltd v. Liquor Licensing Court*[17] where the invocation of the *Kable* principle was also rejected by the High Court. However, in *International Finance Trust Company Limited v. New South Wales Crime Commission*,[18] the impugned provision of the Criminal Assets Recovery Act 1990 (NSW) was invalidated by the High Court applying the *Kable* principle. According to French CJ, the impugned provision amounted to directing the court 'as to the manner in which it exercises its jurisdiction'.[19]

The *Kable* principle was recently invoked successfully before the High Court in *The State of South Australia v. Totani*.[20] To combat the criminal activities of motorcycle gangs in South Australia, the Serious and Organised Crime (Control) Act 2008 (SA) empowers the state attorney-general, upon the application of the state police commissioner, to make a declaration in respect of an organisation on the basis that its members associate for the purpose of engaging in 'serious criminal activity' and that the organisation represents a risk to public safety and order in the state. The High Court determined that the provision in the legislation (s 14(1)) which states that the Magistrates Court of South Australia, pursuant to an application by the state police commissioner, 'must' make a control order against a person 'if the Court is satisfied' that that person is a member of a declared organisation, to be invalid. The legislation was so confining in terms of the exercise of the discretionary judgment of the Magistrates Court that the Court could be seen to be 'acting at the behest of the executive'. The majority judges found that s 14(1) enlisted the Magistrates

15 *Ibid*, at [52].
16 *Ibid*, at [7].
17 (2009) 237 CLR 501.
18 (2009) 240 CLR 319.
19 *Ibid*, at [55]. See *Re Criminal Proceeds Confiscation Act 2002* [2004] 1 Qd R 40 where the Queensland Court of Appeal applied the *Kable* principle to invalidate the impugned s 30 of the Criminal Proceeds Confiscation Act 2002 (Qld).
20 [2010] HCA 39.

Court to implement legislative and executive policy, forcing it to act in a manner incompatible with, or repugnant to, the Court's 'institutional integrity'. In consequence, the High Court found that the independence of the Magistrates Court was impinged.

On the other hand, the challenge to the validity of a piece of federal legislation based on Chapter III of the Constitution was rejected by a majority of the High Court in *Thomas v. Mowbray*.[21] The impugned law under scrutiny by the Court empowered the making by a Federal Magistrate of an interim control order imposing various specified obligations, prohibitions and restrictions upon the plaintiff (Mr Thomas). Gleeson CJ observed that the exercise of such a power 'independently, impartially and judicially, especially when such powers affect the liberty of the individual, would ordinarily be regarded as a good thing, not something to be avoided.'[22] French CJ in *Totani* differentiated *Thomas v. Mowbray* by pointing out that the issues canvassed in the latter case were different: 'whether the power conferred on a court …was judicial power, whether the Code authorised its exercise in a manner contrary to Ch III and whether there was a head of legislative power to support it'.[23] More importantly, the statutory regime in *Thomas v. Mowbray* 'does not purport to impose any obligation upon a court to make a control order upon the basis of an executive determination of the court'.[24] French CJ explained: 'The court cannot make such an order unless it is satisfied, on the balance of probabilities, that to do so would substantially assist in preventing a terrorist act or that the person in question has provided training to, or received training from, a listed terrorist organisation.'[25]

In a 2010 landmark decision in *Kirk v. Industrial Court (NSW)*,[26] the High Court ruled that State legislation 'which would take from a State Supreme Court power to grant relief on account of jurisdictional error is beyond State legislative power'.[27]

---

[21] (2007) 233 CLR 307.

[22] *Ibid*, at [17]. Gleeson CJ's observations reflected the sentiments of the majority in *Grollo v. Palmer* (1995) 184 CLR 348, 367 regarding federal legislation authorising federal judges to issue telephone interception warrants: 'It is precisely because of the intrusive and clandestine nature of interception warrants and the necessity to use them in today's continuing battle against serious crime that some impartial authority accustomed to the dispassionate assessment of evidence and sensitive to the common law's protection of privacy and property…, be authorised to control the official interception of communications.'

[23] [2010] HCA 39, at [39].

[24] *Ibid*.

[25] *Ibid*.

[26] (2010) 239 CLR 531.

[27] *Ibid*, at [100] (per French CJ, Gummow, Hayne, Crennan, Kiefel and Bell JJ).

III. Protecting the 'Reputational Capital' of the Courts

By deploying the separation of judicial power, the High Court in *Wilson v. Minister for Aboriginal & Torres Strait Islander Affairs*[28] invalidated the appointment by a minister of a Federal Court judge (Mathews J) as a reporter entrusted with the function of reporting on Aboriginal heritage issues. These issues arose from a controversial proposal to build a bridge at Hindmarsh Island, South Australia. It was accepted that she was simply appointed as an individual to perform the reporting function. The invocation of the *persona designata* doctrine was no longer sufficient to render her appointment valid. The High Court, applying an additional 'incompatibility' test, held that the performance of such a function by a judge 'places the judge firmly in the echelons of administration, liable to removal by the Minister before the report is made and shorn of the usual judicial protections, in a position equivalent to that of a ministerial adviser.'[29]

The High Court of Australia elucidated 'the incompatibility condition' in the following manner: 'no function can be conferred that is incompatible either with the judge's performance of his or her judicial functions or with the proper discharge by the judiciary of its responsibilities as an institution exercising judicial power.'[30] In *Wilson v. Minister for Aboriginal & Torres Strait Islander Affairs* the Court held that, in determining constitutional incompatibility, the statute or the measures taken pursuant to the statute must be examined in order to determine, first, whether the function is an integral part of, or is closely connected with, the functions of the legislature or the executive government. There is no constitutional incompatibility if the function is not closely connected with the legislature or the executive government. The next step requires an answer to be given to the question whether the function is required to be performed independently of any instruction, advice or wish of the legislature or the executive government, other than a law or an instrument made under a law. In the absence of an affirmative answer there is a breach of the separation. If the answer is in the affirmative, it needs further to be asked whether any discretion purportedly possessed by the Ch III judge is required to be exercised on political grounds, that is, 'on grounds that are not confined by factors expressly or impliedly prescribed by law'.[31]

---

28 (1996) 189 CLR 1.
29 (1996) 189 CLR 1, at [25].
30 *Grollo v. Palmer* (1995) 184 CLR 348.
31 *Ibid*, at 16 (per Brennan CJ, Dawson, Toohey, McHugh and Gummow JJ).

IV. The Executive and Judicial Selection

A topic of increasing interest in Australia relates to the process of selecting judges. The current process in relation to judicial appointments has been criticised as being 'unstructured' and that 'the criteria for making appointments are not defined'.[32] Judicial appointments at both federal and State levels are decisions by the executive arm of government. The only statutory requirement for consultation relates to the appointment of High Court judges (s 6 of the High Court of Australia Act 1979 (Cth)). When a vacancy arises in the High Court, the federal Attorney-General shall, before an appointment is made, consult with the Attorneys-General of the States. Judges of the High Court and other federal courts are appointed by the federal government while judges of the State courts are appointed by the relevant State government.

There have been calls from time to time for reforming the process of selecting judges. The judicial appointment process has been described as 'opaque' and one which involves 'unfettered executive discretion'.[33] To date there is still no desire on the part of most State governments or the federal government to create a standing judicial appointments commission.[34] However, in May 2008, the federal government announced the creation of an advisory panel to 'help screen prospective members of the Federal Court and draw up a short list' for the federal Attorney-General.[35] Another advisory panel was established in relation to the Federal Magistrates Court.[36] These advisory panels are not regulated by statute and a different government in power may choose to jettison such panels. Moreover, there is no way of knowing whether the federal Attorney-General, in bringing the recommendations to the cabinet, has ignored the list drawn up by the advisory panels. While the new panels have

---

[32] Sir G. Brennan, 'The Selection of Judges for Commonwealth Courts', *Papers on Parliament Number 48* (January 2008), 1.

[33] R. Sackville, 'The Judicial Appointment Process in Australia', (2007) 16 *Journal of Judicial Administration* 125, 137.

[34] See J. M. Williams, 'Judicial Independence in Australia' in Peter H Russell and David M O'Brien (eds), *Judicial Independence in the Age of Democracy* (Charlottesville and London 2001), 173 at 186.

[35] The advisory panel for appointment to the Federal Court comprised of the following: Sir Gerard Brennan (a former Chief Justice of the High Court), the Hon. Jane Matthew (a former Judge of the Federal Court), Mr Ian Govey (the deputy secretary of the Commonwealth Attorney-General's Department) and the Hon. Michael Black (current Chief Justice of the Federal Court). M. Pelly, 'Ex-chief justice to judge judges' *The Australian*, 26 May 2008, 5.

[36] The advisory panel for the Federal Magistrates Court comprised of the following: Chief Federal Magistrate John Pascoe, the Hon. Sue Morgan (former Family Court Judge) and a senior departmental officer — Pelly, *Ibid.*

been described as 'a step in the right direction' disquiet has also been expressed over the deficiencies of the new process:

> [T]here is nothing to prevent the Government appointing new judges who have been rejected by its own experts. Worse, the new system has not been accompanied with a mechanism that ensures the public will know if the experts have been bypassed or ignored.[37]

V. Appointment of Acting Judges

There have been some concerns about the increasing number of acting judges which have been appointed in some State courts.[38] A challenge was mounted in the High Court for the first time raising the issue of the validity of a law empowering the appointment of acting judges in *Forge v. Australian Securities and Investments Commission*.[39] The challenge drew on the principle established in *Kable v. Director of Public Prosecution*[40] that a State Parliament cannot legislate to confer on a State court a function which 'substantially impairs its institutional integrity'[41] and which renders it incompatible with its role as a repository of federal jurisdiction. It was generally argued that as State Supreme Courts and other State courts are contemplated as repositories of federal jurisdiction, they must be capable of answering the description of 'courts'. The appointment of acting judges *per se* does not 'deprive the body of the character of a court, or of the capacity to satisfy the minimum requirements of judicial independence'.[42] Gleeson CJ, Gummow, Hayne, Crennan, Callinan and Heydon JJ dismissed the challenge to the validity of the appointment of the acting judge in *Forge*.

Gummow, Hayne and Crennan JJ, in a joint judgment, sounded a caution about a series of acting appointments so extensive that it would 'distort' the character of a court. They said that the institutional integrity of State Supreme Courts is not inevitably compromised by the appointment of an acting judge. However, the institutional integrity of the body 'may be distorted by such appointments if the informed observer may reasonably conclude that the institution no longer is, and no longer appears to be, independent and

[37] 'Reform falls short' (editorial), *The Weekend Australian*, 31 May – 1 June 2008, 16.

[38] The recent appointment of a magistrate to the position of an acting judge of the County Court of Victoria (Judge Barbara Cotterell) led to highly publicised disquiet over the notion of 'temporary judges'. See S. Butcher, 'Part-time judge not so welcome', *The Age*, 16 May 2008, 1; 'Judges shall be seen to act without fear or favour' (editorial), *The Age*, 19 May 2008, 10.

[39] (2006) 228 CLR 45.

[40] (1996) 189 CLR 51. See H.P. Lee, 'The *Kable* Case: A Guard-Dog that Barked But Once?' in G. Winterton (ed), *State Constitutional Landmarks* (Sydney 2006), 390.

[41] (2006) 228 CLR 45, at [40], per Gleeson CJ.

[42] *Ibid*, at [42].

impartial as, for example, would be the case if a significant element of its membership stood to gain or lose from the way in which the duties of office were executed.'[43]

In order to establish that 'distortion' has occurred, Gummow, Hayne and Crennan JJ said that regard would be had to the persons appointed, the length of their appointments, what they have to do and the reasons for the necessity to make acting appointments.[44] They regarded the setting of some numerical boundary as amounting to the pursuit of an illusion. Kirby J, who dissented, viewed the practice as 'inimical to true judicial independence and impartiality'.[45]

VI. Judicial Immunity

In 2005, the High Court of Australia dealt with an appeal from a decision of the Supreme Court of Queensland which dismissed an appeal brought by Ms Diana Fingleton against her conviction following a trial before Helman J and a jury. Described by Kirby J of the High Court as an 'extraordinary case', *Fingleton v. The Queen*[46] highlighted the protection and immunity conferred upon magistrates in the State of Queensland. Kirby J observed:

> In a sense, this appeal illustrates a clash between two principles important to the proper administration of justice. Each of these principles is reflected in the Queensland legislation invoked before this Court. On the one hand, there is the principle providing an immunity to judicial officers in respect of things done and omitted to be done in the exercise of their functions as such. That principle, together with protected tenure in office, reinforces the independence of mind and action of judicial officers, essential to the proper discharge of their functions. On the other hand, there is a further principle that forbids anyone from causing, or threatening to cause, injury or detriment to a witness in judicial proceedings. Self-evidently, judicial proceedings would be undermined, and their just and lawful outcome frustrated, if, without reasonable cause and in retaliation against a person for becoming a witness, threats or other detriments were occasioned to such a witness.[47]

Ms Fingleton, as the Chief Magistrate of Queensland, decided in July 2002 to transfer a magistrate (Anne Thacker) from Brisbane to Townsville. Ms Thacker applied for a review of this determination of the Chief Magistrate by a judicial committee established by the Magistrates Act 1991 (Qld). Ms Thacker also

---

[43] *Ibid*, at [93].
[44] *Ibid*, at [101].
[45] *Ibid*, at [125].
[46] [2005] 227 CLR 166.
[47] *Ibid*, at [130].

sought assistance from the Magistrates Association. Mr Gribbin, the Association vice-president and who was also a co-ordinating magistrate provided an affidavit in support of Ms Thacker. Friction arose between Ms Fingleton and Mr Gribbin regarding an item in an agenda the latter was circulating for a meeting of co-ordinating magistrates without the former's knowledge. A day before the meeting Ms Fingleton sent an email to Mr Gribbin calling on him to show cause why she should not exercise her power to remove him from the position of co-ordinating magistrate. In her email letter, Ms Fingleton sought an explanation as to why Mr Gribbin saw it fit to supply the supporting affidavit. She also considered his act of circulating the agenda item as an act of disloyalty.

Ms Fingleton was found guilty in the court of first instance of engaging in retaliatory conduct against a witness 'without reasonable cause'. She was sentenced to twelve months imprisonment. The sentence was varied by the Court of Appeal which suspended it for an operational period of two years after she had served six months. She resigned as Chief Magistrate prior to her application to the High Court for special leave to appeal. By the time the appeal to the High Court was heard she had served six months of imprisonment. In the appeal before the High Court, the immunity issue was raised for the first time. Kirby J found it 'surprising that the question of immunity did not occur to anyone earlier.'[48]

The Magistrates Act 1991 (Qld) empowered the Chief Magistrate to nominate and also to remove co-ordinating magistrates. The High Court found that the Chief Magistrate was protected by the immunity provided by s 21A of the Act. That section provided:

> A magistrate has, in the performance or exercise of an administrative function or power conferred on the magistrate under an Act, the same protection and immunity as a magistrate has in a judicial proceeding in a Magistrates Court.

The Chief Magistrate was conferred a range of administrative functions or powers under the Magistrates Act 1991 (Qld), such as 'the nomination of co-ordinating Magistrates, the allocation of Magistrates to particular localities and the power of reprimand'. The High Court, in consequence, quashed her conviction.

Attention was drawn to s 30 of the Criminal Code (Qld), which provides:

> Except as expressly provided by this Code, a judicial officer is not criminally responsible for anything done or omitted to be done by the judicial officer in the exercise of the officer's judicial functions, although the act done is in excess of the officer's judicial authority, or although the officer is bound to do the act omitted to be done'.

---

48 *Ibid*, at [136].

Gleeson CJ said that it was clear that s 30 of the Code aided 'the independent and impartial administration of justice; the exercise of judicial functions without fear or favour'.[49] He also added that s 21A of the Magistrates Act 1991 (Qld) extended the s 30 immunity beyond the exercise by magistrates of judicial functions to the exercise of administrative functions and that its purpose was related to the independence of the magistracy. He said that, within any court, 'the assignment of a judicial officer to a particular case, or a particular kind of business, or a particular locality, is a matter intimately related to the independent and impartial administration of justice'.[50] Gleeson CJ added:

> If a Chief Magistrate could be called to account, in civil or criminal proceedings, for decisions about how Magistrates Courts arrange their business, or about the assignment of magistrates to cases, or classes of case, the capacity for the erosion of independence is obvious.[51]

Kirby J stated forcefully that, because the immunity provided 'a complete answer', Ms Fingleton should not have been charged, still less tried, let alone convicted of that offence.[52]

Ms Fingleton was awarded a $475,000 ex gratia compensation payment in 2005 by the Queensland State government.[53]

VII. The Courts and the Media

While the Australian people are welded to maintenance of judicial independence, there is also growing acceptance of the proposition that the judiciary is not fully insulated from criticisms. Casting the judiciary into the spotlight of public scrutiny is no bad thing. The occasional expressions of outrageous or insensitive remarks by some judicial officers, made for instance during the course of a trial, are reported widely by the media. These occasional episodes press home the point that comments from the bench must be weighed carefully.

The courts and their proceedings feature regularly in the print, radio and electronic media. This is a manifestation of the 'open justice' principle which is a fundamental underpinning of any democratic polity. In general, the media

[49] *Ibid*, 190.
[50] *Ibid*.
[51] *Ibid*, 191.
[52] *Ibid*, at [171].
[53] *The Weekend Australian*, 20–21 September 2008, p 3. Ms Fingleton in 2010 'accepted a separate and undisclosed payout after agreeing to settle a $2.3 million damages claim against some of the biggest names in the law in Queensland, who were involved in both the defence and prosecution at her trials': *The Weekend Australian*, 25–26 September 2010, p10.

gives prominence to trials which tend to capture the interest of the public, to controversial statements or remarks made by a judge either during court proceedings or extracurially, and to perceived 'misconduct' of judges. The glare of publicity is one of the acknowledged modes of ensuring judicial accountability. There is a fine line to be drawn between critical reporting of court proceedings and reporting which amounts to a denigration of the judicial institution. In the case of the latter, unconstrained ongoing denigration of or attacks on judges can result in an erosion of judicial independence and undermine public confidence in the courts.

Australian courts have become increasingly aware of the importance of contributing to a better understanding of the functioning of the courts. A number of courts have appointed a public information officer or media liaison officers as part of that contribution. Some courts have adopted the practice of providing brief summaries of judgments to facilitate a better comprehension of judicial reasoning behind various judgments.

There have been occasions where tension has arisen because some courts felt they were the target of a deliberate campaign by particular newspapers to denigrate them. There have been a few occasions when resort was made to the Australian Press Council in order to ensure a more balanced reporting.

For example, in 2005, the then Attorney General of the State of New South Wales (the Hon Bob Debus) brought a complaint against a daily newspaper, *The Australian*, to the Australian Press Council over a series of articles published by the newspaper. The headings of these articles will give a flavour of the thrust of the articles: 'No justice in judges' seven-week break', 'Courts' long break "unfair" to prisoners', 'Chief Justice vows to act on judges' holidays', 'Court defensive over backlog', 'On or off, judges don't lose on holiday time', 'Legal nitpicking won't answer judges' critics', 'Tassie tops supreme court backlog', and 'Long-winded and expensive justice'. Originally, the Attorney-General claimed that *The Australian* 'had conducted a campaign of denigration of the judiciary' which involved an 'emerging pattern of bias, misrepresentation and suppression of relevant facts'. After receiving the newspaper's response to the complaint, the Attorney-General withdrew this aspect of the complaint. In the end, the Australian Press Council upheld the Attorney-General's complaint on three specific issues relating to a failure to take sufficient steps to check the accuracy of some particular claims, a lack of fairness and balance in the newspaper's treatment of material arising from a report of the Productivity Commission, and the misleading nature of another article. The concluding paragraph of the Australian Press Council's Adjudication No. 1300 reads:

> The Press Council emphasises that it is the right of any newspaper to subject any institution to vigorous scrutiny. It must also be pointed out that the complainant does not challenge this right. Given that the courts are central to the administration

> of justice, subjecting them to the glare of publicity will ensure transparency and accountability in relation to their operation. Equally, the Press Council draws the attention of newspapers to the need to maintain confidence in the courts and the rule of law in their presentation of court-related matters. The exercise of the newspaper's right to scrutinise does not give it *carte blanche* to report on the activities of a court in any manner it likes. Like any other entity in society, the courts are entitled to be reported in a fair and balanced manner, and in a manner that accords with the Statement of Principles of the Press Council.[54]

On another occasion, the Australian Press Council upheld a complaint against *The West Australian* over the linking headlines on two court reports. One report dealt with a motor-cyclist who had been killed while the other dealt with a man who had been deliberately run over and severely injured. The full-page coverage had the main headline 'The courts of injustice'. The sub-headline of the first report was 'One judge says a man's life is worth less than five years' while the second was '…despite another saying an injury is worth six'.[55]

The complainant, the Public Information Officer for the West Australian Courts, claimed that the headlines were 'inflammatory and emotive' and not supported by the stories themselves. In Adjudication No 1290 (June 2005), the Press Council held 'that the opinion expressed in the main headline was inappropriate in court reporting'. It added that this would have been acceptable in an editorial on the matter, or in an opinion sidebar to the two reports. The Adjudication concluded:

> Further the Council points out that although there is a widespread temptation to compare one court result or sentence with another, the circumstances are rarely, if ever, exactly the same. Although comparisons can be legitimate, great care should be exercised in them by reporters, sub-editors and editors[56]

It is rare for a newspaper to be sued in defamation by a judicial officer in Australia. Exposure to public scrutiny comes with the territory when a person decides to accept a judicial appointment. Nevertheless, when criticism becomes defamatory of a member of the judiciary, the newspaper publishing the criticism is not immune from civil liability.[57]

VIII. Conclusion

It can be said that Australian courts continue to command the respect of the Australian people as highly independent and impartial bodies. To counter

---

[54] Australian Press Council, Adjudication No. 1300, June 2005.
[55] Australian Press Council, Adjudication No. 1290, June 2005.
[56] *Ibid.*
[57] See e.g. *Herald & Weekly Times Ltd & Bolt v. Popovic* (2003) 9 VR 1.

contemporary challenges to the independence of the courts by executive or legislative measures which would tend to undermine or erode their institutional integrity, the courts can ultimately resort to doctrinal weapons, such as the separation of judicial power and the principle in *Kable*. This approach is reflected very lucidly in the opening paragraph of the lead judgment of French CJ in *Totani*:

> Courts and judges decide cases independently of the executive government. That is part of Australia's common law heritage, which is antecedent to the Constitution and supplies principles for its interpretation and operation. Judicial independence is an assumption which underlies Ch III of the Constitution, concerning the exercise of the judicial power of the Commonwealth. It is an assumption which predates Federation....It is a requirement of the Constitution that judicial independence be maintained in reality and appearance for the courts created by the Commonwealth and for the courts of the States and Territories.[58]

Australian judges are robust enough to warn politicians to keep off their judicial patch.[59] At the same time, Australian courts render themselves accountable through the operation of the 'open court' principle, the obligation to give reasons for decisions, the application of the apprehension of bias rule and the exercise of oversight by the superior courts over the inferior courts.

---

[58] [2010] HCA 39, at [1].

[59] See E. Campbell and H.P. Lee, 'Criticism of Judges and Freedom of Expression' (2003) 8 *Media & Arts Law Review* 77.

CHAPTER TWENTY SEVEN

SHRINKING LEGAL AID, UNREPRESENTED LITIGANTS AND JUDICIAL INDEPENDENCE

*Avrom Sherr**

I. Introduction

This Chapter considers how the role of the judiciary changes when the judge enters the arena in order to balance the position between conflicting parties. It investigates how judicial independence may suffer when one litigant is unrepresented. As a result of reductions in public funding the number of unrepresented litigants is likely to increase further. It considers in some detail how the role and independence of the judge may be affected in such circumstances of inequality of arms.

The Decline of Legal Aid

By the turn of the millennium, in advance of the "credit crunch", even the jurisdictions which had well developed systems of Legal Aid were showing a reluctance to continue public funding of legal services at previous levels. The cost of legal services seemed to be rising disproportionately when compared with other public services. In general, the paraphernalia of post -war welfarism was slowly being dismantled, as political views moved away from state support and smaller proportions of the population were covered by assistance.

> In the 1990s it became increasingly clear that countries with highly developed public legal aid programmes faced similar challenges. Expenditure was rising faster than inflation, declining numbers of poorer citizens were receiving assistance, the cost to recipients was increasing, the scope of available services was being reduced, and new problems in the quality of service delivery were emerging. Governments and public administrators in many developed countries were reforming the role of the welfare state, and often requiring new justifications for existing levels of public funding of citizens' legal aid schemes. Many governments cast increasingly critical glances at the management of legal aid, and were sceptical of the inability of providers to reduce the cost of legal services delivery.[1]

---

* Institute of Advanced Legal Studies, University of London. With grateful thanks for research assistance to Marc Mason, and to Professor Shimon Shetreet and the judicial independence project for research support in funding the Jerusalem conference, March 2008.

[1] Alan Paterson and Avrom Sherr (2004) 'Legal aid and globalisation', *International Journal of the Legal Profession*, **11: 3,** 157–158.

With the beginning of the new millennium even governments on the political left were concerned about the effects of rising costs in criminal legal aid which were beginning to impinge on funds available for civil and family needs.

> The overall cost of our legal aid scheme has grown considerably in recent years, up from around 2.2 billion euros to nearly 3 billion euros in 2004. What has happened is a 37% rise in criminal legal aid spending, compared to a 24% decline for civil and family spending, excluding asylum.[2]

This position in the UK is similarly reflected elsewhere. Ontario, Canada in the early 1990s is a good example of what was happening across the common law world. Funding for the clinic system was frozen in 1992, despite the fact that large areas of the province were still without clinical law services. In 1994, the Ontario government capped funding for the legal aid certificate programme. Over the next couple of years, certificated services dropped significantly. In 1996–97, Ontario Legal Aid issued approximately 75,000 legal aid certificates, a reduction of more than 150,000 certificates from just a few years earlier.[3]

And in the UK, although the actual amount of expenditure was generally on the increase, over the period 2000 to 2007 the number of acts of assistance given to individual clients was generally declining (see Table 1 below).

Table 1: Publicly-funded legal services in England & Wales – Activity and Expenditure, 2000–2007[4]

Publicly funded legal services	2000/01	2001/02	2002/03	2003/04	2004/05	2005/06	2006/07
Total net expenditure (£m)	£1,664.3	£1,716.9	£1,908.5	£2,076.4	£2,038.0	£2,027.8	£1,980.3
Total Acts of Assistance (thousands)	*3,426.0*	*2,817.2*	*2,657.8*	*2,632.9*	*2,435.5*	*2,606.6*	*2,658.6*

II. Adversarial and Inquisitorial Models

As a result, the new Ministry of Justice for England and Wales called in 2007 for a careful analysis of the way in which different countries managed the cost

[2] Vera Baird, Minister in the Department of Constitutional Affairs, England and Wales June 2007 http://www.justice.gov.uk/news/sp060607.htm Accessed 6th August 2010

[3] Legal Aid Ontario Website. http://www.legalaid.on.ca/en/about/historical_overview.asp Accessed 6th August 2010

[4] Adapted from Table 11.4 of Judicial and Court Statistics 2006 at p 176 (Ministry of Justice Nov 2007 http://www.justice.gov.uk/docs/judicial-court-stats-2006-tag.pdf)

Table 2: Public Expenditure on Courts and Legal Aid per inhabitant.[5] (Note that the legal aid budget only includes money granted to parties and lawyers, and does not include the cost of legal aid administration)

	Court budget per inhabitant in euro	Legal aid budget per inhabitant in euro
Andorra	49,58	3,40
Armenia	1,03	0,01
Austria	69,63	1,67
Azerbaijan	0,64	0,02
Belgium	64,41	3,90
Bulgaria	3,53	0,14
Croatia	30,43	included in court budget
Czech Republic	21,02	0,84
Denmark	29,80	7,25
Estonia	12,24	1,09
Finland	41,05	9,98
France	28,35	4,64
FYROMacedonia	6,95	0,22
Georgia	0,83	not reported
Germany	53,15	5,59
Hungry	27,00	not reported
Iceland	32,39	3,56
Ireland	22,21	13,96
Italy	45,98	0,78
Latvia	6,70	0,30
Liechtenstein	224,08	53,92
Lithuania	9,63	0,46
Malta	23,53	0,04
Moldova	0,80	0,03
Netherlands	41,01	12,66
Norway	39,33	18,03
Poland	17,33	0,43
Portugal	46,98	2,94
Romania	5,40	0,08
Russian Federation	4,62	0,01
Slovak Republic	11,24	0,11
Slovenia	51,42	not reported
SM-Serbia	20,01	not reported
Spain	23,52	not reported
Sweden	44,44	11,59
Switzerland	102,66	7,00
Turkey	3,66	0,13
Ukraine	2,31	0,01
UK- England & Wales	16,89	53,8
UK- Northern Ireland	11,87	18,73
UK- Scotland	not reported	43,11

[5] Source: European Judicial Systems 2002. Facts and figures on the basis of a survey conducted in 40 Council of Europe Member States: European Commission for the Efficiency of Justice (CEPEJ) http://www.coe.int/t/dg1/legalcooperation/cepej/evaluation/default_EN.asp

of assisting litigants who could not afford legal services. Some striking differences appeared in the approach of the different judicial families. Adversarial countries in general spent more on their legal aid for legal representation, whilst jurisdictions working under the inquisitorial model spent more on their courts, judicial systems and judicial time.

A good comparison in Table 2 above is the relative costs of Germany and England and Wales, per capita. When both court and representation costs are added together, a similar amount is spent in total per capita in both countries: 58.74 Euros in Germany and 70.69 Euros in England and Wales. However, the larger amount in Germany is spent on the courts system, whereas the larger amount in England and Wales is spent on legal representation. It is also interesting to note that, as would be expected, the Netherlands, with a system closer to the legal aid of the UK, has a greater spend on legal representation than Germany, but less than England and Wales. On the other hand the amount spent in the Netherlands on courts is greater than that of England and Wales.

It is clear from these figures and previous work on the two families of the law[6] that there are two ways to make the business of the courts progress. In the adversarial world, usually with common law jurisdiction, assistance in court for litigants is given by legal representatives who may be funded by legal aid. Alternatively, in the inquisitorial system, where there may be less legal aid and representation, assistance in some form at least in terms of developing the case can be provided by the court itself. In all systems, if legally aided representation is in decline then the involvement of the court in assisting litigants is likely to increase, if only in order to move the business of the court along. However, this may cause a considerable difficulty for the court and for its judges – how can the judge (especially within an adversarial system) assist one litigant disproportionately from the other? And if a litigant is to be assisted in any way by the judge, does this not cause problems for judicial independence?

III. Unrepresented Litigants

So, does current research show any difference in approach as a result of a growth in unrepresented litigants? And, if so, how is this affecting the behaviour of the judges in these particular cases? A study in 2007 in civil and family courts of England and Wales showed the current numbers of unrepresented parties.

[6] See e.g. M Damaška, The Faces of Justice and State Authority: A Comparative Approach to the Legal Process (New Haven, Yale University Press, 1986).

> Nearly a third of ancillary relief cases and half or more of all other types of family case (adoption, contact/residence cases, divorce and injunctions) involved parties who were unrepresented for part or (more usually) all of their case. In civil cases, between 80 and 90 per cent of claimants were represented, but a majority of individual defendants were unrepresented (only 15% of individual defendants in civil cases in county courts were represented).[7]

Family cases can be emotional and difficult; balancing desires to have contact with children against the financial needs of both partners and the children of the family, can produce complex negotiations and apparently hard decisions. The involvement of judges in any partisan assistance in the midst of such situations can produce a sense of unfairness in the courtroom. These would be difficult situations. Stepping down from the higher world of the judges' bench and entering into the battle may prove difficult for judges to handle and for the parties to understand.

Informal procedures can produce uncertainty in the court or tribunal. Although they may be the basis of mediation and other alternative dispute resolution procedures, there can be misunderstandings about roles, relevance, and context when it is the judge or tribunal chair who becomes involved more informally inside litigation.

> Hidden legalism emphasizes judges' attention to official law, but when the parties' participation is informal, the judge may also enter the discussion in an informal way rather than remain a passive evaluator. Moreover, if the parties realize that the judge, despite the style of her participation, is attending to official law, they will, while proceeding in an apparently informal manner, be sure that necessary legal ground is covered and that appropriate legal arguments are made. If only one party realizes that an informal judicial style does not mean that the substantive law has been relaxed, that party will be at a substantial advantage.[8]

It becomes important to understand the nature of judicial behaviour in proceedings which become less formal.

IV. Judges in Informal Proceedings

How do judges tend to behave in these more informal situations? There is little training given to judges in balancing the role of the scrupulously fair arbiter with that of a more partial representative; making unbiased judgment at the same time as having to consider whether the position of one side of the

[7] Richard Moorhead, 'The Passive Arbiter: Litigants in Person and the Challenge to Neutrality', Socio Legal Studies (2007) 16, 405.

[8] Richard Lempert, 'The Dynamics of Informal Procedure: The Case of a Public Housing Eviction Board' Law & Society Review (1989) 23(3) 347at p391.

argument has been sufficiently well served in the absence of representation. In her 1997 work on Tribunals Genn pointed out the unreasonable expectations society has of judges, including the Tribunal Chairs, in circumstances in which there is no legal aid for representation.

> They are presumed to possess an awe-inspiring range of skills and qualities. They have expert knowledge of their field and can unravel complicated regulations and case law without the assistance of representation; can hear and evaluate evidence that would be excluded in conventional courts as unreliable (e.g. hearsay) and be capable of giving it due weight; they can assess the credibility of witnesses and the value of written evidence; assist unrepresented parties and compensate for lack of representation by interventionist (inquisitorial) behaviour; and they are able to reach consistent, reasoned decisions in accordance with law without bias, without technicality, and with speed.[9]

Even if it were possible to take for granted this set of imagined "superskills" for each judge, there are still further important issues which need attention, "Even if chairs succeed in obtaining the information they think they require, there may still be scope for creative argument on the application of regulations which they are unlikely to undertake on behalf of an unrepresented appellant"[10] It is not only the questioning of a litigant in order to present all the facts to the court for understanding and judgment, but also the problem then of balancing the need to develop proper argumentation on behalf of the unrepresented litigant without taking over the case or giving the appearance of partiality or unfairness.

> Some [Tribunal chairs] felt that it was difficult to perform the roles of adjudicator and representative at the same time. They also feared that where only one party was represented, giving assistance to the unrepresented party might be perceived as partiality... The contribution of representatives is to overcome these disadvantages... In the absence of representation, tribunal chairs bear responsibility for the fairness of the proceedings, although there are few immediate controls on their behaviour and there is no formal monitoring of their performance.[11]

Lon Fuller sets out the difficulties of working on both sides of the bench in the adversarial system in his Forms and Limits of Adjudication, a classic Harvard Law Review article in 1978. It is referred to as "the Common Law conundrum" since within the common law approach, "the integrity of the adjudicative process itself depends upon the participation of the advocate. This becomes apparent when we contemplate the nature of the task assumed by an arbiter who attempts to decide a dispute without the aid of partisan advocacy. Such an

[9] Hazel Genn 'Tribunals and Informal Justice' Modern Law Review (1993) 56, 393.
[10] Genn ibid
[11] Genn ibid

arbiter must undertake, not only the role of judge, but that of representative for both of the litigants. Each of these roles must be played to the full. When he resumes his neutral position he must be able to view with distrust the fruits of this identification and be ready to reject the products of his own best mental efforts. The difficulties of this undertaking are obvious. If it is true that a man in his time must play many parts, it is scarcely given to him to play them all at once."[12]

And Moorhead takes up the same argument in his study of litigants in person in 2007. He suggests that there can be a clash between passivity and even-handedness in the public perception of what happens in court,

> The raw interface between social and legal definitions of fairness calls into question the legitimacy of legal process as a fair resolver of disputes. The risks of substantive injustice force judges from the relative safety of passivity towards a degree of intervention that seeks to reconcile two competing demands: the needs of the unrepresented litigant for help and the needs of all parties for a system that is perceived as even-handed.[13]

He also detects the possibility of a professional bias in supporting the lawyers whose work is to represent litigants before the court. Many judges will themselves also be, or will have been, lawyers who act as court representatives. Not only do they assist the work of the court but they are part of the same circle which feeds itself, "In the moral economy, the unrepresented litigant had chosen to appear without counsel and so must 'live with the consequences' (Engler, 1999). In the professional economy, judges wanted to protect themselves against encouraging non-representation and doing lawyers out of work which was deservedly theirs. Under this view, 'the court's primary goal seems to be to deter litigants from "by-passing" lawyers"[14]

It is also immensely difficult to develop the relevant facts of a case with some economy of time without legal representation. And the pressures of court time can lead to poor decisions on policing relevance: "Pre-determination of relevance raises problems. Criticisms of premature diagnosis during professional interviews (Sherr, 1986) may apply also to judges. There is a question mark over the ability of anyone, even skilled judges, to know, often from defective paperwork, what the litigant's case is. Psychological study of decision making has shown a link between high knowledge groups, over-confidence and poor

[12] Lon Fuller, The Forms and Limits of Adjudication, (1978) 92 Harvard L Rev 353 (Cited in Genn 1993)

[13] Moorhead, The Passive Arbiter: Litigants in Person and the Challenge to Neutrality, Social Legal Studies 2007

[14] Moorhead, ibid

decision making (Arkes et al., 1988[15]) even in judicial contexts (Dhami, 2005, looks at magistrates)."[16]

Judges therefore, like the magistrates in Dhami's[17] research and the lawyers in Sherr[18] may jump to early conclusions which might be quite wrong. And since the decisions may not be articulated till the end of the case there may be no time or opportunity for an unrepresented defendant to correct such issues. Aiming to anticipate some of these problems by manipulating the normal course of procedure could also have some unintended consequences,

> Changing the order of hearings in other ways was also a common way of dealing with problems. Judges saw this as managing the process so that unrepresented litigants could respond to what their opponents said, rather than having to go first unaided. Similar changes to the evidence-giving process were made. These approaches aim to teach (in a very short period of time) the litigant some of the conventions of advocacy. They also permit the litigant's opponent to set the agenda for the hearings. Such an approach also privileged, in the eyes of litigants, the role of lawyers.[19]

Judges therefore seemed to dignify process above substantive justice as a means of balancing the needs of the parties and the system of justice. This approach seems to accord with the concept of being an umpire of procedural fairness. This is well exemplified again in their comments about dealing with points of law: "A particular area of tension for judges was the extent to which they intervened to raise points of law 'for' unrepresented litigants. Our judges generally stated that they did this where they could, with a certain wariness of their position as adjudicators, and an awareness of the limits of their own legal knowledge. Again the language indicated a conflicted situation. As one judge said, 'They say that you're not supposed to descend into the arena. But, if I became aware of the fact that some situation did give rise to a question of law, I would mention it to the parties, in fairness to both.' Balancing a role as passive arbiter against the need to deal with cases justly thus caused problems. Judges tended to interpret the duty to do justice in terms of process, rather than substance: maximizing the opportunities for unrepresented litigants to get help rather

---

[15] Arkes, Hal, Robyn M. Dawes and Caryn Christensen (1988) 'Factors Influencing the Use of a Decision Rule in a Probalistic Task', pp. 175 in J. Dowie and A. Elstein (eds) Professional Judgement: A Reader in Clinical Decision Making. Cambridge: Cambridge University Press, pp. 163–180.

[16] Moorhead op. cit. at 14.

[17] Dhami, M. K. (2005) From Discretion to Disagreement: Explaining Disparities in Judges' Pretrial Decisions, Behavioural Sciences and the Law, 23, 367–386 (2005).

[18] Sherr, A., (1986) Lawyers and Clients the First Meeting. *The Modern Law Review*, **49 (3)**, 323–357.

[19] Moorhead, op. cit. at 14.

than ensuring the dispute was adjudicated using a full and proper account of the law."[20]

It may be easier to bring about procedural fairness, which is wholly in the control of the court, than substantive fairness which may be more a matter of judgement and will have different biases. Yet, even here there were some differences of opinion among the judges whose behaviour seemed not always to be consistent, but based on pragmatism and what *seemed* to be correct. "The approach was pragmatic and inconsistent. Some were much more comfortable, explicitly guiding litigants on the law, others felt that was contrary to their role. Most recognized that in more or less extreme cases they would intervene to raise legal points against represented parties. For the most part, however, judges intervened in subtle ways which sought to accommodate intervention with a model of passive neutrality. Shifting turn taking, controlling relevance, and reframing cross-examination are all characterized by a somewhat reactive response to the issues a litigant raises. Some strayed into more proactive territory: identifying issues that the litigant needed, rather than wanted, to cover in cross-examination for instance, but for the most part a strategy of adjournment for advice was operated where the judge felt the intervention demanded by the situation took him or her beyond the judicial role. This is a convenience for the judge but it is of questionable benefit to the litigant; where they are unrepresented out of necessity, their ability to get assistance is limited, as many of the judges recognized."[21] So litigants might be adjourned to get help even where the judge was aware that help was unlikely.

In all, as pointed out by Moorhead and Sefton[22], the independence of the judiciary was affected where there were litigants in person in many ways. Judges found themselves subject to the tensions between promoting the procedure of neutral arbitration and the need to produce substantive justice; between appearing as a neutral arbiter and being neutral advocate; between brokering agreements and actual decision making. It was clear that these issues might well play out differently in the different approaches of adversarial and inquisitorial systems. They noted the tendency to change procedure to accommodate unrepresented litigants, for example by re-ordering the procedure and by acting as an intermediary in witness handling. However this was a demonstration of a preference for procedural over substantive fairness (as suggested by the strategy of adjourning to allow an unrepresented defendant time for seeking

[20] Moorhead, ibid

[21] Moorhead, ibid

[22] Richard Moorhead and Mark Sefton. 'Litigants in Person: Unrepresented Litigants in First Instance Proceedings' DCA Research Series 2/05 (2005) http://www.dca.gov.uk/research/2005/2_2005.pdf

advice when no such advice was available to them). There was also a reliance on the other side's solicitor or counsel both for the structure of proceedings and, to some extent, legal knowledge , emphasising counsel's duty to the court to disclose adverse case law. Even if the attempt was to assist the litigant in person, all of this seemed to result in perceptions that the lawyer and judge set the agenda. Unrepresented litigants often perceived unfairness owing to a lack of understanding of procedure and relevance. It also had the effect of shifting more of the cost burden onto the represented party. These effects in general would not assist in the promotion of judicial independence in such proceedings.[23]

V. Conclusions

Public funding in the developed world is likely to decrease further. Whilst the relatively "developed world" of existing European Union members is shedding its public funding burden it is still demanding a level of legal aid from aspiring applicants, and globalization is also spreading the demands for "Western" systems of justice[24] whilst those systems decrease their own spend on public funding for legal representation. And the actual effects of unrepresented litigants in the courts and tribunals is well described above. Judicial independence is under attack from within the system and judges have little training and ability to carry out the different roles simultaneously or even sequentially.

Moorhead and Sefton[25] rehearse possible solutions to these difficulties. One obvious solution, also suggested by the financial costs information shown above, is to move common law systems more over to an inquisitorial approach, with the judge more able to ask questions and enter into the fray. It has been suggested that the Woolf Reforms of Civil procedure in the 1990s were aimed at such a development[26]. However, a move of this nature is complex. It is not possible to carry out "legal transplants"[27] from one system to another without considering the wider inherent process and culture. It would, for example, also

---

[23] But Moorhead and Sefton also noted that Judges also suffered from an inability to help litigants, even if they wished to do so, either due to their own limited legal knowledge, or their awareness of the proper judicial role.

[24] Sherr, Avrom (2009) International Trends in Legal Aid. International Symposium on Legal Aid. Korea November 2009.

[25] Ibid.

[26] Jolowicz, J.A. (1998) The Woolf Report and the adversary system. C.J.Q. 1996, **15(Jul),** 198

[27] Nelken, David (2002) Legal Transplants and Beyond: of Disciplines and Metaphors in A.J. Harding and E. Orucu (Eds) Comparative Law in the 21st Century, pp 19–34, London: Kluwer Academic.

be necessary to develop the "dossier" approach, to encourage more background help to litigants, to appoint an "expert" tribunal member together with the judicial chair and inevitably to change the entire process of litigation.

It would help if judges or tribunal chairs placed in these difficult positions could acknowledge the problem more openly before the court and to the litigants concerned. However, this approach by itself is unlikely to solve the problem. The result is more likely to be that unrepresented litigants will feel more pressured to contact a lawyer to represent them; and feel that the judicial system is biased in favour of lawyer representation.

It would also help if more Legal Aid type assistance or other forms of assistance for litigants could be developed. Whereas better funding is unlikely as noted above, some interesting systems of communal self–help are developing in California and elsewhere[28]. It is possible that these more limited interventions might assist litigants in understanding the procedure a little more and preparing them for what will happen in court.

And the law and procedure could themselves be simplified, as is also being developed in California in relation to family law[29]. However it is not always possible to make complex issues simple, and further, cases and lawyer involvement have the tendency to produce complications. It can take a generation or more to work through and adopt wholesale changes to the law and procedure. Even the lawyers may adopt "professional capture" of the system and turn it into their own arena, as seems to be happening in some areas in relation to mediation[30].

Knowing and acknowledging the effects on judicial independence are an important first step in maintaining judicial approach and status. Developing better means to handle the difficulties as the numbers of unrepresented litigants grows, is the next stage in development.

---

[28] Hough, Bonnie (2010) *Developing the Continuum of Civil Legal Services in California – Expanding Systems to Maximize Funds for Representation.* Paper delivered at the Legal Services Research Centre International Conference 2010, Cambridge 1st July 2010.

[29] Ibid

[30] Genn, H. (2008)Judging Civil Justice. Cambridge; Cambridge University Press. Abel, R. (1988) The Legal Profession in England and Wales. Oxford: Basil Blackwell.

CHAPTER TWENTY EIGHT

THE NORTHERN IRISH JUDICIARY IN TIMES OF CRISIS: THE DIPLOCK COURTS

*Sophie Turenne**

In 1972, the British government took direct control of Northern Ireland affairs and implemented a new security strategy to deal with the severe civil strife, known as "the Troubles", which has plagued Northern Ireland's history. The British government chose to regard the terrorists as ordinary criminals (a policy which would also have implications for those detained in prison who wished to be regarded as political prisoners) and thus paramilitary offenders were tried in the criminal courts rather than made subject to internment.[1] Among the many emergency measures adopted in 1973, a two-tier criminal justice system was created, with "scheduled" offences leading to trial by a single judge without a jury, while trial by jury for "non-scheduled" offences was maintained.[2] The non-jury trials, known as the Diplock courts[3], were justified by concerns of juror intimidation and "the danger of perverse convictions by partisan jurors".[4] But they were also reminiscent of authoritarian regimes, where judicial activism is contained by fragmenting the judicial system with exceptional courts.[5]

---

* Sophie Turenne, M.A. (Cantab.), Ph.D. (Paris II Panthéon-Assas), is Neil Allam/Clifford Chance Lecturer at the Faculty of Law, University of Cambridge. She is a Fellow of Murray Edwards College, Cambridge.

[1] In recognition of the political nature of the conflict, the 1998 Belfast Agreement permitted the release of all prisoners convicted under the Diplock system.

[2] Although the Diplock courts were abolished in 2007, Northern Ireland continues to allow non-jury trials for suspected members of paramilitary organizations, see the Justice and Security (Northern Ireland) Act 2007. The power to refer paramilitary suspects to non-jury, Diplock-type trial was extended for a further two years in 2009, see the Justice and Security (Northern Ireland) Act 2007 (Extension of duration of non-jury trial provisions) Order 2009.

[3] They were part of the recommendations of the Commission chaired by Lord Diplock, *Report of the Commission to Consider Legal Procedures to Deal with Terrorist Activities in Northern Ireland* (Cmnd. 5185; 1972).

[4] There was evidence of intimidation of witnesses at the time, though probably less intimidation of jurors than suggested. In a small community, it was easy to find out who was on a jury, see J. Jackson, interview by G. Greig, *The Scotsman* (14 August 2007).

[5] T. Ginsburg and T. Moustafa (eds), *Rule by Law. The Politics of Courts in Authoritarian Regimes* (New York 2008), pp. 17–18.

However, unlike in most authoritarian regimes, the regular court hierarchy, the Court of Appeal, had jurisdiction over the "Diplock cases", in order to guarantee compliance with the minimum requirements of the rights to a fair trial under article 6 ECHR. Such institutional framework shapes and explains the judicial role that developed the Diplock courts until they were virtually abolished in 2007 (I). Judicial power was contracted, rather than expanded, and the judiciary was accused of failing to support of the rights of an individual. Indeed, the Diplock courts did demonstrate a "compulsion of legality" in the words of Dyzenhaus[6], that is, a compulsion to justify all acts of state as having legal warrant. Judges may have been aware that they risked their ability to safeguard rights if they attempted to challenge the regime's core legal mechanisms for maintaining political control[7] (II). Nonetheless, a "compulsion of legality" need not be limited to the assertion of the mere appearance of legality; and indeed on occasions the judiciary aimed to enforce the rule of law in the sense of procedural fairness.[8] The judges were able to uphold a certain set of common law principles during the emergency period – as discussed below – and did not abdicate their independence (III). They had a limited ability to safeguards individual rights but did strike, on occasion, against the will of the political regime.

I. The Institutional Framework

1. *The Emergency Legislation*

The Northern Ireland emergency legislation made no exception to the practice that, in times of crisis, the State will make new offences and seek to maximise

[6] D. Dyzenhaus, "Legality in a Time of Emergency" (2008) 24 *Windsor Review of Legal and Social Issues* 1, p. 3; see also D. Dyzenhaus, *The Constitution of Law – Legality in a Time of Emergency*. Cambridge (Cambridge 2006).

[7] T. Ginsburg and T. Moustafa, *ibid.*, p. 18. "If, instead of convicting people on the basis of the emergency legislation, judges had chosen choose to reassert the traditional criminal process, they may have released a number of serious offenders into the community, and this would not have improved the public confidence in the courts either", J. Jackson, "Paradoxes of Law and Professional Decision Making in Common Law Criminal Systems" (2001) 1 Revue Internationale de Droit Pénal 579, p. 587.

[8] See T.R.S Allan, "The Rule of Law as the Rule of Reason: Consent and Constitutionalism" (1999) 115 Law Quarterly Review 221; T. Bingham, "The Rule of Law" (2007) 66 Cambridge Law Journal 67; T.R.S. Allan, *Constitutional Justice: A Liberal Theory of the Rule of Law* (Oxford 2001) and M. Walters, "The Common Law Constitution and Legal Cosmopolitanism" in D. Dyzenhaus (ed.), *The Unity of Public Law* (Oxford 2004), ch. 16. Whether the attitude of the judiciary could or ought to have been different is an issue which cannot be considered here, but see D. Dyzenhaus, note 6 above; R. Posner, *Not a Suicide Pact: The Constitution in a Time of National Emergency* (New York 2007); E. Posner and A. Vermeule, *Terror in the Balance: Security, Liberty and the Courts* (Oxford 2007).

convictions of those whose activities seek to undermine the system.[9] The (Emergency Provisions) Act 1973 ("EPA")[10] created a juryless court for paramilitary suspects, some other "scheduled offences"[11] and for these trials it provided for less stringent rules for the admissibility of evidence.[12] All alleged offences by known paramilitary members were included, however trivial, and the legislation also included executive powers to proscribe organizations. Wide powers to stop, question, and arrest suspects were also introduced.

2. *A Small Judiciary*

The judicial role in Northern Ireland is a small-sized judiciary, with a small-sized legal profession. The Lord Chief Justice acts as president of the Court of Appeal on both the criminal and civil sides, and there are 10 High Court Judges and three Lord Justices of Appeal.[13] At County Court level, there are 15 judges. All judges down to county court level may preside in the Crown Court, where both Diplock cases and ordinary jury trials will be heard. All judges, at least until 2007, lived under constant security, though five have been murdered since 1973. This includes the Lord Chief Justice Gibson, who was killed by the IRA in 1987. This followed his acquittal of four policemen in a contested "shoot to kill" case, which he had accompanied with the observation that the dead IRA suspects had been brought to justice, "in their case the final courts of justice".[14]

---

[9] T. Hadden, "Judicial Roles and the Criminal Process during States of Emergency: A Framework for Analysis" in S. Doran and J. Jackson (eds), *The Judicial Role in Criminal Proceedings* (Oxford 2000), p. 205; O. Gross and F. Ní Aoláin, *Law in Times of Crisis. Emergency Powers in Theory and Practice* (Cambridge 2006) and K. Boyle, T. Hadden and P. Hillyard, *Ten Years on in Northern Ireland: the Legal Control of Political Violence* (London 1980).

[10] The EPA was amended in 1975, reenacted in 1978, 1987, 1991 and 1998. It applied only in Northern Ireland.

[11] See now Terrorism Act 2000, sch. 9. The "scheduled offences" were not necessarily confined to terrorist activity. Defendants who were charged with scheduled offences would generally be denied bail, even if they were not suspected members of paramilitary organisations. Typically they could expect to spend some 18 months in custody before charges went to trial – a marked difference from those accused of non-scheduled offences. Further, there was no case management culture as is familiar today, and there was therefore no way in which a trial judge might pressurise the prosecution to hurry its preparation. Suspects who were subject to long delays were said to be subject to "internment by remand".

[12] It should be said, however, that jury trials are often associated with rules of admissibility that may exclude some types of evidence (such as hearsay evidence or evidence of the bad character of the accused) on the grounds that jury may out undue weight upon them. So it would not come as a surprise to evidence lawyers that a move to trial without jury might coincide with a regime which in principle allows more prosecution evidence to be admitted. In that situation, a judge would be trusted to attach the proper weight to it and this could be scrutinised since, unlike a jury, he would have to give reasons for his verdict.

[13] B. Dickson, *The Legal System of Northern Ireland*, 5th ed. (Belfast 2005), pp. 39–43.

[14] A. Jennings (ed.), *Justice Under Fire: The Abuse of Civil Liberties in Northern Ireland*, 2nd ed. (London 1990).

The context of a divided community acutely raises the question to which community the judge is accountable. The judiciary had traditionally been identified as drawn mainly from the Protestant Unionist majority.[15] But from the 1980s, the composition of the bench gradually began better to reflect the balance of religious persuasion in society.

3. *The Role of the "Diplock Judge"*

The most enduring point of controversy lies in the extent to which a single judge can fairly balance the requirements of law and fact. In a jury trial, judges act as gatekeepers of evidence by withholding irrelevant or prejudicial information from the jury. In the Diplock courts, by contrast, the judge is aware of all evidence, and he or she has to decide both on its admissibility and on guilt on the basis of evidence he or she had admitted, but forgetting that which he has excluded. Judicial practice, however, added some safeguards to this system.[16] It was, for example, common for a different judge to conduct the *voir dire* from the judge who would himself be trying the substantive issues in the trial.[17]

In any event, many "Diplock judges" claimed that they approached cases with a "judicial attitude" regardless of the often conflicting pressures from both the state and the public.[18] Lord Lowry, the former Lord Chief Justice of Northern Ireland, considered that the non-jury trial in the earlier days of the "Troubles" had led to some perverse verdicts on account of what he tactfully called the jury's "emotional" bias.[19] But judges were then accused of becoming case-hardened over-time, that is, "more cynical of defense claims of innocence and more prosecution-prone in their decisions".[20]

---

[15] K. Boyle, T. Hadden, P. Hillyard, *Law and State: the Case of Northern Ireland (*London 1975), pp. 12–13.

[16] R. Lowry, "National Security and the Rule of Law" (1992) 26 Israel Law Review 117, p. 131. It should perhaps be noted that lay magistrates are trusted with this difficult exercise too, albeit only in minor cases.

[17] *McKeown* [2005] N.I. 301 CA (Crim Div) Crown Ct (Belfast); M. Bisgrove, "Judges as Tribunals of Fact: To What Extent do the Provisions for a Defendant to be Tried on Indictment by a Judge Sitting Without a Jury Conflict With the Defendant's Right to a Fair Trial Where Issues of PII are Present?" (2010) 9 Criminal Law Review 702, p. 707.

[18] J. Jackson and S. Doran, *Judge without Jury: Diplock Trials in the Adversary System* (Oxford 1993), p. 228. They also argued that the lack of a jury resulted in an adversarial deficit for the accused, *idem*, ch. 10; S. Doran, J. Jackson, M. Seigel, "Rethinking Adversariness in Non-jury Criminal Trials" (1995–6) 23 American Journal of Criminal Law 2.

[19] R. Lowry, *ibid.*, pp. 132–133.

[20] M. P. O'Connor and C. M. Runmann, "Into the Fire: How to Avoid Getting Burned by the Same Mistakes Made Fighting Terrorism in Northern Ireland" (2003) 24 Cardozo Law Review 1657.

We shall now assess the impact of the pressures exerted on judges through three distinct examples since, "apart from tradition, the justification for dispensing with a jury must be found, if found at all, in the performance of the judge, as assessed objectively and by the public."[21]

II. The Occasional Strike from the Judiciary

In the early 1980s, more than 350 cases a year were being prosecuted in Diplock courts. In 1985, more than 40% of serious cases were tried this way; but this proportion declined. In 1995 about 30% of them; in 2005, only some 5% of serious cases were tried in this way seemingly because fewer serious offences seem to be committed, detected and prosecuted.[22] The average annual roll of Diplock courts has dropped to 64 since 2001.

1. *Confessions*

In the 1970s, the Diplock courts were seen as rubber-stamping confessions which were highly dubious, following some brutal interrogation techniques and some changes to the rules of evidence in favour of the prosecution.[23] The statutory standard of admissibility of confession set in 1973 was a significant departure from the common law test of voluntariness. The sole criterion of admissibility was that the court should be satisfied that no torture or inhuman or degrading treatment had prompted it.[24] Although the Court of Appeal interpreted this phrase to cover any degree of physical violence[25], and Parliament later amended the wording to reflect this,[26] this narrow approach nonetheless encouraged questionable interrogation techniques. The security forces switched from questioning during internment to specialized interrogations centres for terrorists suspects; and here suspects were held incommunicado.The courts

---

[21] R. Lowry, *ibid.*, p. 130.

[22] The annual average having dropped from about 1,000 at the peak of the Troubles in the 1970s to about 400 in 1995, see J. Jackson and S. Doran, "Diplock Courts: a Model for British Justice?" *The Independent* (13 September 1995).

[23] There was no duty on the prosecution to disclose incriminatory evidence. They were not obliged to make available to the defence all and any evidence that might assist the defence case.

[24] In 1978, the European Court of Human Rights condemned various interrogation techniques in breach of Art. 3 for being inhuman and degrading, though not torture, see *Ireland v. UK* (1978) 2 EHRR 25. The Baker Report also estimated that confession forms the mainstay of the prosecution case in around 80% of cases, *Review of the Operation of the Northern Ireland (Emergency Provisions) Act 1978* (Cmnd. 9222; 1984), at para. 195. See Northern Ireland (Emergency Provisions) Act 1996, s. 12, and note the wider test in England and Wales, Police and Criminal Evidence Act 1984, ss. 76–78.

[25] *R. v. O'Halloran* [1979] N.I. 45 (*per* Lord Lowry at [47]).

[26] Northern Ireland (Emergency Provisions) Act 1987, s.11 (2).

did decide that there was still a *discretion* to exclude confessions which were not voluntarily obtained, but this discretion was rarely used,[27] and in a familiar nod to legislative supremacy, it was said indeed that the discretion could not be routinely used else it would directly undermine the statutory test.[28] Importantly, the judges themselves had a limited ability to evaluate the credibility of the defendant's allegations of ill-treatment against the denialsof the police. They often found it impossible to believe either the police or the defendant[29] – and on occasions such as those, sometimes gained a new insight into the difficulties of fact-finding which they were accustomed to leave to juries.

2. *Supergrass Evidence*

As judges eventually "toughened up" the admissibility rules on confessions, they also eventually "toughened up" on the widespread use of uncorroborated evidence of an accomplice, or "supergrass" evidence. Between November 1981 and 1983, almost 600 suspects were arrested on the evidence of 19 Republicans and 8 loyalists supergrasses.[30] The judges thus found themselves deciding several serious charges where the main evidence was given by know offenders, whilst it was not always clear what their incentives for giving testimony might be. Nonetheless the judges for a long time appeared willing to convict on uncorroborated testimony. It is true that, at the common law of the time, the judges had to warn the jury of the dangers of relying on uncorroborated evidence of accomplices. Thus, in Diplock courts, they would make it clear that they had reminded themselves of this when they gave judgment. But sometimes this seemed to take the form of little more than a ritual incantation on the evidence of offenders who had (on bases that were by no means always clear) been granted complete or partial immunity. At common law, the trial judge was required to warn the jury of the danger of relying on such evidence in the absence of corroboration. Whilst the judges did consider the propriety of the use of uncorroborated accomplice evidence as a method of conviction,[31] nonetheless they appeared willing to convict on uncorroborated testimony, albeit remembering to mention in their judgments that they had borne in mind the potential dangers of doing so.

---

[27] J. Jackson, "Many Years on in Northern Ireland: the Diplock Legacy" (2009) 60 Northern Ireland Law Quarterly 213.

[28] *R. v. Tohill* [1974] N.I.J.B. (Mar.).

[29] J. Jackson, "Many Years on in Northern Ireland: the Diplock Legacy", *ibid.*

[30] S. Greer, *Supergrasses: Informers and Anti-Terrorists Law Enforcement in Northern Ireland* (Oxford 1995), p. 57.

[31] See, *e.g.*, *R. v. Gibney* (1983) 13 N.I.J.B. 7–8.

The judges' attitude was criticised in an unofficial report in 1983 by Lord Gifford[32], who concluded that, in handling "the supergrass issue", the common law standards of fairness and due process had not been followed. From 1983, the courts were less prepared to convict on uncorroborated evidence, and this was reflected by the Court of Appeal which laid down the "sternest criteria" to be applied in such cases.[33] The authorities, as a result of the resistance of the courts in cases where supergrass evidence underpinned the prosecution case, started to rely more heavily on forensic evidence. Observers have emphasized how the initial success of the supergrass system (in terms of numbers of prosecutions) can be attributed to an uncritical judiciary which subsequently realised its mistake and about-turned, destroying the phenomenon it had initially tolerated.[34] This was the triumph of the (substantive) rule of law over a dubious policy on the grounds of those enforcing the law,[35] which was perhaps in part directed at causing wider mistrust within the terrorist community.

3. *The Right to Silence*

The Emergency legislation allowed a trial judge to draw certain inferences from silence during interrogation and trial.[36] This was particularly detrimental to defendants in the Diplock courts due to the heavy pressure put upon them to confess. But the government contended that this restriction was required as hardened criminals were not co-operating with investigations by remaining silent (a claim that would be later made by the British government about *all* criminal suspects). However, in the absence of immediate access to legal advice for suspects, such inferences shifted the balance of power in police-suspect encounters significantly towards the police: now suspects had to decide for themselves whether speaking was better than silence – and speaking, say in order to give an innocent explanation to the instant accusation, might easily involve inadvertently admitting to any one of a number of special emergency offences (for example, it was never entirely clear how one became a "member" of a proscribed organisation). A study in 2000 showed that judges were not drawing inferences from silence in order to fill a large evidential deficit in the

---

[32] T. Gifford, *Supergrasses: the Use of Accomplice Evidence in Northern Ireland* (London 1984).

[33] *R. v. Crumley and others* [1986] 7 N.I.J.B. 1 (*per* Lord Lowry at [13]).

[34] *Committee on the Administration of Justice* ("CAJ"), *War on Terror: Lessons from Northern Ireland* (Belfast 2008).

[35] S. C. Greer, "The Rise and Fall of the Northern Ireland Supergrass System" (1987) Criminal Law Review 663, p. 665.

[36] Criminal Evidence (Northern Ireland) Order 1988.

prosecution case.[37] It was left to the European Court of Human Rights to insist in *Murray v. United Kingdom* that although the right to silence is not absolute, when combined with the absence of immediate access to a lawyer, it was incompatible with the concept of a fair trial.[38] Subsequently, such inferences could only be drawn after an accused had had access to legal advice. It may be possible to criticize the Northern Irish judiciary for not deciding this for themselves, but it should be said that the requirement that legal advice be offered had also been missing from the English legislation (s. 34 Criminal justice and Public Order Act 1994) which had to be amended accordingly after the same *Murray* decision.

III. The Emergency Taint on Judicial Independence

As shown above, the "Diplock judges" did not wholly succumb to being a factory for convictions, in a way in which the English magistracy is often accused. To support this further, the broad statistics fail to show any dramatic drop in the acquittal rate. Even at the height of the Troubles, the Diplock courts were acquitting 40–45 per cent of defendants before them, which is a high proportion of cases even though still a lower percentage than is generally found in jury trials in Northern Ireland.[39] It is also relevant that there have been, until now, few convictions reviewed by the Criminal Cases Review Commission that were referred for retrial.[40]

Peter Smith QC, former Deputy Judge of the High Court of Justice, even believes that the use of trials without juries in the Diplock courts was "reasonably successful" as a solution to the intimidation of jurors in Northern Ireland.[41] In particular, the loss of a jury was compensated with the requirement for judges to give reasons for convictions, as well as granting an automatic right of appeal to a three-judges court of appeal against any conviction.[42] Once convicted, the defendant was in a stronger position than someone convicted by a jury, who normally needs leave to appeal and cannot point to deficiencies in jury reasoning (for none is provided). It is also arguable that the requirement to give reasons constrained judicial decision-making much more than jury

[37] J. Jackson, M. Wolfe and K. Quinn, *Legislating Against Silence: The Northern Ireland Experience* (Belfast 2000), ch. 6.
[38] *John Murray v. U.K.* (***1996***) 22 EHRR 29.
[39] J. Jackson, "Many Years on in Northern Ireland: the Diplock Legacy", *ibid.*, p. 220.
[40] Though this is another uncertain measure of success, since many prisoners were released early in the wake of the "Good Friday" agreement in 1998.
[41] CAJ, *ibid.*
[42] Northern Ireland (Emergency Provisions) Act 1996, s. 14. In practice judges also gave reasons for acquittals.

decision-making. The readiness of the Court of Appeal to quash convictions in the supergrass cases of the mid-1980s shows the Northern Irish judiciary using their powers of scrutiny to the full.[43]

Judicial independence, in the sense of institutional autonomy from the executive, did exist, as emphasized by Lord Lowry in 1992, as he referred to the rule of law prevailing "amid the clash of arms".[44] But institutional autonomy exists in more than a few authoritarian states too, as it can be politically advantageous to maintain a formal judicial independence if judicial compliance has been gained without having to attack judicial autonomy.[45] In democratic and authoritarian states alike, formal institutional autonomy is a necessary condition for the maintaining of judicial authority. But it is insufficient by itself; all agents in the process must be accountable. Thus the "compulsion of legality" of the "Diplock judges" did not compensate for the lack of effective accountability mechanisms in the pre-trial process, both at a formal institutional level and in the administration of justice as a whole. There was no truly independent complaints mechanism against the police and army; and there were no codes of conduct, guidelines and regulations for access to lawyers, training etc.[46]

This may be why, in public perception, the Diplock courts were still associated with the state and were therefore "widely hated"[47], being viewed as partisan and oppressive.[48] For several years, IRA members refused to participate in their trials (refusing even to plead) though this was in part directed against the wider policy of processing them through the criminal courts altogether (regardless of the tribunal). The human rights-organisation Committee for the Administration of Justice concluded in 2008 that "The close relationship between the police, the state and the judiciary tends to undermine the critical independence that judges should have".[49] It is true that they tended to believe the police and security forces in cases of use of force,[50] including an acquittal where they shot unarmed people who were fleeing.[51] But it should be said that one of these decisions was affirmed in London by the House of Lords[52],

---

[43] S. Doran and J. Jackson, "The Judicial Role in Northern Ireland" in C. Munro and M. Wasik (eds), *Sentencing, Judicial Discretion and Training* (London 1992), p. 56.

[44] R. Lowry, *ibid.*, p. 119.

[45] T. Ginsburg and T. Moustafa, *ibid.*, p. 16.

[46] CAJ, *ibid.*

[47] J. Jackson and S. Doran, "Diplock courts: a Model for British Justice?", *ibid.*

[48] CAJ, *ibid.*

[49] CAJ, *ibid.*

[50] See, *inter alia*, A. Jennings, note 14 above, on some of the more hotly disputed cases, including the ill-fated Stalker inquiry into the alleged shoot to kill policy.

[51] *R. v. Macnaughton* [1975] N.I. 203, *R. v. Jones* [1975] 2 N.I.J.B.

[52] *Attorney-General for Northern Ireland's reference (No 1 of 1975)* [1977] A.C. 105; C. Gearty, "The Cost of Human Rights: English Judges and the Northern Ireland Troubles" (1999) Current Legal Problems 19.

and that the problems of securing effective legal control in such cases are also evident in countries with trial by jury.

The judiciary was helped by an independent Bar, whose reputation for non-partisan representation remained intact.[53] They were also helped by international human rights organizations whose criticisms of the lack of safeguards during the pre-trial process, such as the curtailing of the right to silence, were constant – when most lawyers remained publicly silent.[54] The Diplock courts therefore appear to have survived on the basis of "a combination of legal professional norms and ethics, but also exposure to international human rights norms".[55]

IV. Conclusion

So was Lord Diplock's legacy good for justice and good for Northern Ireland?[56] The emergency legislation severely undermined public confidence in the administration of justice and the rule of law. The Diplock courts were part of the package of emergency measures, and so became associated with it and were perceived to operate to a different standard of justice than trials by jury.[57] But it is difficult to point to any significant respect in which terrorist suspects tended to fare better in English courts, and the most notorious miscarriages of justice in the United Kingdom (the Birmingham Six, Guildford four) occurred in English courts. Crucially, the quality of sentencing and process in the Diplock courts did not differ greatly from that of the ordinary courts.

The new Justice and Security (Northern Ireland) Act 2007 retains a provision for the Northern Ireland director of public prosecutions ("DPP") to issue

[53] J. Jackson, "Many Years on in Northern Ireland: the Diplock Legacy", *ibid.*, p. 221. Lord Lowry also emphasized the role of a strong Bar, *ibid.* See also K. McEvoy, "Law, Struggle, and Political Transformation in Northern Ireland" (2000) 27 Journal of Law and Society 542, pp. 551–553.

[54] J. Jackson, "Many Years on in Northern Ireland: the Diplock Legacy", *ibid.*, p. 223.; Amnesty International, *Northern Ireland: Fair Trial Concerns in Northern Ireland: the Right of Silence* (1992). On the lack of engagement from the judiciary and lawyers, see S. Livingston, "And Justice for All? The Judiciary and the Legal Profession in Transition" in C. Harvey (ed.), *Human Rights, Equality and Democratic Renewal in Northern Ireland* (Oxford 2001), pp. 131–162. The Human Rights Act 1998 has facilitated access to European Convention rights, and it is hoped that a Bill of Rights for Northern Ireland, currently under discussion, "will assist in establishing a context where the state's response to terrorism will be constrained within a legal framework of respect for human rights", CAJ, *ibid.*

[55] J. Jackson, "Many Years on in Northern Ireland: the Diplock Legacy", *ibid.*, p. 218.

[56] J. Jackson, "Many Years on in Northern Ireland: the Diplock Legacy", *idem*, pp. 225–229.

[57] J. Jackson, "Paradoxes of Law and Professional Decision Making in Common Law Criminal Systems", *ibid.*, p. 586. The emergency powers became part of the problem rather than the solution, see B. Dickson, "Northern Ireland Emergency Legislation – the Wrong Medicine?" (1992) Public Law 592.

a certificate in a case where it is felt a non-jury trial is appropriate. So the Diplock courts remain, in the sense that the non-jury option is still available.[58] The discretion is with the DPP[59] and the lack of judicial review of his decisions, except in exceptional circumstances, raised concerns from the United Nations Human Rights Committee.[60]

However, the acceptance of non-jury trials is growing in some common law jurisdictions. Even in the motherland, the Criminal Justice Act 2003 has exported the Diplock mode of trial to England and Wales in cases where there is a real danger of jury tampering.[61] Recent research further supports the efficiency of juries, showing in particular no evidence of racial bias.[62] However, the same research warns that experiences of juries cannot safely be transposed to other jurisdictions. If there were real grounds to suppose that juries could not be effectively protected from intimidation in Northern Ireland in terrorist trials – and it seems that there were – then Diplock courts proved to be a workable response to civil disorder and terrorism.

---

[58] The special rules governing the admissibility of confessions have however disappeared. Similarly, the 'scheduling' mechanism been replaced by a greater presumption in favour of trial by jury. Between July 2007 and July 2009 the DPP issued certificates for 41 cases to be tried by Diplock-type non-jury courts.

[59] The broad statutory test to determine whether a criminal case should be referred to the new Diplock-type courts limits the DPP's discretion very minimally, see the Justice and Security (Northern Ireland) Act 2007, *ibid.*

[60] The Human Rights Commissioner has noted the lack of obligation on the director to provide "objective and reasonable grounds" when applying different rules of criminal procedure, which is contrary to Article 14 of the ICCPR, see J. Jackson, "Many Years on in Northern Ireland: the Diplock Legacy", *ibid.*, p. 229. See also Lord Carlile of Berriew's recommendations, "Non-Jury Trial in Northern Ireland" in *Replacement Arrangements for the Diplock Court System. A Consultation Paper* (Belfast, 2006), Annex A.

[61] Criminal Justice Act 2004, s. 44. This provision was extended to Northern Ireland on 8 January 2007, see Crown Court (Amendment) Rules (Northern Ireland) 2006. See also *R. v. T* [2009] EWCA (Crim) 1035; [2010] 1 WLR 630 (CA Crim Div), comment by N. Taylor (2010) Criminal Law Review 82.

[62] C. Thomas, *Are Juries Fair?* (London 2010).

CHAPTER TWENTY NINE

THE CHALLENGE OF JUDICIAL INDEPENDENCE AND THE EXPERIENCE OF PAKISTAN

*Mr. Justice Tassaduq Hussain Jillani**

I. The Beginnings

Pakistan came into being as an independent State in August 1947 having a legacy of colonial rule. Its march towards constitutionalism was preceded by a chequered history of constitution making, political instability, martial laws and its concomitant periods of constitutional deviation and finally the epoch making struggle of the Judges, the bar and the civil society in defence of the rule of law under the constitution.

1. *Constitution Making and the Wages of Constitutional Deviations*

Initially the nascent State continued to be governed under the Indian Independence Act, 1947 read with Government of India Act 1935[1] till March 1956 when the first Constitution[2] was promulgated. In October 1958, the

* Mr. Justice Tassaduq Hussain Jillani is a Judge of the Pakistani Supreme Court. In 1974, he started practice at District Courts, Multan. He was appointed as Assistant Advocate General Punjab in July, 1979; and enrolled as an Advocate of the Supreme Court of Pakistan in 1983. Justice Jillani took an oath as a Judge of Lahore High Court on August 7, 1994 and in July 2004 he was elevated to the Supreme Court of Pakistan where he served till the imposition of the state of emergency on November 3, 2007. General Musharraf suspended the constitution and prescribed a special oath of loyalty to himself and those who did not take oath were declared ceased to be judges. Mr. Justice Jillani was one of those who did not take fresh oath and was made dysfunctional. He was made to rejoin the court after the assumption of office by the elected government and resignation of General Musharraf. In July 2008, he was invited by American Bar Association (ABA) to receive the 2008 the Rule of Law Award on behalf of Judges in Pakistan who demonstrated courage in defending the Rule of Law in the country. He was conferred co-chair on the ABA's World Justice Project. Other co-chairs include Justice Sandra Day O-Conor, Justice Anthony M. Kennedy, Justice Ruth Bader Ginsburg, Justice Stephen G. Breyer, President Jimmy Carter, Madeleine Albright, James A Baker III and William H. Gates, Senior. He was also conferred 'Honorary Doctorate in Humane Letters' at a special Convocation held in Southern Virginia University, Washington in 2007. The Hague Conference has appointed him as the Co-chair of the Working Party on Mediation in Family International Law. The Working Party comprises of Judges and Academics from Europe, United States, Latin America, India and Asia.

[1] Indian Independence Act and Government of India Act, 1935 can be found in 1947 Pakistan Code.

[2] PLD 1956 Statute Part.

constitution was abrogated and the Chief of Army Staff imposed martial law. Then the Supreme Court in its perception was confronted with an unprecedented dilemma of complete arbitrary rule by the military in the event of non-validation of the coup d'etat on the one hand and on the other of ceding some power to the military with a view to ensure that the country was back on rails of constitutional governance. It *(in State v. Dosso)*[3] validated the imposition of martial law by invoking the Kelsenian theory and held that, "a victorious revolution was itself a law creating fact." Although the application of Kelsenian theory in the facts and circumstances of that case has been a subject of critical comment but the silver lining was that the judgment unequivocally declared that the country would continue to be governed as nearly as possible under the Constitution which stood abrogated.

The martial law was lifted in 1962 and the country was given a new constitution which unlike the previous one envisaged a presidential form of government. There was constitutional democracy till March 1969 when the country plunged into yet another constitutional and political crisis leading to the imposition of second martial law and the constitution was abrogated by General Muhammad Yahya Khan. However, in 1970, he had to hold elections which unleashed political forces which could not arrive at a consensus on issue of provincial autonomy and the country confronted an existential crisis; those elected from Eastern Wing of the country (East Pakistan) demanded a level of provincial autonomy which to the leaders of the Western Wing (West Pakistan) amounted to secession. Inclined towards the latter view, General Yahya treated it as a law and order situation, attempted to curb the turbulence from that angle which led to war with India who lent an easy hand to those who wanted secession which ultimately paved the way for the creation of a separate state called Bangladesh in 1972. The Chief Martial Law Administrator (General Mohammad Yahya Khan) was forced to hand over power to the political party which commanded majority amongst parliamentarians elected from the West Pakistan i.e. which now constitute Pakistan and late Zulfiqar Ali Bhutto became the President.

The issue of legality of martial law (imposed by General Yahya Khan) once again came under consideration before the Supreme Court (in the famous *Asma Jillani's case*)[4]. Declaring it to be illegal and dubbing the Chief Martial Law Administrator as 'usurper', the Court revisited the law laid down by it in the earlier judgment (*State v. Dosso supra*) and held that the Kelsenian theory had been wrongly applied; that no valid law comes into force from

---

[3] State v. Dosso (PLD 1958 SC (Pak) 533).
[4] Miss Asma Jillani v. Govt. of Punjab and another (PLD 1972 SC 139).

"the foul breath or smeared pen of a person guilty of treason against the national order."

2. *The Constitution, Abrogation and "State Necessity"*

In 1973, the Parliament unanimously passed a new constitution and it was because of its wide approval and acceptance that it continues to be the constitution of the country till date. In early 1977 first general elections were held under an elected government. But on account of serious allegations of rigging, there were country wide agitations which prompted the army to take over on the ground of what it described as preventing country's descent towards anarchy. The then Chief of Army Staff General Muhammad Zia-ul-Haq dissolved the assemblies, dismissed the government and the constitution was declared to be 'held in abeyance'. The Courts were put to test once again. The Supreme Court validated the action (in *Begum Nusrat Bhutto's case*)[5] on the grounds of "State necessity" and the principle of *salus populi suprema lex*. The Court found that on account of massive rigging in 1977 elections, the State machinery had crumbled down and the constitution did not provide remedy. This period of constitutional deviation continued till 1985 when the constitution was revived with the 8th Amendment which was approved by the Parliament by 2/3rd majority. In August 1988, General Zia-ul-Haq died in an air crash. The crash brought a sudden change in political landscape and from the said year till 1999 the country was ruled by democratically elected governments. In October 1999, the then Prime Minister dismissed the Chief of Army Staff General Pervaiz Musharaff but the latter reacted and took over the reigns of the government, suspended the constitution and dissolved the national assembly. The vires of action taken by the Chief of Army Staff were challenged in court and it was subjudice before the Supreme Court when a new Provisional Constitution Order (PCO) was promulgated by General Musharraf which prescribed a special oath for the Judges of the Supreme Court and High Courts and those who did not take oath were laid off. As a consequence of that, several Judges of the Supreme Court and High Courts were 'declared' to have ceased to be Judges. This included the then Chief Justice of Pakistan Mr. Justice Saeed-uz-Zaman Siddiqui. The Constitutionality of these actions was adjudicated upon by the Supreme Court (in *Zafar Ali Shah's* case)[6]. The Court validated Military takeover as according to it the machinery

[5] Begum Nusrat Bhutto v. Chief of Army Staff and Federation of Pakistan (PLD 1977 SC 657).

[6] Syed Zafar Ali Shah v. General Pervez Musharraf, Chief Executive of Pakistan (PLD 2000 SC 869).

of the government had completely broken down and to safeguard country's integrity it was necessary.

II. Defending the Constitution through Judicial Independence

The Supreme Court allowed General Pervaiz Musharraf a period of three years for the purpose of achieving his declared objectives and for that limited period, in the interest of "State necessity" and for the "welfare of the people", entitled him to perform certain acts including the power to amend the constitution. As the constitution was in 'abeyance', the General in order to acquire political legitimacy issued the Referendum Order on 30.4.2002 and got himself elected as President for five years in an uncontested and highly controversial referendum. Towards the close of three years granted by the Supreme Court, he brought the 17th Amendment to the Constitution which was approved by the Parliament as revival of the Constitution and lifting of the proclamation of emergency imposed by him in October 1999 was made conditional to approval of the 17th Amendment by the Parliament. The said amendment sanctified the election of President Musharraf through the afore-referred referendum. In October 2007 when the five years term of office of President was to expire, he wanted to contest for the second term and he knew that it was not possible under the constitution without a compliant Chief Justice. He decided to get rid of him. On 9th of March, 2007, he asked the Chief Justice to resign as according to him he had received complaints of misconduct against him. On his refusal, he suspended the Chief Justice (though there was no provision in the Constitution to that effect) and filed a reference of alleged misconduct against him before the Supreme Judicial Council. This sparked off a countrywide protest against the General and in favour of the Chief Justice led by the Bar Associations. The Chief Justice challenged the reference filed against him before the Supreme Court which was allowed (by a Bench of 13 members of which author was a member) and he was reinstated. This judgment of the Supreme Court not only hurt General's ego, but aggravated his fears as also the sense of insecurity. In the meanwhile, his eligibility to contest presidential elections was challenged in the Supreme Court (an 11 Members Bench) in *Wajihuddin v. The State*. The issues involved in the said petition were two fold: (i) whether General Pervaiz Musharraf (who was still holding the office of Chief of Army Staff) could contest the elections notwithstanding the Constitutional restraint that no holder of public office could contest the elections unless a period of two years has elapsed between his retirement and the elections; (ii) whether the Assemblies whose term was to expire in two months time could be the electoral college or the succeeding Assemblies in view of Article 43 of the Constitution. I was part of the 11-Members Bench which was hearing the case. The arguments dragged on and when the polling day approached nearer, the petitioner made a prayer to stay the elections. The Court did not grant stay order against the election because if that was done, the composition of the electoral college for President's elections would have undergone change as the term of one of the Provincial Assemblies (which was one of the components of the electoral college for the President) was about to expire (Province of Khyber Pakhtoonkhaw). The Court allowed him to contest the elections with the rider that the Election Commission of Pakistan shall not notify the result till the final disposal of the petition pending before the Supreme Court. With this court order, he thought his apprehensions regarding the Supreme Court were coming true and planned to resort to extra constitutional measures once again. Sensing the move, on 2nd of November, 2007, the counsel for the petitioner who happened to be the President of Supreme Court Bar Association as well, (Mr. Aitzaz Ahsan) filed an application for issuance of a restraint order against General Musharraf, Chief of Army Staff, not to pass any order which had the effect of suspending the constitution or changing the composition of the court. In the afternoon of 3rd of November, 2007, the word went around in the Capital city Islamabad that martial law was being imposed. The Chief Justice of Pakistan with the available Judges in the city assembled in the afternoon (7-Members) and passed the restraining order to the effect that the President and Prime Minister shall not pass any order contrary to judicial independence; no judge of the Supreme Court or High Court shall take oath under the Provisional Constitution Order and all military authorities were also restrained from acting on such an Order.

Notwithstanding the order passed by the Supreme Court, General Musharraf, imposed the "State of Emergency", directed once again the Constitution to be 'held in abeyance' (for which there was no provision in the constitution), issued a provisional constitution order prescribing a special oath of loyalty (to himself) for judges of the superior courts with the stipulation that those who did not take oath would cease to be Judges. Out of the 18 Judges of the Supreme Court, 13 including myself did not take oath and out of 93 Judges of the High Courts from all over the four Provinces of the country, 61 did not take oath. All such judges were not only declared ceased to be Judges, but most of them were detained in their own homes.

Those who did not take oath were motivated by no reason other than defending the Constitution and upholding the Rule of Law. Temerity and lure of prestigious offices were shunned for a higher principle. They believed that the court is the keeper of the conscience. And the conscience is the Constitution[7].

---

[7] Bruce Allen Murphy, Wild Bill: The Legend and Life of William O. Douglas 362–68 (2003).

The imposition of 'State of Emergency' was sought to be justified on the ground that the country was a "frontline State" in the war against terror; that the courts were "letting off" accused involved in terror related offences and that the judiciary was out to "derail the system" by such frequent interventions. This unprecedented assault on judiciary was a great blow to its independence, the rule of law and due process. The President of the Supreme Court Bar Association (Mr. Aitzaz Ahsan) in his two articles published in Newsweek[8] deprecated the detention of the Chief Justice (who was awarded Medal of Freedom by Harvard Law School) and other Judges and how it adversely affected the war against terror. He said, "The United States has every reason to worry about terrorism and instability in Pakistan. But allowing Musharraf to continue arresting judges and peaceful protesters will only strengthen the terrorist's hand. If we lock up our judges and subvert the legal process, then those who believe in a more brutal kind of justice will triumph". The international civil society including the Bar Associations and media launched a world wide movement against regime's impunity and for restoration of judiciary. The members of American Bar Association under the leadership of its President William Neukom came out on the streets to press for their demand[9]. Initially, the Western countries thought, perhaps, General Musharraf had a point. However, they soon discovered that his policies were counter productive and self-serving. Meanwhile, in U.S. Barak Obama was elected President. He realized his predecessor's flawed approach and stopped extending support to Musharraf which ultimately was one of the factors which led to latter's exit.

The General had a mind to prolong the State of Emergency. But certain political developments alluded to in the preceding para within and without Pakistan forced him to lift the State of Emergency and hold elections. One of such developments was the assassination of Mohtarma Benazir Bhutto on 27.12.2007.

After the general elections in February 2008, the Constitution was restored and an elected Government revived. General Musharraf resigned, and there was a growing demand for restoration of the Judges who had been removed from the Constitutional Courts. In September 2008, several of the deposed Judges were made to rejoin the Court (including the author), and finally, on 16 March 2009, the Chief Justice of Pakistan, Mr. Justice Iftikhar Muhammad

---

[8] 'Pakistan's Forgotten Man' Newsweek, February 2, 2008 and 'Justice for our Justice' Newsweek, June 21, 2008.

[9] Sindh High Court Bar Association v. Federation of Pakistan (PLD 2009 SC 879 at page 1089 para 116).

Chaudhry and the remaining deposed Judges were re-instated by the Prime Minister of Pakistan.

In countries deficit of constitutional culture, pressures visible and invisible have been exerted on judges to ensure their subservience to the Executive. Historically, assaults on judiciary have taken place in several jurisdictions and invariably they have been motivated by political considerations. During Muslim rule in medieval India, judicial independence was a highly valued trait. However, the conflict between the King and the court too was part of judicial history of those times. In 1248, the Chief Justice of Delhi was removed by the King; was tried on charges of high treason and executed. But the upright Chief Justice was a popular figure and so strong was people's reaction, that it ignited a rebellion and the King was executed by the rebels[10]. Assaults on judiciary mostly failed because they underpin a low moral ground and people have always valued an independent judiciary. As rightly remarked by Barry Friedman. 'From 200 years of challenges to judicial independence, some fairly clear lessons have emerged. First, attacks on the judiciary throughout history are inevitably political. By this I mean they are launched to express dissatisfaction with the content of particular judicial decisions. Second, those attacks have come from every point on the ideological spectrum. Third, virtually every technique one might think of to limit judicial decision making has already been suggested or tried. Finally, and most important, almost invariably challenges to judicial independence fail, because the public does not support them. Once the citizens of this country pay attention to the debate, they are approving of judicial independence and disapproving of attacks on it. Unquestionably this popular sentiment has grown over the course of the more than two centuries of attacks on the federal judiciary. In the rare instances in which Congress has taken steps to influence judicial decision making, the almost invariable public response has been regret[11].

During the 1988 Malaysian constitutional crisis, Tun Haji Mohamed Salleh bin Abas, a former Lord President of the Federal (later Supreme) Court of Malaysia, was suspended by Mahatir and attempts by the judiciary to have him restored were effectively thwarted by the Executive. The silver lining in the case of suspension of Pakistan's Chief Justice has been that although in a period of one year he was twice suspended, physically restrained from going to the office, yet he was restored initially by an independent judiciary and second by the movement spearheaded by the lawyers, civil society and media. They had overwhelming support of the people.

---

[10] 'The Administration of Justice in Medieval India' by Muhammad Basheer Ahmad, Page 108.

[11] Attacks on Judges: Why They Fall—http://www.ajs.org/cji/cji_attacks.asp

III. Restoration & March towards Constitutionalism

After resumption of office, the Chief Justice of Pakistan, Mr. Justice Iftikhar Muhammad Chaudhry reviewed the judgment[12] whereby during the interregnum (when he was deposed), the *de facto* Chief Justice had validated the unconstitutional acts of General Pervaiz Musharraf taken on 3rd of November, 2007. On 31st of July 2009, a 14-Member Bench of the Supreme Court comprising Judges who had not taken oath under P.C.O. (including the author), set aside the judgment which had validated General Musharraf's emergency and declared that[13] the Provisional Constitution Order issued by General Musharraf as Army Chief on 3rd of November, 2007 was ultra vires of the Constitution and all Judges who were retired/laid off for not taking oath under the said Order, were declared never to have been retired, the Judges who had taken oath under the P.C.O. (Provisional Constitution Order) were directed to be proceeded against on charges of misconduct and the code of conduct of Superior Court Judges was amended to provide that any Judge supporting an unconstitutional functionary would be guilty of misconduct.

IV. Judiciary & Enforcement of Human Rights

Persistent judicial deference to military takeovers prior to November 2007 has been subjected to adverse comment by jurists, members of the bar and leaders of public opinion. However, judicial review of military interventions is just one facet of the court's role in enforcement of fundamental rights and the ambit of constitutional law in Pakistan. There is a bigger area of litigation both public and private, where courts have demonstrated independence, vision and a deep commitment to the rule of law. The founding fathers of the 1973 Constitution laid down the foundations of a liberal democracy not only through its very Preamble but also in various specific provisions in the Constitution. In the Preamble, it has, *inter alia*, been mandated that the "State shall exercise its powers and authority through the chosen representatives of the people; wherein the principles of democracy, freedom, equality, tolerance and social justice, as enunciated by Islam, shall be fully observed; wherein adequate provision shall be made for the minorities freely to profess and practise their religions and develop their cultures; *and wherein the independence of the judiciary shall be fully, secured*." (Emphasis is supplied).

---

[12] Tikka Iqbal Muhammad Khan v. General Pervez Musharraf (PLD 2008 SC 178).
[13] Sindh High Court Bar Association v. Federation of Pakistan (PLD 2009 SC 879).

To ensure judicial independence, the Constitution embodied special provisions. It stipulated that, "the Judiciary shall be separated progressively from the Executive within a specific period[14]" The purpose of this provision was to secure complete independence of judiciary untrammelled by any executive encroachment and wherever the executive was found to be intermeddling with judicial functions, it was provided that judiciary would be extricated from that interference within a period specified in the Constitution. When the judiciary was not separated from the Executive by the said cut-off date, the Sindh High Court exercising its constitutional jurisdiction, directed the government to do so which judgment was upheld by the Supreme Court[15]. The Court spelt out the parameters of judicial independence in terms as under:-

(a) That every judge is free to decide matters before him in accordance with his assessment of the facts and his understanding of law without improper influences, inducements or pressures, direct or indirect, from any quarter, or for any reason; and
(b) That the judiciary is independent of the Executive and Legislature, and has jurisdiction, directly or by way of review, over all issues of judicial nature[16].

It was only after this judgment that Judicial Magistrates were separated from the Executive. It is at this level of judicial hierarchy where almost 80% of the litigation originates and is decided[17]. The constitutional provision which has been given effect to by judicial verdict is not only in accord with the fundamental rights guaranteed under the Constitution but also reflects the spirit of Article 14.1 of the International Covenant on Civil and Political Rights which mandates

> All persons shall be equal before the courts and tribunals. In the determination also of any criminal charge against him, or his rights and obligations in a suit of law, everyone shall be entitled to a fair and public hearing by a competent, independent and impartial tribunal established by law.

The courts particularly the Supreme Court in several judgments have given liberal interpretation to fundamental rights provisions of the Constitution and thereby promoted the Rule of Law and democratic norms. In one case the Supreme Court interpreted the right to freedom of association to include the right of a political party to keep functioning[18]. It further expanded this right by

---

[14] Article 175(3) of the Constitution.
[15] Govt. of Sindh v. Sharaf Faridi (PLD 1994 SC 105).
[16] Government of Sindh v. Sharaf Faridi and others (PLD 1994 SC 105 at p. 107, 115, 116).
[17] A Chart showing Organization and strength of Judicial Hierarchy is attached with this paper.
[18] Abul Alamaudoodi v. the State, PLD 1964 SC 673 (Pak).

holding that a political party, if in power, has the right to complete its term unless its Government is ousted under the Constitution[19]. Notwithstanding the 8th Amendment to the Constitution which had the effect of depriving certain political rights in a democracy, the Supreme Court interpreted fundamental rights provisions, directive principles of state policy and the Objective Resolutions[20] in a dynamic and purposive manner. In *Benazir Bhutto's case*[21], the Court in a landmark judgment upheld the principles of rule of law and liberal democracy in observing that while interpreting the Court, "must receive inspiration from the triad of provisions which saturate and invigorate the entire Constitution, namely, the Objectives Resolution (Article 2-A), the Fundamental Rights and the directive principles of State policy so as to achieve democracy, tolerance, equality and social justice according to Islam."

In certain cases, the superior courts acted as "social engineers" and catalysts of social change. Pakistan is a male dominated society where instances are not lacking when women were deprived of their right to inherit property, despite the mandate of law, through involuntary surrender. There have been instances when adult women were denied the right to marry a person of their choice or when they were given in marriage without their consent. The court, when called upon to decide such matters, laid down law, which had the effect of changing the unjust customs and mores. For instance, in a case of denial of right to inherit property, the Supreme Court held that this being a gross violation of fundamental right of a socially disadvantaged gender, claims could be filed even long after expiry of the prescribed period of limitation[22].

Similarly, there was a socially sanctified tradition under which even a sui-juris woman could not marry without permission of her guardian. In a case where an adult girl married a person of her choice, her father, relying on a document evidencing a fake and illegal marriage with her cousin, launched criminal prosecution for adultery against her, and she was arrested. The matter was brought before the High Court; it not only declared counter marriage as illegal but quashed the criminal proceedings[23].

In certain remote areas of our country there is a custom of giving young and even minor girls in marriage as a settlement in blood feuds. The Supreme Court interfered in such cases, the state functionaries were reprimanded for

---

[19] Nawaz Sharif v. President of Pak (PLD 1993 SC 473 (Pak).

[20] Article 2-A: It laid down the socio-economical and political vision for the polity. It was passed by all political parties in 1949, but was made substantive part of the Constitution by insertion of Article 2-A to the Constitution through the 8th Amendment in 1985.

[21] Benazir Bhutto v. Federation of Pakistan (PLD 1988 SC 416).

[22] PLD 1970 SC 1 (Pak).

[23] Humaira v. State PLD 1999 Lahore 494 (Pak).

apathy, and a direction was issued to the government to take preventive and punitive action in such cases. Because of the court interventions, the law was amended, and now it is a Penal offence to give a young girl in marriage as a settlement of a blood feud.

In terrorism related cases, the Supreme Court has been particularly strict. It upheld the Anti Terrorism Act by holding that the legislature could pass a special law to cater for such heinous crimes[24]. It chided the High Court for being too liberal in cases under the Anti Terrorist Laws[25]. The court has always maintained, however, that while investigating such cases, canons of due process should be duly observed. Because when the law enforcement agencies roughshod the law in the name of terror, it amounts to playing on the wicket of the terrorists who wreak violence in disregard to law. The role of the judiciary in a constitutional democracy is to protect the liberty, the due process and the Rule of Law.

Conscious of the fact that the independence of judiciary is inextricably linked with the appointment and selection process of judges and with a view to ensure judicial autonomy in the process, the Constitution originally mandated the appointment of Judges of High Court by the President after consultation (a) with the Chief Justice of Pakistan; (b) with the Governor concerned and (c) except where the appointment is that of Chief Justice of High Court, with the Chief Justice of the concerned High Court. This mode of appointment has now been changed through 19th Amendment[26] whereby the appointments are made by the President but through a two tier process i.e. a Judicial Commission[27] headed by the Chief Justice of Pakistan recommends the names of candidates for appointment to the Parliamentary Committee[28]. The Committee can confirm the recommendations made and send the names to the President for appointment within a period of 14 days of the nomination received and if no decision is taken by the Parliamentary Committee, the names shall be deemed to have been confirmed for formal appointment by the President. The Committee may not confirm the nominations by 3/4th of its

---

[24] Mehram Ali v. Federation of Pakistan (PLD 1998 SC 1445 (Pak).

[25] Mirza Shaukat Baig v. Shahid Jamil (PLD 2005 SC 530 (Pak) 14.

[26] Assented by President on 1.1.2011 and published in Official Gazette on 4.1.2011.

[27] Article 175-A—Judicial Commission consisting of Chief Justice of Pakistan (chairman), two most senior Judges of the Supreme Court, a former Chief Justice or a former Judge of the Supreme Court, Federal Minister for Law and Justice, Attorney General for Pakistan and a senior Advocate of the Supreme court to be nominated by Pakistan Bar Council.

[28] Parliamentary Committee consisting of four members from the Senate and four members from the National Assembly, out of the eight members, four shall be from the Treasury Benches, two from each House and four from the Opposition Benches, two from each House.

total membership and in that eventuality, the Judicial Commission is required to send fresh nominations. I would not like to comment any further with regard to the change in the appointment process as the matter is subjudice before a Bench of which I am a member but suffice it to say that according to the proponents of this amendment, under the newly added provision, the names of candidates for appointment to the Supreme court and High Court are to originate within the Judicial Commission and the Parliamentary Committee is given a cut-off period (14 days) within which it has to decide to confirm or not to confirm the recommendations made failing which the nominations would be deemed to have been confirmed. Its detractors, on the other hand, find it flawed, as according to their understanding, the parliamentary Committee has been given a veto power which is likely to politicize the appointment process and thereby impair judicial independence.

Yet another provision which buttresses judicial independence is the clog on parliamentary power that it can legislate on any item in the Federal Legislative List except the Supreme Court i.e. the powers of the Supreme Court can be enlarged and not curtailed[29]. To insulate the judiciary from any discussion or controversy in the Parliament, it has been specifically provided in the Constitution that no discussion shall take place in the Parliament with respect to the conduct of a Judge of Supreme Court or of High Court in the discharge of his duties[30].

The judiciary has also been given financial autonomy by providing that all expenditure on judiciary would be charged upon the Federal Consolidated Fund and Provincial Consolidated Fund in terms of Article 81 and 121 of the Constitution and such expenditure shall be immune from discussion or vote in the Parliament[31]. The Constitution also provides security of tenure for the Judges of the High Courts and Supreme Court. There is a retirement age i.e. in case of Judges of High Court it is 62 years and in case of Judges of Supreme Court, it is 65 years. The Judges can only be removed on the ground of misconduct by a Supreme Judicial Council headed by the Chief Justice of Pakistan and comprising serving Judges[32].

With a view to ensure that the orders passed by the Supreme Court are given effect to, the Constitution commands that all executive and judicial authorities throughout Pakistan shall act in aid of the Supreme Court[33].

---

[29] Entry No. 55 of Part I in the 4th Schedule to the Constitution.
[30] Article 68 of the Constitution.
[31] Article 82 of the Constitution of Islamic Republic of Pakistan.
[32] Article 209 of the Constitution of Islamic Republic of Pakistan.
[33] Article 190 of the Constitution of Islamic Republic of Pakistan.

V. Ideological Moorings and Common Law Traditions

The textual assertions and other seminal values enshrined in the Constitution suggest that both institutional and functional independence of judiciary was sought to be secured by the constitution makers. However, the practical application of these provisions has depended besides the character of the individual Judge, on other factors as well. In Pakistan some of the factors which have supplemented these provisions and given them practical meaning are the ideological moorings of the State, the Common Law traditions of the rule of law, the international conventions on human rights and the courageous role played by the bar as also the independent media. They constitute the prime elements of "constitutional culture"[34] which sustain judicial independence and the rule of law.

Although Muslim history is mostly replete with arbitrary rulers but at conceptual plane dispensation of justice through judicial independence has been given the status of divine virtue in Islam and the traditions of its application in golden periods of Muslim history abound. As per Holy Quran, to dispense justice without fear is a command from the Almighty:

> Allah commands you to deliver whatever you have been entrusted with to their rightful owner and whenever you judge between people, judge with justice. Most excellent is what Allah exhorts you to do. Allah hears all and see all. (4:58)

Justice is one of the cherished goals in all religions. Reiterating the Quranic command, Prophet Muhammad(PBUH) once said, "a moment of justice delivered is more valued than sixty nights of worship[35]."

Pakistan's colonial legacy bequeathed a reservoir of common law traditions. The history of attainment of judicial independence in England, the effect of Justice Cook's stand against the King in defence of the rule of law in 1616, the passage of the Act of Settlement whereby the statutory recognition to the principle of judicial independence was given for the first time and the adoption of Magna Carta are some of the milestones which shaped institutions and contributed towards the growth of rule of law and judicial independence in India under the British rule. Some of these values, traditions and institutions were also inherited by Pakistan.

---

[34] 'Toward a General Theory' by Peter H. Russell in 'Judicial Independence in the Age of Democracy: Critical Perspectives from around the World' edited by Peter H. Russell and David M. O'Brien, Page No.5.

[35] "KASHFUL KHIFA" Volume II by Ahmad Alqlash as quoted by Justice Tassaduq Hussain in his article titled as, "Democracy and Islam: An Odyssey in Braving the Twenty-first Century" published in Brigham Young University Utta,.

The Role of the Bar, Civil Society & Media:

The role played by the Bar has been a source of immense strength for advancement of constitutionalism in the country. The empirical research indicates that not only in Pakistan but in several other jurisdictions, lawyers have played seminal role in mobilizing public opinion to defend the rule of law and judicial independence. According to Terence C. Halliday, "the national case studies establish, first, that in widely varying times and places lawyers mobilize frequently on behalf of political liberalism; second, that in various configurations lawyers are often but not invariably joined by other legal professions, including judges and legal academics, and occasionally prosecutors and state lawyers, and third, that on many occasions this mobilization is associated with the obtaining, consolidating, or protecting of basic legal freedoms[36]." In Pakistan the Bar Associations are highly organized bodies and they exert influence in politics and public sphere through lobbying, resolutions and even taking out processions. Their services in defence of the rule of law have been recognized by various bar associations around the world. In 2008, the American Bar Association awarded its 2008 the Rule of Law Award to the Judges and lawyers, "for their courage in defending the rule of law" and the author was invited to receive the award on behalf of Judges.

Chief Justice William Rehnquist of the Unites States Supreme Court once remarked, "Justice is too important a matter to be left to the judges, or even to the lawyers; the American people must think about, discuss, and contribute to the future planning of their courts[37]." This aptly describes the role which the civil society and media have played in promoting judicial independence and the rule of law at various levels. "The media offer great potential to spearhead and to amplify the campaigns of other groups for the rule of law. In principle, they can broadcast points of view, call to arms, mobilize publics and mediate public exchanges among the legal complex, civil society and publics[38]." In Pakistan they have been catalyst in creating greater awareness among the public regarding issues which impinge their basic rights and freedoms, in highlighting the importance of judicial independence and the rule of law. In the judicial crisis of 2007, judiciary in Pakistan led by its Chief Justice in an unprecedented move stood up against assault on its independence and it was the

[36] 'The fight for basic legal freedoms: Mobilization by the legal complex' by Terence C. Halliday in 'Global Perspectives on the Rule of Law by James J. Heckman, Robert L. Nelson and Lee Cabatingan, Page # 211.

[37] 'Civil Society Contributions to Judicial Independence' by Stephen Golub, in 'Guidance for Promoting Judicial Independence and Impartiality' Revised Edition January 2002.

[38] 'The fight for basic legal freedoms: Mobilization by the legal complex' by Terence C. Halliday in 'Global Perspectives on the Rule of Law by James J. Heckman, Robert L. Nelson and Lee Cabatingan, Page # 226.

media which brought the issue to public focus in a manner which energized and mobilized all the stake holders to rise in defence of the rule of law. The judiciary for the first time refused to validate the imposition of an unconstitutional state of emergency. General Musharraf attempted to foist a pliable judiciary after suspending the Chief Justice but on account of the activist civil society and the media educating the public, there was a massive condemnation of General's act and support for the Chief Justice. Never before the lawyers, the members of the civil society and the public at large came out on streets in defence of judiciary and the rule of law. This awareness augurs well for sustenance of the values and institutions which the constitution enshrines.

VI. Judiciary as a Catalyst of Social Change

Pakistan has a declared State religion. But there is a comprehensive chapter in the Constitution on Fundamental Rights which includes freedom of religion. The Courts through their judgments have endeavoured to ensure that the enjoyment of this right does not lead to a myopic view of religion or infringes a similar right of other religious minorities or that it does not violate the fundamental rights' provisions of the Constitution. A recent case in point is that of Hisba Bill (Law of accountability under Sharia) where a Provincial Assembly passed a law to enforce a parallel system of accountability and dispensation of justice in the name of Islam. The Court declared it as violative of the Constitution and directed the Governor of the said Province not to give assent to it[39].

The courts while dispensing justice have generally tried to balance the principle of judicial independence with canons of judicial restraint. The courts and in particular the Supreme Court has broadly kept three considerations in view. First, that Judiciary is one of the three organs of the state, and good governance is possible only if they remain within their defined limits. Second, the law may not keep pace with the changing times and may not respond to every situation. The Court has a role to bridge the gap between the law and the society[40]. This consideration is particularly relevant to the powers of the Supreme Court under Article 184 (3) of the Constitution. Third, the court has been conscious that as a member of the United Nations and being part of a global community, Pakistan has certain obligations under the international law. It is an interdependent world. Any activity within the country that has or has a potential to

[39] PLD 2005 SC 873 (Opinion of Supreme Court in Reference No. 2 of 2005 on Hasba Bill Case).

[40] Justice Barak, supra FN 19.

have nexus with a crime committed outside the country, be it a financial crime or an act of terror, has to be brought to justice under the law.

The Supreme Court (under Article 184(3) of the constitution in its attempt to ensure substantive justice has given an extended meaning to the fundamental right of right to life[41]. The Court held that life has a larger concept which includes the right of enjoyment of life, maintaining adequate level of living for full enjoyment of freedom and rights[42]. To ensure pollution free environment, the court declared that any action which may create hazards to life will be encroachment on personal rights to enjoy the life according to law[43]. The conviction by a Military Court not empowered to try under the law was held to be violative of Article 9 of the Constitution[44]. The Court annulled the privatization of Pakistan Steel Mills Corporation as the process lacked transparency and was found to be against public policy and national interest[45]. In yet another case, the Court upheld the institutional authority and observed that, "a nation which fails to respect the institutions falls in grace, decays, splits and is condemned in history. A society bereft of stable institutions would be at odds with itself[46]."

Every Judge, be it of the High Court or the Supreme Court, before he enters the mantle of his calling, makes an oath that he/she will abide by the code of conduct issued by the Supreme Judicial Council; will not allow his/her personal interest to influence official conduct or official decisions; will preserve, protect and defend the Constitution of the Islamic Republic of Pakistan.

Epilogue

These solemn affirmations reflect the vision and promise of judicial independence in Pakistan. The spirit of this oath echoes in the code of conduct at every level of judicial hierarchy. In launching the movement for restoration of judiciary and its independence, by risking their lives and livelihood, the lawyers, the civil society and public at large demonstrated that "Liberty lies in the hearts of men and women[47]". Through their blood and sweat, they have given life and meaning to the "constitutional culture" of which they were accused of being

[41] Article 9 of the Constitution.
[42] The Employee of Pakistan Law Commission Islamabad v. Ministry of Works (1994 SCMR 1548).
[43] Ms. Shehla Zia v. WAPDA (PLD 1994 SC 693).
[44] Sh. Liaquat Hussain v. Federation of Pakistan (PLD 1999 SC 504).
[45] Watan Party v. Federation of Pakistan (PLD 2006 SC 697).
[46] Pakistan Medical and Dental Council v. Ziauddin Medical University (Civil Appeal No. 2206 of 2005).
[47] Famous quote by Learned Hand in "The Spirit of Liberty" a speech at "I am an American Day" ceremony, Central Park, New York City (21 May 1944).

bereft. The moral high ground of political sovereign's victory in the battle for the rule of law has placed the judiciary under a debt, a challenge and a vigil. The future of judicial independence in the polity would be defined in how this debt is discharged, how the challenge is met and how eternal is the vigil.

ORGANISATION AND STRENGTH OF JUDICIAL HIERARCHY

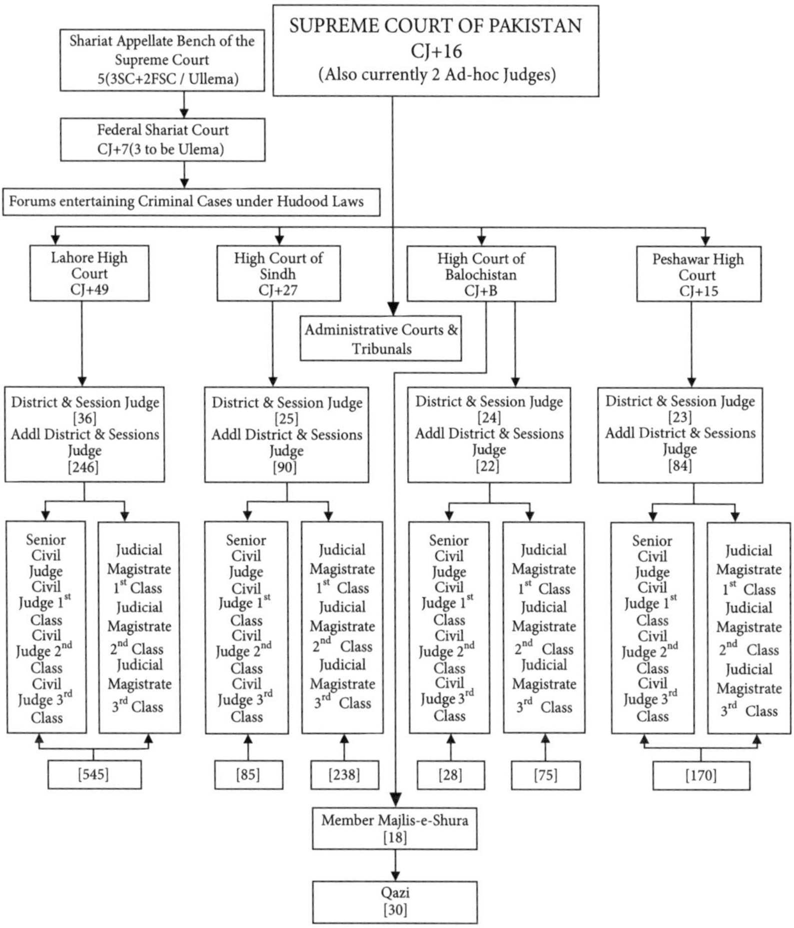

Note:

1. In Punjab, 55 District & Sessions Judges, 34 Additional District & Sessions Judges and 23 Senior/Civil Judges and Judicial Magistrates are working on ex cadre posts.
2. In Sindh, 42 District & Sessions Judges, 9 Additional District & Sessions Judges and 8 Senior/Civil Judges and 11 Judicial Magistrates are working on ex cadre posts.
3. In Balochistan, 5 District & Sessions Judges, 4 Additional District & Sessions Judges, 7 Senior/Civil Judges and Judicial Magistrates are working on ex cadre posts.
4. In NWFP, 31 District & Sessions Judges, 19 Additional District & Sessions Judges and 17 Senior/Civil Judges and Judicial Magistrates are working on ex cadre posts.

CHAPTER THIRTY

THE RELEVANCE FOR BRAZIL OF INTERNATIONAL STANDARDS OF JUDICIAL INDEPENDENCE

Ada Pellegrini Grinover

I. The Brazilian Legal System

Brazil is considered to have a legal system of "civil law", but one can also find many concepts of "common law" in it. Enrico Tullio Liebman, who deeply studied the Brazilian law during his stay in São Paulo, where he sheltered from the war, said that the Brazilian legal system blended the features of both systems.

In 1981, as from the Republic, the Brazilian federation was inspired by the North-Americans in order to create the Brazilian Constitution and, therefore, some concepts of the procedural law have also been directly taken from the common law. In the same way, we do not have the administrative jurisdictions and, as it happens in the United States, the ordinary courts are competent for whichever type of lawsuit or of issue. Also, we have learned from the United States that several writs can be regarded as instruments of constitutional guarantee: the "habeas corpus", for the protection of the personal freedom even as a preventive measure; the injunction, for the protection of the rights different from those regarding freedom and even against the illegal or abusive jurisdictional act. As from the 1988 Constitution, the "habeas data" was created for the protection of the information data. The 1934 Constitution included the popular actions. In Brazil the popular actions are corrective, that is, the lawsuit is filed against the administration for the protection of the public goods and values. We have a constitutional control, like in the USA, either diffuse or concentrated; therefore, the judges may or may not apply the law if they consider it constitutionally legal or illegal. Similar is the direct action of constitutional legitimacy, which is the Federal Supreme Court's competence and was based on the American Supreme Court's actions.

II. The Powers of the Brazilian Judge

The Brazilian judge holds strong powers. First of all, I would remember the legislative introduction of the so-called mandatory provisions – largely corresponding to the injunctions – initially in the field of the diffuse and collective rights or interests and, then, as a general rule of the procedural system, based on a new rule of 1996, which regulated the obligations to do or not to do. Those must be put into effect in a specific way, either by means of indirect constraint, like the *astreintes*, or by means of direct constraint imposed by the judge, who can change the provision of the sentence into another provision specifically meant to reach the results that would have been obtained if the obligation had been implemented. An example concerning the environment would be the obligation of a company to prevent pollution. The judge can apply the *astraintes* or, at the same time, he can transform the negative obligation of not polluting into a positive one of installing a filter. If this task is not accomplished, the judge can go beyond and determine that a third party installs the filter at the expenses of the party. In case this cannot be done either, the closing of the plant shall be determined. Another example could be the anticipated protection as a general principle of the legal system with characteristics that differ from those of the provisional protection because it is a matter of anticipating effectively, partially or totally, the effects of the decision. Also in this matter the judge holds strong discretionary powers, although the law evidently establishes the conditions and the limits of the anticipated protection.

One can notice that the Brazilian judge, even without having the defining function of the North American judge, has been invested with large discretionary powers. The Brazilian legislator, influenced by the procedural law scholars that were in charge of the changes, invested the judge with confidence, maybe because the work can be very well controlled. The Appellate Court can immediately suspend the anticipated protection determined by the judge of the trial court and an injunction against the jurisdictional act would be adequate to this situation.

That confidence is based on a political position since Brazil, like many countries in Latin America, is hostile and suspicious concerning the government – given to previous authoritarian governments. However, people have much confidence in the judge and in the administration of the justice. Naturally, there are controls and limits like those that refer to the application of the principle of reazonability, a not written constitutional principle and considered a principle of necessity and adequacy between the means and the goals.

In this context it is important to assure the independence and the impartiality both of the Judiciary as a whole as well as of each judge individually. The Brazilian Constitution is in charge of this.

III. The Independence and the Impartiality of the Judiciary in Brazil

The condition of the Judiciary as the protector of the individual freedom can only be preserved through its independence and impartiality. Thus, it is extremely important to analyze the guarantees that the Brazilian Constitution established in order to save that impartiality and independence.

Some guarantees refer to the Judiciary considered as a whole and are intended to defend it from the influence of the other branches – the government and the Legislative. Other guarantees, however, refer directly to the organs of the Judiciary and particularly to the judges.

Those guarantees correspond to the *political independence* of the Judiciary and its organs and are characterized by the self-governing of the bench, the security of tenure, unremovability, irreducible earnings and the prohibition to perform certain activities, which will assure the parties of the judges' impartiality.

Based on the political independence there is also the judges' *juridical independence*, which exempts them from any kind of hierarchical subordination in their professional activities: the judges are dependent only on the law and are totally free to work on their decisions and to follow the dictates of their own conscience.

The juridical independence, however, does not exclude the censorious activity of the disciplinary organs of the bench over the administrative aspects of the judges' behaviour.

IV. The Guarantees of the Judiciary as a Whole

The Brazilian Constitution assures the Judiciary of the prerogative of self-governing by applying normative and administrative action of self-organization and self-regulation.

According to the Brazilian Constitutional order, the guarantee of self-governing includes not only the administrative but also the financial autonomy, which means that the courts have the prerogative to make and control their own budget.

Then, the courts have some tasks such as to nominate their controlling organs and prepare their statutes[1]; to organize their secretariats and supporting services as well as of all their related courts[2]; to provide the judges' positions[3]; to plan the creation of new courts[4]; to provide the jobs which are necessary to run the judiciary[5]; to be in charge of the vacation or leave of absence of their members, judges or agents[6].

1 article 96, item I, a of the Constitution
2 article 96, item I, b of the Constitution
3 article 96,item I, c of the Constitution
4 article 96, item I, d of the Constitution
5 article 96, item I, e of the Constitution
6 article 96, item I, f of the Constitution

The Supreme Court of Brazil, the Courts of Appeals and the Supreme Courts of the States have the power to change the number of members in the inferior courts because of their legislative initiative[7]. They can also create and extinguish jobs and positions as well as determine the earnings of their members and judges and the cost for their supporting services and for their related courts[8]. They are allowed to create or extinguish the inferior courts[9] and to change the judiciary's organization and divisions[10].

The guarantees in the article 96 of the Constitution basically aim at establishing the independence of the judiciary towards the other governmental branches. This independence is absolute considering the performance of their professional activities. However, it does not apply to the Judiciary's organization, which usually depends on the Government or the Legislative and, sometimes, on both.

Concerning to the Supreme Court and the Federal Court of Appeals the judges are appointed by the Government with the approval of the Senate.

That is why the independence of the Judiciary is absolute as far as their activities are concerned but it is not absolute concerning to establishing some courts.

V. The Guarantees for the Judges

To start a career in Brazil, the applicants are supposed to go through an exam and the analysis of their background. Their political guarantees complement those of the Judiciary as a whole.

There are two kinds of guarantees for the judges. On one hand, there are the guarantees intended to protect the judges' independence, even towards other organs of the Judiciary. On the other hand, there are certain impediments that provide the conditions of impartiality and protect the judges against themselves; consequently, the parties are granted the assurance that the judges' performance will be impartial.

The former guarantee (independence) is represented by the tenure, unremovability and irreducible earnings[11]. The latter (the impediments that grant the impartiality) is listed in the paragraph of the article 95 in the Constitution.

---

[7] article 96, item II, a of the Constitution
[8] article 96, item II, b of the Constitution
[9] article 96, item II, c of the Constitution
[10] article 96, item II, d of the Constitution
[11] article 95

Those guarantees for the judges include only the bench. The jury, the Justice of the Peace, the arbitrators and the conciliators are out.

VI. Guarantees of Independence

Tenure means that the judges will keep their position unless a *judicial decision* states otherwise[12]. There is a difference between tenure (ensured by the Constitution for the judges, members of the Prosecution Department and Audit Court) and the job stability that is granted to the other civil servants[13], which means that they will keep their position unless a judicial decision *or an administrative proceeding* determines otherwise.

The first degree judges are granted the tenure two years after starting their professional activities and may be dismissed during that time in case there is a decision from the court they work for[14]. This is because there is no prerequisite to work in a juridical profession before being approved in the entrance exam.

The tenure does not prevent the judges from retiring compulsorily because of public interest, or because they become seventy years old, or because of a disabling disease[15], or even because two thirds of the members of the court voted for a judge's temporary withdrawal from work, in the case which they still have the right of defense[16].

To require that a judge is temporarily withdrawn from work or that a judge retires as per the steps of the article 93, item VIII of the constitution, the Judiciary will start an administrative proceeding, which may be subject to a jurisdictional revision in view of a judicial decision. The same happens when the judges are dismissed while on probation[17]. Unremovability means that the judges may not be removed from one place to another unless they consent to it[18].

The unremovability comprehends the degree, the venue, the jurisdiction, the judicial section, the position, the court and the division. For the unremovability there is not any possibility of exception without the judges' consent, not even in case of a promotion. However, if it is the case of public interest and if it is approved by two thirds of the court's permanent members, the consent is unnecessary.

---

12 article 95, item I
13 article 41, paragraph 1
14 article 95, item I of the constitution
15 article 93, item VI
16 article 93, item VIII
17 article 95, item I
18 article 95, item II

For the removal and temporary withdrawal from work, the rules are the same, that is, it depends on an administrative decision which is subject to a jurisdictional revision by means of a lawsuit.

The issue of irreducible earnings ensured by the article 95, item III does not avoid tax collection, according to the rule[19].

VII. Impediments as Guarantees of Impartiality

The judges' constitutional impediments refer to the prohibitions that aim at providing the judges with better conditions of impartiality and, consequently, those conditions will represent a guarantee for the litigants.

Except for teaching, the paragraph in article 95 of the Constitution does not allow the judges to have another job or position even if they are temporarily withdrawn from work (item I). Also, the judges are forbidden to: receive, by no means, costs or incentive in a lawsuit (item II); act for a political party (item III); "receive, under no excuse, support or contributions from individual persons or private or public legal entities, except for the situations allowed by the law" (item IV); "to act as an attorney in the court they quit, within two years from the date they left their job, because of retirement or dismissal" (item V – this is a rule called "quarantine")

The National Council of Justice is responsible for the enforcement of the impediments and accomplishments of the duties assigned to the judges. The Council has strong censorious and disciplinary power over the judges[20]. The Council may be called for by any interested person or by the Justice Complaints Department, which will receive and be in charge of the complaints lodged against irregular procedures[21].

VIII. The Relevance for Brazil of International Standards of Judicial Independence

In the first place it is worth observing that almost all the international standards of judicial independence, as approved in the draft, are duly covered by the Brazilian Constitution, which is adjusted to those standards.

However, there are still some points for which the above mentioned international standards of judicial independence, as approved in the draft, may be

[19] articles 150, item II and 153, item III
[20] article 92, item I-A of the Constitution
[21] article 103 B, paragraph, items II and III paragraph 5, item I and paragraph 7

useful in Brazil, boosting reforms which can assure more and more the independence and impartiality of the Judiciary and the judges. That is what will be analyzed next.

1. *The Budget of the Judiciary*

In Brazil the Judiciary has the prerogative to elaborate the budget (article 99) and, then, to deal with the endowments. But the proposal is not binding. The budget is made and presented by the government to the Legislative for approval. This way, costs are usually cut by the government and, consequentially, the Judiciary, as a whole, go trough difficult financial situations; therefore, some of the principles in the approved draft of international standards cannot be applied (2.20, 2.21).

2. *The Media and the Judiciary*

The principles established by the approved draft for this issue are very useful for Brazil. The media do not restrain any publications towards pending cases or criticism of judicial decisions. Some judges are used to having interviews directly with the general media. A spokesperson assigned by the courts is not typical in Brazil (6.1, 6.2, and 6.3).

3. *The Judges' Standards of Conducts*

The Brazilian judges do not have other professional activities, except for teaching. But a rule as nr 7.4 of the approved draft can be very useful.

4. *Contact with a Party*

Although the rule nr 21.2, part "B" of the approved draft is intended only for the international judges[22], I think that it should be applied to the judges in general. In Brazil, it is common that the parties hand in, before the judgment, a brief to the court's members. Those briefs are not submitted to disclosure to the court and to the other party. Number 21.2 "B" is very useful for the Brazilian courts.

IX. Conclusion

In Brazil, it is certain that the constitutional guarantees for the Judiciary and for the judges adequately assure their independency and impartiality and most

[22] - Por sugestão da Autora, a regra passou a constar também em relação aos juízes nacionais (Parte A, n. 7.11).

of the rules coincide with those established in the international standards of judicial independence as approved in the draft.

However, there are some topics of the international standards that may be taken in order to improve the independence and impartiality of the Judiciary and the Brazilian judges.

They are: the budget of the judiciary, the media and the judiciary, some standards of conduct of the judge, and the contact between the judge and a party.

CHAPTER THIRTY ONE

THE ROLE OF LAW IN SOCIETY IN DEVELOPING COUNTRIES

*Chandra R. de Silva**

This chapter[1] makes three fairly simple and related propositions: a) that in developing countries[2] there is a greater dissonance between formal legal systems and society than in developed countries, b) that paradoxically, greater burdens are placed on the generally weaker legal systems in these developing countries, and finally c) that legal systems play a larger formative role in developing countries than in developed countries. It will then consider some implications of these propositions. The chapter will not deal with the interactions of law and society in areas of intense political turmoil, and questions of law and society in repressive societies.

David Nelken, in a paper delivered at the Annual Drapkin Conference at the Faculty of Law at Hebrew University, Jerusalem analyzed the contribution of social sciences to law.[3] He pointed out that most of us agree that social scientists provide both theoretical insights and empirical findings which enable judges to understand social conditions. Social science is an analytic tool in the law, and familiarity with it will heighten the lawyer's professional effectiveness and sharpen the legal scholar's insight. But he also pointed out that the purposes of law, and those of the social sciences, are very different, and warned against too ready an acceptance of the theoretical assumptions of social sciences. As a social scientist, I remind you of his caution.

The ensuing analysis of the role of law in developing countries requires that special care be given to maintaining the principle and culture of judicial independence in these countries.

---

* Chandra R. de Silva is Professor of History and Special Assistant to the Provost at Old Dominion University. He has written extensively on contemporary education, ethnicity and politics in Sri Lanka.

[1] This is a revised version of the 2010 Daniel Jacobson Lecture delivered at the Hebrew University, Jerusalem on May 16, 2010.

[2] The use of the terms 'developing' and 'developed' in this article should not be taken to imply a stance in the debate on the nature of development. The terms are simply used to indicate different levels of wealth and for the purpose of this article the terms 'underdeveloped' and 'developed' could be substituted without prejudice to the argument.

[3] Paper presented on March 13, 2001. For the text, *see* David Nelken, *Beyond Law in Context, Developing a Sociological Understanding of Law*, (Farnham: Ashgate, 2009) pp. 193–212.

I. The Story of Ameena: An Illustrative Case Study

On August 10, 1991, on a flight from Hyderabad (India) to Delhi (on the way to Riyadh), Ameena, a child of 10–12 years of age was seen crying and passengers reported this to the airhostess. The child told the airhostess (Amrita Ahuwalia) that she had been married in her native city of Hyderabad, without her consent to the sixty-year old man seated beside her, Yahya Mohammed al-Sageih, a Saudi national. It later came out that al-Sageih had arrived in Hyderabad on July 28, and met Ameena's family on August 7 through a marriage broker. They were married the next day. When the plane landed in Delhi, the airhostess complained to the authorities, and the police arrested al-Sageih. Ameena was produced before a magistrate who sent her temporarily to a destitute women's home (*Nari Nikethan*). According to her passport and her marriage certificate, her age was listed as 35. The parents claimed that she was 18. A medical exam and Ameena's own statements suggested that she was eleven or twelve. al-Sageih was said to have paid the father, Badruddin, Rs. 6000 as marriage settlement (*mehr*).

Media frenzy resulted. Airhostess Ahuwalia petitioned for custody of Ameena. Women's groups (*Saheli* and *Janwadi Mahila Samithi*) protested at placing her in a destitute women's home and applied for custody of Ameena. al-Sageih was granted bail on condition he did not leave the country and found refuge in the Saudi Arabian embassy in Delhi. When Ameena was produced in the magistrate's court on August 13, the court moved her to a short-term home, and directed the Juvenile Justice Court to decide on an appropriate residence. Ameena then wanted to return to her parents. The father was a three-wheeler scooter driver with eight children who lived in a poverty-stricken neighborhood in Hyderabad. Ameena was the second of five daughters. The parents came to Delhi on August 29 and filed a petition for their daughter, claiming that the marriage was in accordance with Muslim law. The court rejected all petitions for custody on September 3, and ordered that Ameena should be kept in a home for children for three months. By December 5, the three months had gone by and the Juvenile Justice Board was no nearer a solution. The Delhi High Court intervened and requested for swift action. On March 4, 1992, the Juvenile Justice Board found the parents 'unfit,' and ordered that Ameena should be transferred to a service home in Hyderabad for three years. However, a two-justice bench of the Delhi High Court intervened again. On March 11, 1992, the judges ascertained from Ameena that she wished to go home, and questioned the father on his willingness to take custody. The father, Badruddin, produced affidavits from respectable Hyderabad citizens, and on March 12, the court ordered the return of Ameena to her parents subject to monitoring of Ameena's welfare by the magistrate's court in Hyderabad.

Meanwhile Delhi city police filed criminal charges against al-Sageih and the parents under the Indian Penal Code for abduction (Section 366), cheating and forgery and using forged documents (Sections 420, 467, & 486), sale of a minor for prostitution (Section 372), purchase of a minor for prostitution (Section 373) and conspiracy for these offences (Section 120), as well as section 4 of the Child Marriage Restraint Act (1928 as amended in 1978).[4] The parents were arrested in Hyderabad on the criminal case and released on bond on January 3, 1992. The criminal case against al-Sageih and the parents continued independent of the custody issue. The three accused appeared before the city magistrate on February 21, 1992 and the case, referred to the Sessions Court, resumed on September 9. Al-Sageih's defense counsel, Irshad Ullah Khan argued that Ameena was not coerced, and that the marriage was valid under Muslim personal law. The court ruled against him, and let the prosecution proceed, but on November 17, Ameena appeared in court and (in the judge's chambers) insisted that she had consented to the marriage and testified that her age was 16 or 17 though she did not know her date of birth. This weakened the prosecution case and in July 1993, al-Sageih jumped bail and fled to Saudi Arabia. The case fizzled out.

Ameena did not benefit from the publicity. She could not attend the technical schools established to give opportunities for Muslim girls in Hyderabad because she was in *purdah*.[5] Some lawyers advocated criminalizing child marriages and punishing the parents, but child marriage is widespread in India (In 2009, the average age of females at marriage in India was 21 years).

II. The dissonance Between Law and Society in Developing Countries

One of the issues that the story of Ameena touches is the question of legal pluralism or the question of what law or whose law? In many developing countries (as well as in a few developed countries) there is a conflict between 'local customs' sanctioned by long usage and social acceptance, as against laws imposed by the state and by international obligations of the state. [6] Customs are hard to override because they are bound with culture and involve a sense of obligation

[4] The revised law prescribes the minimum age for marriage as 18 for women and 21 for men.

[5] The practice of preventing women being seen by men (other than their husbands) through seclusion and by requiring women to cover their bodies and conceal their form.

[6] Shimon Shetreet, *Law and Social Pluralism, op. cit.*, pp. 305–306. "In the beginning it is a behaviour in certain situations by a certain group. Finally, a custom is formed out of the expected behaviour, and this behaviour becomes binding and enforceable."

and duty. One of the basic questions that arise here is whether the state is the only source of law or as Neil MacCormick argued more than a decade ago, is 'law' only one set of multiple 'institutional normative orders' that influence human behaviour?[7] If we move away from a monistic view of law (that all legal norms derive from a single common basic source)[8] to an understanding that law has many legitimate sources, then a question arises on the extent to which norms relating to human and individual rights should be imposed, even at the expense of changing culture.

This question is complicated by the development of measures for the protection of human rights at the international level. Early international concern relating to human rights came in a limited way with protections for discrimination against minorities under the mandate system of the League of Nations. However, contemporary international human rights law truly emerged only after the charter of the United Nations (UN) specified that promoting and encouraging human rights was one of the purposes of that organization. Article 56 of the UN Charter required member states to cooperate with the UN in the promotion of human rights. The adoption of human rights conventions culminated in two major International Covenants in 1966. Since then, the United Nations has placed considerable pressure on individual member states through the adoption of a large number of human rights treaties and through action by regional organizations in Europe, the Americas and Africa.[9]

The debate in developing countries relating to this matter is complex. Most would argue that systems of justice must be built on existing cultural foundations. Jurisprudence should be textured into the life of people to define the good life. One of the disputes relates to the extent to which we should do this. But should the customs of a community or community rights be protected, if they violate individual rights? This is what Muslim traditionalists argued in

[7] For a discussion see Neil MacCormick, Institutional Normative Order: A Conception of Law, *Cornell Law Review*, 82 (1997) pp. 1051–1063; William Ewald, Symposium: Comment on MacCormick, *Cornell Law Review*, 82 (1997) pp. 1071–1079 and Neil MacCormick, Institutions and Law Again, *Texas Law Review*, 77 (1999) pp. 1429–1441.

[8] According to Kelsen, a key advocate of monism, national legal systems derive their legitimacy from the principle of sovereignty. *See* Hans Kelsen, *Introduction to the Problems of Legal Theory*, trans. Bonnie Litschewski Paulson & Stanley L. Paulson (Oxford: Oxford University Press, 1992) pp. 61–62. In contrast, dualism views domestic laws and institutions as emanating from domestic legal systems with its own basic norms as distinct from supra-national norms. It is also possible to posit a third pluralist view that envisages multiple systems of law operating in a single unit.

[9] For recent surveys see Thomas Buergenthal, Centennial Essay: The Evolving International Human Rights System, *American Journal of International Law*, 100 (October 2006) pp. 783–807 and Yuval Shany, How Supreme is the Supreme Law of the Land?: Comparative Analysis of the Influence of International Human Rights Treaties upon the Interpretation of Constitutional Texts by Domestic Courts, *Brooklyn Journal of International Law*, 31(2) 2005 pp. 341–404.

India in the Ameena case. On the other hand, Ghanian writer, Kwasi Wiredu argues that there are limits to the protection of customs and practices because rights violations cannot be "rationalized by appeal to any authentic aspect of African politics".[10] Therefore, in his view, cultural traditions cannot be used to justify violations of individual rights but should be used to give local reinforcement and greater legitimacy to human rights. This was the argument posed by women's rights advocates in the Ameena case.

Compromises are hard to find. The most famous legal battle in this area occurred in India and is best known through the Shah Bano case in India.[11] Under provisions of the Indian Constitution, changing customary marriage and inheritance practices have been limited to certain areas, when existing practice was deemed to be against the good of the people or of the individual. One such instance is the outlawing of polygamy for Hindus. Two cases in Kerala in the 1990s[12] have led to laws that equalized grounds for divorce among Christians across gender and included a provision for divorce by mutual consent.[13] However, Muslims have remained under Muslim personal law in India in areas such as marriage, divorce and inheritance. When Shah Bano applied and received an order from the courts for maintenance beyond what was sanctioned by Muslim personal law in 1985, Muslim traditionalists were strong enough politically, to reverse that decision through the Muslim Women (Protection of Rights on Divorce) Act.[14]

However, challenges to personal law in India have continued. In the *Sarla Mudgal* case (1995)[15] it was ruled that conversion to Islam cannot be used as a way to circumvent the law on bigamy. In the 2002 *Daghu Pathan* case[16] where

---

[10] Kwasi Wiredu, An Akan Perspective on Human Rights, *Human Rights in Africa: Cross-Cultural Perspectives,* ed. Abdullahi Ahmed An-Naim and Francis M. Deng (Washington DC: Brookings Institute, 1990) pp. 243–260 (260).

[11] Mohammad Ahmed Khan v. Shah Bano Begum (AIR 1985 SC 945). On the implications of the Shah Bano case for national politics in India, see Veena Das, *Critical Events: An Anthropological Perspective on Contemporary India,* (Delhi: Oxford University Press, 1997).

[12] *Ammini E. J. v. Union of India* AIR 1995 Kerala 252; *Mary Sonia Zachariah v. Union of India* (1990) (1) KLT 130.

[13] *The Indian Divorce (Amendment) Act* No 49 of 2001 (See Section 10 for equal grounds for divorce for men and women and Section 10A for divorce by mutual consent); *The Christian Marriage (Amendment) Act* No 49 of 2001.

[14] *The Muslim Women (Protection of Rights on Divorce) Act, 1986, Act No. 25 of 1986* [19th May, 1986.] However, under this act, the maintenance orders provided by the courts to Muslim women have risen considerably. Flavia Agnes, The Supreme Court, the Media and the Uniform Civil Code Debate in India, *The Crisis of Secularism in India,* ed. Anurudha Dingwaney Needham and Rajeswari Sunder Rajan (Durham: Duke University Press, 2007) p. 311.

[15] *Sarla Mudgal (Smt.) President, Kalyani and Others v. Union of India and Others,* 1995 3 SCC.

[16] *Daghu v. Rahimbi Daghu Pathan and Others* II (2002) Divorce and Matrimonial Cases 315 (FB) Bombay High Court. The idea that divorce was not an unregulated right was reaffirmed in *Shamin Ara v. State of UP and Another* 2002 SOL Case no 514.

the Muslim husband denied liability for maintenance under Muslim law stating that he had divorced his wife through triple *talaq*,[17] the Bombay High Court ruled that "mere pronouncement of talaq by the husband or merely declaring his intentions or his acts of having pronounced the talaq are not sufficient and does not meet the requirement of the law. In every such exercise of the right to talaq, the husband is required to satisfy the preconditions of arbitration for reconciliation and the reasons for talaq".[18] However, judges have been proceeding with care because in another case,[19] the Indian Supreme Court ruled that the removal of gender discrimination through changes in personal law was in the province of the legislature.

The issue of personal law is not confined to India. Consider the Muslim community in South Africa which has long administered portions of its personal laws through its own set of informal religious tribunals, laws which are not subject to review by the South African civil court system. In response to this situation, the South African Law Reform Commission published Discussion Paper 101 in 2001 that contained a Draft Bill on Islamic Marriages,[20] which included provisions regarding the recognition of, and dissolution of, Muslim marriages in South Africa, the status and capacity of spouses in these marriages, custody of and access to minor children, maintenance, and proprietary consequences. The purpose of the draft bill was to relieve the hardship caused by the non-recognition of Muslim marriages in South Africa. Admittedly this proposal had its limitations, including the provision that the proposed law was applicable to a marriage only if the parties choose that option.[21] However, the bill was seen as controversial and made no progress. Meanwhile, the situation on the ground brought up a case which, although it dealt with inheritance, had implications on personal law. In July 2009, the Constitutional Court of South Africa was confronted with the question as to whether all widows of a polygynous Muslim marriage are entitled to compensation if the husband dies intestate.[22] On the death of the intestate husband Ebrahim Hassam in 2001, the first wife Fatima Hassam asked that the executor of the estate recognize her marriage. The executor refused because the Intestate Succession Act No. 81 of 1987 did not recognize marriages under Muslim law. Fatima Hassam appealed to

[17] The divorce process by which the husband pronounces the *talaq*, the formula of repudiation, thrice. The first two times it is pronounced, it may be withdrawn. But the third time it is pronounced, the divorce is final.

[18] Quoted from Vrinda Narain, *Reclaiming the Nation: Muslim Women and the Law in India*, (Toronto: University of Toronto Press, 2007) p. 120.

[19] *Ahmedabad Women's Action Group vs Union of India* (1997) 3 SCC 573

[20] SALC *Islamic Marriages and Related Matters* (Discussion Paper 101) 49.

[21] Cl 2(1). Cl 5 lists the requirements for a valid Muslim marriage.

[22] CCT 83/08 [2009] ZACC 19 *Fatima Gabie Hassam vs John Hermanus Jacob No et. al.*

the Western Cape High Court which declared that Section 1(4) (f) of the Intestate Succession Act was unconstitutional. The case eventually went to the Constitutional Court. Judge Bess Nkabinde, with the concurrence of all 10 other judges of the court, ruled that the act should be read as though the words "or spouses" appeared after the word "spouse" wherever it appeared in section 1 of the act. "By discriminating against women in polygynous Muslim marriages on the grounds of religion, gender and marital status" said Judge Nkabinde, "the act clearly reinforces a pattern of stereotyping and patriarchal practices that relegates women in these marriages to being unworthy of protection". The judge was careful not to rule on the legality of polygynous marriages, but stated that given that they exist, ignoring such marriages in intestate legislation "works to the detriment of Muslim women and not Muslim men."[23] Here was an instance where the recognition of Muslim personal law helped to end a discriminatory practice in inheritance. Clearly many other anomalies remain. For instance in South Africa, a Muslim woman who wishes to divorce may be unable to do so by way of the religious tribunals, but the South African civil courts may also not hear her case, as they might consider the underlying marriage to be invalid, having been consecrated outside of the South African civil system.[24]

Some writers have pointed out that laws in this area could lead to complex issues. For example, an Indian Court's upholding of the right of the Borah community to exclude a member[25] could protect the rights of that religious community but interfere with an individual's freedom to adhere to a religion. If a faith cannot manage its own affairs, its existence is threatened, but if the believer is deprived of the right to belong, his religious freedom is compromised. The problem is whether social consensus justifies a law that might infringe on individual rights and on equality.

There is also the issue that in many developing countries, 'custom' is difficult to define. In parts of Africa when customary law was codified, what was adapted was codified after encounters with European law.[26] Once it was codified, it ceased to change with changes in the community. This is why Barbara Oomen, writing about Sekhukhune in northern South Africa, distinguishes between customary law and living law. Official customary law in South Africa

---

[23] *Ibid.* [31]

[24] C. Rautenbach, "Some Comments on the Current (and Future) Status of Muslim Personal Law in South Africa" 2004(2) *Potchefstroom Electronic Law Journal*, available at http://www.puk.ac.za/opencms/export/PUK/html/fakulteite/regte/per/issues/2004_2__rautenbach_sum.pdf pp. 1–2.

[25] Rajeev Dhavan, An Introduction, in Shimon Shetreet, *Law and Social Pluralism, op. cit.*, p. lxxviii

[26] K. Mann and R. Roberts, *Law in Colonial Africa* (Portsmouth, NH, Heinemann, 1991).

is a written record of local law dating from colonial and apartheid times. Oomen distinguishes between codified customary law and stated customary law (unchanging traditional law as explicated by contemporary elders). She also distinguishes both of these from 'living law,' which include legal norms that are evolving.[27] Keebt von Benda-Beckmann calls these changing norms, 'unnamed local norms.'[28]

Therefore, developing countries are faced with formulating laws that are in consonance with preexisting customary norms and need to reconcile the new laws with existing notions of what is permissible and just. In many cases, they are also confronted with the issue of a set of codified customs that, because they were codified in colonial times, have no longer kept up with living practices. Sometimes people prefer the traditional systems of law because they emphasize harmony and restorative justice; for instance in Timor Leste, a rape victim, stigmatized and unable to find a husband, will find more consideration given to her economic future in the traditional system than in the adversarial court system. Therefore, it is not just the law that needs to be looked at, but, also the ways in which that law serves the needs of the individuals and the community. Afghan *jirgas* and *shuras* resolve disputes through restorative measures and formal apologies.[29] There may be ways to integrate such institutions to formal systems.[30] Should such systems be recognized but restricted? Alternatively should the formal systems incorporate some customary practices?[31]

There are many models across the developing world. In Timor Leste, the traditional system is allowed to operate provided it does not conflict with formal law and the constitution. In Afghanistan, it is unregulated. However, in Southern Sudan as well as in Nigeria and South Africa, customs 'repugnant' to principles of equity, good conscience and written law are not enforced.

[27] *Ibid.*, p. 169

[28] Keebet von Benda-Beckmann, The Environment of Disputes, *The Dynamics of Power and the Rule of Law: Essays on Africa and Beyond in Honour of Emile Adriaan B. van Rouveroy van Nieuwaal,* ed. Winn van Binsbergen (Leiden: African Studies Centre, 1998) pp. 241.

[29] See www.TheILF.org The Customary Laws of Afghanistan, September 2004; Ali Wardak, Building a Post-War Justice System in Afghanistan, *Crime, Law and Social Change*, 41, 2004, pp. 319–341.

[30] For example, the incorporation of the *gacaca* system in Rwanda after the genocide on which see Alan Erin Tiemessen, After Arusha: Gacaca Justice in Post-Genocide Rwanda, *African Studies Quarterly,* 8 (1) Fall 2004, pp. 57–76.

[31] Jane Stromseth, David Whippen and Rosa Brooks, *Can Might Make Rights?: Building the Rule of Law After Military Interventions,* (Cambridge, Cambridge University Press, 2006) pp. 334–339.

III. The Greater Burdens on Legal Systems in Developing Countries

People do not necessarily engage in disputes because they want to settle them. Some may wish to do so. Others might have political or personal reasons or might simply wish to tell their story. In developed countries, there are many other forums for some of these activities. In developing countries, people come to legal systems to provide an arena for all of these needs. One of the advantages in having multiple and parallel judicial systems is that it enables this need to be catered to. In parts of South Africa people have a choice between customary courts, magistrates courts, community police forums, community conciliation organizations and a council set up by the municipality. This might be why individuals go 'forum shopping'. For instance, paralegals in rural areas of Sierra Leone have helped people to choose between alternative systems. Legal aid is also important because people who might be familiar with local and customary systems may be less aware of formal legal systems. When people migrate to cities for various reasons, they often resolve disputes outside the formal system of courts.[32]

In other words, the argument is that legal systems in developing countries are expected to perform some functions that they are not burdened with in the developed world. To some extent, this is what Amy S. Tsanga[33] was hinting at when she argued that the current approaches to giving legal advice in Africa through paralegals, community legal education and training of persons to lead legal education in the community need to be replaced with a more holistic one – one that engages the cultural assumptions on which customary law is based.

For many in developing countries, there is no real choice. In Timor Leste, people resort to customary conflict resolution practices through Lia-nains or custodians of traditional law because they are more accessible, cheaper and more familiar.[34] Traditional mechanisms through community elders thrive in Sierra Leone especially because courthouses exist only in urban centers.

---

[32] *Ibid.*, pp. 332–333 gives example of human rights clinic at Fourah Bay College, Freetown, Sierra Leone working to ensure free judicial representation and access to education. It was set up by a group of law professors and students.

[33] Amy S. Tsanga, 'Reconceptualizing the Role of Legal Information Dissemination in the Context of Legal Pluralism in African Settings,' *Human Rights, Plural Legalities and Gendred Realities: Paths are Made by Walking,* eds. Anne Hellum, Julie Stewart, Sardar Ali and Amy Tsanga (Harare, Weaver Press, 2007) pp. 437–460.

[34] Tanya Hole and Rod Nixon, Reconciling Justice: "Traditional" Law and State Judiciary in East Timor, (Report for US Institute for Peace 2003) http://www.jsmpminihub.org/Traditional%20Justice/Indextraditional.htm; David Mearns, Looking Both Ways: Models for

Some developing countries have seen efforts to cope with these demands through existing systems. In India, Justice P. N. Bhagwati's solution was a simplification of legal remedies at the Supreme Court level. There a letter could be equated to a fundamental rights petition (epistolary jurisdiction) and social action groups were given the right to intervene on behalf of those who are, due to poverty or of deprivation, unable to seek legal redress.[35] No longer was legal standing confined to a person who has suffered or is threatened with a legal injury. This was combined with fact-finding commissions appointed by the court an interim orders to state agencies to afford relief to victims.[36] Upendra Baxi argues that this is more than 'public interest litigation' in the US because social action litigation addresses issues of fundamental rights (e.g. interpreting Article 21 of the Constitution protecting life and liberty into a due process clause). However, this leads to the overloading of court dockets and the opposition from lawyers who see their cases delayed.[37] On the other hand, there is a great deal of resistance to such moves in other countries. For example, in Sri Lanka, the Supreme Court has accepted a narrower role, and in *Seneviratne v. University Grants Commission* ruled that Directives of State Policy can be used to justify unequal treatment of groups.[38]

There is also the challenge that customary courts might provide for social needs, but they might have questionable processes privileging men over women. For example, *jirgas*[39] in Pashtun areas in Afghanistan may resolve a rape case by ordering the alleged perpetrator to supply a young girl from his family who might be forced to marry into the victim's family. The Limbe customary court decision in Cameroon that rejected the application for divorce of a woman, who eventually won her case on grounds of cruelty and desertion in a civil court in the case of *Njang vs Njang* (1991) is another example.[40]

Justice in East Timor, (American Legal Resources International 2002) http://www.jsmpminihub.org/Traditional%20Justice/Indextraditional.htm and other documents at this site.

[35] P. N. Bhagwati, Social Action Litigation: The Indian Experience, *The Role of the Judiciary in Plural Societies,* ed. N. Tiruchelvam and R. Coomaraswamy, (New York: St Martin's Press) 1987, p. 24–27.

[36] *Bhandua Mukti Morcha v. Union of India and Others* AIR 1984 Supreme Court 802 where the Supreme Court appointed Dr. Patwardhan, a sociologist of the IIT to investigate working conditions in the Faridabad stone quarries.

[37] Upendra Baxi, Taking Suffering Seriously: Social Action Litigation in the Supreme Court of India, *The Role of the Judiciary in Plural Societies, op. cit,* pp. 32–60.

[38] Radhika Coomaraswamy, The Sri Lankan Judiciary and Fundamental Rights, *The Role of the Judiciary in Plural Societies, op. cit.,* p. 117.

[39] A tribal assembly of elders

[40] *Ibid.,* pp. 26–27.

IV. The Formative Impact of Legal System in Developing Countries

We also need to recall that law can modify culture as well. For instance, a study of the Domestic Violence Act (1991) in Trinidad indicates that the very passage of a law according to which a victim (spouse, guardian/child/parent or other dependent) could ask for relief through a short application form filled at the courthouse has had a positive impact on domestic violence. Within three years there were 8000 filings for protection. Only 39% of requests for restraining orders were granted. This is partly because some withdraw cases due to family pressure or economic need (employers might not give leave from work to attend domestic violence cases; cases are delayed and victims have to come to court several times), and there are reconciliations. Also some accused give pledges not to harass the victims. Magistrates prefer reconciliation, especially if there are children in the family. Although the Act succeeded only moderately because it did not protect all (abused children come rarely to court, nor do the elderly), it did raise the level of public awareness and a new cultural awareness emerged. What was once a private matter now became a 'public' concern.[41] The police could begin to encourage victims to go to court.

In other words, law fashions society and regulates conduct through penalties for violations.[42] It influences conduct by demarcating what is socially acceptable. However, I would like to introduce two notes of caution. First, when scholars examine the interaction of law and society, they try to view particular disputes within broadly accepted norms of rights and justice. I agree with many of these norms, for example, those relating to child marriage or domestic violence. However, I recognize that some of the norms which I accept are themselves interpretations, and we need to pay some attention to what happens when particular narratives, especially minority narratives, cannot be generalized or fitted into the structure. Should the legal traditions of minority groups be seen simply as outdated structures, and if so, what impact could that interpretation have on their culture and identity? To what extent can law reconstitute religious belief by outlawing its practices?[43] Therefore, following earlier scholars, I maintain that it is as useful to look at the ways in which law

[41] Mindie Lazarus-Black, Law and the Pragmatics of Inclusion: Governing Domestic Violence in Trinidad and Tobago, *American Ethnologist,* 28 (2) 2001, 388–416.

[42] Franz von Benda-Beckmann, Legal Anthropology, Legal Pluralism and Islamic Law, *The Dynamics of Power and the Rule of Law: Essays on Africa and Beyond in Honour of Emile Adriaan B. van Rouveroy van Nieuwaal,* ed. Winn van Binsbergen, (Leiden: African Studies Centre, 1998) pp. 259.

[43] Upendra Baxi, Siting Secularism in the Uniform Civil Code: A "Riddle Wrapped Inside an Enigma," *The Crisis of Secularism in India, op. cit.* p. 270.

constitutes or structures society as it is to look upon law as a sector fulfilling the demands within society.[44]

I would also like to stress the value of looking carefully at the cultural meaning of both law and society. Society is a text to be interpreted, and for some, signs take on their own meanings, referring not to underlying social realities but to their own reality. Law is thus not only a technical means to an end but a story we tell about ourselves. Legal communications reinforce identifications and activate memories. Law is an authoritative search for meaning because it is about conversation and authority, authorizing who says what, when and why.[45] To ensure commitment, local actors need "to own the process of justice".

V. Conclusion

The major arguments I have made in this chapter are, that in developing countries (in contrast to the situation in developed countries) there is a greater dissonance between the formal legal system and society, greater burdens are placed on legal systems and that legal systems have played a larger formative role. In addition, there is the issue of external pressure for change that is greater for many developing countries than for others.[46] If we keep in mind that our laws, like our social norms, constitute a story we tell about ourselves, reconciling these external pressures with local traditions is yet another challenge confronting these countries.

All these arguments lead to a further general conclusion of the importance of judicial independence and impartiality in developing countries.

[44] R. Gordon, Critical Legal Histories, *Stanford Law Review*, 36, 1984; A. Hunt, *The Constitutive Theory of Law*, (London, Routledge) 1993.

[45] J. Boyd White, *Justice as Translation: An Essay in Cultural and Legal Criticism*, (Chicago: University of Chicago Press, 1990).

[46] For instance see Morag Goodwin and Kate Rose-Sender, Linking Corruption and Human Rights: An Unwelcome Addition to the Development Discourse in F. Coomans et al. (eds.), *Corruption and Human Rights*, (Intersentia, forthcoming).

CHAPTER THIRTY TWO

THE SUPREME COURT AND THE SUPREMACY OF THE JUDICIARY IN INDIA

*K. K. Venugopal**

The Constitution of India, as finally adopted on 26 November, 1949, made it abundantly clear that it was the desire of the founding fathers that they should bring into existence a powerful and independent court which would implement the socialist objectives engrafted into the Constitution. In his welcome address at the inaugural function of the new Supreme Court, the first Attorney General of India, M.C. Setalvad said:[1]

> It can truly be said that the jurisdiction and powers of this Court, in the nature and extent, are wider than those exercised by the highest court of any country in the Commonwealth or by the Supreme Court of the United States.

At the same time, a sober note was struck by Chief Justice Kania:[2]

> As it is often stated, in cases of hardship the court tries its best to do justice between the parties, but if a clear provision of law exists, it has to administer the law and not make one. The court is thus working in co-operation with the legislature and at no time, its work can be considered obstructive and its attitude antagonistic.

While many of the founding fathers were confident that the conferment of vast powers on the Supreme Court would not militate against its remaining an equal and co-ordinate organ of the State along with the executive and the legislative branches, some, however, had misgivings. At the time of the framing of the Constitution, a member of the Constituent Assembly, T.T. Krishnamachari, expressed dark forebodings with the following words:

> It might be that by giving the judiciary an enormous amount of power – a judiciary which may not be controlled by any legislature in any manner except by the means of ultimate removal – we may perhaps be creating a Frankenstein monster which could nullify the intentions of the framers of the Constitution. I have in mind the difference that was experienced in another country.

---

* Senior Advocate, Supreme Court of India

[1] Proceedings at the Inaugural Sitting of the Supreme Court of India in the Court House, New Delhi [1950] SCR 1, at 3 (28 January 1950).

[2] *Ibid.*, at 9.

Sir Alladi Krishnaswamy Ayyar, another member of the Constituent Assembly, too struck an ominous note when he declared:

> The doctrine of independence is not to be raised to the level of a dogma so as to enable the judiciary to function as a kind of super-legislature or super-executive.

B.N. Rau, the Constitutional Adviser, also had his doubts about arming the Supreme Court with such vast powers. His warning to the Constituent Assembly was:

> The courts, manned by an irremovable judiciary not so sensitive to public needs in the social or economic sphere as the representatives of a periodically elected legislature will, in effect, have a veto on legislation exercisable at any time and at the instance of any litigant.

Traditionally, it has not been uncommon for a completely independent judiciary to be looked at with suspicion by the executive, the fear being that the courts may set themselves up above the law or as a third house of parliament. To quote from Justice Frankfurter of the US Supreme Court: *"All power is, in Madison's phrase, of an encroaching nature and judicial power is not immune against this human weakness."*[3]

I. Early Years of Conflict

In the first two decades after the framing of the Constitution, a large number of land reform laws were declared unconstitutional by the Supreme Court. These decisions arose out of a clash between, on the one hand, the government's desire to introduce measures aimed at ensuring social justice and creating an egalitarian society, and, on the other hand, the Constitution's promise of the right to property guaranteed under Articles 19(1)(f) and 31. If the constitutional scheme was to bring into existence an independent and fearless judiciary and *ex facie* the judiciary was given the power to strike down laws which are inconsistent with the Constitution, the only alternative left to Parliament was to neutralise the judgment of the Supreme Court through constitutional amendment.

By 1966, Parliament passed as many as twenty amendments to the Constitution (being only slightly fewer than the amendments made to the US Constitution over the course of two hundred years of its existence) to neutralise

[3] *Trop v. Dulles* 356 US 86 [1958].

the judgments of the Supreme Court of India. This prompted Chief Justice Hidayatullah to say:[4] *"In our country, amendments so far have been made only with the object of negativing Supreme Court decisions..."*

Mohan Kumaramangalam, then Union Minister of Steel, in a monograph titled 'Judicial Appointments' dealing with the period after 1967 wrote:

> The experience of the last six years, an unfortunate period of virtual confrontation between the judiciary and Parliament, of confusion and uncertainty in the law, has to be understood and correct conclusions drawn from it.

II. The 'Basic Structure' Doctrine

Matters came to a head when the Supreme Court pronounced its judgment in the *Kesavananda Bharati case.*[5] The case was a culmination of a series of decisions relating to limitations on the power of amending the Indian Constitution. The Supreme Court declared that the power to amend the Constitution under Article 368[6] was not absolute, but subject to the implied limitation that the amendments could not abrogate or destroy the very foundation on which the Constitution rested.[7] In this judgment and in subsequent decisions some illustrations of those aspects that constitute the basic structure of the Constitution were set out, but the Court declared that these were not exhaustive.[8] Parliament was, as a consequence, unable to conclude with certainty whether a proposed amendment would pass judicial scrutiny or not. Some aspects of the Constitution declared as constituting the "basic structure" were the rule of law,[9] the supremacy of the Constitution,[10] the republican and democratic form of government,[11] separation of powers between the legislature, the executive and the judiciary,[12] the federal character of the Constitution,[13] the sovereignty

[4] In *Golak Nath v. State of Punjab* AIR 1967 SC 1643.

[5] *His Holiness Kesavananda Bharati v. State of Kerala and Others* AIR 1973 SC 1461.

[6] *See* http://indiacode.nic.in/coiweb/welcome.html for the text of Article 368 of the Constitution of India, Part XX, Amendment of the Constitution.

[7] *Supra. n.5.*

[8] Also *see Indira Gandhi v. Raj Narain* 1975 [Supp] SCC 1, *Kihoto Hollohan v. Zachillhu* 1992 Supp (2) SCC 651.

[9] Supra n.5.

[10] *Ibid.*

[11] *Ibid.*

[12] *Ibid.*

[13] *Ibid.*

of India, and by later judgments, the powers of judicial review.[14] If judicial review were to be part of the basic structure of the Constitution, it would follow that the judgment in *Kesavananda Bharati* could not be neutralised by any amendment to the Constitution and nor could the scope of judicial review, as declared by the Court, be whittled down.[15]

III. The Emergency Years

Attempts were made to neutralise the judgment in *Kesavananda Bharati,* but these failed. The confrontation between the executive and Parliament on the one hand and the judiciary on the other came to a head when a state of Emergency was declared on 26 June 1975. The fundamental right to life and liberty stood suspended. On 28 October 1976, H.R. Gokhale, then Union Minister for Law, made a frontal attack on the Supreme Court of India by repeating, without acknowledging, words spoken by Franklin Delano Roosevelt when parts of the New Deal were declared unconstitutional. He said:[16]

> An atmosphere of confrontation was sought to be created by those whose duty it was to see that they did not encroach upon the field which did not legitimately belong to them. Nothing should be left undone now to ensure that such a situation did (sic, does) not recur. If even after the amendment confrontation continues, then I think it will be a bad day for the judiciary.

And again:

> We are trying to save them from the temptation to intrude into powers which do not belong to them. What we are doing today is not to save the people from the judges but really enabling the judges to save them from themselves.

These threats never came to be carried out. But the Emergency tested the very fibre of the higher judiciary in India. It is a sad commentary on the Supreme Court that it failed to assert the leadership which was expected of it by the public and the High Courts of the country. On the contrary, where judges of the High Courts, in the teeth of the threat of transfer from one High Court to another, were prepared to assert their independence by releasing political

---

[14] *Minerva Mills* v. *Union of India,* (1980) 3 SCC 625, *P. Sambamurthy* v. *State of Andhra Pradesh,* (1987) 1 SCC 362, *Kihoto Hollohan* v. *Zachillhu,* 1992 Supp (2) SCC 51 and *L.Chandra Kumar* v. *Union of India,* (1997) 3 SCC 261.

[15] Section 55 of the Constitution (42nd Amendment) Act, 1976 sought to introduce two provisions in Article 368 of the Constitution in an attempt to negate the effect of the *Kesavananda Bharati* judgment. The challenge to this insertion was struck down as unconstitutional in *Minerva Mills* v. *Union of India,* (1980) 3 SCC 625, where the *Kesavananda* dictum was reiterated.

[16] K.K. Venugopal, "Supreme Court and the Common Man" The Hindu (19 December 2003).

detenues, the Supreme Court, during that turbulent period, would routinely stay their release from jails all over the country.

The Supreme Court reached its nadir when it delivered its judgment in the *ADM Jabalpur case*[17] on 28 April 1976. The Court declared that along with the Proclamation of Emergency, the very right to life under Article 21 of the Constitution stood suspended. Of the five judges on the Bench that decided the case, there was but one lone and fearless dissenting voice, that of Justice H.R. Khanna, that lamented the loss of personal liberty in the face of arbitrary State action. Justice Khanna carved a name for himself in India's constitutional history by stating, in his now legendary dissent, that if the majority's view were to be accepted, any official, even a head constable, could capriciously arrest and detain a person indefinitely or even deprive him of his life without authority of law, with the aggrieved person not being able to seek any relief from the courts against such detention during the period of the Emergency.

In the course of the next thirty years, beginning with the electoral debacle in March 1977, resulting in the political party in power during the Emergency being swept out of power, a resurgent Supreme Court made amends for its failures during the Emergency by carving out for itself an undoubted position of primacy among the three organs of the State. Judgment after judgment was delivered by which the Supreme Court garnered for itself such vast powers that at a certain stage it was difficult to distinguish between the judgments which were adjudicatory in nature and those which encroached upon the areas reserved by the Constitution to Parliament and the executive.

IV. The Beginnings of an Activist Court

The 1980s saw the Supreme Court embark upon a period of judicial activism unparalleled in the history of any democracy in the world. In doing so, it compelled obedience to its will through its power of contempt. India has a vast population of disadvantaged sections of society, who on account of poverty, illiteracy and ignorance are unable to have access to justice. The Court devised the tool of 'public interest litigation' which did away with the limitations of *locus standi*, permitting a non-governmental organisation or a lawyer to espouse the cause of an individual or group which was unable to approach the Court to seek relief for itself.[18] The Court declared in no uncertain terms that

---

[17] *ADM Jabalpur v. Shivkant Shukla* AIR 1976 SC 1207.
[18] *S.P. Gupta v. Union of India* AIR 1982 SC 149.

the confines of the adversarial system could not trammel its powers. As a result, it forged remedies and brought about dramatic and far-reaching changes in the areas of prison justice,[19] environment,[20] right to legal aid,[21] right against sexual harassment,[22] etc. There was no area of human endeavour in regard to which the Supreme Court did not seek to bring its judicial activism to bear to bring relief to those whose rights had been infringed.

Article 21 of the Constitution declares that "no person shall be deprived of his life or personal liberty except according to procedure established by law". The Supreme Court held that the right to life was not a right to mere animal existence, but a right to live with human dignity.[23] It expanded the scope of this basic right to include the right to go abroad,[24] the right to reputation,[25] the right to shelter,[26] the right to privacy,[27] the right to education[28] and the right to a clean and healthy environment.[29]

The techniques which the court adopted for achieving these results were many. It appointed committees to investigate and report on public interest petitions complaining of environmental degradation of forests, rivers and lakes. It called upon expert bodies of the Government or the private sector to submit solutions for remedying the serious health hazards caused by the emission of noxious gases from motor vehicles in the cities. It laid down guidelines for preventing sexual harassment of women at the work place,[30] until such time as the legislature passed a law for the said purpose. So too for regulating the adoption of Indian children by foreign parents.[31]

These interventions by the Court are the logical consequence of the holding that the right to life comprehends a multitude of rights including the right to a pollution-free environment. The proceedings before the Court were often declared to be non-adversarial in character. The Court would summon a

[19] *Sunil Batra v. Delhi Administration* [1978] 4 SCC 494, *Hussainara Khatoon v. Home Secretary, State of Bihar* AIR 1979 SC 1360.
[20] *Vellore Citizens Welfare Forum v. Union of India* [1996] 5 SCC 647, *Subhash Kumar v. State of UP* [1991] 1 SCC 598.
[21] *M.H. Hoskot. v. State of Maharashtra* [1978] 3 SCC 544.
[22] *Vishakha v. State of Rajasthan* [1997] 6 SCC 241.
[23] *Olga Tellis v. Bombay Municipal Corporation* AIR 1986 SC 180.
[24] *Satwant Singh Sawhney v. D. Ramarathnam* AIR 1967 SC 1836.
[25] *Kiran Bedi v. Committee of Inquiry* [1989] 1 SCC 494.
[26] *Shanti Star Builders v. N.K. Totame* [1990] 1 SCC 520.
[27] *Gobind v. State of M.P.* [1975] 2 SCC 148.
[28] *Pradeep Jain v. State of U.P.* AIR 1984 SC 240, *Mohini Jain v. State of Karnataka* [1992] 3 SCC 666; *J.P. Unnikrishnan* v. *State of Andhra Pradesh*, (1993) 4 SCC 111.
[29] *Subhash Kumar v. State of UP* [1991] 1 SCC 598.
[30] *Vishakha v. State of Rajasthan* [1997] 6 SCC 241.
[31] *Lakshmi Kant Pandey v. Union of India* [1984] 2 SCC 244.

Secretary to the Government to participate in the hearing, in addition to his counsel, so that it could consider the difficulties experienced by Government, and a solution could be found. The Court was able to assert its will because of public acceptance of its judgments in the field of enforcing fundamental rights through public interest litigation. Along with this was the awareness that the Court could, if required, ensure implementation of its orders by taking recourse to its contempt power.

V. Supreme Organ

In its issue of 18 March 1996, *Time* magazine published the following statement by Justice P.N. Bhagwati, former Chief Justice of India: "*The (Indian) Supreme Court today is the most powerful court in the world.*" The article proceeded to state:

> Nowadays, Indians are less likely to rely on politicians for redress of their grievances than on the Supreme Court, as from garbage disposal to the removal of polluting factories from the vicinity of Taj Mahal, hardly any matter seems beyond the Court's purview.

The Supreme Court of India has, over the years, evolved into a very powerful and respected Constitutional Court. An activist Supreme Court today enjoys popular legitimacy. It is seen as the most credible institution, having the will and the wherewithal to tackle the ills plaguing the community. At the same time, questions have been raised about its encroachment into the realm of legislative and executive functions.

It is true that there are areas where the exact scope and extent of the court's role require closer scrutiny and consideration. However, the Court's activist approach has to be viewed in the backdrop of executive apathy and indifference and the lack of political and legislative will. In one prominent recent case, the lustrous marble of Taj Mahal in Agra was progressively yellowing because of the pollution created by a large number of industries in the area. The Supreme Court was able to single-handedly salvage this ancient Indian monument from deterioration.[32] The survival of the Taj Mahal is owed to the statesmanship of a Supreme Court judge who directed that no polluting industry would be permitted in its vicinity.

In very many of the cases adjudicated, the Supreme Court was able to achieve dramatic results through its activism. The relocation of polluting industries

---

[32] *M.C. Mehta* v. *Union of India*, AIR 1997 SC 734

outside Delhi, the cleansing of the River Yamuna and the conversion of motor-vehicles in Delhi from petrol to a cleaner fuel, namely, Compressed Natural Gas are all such examples, but the most striking one is the directive to the Government to re-open the closed Public Distribution Shops and supply surplus food grains through the public distribution system to people living below the poverty line.[33] Surely, no other court in the world could have achieved all this by which, not hundreds, or thousands, but hundreds of thousands of people were benefited.

VI. Analysing the Supreme Court's Role in the Indian Polity

Looking back at the last six decades, one could say with pride that here is an apex court which has not hesitated to innovate and improvise so that the poor and the disadvantaged people realise their basic and fundamental rights. The traditional confines of the law have not constricted the Court's power to mould the relief that it could give.

The pre-eminence of the judiciary today, relative to the executive and legislature in India, may not be an unique phenomenon. Scholars have noted that since the end of the Second World War, the importance of the judiciary in various democracies has increased and there is a strong trend towards the "constitutionalisation of democratic politics".[34] The increasing urge to turn to the judiciary to solve pressing social problems has prompted many to ask if the separation of powers has become blurred and if judges have not taken on too much power.[35]

Courts globally have been asserting themselves to whittle down the area of non-justiciability. For instance, the Supreme Court of Israel recently considered a petition in which it was asked to rule whether the security fence erected by the government separating the State of Israel from the areas of Palestinian autonomy was legal. The political aspects of erecting the fence did not prevent the Israeli Supreme Court from adjudicating the dispute between the State and the Palestinian inhabitants.[36] The Court decided that the fence in its location imposed non-proportional injuries on the inhabitants.[37]

---

[33] *People's Union for Civil Liberties* v. *Union of India & Ors.*, W.P.(c) No.196/2011.

[34] Richard Pildes, "The Supreme Court 2003 Term – Foreword: The Constitutionalisation of Democratic Politics" [2004] 118 Harv. L. Rev. 28, 31 cited in Aharon Barak, *The Judge in a Democracy* (Princeton 2006), at xii.

[35] *Ibid.*

[36] H.C. 2056/04, *Beit Sourik Village Council v. The Government of Israel* (unreported, English translation available at www.court.gov.il)

[37] Supra n. 31 at 181–2.

Notwithstanding that the Indian Supreme Court has, on occasion, strayed into the political domain, for example, by deciding in a recent case upon the justiciability of the decision of the Governor of a state not to appoint a Chief Minister,[38] even so, I do not believe we will see Indian courts judicially reviewing matters relating to war and peace, defence of the nation, the line of control between India and Pakistan, the appointment of ambassadors and so on.

Nevertheless, the future certainly holds the potential for some degree of tension between the activist Supreme Court and the other organs of the Indian State. Some would say, however, that tension between the courts and the other branches is natural, even desirable.[39] If the Court's rulings were always satisfactory to the other branches, it would raise suspicion that the Court was not properly fulfilling its role as the sentinel on the *qui vive* in a democracy. Thus criticism of the Court's rulings is proper and benefits the Court itself, for it helps to guard the guardians.

VII. Conclusion

I have no doubt that the conservative school would be aghast at what would appear to be drastic inroads into the executive and legislative domain and would call for judicial restraint. But one has to realize that India has a vast population, exceeding one billion. Though the percentage of illiteracy has gone down from about 88%, when India became independent in 1947, to about 34% as of 2008,[40] yet, in absolute terms, there are almost 300 million people who belong to the disadvantaged sections of society. There is hence a greater imperative for bringing about social justice. If the indifference or apathy of the executive results in violating basic rights, the Constitution has provided the courts with the tools for redressal of the wrongs. A written Constitution provides greater flexibility for interpretation of the concepts enshrined in its provisions, including the interpretation of fundamental rights and the Directive Principles of State Policy.

It is self-evident that judicial restraint and statesmanship are necessary to prevent breaching the principles of separation of powers by the judiciary. At the same time, it will be difficult for the Supreme Court of India to be a silent spectator when the promises held out by the Constitution of extending social justice are not faithfully implemented by the executive and the

[38] *Rameshwar Prasad v. Union of India* [2006] 2 SCC 1 (also known as the *Bihar Assembly case*).

[39] *Supra* n. 31, at 216.

[40] UNICEF, "India Statistics" available at http://www.unicef.org/infobycountry/india_statistics.html

legislatures. If human endeavour can achieve at least a part of what the Constitution has guaranteed to the people, then judicial activism has been the tool with which the courts have made the Constitution and the fundamental rights a reality to India's vast population. It would not be amiss, however, to recall the words of caution uttered by famous American jurist, Justice Cardozo:

> The Judge even when he is free, is still not wholly free. He is not to innovate at pleasure. He is not a knight-errant roaming at will in pursuit of his own ideal of beauty or goodness. He is to draw his inspiration from consecrated principles. He is not to yield to spasmodic sentiment, to vague and unregulated benevolence. He is to exercise a discretion informed by tradition, methodized by analogy, disciplined by system, and subordinated to 'the primordial necessity of order in social life'.

To be able to "cure the illness" before the court without creating any undesirable "side effects" requires great statesmanship and craftsmanship, not to mention incredible foresight. I have no doubt that the Supreme Court and the High Courts have judges possessing statesmanship and craftsmanship who will be able to use their vast powers for the relief of the poor, the illiterate and the disadvantaged millions of India.

PART VI

INTERNATIONAL STANDARDS IN THE MAKING

CHAPTER THIRTY THREE

THE MT. SCOPUS INTERNATIONAL STANDARDS OF JUDICIAL INDEPENDENCE: THE INNOVATIVE CONCEPTS AND THE FORMULATION OF A CONSENSUS IN A LEGAL CULTURE OF DIVERSITY

*Shimon Shetreet**

I. Significance of International Standards in the Development of Innovative Concepts of Judicial Independence and Accountability

For courts to resolve disputes without bias there needs to be judicial independence: the judiciary must be both independent and impartial.[1] Both conditions are necessary in order to avoid the opposing risks of infirmity and tyranny. The risk of infirmity exists when the judiciary is dependent on other branches of government or on public opinion. The risk of tyranny is associated with a biased judiciary and a lack of judicial accountability.[2]

Judicial independence is critical for the proper functioning of civil society. Without impartial and independent dispute resolution, there is no substantive protection of human rights,[3] no true economic security or free market, and no

* LL.B., LL.M. (Hebrew University), M.C.L., D.C.L. (University of Chicago), Greenblatt Professor of International and Public Law, Past Director of the Sacher Institute, Faculty of Law, Hebrew University of Jerusalem.

[1] S. Shetreet, "Models of Constitutional Adjudication," published in *The Legal Cultures of China and Israel – Proceedings of the Legal Conference of Zhengfa University, Beijing University, and Hebrew University* (Zengfa University: 2005) [hereinafter Shetreet, "Models of Constitutional Adjudication"].

[2] For examples of tyranny, see Human Rights Watch, *Rigging the Rule of Law: Judicial Independence Under Siege in Venezuela*, Volume 16, No. 3(B) (June 2004) reporting some of allegations of judicial bias in Venezuela. For instance, Attorney General Isaías Rodríguez in May 2004 is reported as describing how, in the past, the country's top administrative court set fees for resolving different kinds of cases. See F. Cross, "Thoughts on Goldilocks and Judicial Independence" (2003) 64 Ohio State Law Journal 195, which describes how the independent Iranian judiciary's supreme independence resulted in irresponsibility.

[3] SA Beliaev, "The Fundamental Right to an Independent and Impartial Judge (Challenging a Judge)," paper given at the workshop on "Judicial Independence and Incompatibilities of the Office of Judge with Other Activities" held in Bishkek, Kyrgyzstan, 20–21 April 1998, organised by the Council of Europe jointly with the Constitutional Court of Kyrgyzstan.

good government or civil order. The rule of law requires judicial independence as a precondition.[4]

It is against this background that a group of legal academics and professional jurists decided to create a revised set of minimum international standards of judicial independence in 2007. The project was important due to the need to update the standards to the contemporary needs and to develop a set of standards for both national and international judges.

The group held a series of collaborative conferences and workshops during 2007 and 2008 in order to draft and approve the Standards. They achieved their goal in the spring of 2008, when the Standards were approved in their present form by an international conference of experts, in Jerusalem on Mt. Scopus, and they are styled The Mt. Scopus Standards of Judicial Independence.

The Mt. Scopus Standards are based primarily on *The International Bar Association Minimum Standards of Judicial Independence* (for the national judiciary) first adopted in 1982 and *The Burgh House Principles of Judicial Independence in International Law* (for international judges). Inspiration was also drawn from the *Tokyo Law Asia Principles*, the *Montréal Universal Declaration on the Independence of Justice*, the *United Nations Basic Principles on Judicial Independence*, and the *American Bar Association*'s revision of its ethical standards for judges. Academic and current texts provided additional input, as well as the personal experiences of judicial independence experts.

One of the primary texts from which the Mt. Scopus Standards were based, *The International Bar Association Minimum Standards of Judicial Independence*, was confirmed by the International Bar Association (IBA) Project on Minimum Standards of Judicial Independence during the Biennial Convention of the IBA in 1982 in New Delhi, this author served as General Rapporteur of the IBA standards.

The other basic text, from which the Mt. Scopus Standards drew, *The Burgh House Principles of Judicial Independence in International Law*, was the product of the 2004 ILA/PICT Study Group of the International Law Association on

---

[4] HG Heinrich, "The Role of Judicial Independence for the Rule of Law," paper given at the workshop on "Judicial Independence and Incompatibilities of the Office of Judge with Other Activities" held in Bishkek, Kyrgyzstan, 20–21 April 1998, organised by the Council of Europe jointly with the Constitutional Court of Kyrgyzstan; European Committee for Legal Co-Operation, Part B *Draft Explanatory Memorandum* to Part A *Draft Recommendation No. R (94)... Of the Committee of Ministers to Member States on the Independence, Efficiency and Role of Judges* (61st Meeting, 35th Meeting as a Steering Committee, Strasbourg, 31 May to 3 June 1994, para. 3: "The Recommendation of the independence, efficiency and role of judges recognises and emphasises the pre-eminent and significant role played by judges in the implementation of these aims [of the establishment of a constitutionally governed State, the rule of law, and the promotion and protection of human rights and fundamental freedoms]".

the Practice and Procedure of International Courts and Tribunals, in association with the Project on International Courts and Tribunals.

II. The Normative Cycle of Judicial Independence in Historical Perspective

The creation of the culture of judicial independence has been a combined process of national and international developments of concepts and ideas. In its first phase the development of the concept of judicial independence predominantly took place within the domestic national systems. In the later stage, focus shifted to the international level which developed the concept further. In the third phase, the international treaties and jurisprudence began to impact the national legal systems with sometimes significant and even dramatic results.[5]

The inception of the concept of judicial independence was in the domestic scenes of the world. Then, this domestic development creating a culture of judicial independence crossed the national boundaries and impacted the thinking of scholars and political leaders of the international community and brought about the formulation of established principles of judicial independence on the transnational level both regionally and internationally. In this second phase of the development the domestic law concepts of judicial independence which transcended national boundaries became part of the established principles of international law and have been bolstered on the international level. In the successive phase, the international law of judicial independence began to exercise a significant impact on the domestic laws of nations.

England was the scene of the original development of the concept of judicial independence when it enacted the Act of Settlement 1701. The United Kingdom has been significantly influenced in the area of judicial independence in recent decades by the principles of judicial independence developed in the international constitutional documents of human rights. I refer to the significant impact of the jurisprudence of the European Court of Human Rights on the conceptual analysis of the foundations of judicial independence in England and Scotland. This process began in the late 1990's following cases delivered by the European Court of Human Rights before the adoption of the UK Human

[5] For a detailed analysis of this thesis, see Shetreet, "The Normative Cycle of Shaping Judicial Independence in Domestic and International Law: The Mutual Impact of National and International Jurisprudence and Contemporary Practical and Conceptual Challenges" (2009), 10 Chicago J. of International Law 275–332.

Rights Act of 1998. It found its dramatic expression in the transformation into the British national Constitutional system of the European Convention of Human Rights by virtue of the HRA 1998 which came into force in 2000.

This development of the shifting directions of the impact of international law of judicial independence on British domestic law (as contrasted by the earlier phase when the British National law impacted the international law of judicial independence), has further been reinforced by the passing of the Constitutional Reform Act of 2005, which introduced into the British system yet another dramatic reform on the control over the administration of justice in England and Wales. This reform discontinued the anomaly of the position of the Lord Chancellor, one of the oldest officers in the British constitution, entrusted with three capacities – Legislative Executive and Judicial. The Constitutional Reform Act 2005 established new lines of demarcation between the Lord Chancellor and the Judiciary, transferring all the judicial functions to the judiciary and entrusting the Lord Chancellor with what is considered conceptually, administrative and executive matters, rather than judicial.

Thus the United Kingdom illustrates vividly and strikingly the mutual impacts of national and international law and jurisprudence in the area of judicial independence. It shows clearly the cross conceptual fertilization and the mutual impact and ideas that have enriched both international and domestic jurisprudence.

The United Kingdom is a very instructive illustration. Similar development of conceptual cross fertilization in the area of judicial independence has also taken place. This is true in regard to European countries such as Austria.[6] This is evident with regard to the law of the European Union. It is also true with regard to Canada.

The impact of international law on judicial independence has been affected by international human rights treaties which contained principles on fair procedure and on the right to be tried before an impartial and independent tribunal. It was reinforced by judge-made jurisprudence by the international courts. In addition it was also substantially enriched and influenced by a long series of international standards of judicial independence that were drafted by numerous professional non-governmental as well as intergovernmental organizations. The standards developed by these organizations had a very positive impact on the creation of a culture of judicial independence as an established and accepted system of conceptual principles. These principles of judicial independence are essential for ensuring the rule of law, maintaining human rights,

---

[6] See: Walter Rechberger, "The Impact of the ECHR Jurisprudence on the Austrian Practice in the Field of Judicial Independence", chapter 14 this volume.

and securing the continued preservation and development of democratic societies.

This author was privileged to be part of the leadership in the development of one such set of standards of judicial independence, The International Bar Association Code of Minimum Standards of Judicial Independence, which was adopted and confirmed by the IBA convention in 1982 in New Delhi at the end of a three year project with the participation of over 60 international scholars and professionals.

This author is now privileged to serve a General Coordinator of an academic and professional project which developed a revised code of international standards of judicial independence for national and international judges, The Mt. Scopus International Standards of Judicial Independence.[7]

III. International Standards of Judicial Independence

If judicial independence is the means to achieve and sustain the goals of democracy, liberty, and the support of a free market economy, then recognized international standards of judicial independence are the tools necessary to achieve it. International standards are the carrot in the proverbial donkey and carrot analogy: they provide the incentive for societies to strive for levels of judicial independence required in order to achieve democracy, freedom, and a capital market economy.[8] Recognized international standards of judicial independence provide added benefits: they provide a clear statement of judicial independence for protection against the power of unofficial laws[9] that oppose society's best interests.

Traditionally, academics considered judicial independence to consist of only two attributes: personal and substantive independence. However, as both judiciary and academic thought expanded, so has the definition of judicial independence. The judiciary is now seen as being greater than the sum of member judges; it has developed into an important social institution with a significant constitutional role. Parallel with this evolution has been the development of innovative models of judicial independence expanding beyond the personal and substantive independence of individual judges into the realm of the independence of the institutional judicial body. Innovative concepts of judicial

---

[7] See this volume, Part VII, Appendix I.

[8] See S. Shetreet, "The Role and Independence of the Judiciary: Need for an International Code" in SR Mohnot, ed., *Towards a New Global Order – Essays in Honour of Dr. L.M. Singhvi*, at 75–96 (Haravard: 1993).

[9] For a discussion of unofficial laws, see Human Rights Committee of the Bar of England and Wales, *Manual on Rule of Law in Afghanistan* (2006).

independence include the ideas of collective or institutional independence of the judiciary as a body, and internal independence, the independence of the judge *vis a vis* his judicial colleagues and superiors.

In addition, the work on judicial independence has brought about the emergence of two major ideas that have gained support. The first is the principle of the reflective judiciary, and the second is the principle of democratic accountability.[10]

With regard to both the traditional and more modern concepts of judicial independence and accountability, it is important to stress that all models are legitimate, and that none in isolation is a better harbourer of judicial independence than any other. No rational basis exists to the argument that adopting one model over another is anti-democratic or a violation of judicial independence. Rather, all concepts, both traditional and innovative, are means by which systems are able to create models for the judicial review of statutes, for judicial selection, and for the orderly and just delegation of court administration responsibilities.[11]

IV. Personal and Substantive Independence

Personal and substantive independence both relate to the independence of the individual judge. They are necessary in order to protect a judge from fears of personal or professional safety that may influence his or her official duties.[12] Examples of personal independence include security of office, life tenure, and adequate remuneration and pensions. Substantive independence refers to the freedom of judges to perform their official judicial functions independently.[13]

---

[10] For a primary reference, see Shetreet, "Models of Constitutional Adjudication," note 1 above. See also PH Lane, "Fragile Bastion: Constitutional Aspects of Judicial Independence" (Judicial Independence is composed of at least five aspects: (1) non-political appointments to a court; (2) guaranteed tenure and salary; (3) executive and legislative interference with court proceedings or office holders; (4) budgetary autonomy; (5) administrative autonomy).

[11] S. Shetreet, "Significance of International Standards in the Development of Innovative Concepts of Judicial Independence and Accountability" (Paper given at the International Conference on Judicial Independence and the Constitutional Position of the Judiciary Jerusalem, March 18th - 20th, 2008).

[12] Sandra Day O'Connor, "The Importance of Judicial Independence," remarks before the Arab Judicial Forum, Manama, Bahrain, September 15, 2003.

[13] *S. Shetreet, "Judicial Independence: New Conceptual Dimensions and Contemporary Challenges" in S. Shetreet and J. Dechenes, eds.,* Judicial Independence: the Contemporary Debate *(Martinus Nijhoff: 1985) at 594–599 [the edited volume hereinafter* Judicial Independence: the Contemporary Debate"*; L. Atkins, "The Shifting Focus of Judicial Reform: from Independence to Capacity," OSI EU Monitoring and Advocacy Program (EUMAP) http://www.eumap.org/journal/features/2002/aug02/indeptocapacity.*

Section 2.2 (National Judges) of the Mt. Scopus Standards makes the distinction between personal and substantive independence:

> 2.2 Each judge shall enjoy both personal independence and substantive independence:
>
> 2.2.1 Personal independence means that the terms and conditions of judicial service are adequately secured by law so as to ensure that individual judges are not subject to executive control; and
>
> 2.2.2 Substantive independence means that in the discharge of his judicial function, a judge is subject to nothing but the law and the commands of his conscience.

V. Collective Independence

Collective independence is an extension of personal and substantive independence. It developed as a legal theory from the recognition that the judiciary is larger than the sum total of its individual judges, and that this collective body must also be protected from unjustified influence from other branches. Judicial administration and court administration fall under the ambit of collective independence.[14]

> Proper court administration requires appropriate collaboration between the judiciary and other governmental bodies in areas not touching judicial procedural or substantive roles.[15] Shared responsibilities for court administration, for instance, can add an element of democracy.[16]

The Mt. Scopus Standards address this distinction in Sections 2.12 and 2.13 (National Judges) (emphasis added):

> 2.12 *Judicial matters* are exclusively within the responsibility of the Judiciary, both in central judicial administration and in court level judicial administration.
>
> 2.13 The central responsibility for *judicial administration* shall preferably be vested in the Judiciary or jointly in the Judiciary and the Executive.

---

[14] See Shetreet, "Models of Constitutional Adjudication," note 1 above. See also Mollah, "Separation of Judiciary and Judicial Independence in Bangladesh," at 2, available in: http://unpan1.un.org/intradoc/groups/public/documents/apcity/unpan020065.pdf (Visited: Oct 25, 2010).

[15] See the discussion on Internal Independence that follows for a fuller description of administrative, procedural, and substantive judicial roles.

[16] C. DeSilva, "A Recent Challenge to Judicial Independence in Sri Lanka: The Issue of the Constitutional Council", chapter 25 of this volume.

Collective independence is critical. Just as interference with the independence of individual judges is detrimental to the rule of law, interference with the independence of the collective judiciary leads to a diminution of judicial independence. It is difficult, if not impossible, for individual judges to independently discharge their official duties in an atmosphere of collective repression.

> Collective independence refers to the idea that the judiciary shares the responsibility for court administration. There are three primary models of court administration:[17] the exclusive judicial model, where the judiciary is solely responsible for court administration; the exclusive executive model, where the executive is solely responsible for court administration; and the joint executive and judicial model in which both institutions share responsibilities. In addition, there is a fourth model, the mixed model seen in Australia, where the high court's court administration is controlled by the judiciary, and the lower courts' court administration is executive-run.

It is not a violation of judicial independence to have the executive involved in some degree with court administration.

VI. Judicial Appointments

The same approach is relevant with regard to judicial appointments. They can be seen in Sections 2.14 and 4.2 of the Mt. Scopus Standards:

> 2.14 Judicial appointments and promotions by the Executive are not inconsistent with Judicial Independence as long as they are in accordance with Principles 4 [Principles dealing with Judicial Appointments].
>
> 4.2 (a) The principle of democratic accountability should be respected and therefore it is legitimate for the Executive and the Legislature to play a role in judicial appointments provided that due consideration is given to the principle of Judicial Independence.
>
> (b) The recent trend of establishing judicial selection boards or commissions in which members or representatives of the Legislature, the Executive, the Judiciary and the legal profession take part, should be viewed favourably, provided that a proper balance is maintained in the composition of such boards or commissions of each of the branches of government

[17] See the Hon. Mr. Justice Beatson, "Judicial Independence and Accountability", para. 9, for his discussion of the switch in responsibility of court administration, available in: http://www.judiciary.gov.uk/media/speeches/2008/speech-beatson-j-16042008 [hereinafter Beatson, "Judicial Independence and Accountability"].

Safeguards are provided in Section 4.1 (National Judges):

4.1 The method of judicial selection shall safeguard against judicial appointments for improper motives and shall not threaten Judicial Independence.

Sections 11.3 and 11.4 (International Judges) of the Mt. Scopus Standards also provide for the importance and significance in the judicial selection process:

11.3 Procedures for the nomination, election, and appointment of judges should be transparent and provide appropriate safeguards against nominations, elections and appointments motivated by improper considerations.

11.4 Information regarding the nomination, election and appointment process and information about candidates for judicial office should be made public, in due time and in an effective manner, by the international organisation or other body responsible for the nomination, election and appointment process.

VII. Internal Independence

Internal judicial independence requires that with regard to certain types of adjudicative functions, judges be independent from directives or pressures from fellow judges.[18] Adjudicative functions are those official functions for which judges are responsible in the discharge of their official duties. They are threefold: administrative, procedural, and substantive.

Administrative adjudicative functions include managing caseloads, setting hearing dates, organizing judicial workloads, and expediting hearings and resolutions of cases. Procedural adjudicative functions involve the conduct of hearings according to procedural rules and procedures, and ruling on procedural motions. Eventually, judges resolve cases, through their substantive adjudicative functions, which consist of determining findings of fact, applying relevant legal norms to the facts of the case, extending existing legal norms, and creating new doctrines. Internal independence refers to substantive and procedural aspects.

---

[18] Also see S. Shetreet, "Judicial Independence on the Scope of Internal Independence" published in *Judicial Independence Today*, Essays in honor of Justice Giovanni E. Longo (*giuffre editore* 1999) at 345–357.

The Mt. Scopus Standards deal with internal independence in Section 9:

9.1 In the decision-making process, a judge must be independent vis-à-vis his judicial colleagues and superiors.

9.2 Any hierarchical organization of the judiciary and any difference in grade or rank shall in no way interfere with the right of judges to pronounce their judgments freely.

Professor Cappelletti viewed administrative and procedural adjudicative functions as analogous.[19] However, as the types of duties involved with each of the two types of functions are distinct, it is useful to categorize them separately. This distinction is of particular importance in the discussion of internal judicial independence, which demands more independence with regard to procedural than administrative functions, as illustrated in the case of Chandler.[20]

The scope of internal judicial independence is connected to the doctrine of binding precedent, which exists in different forms in different jurisdictions and legal systems. Many civil law countries define substantive internal judicial independence as including judicial independence from superior court decisions. An instructive example is Germany, where, with some exceptions, judges are free from the restraints of upper court decisions when rendering judgments. This framework contrasts with that of common law countries, where judges are bound by the decisions of upper courts, and sometimes also of the same in which they are sitting.[21]

VIII. Illustrative Examples of Dilemmas in Case of Diversity

The issue of the political activities of judges has given rise to some problems. In the continent of Europe judges are involved in party politics, but in common law countries they are excluded. The compromise between the two legal cultures is expressed in section 7.1 of the Mt. Scopus standards. It adopted the

---

[19] M. Cappelletti, "Who Watches the Watchmen? A Comparative Study on Judicial Responsibility" (1983) 31 *American Journal of Comparative* Law 1, at pp. 7–9. See Shetreet and Deschenes: "Judicial Independence: The Contemporary Debate, note 13 above.

[20] *Chandler*, 398 US 74

[21] Practice is not always the same as theory. For an interesting comment on how some US Supreme Courts have overturned past decisions regarding the constitutionality of statutes, See A. Maoz, "On the Boundaries of Justiciability: Parliament, Government and Courts" (Paper given at the International Conference on Judicial Independence and the Constitutional Position of the Judiciary Jerusalem, March 18th – 20th, 2008), ff 45, and his references to West Coast Hotel Co. v. Parrish, 300 US 379 (1937) and to Lawrence v. Texas, 539 US 558 (2003) [hereinafter Maoz, "On the Boundaries of Justiciability"].

previous IBA standards, and provides that "Judges shall not hold positions in political parties".

The role of the Lord Chancellor before the Constitutional Reforms Act 2005 gave rise to serious problem concerning executive responsibility for judicial matters and court administration. The Compromise was expressed in 1982 as follows: "Except where such practice is by long and democratic tradition" in section 3 of the IBA code 1982. After 2005, this was no longer necessary in the Mt. Scopus Standards.

IX. Special Issues and Principles Regarding Judicial Appointments exclusionary Model: The Principle of a Fair Reflection of Society

One should distinguish between the inclusionary model and the exclusionary model. The inclusionary model demands that a certain judge, or certain type of judge, be a member of a court, panel, or sit on a specific case. It includes the principle of a fair reflection of society. The exclusionary model requires the exclusion of biased judges.

There is ever-increasing awareness of the importance of the principle of a fair reflection of society. It is illustrated by legislation and conventions which demand that judges with certain characteristics be members of a bench of a particular court, by federal and multi-cultural countries where the constituent political units, cultures or geographical regions are expected to be reflected on the bench, and by constitutional changes such as the UK's *Constitution Reform Act 2005*[22] requiring diversity in the process of judicial appointments.

Canada offers an instructive example of both legislated and non-legislated geographical reflectiveness. By statute, three of nine of the just˙ es of its highest court, the Supreme Court of Canada, are drawn from Quebec, and by convention three are selected from Ontario, two from the western provinces, and one from the Atlantic Provinces.[23] Canadians believe that this formula helps ensure that the diversity of Canadian society is best reflected in the country's highest court.[24] The ad hoc judge procedure in the International Court of Justice[25] is another established practice of the inclusionary model.

---

22 See *UK Constitutional Reform Act 2005*

23 See s. 30(2) of the *Supreme Court Act (Canada).*

24 I. Cotler, "The Supreme Court Appointment Process: Chronology, Context and Reform," chapter 18 of this volume.

25 For a discussion of *ad hoc* judges in the International Court of Justice, see Pettiti, "Independence of International Judges," in Shetreet and Deschenes: "Judicial Independence: The Contemporary Debate", note 13 above..

Geographical and cultural reflection is maintained in Great Britain's Supreme Court formerly the House of Lords, which always has one judge from Scotland and one from Northern Ireland.

Fair reflection can be socially-based, often rooted in criticism directed at the social composition of the judiciary, traditionally drawn predominantly from the upper middle class. England, Canada, Greece, France and Germany are sensitive to this issue, as are African countries, where regional, tribal and cultural considerations are necessary to maintain at least appearances of impartiality and the confidence in the courts of diverse segments of society.

The principle of fair reflection of society is an adequate conceptual remedy to the problem of an unbalanced judicial composition, whether upon ideological, social, cultural, geographical, or other grounds. Fair reflection builds the judiciary's credibility, and public confidence in its functions. This is because the judiciary is also a branch of government, not merely a dispute resolution institution, and therefore there is value in it sharing the diversity of the society from which it is drawn. Fair reflection is also important in order to ensure balanced panels in appellate courts, particularly in cases with public or political overtones.

A reflective judiciary is an imperative factor for maintaining the important value of public confidence in the courts. Although the over-emphasis on personal judicial biases pays insufficient credit to the balancing effect of social controls, system factors and institutional traditions, it cannot be denied that all judges view the world to some degree through their own individually-tinted glasses.[26] Thus a reflective judiciary is required. The process and standards of judicial selection must ensure fair reflection of social classes, ethnic and religious groups, ideological inclinations and, where appropriate, geography. The reflection should be fair rather than strictly numerical or proportional.[27] Likewise, compliance with the principle of a fair reflection of society must be premised foremost on maintaining impeccable judicial professional standards and moral values. Again turning to Canada, the selection of Supreme Court of Canada justices is based first and foremost on merit, and only after this criterion has been satisfied, are personal and reflective qualities weighed.[28]

---

[26] S. Shetreet, "On Assessing the Role of Courts in Society", 10 Manitoba L.J. 355, at 399–402 [hereinafter Shetreet, "Assessing the Role of Courts"]; DR Pinello, "Linking Party to Judicial Ideology in American Courts: A Meta-Analysis," (20:3) *The Justice System Journal* (1999) at 219–54 (judges' party affiliations account for between 31% and 48% of ideological variance).

[27] Shetreet, "Models of Constitutional Adjudication," note 1 above.

[28] Cotler, "Supreme Court Appointment Process," note 24 above.

The Mt. Scopus Standards (International Judges) Section 11.2 shares this sentiment:

> 11.2 While procedures for nomination, election and appointment should consider fair representation of different geographic regions and the principal legal systems, as appropriate, as well as of female and male judges, appropriate personal and professional qualifications must be the overriding consideration in the nomination, election and appointment of judges.

The concept of a reflective judiciary is applicable too to the panel compositions in specific cases. The doctrine of fair reflection demands balanced panels, hence promoting neutrality. Judges with convictions or experiences that strongly identify them with a particular side should refrain from sitting in cases that might lead the public to question their neutrality.[29]

Section 2.15 of the Mt. Scopus Standards provide for a fair reflection of society:

> 2.15 The process and standards of judicial selection shall give due consideration to the principle of fair reflection by the judiciary of the society in all its aspects.
>
> 2.15.1 Taking into consideration the principle of fair reflection by the judiciary of the society in all its aspects, in the selection of judges, there shall be no discrimination on the grounds of race, colour, gender, language, religion, national or social origin, property, birth or status, subject however to citizenship requirements.

Section 2.17 also speaks of a fair reflection:

> 2.17 The process and standards of judicial selection shall give due consideration to the principle of fair reflection by the judiciary of the society in all its aspects.

It is important to distinguish "reflection", which refers to members of the judiciary mirroring certain characteristics of the population, from "representation", which implies loyalty and continued contacts and links to segments of

---

[29] Shetreet, "Assessing the Role of Courts," note 26 above; Shetreet and Deschenes Judicial Independence: The Contemporary Debate, note 13 above, at pp. 401.

the population. We speak of judicial reflection rather than of representation for we expect judges after their appointment to be completely independent, without loyalties to the sector in society from which they were drawn. This contrasts with the representative nature of members of parliament, who are expected after their election to office to keep contacts with the people who elected them and to promote their constituents' often self-serving interests. In addition, whereas democratic representation should be numerically-based, the judicial reflection of society is based on fairness rather than numbers.

X. Exclusionary Model

The Exclusionary Model states that in certain circumstances, a judge must be disqualified from sitting on a court, panel, or case, on account of personal associations and therefore displaying a real or perceived bias.[30] Perceived bias might also occur on account of a judge giving an opinion on a matter in public, and later being asked to sit on a case dealing with this subject.[31] Similar disqualification of a judge from sitting in a case could result from outside activities of the judge.[32] This is the neutral judge principle.[33] Although based on an opposing principle to that of the inclusionary model, the exclusionary model equally bolsters judicial independence.

There is a risk that the exclusionary model may be used to disqualify judges for improper reasons. It is therefore important to minimize the need to implement this model. One way of achieving this is through restricting judges' outside activities, thus decreasing the reasons for disqualification.[34]

In the Mt. Scopus Standards both disqualification and restrictions on judges' outside activities are provided in Section 7 (National Judges) and in Sections 18 through 20 (International Judges).[35]

---

[30] Shetreet, "Models of Constitutional Adjudication," note 1 above.

[31] Beatson, "Judicial Independence and Accountability," note 17 above, paras. 16–17, outlines this issue and the potential problems of judges speaking in parliament on "aspects of the administration of justice that are of general interest and concern and upon which it is appropriate for judges to comment."

[32] S. Shetreet, "Standards of Conduct of International Judges: Outside Activities" *The Law and Practice of International Courts and Tribunals 2* (Kluwer Law International: Netherlands, 2003) p. 127 [hereinafter Shetreet, "Outside Activities"].

[33] See W Habscheid, "Les Princies Fondamentau" in W Habscheid (ed.), *Effectiveness of Judicial Protection and Constitutional Order* (Gieseking 1983) 161, at pp. 169–172.

[34] See Shetreet, "Outside Activities", note 32 above; see also S. Shetreet, "Judicial Independence and Freedom of Expression", in JR Harper, ed., *Global Law Practice* (Kluwer Law International, 50th Anniversary of the International Bar Association Volume: 1997) at 8–45; see also ABA *Model Code of Judicial Conduct* (February 2007).

[35] See this volume, Part VII Appendix I.

XI. Methods of Judicial Selection and the Models of Constitutional Adjudication

Democratic accountability requires that the other branches take part in the process of judicial appointments. The method of judicial selection must be considered when building its model of constitutional adjudication.[36] Thus, jurisdictions whose methods of judicial selection include democratic input and an element of accountability are morally justified in adopting an adjudicative model of constitutional adjudication that gives the court the power to invalidate unconstitutional statutes.[37]

In contrast, models of judicial selection that base appointments on professional qualifications in the absence of democratic input should adopt one of the following two models of constitutional adjudication. The first model provides that judgments regarding legislative constitutionality are declaratory only, with no judicial power to invalidate offending statutes.[38] The second model provides that the court has the power to invalidate offending statutes, but this power is counterbalanced by the democratic parliament's override ability.[39]

There exists also the model of drafting a jurisdiction's constitution in a very detailed and precise manner in order to guide judges in their exercise of judicial review of the constitutionality of statutes.[40] Although good in theory, this model is not realistic in practice, for constitutions tend to be drafted in broad terms leaving wide discretion to the judiciary. This issue is compounded when judges use methods of interpretation not closely linked to the text, but rather to its purpose and the values of the system.[41]

Models of constitutional adjudication can be classified as follows: The first model is the Adjudicative Model: the US Model. One of the most significant traditions of judicial review originates in the United States, where the courts

---

[36] S. Shetreet, "Judicial Appointments: Standards and Process" (2003) 8 *Hamishpat Law Review* 357–404 (Hebrew).

[37] This is the USA model.

[38] This is the UK model.

[39] This is the Canadian model. See Rosenberg & Perrault, "Ifs and Buts in Charter Adjudication: The Unruly Emergence of Constitutional Exemptions in Canada" (2002) 16 *S.C.L.R.* (2d) 375; Sankoff, "Constitutional Exemptions: Myth or Reality?" (1999–2000), 11 *N.J.C.L.* 411; RH Bork, "Coercing Virtue: The Worldwide Rule of Judges," AEI Bradley Lecture (Washington) (2003).

[40] Paul P Craig, *Administrative Law* (London, 3ed., 1994), at 3, and Stewart, Richard B., "The Reformation of Administrative Law" 88 *Harv. L.R.* 1667 (1974–5).

[41] For the objective method of interpretation see A. Barak, *Constitutional Interpretation*, 165 (1993) (Hebrew), A. Barak, *Purpose Oriented Interpretation*, 239 (2003) (Hebrew). For the purpose-oriented approach in the Canadian context see: Schachter; Vriend v. Alberta, [1998] 1 S.C.R. 493; R. v. Sharpe, [2001] 1 S.C.R. 45, 2001 SCC 2, R. v. Ferguson, 2008 SCC 6.

are authorized to determine whether statutes are constitutional, and if they are not, to strike them down.[42] The power of judicial review is exercised by all levels of court, with final decisions resting with the Supreme Court, which is the court of last resort.[43]

The second model is the Adjudicative Model with Legislative Override: the Canadian Model. The Canadian judicial review resembles the American model in that it combines the judicial review of laws with the comprehensive review of executive branch actions. However, in Canada, the legislature has the power to override a judicial striking-down of an unconstitutional law. This override power is restricted, for it is valid for renewable five-year periods only, and the offending law must contain a statement that the override power has been used. For political reasons use of the override power has been restrained.

The third model is the Declaratory Model: the UK Model. The declaratory model of judicial review empowers the court only to declare that the challenged statute is constitutionally incompatible. It is parliament, not the courts, that decides whether the offending legislation will be struck down. This model is one solution to the dilemma of an unaccountable judiciary adjudicating constitutional questions.[44]

The UK has adopted this model with regard to conflicts between its legislation and the European Convention on Human Rights. The UK *Human Rights Act 1998* reads:

4. Declaration of incompatibility

> ...
>
> (2) If the court is satisfied that the provision is incompatible with a Convention right, it may make a declaration of that incompatibility.
>
> ...
>
> (6) A declaration under this Section ("a declaration of incompatibility")—
> (a) does not affect the validity, continuing operation or enforcement of the provision in respect of which it is given; and
> (b) is not binding on the parties to the proceedings in which it is made.[45]

The fourth model of constitutional adjudication is the Separate Constitutional Court: the German, and Italian Models. The European model adopted by

---

[42] Shetreet, "Models of Constitutional Adjudication," note 1 above. For a perspective that disagrees with this ability, RH Bork, "Coercing Virtue: The Worldwide Rule of Judges," AEI Bradley Lecture (Washington) (2003).

[43] See *Marbury V. Madison*, 5 US 137 (1803), *Dred Scott v. Sanford* 60 U.S. 393 (1856), *Lochner v. New York* 198 U.S. 45 (1905), *Lawrence v. Texas* 539 U.S. 558 (2003).

[44] UK examples are *Wilson v. First County Trust Ltd* and *Bellinger v. Bellinger* [2003] UKHL 21.

[45] *Human Rights Act 1998* (1998 Chapter 42).

Germany, Italy and others, entrust judicial review to special constitutional courts that meet requirements of democratic accountability by providing special procedures for selection of the members of the separate constitutional courts.[46] In view of the recognition that constitutional adjudication, this requires a wider value-oriented approach, and in view of the fact that the European career judiciary in the ordinary court system cannot ensure democratic accountability in an adequate manner.[47] Normally, the process of election of members of the separate constitutional court takes place in the legislation and is different from the political role than the process of appointment in the ordinary system, which is purely professional and rooted in a career judiciary.[48]

France adopted the model of the Prior Review of Legislation. In France, judges review of the constitutionality of a proposed statute takes place before it is passed by Parliament. In the other more common models, judicial review is exercised after legislation is passed.[49] In recent years France also allows post legislation judicial review.

Another parameter of classification is the judicial forum exercising the judicial review. In this regard we distinguish between the centralised model where only one, usually the highest court of the country, may exercise judicial review of statutes, and the decentralised model, where every court engages in constitutional adjudication, with the court of final resort having the final judgment. Germany is an example of the first model, whereas the United States of the second.

XII. Judicial Review and Democratic Accountability

The requirement for judicial accountability comes from the principle of constitutionality.[50] Underlying this principle of constitutionality is the belief, accepted by most systems of government, that under certain circumstances it

---

[46] Shetreet, "Models of Constitutional Adjudication," note 1 above.

[47] This is the reason for the criticism regarding the absence of time limitation for the term of office of federal justices. See J. Resnik, "Judicial Selection and Democratic Theory: Demand, Supply And Life-Tenure", 26 *Cardozo Law Review*, 579 (2005); DR Stras and RW Scott, "Retaining Life Tenure: The Case for a Golden Parachute" 83 *Washington University Law Quarterly* (2006).

[48] Shetreet, Judicial Independence: The Contemporary Debate, note 13 above; J. Bell, *Judiciaries Within Europe: A Comparative Review* (Cambridge 2006).

[49] "Models of Constitutional Adjudication," note 1 above.

[50] See Yoav Dotan "Judicial Review within a Constitution: The Issue of accountability – A Comparative Look"; see also s. 52(1) of Canada's *Constitution Act, 1982*: "The Constitution of Canada is the supreme law of Canada, and any law that is inconsistent with the provisions of the Constitution is, to the extent of the inconsistency, of no force or effect."

is justifiable to limit the legislative branch's power.[51] Judicial review is often widely accepted in jurisdictions where other branches of government are less trusted.[52]

There are dilemmas with regard to the democratic legitimacy of constitutional adjudication, and how constitutional disputes are settled in a society.[53] A counterweight to the discretionary decisions of a democratically representative legislative branch is the constitutional power of judicial review. This balance must be buttressed by firm rules aimed at preventing a judicial abuse of this supervisory power.[54] Rules are required in order to counteract the inherent problems that are interwoven with the arguably non-democratic accountability of judicial review.[55]

The American attempt to solve this dilemma was to increase judicial accountability by introducing democratic elements into judicial appointments

---

[51] See *Public Committee Against Torture in Israel v. The State of Israel* (HCJ); A.N. Guiora and E.M. Page, " Going Toe to Toe: President Barak's and Chief Justice Rehnquist's Theories of Judicial Activism". There are also dissenting voices. For a discussion of these dissenting voices see *contra* S. Goldstein, "The Rule of Law vs. The Rule of Judges: a Brandeisian Solution" (Paper given at the International Conference on Judicial Independence and the Constitutional Position of the Judiciary Jerusalem, March 18th – 20th, 2008): "The proponents of strong judicial activism see it as a necessary mechanism to protect the "rule of law" while the opponents see the same phenomenon not as protecting the rule of law, which, of course, is not self-executing, but rather as creating the "rule of judges." See also "On the Boundaries of Justiciability" *supra* note 21: "The independent judiciary, which is absent political accountability, is indeed suitable for this purpose [of examining the constitutionality of laws]".

[52] KK Venugopal, "The Supreme Court and Judicial Supremacy," (Paper given at the International Conference on Judicial Independence and the Constitutional Position of the Judiciary Jerusalem, March 18th – 20th, 2008), See chapter 32 this volume; AP Grinover, "The Relevance for Brazil of International Standards of Judicial Independence," (Paper given at the International Conference on Judicial Independence and the Constitutional Position of the Judiciary Jerusalem, March 18th – 20th, 2008), See chapter 30 this volume.

[53] See for example R. Gavison "The Constitutional Revolution: Description of Reality or a Self-Fulfilled Prophecy" (1997) 28 Mishpatim 21, at 28–32; Y. Dotan, "Constitution for Israel? The Constitutional Dialogue after the Constitutional Revolution" (1997) 28 *Mishpatim* 149; Bruce Ackerman, "The Storrs Lectures – Discovering the Constitution" (1984) 89 *Yale L.J.* 1013, Sunstein Cass "Constitutionalism and Secession" (1991) 58 *U. Chicago L.R.* 633.

[54] See S. Shetreet, "The Discretionary Power of the Judge" in M. Storme and B. Hess, eds., *Discretionary Power of the Judge: Limits and Control*, 73 – 116 (Procedure Gent 2000) (Kluwer 2003). (On the occasion of the 500th Anniversary of the University of Gent and 50th Anniversary of the International Association of Procedural Law).

[55] One issue related to the non-democratic accountability of judges and constitutional adjudication is the issue of constitutional exemptions, whereby when a law that is constitutional in most of its applications generates an unconstitutional result in a small number of cases, it might be advantageous to grant a constitutional exemption in these cases than to strike down the law as a whole. There is mixed opinion as to whether this approach is good or not. The Supreme Court of Canada in its 2008 decision R. *v.* Ferguson, 2008 SCC 6 stated that: "... while the availability of constitutional exemptions for mandatory minimum sentencing laws has not been conclusively decided, the weight of authority thus far is against them and sounds a cautionary note" (para. 48).

at the federal and state ordinary court levels.[56] In contrast, models adopted by France, Germany and Italy entrust judicial review not to ordinary courts, but rather to democratically accountable constitutional courts with special selection procedures.[57]

The Mt. Scopus Standards discuss judicial appointments and democratic accountability in Sections 2.14 and 4.2:

The principle of democratic accountability should be respected and therefore it is legitimate for the legislature to play a role in judicial appointments and central administration of justice provided that due consideration is given to the principle of judicial independence.

Mt. Scopus Standards also provide that:

4.2 b) The recent trend of establishing judicial selection boards or commissions in which members or representatives of the Legislature, the Executive, the Judiciary and the legal profession take part, should be viewed favourably, provided that a proper balance is maintained in the composition of such boards or commissions of each of the branches of government

The Common Law Model is also designed to respond to the lack of accountability in the judiciary. It focuses on restricting the scope of judicial review and abstention from rigid constitutions. Rigid constitutionalism is present in federal common law states including Canada and Australia, in order to regulate federal relationships and hierarchies. In these countries, the process of judicial appointment is characterized by limited democratic input.[58] Sometimes, in an effort to counteract the lack of public accountability, the power of judicial review is balanced by the legislative override power, as is seen in the Canadian model.

---

[56] See also J. Resnik, *"Judicial Selection and Democratic Theory: Demand, Supply And Life-Tenure"* (2005) 26 *Cardozo Law Review* 579.

[57] Shetreet, "Models of Constitutional Adjudication," note 1 above.

[58] D. Williams, "The Judicial Appointment Process", 2004 NZ L.R. 39, p. 34–44, 47–48; M. Bhattacharya & R. Smyth, "The Determinations of Judicial Prestige and Influence: Some Empirical Evidence from the High Court of Australia" 30 *J. Legal Studies* 223 (2001) p. 229–232; S. de Smith & R. Brazier, "Constitutional and Administrative Law, 7th ed. (London: 1994) at 398.

XIII. Main Judicial Function in Society: Dispute Resolution

The Mt. Scopus Standards in Section 1.2 express a very clear idea on the main role of the court in society. The Mt. Scopus Standards recognise that court must support human rights and maintain the rule of law. However, their main function is to resolve disputes.[59]
The function of the court is as follows:

1.1. To resolve disputes and to administer the law impartially between persons and between persons and public authorities;
1.2. To promote, within the proper limits of the judicial function, the observance and the attainment of human rights; and
1.3. To ensure that all people are able to live securely under the rule of law.[60]

The main function of the courts is to resolve disputes and to do justice, but due to the expanding role of the judiciary in society[61], the secondary roles of the judiciary have received increased attention. This increasing judicialization is in part a result of social developments, such as the massive industrialization or the expansion of the welfare state. Wide-ranging primary and secondary legislation has been enacted, and consequently there has been a corresponding expansion in litigation against government services, as well as the development of social rights in the welfare state. In addition, collective procedures, such as the American class action, or the French "action collective" have developed, which have brought about a "massification" of the law, transforming the traditional two-party litigation into a major multi-party complex litigation.[62]

---

[59] Justice Aharon Barak, "Foreword: A Judge on Judging: the Role of a Supreme Court in a Democracy", 116 *Harv. L. Rev.* 16 (2002), Expressed the view that the judge has two functions: development of the law and protecting the constitution and democracy

[60] Montréal Declaration, Part VII, Appendix VIII this volume.
Recall competing values of judicial independence and judicial accountability: "As phrased by a Canadian judge, Mr. Justice Riddell, commenting on an arrangement of divisions of labour among the judges, 'Judges are the servants, not the masters of the people.' Servants are accountable, so are judges." From Shetreet, Judicial Independence: The Contemporary Debate, note 13 above, at pp. 593, referring to *Davis Acetylene Gas Co. v. Morrison*, (1915) 34 O.L.R. 155, 23 D.L.R. 871 (C.A.).

[61] See further: M. Cappelletti, "Who Watches the Watchmen? A Comparative Study on Judicial Responsibility" 31 *American Journal of Comparative* Law (1983) 1, at 7–9. For further discussion on the increasing judicial role in society, see E. Vescovi, "La Independencia de la Magistratura en la Evolucion Actual del Derecho", in W. Habscheid (ed.), *Effectiveness of Judicial Protection and Constitutional Order* (1983) 161, at 169–72.

[62] For an examination of the massification of the judicial system in criminal cases, see D.H. Whitbread (ed.), *Mass Production Justice and Constitutional Idea* (1970) 1. Massification occurs in civil cases as well.

While these above-mentioned developments may be seen as natural and objective, there are also causes for increased judicialization that may be termed "convenience-based processes of judicialization". This refers to the judicialization of issues largely for the political convenience of the other branches of government.[63] A similar trend may be observed in Israel, where the relative role of the executive has declined, whereas the judicial role has increased. Two major processes are taking place. First, the realization of the public that the ordinary bureaucratic and political institutions are failing to solve issues has diverted the public to seek judicial redress where these other institutions have failed. Secondly, the executive has sometimes intentionally shifted questions to the courts in order to secure a judicial resolution of disputes which are economic or political in nature, to avoid having to pay the political price of the decision.

Section 1 of the Mt. Scopus standards expresses the view that the main function of the courts in society is to resolve disputes. The secondary functions are to protect democracy, to defend the constitution and to promote the rule of law and human rights. The idea is that the predominant role of the judiciary is private litigation of cases, initiated mostly by private citizens and corporations rather than public interest litigation initiated by civil rights groups and social organizations. The additional functions, which must be recognized as well, should remain in proportion.

The judiciary cannot invest disproportionate resources to the public interest litigation at the expense of private litigation and the classic function of dispute resolution.

XIV. The Principle of Pre-determined Plan for Case Assignments

Methods of case assignment are not merely administrative in nature. They have constitutional and doctrinal ramifications. In Continental Europe, the principle of the natural judge is widely accepted.

The doctrinal principle with regard to case assignment to judges provides that cases to judicial panels or individual judges should be assigned based on a predetermined plan. This is required in order to avoid the possibility of conscious judge selection in the case assignment based on the content of the cases or the identity of the parties in the cases.

The system for assigning cases should be sophisticated enough to prevent the phenomenon of "judge shopping" – that is, the use, by one or both parties,

[63] As Sir Ninian Stephen wrote, in "Judicial Independence – A Fragile Bastion", in S. Shetreet and J. Deschenes (eds.), *Judicial Independence: The Contemporary Debate* (Dordrecht 1985) 529, at 543 note 1 above.

of procedural tactics, so that their case will be heard before a judge or a panel which they feel to be more favourable to their cause.[64]

The "natural judge" principle requires that courts be constituted prior to the beginning of the trial, thus in the assignment of a judge there is no possibility of one judge being preferred, due to an internal system of judicial dependence. The application of this principle ensures absolute neutrality and randomness with respect to the composition of the judicial panel in any particular case. The "natural judge" principle, first introduced in France (*juge naturel*), is accepted in countries in continental Europe. It clearly enhances public confidence in the court system, since it removes suspicions that the outcome of a specific case can be influenced through deliberate judge selection.[65]

No equivalent principle prevails in common law countries. These countries allow the rejection of a specific judge on the grounds of bias.[66] However, this rule is insufficient and only applies in cases of suspicion of judicial bias, i.e., a specific, negative situation. Case assignment in Common Law countries is a matter for the head of the court (chief justice or president), or it falls within the collective power of the judges of the court, but no substantive principles guide the case assignment, except the general values of efficiency and impartiality, and appearance of justice.[67] The "natural judge" principle, on the other hand, guarantees fairness and neutrality from the very beginning, with respect to the composition of the court.

Needless to say, if by pure chance a judge who is suspected of being biased is selected, there is a provision for his removal from the case, based on well defined procedure.[68] International standards of judicial independence express recognition of the necessity of a practice of a pre-determined case assignment

---

[64] The *St. John's Hospice* affair (A.P. (Appeal Petition) 94, 95, 96/90 *The Greek Orthodox Patriarch of Jerusalem v. Matosian* (not yet published), was a case which dealt with the transfer of immovable property in the Old City of Jerusalem. It attracted a wide range of media coverage due to the heavy political charge attached to it. At one particular stage, the attorneys for the buyers wanted to apply for an urgent remedy from the court. However, at the same time, the judge on duty was one who had already previously handed down a decision against the buyers in the same matter. Therefore, they did not want "to be in need of her services." They waited until midnight on the evening when the judges on duty were to be changed, applied to the new judge on duty, and, without revealing to him the chain of events, were awarded the requested remedy. When the affair became known, the President of the District Court of Jerusalem, in whose jurisdiction this judge shopping was occurring, took a most exceptional step and on a panel including himself, the preferred judge and the undesired judge, the entire proceeding was invalidated.

[65] Shimon Shetreet, Judicial Independence – The Contemporary Debate, note 13 above.

[66] *See* S. Shetreet, "Developments in Constitutional Law" (1990) 24 *Isr. L. Rev*. 368–430.

[67] Shetreet, *Judicial Independence—The Contemporary Debate,* note 13 above, at 618.

[68] Shimon Shetreet, *Justice in Israel, A Study of the Israeli Judiciary* (Martinus Nijhoff,1994) 174–175.

and support a departure from the Common Law approach of total absence of doctrinal limitations in case assignments.[69] The right to a "natural judge" or to "a lawful judge" (*gesetzlicher Richter*) in the German legal tradition is older than the actual existence of Germany as a national state and can be traced back to the 19th century. It has become part of the German constitution and therefore the legislature is bound to uphold it. In Germany, the principle is explicitly provided for in section 101(1) of the Basic Law (*Grundgsetz*). Moreover, it is also possible to apply directly to the federal Supreme Court in Germany with a claim that the said principle, lawful judge (*gesetzeiden richter*) contained in section 101(1), has been violated.

The judiciary determines which judge will preside over a specific case mainly by using an internal method of case assignment. The rule is that the determination of an individual judge sitting on a specific case must be through quasi-automatic methods, such as random choice, without any real discretion left to the case allocation plan which is the process of individualization of the general legal norms.[70]

In the United States, the element of efficiency is emphasised and there exist two principal methods for assigning cases: the individual list method, in which one judge deals with each case from beginning to end; and the master calendar method, in which each case is placed into a pool, where one judge hears the case at a particular stage, after which it is placed back into the pool, to be assigned to a different judge who hears it at its next stage.[71] Unlike in Germany, more than a few circuit courts in the United States have rejected arguments about the constitutional right to random assignment.[72] However some circuits were more sympathetic for arguments of this sort.[73]

Under all methods of case assignment to the judges, the responsibility for the management of case assignment must rest with the heads of the courts, to assume the fair operation of the system and to also give the appearance of justice.[74]

It is important to mention that international standards of judicial independence express cognition of the necessity of a practice of a predetermined plan

---

[69] Shetreet, Judicial Independence – The Contemporary Debate, note 13 above, at pp. 617–620.

[70] Id.

[71] E.C. Friesen, E.C. Gallas and N.M. Gallas, *Managing the Courts* (New York, 1971) pp. 182–184.

[72] See Jonathan L. Entin, "The sign of 'the four': judicial assignment and the rule of law" (1998) 68 Mississippi Law Journal 369–389.

[73] Id. at 375–376. For a discussion about difficulties created by pre-determined plan, see Id. at 377–379.

[74] See article 2.43 of the Montreal Declaration, Part VII, Appendix VIII in this volume.

for case assignment, and support a departure from the Common Law approach of the total absence of doctrinal limitations in case assignments. The IBA Standards (11(a)) provide that "division of work among judges should ordinarily be done under a predetermined plan, which can be changed in certain clearly defined circumstances." The Syracuse Principles (Art. 19) and the Montreal Declaration (Article 2.43) provide that assignment of cases must be done "in accordance with law or rules of court". The IBA Standards are formulated in a more express wording, but the Syracuse and Montreal texts assume that case assignment will be subject to certain rules.

The Mt. Scopus Standards also require a predetermined plan for the distribution of cases among the judges, and by that they are closer to the continental method. The following articles refer to this issue:

2.18. Division of work among judges should ordinarily be done under a predetermined plan, which can be changed in certain clearly defined circumstances.

2.18.1. In countries where the power of division of judicial work is vested in the chief justice, it is not considered inconsistent with judicial independence to accord to the chief justice the power to change the predetermined plan for sound reasons, preferably in consultation with the senior judges when practicable.

2.18.2. Subject to 3.18.1, the exclusive responsibility for case assignment should be vested in a responsible judge, preferably the President of the Court.

PART VII

TEXT OF THE INTERNATIONAL STANDARDS OF JUDICIAL INDEPENDENCE

APPENDIX I

MOUNT SCOPUS INTERNATIONAL STANDARDS OF JUDICIAL INDEPENDENCE* 2008

Preamble

These Revised standards are approved in recognition of the need for the revision of the guidelines of general application to contribute to the independence and impartiality of the judiciary, with a view to ensuring the legitimacy and effectiveness of the judicial process;

In formulating these standards due regard has been given to the IBA Minimum Standards on Judicial independence 1982 and the UN Basic Principles of Judicial Independence 1985 and the long series of sets of other international rules and standards relating to judicial independence and the right to a fair trial; and *The Burgh House Principles of Judicial Independence in International Law* (for the international judiciary). Inspiration has also been drawn from the *Tokyo Law Asia Principles*; the *Montréal Universal Declaration on the Independence of Justice*; *Council of Europe Staetements on judicial independence* particularly Recommendation of the Committee of Ministers to Member States on the independence, efficiency and role of judges. Council of Europe *1998*[1], *The Bangalore Principles of Judicial Conduct* November 2002,[2] and the *American Bar Association*'s revision of its ethical standards for judges.

The Standards were drafted bearing in mind the special challenges facing the judiciary in view of the challenges and problems in both the national and international spheres.

An updated comprehensive revision of minimum standards for judicial independence is called for in order to give appropriate response to the developments and challenges regarding the position of courts and judges in contemporary society. This revision is important to enable the judiciary to play a role in the adequate protection of human rights and in the operation of an efficient and fair market economy with a human face in the era of globalisation.

The standards give due consideration particularly to the fact that that each jurisdiction and legal tradition has own characteristics that must be recognised. It is also recognized that in the international judiciary each court or tribunal has its unique features and functions and that in certain instances judges serve on a part-time basis or as *ad hoc* or *ad litem* judges.

---

* The Mt. Scopus Standards are available online in: http://law.huji.ac.il/eng/segel.asp?staff_id=15&cat=441

[1] http://www.coe.int

[2] adopted by *Judicial Group on Strengthening Judicial Integrity*, AJA, http://www.ajs.org

I. National Judges

1. The Significance of the Independence of the Judiciary

1.1. An independent and impartial[3] judiciary is an institution of the highest value in every society[4] and an essential pillar of liberty[5] and the rule of law.

1.2. The objectives and functions of the judiciary shall include:

1.2.1.1. To resolve disputes and to administer the law impartially between persons and between persons and public authorities;

1.2.1.2. To promote, within the proper limits of the judicial function, the observance and the attainment of human rights; and

1.2.1.3. To ensure that all people are able to live securely under the rule of law.[6]

2. The Judiciary[7] and the Executive

2.1. The Judiciary as a whole shall be independent.

2.2. Each judge shall enjoy both personal independence and substantive independence:[8]

2.2.1. Personal independence means that the terms and conditions of judicial service are adequately secured by law[9] so as to ensure that individual judges are not subject to executive control; and

---

[3] Stating this in the body of the standards themselves in addition to the preamble helps stress the section's importance and ensures that it is more easily referred to.

→ This is preferred to the first version as it describes exactly what elements are required in the Judiciary

→ Tokyo Law Asia Principles. Stating this in the body of the standards themselves rather than in a preamble helps stress the section's importance and ensures that it is more easily referred to.

[5] Preamble, Montréal Declaration.

[6] Montréal Declaration.

→ Recall competing values of judicial independence and judicial accountability: "As phrased by a Canadian judge, Mr. Justice Riddell, commenting on an arrangement of divisions of labour among the judges, 'Judges are the servants, not the masters of the people.' Servants are accountable, so are judges." From Shetreet, *Judicial Independence: The Contemporary Debate*, at 593, referring to *Davis Acetylene Gas Co. v. Morrison*, (1915) 34 O.L.R. 155, 23 D.L.R. 871 (C.A.).

[7] The focus is really on the relationship with the judiciary as a whole, rather than with individual judges.

[8] Although substantive independence warrants wide protection, it is not without boundaries. Judges must exercise their powers subject to the general limit of mutual respect between the various branches of the government and accepted lines of demarcation of their respective responsibilities. The mutual respect is expressed in judge-made rules, including the rule that courts will not engage in the adjudication of unjusticiable issues, such as political questions: Shetreet, Judicial Independence: New Conceptual Dimensions and Contemporary Challenges, in Shetreet and Descenes *Judicial Independence: The Contemporary Debate* at 635.(1985)

[9] To clarify that these important conditions must be legally entrenched.

2.2.2. Substantive independence means that in the discharge of his judicial function, a judge is subject to nothing but the law and the commands of his conscience.

2.3. The Judiciary as a whole shall[10] enjoy collective independence and autonomy vis-à-vis the Executive.

2.4. Judicial appointments and promotions by the Executive are not inconsistent with judicial independence as long as they are in accordance with Principles 4.

2.5. No executive decree shall reverse specific court decisions, or change the composition of the court in order to affect its decision-making.[11]

2.6. The Executive may only participate in the discipline of judges by referring complaints against judges, or by the initiation of disciplinary proceedings, but not by the adjudication of such matters.

2.7. The power to discipline or remove a judge must be vested in an institution which is independent of the Executive.

2.8. The power of removal of a judge shall preferably be vested in a judicial tribunal.

2.9. The Executive shall not have control over judicial functions.

2.10. Rules of procedure and practice shall be made by legislation or by the Judiciary in cooperation with the legal profession, subject to parliamentary approval.

2.11. The state shall have a duty to provide for the execution of judgments of the Court. The Judiciary shall exercise supervision over the execution process.

2.12. Judicial matters are exclusively within the responsibility of the Judiciary, both in central judicial administration and in court level judicial administration.

2.13. The central responsibility for judicial administration shall preferably be vested in the Judiciary or jointly in the Judiciary and the Executive.

2.14. The principle of democratic accountability should be respected and therefore it is legitimate for the legislature to play a role in judicial appointments and central administration of justice provided that due consideration is given to the principle of judicial independence.

2.15. The process and standards of judicial selection shall give due consideration to the principle of fair reflection by the judiciary of the society in all its aspects.[12]

---

[10] Adds mandatory language.

[11] Montréal Declaration section 2.08.

[12] Montréal Declaration section 2.13. See also Shetreet, *Judicial Independence: The Contemporary Debate*, at 401.

2.15.1. Taking into consideration the principle of fair reflection by the judiciary of the society in all its aspects, in the selection of judges, there shall be no discrimination on the grounds of race, colour, gender, language, religion, national or social origin, property, birth or status, subject however to citizenship requirements.[13]

2.16. Candidates for judicial office shall be individuals of integrity[14] and ability, well- trained in the law. They shall have equality of access to judicial office.[15]

2.17. It is the duty of the state to provide adequate financial resources to allow for the due administration of justice.

2.18. Division of work among judges should ordinarily be done under a predetermined plan, which can be changed in certain clearly defined circumstances.

2.18.1. In countries where the power of division of judicial work is vested in the chief justice, it is not considered inconsistent with judicial independence to accord to the chief justice the power to change the predetermined plan for sound reasons, preferably in consultation with the senior judges when practicable.

2.18.2. Subject to 3.18.1, the exclusive responsibility for case assignment should be vested in a responsible judge, preferably the President of the Court.

2.19. The power to transfer a judge from one court to another shall be vested in a judicial authority according to grounds provided by law and preferably shall be subject to the judge's consent, such consent not to be unreasonably withheld.

2.20. Judicial salaries and pensions shall be adequate at all times, fixed by law, and should be periodically reviewed independently of Executive control.

2.21. The position of the judges, their independence, their security of tenure, and their adequate remuneration shall be entrenched constitutionally[16] or secured by law.

2.22. Judicial salaries, pensions, and benefits[17] cannot be decreased during judges' service except as a coherent part of an overall public economic measure.

---

[13] Montréal Declaration
→ "Political opinion" is also taken from PH Lane, *Fragile Bastion: Constitutional Aspects of Judicial Independence* (judicial independence is composed of at least five aspects: (1) non-political appointments to a court; (2) guaranteed tenure and salary; (3) executive and legislative interference with court proceedings or office holders; (4) budgetary autonomy; (5) administrative autonomy.

[14] Montréal Declaration section 2.11.

[15] Exact wording of the Montréal Declaration, section 2.11.

[16] UN Basic Principles.
→ Change suggested in order to provide additional flexibility, and also to stress how this is an important enough issue to be constitutionally entrenched.

[17] In the interests of completeness.

2.23. The Ministers of the government shall not exercise any form of pressure on judges, whether overt or covert, and shall not make statements which adversely affect the independence of individual judges, or of the Judiciary as a whole.

2.24. The power of pardon shall be exercised cautiously so as to avoid its use as an interference with judicial decision.

2.25. The Executive shall refrain from any act or omission which pre-empts the judicial resolution of a dispute, or frustrates the proper execution of a court judgment.

2.26. The Executive shall not have the power to close down, or suspend, or delay, the operation of the court system at any level.

3. The Judiciary[18] and the Legislature

3.1. The Legislature shall not pass legislation which reverses specific court decisions.

3.2. Legislation introducing changes in the terms and conditions of judicial service shall not be applied to judges holding office at the time of passing the legislation unless the changes improve the terms of service and are generally applied.[19]

3.3. In case of legislation reorganising or abolishing courts, judges serving in these courts shall not be affected, except for their transfer to another court of the same or materially comparable[20] status.

---

[18] The focus is really on the relationship with the judiciary as a whole, rather than with individual judges.

[19] In order to prevent "rewarding" specific judges.

→ The US Constitution's Compensation Clause guarantees federal judges a "Compensation, which shall not be diminished during their Continuance in Office." *U.S. Const.*, Art. III, §1.

→ See *US v. Hatter* (99–1978) 532 U.S. 557 (2001) 203 F.3d 795: Congress is prohibited from singling out judges for specially unfavourable taxation treatment, although it is permitted to impose a "non-discriminatory tax laid generally" upon judges and other citizens.

→ See *United States v. Will*, 449 U.S. 200, 220–21 (1980): though Congress may not rescind a salary increase for judges once it has gone into effect - that would be a diminishment of compensation - Congress is under no constitutional obligation to grant salary increases.

→ See *Evans v. Gore*, 253 U.S. 245, 253 (1920): The imposition of a new federal tax that has the effect of reducing the judicial compensation of judges already in office is unconstitutional.

→ But see *O'Malley v. Woodrough*, 307 U.S. 277 (1939): an income tax levied against the judicial salary of judges who took office after the levy is in effect is constitutional, when the taxing measure is of general, non-discriminatory application to all earners of income.

[20] To provide for situations such as those that occurred in Ontario when the entire court structure was reorganized.

3.4. Everyone shall have the right to be tried expeditiously by the established ordinary courts or judicial tribunals under law, subject to review by the courts.[21]

3.5. Part-time judges should be appointed only with proper safeguards secured by law.

3.6. The Legislature may be vested with the powers of removal of judges, upon a recommendation of a judicial commission or pursuant to constitutional provisions or validly enacted legislation.[22]

4. Terms and Nature of Judicial Appointments

4.1. The method of judicial selection shall safeguard against judicial appointments for improper motives[23] and shall not threaten judicial independence.

4.2. a) The principle of democratic accountability should be respected and therefore it is legitimate for the Executive and the Legislature to play a role in judicial appointments provided that due consideration is given to the principle of Judicial Independence.

b) The recent trend of establishing judicial selection boards or commissions in which members or representatives of the Legislature, the Executive, the Judiciary and the legal profession take part, should be viewed favourably, provided that a proper balance is maintained in the composition of such boards or commissions of each of the branches of government.

4.3. Judicial appointments should generally be for life, subject to removal for cause and compulsory retirement at an age fixed by law at the date of appointment.

4.3.1. Retirement age shall not be reduced for existing judges.[24]

4.4. Promotion of judges shall[25] be based on objective factors, in particular merit,[26] integrity and experience.[27]

---

[21] For a discussion of this issue, see Shetreet, *Judicial Independence: The Contemporary Debate*, at 616.

[22] In order to try to prevent situations such as those that occurred in Ecuador in April 2007 when Congress removed all nine judges of the Constitutional Court in a retaliatory measure, contrary to the Ecuadorian constitution which provides that judges of the Constitutional Court can only be removed by impeachment: Human Rights Watch, *Ecuador: Removal of Judges Undermines Judicial Independence* (May 11, 2007).

[23] Montréal Declaration.

[24] See Shetreet, Judicial Independence: New Conceptual Dimensions and Contemporary Challenges, in Shetreet and Descenes *Judicial Independence: The Contemporary Debate*, at 607 (1985) reporting that in Bangladesh, in 1977 an ordinance was passed bringing down the retirement age from 65 to 62 years with immediate effect. This resulted in the retirement of two distinguished judges. This was in fact a legislative removal of these two judges though it was in theory a general statute.

[25] In order to make this mandatory.

[26] "Merit" is broader than "ability".

[27] UN Basic Principles.

→ Montréal Declaration provides: "Promotion of a judge shall be based on an objective assessment of the candidate's integrity and independence of judgment, professional competence, experience, humanity and commitment to uphold the rule of law."

4.5. Judicial appointments and promotions shall be based on transparency of the procedures and standards and shall be based on professional qualifications, integrity, ability and efficiency.

4.6. Judges should not be appointed for probationary periods except in legal systems in which appointments of judges do not depend on having practical experience in the profession as a condition of appointment, and provided that permanent appointment will be granted on merit.[28]

4.7. The institution of temporary judges should be avoided as far as possible except where there exists a long historic democratic tradition.

4.8. Part-time judges should be appointed only with proper safeguards secured by law.

4.9. The number of the members of the highest court should be fixed, with the exception of courts modeled after the courts of cassion, and in the case of all courts, should not be altered for improper motives.

5. Judicial Removal and Discipline

5.1. The proceedings for discipline and removal of judges[29] shall be processed expeditiously and fairly[30] and shall ensure fairness to the judge including adequate opportunity for hearing.

5.2. With the exception of proceedings before the Legislature[31], the procedure for discipline should be held *in camera*. The judge may however request that the hearing be held in public[32] and such request should be respected, subject to expeditious, final and reasoned disposition of this request by the disciplinary tribunal. Judgments in disciplinary proceedings, whether held in camera or in public, may be published.[33]

5.3. All of the grounds for the discipline, suspension and removal of judges shall be entrenched constitutionally or fixed by law and shall be clearly defined.

5.4. All disciplinary, suspension and removal[34] actions shall be based upon established standards of judicial conduct.[35]

5.5. A judge shall not be subject to removal, unless by reason of a criminal act or through gross or repeated neglect or serious infringements of disciplinary rules or physical or mental incapacity he has shown himself manifestly unfit

---

[28] Scottish temporary judges cases Starrs and Chalmers v. D. F. Linlithgow 2000 S. L. 2; Clancy v. Caird 2000 Scottish Law Times, The Bailiff Judicial Appointments (Scotland) Act 2000.

[29] The UN Basic Principles adds "in his/her judicial and professional capacity." This wording was not added here to prevent personal suits being lodged against judges as a back-door method of interfering with their independence.

[30] UN Basic Principles.

[31] Montréal Declaration section 2.36.

[32] Montréal Declaration section 2.36.

[33] Montréal Declaration section 2.36.

[34] Inclusive.

[35] Montréal Declaration section 2.34. Broad.

to hold the position of judge. The grounds for removal shall be limited to reasons of medical incapacity or behaviour that renders the judge unfit to discharge their duties.[36]

5.6. In systems where the power to discipline and remove judges is vested in an institution other than the Legislature, the tribunal for discipline and removal of judges shall be permanent, and be composed predominantly of members of the Judiciary.

5.7. The head of the court may legitimately have supervisory powers to control judges on administrative matters.

6. The Media and the Judiciary

6.1. It should be recognized that judicial independence does not render judges free from public accountability, however, the media and other institutions should show respect for judicial independence and exercise restrain in criticism of judicial decisions.[37]

6.2. While recognising the general right of freedom of expression of all citizens, a judge should not interview directly with the general media. If a judge needs to respond to the media in regard to a media report or inquiry, it shall be done via a spokesperson assigned by the court or a judge specifically assigned by the court for this purpose. In exceptional circumstances a judge may respond directly to the media if that judge's direct response will prevent an irreparable damage.

6.3. The media should show responsibility and restraint in publications on pending cases where such publication may influence the outcome of the case.

6.4. A judge shall not knowingly, while a proceeding is, or could come before the judge, make any comment that might reasonably be expected to affect the outcome of such proceeding or impair the manifest fairness of the process. Nor shall the judge make any comment in public or otherwise that might affect the fair trial of any person or issue.[38]

7. Standards of Conduct[39]

7.1. Judges may not serve in Executive or Legislative functions, including as:

7.1.1. Ministers of the government; or as

7.1.2. Members of the Legislature or of municipal councils.

---

[36] UN Basic Principles.

[37] See discussion by Julie Debeljak, *Judicial Conference of Australia, Uluru, April 2001: Judicial Independence: A Collection of Material for the Judicial Conference of Australia* regarding the consequences of inappropriate public criticism (it leaves judges having to choose between being silent leading to a potential decrease in public confidence in the judiciary, or else inappropriately being drawn into public criticism).

[38] Bangalore Principles.

[39] Human Rights Watch, *Rigging the Rule of Law: Judicial Independence Under Siege in Venezuela*, Volume 16, No. 3(B) (June 2004) reporting some of allegations of judicial bias in

7.2. Judges shall not hold positions in political parties.

7.3. A judge, other than a temporary or part-time judge, may not practice law.

7.4. A judge should refrain from business activities and should avoid from engaging in other remunerative activity,[40] that can affect the exercise of judicial functions or the image of the judge, except in respect of that judge's personal investments, ownership of property, the business activities or ownership of property of family members[41], or that judge's teaching at a university or a college.

7.5. A judge should always behave in such a manner as to preserve the dignity of the office and the impartiality, integrity and independence of the Judiciary.

7.6. Judges may be organized in associations designed for judges, for furthering their rights and interests as judges.

7.7. Judges may take appropriate action to protect their judicial independence.[42]

7.8. A judge shall disqualify himself or herself from participating in any proceedings in which the judge is unable to decide the matter impartially or in which it may appear to a reasonable observer that the judge is unable to decide the matter impartially.

7.9. Such proceedings include, but are not limited to, instances where

a) the judge has actual bias or prejudice concerning a party or personal knowledge of disputed evidentiary facts concerning the proceedings;

b) the judge previously served as a lawyer or was a material witness in the matter in controversy; or

c) the judge, or a member of the judge's family, has an economic interest in the outcome of the matter in controversy:
Provided that disqualification of a judge shall not be required if no other tribunal can be constituted to deal with the case or, because of urgent circumstances, failure to act could lead to a serious miscarriage of justice [43]

7.10. A case should not be withdrawn from a particular judge without valid reasons, such as cases of serious illness or conflict of interest. Any such reasons and the procedures for such withdrawal should be provided for by law and

---

Venezuela. For instance, Attorney General Isaías Rodríguez in May 2004 allegedly described how the country's top administrative court in the past established set fees for resolving different kinds of cases.

[40] ABA Model Code of Judicial Conduct (February 2007), Canon 4, Article D(2).

[41] ABA Model Code of Judicial Conduct (February 2007), Canon 4, Article D(2) discusses family.

[42] This is how the section appears in the Montréal Declaration, section 2.09.

[43] Bangalore Principles.

may not be influenced by any interest of the government or administration. A decision to withdraw a case from a judge should be taken by an authority which enjoys the same judicial independence as judges.[44]

7.11. Judges shall discourage *ex parte* communications from parties and except as provided by the rules of the court such communications shall be disclosed to the court and to the other party.

8. Securing Impartiality and Independence[45]

8.1. A judge[46] shall enjoy immunity from legal actions in the exercise of his official functions.[47]

8.2. A judge shall not sit in a case where there is a reasonable suspicion of bias or potential bias.[48]

8.3. A judge shall avoid any course of conduct which might give rise to an appearance of partiality.

8.4. The state shall ensure that in the decision-making process, judges should be independent and be able to act without any restriction, improper influence, inducements, pressures, threats[49] or interferences, direct or indirect, from any quarter or for any reason. The law should provide for sanctions against persons seeking to influence judges in any such manner. Judges should have unfettered freedom to decide cases impartially, in accordance with their conscience and their interpretation of the facts, and in pursuance of the prevailing rules of the law. Judges should not be obliged to report on the merits of their cases to anyone outside the judiciary [50]

9. The Internal Independence of the Judiciary

9.1 In the decision-making process, a judge must be independent vis-à-vis his judicial colleagues and superiors.

---

[44] Recommendation No.R(94)12). of the committee of Ministers of the Council of Europe to Memner States.

[45] See Cyrus Das and K. Chandra, Editors, *Judges and Judicial Accountability*, Universal Law Publishing Company Ltd., Delhi.

[46] This does not exclude the possibility that the state may be liable for the gross negligence of a judicial officer.

[47] Consider a 1988 Italian law which was designed to, within certain limit, render judges accountable for damages caused by serious fault in the exercise of their functions: see Giovanni E. Longo, "The Human Right to an Independent Judiciary: International Norms and Denied application before a Domestic Jurisdiction," *St. John's Law Review* (Winter 1996).

[48] "It is most important that the judiciary be independent and be so perceived by the public. The judges must not have cause to fear that they will be prejudiced by their decisions or that the public would reasonably apprehend this to be the case": Howland, CJ, *R. v. Valente* 2 C.C.C. (3d) 417, at 423 (1983).

[49] Including physical threats to injure or to kill.

[50] Recommendation No.R(94)12 of the committee of Ministers of the Council of Europe to Memner States.

9.2 Any hierarchical organization of the judiciary and any difference in grade or rank shall in no way interfere with the right of judges to pronounce their judgments freely.[51]

II. International Judges

The following text on minimum standards for the independence of the international judiciary is based, with minor amendments, on the Burgh House Principles on the Independence of the International Judiciary which were formulated by the Study Group of the International Law Association on the Practice and Procedure of International Courts and Tribunals.

10. Independence

10.1 The international courts and the judges shall exercise their functions free from direct or indirect interference or influence by any person or entity.

10.2 This freedom of the judges and courts shall apply both to the judicial process in pending cases, including the assignment of cases to particular judges, and to the operation of the court and its registry.

10.3 The court shall be free to determine the conditions for its international administration, including staff recruitment policy, information systems and allocation of budgetary expenditure.

10.4 Deliberations of the court shall remain confidential.

10.5 All Judges of international courts and tribunals shall adhere to the principle that a judges who are nationals of a member state of the organisation establishing the court or tribunal when exercising judicial discretion and function shall engage in fair and independent adjudication of the case and by no means in representation of the member state.

11. Nomination, Election and Appointment

11.1 In accordance with the governing instruments, judges shall be chosen from among persons of high moral character, integrity and conscientiousness who possess the appropriate professional qualifications, competence and experience required for the court concerned.

11.2 While procedures for nomination, election and appointment should consider fair representation of different geographic regions and the principal legal systems, as appropriate, as well as of female and male judges, appropriate personal and professional qualifications must be the overriding consideration in the nomination, election and appointment of judges.

11.3 Procedures for the nomination, election, and appointment of judges should be transparent and provide appropriate safeguards against nominations, elections and appointments motivated by improper considerations.

---

[51] Montréal Declaration section 2.03.

11.4 Information regarding the nomination, election and appointment process and information about candidates for judicial office should be made public, in due time and in an effective manner, by the international organisation or other body responsible for the nomination, election and appointment process.

11.5 For the promotion of the independence of judges it is preferable that appointment of judges to the international courts and tribunals shall be for one long term and shall not be open for re-election.

12. Security of Tenure

12.1 Judges shall have security of tenure in relations to their term of office. They may only be removed from office upon specified grounds and in accordance with appropriate procedures specified in advance.

12.2 The governing instruments of each court should provide for judges to be appointed for a minimum term to enable them to exercise their judicial functions in an independent manner.

13. Service and Remuneration

13.1 Judges' essential conditions of service shall be enumerated in legally binding instruments.

13.2 No adverse changes shall be introduced with regard to judges' remuneration and other essential conditions of service during their terms of office.

13.3 Judges should receive adequate remuneration which should be periodically adjusted in line with any increases in the cost of living at the seat of the court.

13.4 Conditions of service should include adequate pension arrangements.

14. Privileges and Immunities

14.1 Judges shall enjoy immunities equivalent to full diplomatic immunities, and in particular shall enjoy immunities from all claims arising from the exercise of their judicial functions.

14.2 The court alone shall be competent to waive the immunity of judges; it should waive immunity in any case where, in its opinion, the immunity would impede the course of justice and can be waived without prejudice to the exercise of the judicial function.

14.3 Documents and papers of the courts, judges and registry, in so far as they relate to the business of the court, shall be inviolable.

14.4 The state in which an international court has its seat shall take the necessary measures to protect the security of the judges and their families, and to protect them from adverse measures related to the exercise of their judicial function.

15. Budget

15.1 States, parties and international organisations shall provide adequate resources, including facilities and levels of staffing, to enable courts and the judges to perform their functions effectively.

16. Freedom of Expression and Association

16.1 Judges shall enjoy freedom of expression and association. These freedoms must be exercised in a manner that is compatible with the judicial function and that may not affect or reasonably appear to affect judicial independence or impartiality.

16.2 Judges shall maintain the confidentiality of deliberations, and shall not comment extra-judicially upon pending cases.

16.3 Judges shall exercise appropriate restrain in commenting extra-judicially upon judgements and procedures of their own and other courts and may upon any legislation, drafts, proposals or subject-matter likely to come before their court.

17. Extra-Judicial Activity

17.1 Judges shall not engage in any extra-judicial activity that is incompatible with their judicial function or the efficient and timely functioning of the court of which they are members, or that may affect or may reasonably appear to affect their independence or impartiality.

17.2 Judges shall not exercise any political function.

17.3 Each court should establish an appropriate mechanism to give guidance to judges in relation to extra-judicial activities, and to ensure that appropriate means exist for parties to proceedings to raise any concerns.

18. Past Links to a Case

18.1 Judges shall not serve in a case in which they have previously served as agent, counsel, advisor, advocate, expert or in any other capacity for one of the parties, or as a member of a national or international court or other dispute settlement body which has considered the subject matter of the dispute or in a case where they had previously commented or expressed an opinion concerning the subject matter in a manner that is likely to affect or may reasonably appear to affect their independence or impartiality.

18.2 Judges shall not serve in a case with the subject matter of which they had other forms of association that may affect or may reasonably appear to affect their independence or impartiality.

19. Past Links to a Party

19.1 Judges shall not sit in any case involving a party for whom they have served as agent, counsel, advisor, advocate or expert within the previous three years or such other period as the court may establish within its rules; or with whom they have had any other significant professional or personal link within the previous three years or such other period as the court may establish within its rules.

20. Interest in the Outcome of a Case

20.1 Judges shall not sit in any case in the outcome of which they hold any material personal, professional or financial interest.

20.2 Judges shall not sit in any case in the outcome of which other persons or entities closely related to them hold a material, personal, professional or financial interest.

20.3 Judges must not accept any undisclosed payment from a party to the proceedings or any payment whatsoever on account of a judge's participation in the proceedings.

21. Contact with a Party

21.1 Judges shall exercise appropriate caution in their personal contacts with parties, agents, counsel, advocates, advisors, and other persons and entities associated with a pending case. Any such contacts should be conducted in a manner that is compatible with the judicial function and that may not affect or reasonably appear to affect the judge's independence and impartiality.

21.2 Judges shall discourage *ex parte* communications from parties and except as provided by the rules of the court such communications shall be disclosed to the court and to the other party.

22. Post-Service Limitations

22.1 Judges shall not serve in a case with the subject-matter of which they have had any other form of association that may affect or may reasonably appear to affect their independence or impartiality.

22.2 Judges shall not seek or accept, while they are in office, any future employment, appointment or benefit, from a party to a case on which they sat or from any entity related to such a party that may affect or may reasonably appear to affect their independence or impartiality.

22.3 Former judges shall not, except as permitted by rules of the court, act in any capacity in relations to any case on which they sat during their judicial term of office.

22.4 Former judges shall not act as agent, counsel, advisor or advocate in any proceedings before the court on which they previously served for a period of three years after they have left office or such other period as the court may establish and publish.

22.5 Former judges should exercise appropriate caution as regards the acceptance of any employment, appointment or benefit, in particular from a party to a case on which they sat or from any entity related to such a party.

23. Disclosure

23.1 Judges shall disclose to the court and, as appropriate, to the parties of the proceedings any circumstances which come to their notice at any time by virtue of which any of Principles 16 to 22 apply.

23.2 Each court shall establish appropriate procedures to enable judges to disclose to the court and, as appropriate, to the parties to the proceedings matters that may affect or may reasonably appear to affect their independence or impartiality in relations to any particular case.

24. Waiver

24.1 Notwithstanding Principles 16 to 22, judges shall not be prevented from sitting in a case where they have made appropriate disclosure of any facts bringing any of those Principles into operation, where the court expresses no objections and the parties give their express and informed consent to the judge acting.

25. Withdrawal or Disqualification

25.1 Each court shall establish rules of procedure to enable the determination whether judges are prevented from sitting in a particular case as a result of the application of these Principles or for reasons of incapacity. Such procedures shall be available to a judge, the court, or any party to the proceedings.

26. Misconduct

26.1 Each court shall establish rules of procedure to address a specific complaint of misconduct or breach of duty on the party of a judge that may affect independence or impartiality.

26.2 Such a complaint may, if clearly unfounded, be resolved on a summary basis. IN any case where the court determines that more detailed investigation is required, the rules shall establish adequate safeguards to protect the judges' rights and interests and to ensure appropriate confidentiality of the proceedings.

26.3 The governing instruments of the court shall provide for appropriate measures, including the removal from office of a judge.

26.4 The outcome of any complaint shall be communicated to the complainant.

27. Ad Hoc Judges

27.1 An *ad hoc* judge in an international court or tribunal must act conscientiously and independently in the adjudication of the case to which that judge was assigned to sit.

27.2 The restrictions and provisions applicable to full-time international judges regarding past links, extra-judicial activities, post-service limitations, and security of tenure shall not apply to *ad hoc* judges.

Amendments to The Mt Scopus International Standards of Judicial Independence Approved in Vienna 21st May 2011

Add a paragraph in Section 1.3 as follows

1.3 It is vital that supranational and international Tribunals respect the fundamental principles of the legal systems of the Member States and to that end acknowledge the collegiality of the traditions of the courts of both the municipal and extra municipal courts.

Add to Section 7

7.12. Except in cases of legitimate consultations a Judge shall not approach other judges not sitting with him on the same panel on pending cases.

Add to section 4

4.10. Legislatures should formulate special procedures for the appointment of Chief Justices and Presidents of courts.

Add Section 9A

9A. ADMINISTRATIVE ADJUDICATORS

Administrative adjudicatory officers

9A.1—Definitions
In this section the term administrative adjudicators means — Administrative officers exercising judicial functions in agencies but are not part of the regular court system.

9A.2. Except as provided below, the standards applicable to national judges shall apply to administrative adjudicators.

9A.3. Administrative officers exercising judicial functions - hereinafter administrative adjudicators - may be appointed by the executive on merit according to the general principles in section 4.4 and section 4.5.

9A.4. Administrative adjudicators may be appointed for probationary periods provided the decision whether to make a permanent appointment is based on merit.

9A.5. Compensation of administrative adjudicators shall not be reduced except as part of a general economic measures applied to the country as a whole.

9A.6. Administrative adjudicators may be removed only for good cause, to be specified by law, and only after a fair hearing.

9A.7. Administrative adjudicators shall not exercise or be assigned non-adjudicatory functions in the same or a related matter in which they perform adjudicatory functions.

9A.8. Decisions of administrative adjudicators, including factual findings and legal conclusions, shall be subject to review by the agency that administers the program under which the matter arises and also may be subject to judicial review according to law.

9A.9. The executive shall not interfere in the substantive decision-making of administrative adjudicators.

9A.10. Administrative adjudicators shall be subject to evaluation according to objective criteria that are related to promoting uniform decisional standards.

Appendix 1

Officers and Conferences of the International project on judicial independence

1. *General Coordinator, International Project on Judicial Independence*

Professor Shimon Shetreet, Director Sacher Institute of Comparative Law, and Greenblatt Professor of Public and International Law, Hebrew University of Jerusalem.

2. *Co Chairs of the international conference on Judicial Independence in International Law Jerusalem 26–27 June 2007*

Professor Shimon Shetreet, Director Sacher Institute of Comparative Law, and Greenblatt Professor of Public and International Law, Hebrew University of Jerusalem,
Professor James R. Crawford, Faculty of Law, University of Cambridge

3. *Officers of the international conference on Judicial Independence for the Drafting of the International Standards of Judicial Independence Zurich Area Conference 30 November –1st of December 2007*

Professor Shimon Shetreet, Co Chair of the Conference. Director, Sacher Institute of Comparative Law, and Greenblatt Professor of Public and International Law, Hebrew University of Jerusalem,
Professor Christopher F. Forsyth, Co Chair of the Conference. Director Centre of Public Law, Faculty of Law, University of Cambridge
Professor Marcel Storme, Emeritus Professor, Ghent University, Past President of the World Association of Procedural Law, Leader of the Discussions
HE Markus Buechel, Chair of the Local Organising Committee

4. *Co Chairs of the international conference on Judicial Independence and the Constitutional Position of the Judiciary Jerusalem 18–20 2008*

Professor Shimon Shetreet, Co Chair of the Conference. Director, Sacher Institute of Comparative Law, and Greenblatt Professor of Public and International Law, Hebrew University of Jerusalem.
Professor Christopher F Forsyth, Co Chair of the Conference. Director Centre of Public Law, Faculty of Law, University of Cambridge

5. *Co Chairs of the international conference on Judicial Independence and the Constitutional Position of the Judiciary Krakow November 2008*

Professor Shimon Shetreet, Co Chair of the Conference. Director, Sacher Institute of Comparative Law, and Greenblatt Professor of Public and International Law, Hebrew University of Jerusalem.
Prof. Dr. Fryderyk Zoll, Faculty of Law, Jagelonian University, Krakow

6. *Co Chairs of the international conference on the The Culture of Judicial independence – Conceptual Foundations and Practical Challenges University of Cambridge 14–16 August 2009*

Professor Shimon Shetreet, Co Chair of the Conference. Greenblatt Professor of Public and International Law, Hebrew University of Jerusalem, past Director, Sacher Institute of Comparative Law.
Professor Christopher F Forsyth, Co Chair of the Conference. Director Centre of Public Law, Faculty of Law, University of Cambridge.

7. *Co Chairs of the international conference on Judicial Independence; Judicial Independence in Crisis Time – Implementing judicial independence in multi cultural societies and in times of crisis. University of Utah 1–3 October 2010*

Professor Shimon Shetreet, Co Chair of the Conference. Greenblatt Professor of Public and International Law, Hebrew University of Jerusalem, past Director, Sacher Institute of Comparative Law.
Dean Hiram Chodosh, Co Chair of the Conference. Dean School of Law, University of Utah
Prof. Wayne McCormack, Co Chair of the Conference. Dean School of Law, University of Utah

8. *Co Chairs of the international conference on Judicial Independence and International Trade in a Global Economy. University of Vienna 20–22 May 2011*

Professor Shimon Shetreet, Co Chair of the Conference. Greenblatt Professor of Public and International Law, Hebrew University of Jerusalem, past Director, Sacher Institute of Comparative Law,
Prof Walter Rechenberger, Co Chair of the Conference, Faculty of Law, University of Vienna

9. *Members of the Consultation Group of the International Project of Judicial Independence*

Dr Cyrus Das, Former President of the Bar of Malaysia
Dr. Anat Scolnicov, Deputy Director, Centere of Public Law, University of Cambridge
Prof. Dr. Fryderyk Zoll, Faculty of Law, Jagelonian University, Krakow
Prof. Yuval Shany, Faculty of Law, Hebrew University of Jerusalem
H.E. Advocate Markus Buechel, Senior Lawyer, Liechtenstein
Justice Tassaduq Hussain Jillani, Judge of the Supreme Court of Pakistan
Prof. Yitzhak Hadari, Tel Aviv University, Natanya College Law
Professor Maimon Schwarzschild, Faculty of Law, University of San Diego
Professor Ada Pellegrini Grinover, Brazil
Professor Albert Chen, Professor of Law, Hong Kong University
Professor Andreyj J. Zoll, Former President of Constitutional Court of Poland
Professor Anton Cooray, The School of Law, City University of Hong Kong
Professor Bernhard Ehrenzeller, Universität St.Gallen

Professor Bryant G. Garth, American Bar Foundation
Professor Chandra R De Silva, Dean, College of Arts and Letters at Old Dominion University
Professor Christopher F Forsyth, Director Centre of Public Law, Faculty of Law University of Cambridge
Professor Daniel Thurer, Universität Zürich
Professor David Feldman, Chairman of the Faculty Board of Law, Faculty of Law University of Cambridge
Professor Asher Maoz, Tel-Aviv University, Faculty of Law
Professor Dr. Burkhardt Hess, University of Heidelberg
Professor Yoav Dotan, Dean Faculty of Law Hebrew University
Dr. Tomer Braude, Faculty of Law Hebrew University
Professor Dr. Francisco Ramos Mendez, Univ of Barcelona
Professor Dr. Paul Oberhammer, Universität Zürich
Professor Dr. Winfried Brugger, Universitat Heidelberg
Professor Frank Bates, School of Law, University of Newcastle Australia
Paul Morris, Barrister York UK
Prof. Sir Louis Blom-Cooper, UK
Professor Federico Carpi, President of the World –Association of Procedural Law
Professor Garry D. Watson, Osgoode Hall Law School, York University
Professor Gary J Simson, Dean, Case Western Reserve University
Professor Joseph Weiler, New York University
Professor Walter Habscheid, Prof Emeritus, University of Zurich
Professor Hans Walter Fasching, Austria
Professor Hiram Chodosh, Dean, S.J. College of Law, the University of Utah
Professor Hoong Phun ('H.P.') Lee, Deputy Dean, Faculty of Law, Monash University
Professor James Nemeth, Eotvos Lorand University, Hungary
Professor James R Crawford, Faculty of Law, University of Cambridge
Professor John Anthony Jolowicz, Trinity College, University of Cambridge
Professor John Bell, Faculty of Law, University of Cambridge
Professor Jonathan Entin, Case Western Reserve University School of Law
Professor Keith Uff, Executive Secretary General, International Association of Procedural Law, Professor, Faculty of Law, University of Birmingham
Professor KK Venogopal, Senior Advocate of the Supreme Court India
Professor Konstantinos D. Kerameus, University of Athens Greece
Professor Marcel Storme, Ghent University, Past President of the World -Association of Procedural Law
Professor Martin Friedland, Faculty of Law, University of Toronto
Professor Masahisa Deguchi, Faculty of Law, Ritsumeikan University
Professor Michel Rosenfeld, Benjamin N. Cardozo School of Law, Yeshiva University
Professor Moshe Hirsh, Faculty of Law, Hebrew University of Jerusalem
Professor Neil H. Andrews, University of Cambridge, Clare College
Professor Neil James Williams, University of Melbourne,
Professor Nikolas Klamaris, University of Athens
Professor Oscar G. Chase, New York University School of Law
Professor Pelayia Yessiou-Faltsi, Faculty of Law, Aristotle University of Thessaloniki
Professor Per Henrick Lindblom, Faculty of Law, Uppsala University Juridicum
Professor Peter Gilles, Institut fur Rechtsvergleichung Johann Wolfgang Goethe Universitat

Professor Peter Gottwald, Universitat Regensburg, Secretary General World association of procedural Law
Professor John Anthony Jolowicz University of Cambridge
Professor Roger Perrot, Université de Paris
Professor Ruth Lapidot, Faculty of Law Hebrew University of Jerusalem
Professor Sean McConville, Professor of Law and Professorial Research Fellow School of Law Queen Mary College, University of London
Professor Shimon Shetreet, Director, Sacher Institute of Comparative Law Hebrew University of Jerusalem
Professor Stephen Goldstein, Emeritus Professor, Hebrew University of Jerusalem
Professor Stephen Marks, Francois-Xavier Bagnoud Professor of Health and Human Rights Department of Population and International Health Harvard School of Public Health.
Professor Vernon Bogdanor, Oxford University
Professor Walter H. Rechberger, University of Vienna
Professor Walther J. Habscheid, Emeritus Professor, University of Geneva and University of Zurich
Professor Yasuhei Taniguchi Tokyo Japan
Professor Yoav Dotan, Dean Faculty of Law Hebrew University of Jerusalem
Professor Zhivko Stalev, Bulgaria

Appendix 2

International Law Association Study Group on the Practice and Procedure of International Courts and Tribunals on the Independence of International Judges

1. *Co-Chairs*

Philippe Sands, Professor of Law, University College London; Co-Director, Project on International Courts and Tribunals
Campbell McLachlan, Professor, Deputy Dean, School of Law, Victoria University of Wellington

2. *Members*

Laurence Boisson de Chazournes, Professor of International Law, University of Geneva
Rodman Bundy, Frere Cholmeley Eversheds, Paris,
James Crawford, Whewell Professor of International Law, Cambridge University,
Hans van Houtte, Professor of International Law, Katholieke Universiteit Leuven,
Mojtaba Kazazi, United Nations Compensation Commission,
Francisco Orrego Vicuna, Professor of International Law, University of Chile,
Alain Pellet, Professor of International Law, Université Paris X Nanterre
Davis Robinson, LeBoeuf, Lamb, Greene & MacRae,
Soli Sorabjee, Attorney General of India,
Margrete Stevens, Senior Counsel, International Centre for Settlement of Investment Disputes

APPENDIX II

DRAFT STANDARDS OF THE MT. SCOPUS STANDARDS OF JUDICIAL INDEPENDENCE

The following text is the proposed draft standards presented by Professor Shimon Shetreet, the general coordinater of the project on judicial independence to the conference held in Vaduz on 30th November to 2nd December 2007.* Based on this draft the participants in the Vaduz conference approved the final text which was presented and confirmed in Jerusalem in March of 2008 and styled Mount Scopus Standards of Judicial Independence.

- These Draft Revised Standards are based on the following:
  - National Judges: The International Bar Association Code of Minimum Standards of Judicial Independence.[1]
  - Jurors: The Universal Declaration on the Independence of Justice (the "Montréal Declaration").[2]
  - Assessors: The Montréal Declaration.
- Suggested changes or additions from the original text are indicated in boxes.
- International Judges and the Burgh House Principles are being presented by Professor Yuval Shany.

---

* I am greatful to Sat Sung Kelman for her valuable assistance in preparing the draft.

[1] The International Bar Association (WA) Project on Minimum Standards of Judicial Independence was initiated by the Committee on the Administration of Justice, at the 18th Biennial Convention of the I.B.A. held at Berlin in 1980. Dr. Shimon Shetreet of the Hebrew University of Jerusalem was entrusted with the position of General Rapporteur of the Project, and Chief Justice Leonard King of South Australia was appointed General Coordinator of the Project. The General Rapporteur distributed General Guidelines for National Rapporteurs. Leading jurists from some thirty countries submitted reports to the Rapporteur General. The aim of the Project was to develop International Minimum Standards of Judicial Independence.

[2] In June 1983 the First World Conference on the Independence of Justice was held in Montréal at the Queen Elizabeth Hotel under the leadership of Chief Justice Jules Deschênes, as he then was. Justice Deschênes, succeeded in the difficult task of gathering under one roof about 130 distinguished jurists representing some 20 international organisations, in order to approve a Universal Declaration on the Independence of Justice.

Suggested new section A (Version 1):
- A The significance OF the independence of THE JUDICIARY[3]

Suggested new section A (Version 2):
- IMPORTANCE AND OBJECTIVE[4] OF THE JUDICIARY

Suggested new section B (Version 1):
- The Judiciary is an institution of the highest value in every society[5] and one of the essential pillars of liberty.[6]

Suggested new section B (Version 2):
- An independent and impartial[7] judiciary is an institution of the highest value in every society and an essential pillar of liberty and the rule of law.

Suggested new section C (Version 1):
- The free exercise of fundamental human rights as well as peace between nations can only be secured through respect for the rule of law.[8]

[3] Tokyo LawAsia Principles. This is one of the few international standards that explicitly states the importance of the judiciary in the opening section. Stating this in the body of the standards themselves rather than in a preamble helps stress the section's importance and ensures that it is more easily referred to.

[4] Further clarification.
- → Tokyo LawAsia Principles. Stating this in the body of the standards themselves rather than in a preamble helps stress the section's importance and ensures that it is more easily referred to.

[6] Preamble, Montréal Declaration.

[7] Stating this in the body of the standards themselves rather than in a preamble helps stress the section's importance and ensures that it is more easily referred to.
- → This is preferred to the first version as it describes exactly what elements are required in the Judiciary

[8] Preamble, Montréal Declaration.
- → See also Howard, CJ, in *R. v. Valente*, 2 C.C.C. (3d) 417, at 423 (1983): "Judicial independence, like the rule of law, is one of the corner stones of our legal system. The courts stand between the state and the individual to maintain the supremacy of the law. They safeguard the rights of the individual and ensure that there is no interference with his or with her liberty which is not justified by the laws."
- → See also Susan Rose-Ackerman "An Independent Judiciary and the Control of Corruption" (2007) (A necessary condition for the rule of law is an independent and competent judiciary, and the independence of the judiciary is associated with higher levels of political and economic freedom, stronger economic growth, and more developed credit markets).

Suggested new section D (Version 1):
- The objectives and functions of the judiciary shall include:
  - To resolve disputes and to administer the law impartially between persons and between persons and public authorities;
  - to promote, within the proper limits of the judicial function, the observance and the attainment of human rights;
  - to ensure that all people are able to live securely under the rule of law.[9]

Suggested new section E (Version 1):
- All states and courts must, within the scope of their competence, seek to promote the lofty objectives set out in the Charter of the United Nations, the Universal Declaration of Human Rights, the International Covenant on Economic, Social and Cultural Rights, the International Covenant on Civil and Political Rights, the Optional Protocol to the latter Covenant and other pertinent international. instruments, objectives which embrace the independence of the administration of the justice.[10]
- Such independence must be guaranteed to international judges, national judges, lawyers, jurors and assessors.[11]

Suggested new section F (Version 1):
- The foundations of the independence of justice and the conditions of its exercise may benefit from restatement.[12]

---

[9] Montréal Declaration.
→ Recall competing values of judicial independence and judicial accountability: "As phrased by a Canadian judge, Mr. Justice Riddell, commenting on an arrangement of divisions of labour among the judges, 'Judges are the servants, not the masters of the people.' Servants are accountable, so are judges." From Shetreet, *Judicial Independence: The Contemporary Debate*, at 593, referring to *Davis Actylene Gas Co. v. Morrison*, (1915) 34 O.L.R. 155, 23 D.L.R. 871 (C.A.).

[10] Preamble, Montréal Declaration.

[11] Preamble, Montréal Declaration.

[12] Preamble, Montréal Declaration.
→ During one of the plenary sessions during the drafting of the IBA standards it was agreed that the standards, as amended, were to be subject to periodic review as circumstances might require.

I. Judges and the Executive

Suggested revision G (Version 1):
- ~~JUDGES~~ THE JUDICIARY[13] AND THE EXECUTIVE

Suggested new section H (Version 1):
- The Judiciary as a whole shall be independent.

Suggested new section H (Version 2):
- Without detracting from the principle of democratic accountability, the Judiciary as a whole should be independent.

1.
   a) Individual judges should enjoy personal independence and substantive independence.[14]

Suggested revision I (Version 1):
- Each judge shall enjoy both personal independence and substantive independence.[15]

Suggested revision I (Version 2):
- It is critical for the functioning of an independent judiciary that individual judges ~~should~~ enjoy both personal independence and substantive independence.[16]

   b) Personal independence means that the terms and conditions of judicial service are adequately secured, so as to ensure that individual judges are not subject to executive control.

---

[13] The focus is really on the relationship with the judiciary as a whole, rather than with individual judges.

[14] **Should a limit be suggested to substantive independence?** Although substantive independence warrants wide protection, it is not without boundaries. Judges must exercise their powers subject to the general limit of mutual respect between the various branches of the government and accepted lines of demarcation of their respective responsibilities. The mutual respect is expressed in judge-made rules, including the rule that courts will not engage in the adjudication of injusticiable issues, such as political questions: Shetreet, *Judicial Independence: The Contemporary Debate* at 635.

[15] Change suggested for the purposes of clarification.

[16] Change suggested in order to stress the importance of this condition.

Suggested revision J (Version 1):
- Personal independence means that the terms and conditions of judicial service are adequately secured by law[17] so as to ensure that individual judges are not subject to executive control.

c) Substantive independence means that in the discharge of his judicial function, a judge is subject to nothing but the law and the commands of his conscience.

2. The judiciary as a whole should enjoy autonomy and collective independence[18] vis-à-vis the Executive.

Suggested revision K (Version 1):
- The Judiciary as a whole ~~should~~shall[19] enjoy and collective independence and autonomy vis-à-vis the Executive.

Suggested revision K (Version 2):
- The Judiciary as a whole ~~should~~shall enjoy autonomy and collective independence vis-à-vis the Executive with regard to procedural and substantive elements.[20]

3.

a) Participation in judicial appointments and promotions by the Executive or Legislature is not inconsistent with judicial independence, provided that appointments and promotions of judges are vested in a judicial body, in which members of judiciary and the legal profession form a majority.

[17] To clarify that these important conditions must be legally entrenched.

[18] Judicial independence is not confined to the individual judge and his substantive and personal independence, but also includes the collective independence of the judiciary as a whole. The concept of collective judicial independence may require a greater measure of judicial participation in the central administration of the courts including the preparation of budgets for the courts, and depending on one's view of the nature of judicial independence, the extent of judicial participation may range from consultation, or joint responsibility with the executive, or exclusive judicial responsibility in some matters. See Shetreet, "The Administration of Justice: Practical Problems, Value Conflicts and Changing Concepts," 13 *UBC L. Rev.* 52 at 57–62 (1979) and Shetreet, "Judicial Independence," *Lisbon Background Paper*, at 6 (1981).

[19] Adds mandatory language.

[20] The principle of democratic accountability permits the executive to have a role in central court administration. See Shetreet, *Judicial Independence: The Contemporary Debate*, at 598. See also See S. Shetreet, "Judicial Responsibility," in *Israeli Reports to the XIth International Congress of Comparative Law*, 88, 88–89 (S. Goldstein, Editor, 1982). See M. Cappelletti, "Who Watches the Watchmen? A Comparative Study on Judicial Responsibility," 31 *Am. J. Comp. L.* 1 (1983), generally accepting the thesis.

Amended in New Delhi:

(a) Judicial appointments and promotions by the Executive are not inconsistent with judicial independence in pursuance with sections II and JJ

> Suggested revision L (Version 1):
>
> - ~~Participation in judicial appointments and promotions by the executive or legislature is not inconsistent with judicial independence provided that appointments and promotions of judges are vested in a judicial body in which members of judiciary and the legal profession form a majority~~. Both the executive and the judiciary should be involved in judicial appointments, with the executive forming the majority. It is not inconsistent with judicial independence for the legislature to also be involved.[21]

b) Appointments and promotions by a non-judicial body will not be considered inconsistent with judicial independence in countries where, by long historic and democratic tradition, judicial appointments and promotion operate satisfactorily.

> Suggested revision M (Version 1):
>
> - Appointments and promotions solely[22] by a non-judicial body will not be considered inconsistent with judicial independence in countries where, by long historic and democratic tradition, judicial appointments and promotion operate satisfactorily.

Amended in New Delhi:

b) Except for countries where by long historic and democratic tradition judicial appointments operate satisfactorily, judicial participation in the process of judicial appointments and promotions, whether by judicial commission or otherwise, is imperative for the maintenance of judicial independence.

> Suggested revision N (Version 1):
>
> - Except for countries where by long historic and democratic tradition judicial appointments operate satisfactorily, a fair but not dominant judicial ~~participation~~ role in the process of judicial appointments and promotions, whether by judicial commission or otherwise, is imperative for the maintenance of judicial independence.

> Suggested new section O (Version 1):
>
> - No executive decree shall reverse specific court decisions, nor to change the composition of the court to affect its decision-making.[23]

---

21 In order to be consistent with the principle of democratic accountability.

22 In order to be consistent with the previous amendment.

23 Montréal Declaration section 2.08.

a) The Executive may only participate in the discipline of judges, in referring complaints against judges, or in the initiation of disciplinary proceedings, but not the adjudication of such matters.

b) The power to discipline or remove a judge must be vested in an institution which is independent of the Executive.

c) The power of removal of a judge shall preferably be vested in a judicial tribunal.

d) The Legislature may be vested with the powers of removal of judges, upon a recommendation of a judicial commission.

> Suggested revision P (Version 1):
> - The Legislature may be vested with the powers of removal of judges, ~~preferably~~ upon a recommendation of a judicial commission or pursuant to constitutional provisions or validly enacted legislation.[24]

5. The Executive shall not have control over judicial functions.
6. Rules of procedure and practice shall be made by legislation or by the Judiciary in cooperation with the legal profession, subject to parliamentary approval.
7. The state shall have a duty to provide for the execution of judgments of the Court. The Judiciary shall exercise supervision over the execution process.

> Suggested new section Q (Version 1):
> - The State shall not frustrate the execution of judgments of the Court.

8. Judicial matters are exclusively within the responsibility of the Judiciary, both in central judicial administration and in court level judicial administration.
9. a) The central responsibility for judicial administration shall preferably be vested in the Judiciary or jointly in the Judiciary and the Executive.

> Suggested revision R (Version 1):
> - ~~The central responsibility for judicial administration shall preferably be vested in the Judiciary or jointly in the Judiciary and the Executive~~
>
> b) The principle of democratic accountability should be respected and therefore it is legitimate for the legislature to play a role in judicial appointments and central administration of justice provided that due consideration is given to the principle of judicial independence.

---

[24] In order to try to prevent situations such as those that occurred in Ecuador in April 2007 when Congress removed all nine judges of the Constitutional Court in a retaliatory measure, contrary to the Ecuadorian constitution which provides that judges of the Constitutional Court can only be removed by impeachment: Human Rights Watch, *Ecuador: Removal of Judges Undermines Judicial Independence* (May 11, 2007).

10. It is the duty of the state to provide adequate financial resources to allow for the due administration of justice.

11.
  a) Division of work among judges should ordinarily be done under a predetermined plan, which can be changed in certain clearly defined circumstances.

> Suggested new section S (Version 1):
> - The trial judge should have sole power over procedural judicial matters with regard to his or her case load.
>
> Suggested new section S (Version 2):
> - The trial judge should have sole power over procedural judicial matters, even over the President of the court and other judges.

> Suggested new section T (Version 1):
> - The trial judge should have sole power over substantive judicial matters with regard to his or her case load.
>
> Suggested new section T (Version 2):
> - The trial judge should have sole power over substantive judicial matters, even over the President of the Court and other judges.

  b) In countries where the power of division of judicial work is vested in the chief justice, it is not considered inconsistent with judicial independence to accord to the chief justice the power to change the predetermined plan for sound reasons, preferably in consultation with the senior judges when practicable.

> Suggested revision U (Version 1):
> - Delete this entire section.

  c) Subject to (a), the exclusive responsibility for case assignment should be vested in a responsible judge, preferably the President of the Court.

12. The power to transfer a judge from one court to another shall be vested in a judicial authority and preferably shall be subject to the judge's consent, such consent not to be unreasonably withheld.

13. Court services should be adequately financed by the relevant government.

> Suggested revision V (Version 1):
> - Court services should be adequately financed by the relevant government branches.

14. Judicial salaries and pensions shall be adequate at all times fixed by law, and should be periodically reviewed independently of Executive control.

> Suggested revision W (Version 1):
> - Judicial salaries, ~~and~~ pensions, and benefits[25] shall be fixed in law, adequate, and should be regularly adjusted regularly adjusted to account for price increases independently of Executive control.

15.

a) The position of the judges, their independence, their security, and their adequate remuneration shall be secured by law.

Amended in New Delhi:

(a) The position of the judges, their independence, and their adequate remuneration shall be secured by law.

> Suggested revision X (Version 1):
> - The position of the judges, their independence, their security of tenure, and their adequate remuneration shall be entrenched constitutionally[26] or secured by law.

> Suggested revision X (Version 2):
> - The position of the judges, their independence, their security of tenure, and their adequate remuneration shall be entrenched constitutionally[27] or secured by law. It is the duty of all governmental and other institutions to respect and observe the independence of the judiciary.[28]

b) Judicial salaries cannot be decreased during the judges' service except as a coherent part of an overall public economic measure.

> Suggested revision Y (Version 1):
> - Judicial salaries, pensions, and benefits[29] cannot be decreased during judges' service except as a coherent part of an overall public economic measure.

---

[25] In the interests of completeness.

[26] UN Basic Principles.
→ Change suggested in order to provide additional flexibility, and also to stress how this is an important enough issue to be constitutionally entrenched.

[27] UN Basic Principles.
→ Change suggested in order to provide additional flexibility, and also to stress how this is an important enough issue to be constitutionally entrenched.

[28] UN Basic Principles.
→ Change suggested in order to emphasize the state's obligation to respect judicial independence.

[29] In the interests of completeness

16. The Ministers of the government shall not exercise any form of pressure on judges, whether overt or covert, and shall not make statements which adversely affect the independence of individual judges, or of the Judiciary as a whole

17. The power of pardon shall be exercised cautiously so as to avoid its use as an interference with judicial decision.

18.
   a) The Executive shall refrain from any act or omission which pre-empts the judicial resolution of a dispute, or frustrates the proper execution of a court judgment.
   b) The Executive shall not have the power to close down, or suspend, the operation of the court system at any level.

II. Judges and the Legislature

> Suggested revision Z (Version 1):
> ~~JUDGES~~THE JUDICIARY[30] AND THE LEGISLATURE

19. The Legislature shall not pass legislation which reverses specific court decisions.

> Suggested revision AA (Version 1):
> - The Legislature shall not pass legislation which retroactively revises or reverses specific court decisions.
>
> Suggested revision AA (Version 2):
> - The Legislature shall not pass legislation which retroactively revises or reverses specific[31] court decisions.
>
> Suggested revision AA (Version 3):
> - The Legislature shall not pass legislation which retroactively revises or reverses ~~specific~~ court decisions except as pursuant to constitutionally-enacted override legislation.[32]

> Suggested new section BB (Version 1):
> - No legislation shall attempt retroactively, to reverse specific court decisions, nor to change the composition of the court to affect its decision-making.[33]

[30] The focus is really on the relationship with the judiciary as a whole, rather than with individual judges.

[31] **Consider the UN Principles which prohibit any "revision" of court decisions (section 4).**

[32] Adds escape clause. **Consider whether this is desirable.**

[33] Montréal Declaration section 2.08.

Suggested new section CC (Version 1):
- The override legislation referred to in Section _____ shall apply to court decisions generally, and not to one or more specific court decision(s).

20.

a) Legislation introducing changes in the terms and conditions of judicial services shall not be applied to judges holding office at the time of passing the legislation unless the changes improve the terms of service.

Suggested revision DD (Version 1):
- Legislation introducing changes in the terms and conditions of judicial service shall not be applied to judges holding office at the time of passing the legislation unless the changes improve the terms of service and are generally applied.[34]

b) In case of legislation reorganizing courts, judges serving in these courts shall not be affected, except for their transfer to another court of the same status.

Amended in New Delhi:

b) In case of legislation abolishing courts, judges serving in these courts shall not be affected, except for their transfer to another court of the same status.

Suggested revision EE (Version 1):
- In case of legislation reorganising or abolishing courts, judges serving in these courts shall not be affected, except for their transfer to another court of the same status.

---

[34] In order to prevent "rewarding" specific judges.
- → The US Constitution's Compensation Clause guarantees federal judges a "Compensation, which shall not be diminished during their Continuance in Office." *U.S. Const.*, Art. III, §1.
- → See *US v. Hatter* (99–1978) 532 U.S. 557 (2001) 203 F.3d 795: Congress is prohibited from singling out judges for specially unfavourable taxation treatment, although it is permitted to impose a "non-discriminatory tax laid generally" upon judges and other citizens.
- → See *United States v. Will*, 449 U.S. 200, 220–21 (1980): though Congress may not rescind a salary increase for judges once it has gone into effect – that would be a diminishment of compensation – Congress is under no constitutional obligation to grant salary increases.
- → See *Evans v. Gore*, 253 U.S. 245, 253 (1920): The imposition of a new federal tax that has the effect of reducing the judicial compensation of judges already in office is unconstitutional.
- → But see *O'Malley v. Woodrough*, 307 U.S. 277 (1939): an income tax levied against the judicial salary of judges who took office after the levy is in effect is constitutional, when the taxing measure is of general, non-discriminatory application to all earners of income.

Suggested revision EE (Version 2):
- In case of legislation reorganising or abolishing courts, judges serving in these courts shall not be affected, except for their transfer to another court of the same or materially comparable[35] status.

Suggested new section FF (if Version 2, above, is accepted) (Version 1):
- In the case of a transfer to a materially comparable court, approval of the judiciary is required in advance of such transfer.[36]

21. A person shall have the right to be tried by the ordinary courts of law, and shall not be tried before *ad hoc* tribunals.[37]

Suggested restatement GG (Version 1):[38]

- No ad hoc tribunals shall be established;
- Everyone shall have the right to be tried expeditiously by the established ordinary courts or judicial tribunals under law, subject to review by the courts;[39]
- Some derogations may be admitted in times of grave public emergency which threatens the life of the nation but only under conditions prescribed by law, and only to the extent strictly consistent with internationally recognized minimum standards and subject to review by the courts;
- In such times of emergency:
  - Civilians charged with criminal offences of any kind shall be tried by ordinary civilian courts, expanded where necessary by additional competent civilian judges;
  - Detention of persons administratively without charge shall be subject to review by ordinary courts by way of habeas corpus or similar procedures, so as to insure that the detention is lawful, as well as to inquire into any allegations of ill—treatment;
- The jurisdiction of military tribunals shall be confined to military offences committed by military personnel. There shall always be a right of appeal from such tribunals to a legally qualified appellate court.[40]

---

[35] To provide for situations such as those that occurred in Ontario when the entire court structure was reorganized.
[36] Adds safeguards.
[37] See James Crawford, "The Independence of the Judiciary in International Law".
[38] Montréal Declaration, section 2.06.
[39] For a discussion of this issue, see Shetreet, *Judicial Independence: The Contemporary Debate*, at 616.
[40] Cf. Chief Justice Bora Laskin, *MacKay v. The Queen* (1980) 54 C.C.C.(2d) 129,114 D.L.R.(3d) 393, at 40 1-2: "the military judge is not suited because of his close involvement with the prosecution and with the entire military establishment" (dissenting opinion).

Suggested new section HH (Version 1):
- Tribunals that do not use the duly established procedures of the legal process shall not be created to displace the jurisdiction belonging to the ordinary courts or judicial tribunals.[41]

III. Terms and Nature of Judicial Appointments

Suggested new section II (Version 1):
- The method of judicial selection shall safeguard against judicial appointments for improper motives.[42] And shall not threaten judicial independence.

Suggested new section JJ (Version 1):
- The principle of democratic accountability should be respected and therefore it is legitimate for the Executive and the Legislature to play a role in judicial appointments provided that due consideration is given to the principle of Judicial Independence.

22.
  a) Judicial appointments should generally be for life, subject to removal for cause and compulsory retirement at an age fixed by law at the date of appointment.
  b) Retirement age shall not be reduced for existing judges.[43]

Suggested new section KK (Version 1):
- Promotion of judges, wherever such a system exists, should be based on objective factors, in particular ability, integrity and experience.[44]

Suggested new section KK (Version 2):
- Promotion of judges, wherever such a system exists, ~~should~~ shall[45] be based on objective factors, in particular ability integrity and experience.

---

[41] UN Basic Principles.

[42] Montréal Declaration.

[43] See Shetreet, *Judicial Independence: The Contemporary Debate*, at 607 which describes that in Bangladesh, in 1977 an ordinance was passed bringing down the retirement age from 65 to 62 years with immediate effect. This resulted in the retirement of two distinguished judges. This was in fact a legislative removal of these two judges though it was in theory a general statute.

[44] UN Basic Principles.
→ Montréal Declaration provides: "Promotion of a judge shall be based on an objective assessment of the candidate's integrity and independence of judgment, professional competence, experience, humanity and commitment to uphold the rule of law."

[45] In order to make this mandatory.
→ Preferred over the previous version.

> Suggested new section KK (Version 3):
> - Promotion of judges ~~should~~ shall be based on objective factors, in particular ~~ability~~ merit,[46] integrity and experience.

23.
  a) Judges should not be appointed for probationary periods except for in legal systems in which appointments of judges do not depend on having practical experience in the profession as a condition of appointment.[47]

> Suggested revision LL (Version 1):
> - Judges should not be appointed for ~~probationary~~ temporary periods except in legal systems in which appointments of judges do not depend on having practical experience in the profession as a condition of appointment provided that provided that permanent appointment will be granted on merit.[48]
>
> Suggested revision LL (Version 2):
> - Judges should not be appointed for ~~probationary~~ temporary periods except for in legal systems in which appointments of judges do not depend on having practical experience in the profession as a condition of appointment. However, in no case shall a judge from a lower court be appointed to a higher court.

  b) The institution of temporary judges should be avoided as far as possible except where there exists a long historic democratic tradition.

24. The number of the members of the highest court should be fixed and should not be altered for improper motives.[49]
25. Part-time judges should be appointed only with proper safeguards.

> Suggested revision MM (Version 1):
> - Part-time judges should be appointed only with proper safeguards secured by law.

[46] "Merit" is broader than "ability".
→ Preferred over the previous version

[47] Probationary appointments are considered inconsistent with judicial independence, except for legal systems where judges are appointed without prior practical experience (See Shetreet, *Judicial Independence: The Contemporary Debate*).

[48] Scottish sheriffs case

[49] exception –cour de cassasion

THE FOLLOWING 3 articles should be moved to the beginning of this chapter afer section on democratic accountability

Suggested new section NN (Version 1):
- The process and standards of judicial selection shall give due consideration to the principle of fair reflection by the judiciary of the society in all its aspects.[50]

Suggested new section OO (Version 1):
- In the selection of judges, there shall be no discrimination of the grounds of race, colour, gender, language, religion, political or other opinion, national or social origin, property, birth or status, subject however to citizenship requirements.[51]

Suggested new section OO (Version 2):
- Taking into consideration the principle of fair reflection by the judiciary of the society in all its aspects, in the selection of judges, there shall be no discrimination on the grounds of race, colour, gender, language, religion, national or social origin, property, birth or status, subject however to citizenship requirements.

26. Selection of judges shall be based on merit.

Suggested revision PP (Version 1):
- Selection of judges shall be based on merit and integrity.[52]

Suggested revision PP (Version 2):
- Selection of judges shall be based on merit, integrity, and experience in the law.

Suggested revision PP (Version 3):
- Candidates for judicial office shall be individuals of integrity and ability, well-trained in the law. They shall have equality of access to judicial office.[53]

---

[50] Montréal Declaration section 2.13. See also Shetreet, *Judicial Independence: The Contemporary Debate*, at 401.

[51] Montréal Declaration
→ "Political opinion" is also taken from PH Lane, *Fragile Bastion: Constitutional Aspects of Judicial Independence* (judicial independence is composed of at least five aspects: (1) non-political appointments to a court; (2) guaranteed tenure and salary; (3) executive and legislative interference with court proceedings or office holders; (4) budgetary autonomy; (5) administrative autonomy.

[52] Montréal Declaration section 2.11.

[53] Exact wording of the Montréal Declaration, section 2.11.

IV. Judicial Removal and Discipline

27. The proceedings for discipline and removal of judges should ensure fairness to the judge and adequate opportunity for hearing.

Suggested revision QQ (Version 1):
- The proceedings for discipline and removal of judges[54] shall be processed expeditiously and fairly[55] and shall ensure fairness to the judge and adequate opportunity for hearing.

Suggested revision QQ (Version 2):
- The proceedings for discipline and removal of judges shall be processed expeditiously and fairly under an appropriate procedure[56] and should ensure fairness to the judge and adequate opportunity for hearing.

28. The procedure for discipline should be held in camera. The judge may however request that the hearing be held in public, subject to a final and reasoned disposition of this request by the Disciplinary Tribunal. Judgments in disciplinary proceedings, whether held in camera or in public, may be published.[57]

Amended in New Delhi:

The procedure for discipline should be in camera; however, judgments in disciplinary proceedings may be published.

Suggested revision RR (Version 1):
- With the exception of proceedings before the Legislature,[58] the procedure for discipline should be held *in camera*; however, judgments in disciplinary proceedings may be published.

Suggested revision RR (Version 2):
- With the exception of proceedings before the Legislature, the procedure for discipline should be held *in camera*; however, judgments in disciplinary proceedings, whether held *in camera* or in public,[59] may be published.

---

[54] The UN Basic Principles adds "in his/her judicial and professional capacity. This wording was not added here to prevent personal suits being lodged against judges as a back-door method of interfering with their independence.

[55] UN Basic Principles.

[56] UN Basic Principles.

[57] Background to this section: During one of the plenary sessions, on October 22, 1982, Chief Justice Deschênes (Canada) undertook the drafting of an amendment to this Section, in respect of which agreement was reached that a judge could waive a hearing in camera, but that such hearing should not automatically be held in public without reasons from the disciplinary tribunal.

[58] Montréal Declaration section 2.36.

[59] Montréal Declaration section 2.36.

Suggested revision RR (Version 3):
- With the exception of proceedings before the Legislature, the procedure for discipline should be held *in camera*. The judge may however request that the hearing be held in public, subject to final and reasoned disposition of this request by the disciplinary tribunal. Judgments in disciplinary proceedings, whether held in camera or in public, may be published.[60]

Suggested revision RR (Version 4):
- With the exception of proceedings before the Legislature, the procedure for discipline should be held *in camera*. The judge may however request that the hearing be held in public and such request should be respected, subject to expeditious, final and reasoned disposition of this request by the disciplinary tribunal. Judgments in disciplinary proceedings, whether held in camera or in public, may be published.

29.
a) The grounds for removal of judges shall be fixed by law and shall be clearly defined.

Suggested revision SS (Version 1):
- The grounds for the discipline, suspension and removal of judges shall be fixed by law and shall be clearly defined.

Suggested revision SS (Version 2):
- The grounds for the discipline, suspension and removal of judges shall be entrenched constitutionally[61] or fixed by law and shall be clearly defined.

Suggested revision SS (Version 3):
- All ~~The~~[62] grounds for the discipline, suspension and removal of judges shall be entrenched constitutionally or fixed by law and shall be clearly defined.

Suggested revision SS (Version 4):
- All of the ~~The of the~~ grounds for the discipline, suspension and removal of judges shall be entrenched constitutionally or fixed by law and shall be clearly defined.

b) All disciplinary actions shall be based upon standards of judicial conduct promulgated by law or in established rules of court.

---

[60] Montréal Declaration section 2.36.

[61] Stresses its importance.
→ Preferred over the previous version.

[62] To be more inclusive.
→ Preferred over the previous version.

Suggested revision TT (Version 1):
- All disciplinary, suspension and removal[63] actions shall be based upon standards of judicial conduct promulgated by law or in established rules of court.

Suggested revision TT (Version 2):
- All disciplinary, suspension and removal actions shall be based upon accepted[64] standards of judicial conduct ~~promulgated by law or~~[65] in established rules of court.

Suggested revision TT (Version 3):
- All disciplinary action shall be based upon established standards of judicial conduct ~~promulgated by law or in established rules of court~~.[66]

Suggested revision TT (Version 4):
- All disciplinary, suspension and removal[67] actions shall be based upon established standards of judicial conduct ~~promulgated by law or in established rules of court~~.

30. A judge shall not be subject to removal unless, by reason of a criminal act or through gross or repeated neglect or physical or mental incapacity, he has shown himself manifestly unfit to hold the position of judge. The grounds for removal *shall be limited to reasons of medical incapacity or behaviour that renders them unfit to discharge their duties.*[68]

Suggested revision UU (Version 1):
- A judge shall not be subject to removal unless by reason of a criminal act, an offence involving moral turpitude,[69] or through gross or repeated neglect or physical or mental incapacity he has shown him manifestly unfit to hold the position of judge.

Suggested revision UU (Version 2):
- A judge shall not be subject to removal unless by reason of a criminal act, an offence involving moral turpitude, or through gross or repeated neglect or physical or mental incapacity he has shown him ~~manifestly~~[70] unfit to hold the position of judge.

---

[63] UN Basic Principles.
- → More inclusive.
- → Arguably "suspension" and "removal" fall under "disciplinary", but listing them separately eliminates doubt.

[64] To fit with the following footnote.

[65] The UN Basic Principles does not include "promulgated by law".

[66] Montréal Declaration section 2.34. Broad.

[67] More inclusive.

[68] UN Basic Principles.
- → Taken with the previous footnote, protects judges.
- → Preferred over the earlier version.

[69] Broadens.

[70] Higher standard.

31. In systems where the power to discipline and remove judges is vested in an institution other than the Legislature, the tribunal for discipline and removal of judges shall be permanent, and be composed predominantly of members of the Judiciary.

32. The head of the court may legitimately have supervisory powers to control judges on administrative matters.

V. The Media and the Judiciary

33. It should be recognized that judicial independence does not render judges free from public accountability, however, the media and other institutions should show respect for judicial independence and exercise restrain in criticism of judicial decisions..[71]

34. A judge should not interview directly with the general media. If a judge needs to respond to the media in regard toia media report or inquiry, it shall be done via a spokesperson assigned by the court or a judge specifically assigned by the court. In exceptional circumstances may respond directly to the media if his or her direct response will prevent an irreparable cdamage.

35. The media should show restraint in publications on pending cases where such publication may influence the outcome of the case.

Suggested revision VV (Version 1):
- The media should show responsibility and restraint in publications on pending cases where such publication may influence the outcome of the case.

VI. Standards of Conduct[72]

36. Judges may not, during their term of office, serve in Executive functions, such as ministers of the government, nor may they serve as members of the Legislature or of municipal councils, unless by long historical traditions these functions are combined.

---

[71] See discussion by Julie Debeljak, *Judicial Conference of Australia, Uluru, April 2001: Judicial Independence: A Collection of Material for the Judicial Conference of Australia* regarding the consequences of inappropriate public criticism (it leaves judges having to choose between being silent leading to a potential decrease in public confidence in the judiciary, or else inappropriately being drawn into public criticism).

[72] Human Rights Watch, *Rigging the Rule of Law: Judicial Independence Under Siege in Venezuela*, Volume 16, No. 3(B) (June 2004) describes some of allegations of judicial bias in Venezuela. For instance, Attorney General Isaías Rodríguez in May 2004 allegedly described how the country's top administrative court in the past established set fees for resolving different kinds of cases.

Suggested revision WW (Version 1):
- Judges may not, ~~during their term of~~ office,[73] serve in Executive functions, such as ministers of the government, nor may they serve as members of the Legislature or of municipal councils,

37. Judges may serve as chairmen of committees of inquiry in cases where the process requires skill of fact-finding and evidence-taking. ERASE THIS SECTION ALTOGETHER
38. Judges shall not hold positions in political parties.
39. A judge, other than a temporary judge, may not practice law during his term of office.[74]

Suggested revision XX (Version 1):
- A judge, other than a temporary or part time jjudge, may not practice law ~~during his term of office~~.[75]

40. A judge should refrain from business activities, except his personal investments, or ownership of property.

Suggested revision YY (Version 1):
- A judge should refrain from business activities, except his personal investments, or ownership of property, or the business activities or ownership of property of his family.[76]

Suggested revision YY (Version 2):
- A judge should refrain from business activities, except his personal investments, or ownership of property, or the business activities or ownership of property of his immediate[77] family.

Suggested revision YY (Version 3):
- A judge should refrain from business activities and should avoid from engaging in other remunerative activity,[78] except in respect of his personal investments, or ownership of property, or the business activities or ownership of property of his family.or teacing in university

[73] Redundant language – if a judge is no longer in office, he or she is no longer a judge.
[74] *R. v. Lippe* [1991] 2 SCR 114 (The municipal court system in Quebec allowed part-time judges to continue to practice law. It was held that the judges were an independent and impartial tribunal.).
[75] Redundant language – see earlier comment.
[76] ABA Model Code of Judicial Conduct (February 2007), Canon 4, Article D(2).discusses family.
[77] More specific. Perhaps a different degree of relation is preferable.
[78] ABA Model Code of Judicial Conduct (February 2007), Canon 4, Article D(2).

Suggested revision YY (Version 4):
- A judge should refrain from business activities and should avoid from engaging in other remunerative activity,[79] except his personal investments, or ownership of property, or the business activities or ownership of property of his immediate[80] family.

Suggested new section ZZ (Version 1):
- Continuing education shall be available to judges.[81]

Suggested new section AAA (Version 1):
- Sufficient resources shall be made available to judges.[82]

Suggested new section BBB (Version 1):
- Judges shall keep themselves informed about international conventions and other instruments establishing human rights' norms, and shall seek to implement them as far as feasible, within the limits set by their national constitutions and laws.[83]

Suggested new section CCC (Version 1):
- Judges shall ensure the fair conduct of the proceeding and inquire fully into any allegation made of a violation of the rights of a party or of a witness.[84]

Suggested new section DDD (Version 1):
- Judges shall accord respect to members of the Bar.[85]

41. A judge should always behave in such a manner as to preserve the dignity of his office and the impartiality integrity and independence of the Judiciary.

[79] ABA Model Code of Judicial Conduct (February 2007), Canon 4, Article D(2).
[80] See earlier footnote regarding the preferred degree of relation.
[81] Montréal Declaration section 2.15.
[82] PH Lane, *Fragile Bastion: Constitutional Aspects of Judicial Independence.*
[83] Montréal Declaration section 2.48.
[84] Montréal Declaration section 2.45.
[85] Montréal Declaration section 2.46.

Suggested revision EEE (Version 1):
- A judge is like other citizens entitled to freedom of expression, belief, association and assembly; provided, however, that in exercising such rights,[86] a judge should always behave in such a manner as to preserve the dignity of his office and the impartiality and independence of the Judiciary.

Suggested revision EEE (Version 2):
- A judge is like other citizens entitled to freedom of expression, belief, association and assembly; provided, however, that in exercising such rights, a judge shall ~~should~~ always behave in such a manner as to preserve the dignity of his office and the impartiality and independence of the Judiciary.

Suggested revision EEE (Version 3):
- A judge is like other citizens entitled to freedom of expression, belief, association and assembly; provided, however, that in exercising such rights, a judge shall ~~should~~ always behave in such a manner as to preserve the dignity of his office and the impartiality, integrity,[87] and independence of the Judiciary.

Suggested new section FFF (Version 1):
- A judge shall avoid impropriety and the appearance of impropriety.[88]

Suggested new section GGG (Version 1):
- A judge shall be both objectively and subjectively impartial.[89]

Suggested new section HHH (Version 1):
- Objective impartiality means that judges shall decide matters before them on the basis of facts and in accordance with the law, without any restrictions, improper influences, inducements, pressures, threats or interferences, direct or indirect, from any quarter or for any reason.[90]

---

[86] UN Basic Principles.
→ To put the balancing of these rights up, front, and centre.

[87] ABA Model Code of Judicial Conduct (February 2007).

[88] ABA Model Code of Judicial Conduct (February 2007).
→ Preferred over the previous version.

[89] See *McGonnell v. UK*, ECHR judgment of 18 February 2000, Application No. 28488/95 (A bailiff with executive and legislative rules as the representative of the Crown. was not impartial, despite the lack of any proof of actual bias.) Refer also to *Re Pincohet,* HL, 15 January 1999 (Lord Hoffmann's links with Amnesty were such to give the appearance of possible bias due to his links with Amnesty International. Lord Browne-Wilkinson: "The rationale of the whole rule is that a man cannot be a judge in his own cause".) and *De Haan*, ECHR – judgment of 26 August 1997, Reports 1997–IV, pp. 1392, 1393 (Judge was called upon to decide upon an objection for which he himself was responsible.).

[90] UN Basic Principles.

Suggested new section III (Version 1):
- Subjective impartiality means that there is no appearance of lack of judicial neutrality.

42. Judges may be organized in associations designed for judges, for furthering their rights and interests as judges.

43. Judges may take collective action to protect their judicial independence and to uphold their position.

Suggested revision JJJ (Version 1):
- Judges may take appropriate action to protect their judicial independence ~~and to uphold their position~~.[91]

VII. Securing Impartiality and Independence[92]

44. A judge shall enjoy immunity from legal actions, and the obligation to testify concerning matters arising in the exercise of his official functions.

Amended in New Delhi:

A judge[93] shall enjoy immunity from legal actions in the exercise of his official functions.[94]

Suggested revision KKK (Version 1):
- A judge shall enjoy immunity from legal actions in the exercise of his official functions, including from improper acts or omissions in the exercise of his judicial functions.[95]

Suggested revision KKK (Version 2):
- A judge shall enjoy immunity ~~from legal actions and the obligation to testify in matters arising in the exercise~~ from suit or harassment for acts and omissions in his official capacity ~~functions~~.[96]

---

[91] This is how the section appears in the Montréal Declaration, section 2.09.

[92] See Cyrus Das and K. Chandra, Editors, Judges and Judicial Accountability, Universal Law Publishing Company Ltd., Dehli.

[93] This does not exclude the possibility that the state may be liable for gross negligence of a judicial officer.

[94] Consider a 1988 Italian law which was designed to, within certain limit, render judges accountable for damages caused by serious fault in the exercise of their functions: see Giovanni E. Longo, "The Human Right to an Independent Judiciary: International Norms and Denied application before a Domestic Jurisdiction," *St. John's Law Review* (Winter 1996).

[95] UN Basic Principles.

[96] Montréal Declaration, section 2.24.

45. A judge shall not sit in a case where there is a reasonable suspicion of bias or potential bias.[97]

Suggested revision LLL (Version 1):
- A judge shall not sit in a case where there is a reasonable suspicion of bias or potential bias unless there is no provision for calling another in, or where no one else can take that judge's place.[98]

Suggested new section MMM (Version 1):
- The judiciary shall be bound by professional secrecy with regard to their deliberations and to confidential information acquired in the course of their duties other than in public proceedings.[99]

46. A judge shall avoid any course of conduct which might give rise to an appearance of partiality.

Suggested new section NNN (Version 1):
- A judge shall not abuse the prestige of judicial office to advance the personal or economic interests of the judge or other, or allow others to do so.[100]

VIII. The Internal Independence of the Judiciary

47. In the decision-making process, a judge must be independent vis-à-vis his judicial colleagues and superiors.

Suggested revision OOO (Version 1):
- In the decision-making process, a judge must be independent vis-à-vis his judicial colleagues and superiors. Any hierarchical organization of the judiciary and any difference in grade or rank shall in no way interfere with the right of judges to pronounce their judgments freely.[101]

---

[97] "It is most important that the judiciary be independent and be so perceived by the public. The judges must not have cause to fear that they will be prejudiced by their decisions or that the public would reasonably apprehend this to be the case: Howland, CJ, *R. v. Valente* 2 C.C.C.(3d) 417, at 423 (1983).

[98] Williams v. US (US Supreme Court) No. 01-175. Decided March 4, 2002: "the law requires judges to decide cases in which they have a self-interest where, as here, " 'no provision is made for calling another in, or where no one else can take his place.' " (quoting *Will*, 449 U.S., at 214, quoting *Philadelphia* v. *Fox*, 64 Pa. 169, 185 (1870)). (US Supreme Court deciding a case involving judge salaries).

[99] UN Basic Principles.
→ Required for impartiality.

[100] ABA Model Code of Judicial Conduct (February 2007).

[101] Montréal Declaration section 2.03.

JURORS[102]

IX. Selection of Prospective Jurors

48. The opportunity for jury service shall be extended without distinction of any kind by reason of race, colour, sex, language, religion, political or other opinion, national or social origin, property, birth or status, subject however to citizenship requirements.

Suggested new section PPP (Version 1): - Reflective and impartial juries are important components of an independent and impartial justice system.

49. The names of prospective jurors shall be drawn from a jury source list compiled from one or more regularly maintained lists of persons residing in the court's jurisdiction.
50. The jury source list shall be representative, and shall be as inclusive of the adult population in the jurisdiction, as is feasible.
51. The Court shall periodically review the jury source list for its representativeness and inclusiveness. Should the Court determine that improvement is needed in the representativeness or inclusiveness of the jury source list, appropriate corrective action shall be taken.
52. Random selection procedures shall be used at all stages throughout the jury selection process except as provided herein.
53. The frequency and the length of time that persons are called upon to perform jury service and to be available therefore, shall be the minimum, consistent with the needs of justice.
54. All automatic excuses or exemptions from jury service shall be eliminated.
55. Eligible persons who are summoned may be excused from jury service only for valid reason by the court, or with its authorization.

X. Selection of a Particular Jury

56. Examination of prospective jurors shall be limited to matters relevant to determining whether to remove a juror for cause, and to exercising peremptory challenges.
57. If the judge determines during the examination of prospective jurors, that an individual is unable or unwilling to hear the particular case at issue fairly and

[102] Unless otherwise indicated, the sections relating to Jurors are from the Montréal Declaration.

impartially, the individual shall be removed from the panel. Such a determination may be made on motion of a party or on the judge's own initiative.[103]

58. In jurisdictions where peremptory challenges are permitted, their number and the procedure for exercising them shall be uniform for the same type of case.
59. Peremptory challenges shall be limited to a number no larger than necessary,[104] to provide reasonable assurance of obtaining an unbiased jury.

XI. Administration of the Jury System

60. The responsibility for administration of the jury system shall be under the control of the judiciary.
61. The notice summoning a person to jury service shall be in writing, easily understandable, and delivered sufficiently in advance.
62. Courts shall employ the services of prospective jurors, so as to achieve the best possible use of them with a minimum of inconvenience.
63. Courts shall provide adequate protection for jurors from threat and intimidation.

> Suggested revision QQQ (Version 1):
> - Courts shall provide ~~adequate~~ appropriate[105] protection for jurors from threat and intimidation.

64. Courts shall provide an adequate and suitable environment for jurors, and jury facilities shall be arranged to minimize contact between jurors and parties, counsel and the public.

> Suggested revision RRR (Version 1):
> - Courts shall provide an ~~adequate~~ appropriate[106] and suitable environment for jurors, and jury facilities shall be arranged to minimize contact between jurors and parties, counsel and the public.

65. Persons called for jury service shall receive a reasonable allowance.

---

[103] **Should there be a penalty for a prospective juror's intentional fair and impartial hearing of the case in order to avoid jury service?**

[104] **Consider making this phrasing more specific.**

[105] "Adequate" is too low a standard. Consider the definition of "adequate" (from Webster's Dictionary) (emphasis added):

1: sufficient for a specific requirement <*adequate* taxation of goods>; *also* : **barely sufficient or satisfactory** <her first performance was merely *adequate*>

2: lawfully and reasonably sufficient <*adequate* grounds for a lawsuit>

If the role of juror is to be respected, conditions must be appropriate and comfortable.

[106] See previous footnote.

66. Employers shall be prohibited from penalizing employees who are called for jury service.

> Suggested revision SSS (Version 1):
> - Employers shall be prohibited from penalizing employees who are called for jury service, and the legislature shall enact laws punishing any such penalization.[107]

XII. Jury Consideration and Deliberations

67. Procedures shall be provided to prevent a trial from being terminated because of unforeseen circumstances which would reduce the number of jurors.

68. Courts shall provide some form of orientation or instruction to persons called for jury service, to increase prospective jurors' understanding of the judicial system, and prepare them to serve competently as jurors.

69. In simple language the trial judge shall: i) directly following empanelment of the jury, give preliminary explanations of the jury's role and of trial procedures; and ii) prior to commencement of deliberations, direct the jury on the law.

> Suggested revision TTT (Version 1):
> - In simple and understandable language the trial judge shall: i) directly following empanelment of the jury, give preliminary explanations of the jury's role and of trial procedures; and ii) prior to commencement of deliberations, direct the jury on the law.

70. A jury's deliberations shall be held in secrecy. Jurors shall not make public the reasons for their decisions.

> Suggested revision UUU (Version 1):
> - A jury's deliberations shall be held in secrecy. Jurors shall not make public the reasons for their decisions, and there shall be court rules enforcing this requirement.[108]

71. a) A jury shall be sequestered only for the purpose of insulating its members from improper information or influence.

---

[107] Puts teeth into this important prohibition.
[108] Many jurors do not appreciate the gravity of this requirement.

Suggested revision VVV (Version 1):
- A jury shall be sequestered only for the purpose of insulating its members from improper information or influence or when otherwise required in the interests of justice.[109]

b) Standard procedures shall be promulgated to make certain that the inconvenience and discomfort of the sequestered jurors are minimized.

ASSESORS[110]

XIII. Status

72. In defining assessor, the following shall be considered: In general, on certain judicial, quasi-judicial bodies or administrative tribunals, the assessor sits with a judge, magistrate or other jurist, to assist him in his duties. In most cases he is a person who does not necessarily have legal training, but who has some specific professional qualification or socio-economic expertise, that pertains to the subject-matter under consideration.
73. In some cases, the assessor shares with his legally-trained colleague, responsibility for the decision to be rendered: this then becomes a multi-disciplinary judicial or quasi-judicial body.

XIV. Appointment

74. Unless he is selected by the parties unanimously, the assessor shall be appointed by a neutral authority not involved in the dispute.
75. Unless agreed upon by the parties or provided by law, the assessor shall be paid according to the decision of a neutral authority not involved in the dispute.
76. The assessor shall be selected for reasons of integrity and competence especially relevant to the matter to be considered by him.
77. The assessor shall enjoy a tenure which guarantees his independence; if he serves on a permanent basis he shall be guaranteed security, adequate remuneration and conditions of service.
78. Before commencing his duties, the assessor shall take an oath or affirmation of office.

---

[109] For instance, in highly sensitive cases where there is a concern about one or more jury members leaking information.
[110] Unless otherwise indicated, the sections relating to Assessors are from the Montréal Declaration.

XV. Exercise of Mandate

79. In the decision-making process, the assessor shall be free from any order or instruction by the authority which has appointed him, by the parties or by the professional associations to which he belongs.

80. The assessor shall have the right to participate in the decision with complete freedom and independence in the area of his jurisdiction.

81. The assessor shall behave in such a manner as will maintain the dignity of his position and the impartiality and independence of justice.

82. The assessor shall not sit in a case where a reasonable apprehension of bias on his part may arise.

> Suggested revision WWW (Version 1):
> The assessor shall not sit in a case where there is a reasonable suspicion ~~apprehension~~ of bias or potential bias ~~on his part may arise~~.[111]
>
> Suggested revision WWW (Version 2):
> The assessor shall not sit in a case where there is a reasonable suspicion ~~apprehension~~ of bias or potential bias ~~on his part may arise~~ unless there is no provision for calling another in, or where no one else can take that judge's place.[112]

83. The assessor shall be free to withdraw for generally accepted reasons.

XVI. Powers and Immunity

84. The assessor shall be vested with the authority, immunity and powers necessary to carry out his duties.

85. The assessor shall not be sued or harassed for acts and omissions in his official capacity.

XVII. Dismissal

86. The assessor shall not be dismissed in the course of his mandate except for incapacity or misbehaviour.[113]

> Suggested new heading XXX (Version 1):
> - ARBITRATORS

---

[111] To be consistent with the mirror section for judges.

[112] To be consistent with the suggested revision in the mirror section for judges.

[113] **Consider who should decide whether there has been incapacity or misbehaviour by the assessor.**

Suggested new section YYY (Version 1):
- It is appropriate to have arbitrators arbitrate legal disputes subject to the duty to insure impartiality, ensure fair procedure, and ensure the rules of natural justice including the right of hearing and refraining from conflicts of interest.

XVIII. International Judges

This section will be presented by Prof Yuval Shany based on the Burgh House Principles and additional amendments and revisions.

APPENDIX III

INTERNATIONAL BAR ASSOCIATION CODE OF MINIMUM STANDARDS OF JUDICIAL INDEPENDENCE

THE JERUSALEM APPROVED STANDARDS AS ADOPTED IN THE PLENARY SESSION OF THE 19TH IBA BIENNIAL CONFERENCE HELD ON FRIDAY, 22ND OCTOBER 1982, IN NEW DELHI, INDIA.

I. Judges and the Executive

1. (a) Individual judges should enjoy personal independence and substantive independence.

   (b) Personal independence means that the terms and conditions of judicial service are adequately secured, so as to ensure that individual judges are not subject to executive control.

   (c) Sustantive independence means that in the discharge of his judicial function, a judge is subject to nothing but the law and the commands of his conscience.

2. The judiciary as a whole should enjoy autonomy and collective independence vis-a-vis the Executive.

3. (a) Participation in judicial appointments and promotions by the Executive or Legislature is not inconsistent with judicial independence, provided that appointments and promotions of judges are vested in a judicial body, in which members of judiciary and the legal profession form *a* majority.

   (b) Appointments and promotions by a non-judicial body will not be considered inconsistent with judicial independence in countries where, by long historic and democratic tradition, judicial appointments and promotion operate satisfactorily.

4. (a) The Executive may participate in the discipline of judges, only in referring complaints against judges, or in the initiation of disciplinary proceedings, but not the adjudication of such matters. The power to discipline or remove a judge must be vested in an institution which is independent of the Executive.

   (b) The power of removal of a judge should preferably be vested in a judicial tribunal.

   (c) The Legislature may be vested with the powers of removal of judges, preferably upon a recommendation of a judicial commission.

5. The Executive shall not have control over judicial functions.

6. Rules of procedure and practice shall be made by legislation or by the Judiciary in cooperation with the legal profession, subject to parliamentary approval.
7. The state shall have a duty to provide for the execution of judgments of the Court. The Judiciary shall exercise supervision over the execution process.
8. Judicial matters are exclusively within the responsibility of the Judiciary, both in central judicial administration and in court level judicial administration.
9. The central responsibility for judicial administration shall preferably be vested in the Judiciary or jointly in the Judiciary and the Executive.
10. It is the duty of the state to provide adequate financial resources to allow for the due administration of justice.
11. (a) Division of work among judges should ordinarily be done under a predetermined plan, which can be changed in certain clearly defined circumstances.

    (b) In countries where the power of division of judicial work is vested in the chief justice, it is not considered inconsistent with judicial independence to accord to the chief justice the power to change the predetermined plan for sound reasons, preferably in consultation with the senior judges when praticable.

    (c) Subject to (a), the exclusive responsibility for case assignment should be vested in a responsible judge, preferably the President of the Court.
12. The power to transfer a judge from one court to another shall be vested in a judicial authority and preferably shall be subject to the judge's consent, such consent not to be unreasonably withheld.
13. Court services should be adequately financed by the relevant government.
14. Judicial salaries and pensions shall be adequate, and should be regularly adjusted to account for price increases independently of Executive control.
15. (a) The position of the judges, their independence, their security, and their adequate remuneration shall be secured by law.

    (b) Judicial salaries cannot be decreased during the judges' service except as a coherent part of an overall public economic measure.
16. The Ministers of the government shall not exercise any form of pressure on judges, whether overt or covert, and shall not make statements which adversely affect the independence of individual judges, or of the Judiciary as a whole.
17. The power of pardon shall be exercised cautiously so as to avoid its use as an interference with judicial decision.
18. (a) The Executive shall refrain from any act or omission which pre-empts the judicial resolution of a dispute, or frustrates the proper execution of a court judgment.

    (b) The Executive shall not have the power to close down, or suspend, the operation of the court system at any level.

II. Judges and the Legislature

19. The Legislature shall not pass legislation which retroactively reverses specific court decisions.

20. (a) Legislation introducing changes in the terms and conditions of judicial services shall not be applied to judges holding office at the time of passing the legislation, unless the changes improve the terms of service.

    (b) In case of legislation reorganising courts, judges serving in these courts shall not be affected, except for their transfer to another court of the same status.

21. A citizen shall have the right to be tried by the ordinary courts of law, and shall not be tried before ad hoc tribunals.

III. Terms and Nature of Judicial Appointments

22. (a) Judicial appointments should generally be for life, subject to removal for cause and compulsory retirement, at an age fixed by law at the date of appointment.

    (b) Retirement age shall not be reduced for existing judges.

23. (a) Judges should not be appointed for probationary periods except for in legal systems in which appointments of judges do not depend on having practical experience in the profession as a condition of appointment.

    (b) The institution of temporary judges should be avoided as far as possible except where there exists a long historic democratic tradition.

24. The number of the members of the highest court should be rigid and should not be subject to change, except by legislation.

25. Part-time judges should be appointed only with proper safeguards.

26. Selection of judges shall be based on merit.

IV. Judicial Removal and Discipline

27. The proceedings for discipline and removal of judges should ensure fairness to the judge, and adequate opportunity for hearing.

28. The procedure for discipline should be held in camera. The judge may however request that the hearing be held in public, subject to a final and reasoned disposition of this request by the Disciplinary Tribunal. Judgments in disciplinary proceedings, whether held in camera or in public, may be published.

29. (a) The grounds for removal of judges shall be fixed by law and shall be clearly defined.

(b) All disciplinary action shall be based upon standards of judicial conduct promulgated by law, or in established rules of court.

30. A judge shall not be subject to removal unless, by reason of a criminal act or through gross or repeated neglect or physical or mental incapacity, he has shown himself manifestly unfit to hold the position of judge.

31. In systems where the power to discipline and remove judges is vested in an institution other than the Legislature, the tribunal for discipline and removal of judges shall be permanent, and be composed predominantly of member of the Judiciary.

32. The head of the court may legitimately have supervisory powers to control judges on administrative matters.

V. The Press, the Judiciary and the Courts

33. It should be recognised that judicial independence does not render the judges free from public aCcountability, however, the press and other institutions should be aware of the potential conflict between judicial independence and excessive pressure on judges.

34. Subject to Standard 41, judges may write articles in the press, appear on television and give interviews to the press.

35. The press should show restraint in publications on pending cases where such publication may influence the outcome of the case.

VI. Standards of Conduct

36. Judges may not, during their term of office, serve in Executive functions, such as ministers of the government, nor may they serve as members of the Legislature or of municipal councils, unless by long historical traditions these functions are combined.

37. Judges may serve as chairmen of committees of inquiry in cases where the process requires skill of fact-finding and evidence-taking.

38. Judges shall not hold positions in political parties.

39. A judge, other than a temporary judge, may not practice law during his term of office.

40. A judge should refrain from business activities, except his personal investments, or ownership of property.

41. A judge should always behave in such a manner as to preserve the dignity of his office and the impartiality and independence of the Judiciary.

42. Judges may be organized in associations designed for judges, for furthering their rights and interests as judges.

43. Judges may take collective action to protect their judicial independence and to uphold their position.

VII. Securing Impartiality and Independence

44. A judge shall enjoy immunity from legal actions, and the obligation to testify concerning matters arising in the exercise of his official functions.

45. A judge shall not sit in a case where there is a reasonable suspicion of bias or potential bias.

46. A judge shall avoid any course of conduct which might give rise to an appearance of partiality.

VIII. The Internal Independence of the Judiciary

47. In the decision-making process, a judge must be independent vis-a-vis his judicial colleagues and superiors.

Note: The above standards are subject to periodic review by the appropriate committee or committees of the International Bar Association and amendment from time to time by the International Bar Association in plenary session as circumstances may warrant or require.

Appendix
Text of Jerusalem Approved Standards which were Amended in New Delhi

(Remaining Jerusalem Standards were approved without change.)

3. (a) Judicial appointments and promotions by the Executive are not inconsistent with judicial independence.

   (b) Except for countries where by long historic and democratic tradition judicial appointments operate satisfactorily, judicial participation in the process of judicial appointments and promotions, whether by judicial commission or otherwise, is imperative for the maintenance of judicial independence.

15. (a) The position of the judges, their independence, and their adequate remuneration shall be secured by law.

20. (b) In case of legislation abolishing courts, judges serving in these courts shall not be affected, except for their transfer to another court of the same status.

28. The procedure for discipline should be in camera; however, judgments in disciplinary proceedings may be published.

44. A judge shall enjoy immunity from legal actions in the exercise of his official functions.

APPENDIX IV

UN BASIC PRINCIPLES ON THE INDEPENDENCE OF THE JUDICIARY

Adopted by the Seventh United Nations Congress on the Prevention of Crime and the Treatment of Offenders held at Milan from 26 August to 6 September 1985 and endorsed by General Assembly resolutions 40/32 of 29 November 1985 and 40/146 of 13 December 1985

Whereas in the Charter of the United Nations the peoples of the world affirm, inter alia, their determination to establish conditions under which justice can be maintained to achieve international co-operation in promoting and encouraging respect for human rights and fundamental freedoms without any discrimination,

Whereas the Universal Declaration of Human Rights enshrines in particular the principles of equality before the law, of the presumption of innocence and of the right to a fair and public hearing by a competent, independent and impartial tribunal established by law,

Whereas the International Covenants on Economic, Social and Cultural Rights and on Civil and Political Rights both guarantee the exercise of those rights, and in addition, the Covenant on Civil and Political Rights further guarantees the right to be tried without undue delay,

Whereas frequently there still exists a gap between the vision underlying those principles and the actual situation,

Whereas the organization and administration of justice in every country should be inspired by those principles, and efforts should be undertaken to translate them fully into reality,

Whereas rules concerning the exercise of judicial office should aim at enabling judges to act in accordance with those principles,

Whereas judges are charged with the ultimate decision over life, freedoms, rights, duties and property of citizens,

Whereas the Sixth United Nations Congress on the Prevention of Crime and the Treatment of Offenders, by its resolution 16, called upon the Committee on Crime Prevention and Control to include among its priorities the elaboration of guidelines relating to the independence of judges and the selection, professional training and status of judges and prosecutors,

Whereas it is, therefore, appropriate that consideration be first given to the role of judges in relation to the system of justice and to the importance of their selection, training and conduct,

The following basic principles, formulated to assist Member States in their task of securing and promoting the independence of the judiciary should be taken into account and respected by Governments within the framework of their national legislation and practice and be brought to the attention of judges, lawyers, members of the executive and the legislature and the public in general. The principles have been formulated principally with professional judges in mind, but they apply equally, as appropriate, to lay judges, where they exist.

I. Independence of the Judiciary

1. The independence of the judiciary shall be guaranteed by the State and enshrined in the Constitution or the law of the country. It is the duty of all governmental and other institutions to respect and observe the independence of the judiciary.

2. The judiciary shall decide matters before them impartially, on the basis of facts and in accordance with the law, without any restrictions, improper influences, inducements, pressures, threats or interferences, direct or indirect, from any quarter or for any reason.

3. The judiciary shall have jurisdiction over all issues of a judicial nature and shall have exclusive authority to decide whether an issue submitted for its decision is within its competence as defined by law.

4. There shall not be any inappropriate or unwarranted interference with the judicial process, nor shall judicial decisions by the courts be subject to revision. This principle is without prejudice to judicial review or to mitigation or commutation by competent authorities of sentences imposed by the judiciary, in accordance with the law.

5. Everyone shall have the right to be tried by ordinary courts or tribunals using established legal procedures. Tribunals that do not use the duly established procedures of the legal process shall not be created to displace the jurisdiction belonging to the ordinary courts or judicial tribunals.

6. The principle of the independence of the judiciary entitles and requires the judiciary to ensure that judicial proceedings are conducted fairly and that the rights of the parties are respected.

7. It is the duty of each Member State to provide adequate resources to enable the judiciary to properly perform its functions.

II. Freedom of Expression and Association

8. In accordance with the Universal Declaration of Human Rights, members of the judiciary are like other citizens entitled to freedom of expression, belief, association and assembly; provided, however, that in exercising such rights, judges shall always conduct themselves in such a manner as to preserve the dignity of their office and the impartiality and independence of the judiciary.

9. Judges shall be free to form and join associations of judges or other organizations to represent their interests, to promote their professional training and to protect their judicial independence.

III. Qualifications, Selection and Training

10. Persons selected for judicial office shall be individuals of integrity and ability with appropriate training or qualifications in law. Any method of judicial selection shall

safeguard against judicial appointments for improper motives. In the selection of judges, there shall be no discrimination against a person on the grounds of race, colour, sex, religion, political or other opinion, national or social origin, property, birth or status, except that a requirement, that a candidate for judicial office must be a national of the country concerned, shall not be considered discriminatory.

IV. Conditions of Service and Tenure

11. The term of office of judges, their independence, security, adequate remuneration, conditions of service, pensions and the age of retirement shall be adequately secured by law.

12. Judges, whether appointed or elected, shall have guaranteed tenure until a mandatory retirement age or the expiry of their term of office, where such exists.

13. Promotion of judges, wherever such a system exists, should be based on objective factors, in particular ability, integrity and experience.

14. The assignment of cases to judges within the court to which they belong is an internal matter of judicial administration. Professional secrecy and immunity

15. The judiciary shall be bound by professional secrecy with regard to their deliberations and to confidential information acquired in the course of their duties other than in public proceedings, and shall not be compelled to testify on such matters.

16. Without prejudice to any disciplinary procedure or to any right of appeal or to compensation from the State, in accordance with national law, judges should enjoy personal immunity from civil suits for monetary damages for improper acts or omissions in the exercise of their judicial functions.

V. Discipline, Suspension and Removal

17. A charge or complaint made against a judge in his/her judicial and professional capacity shall be processed expeditiously and fairly under an appropriate procedure. The judge shall have the right to a fair hearing. The examination of the matter at its initial stage shall be kept confidential, unless otherwise requested by the judge.

18. Judges shall be subject to suspension or removal only for reasons of incapacity or behaviour that renders them unfit to discharge their duties.

19. All disciplinary, suspension or removal proceedings shall be determined in accordance with established standards of judicial conduct.

20. Decisions in disciplinary, suspension or removal proceedings should be subject to an independent review. This principle may not apply to the decisions of the highest court and those of the legislature in impeachment or similar proceedings.

APPENDIX V

COMMONWEALTH (LATIMER HOUSE) PRINCIPLES ON THE THREE BRANCHES OF GOVERNMENT

Commonwealth Heads of Government warmly welcome the contribution made by the Commonwealth Parliamentary Association and the legal profession of the Commonwealth represented by the Commonwealth Magistrates' and judges' Association, the Commonwealth Lawyers Association and the Commonwealth Legal Education Association to further the Commonwealth Harare Principles.

They acknowledge the value of the work of these Associations to develop the Latimer House Guidelines and resolve, in the spirit of those Guidelines, to adopt the Commonwealth Principles on the Accountability of and the Relationship Between the Three Branches of Government.

I. Objective

The objective of these Principles is to provide, in accordance with the laws and customs of each Commonwealth country, an effective framework for the implementation by governments, parliaments and judiciaries of the Commonwealth's fundamental values.

1. *The Three Branches of Government*

Each Commonwealth country's Parliaments, Executives and Judiciaries are the guarantors in their respective spheres of the rule of law, *the* promotion and protec- tion of fundamental human rights and the entrenchment of good governance based on the highest standards of honesty, probity and accountability.

2. *Parliament and the Judiciary*

(a) Relations between parliament and the judiciary should be governed by respect for parliament's primary responsibility for law making on the one hand and for the judiciary's responsibility for the interpretation and application of the law on the other hand.

(b) Judiciaries and parliaments should fulfill their respective but critical roles in the promotion of the rule of law in a complementary and constructive manner.

3. *Independence of Parliamentarians*

(a) Parliamentarians must be able to carry out their legislative and constitutional functions in accordance with the Constitution, free from unlawful interference.

(b) Criminal and defamations laws should not be used to restrict legitimate criticism of Parliament; the offence of contempt of parliament should be narrowly drawn and reporting of the proceedings of parliament should not be unduly restricted by narrow application of the defence of qualified privilege.

4. *Independence of the Judiciary*

An independent, impartial, honest and competent judiciary is integral to upholding the rule of law, engendering public confidence and dispensing justice. The unction of the judiciary is to interpret and apply national constitutions and legislation, consistent with international human rights conventions and international law, to the extent permitted by the domestic law of each Commonwealth country.

To secure these aims:

(a) Judicial appointments should be made on the basis of clearly defined criteria and by a publicly declared process. The process should ensure:

Equality of opportunity for all who are eligible for judicial case;

Appointment on merit; and

That appropriate consideration is given to the need for the progressive attainment of gender equity and the removal of other historic factors of discrimination.

(b) Arrangements for appropriate security of tenure and protections of levels of remuneration must be in place.

(c) Adequate resources should be provided for the judicial system to operate effectively without any undue constraints which may hamper the independence sought;

(d) Interaction, if any, between the executive and the judiciary should not compromise judicial independence.

Judges should be subject to suspension or removal only for reasons of incapacity or misbehavior that clearly renders them unfit to discharge their duties.

Court proceedings should, unless the law or overriding public interest otherwish dictates, be open to the public. Superior Court decisions should be published and accessible to the public and be given in a timely manner.

An independent effective and competent legal profession is foundamental to the upholding of the rule of law and the independence of judiciary.

5. *Public Office Holders*

(a) Merit and proven integrity, should be the criteria of eligibility for appointment to public office;

(b) Subject to (a), measures may be taken, where possible and appropriate, to ensure that the holders of all public offices generally reflect the composition of the community in terms of gender, ethunicity, social and religious groups and regional balance.

6. *Ethical Governance*

Ministers, members of Parliament, judicial officers and public office holders in each jurisdiction should respectively develop, adopt and periodically review appropriate guidelines for ethical conduct. These should address the issue of conflict of interest, whether actual or perceived, with a view to enhancing transparency, accountability and public confidence.

7. *Accountability Mechanisms*

(a) Executive Accountability to Parliament
Parliaments and governments should maintain high standards of accountability, transparency and responsibility in the conduct of all public business.

Parliamentary procedures should provide adequate mechanisms to enforce the accountability of the executive to Parliament.

(b) Judicial Accountability
Judges are accountable to the constitution and to the law which they must apply honestly, independently and with integrity. The principles of judicial accountability and independence underpin public confidence in the judicial system and the importance of the judiciary as one of the three pillars upon which a responsible government relies.

In addition to providing proper procedures for the removal of judges on grounds of incapacity or misbehavior that are required to support the principle of independence of the judiciary, any disciplinary procedures should be fairly and objectively administered. Disciplinary proceedings which might lead to the removal of a judicial officer should include appropriate safeguards to ensure fairness.

The criminal law and contempt proceedings should not be used to restrict legitimate criticism of the performance of judicial functions.

(c) Judicial review
Best democratic principles require that the actions of governments are open to scrutiny by the courts, to ensure that decisions taken comply with the Constitution, with relevant statutes and other law, including the law relating to the principles of natural justice.

8. *The law-making process*

In order to enhance the effectiveness of law making as an essential element of the good governance agenda:

There should be adequate parliamentary examination of proposed legislation;

Where appropriate, opportunity should be given for public input into legislative process;

Parliament should, where relevant, be given the opportunity to consider international instruments or regional conventions agreed to by governments.

9. *Oversight of government*

The promotion of zero-tolerance for corruption is vital to good governance. A transparent and accountable government, together with freedom of expression, encourages the full participation of its citizens in the democratic process.

Steps which may be taken to encourage public sector accountability include:

(a) the establishment of scrutiny bodies and mechanisms to oversee Government, enhances public confidence in the integrity and acceptability of Committees. Ombudsmen, Human Rights Commissions, Auditors-General, Anti-corruption commissions, Information Commissioners and similar oversight institutions can play a key role in enhancing public awareness of good governance and rule of law issues. Governments are encouraged to establish or enhance appropriate oversight bodies in accordance with national circumstances.

(b) Government's transparency and accountability is promoted by an independent and vibrant media which is responsible, objective and impartial and which is protected by law in its freedom to report and comment upon public affairs.

10. *Civil Society*

Parliaments and governments should recognize the role that civil society plays in the implementation of the Commonwealth's fundamental values and should strive for a constructive relationship with civil society to ensure that there is broader opportunity for lawful participation in the democratic process.

ANNEX
PARLIAMENTARY SUPREMACY
JUDICIAL INDEPENCE
LATIMER HOUSE GUIDELINES FOR THE COMMONWEALTH
19 JUNE 1998

Guidelines on good practice governing relations between the Executive, Parliament and the Judiciary in the promotion of good governance, the rule of law and human rights to ensure the effective implementation of the Harare Principles.

II. Preamble

Recalling the renewed commitment at the 1997 Commonwealth Heads of Government Meeting at Edinburgh to the Harare Principles and the Millbrook Commonwealth Action Programme and, in particular, the pledge in paragraph 9 of the Harare Declaration to work for the protection and promotion of the fundamental political values of the Commonwealth

- Democracy.
- Democratic processes and institutions which reflect national circumstances, the rule of law and the independence of the judiciary;
- Just and honest government;
- Fundamental human rights, including equal rights and opportunities for all citizens regardless of race, color, creed or political belief, and
- Equality for women, so that they may exercise their full and equal rights.

Representatives of the Commonwealth Parliamentary Association, the Commonwealth Magistrates' and Judges' Association, the Commonwealth Lawyers' Association and

the Commonwealth Legal Education Association meeting at Latimer House in the United Kingdom from 15 to 19 june 1998:
Have resolved to adopt the following Principles and Guidelines and propose them for consideration by the Commonwealth Heads of Government Meeting and for effective implementation by member countries of the Commonwealth.

III. Principles

The successful implementation of these Guidelines calls for a commitment, made in the utmost good faith, of the relevant national institutions, in particular the executive, parliament and the judiciary, to the essential principles of good governance, fundamental human rights and the rule of law, including the independence of the judiciary, so that the legitimate aspirations of all the peoples of the Commonwealth should be met.

Each institution must exercise responsibility and restraint in the exercise of power withing its own constitutional sphere so as not to encroach on the legitimate discharge of constitutional functions by the other institutions.

It is recognised that the special circumstances of small and/or under-resourced jurisdictions may require adaptation of these Guidelines.

It is recognised that redress of gender imbalance is essential to accomplish full and equal rights in society and to achieve true human right.[1] Merit and the capacity to perform public office regardless of disability should be the criteria of eligibility for appointment or election.

IV. Guidelines

1. *Parliament and the Judiciary*

1. the legislative function is the primary responsibility of parliament as the elected body representing the people. Judges may[2] be constructive and purposive in the interpretation of legislation, but must not usurp Parliament's legislative function. Courts should have the power to declare legislation to be unconstitutional and of no legal effect. However, there may be circumstances where the appropriate remedy would be for the court to declare the incompatibility of a statute with the Constitution, leaving it to the legislature to take remedial legislative measures.

2. Commonwealth parliaments should take speedy and effective steps to implement their countries' international human rights obligations by enacting appropriate

[1] The final paragraph does no refer expressly to other forms of discrimination, e.g. on ethnic or religious grounds. There are a number of approaches to the redress of existing imbalances, such as selection based on "merit with bias", i-e. where, for example, if two applicants ore of equal merit, the bias should be to appoint a woman where there exists gender imbalance.

[2] It has been suggested that judges "shall" have a duty to adopt a constructive and purposive approach to the interpretation of legislation, particularly in a human rights context, as indicated in paragraph 3.

human rights legislation. Special legislation (such as equal opportunity laws) is required to extend the protection of fundamental rights to the private sphere. Where domestic incorporation has not occurred, international instruments should be applied to aid interpretation.

3. Judges should adopt a generous and purposive approach in interpreting a Bill of Rights. This is particularly important in countries which are in the process of builing democratic traditions. Judges have a vital part to play in developing and maintaining a vibrant human rights environment throughout the Commonwealth.
4. International law and, in particular, human right jurisprudence can greatly assist domestic courts in interpreting a Bill of Rights. It also can help expand the scope of a Bill of Rights making it more meaningful and effective.
5. While dialogue between the judiciary and the government may be desirable of appropriate, in no circumstances should such dialogue compromise judicial independence.
6. People should have easy and unhindered access to courts, particularly to enfore their fundamental rights. Any existing procedural obstacles to access to justice should be removed.
7. people should also be made aware of, and have access to, other important fora for human rights dispute resolution, particularly Human Rights Commissions, Offices of the Ombudsman and mechnisms for alternative dispute resolution.
8. Everyone, especially judges, Parliamentarians and lawyers, should have access to human rights education.

2. *Preserving Judicial Independence*

a. *Judicial appointments*
Jurisdictions should have an appropriate independent process in place for judicial appointments. Where no independent system already exists, appointments should be made by a judicial services commission (established by the Constitution or by statute) or by an appropriate officer of state acting on the recommendation of such a commission.[3]

The appointment process, whether or not involving an appropriately constituted and representative judicial services commission, should be designed to guarantee the quality and independence of mind of those selected for appointment at all levels of the judiciary.

[3] The Guidelines clearly recognise that, in certain jurisdictions, appropriate mechanisms for judicial appointments not involving a judicial service commission are in place. However, such commissions exist in many jurisdictions, though their composition differs. There are arguments for and against o majority of senior judges and in favour of strong representation of other branches of the legal profession, members or parliament and of civil society in general.

Judicial appointments to all levels of the judiciary should be made on merit with appropriate provision for the progressive removal of gender imbalance and of other historic factors of discrimination.

Judicial appointments should normally be permanent; whilst in some jurisdictions, contract appointments may be inevitable, such appointments should be subject to appropriate security of tenure.[4]

Judicial vacancies should be advertised.

b. *Funding*
Sufficient and sustainable funding should be provided to enable the judiciary to perform its functions to the highest standards. Such funds, once voted for the judiciary by the legislature, should be protected from alienation or misuse. The allocation or withholding of funding should not be used as a means of exercising improper control over the judiciary.[5]

Appropriate salaries and benefits, supporting staff, resources and equipment are essential to the proper functioning of the judiciary.

As a matter of principle, judicial salaries and benefits should be set by an independent body and their value should be maintained.

c. *Training*[6]
A culture of judicial education should be developed.

Training should be organised, systematic and ongoing and under the control of an adequately funded judicial body.

Judicial training should include the teaching of the law, judicial skills and the social context including ethnic and gender issues.

The curriculum should be controlled by judicial officers who should have the assistance of lay specialists.

For jurisdictions without adequate training facilities, access to facilities in other jurisdictions should be provided.

---

[4] The making of non-permanent judicial appointments by the executive without security of tenure remains controversial in a number of jurisdictions.

[5] The provision of adequate funding for the Judiciary must be a very high priority in order to uphold the rule of law, to ensure that good governance and democracy are sustained and to provide for the effective and efficient administration of justice. However, it is acknowledged that a shortfall in anticipated notional income might lead to budgetary constraints. Finance ministries ore urged to engage in appropriate consultations in order to set realistic and sustainable budgets which parliaments should approve to ensure adequate funds are available.

[6] This is an area where the sponsoring associations can play a cost-effective role in co-operation with the Commonwealth Secretariat. Resources need to be provided in order to support the judiciary in the promotion of the rule of law and good governance.

Courses in judicial education should be offered to practicing lawyers as part of their ongoing professional development training.[7]

3. *Preserving the Independence of Parliamentarians*[8]

1. article 9 of the Bill of Rights 1688 is re-affirmed. This article provides:

> that the Freedome of Speech and Debates or Proceedings in Parlyement ought not to be impeached or questioned in any court or place out of Parlyement

2. security of members during their parliamentary term is fundamental to parliamentary independence and therefore:

(a) the expulsion of members from parliament as a penalty for leaving their parties (floor-crossing) should be viewed as a possible infringement of members' independence; anti-deflection measures may be necessary in some jurisdictions to deal with corrupt practices[9];
(b) laws allowing for rthe recall of members during their elected term should be viewed with caution, as a potential threat to the independence of members;
(c) the cessation of membership of a political party of itself should not lead to the loss of a member's seat

3. In the discharge of their functions, members should be free from improper pressures and accordingly:

(a) the criminal law and the use of defamation proceedings are not appropriate mechanisms for restricting legitimate criticism of the government to the parliament.
(b) the defence of qualified privilege with respect to reports of parliamentary proceedings should be drawn as broadly as possible to permit full public reporting and discussion of public affairs;
(c) the offence of contempt of parliament should be drawn as narrowly as possible.

[7] The drafters of the Guidelines did not wish by this provision to impinge on either the independence of the judiciary or the independence of the legal profession. However, in many jurisdictions throughout the Commonwealth, magistrates and judges are given no formal training on commencement of their duties. It was felt that appointees to the bench would benefit from some training prior to appointment in order to make them more aware of the duties and obligations of judicial officers and aid their passage to the bench.

[8] It has been observed that the Guidelines are silent about the elected composition of the popular chamber. In a number of jurisdictions, nominated members may have a decisive influence on the outcome of a vote. If property used, however, the power of nomination may be used to redress, for example, gender imbalance and to ensure representation of ethnic or religious minorities. The role of non-elected senates or upper chambers must also be considered in this context.

[9] There remains controversy about the balance to be struck between anti-floor-crossing measures as a barrier against corruption and the potential threat to the independence of MP.

4. *Women in Parliament*[10]

1. To improve the numbers of women members in Commonwealth parliaments, the role of women within political parties should be enhanced, including the appointment of more women to executive roles within political parties.
2. Pro-active searches for potential candidates should be undertaken by political parties.
3. Political parties in nations with proportional representation should be required to ensure an adequate gender balance on their respective lists of candidates for election. Women, where relevant, should be included in the top part of the candidates lists of political parties. Parties should be called upon publicly to declare the degree of representation of women on their lists and to defend any failure to maintain adequate representation.
4. Where there is no proportional representation, candidate search and/or selection committees of political parties should be gender-balanced as should representation at political conventions and this should be facilitated by political parties by way of amendment to pary constitutions; women should be put forward for safe seats.
5. Women should be elected to parliament through regular electoral processes. The provision of reservations for women in national constitutions, whilst useful, tends to be insufficient for securing adequate and long-term representation by women.
6. Men should work in partnership with women to redress constraints on women entering parliament. True gender balance requires the oppositional element of the inclusion of men in the process of dialogue and and remedial action to address the necessary inclusion of both genders in all aspects of the public life.

5. *Judicial and Parliamentary Ethics*

a. *Judicial Ethics*

(a) A code of Ethics and Conduct should be developed and adopted by each judiciary as a means of ensuring the accountability of judges;

(b) the Commonwealth Magistrates' and Judges' Association should be encouraged to complete its Model Code of Judicial Conduct now in development[11];

---

[10] The emphasis on gender balance is not intended to imply that there are not other issues of equity in representation which need to be considered. Parliament should reflect the composition of the community which it represents in terms of ethnicity, social and religious groups and regional balance. Some countries have experimented with regulation of notional political parties to ensure, for example, that their support is not confined to one regional or ethnic group, a notion which would be profoundly hostile to the political culture in other jurisdictions.

[11] Following discussion of the Guidelines, it has been accepted by the Working Group that a "uniform" Model Code of judicial Conduct is inappropriate. Judicial Officers in each country should develop, adopt and periodically review codes of ethics and conduct appropriate to their jurisdiction. The CMJA will promote that process in its programmes and will serve as a repository for such codes when adopted.

(c) the Association should also serve as a repository of codes of judicial conduct developed by Commonwealth judiciaries, which will serve as a resource for other jurisdictions.

b. *Parliamentary ethics*

(a) Conflict of interest guidelines and codes of conduct should require full disclosure by ministers and members of their financial and business interests;

(b) members of parliament should have privileged access to advice from statutorily-established Ethics Advisors;

(c) whilst responsive to the needs of society and recognizing minority views in society, members of parliament should avoid excessive influence of lobbyists and special interest groups.

6. *Accountability Mechanisms*

a. *Judicial Accountability*

(a) discipline:

(i) In cases where a judge is at risk of removal, the judge must have the right to be fully informed of the charges, to be represented at a hearing, to make a full defence and to be judged by an independent and impartial tribunal.

Grounds for removal of a judge should be limited to:

(A) inability to perform judicial duties and

(B) serious misconduct.

(ii) In all other matters, the process should be conducted by the chief judge of the courts;

(iii) Disciplinary procedures should not include the public admonition of judges. Any admonitions should be delivered in private, by the chief judge.

b) Public Criticism[12]:

(i) Legitimate public criticism of judicial performance is a means of ensuring accountability;

(ii) The criminal law and contempt proceedings are not appropriate mechanisms for restricting legitimate criticism of the courts.

b. *Executive Accountability*

(a) Accountability of the Executive to Parliament

Parliamentary procedures should provide adequate mechanisms to enforce the accountability of the executive to parliament. These should include:

---

[12] In certain jurisdictions, the corruption of the judiciary is acknowledged as a real problem. The recommendations contained in the Guidelines are entirely consistent with the Framework for Commonwealth Principles in Promoting Good Governance and Combating Corruption approved by CHOGM in Durban in 1999. There is some support for the creation of a judicial Ombudsman who may receive complaints from the public regarding the conduct of judges.

(i) a committee structure appropriate to the size of parliament, adequately resourced and with the power to summon witnesses, including ministers. Governments should be required to announce publicly, within a defined time period, their responses to committee reports;
(ii) standing orders should provide appropriate opportunities for members to question ministers and full debate on legislative proposals;
(iii) the public accounts should be independently audited by the Auditor General who is responsible to and must report directly to parliament;
(iv) the chair of the Public Accounts Committee should normally be an opposition member;
(v) offices of the Ombudsman, Human Rights Commissions and Access to Information Commissioners should report regularly to parliament.

(b) Judicial Review

Commonwealth governments should endorse and implement the principles of judicial review enshrined in the Lusaka Statement on Government under the Law.

7. *The Law-Making Process*

1. Women should be involved in the work of national law commissions in the law-making process. Ongoing assessment of legislation is essential so as to create a more gender-balanced society. Gender-neutral language should be used in the drafting and use of legislation.

2. Procedures for the preliminary examination of issues in proposed legislation should be adopted and published so that:

(a) there is public exposure of issues, papers and consultation on major reforms including, where possible, a draft bill;
(b) standing orders provide a delay of some days between introduction and debate to enable public comment unless suspended by consent or a significantly high percentage vote of the chamber; and
(c) major legislation can be referred to a select committee allowing for the detailed examination of such legislation and the taking of evidence from members of the public.

3. Model standing orders protecting members' rights and privileges and permitting the incorporation of variations, to take local circumstances into account, should be drafted and published.

4. Parliament should be serviced by a professional staff independent of the regular public service.

5. Adequate resources to government and non-government backbenchers should b e provided to improve parliamentary input and should include provision for:

(a) training of new members;
(b) secretarial, office, library and research facilities;
(c) drafting assistance including private members' bills.

6. An all-party committee of members of parliament should review and administer parliament's budget which should not be subject to amendment by the executive.

7. Appropriate legislation should incorporate international human rights instruments to assist in interpretation and to ensure that ministers certify compliance with such instruments, on introduction of the legislation.
8. It is recommended that "sunset" legislation (for the expiry of all subordinate legislation not renewed) should be enacted subject to power to extend the life of such legislation.

8. *The Role of Non-Judicial and Non-Parliamentaric Institutions*

1. The Commonwealth Statement on Freedom of Expression[13] provides essential guarantees to which all Commonwealth countries should subscribe.
2. The Executive must refrain from all measures directed at inhibiting the freedom of the press, including indirect methods such as the misuse of official advertising.
3. An independent, organized legal profession is and essential component in the protection of the rule of law.
4. Adequate legal aid schemes should be provided for poor and disadvantaged litigants, including public interest advocates.
5. Legal professional organisations should assist in the provision, through pro bono schemes, of access to justice for the impecunious.
6. The executive must refrain from obstructing the functioning of an independent legal profession by such means as withholding licensing of professional bodies.
7. Human Rights Commissions, Offices of the Ombudsman and Access to Information Commissioners can play a key role in enhancing public awareness of good governance and rule of law issues, and adequate funding and resources should be made available to enable them to discharge these functions. Parliament should accept responsibility in this regard.

Such institutions should be empowered to provide access to alternative dispute-resolution mechanisms.

9. *Measures for Implementation and Monitoring Compliance*

These guidelines should be forwarded to the Commonwealth Secretariat for consideration by Law Ministers and Heads of Government.[14]

---

[13] Since the Guidelines were drafted, the draft Statement on Freedom of Expression has been subject to further consideration and the reference should take account of the new developments. The Commonwealth Heads of Government, in the Coolum Declaration of 5 March 2002, included a commitment to freedom of expression: "We stand united in our commitment to democracy, the rule of law, good governance, freedom of expression and the protection of human rights…"

[14] Under active consideration is the creation of a monitoring procedure outside official Commonwealth processes. This initially may involve on "annual report" on the implementation of the Guidelines in oil Commonwealth jurisdictions, noting "good" and "bad' practice.

If these Guidelines are adopted, an effective monitoring procedure, which might include a Standing Committee, should be devised under which all Commonwealth jurisdictions accept an obligation to report on their compliance with these Guidelines.

Consideration of these reports should form a regular part of the Meetings of Law Ministers and of Heads of Government.

APPENDIX VI

TOKYO PRINCIPLES ON THE INDEPENDENCE OF THE JUDICIARY IN THE LAWASIA REGION

A REPORT OF A SEMINAR HELD IN TOKYO ON 17TH–18TH JULY 1982 OF LAWASIA: THE LAW ASSOCIATION FOR ASIA AND THE WESTERN PACIFIC

I. Introduction

Fall S. Nariman

On 17th–18th July, 1982, the LAW ASIA Human Rights Standing Committee met in Tokyo, Japan for the purpose of discussing the application of the principle of the Independence of the Judiciary in the context of the history and culture of Asian countries. The meeting of the Standing Committee was held in private.

The Committee was honoured by the presence at its meeting of Chief Justice Chandrachud of India, Chief Justice Fernando of the Phillippines, Chief Justice samarakoon of Sri Lanka, and President Suchiva of the Supreme Court of Thailand. It was also honoured by the distinguished presence of the Former President of the Supreme Court of Japan, former Judge Ekizo Fujibayashi, former Supreme Court Judge, former Judge Sakamoto and former Judge Takeda, and the former Chief Justice of the Nagoya High Court, former Judge Yorihiro Natio. The meeting was also attended by eminent Japanese lawyers and professors, including the former Dean of the Law Faculty of Tokyo University, Professor Mikazuki.

Having had the benefit of the experience and wisdom of these eminent jurists, and the advantages of their insight into the functioning of different jUdicial systems, and drawing upon the collective experience of members of LA WASIA in the region, the LAW ASIA Human Rights Standing Committee at its subsequent meeting in Tokyo, formulated the following principles and conclusions.

1. The judiciary is an institution which has, and is seen to be of the highest value in the societies in the countries of the LAW ASIA region.

2. The maintenance of the independence of the judiciary is essential to the attainment of its objectives and the proper performance of its high function.

3. It is the duty of the judiciary to respect and observe the proper objectives and functions of the other institutions of government; it is the duty of those institutions to respect and observe the proper objectives and functions of the judiciary.

4. The objectives and functions of the judiciary in these countries include the following:

   (b) to promote, within the proper limits of the jUdicial function, the observance and the attainment of human rights within its own society;

(c) to administer the law impartially between citizen and citizen and between citizen and state.

5. To enable the judiciary to achieve its objectives and perform its functions, it is essential that those appointed as judges be chosen with due regard to their independence, competence and integrity.

6. It is fundamental to the preservation of the independence of the jUdiciary that it be freed from threats and pressures from any quarter.

7. It is also essential that the judges be provided with the facilities necessary to enable them to perform their functions.

8. It is the duty of the institutions of government to ensure that the judiciary occupies, and is seen to occupy, the position in its society which will enable it to maintain its proper dignity and standing in that society and to achieve its objectives and perform its functions.

9. It is equally the duty of each member of the judiciary to conduct himself/herself in all things in such a way as is consistent with the dignity and standing of his/her office and as will promote the achievement of the objectives and the performance of the functions of the judiciary to which he/she belongs.

10. Appointment of Judges:

(a) There is no single mode of appointment of judges which is essential to their proper appointment. However, the mode adopted should be such as will best promote the appointment of proper persons to the office of a judge, will provide a safeguard against appointments being influenced by inappropriate factors, and will be seen to be directed to the appointment of judges of independence, capacity and integrity.

(b) The structure of the legal profession, and the source from which jUdges are taken within the legal profession, differ in different societies within the LA W ASIA region. In some societies, the jUdiciary is a career service, in others, judges are chosen from the practising profession. Therefore, it is accepted that in different societies, different procedures and safeguards may be seen as of assistance in ensuring the proper appointment of judges.

(c) The Committee has observed that, in some societies, the appointment of judges, by, with the consent of, or after consultation with a Judicial Services Commission has been seen as a means of ensuring that those chosen as jUdges are appropriate for the purpose.

(d) The Committee recommends that the appointment of a Judicial Services Commission, or the adoption of a procedure of consultation with the organized associations of lawyers should be adopted as a means of safeguarding the proper appointment of judges.

Where a Judicial Services Commission is adopted for these purposes, it should be representative of the higher judiciary, and of all concerned in the administration of justice, to an extent that will ensure that its independence and integrity are safeguarded, and are seen to be safeguarded.

ll. Tenure:

(a) The independence of the judiciary must be secured by security of tenure.

(b) The Committee recognises that, in some countries, the tenure of jUdges is sUbject to confirmation from time to time by an electorate or otherwise.

(c) However, the Committee recommends that all jUdges should be appointed for a period related to the attainment of a particular age, and that that period should be applicable to all judges exercising the same jurisdiction.

(d) Judges should be subject to removal from office only for proved incapacity, serious criminal default, or serious misconduct, such as, in each case, makes the judge unfit to be a judge.

(i) The Committee recognises that, by reasons of differences in history and culture, the procedures appropriate for the removal of jUdges may differ in different societies. It recognises, in particular, that removal by parliamentary procedures has traditionally been adopted in some countries. However, the Committee believes that in some areas of the LA W ASIA region, that procedure is unsuitable: it is not appropriate for dealing with some grounds for removal; it is rarely if ever used; and the use of it, other than for the most serious of reasons, is apt to lead to its misuse, and to encourage its use where it should not be used. The Committee believes that there is, in some areas of the LAW ASIA region, a clear consensus within the legal profession that such procedures should be under the control of the senior judges of the particular society.

(ii) Where it is proposed to take steps to secure the removal of a jUdge, there should, in the first instance, be an examination of the reasons suggested for his/her removal, for the purpose of determining whether the formal proceedings for his/her removal should be com menced. Formal proceedings for that purpose should be commenced only if the preliminary examination indicates that there are adequate reasons for taking them. Such formal proceedings should not take place in public, except with the agreement of the Chairman of the body conducting those procedures and of the jUdge in question.

(iii) The abolition of the court of which a jUdge is a member should not be accepted as a reason or an occasion for the removal of a judge.

12. Relationship with the Executive:

(a) The Committee is aware of instances of threats and pressures made or

(i) judges have been transferred from one court to another, or suspended from office for wrong reasons;

(ii) the remuneration or facilities of a judge have been affected because of decisions given by the judge;

(b) Powers which may affect judges in their office, their remuneration or their facilities, must not be used so as to threaten or bring pressure upon a particular judge or judges.

(c) Inducements or benefits should not be offered to, or accepted, by judges, which affect or are apt to affect the performance of their judicial functions.

(i) The Com mittee has been made aware of instances of inducements or benefits offered to judges. Examples have been given where, during or after the tenure of office of the judge, appointments or emoluments have been offered in circumstances in which the judge may have been, or may reasonably be, thought to have been influenced by them.

(ij) The judiciary and the other institutions of government should be conscious of the fact that whether what is done in fact induces a jUdge to act otherwise than he/she" should, it is essential that what is done be not such as to be seen to be an inducement or a benefit to a judge for such a purpose.

(d) It is at all times the duty of a judge to decide matters coming before him/her on his/her own view of the facts and in accordance with the law. It is the duty of the other institutions of government to ensure that he/she is in a position so to do.

13. Remuneration and Facilities:

(a) The Committee is aware of instances in the LAWASIA region, where the facilities, which are now provided to jUdges and to the court system, are below what is the minimum acceptable level at which judges and courts can carry out their functions properly.

(b) The Committee recongizes that there may be economic circumstances in which it is impossible for facilities to be provided to judges and to the court system, at what would otherwise be an appropriate level.

(c) However, a proper system of courts and the proper performance of the judicial functions are each essential to the maintenance of proper values, the rule of law, and the attainment of human rights within a society. The Committee therefore recommends that the provision of such facilities be seen as having a priority of the highest order in the ordering of each society.

14. It is the conclusion of the Committe that these represent the minimum standards necessary to be observed in order to maintain the independence of the judiciary and the functioning of an effective judiciary in the LAW ASIA region."

APPENDIX VII

UNIVERSAL DECLARATION ON THE INDEPENDENCE OF JUSTICE

I. Introduction

The Universal Declaration on the Independence of Justice adopted at Montreal on June 10th, 1983 was not the product of spontaneous generation. Rather, it marked the culmination of a series of efforts which for two years had progressed along a checkered path:

One can readily see that attention had generally been focused on the judiciary, except for the Noto meeting on lawyers. It happens, however, that consideration had started to be given to the topic over twenty years ago by the Sub-Commission on Prevention of Discrimination and Protection of Minorities of the Commission on Human Rights of the United Nations. Interest was revived in 1978 and, on May 2nd 1980, the Economic and Social Council of the United Nations authorized the SubCommission to entrust Dr. L.M. Singhvi, of New Delhi, with the preparation of a Report on "the independence and impartiality of the judiciary, jurors and assessors and the independence of lawyers."

Now a large number of bodies were showing interest in the matter, but they were working more or less separately and there was no commmon forum where they could put their ideas together in order to achieve their common purpose.

The author then suggested to the Noto meeting that such a general Conference be organized to deal with the wider topic as proposed in the UN. The suggestion was received with sympathy and the project was born. A year later the first World Conference on the Independence of Justice convened in Montreal. It was sponsored by seven Canadian organizations and enjoyed the support of the Governments of Canada and of Quebec, and of the International Development Research Centre. Twenty-six international bodies, represented by citizens of thirty-four countries, met on that occasion: they included the United Nations, the four International Courts (which were thus officially gathered for the first time) and organizations with membership in the five continents.

This time the participants were expected to study not only the independence of jUdges or that of lawyers, but more broadly what had been termed significantly "the independence of justice." So in order to cover the field and to tie in with the mandate given to Dr. Singhvi by the UN, the study was split into five chapters: International Judges, National Judges, Lawyers, Jurors and Assessors.

At the end of a week of deliberations at times heated but always courteous, the Conference adopted unanimously – this should be stressed – an ambitious Universal Declaration, in French and in English, which purports to cover the whole field of the independence of justice.

The Preamble recalls the link between justice and liberty, the need for the respect of the rule of law, the respective roles of the national and the international courts, and the need for the guaranteed independence of all actors in the process of justice. Then, follow 142 compact articles, which profess to set out an universally applicable theory of the independence of justice.

It is now hoped that the effort will not prove fruitless and that it will bring closer the adoption by the United Nations of a "Universal Declaration on the Independence of Justice" through which all the peoples of the world may at last see the ideal 0 f justice dawning on the horizon.

II. The Declaration

Unanimously adopted at the final plenary session of the First World Conference on the Independence of Justice held at Montreal (Quebec, Canada) on June 10th, 1983.

Preamble

Whereas justice constitutes one of the essential pillars of liberty;

Whereas the free exercise of fundamental human rights as well as peace between nations can only be secured through respect for the rule of law;

Whereas States have long established courts and other institutions with a view to assuring that justice be duly administered in their respective territories;

Whereas the Charter of the United Nations has established the International Court of Justice as its principal judicial organ in order to promote the peaceful solution of disputes between States, in conformity with the principles of justice and international law;

Whereas the Statute of the International Court of Justice provides that the latter shall be composed of a body of independent judges, elected regardless of nationality, which as a whole shall be representative of the main forms of civilisation and of the principal legal systems of the world;

Whereas various Treaties have established other courts endowed with an international competence, which equally owe exclusive allegiance to the international legal order and benefit from representation of diverse legal systems;

Whereas the jusrisdiction vested in international courts shall be respected in order to facilitate the interpretation, application and progressive development of international law and the promotion of human rights;

Whereas national and international courts shall, within the sphere of their competence, cooperate in the achievement of the foregoing objectives;

Whereas all those institutions, national and international, must, within the scope of their competence, seek to promote the lofty objectives set out in the Charter of the United Nations, the Universal Declaration of Human Rights, the International Covenant on Economic, Social and Cultural Rights, the International Covenant on Civil and Political Rights, the Optional Protocol **to** the latter Covenant and other pertinent international instruments, objectives which embrace the independence of the administration of the justice;

Whereas such independence must be guaranteed to international judges, national judges, lawyers, jurors and assessors;

Whereas the foundations of the independence of justice and the conditions of its exercise may benefit from restatement;

The World Conference of the Independence of Justice recommends to the United Nations on **the** consideration of this Declaration.

1. *International Judges*

Definitions

1.01 In this chapter:

a) "judges" means international judges and arbitrators;

b) "court" means an international court **or** tribunal of universal, regional, community or specialized competence.

Independence

1.02 The international status of judges shall require and assure their individual and collective independence and their impartial and conscientious exercise of their functions in the common interest. Accordingly, States shall respect the international character of the responsibilities of judges and shall not seek to influence them in the discharge **of** these responsibilities.

1.03 Judges and courts shall **be** free in the performance of their duties to ensure that the Rule of Law is observed, and shall not admit influence from any government or any other authority external to their statutes and the interests of international justice.

1.04 When governing treaties give international courts **the** competence to determine their rules of procedure, such rules shall **come** into and remain in force upon adoption by the courts concerned.

1.05 Judges shall enjoy freedom of thought and, in the **exercise** of their duties, shall avoid being influenced by any considerations other than those of international justice.

1.06 The ethical standards required of national judges in the exercise of their judicial functions shall apply to judges of international courts.

1.07 The principles of judicial independence embodied in the Universal Declaration of Human Rights and other international instruments for the protection of human rights shall apply to judges.

1.08 Judges snall promote the principle of the due process of law as being an integral part of the independence of justice.

1.09 No reservation shall **be** made or admitted to treaty provisions relating to the fundamental principles of independence of the judiciary.

1.10 Neither the accession of a state to the statute of a court nor the creation of new international courts shall affect the validity of these fundamental principles.

Appointment

1.11 Judges shall be nominated and appointed, or elected in accordance with governing constitutional and statutory provisions which shall, if possible, not confine the power of nomination to governments or make nomination dependent on nationality.

1.12 Only a jurist of recognized standing shall be appointed or elected to be a judge of an international court.

1.13 When the statute of a court provides that judges shall be appointed on the recommendation of a government, such appointment shall not be made in circumstances in which that government may subsequently exert any influence upon the judge.

Compensation

1.14 The terms of compensation and pension of judges shall be established and maintained so as to ensure their independence. Those terms shall take into account the recognized limitations upon their professional pursuits both during and after their tenure of office, which are defined either by their statute or recognized and accepted in practice.

Immunities and Privileges

1.15 Judges shall enjoy privileges and immunities, facilities and prerogatives, no less than those conferred upon chiefs of diplomatic missions under and recognized by the Vienna Convention on Diplomatic Relations. Only the court concerned may lift these immunities.

1.16 Judges shall not be liable for acts done in their official capacity.

1.17 a) In view of the importance of secrecy of judicial deliberations to the integrity and independence of the judicial process, judges shall respect secrecy in, and in relation to their judicial deliberations;

b) States and other external authorities shall respect and protect the secrecy and confidentiality of the courts' deliberations at all stages.

Discipline and Removal

1.18 All measures of discipline and removal relating to judges shall be governed exclusively by the statutes and rules of their courts, and be within their jurisdiction.

1.19 Judges shall not be removed from office, except by a decision of the other members of the court and in accordance with its statute.

Judges Ad Hoc and Arbitrators

1.20 Unless reference to the context necessarily makes it inapplicable or inappropriate, the foregoing articles shall apply to judges ad hoc and to arbitrators in public international arbitrations.

2. *National Judges*

Objectives and Functions

2.01 The objectives and functions of the judiciary shall include:

a) to administer the law impartially between citizen and citizen, and between citizen and state;

b) to promote, within the proper limits of the judicial function, the observance and the attainment of human rights;

c) to ensure that all peoples are able to live securely under the rule of law.

Independence

2.02 Judges individually shall be free, and it shall be their duty, to decide matters before them impartially, in accordance with their assessment of the facts and their understanding of the law without any restrictions, influences, inducements, pressures, threats or interferences, direct or indirect, from any quarter or for any reason.

2.03 In the decision-making process, judges shall be independent vis-a-vis their judicial colleagues and superiors. Any hierarchical organization of the judiciary and any difference in grade or rank shall in no way interfere with the right of the judge to pronounce his judgment freely.

2.04 The judiciary shall be independent of the Executive and Legislative.

2.05 The judiciary shall have jurisdiction, directly or by way or review, over all issues of a judicial nature.

2.06 a) No ad hoc tribunals shall be established;

b) Everyone shall have the right to be tried expeditiously by the established ordinary courts or judicial tribunals under law, subject to review by the courts;

c) Some derogations may be admitted in times of grave public emergency which threatens the life of the nation but only under conditions prescribed by law, and only to the extent strictly consistent with internationally recognized minimum standards and subject to review by the courts;

d) In such times of emergency:

I. Civilians charged with criminal offences of any kind shall be tried by ordinary civilian courts, expanded where necessary by additional competent civilian judges;

II. Detention of persons administratively without charge shall be subject to review by ordinary courts by way of habeas corpus or similar procedures, so as to insure that the detention is lawful, as well as to inquire into any allegations of ill-treatment;

e) The jurisdiction of military tribunals shall be confined to military offences committed by military personnel. There shall always be a right of appeal from such tribunals to a legally qualified appellate court.

2.07 a) No power shall be exercised so as to interfere with the judicial process.

b) The Executive shall not have control over judicial functions.

c) The Executive shall not have the power to close down or suspend the operation of the courts.

d) The Executive shall refrain from any act or omission which preempts the judicial resolution of a dispute or frustrates the proper execution of a court decision.

2.08 No legislation or executive decree shall attempt retroactively, to reverse specific court decisions, nor to change the composition of the court to affect its decision-making.

2.09 Judges may take collective action to protect their judicial independence.

2.10 Judges shall always conduct themselves in such a manner as to preserve the dignity of their office and the impartiality and independence of the judiciary. Subject to this principle, judges shall be entitled to freedom of belief, expression, association and assembly.

Qualifications, Selections and Training

2.11 Candidates for judicial office shall be individuals of integrity and ability, well-trained in the law. They shall have equality of access to judicial office.

2.12 In the selection of judges, there shall be no discrimination on the grounds of race, colour, sex, language, religion, political or other opinion, national or social origin, property, birth or status, subject however to citizenship requirements.

2.13 The process and standards of judicial selection shall give due consideration to ensuring a fair reflection by the judiciary of the society in all its aspects.

2.14 a) There is no single proper method of judicial selection provided it safeguards against judicial appointments for improper motives.

b) Participation in judicial appointments by the Executive or Legislature is consistent with judicial independence, so long as appointments of judges are made in consultation with members of the judiciary and the legal profession, or by a body in which members of the judiciary and the legal profession participate.

2.15 Continuing education shall be available to judges.

Posting, Promotion and Transfer

2.16 The assignment of a judge, to a post within the court to which he is appointed is an internal administrative function to be carried out by the judiciary.

[Explanatory Note: Unless assignments are made by the court, there is a danger of erosion of judicial independence by outside interference. It is vital that the court not make assignments as a result of any bias or prejudice or in response to external pressures. These comments are not intended to exclude the practice in some countries of requiring that assignments be approved by a Superior Council of the judiciary or similar body.]

2.17 Promotion of a judge shall be based on an objective assessment of the candidate's integrity and independence of judgment, professional competence, experience, humanity and commitment to uphold the rule of law. Article 2.14 shall apply to promotions.

2.18 Except pursuant to a system of regular rotation, judges shall not be transferred from one jurisdiction or function to another without their consent, but such consent shall not be unreasonably withheld.

[Explanatory Note: Unless this principle is accepted, transfer can be used to punish an independent and courageous judge, and to deter others from following his example. This principle is not intended to interfere with sound administrative practices enumerated in the law. Thus exceptions may be made, for example, where a judge in his early years is transferred from post to post to enrich his judicial experience.]

Tenure

2.19 a) The term of office of the judges, their independence, security, adequate remuneration and conditions of service shall be secured by law and shall not be altered to their detriment.

b) Judges, whether appointed or elected, shall have guaranteed tenure until a mandatory retirement age or expiry of their term of office, where such exists.

2.20 The appointment of temporary judges and the appointment of judges for probationary periods is inconsistent with judicial independence. Where such appointments exist, they shall be phased out gradually.

[Explanatory Note: This text is not intended to exclude part-time judges. Where such practice exists, proper safeguards shall be laid down to ensure impartiality and avoid conflict of interests. Nor is this text intended to exclude probationary periods for judges after their initial appointment, in countries which have a career judiciary, such as in civil law countries.]

2.21 a) During their terms of office, judges shall receive salaries and after retirement, they shall receive pensions.

b) The salaries and pensions of judges shall be adequate, commensurate with the status, dignity and responsibility of their office, and be regularly adjusted to account fully for price increases.

c) Judicial salaries shall not be decreased during the judges' term of office, except as a coherent part of an overall public economic measure.

2.22 Retirement age shall not be altered for judges in office without their consent.

2.23 The executive authorities shall, at all times, ensure the security and physical protection of judges and their families.

Immunities and Privileges

2.24 Judges shall enjoy immunity from suit, or harassment, for acts and omissions in their official capacity.

2.25 a) Judges shall be bound by professional secrecy in relation to their deliberations, and to confidential information acquired in the course of their duties other than in public proceedings.

b) Judges shall not **be** requried to testify on such matters.

Disqualifications

2.26 Judges may not serve in an executive or a legislative capacity unless it is clear that these functions are combined, without compromising judicial independence.

2.27 Judges may not serve as chairmen or members of committees of inquiry, except in cases where judicial **skills** are required.

2.28 Judges shall not be active members of, or hold positions in, political parties.

[Explanatory Note: This text is not intended to permit membership of judges in political parties in countries where under law or practice such is excluded, but to lay down standards limiting the scope of judicial involvement in countries where such membership is permissible.]

2.29 Judges may not practice law.

[Explanatory Note: **See** note 2.20.1

2.30 Judges shall refrain from business activities, except as incidental to their personal investments or their ownership of property.

2.31 A judge shall not sit in a case where a reasonable apprehension of bias on his part may arise.

Discipline and Removal

2.32 A complaint against a judge shall be processed expeditiously and fairly under an appropriate practice, and the judge shall **have** the opportunity to comment on the complaint at the initial stage. The examination of the complaint at its initial stage shall be kept confidential, unless otherwise requested by the judge.

2.33 a) The proceedings for judicial removal or discipline, when such are initiated, shall be held before a court or a board predominantly composed of members of the judiciary and selected by the judiciary.

b) However, the power **of** removal may be vested in the Legislature by impeachment or joint address, preferably upon a recommendation of a court or board as referred to in 2.33(a).

[Explanatory Note: In countries where the legal profession plays an indispensable role in maintaining the rule of law and judicial independence, it is recommended that members **of** the legal profession participate in the selection of the members of the **court** or board, and be included as members thereof.

2.34 All disciplinary action shall be based upon established standards of judicial conduct.

2.35 The proceedings for discipline of judges shall ensure fairness to the judge and the opportunity **of** a full hearing.

2.36 With the exception of proceedings before the Legislature, the proceedings for discipline and removal shall be held in camera. The judge may, however, request that the hearing be held in public, subject to a final and reasoned disposition of this request by the disciplinary Tribunal. Judgments in disciplinary proceedings, whether held in camera or in public, may be published.

2.37 With the exception of proceedings before the Legislature or in connection with them, the decision of a disciplinary Tribunal shall be subject to appeal to a court.

2.38 A judge shall not be subject to removal except on proved grounds of incapacity or misbehaviour, rendering him unfit to continue in office.

2.39 In the event that a court is abolished, judges serving in this court shall not be affected, except for their transfer to another court of the same status.

Court Administration

2.40 The main responsibility for court administration shall vest in the judiciary.

2.41 It shall be a priority of the highest order, for the state to provide adequate resources to allow for the due administration of justice, including physical facilities appropriate for the maintenance of judicial independence, dignity and efficiency, judicial and adminstrative personnel, and operating budgets.

2.42 The budget of the court shall be prepared by the competent authority in collaboration with the judiciary. The judiciary shall submit their estimate of the budget requirements to the appropriate authority.

2.43 The judiciary shall alone be responsible for assigning cases to individual judges or to sections of a court composed of several judges, in accordance with law or rules of court.

2.44 The head of the court may exercise supervisory powers over judges on administrative matters.

Miscellaneous

2.45 A judge shall ensure the fair conduct of the trial and inquire fully into any allegation made of a violation of the rights of a party or of a witness, including allegations of ill-treatment.

2.46 Judges shall accord respect to the members of the Bar.

2.47 The state shall ensure the due and proper execution of orders and judgments of the courts; but supervision over the execution of orders and judgments process shall be vested in the judiciary.

2.48 Judges shall keep themselves informed about international conventions and other instruments establishing human rights' norms, and shall seek to implement them as far as feasible, within the limits set by their national constitutions and laws.

2.49 The provisions of Chapter U: National Judges, shall apply to all persons exercising judicial functions, including arbitrators and public prosecutors, unless reference to the context necessarily makes them inapplicable or inappropriate.

3. *Lawyers*

Definitions

3.01 In this chapter:

a) "lawyer" means a person qualified and authorized to practice before the courts, and to advise and represent his clients in legal matters;

b) "Bar association" means the recognized professional association to which lawyers within a given jurisdiction belong.

General Principles

3.02 The legal profession is one of the institutions referred to in the preamble to this declaration. Its independence constitutes an essential guarantee for the promotion and protection of human rights.

3.03 There shall be a fair and equitable system of administration of justice, which guarantees the independence of lawyers in the discharge of their professional duties without any restrictions, influences, inducements, pressures, threats or interferences, direct or indirect, from any quarter or for any reason.

3.04 All persons shall have effective access to legal services provided by an independent lawyer, to protect and establish their economic, social and cultural, as well as civil and political rights.

Legal Education and Entry into the Legal Profession

3.05 Legal education shall be open to all persons with requisite qualifications, and no one shall be denied such opportunity by reason of race, colour, sex, language, religion, political or other opinion, national or social origin, property, birth or status.

3.06 Legal education shall be designed to promote in the public interest, in addition to technical competence, awareness of the ideals and ethical duties of the lawyer, and of human rights and fundamental freedoms recognized by national and international law.

3.07 Programmes of legal education shall have regard to the social responsibilities of the lawyer, including cooperation in providing legal services to the poor and the promotion and defence of economic, social and cultural rights in the process of development.

3.08 Every person having the necessary integrity, good character and qualifications in law shall be entitled to become a lawyer, and to continue in practice without discrimination for having been convicted of an offence for exercising his internationally recognized civil or political rights.

Education of the Public Concerning the Law

3.09 It shall be the responsibility of the lawyer to educate the members of the public about the principles of the rule of law, the importance of the independence of the judiciary and of the legal profession and to inform them about their rights and duties, and the relevant and available remedies.

Rights and Duties of Lawyers

3.10 The duties of a lawyer towards his client include: a) advising the client as to his legal rights and obligations; b) taking legal action to protect him and his interests; and, where required, c) representing him before courts, tribunals or administrative authorities.

3.11 The lawyer, in discharging his duties, shall at all times act freely, diligently and fearlessly in accordance with the wishes of his client and subject to the established rules, standards and ethics of his profession without any inhibition or pressure from the authorities or the public.

3.12 Every person and group of persons is entitled to call upon the assistance of a lawyer to defend his or its interests or cause within the law, and it is the duty of the lawyer to do so to the best of his ability. Consequently the lawyer is not to be identified by the authorities or the public with his client or his client's cause, however popular or unpopular it may be.

3.13 No lawyer shall suffer or be threatened with penal, civil, administrative, economic or other sanctions by reason of his having advised or represented any client or client's cause.

3.14 No court or administrative authoirty shall refuse to recognize the right of a lawyer to appear before it for his client.

3.15 It is the duty of a lawyer to show proper respect towards the judiciary. He shall have the right to raise an objection to the participation or continued participation of a judge in a particular case, or to the conduct of a trial or hearing.

3.16 If any proceedings are taken against a lawyer for failing to show proper respect towards a court, no sanction against him shall be imposed by a judge who participated in the proceedings which gave rise to the charge against the lawyer.

3.17 Save as provided in these principles, a lawyer shall enjoy civil and penal immunity for relevant statements made in good faith in written or oral pleadings, or in his professional appearances before a court, tribunal or other legal or administrative authority.

3.18 The independence of lawyers, in dealing with persons deprived of their liberty, shall be guaranteed so as to ensure that they have free and fair legal assistance. Safeguards shall be built to avoid any possible suggestions of collusion, arrangement or dependence between the lawyer who acts for them and the authorities.

3.19 Lawyers shall have all such other facilities and privileges as are necessary to fulfill their professional responsibilities effectively, including: a) absolute confidentiality of the lawyer-client relationship; b) the right to travel and to consult with their clients freely, both within their own country and abroad; c) the right freely to seek, to receive and, subject to the rules of their profession, to impart information and ideas relating to their professional work; d) the right to accept or refuse a client or a brief.

3.20 Lawyers shall enjoy freedom of belief, expression, association and assembly; and in particular they shall have the right to: a) take part in public discussion of matters concerning the law and the administration of justice, b) join or form freely local, national and international organizations, c) propose and recommend well-considered law reforms in the public interest and inform the public about such matters, and d) take full and active part in the political, social and cultural life of their country.

3.21 Rules and regulations governing the fees and remunerations of lawyers shall be designed to ensure that they earn a fair and adequate income, and legal services are made available to the public on reasonable terms.

Legal Services for the Poor

3.22 It is a necessary corollary of the concept of an independent bar, that its members shall make their services available to all sectors of society, so that no one may be denied justice, and shall promote the cause of justice by protecting the human rights, economic, social and cultural, as well as civil and political, of individuals and groups.

3.23 Governments shall be responsible for providing sufficient funding for legal service programmes for the poor.

3.24 Lawyers engaged in legal service programmes and organizations, which are financed wholly, or in part, from public funds, shall receive adequate remuneration and enjoy full guarantees of their professional independence in particular by:

– the direction of such programmes or organizations being entrusted to an independent board, composed mainly or entirely of members of the profession, with full control over its policies, budget and staff;

– recognition that, in serving the cause of justice, the lawyer's primary duty is towards his client, whom he must advise and represent in conformity with his professional conscience and judgment.

The Bar Association

3.25 There shall be established in each jurisdiction one or more independent and self-governing associations of lawyers recognized in law, whose council or other executive body shall be freely elected by all the members without interference of any kind by any other body or person. This shall be without prejudice to their right to form or join, in addition, other professional associations of lawyers and jurists.

3.26 In order to enjoy the right of audience before the courts, all lawyers shall be members of the appropriate Bar Association.

Function of the Bar Association

3.27 The functions of a Bar Association in ensuring the independence of the legal profession shall be inter alia:

a) to promote and uphold the cause of justice, without fear or favour;

b) to maintain the honour, dignity, integrity, competence, ethics, standards of conduct and discipline of the profession;

c) to defend the role of lawyers in society and preserve the independence of the profession;

d) to protect and defend the dignity and independence of the judiciary;

e) to promote the free and equal access of the public to the system of justice, including the provision of legal aid and advice;

f) to promote the right of everyone to a fair and public hearing before a competent, independent and impartial tribunal, and in accordance with proper procedures in all matters;

g) to promote and support law reform, and to comment upon and promote public discussion on the substance, interpretation and application of existing and proposed legislation;

h) to promote a high standard of legal education as a prerequisite for entry into the profession;

0 to ensure that there is free access to the profession for all persons having the requisite professional competence and good character, without discrimination of any kind, and to give assistance to new entrants into the profession;

j) to promote the welfare of members of the profession and render assistance to a member of his family in appropriate cases;

k) to affiliate with, and participate in, the activities of international organizations of lawyers.

3.28 Where a person involved in litigation wishes to engage a lawyer from another country to act with a local lawyer, the Bar Association shall cooperate in assisting the foreign lawyer to obtain the necessary right of audience.

3.29 To enable the Bar Association to fulfill its function of preserving the independence of lawyers, it shall be informed immediately of the reason and legal basis for the arrest or detention of any lawyer; and for the same purpose the association shall have prior notice for: 0 any search of his person or property, ii) any seizure of documents in his possessions, and iii) any decision to take proceedings affecting or calling into question the integrity of a lawyer. In such cases, the Bar Association shall be entitled to be represented by its president or nominee, to follow the proceedings, and in particular to ensure that professional secrecy is safeguarded.

Disciplinary Proceedings

3.30 The Bar Association shall freely establish and enforce, in accordance with the law, a code of professional conduct of lawyers.

3.31 The Bar Association shall have exclusive competence to initiate and conduct disciplinary proceedings against lawyers on its own initiative or at the request of a litigant. Although no court or public authority shall itself take disciplinary proceedings against a lawyer, it may report a case to the Bar Association with a view to its initiating disciplinary proceedings.

3.32 Disciplinary proceedings shall be conducted in the first instance by a disciplinary committee established by the Bar Association.

3.33 An appeal shall lie from a decision of the disciplinary committee to an appropriate appellate body.

3.34 Disciplinary proceedings shall be conducted with full observance of the requirements of fair and proper procedure, in the light of the principles expressed in this declaration.

4. *Jurors*

Selection of Prospective Jurors

4.01 The opportunity for jury service shall be extended without distinction of any kind by reason of race, colour, sex, language, religion, political or other opinion, national or social origin, property, birth or status, subject however to citizenship requirements.

4.02 The names of prospective jurors shall be drawn from a jury source list compiled from one or more regularly maintained lists of persons residing in the court's jurisdiction.

4.03 The jury source list shall be representative, and shall be as inclusive of the adult population in the jurisdiction, as is feasible.

4.04 The Court shall periodically review the jury source list for its representativeness and inclusiveness. Should the Court determine that improvement is needed in the representativeness or inclusiveness of the jury source list, appropriate corrective action shall be taken.

4.05 Random selection procedures shall be used at all stages throughout the jury selection process except as provided herein.

4.06 The frequency and the length of time that persons are called upon to perform jury service and to be available therefor, shall be the minimum consistent with the needs of justice.

4.07 All automatic excuses or exemptions from jury service shall be eliminated.

4.08 Eligible persons who are summoned may be excused from jury service only for valid reason by the court, or with its authorization.

Selection of a Particular Jury

4.09 Examination of prospective jurors shall be limited to matters relevant to determining whether to remove a juror for cause, and to exercising peremptory challenges.

4.10 If the judge determines during the examination of prospective jurors, that an individual is unable or unwilling to hear the particular case at issue fairly and impartially, the individual shall be removed from the panel. Such a determination may be made on motion of a party or on the judge's own initiative.

4.11 In jurisdictions where peremptory challenges are permitted, their number and the procedure for exercising them shall be uniform for the same type of case.

4.12 Peremptory challenges shall be limited to a number no larger than necessary, to provide reasonable assurance of obtaining an unbiased jury.

Administration of the Jury System

4.13 The responsibility for administration of the jury system shall be under the control of the judiciary.

4.14 The notice summoning a person to jury service shall be in writing, easily understandable, and delivered sufficiently in advance.

4.15 Courts shall employ the services of prospective jurors, so as to achieve the best possible use of them with a minimum of inconvenience.

4.16 Courts shall provide adequate protection for jurors from threat and intimidation.

4.17 Courts shall provide an adequate and suitable environment for jurors, and jury facilities shall be arranged to minimize contact between jurors and parties, counsel and the public.

4.18 Persons called for jury service shall receive a reasonable allowance.

4.19 Employers shall be prohibited from penalizing employees who are called for jury service.

Jury Consideration and Deliberations

4.20 Procedures shall be provided to prevent a trial from being terminated because of unforeseen circumstances which would reduce the number of jurors.

4.21 Courts shall provide some form of orientation or instruction to persons called for jury service, to increase prospective jurors understanding of the judicial system, and prepare them to serve competently as jurors.

4.22 In simple language the trial judge shall: i) directly following empanelment of the jury, give preliminary explanations of the jury's role and of trial procedures; ii) prior to commencement of deliberations, direct the jury on the law.

4.23 A jury's deliberations shall be held in secrecy. Jurors shall not make public, reasons for their decisions.

4.24 a) A jury shall be sequestered only for the purpose of insulating its members from improper imformation or influence.

b) Standard procedures shall be promulgated to make certain that the inconvenience and discomfort of the sequestered jurors are minimized.

5. *Assessors*

Status

5.01 In defining assessor, the following shall be considered: In general, on certain judicial, quasi-judicial bodies or administrative tribunals, the assessor sits with a judge, magistrate or other jurist, to assist him in his duties. In most cases he is a person who does not necessarily have legal training, but who has some specific professional qualification or socio-economic expertise, that pertains to the subject-matter under consideration.

5.02 In some cases, the assessor shares with his legally-trained colleague, responsibility for the decision to be rendered: this then becomes a multidisciplinary judicial or quasi-judicial body.

Appointment

5.03 Unless he is selected by the parties unanimously, the assessor shall be appointed by a neutral authority not involved in the dispute.

5.04 Unless agreed upon by the parties or provided by law, the assessor shall be paid according to the decision of a neutral authority not involved in the dispute.

5.05 The assessor shall be selected for reasons of integrity and competence especially relevant to the matter to be considered by him.

5.06 The assessor shall enjoy *a* tenure which guarantees his independence; if he serves on a permanent basis he shall be guaranteed security, adequate remuneration and conditions of service.

5.07 Before commencing his duties, the assessor shall take an oath or affirmation of office.

Exercise of Mandate

5.08 In the decision-making process, the assessor shall be free from any order or instruction by the authority which has appointed him, by the parties or by the professional associations to which he belongs.

5.09 The assessor shall have the right to participate in the decision with complete freedom and independence in the area of his jurisdiction.

5.10 The assessor shall behave in such a manner as will maintain the dignity of his position and the impartiality and independence of justice.

5.11 The assessor shall not sit in a case where a reasonable apprehension of bias on his part may arise.

5.12 The assessor shall be free to withdraw for generally accepted reasons.

Powers and Immunity

5.13 The assessor shall be vested with the authority, immunity and powers necessary to carry out his duties.

5.14 The assessor shall not be sued or harassed for acts and omissions in his official capacity.

Dismissal

5.15 The assessor shall not be dismissed in the course of his mandate except for incapacity or misbehaviour.

APPENDIX VIII

BANGALORE PRINCIPLES OF JUDICIAL INDEPENDENCE

The Economic and Social Council,

Recalling the Charter of the United Nations, in which Member States affirm, inter alia, their determination to establish conditions under which justice can be maintained to achieve international cooperation in promoting and encouraging respect for human rights and fundamental freedoms without any discrimination,

Recalling also the Universal Declaration of Human Rights, which enshrines in particular the principles of equality before the law, of the presumption of innocence and of the right to a fair and public hearing by a competent, independent and impartial tribunal established by law,

Recalling further the International Covenant on Economic, Social and Cultural Rights and the International Covenant on Civil and Political Rights,[1] which both guarantee the exercise of those rights, and that the International Covenant on Civil and Political Rights further guarantees the right to be tried without undue delay,

Recalling the United Nations Convention against Corruption,[2] which in its article 11 obliges States parties, in accordance with the fundamental principles of their legal systems and without prejudice to judicial independence, to take measures to strengthen integrity and to prevent opportunities for corruption among members of the judiciary, including rules with respect to the conduct of members of the judiciary,

Convinced that corruption of members of the judiciary undermines the rule of law and affects public confidence in the judicial system,

Convinced also that the integrity, independence and impartiality of the judiciary are essential prerequisites for the effective protection of human rights and economic development,

Recalling General Assembly resolutions 40/32 of 29 November 1985 and 40/146 of 13 December 1985, in which the Assembly endorsed the Basic Principles on the Independence of the Judiciary, adopted by the Seventh United Nations Congress on the Prevention of Crime and the Treatment of Offenders, held in Milan from 26 August to 6 September 1985,[3]

Recalling also the recommendations adopted by the Ninth United Nations Congress on the Prevention of Crime and the Treatment of Offenders, held in Cairo from 29 April to 8 May 1995,[4] concerning the independence and impartiality of the judiciary and the proper functioning of prosecutorial and legal services in the field of criminal justice,

---

1 General Assembly resolution 2200 A (XXI), annex.

2 General Assembly resolution 58/4, annex.

3 See *Seventh United Nations Congress on the Prevention of Crime and the Treatment of Offenders, Milan, 26 August-6 September 1985: report prepared by the Secretariat* (United Nations publication, Sales No. E.86.IV.1), chap. I, sect. D.2, annex.

4 See A/CONF.169/16/Rev.1, chap. I, resolution 1, sect. III.

Recalling further that in 2000 the Centre for International Crime Prevention of the Secretariat invited a group of chief justices of the common law tradition to develop a concept of judicial integrity, consistent with the principle of judicial independence, which would have the potential to have a positive impact on the standard of judicial conduct and to raise the level of public confidence in the rule of law,

Recalling the second meeting of the Judicial Group on Strengthening Judicial Integrity, held in 2001 in Bangalore, India, at which the chief justices recognized the need for universally acceptable standards of judicial integrity and drafted the Bangalore Principles of Judicial Conduct,[5]

Recalling also that the Judicial Group on Strengthening Judicial Integrity thereafter conducted extensive consultations with judiciaries of more than eighty countries of all legal traditions, leading to the endorsement of the Bangalore Principles of Judicial Conduct by various judicial forums, including a Round Table Meeting of Chief Justices, held in The Hague on 25 and 26 November 2002, which was attended by senior judges of the civil law tradition as well as judges of the International Court of Justice,

Recalling further Commission on Human Rights resolution 2003/43, on the independence and impartiality of the judiciary, jurors and assessors and the independence of lawyers, in which the Commission took note of the Bangalore Principles of Judicial Conduct and brought those principles to the attention of Member States, relevant United Nations organs and intergovernmental and non-governmental organizations for their consideration,

Recalling Commission on Human Rights resolution 2003/39 on the integrity of the judicial system, in which the Commission emphasized the integrity of the judicial system as an essential prerequisite for the protection of human rights and for ensuring that there was no discrimination in the administration of justice,

1. *Invites* Member States, consistent with their domestic legal systems, to encourage their judiciaries to take into consideration the Bangalore Principles of Judicial Conduct, annexed to the present resolution, when reviewing or developing rules with respect to the professional and ethical conduct of members of the judiciary;
2. *Emphasizes* that the Bangalore Principles of Judicial Conduct represent a further development and are complementary to the Basic Principles on the Independence of the Judiciary, endorsed by the General Assembly in its resolutions 40/32 and 40/146;
3. *Acknowledges* the important work carried out by the Judicial Group on Strengthening Judicial Integrity under the auspices of the United Nations Office on Drugs and Crime, as well as other international and regional judicial forums that contribute to the development and dissemination of standards and measures to strengthen judicial independence, impartiality and integrity;
4. *Requests* the United Nations Office on Drugs and Crime, within available extrabudgetary resources, not excluding the use of existing resources from the regular budget of the Office[6] and in particular through its Global Programme

[5] E/CN.4/2003/65, annex.

[6] This language does not provide a basis for an increase in the regular budget or requests for supplemental increases.

against Corruption, to continue to support the work of the Judicial Group on Strengthening Judicial Integrity;

5. *Expresses appreciation* to Member States that have made voluntary contributions to the United Nations Office on Drugs and Crime in support of the work of the Judicial Group on Strengthening Judicial Integrity;
6. *Invites* Member States to make voluntary contributions, as appropriate, to the United Nations Crime Prevention and Criminal Justice Fund to support the Judicial Group on Strengthening Judicial Integrity, and to continue to provide, through the Global Programme against Corruption, technical assistance to developing countries and countries with economies in transition, upon request, to strengthen the integrity and capacity of their judiciaries;
7. *Also invites* Member States to submit to the Secretary-General their views regarding the Bangalore Principles of Judicial Conduct and to suggest revisions, as appropriate;
8. *Requests* the United Nations Office on Drugs and Crime, within available extrabudgetary resources, not excluding the use of existing resources from the regular budget of the Office,[7] to convene an open-ended intergovernmental expert group, in cooperation with the Judicial Group on Strengthening Judicial Integrity and other international and regional judicial forums, to develop a technical guide to be used in providing technical assistance aimed at strengthening judicial integrity and capacity, as well as a commentary on the Bangalore Principles of Judicial Conduct, taking into account the views expressed and the revisions suggested by Member States;
9. *Requests* the Secretary-General to report to the Commission on Crime Prevention and Criminal Justice at its sixteenth session on the implementation of the present resolution.

ANNEX

Bangalore Principles of Judicial Conduct

WHEREAS the Universal Declaration of Human Rights recognizes as fundamental the principle that everyone is entitled in full equality to a fair and public hearing by an independent and impartial tribunal, in the determination of rights and obligations and of any criminal charge,

WHEREAS the International Covenant on Civil and Political Rights[8] guarantees that all persons shall be equal before the courts and that in the determination of any criminal charge or of rights and obligations in a suit at law, everyone shall be entitled, without undue delay, to a fair and public hearing by a competent, independent and impartial tribunal established by law,

---

[7] This language does not provide a basis for an increase in the regular budget or requests for supplemental increases.

[8] General Assembly resolution 2200 A (XXI), annex.

WHEREAS the foregoing fundamental principles and rights are also recognized or reflected in regional human rights instruments, in domestic constitutional, statutory and common law, and in judicial conventions and traditions,

WHEREAS the importance of a competent, independent and impartial judiciary to the protection of human rights is given emphasis by the fact that the implementation of all the other rights ultimately depends upon the proper administration of justice,

WHEREAS a competent, independent and impartial judiciary is likewise essential if the courts are to fulfil their role in upholding constitutionalism and the rule of law,

WHEREAS public confidence in the judicial system and in the moral authority and integrity of the judiciary is of the utmost importance in a modern democratic society,

WHEREAS it is essential that judges, individually and collectively, respect and honour judicial office as a public trust and strive to enhance and maintain confidence in the judicial system,

WHEREAS the primary responsibility for the promotion and maintenance of high standards of judicial conduct lies with the judiciary in each country,

AND WHEREAS the Basic Principles on the Independence of the Judiciary[9] are designed to secure and promote the independence of the judiciary and are addressed primarily to States,

THE FOLLOWING PRINCIPLES are intended to establish standards for ethical conduct of judges. They are designed to provide guidance to judges and to afford the judiciary a framework for regulating judicial conduct. They are also intended to assist members of the executive and the legislature, and lawyers and the public in general, to better understand and support the judiciary. These principles presuppose that judges are accountable for their conduct to appropriate institutions established to maintain judicial standards, which are themselves independent and impartial, and are intended to supplement and not to derogate from existing rules of law and conduct that bind the judge.

Value 1
Independence

Principle

Judicial independence is a prerequisite to the rule of law and a fundamental guarantee of a fair trial. A judge shall therefore uphold and exemplify judicial independence in both its individual and institutional aspects.

Application

1.01 A judge shall exercise the judicial function independently on the basis of the judge's assessment of the facts and in accordance with a conscientious

[9] See *Seventh United Nations Congress on the Prevention of Crime and the Treatment of Offenders, Milan, 26 August-6 September 1985: report prepared by the Secretariat* (United Nations publication, Sales No. E.86.IV.1), chap. I, sect. D.2, annex.

understanding of the law, free of any extraneous influences, inducements, pressures, threats or interference, direct or indirect, from any quarter or for any reason.

1.02 A judge shall be independent in relation to society in general and in relation to the particular parties to a dispute that the judge has to adjudicate.

1.03 A judge shall not only be free from inappropriate connections with, and influence by, the executive and legislative branches of government, but must also appear to a reasonable observer to be free therefrom.

1.04 In performing judicial duties, a judge shall be independent of judicial colleagues in respect of decisions that the judge is obliged to make independently.

1.05 A judge shall encourage and uphold safeguards for the discharge of judicial duties in order to maintain and enhance the institutional and operational independence of the judiciary.

1.06 A judge shall exhibit and promote high standards of judicial conduct in order to reinforce public confidence in the judiciary, which is fundamental to the maintenance of judicial independence.

Value 2
Impartiality

Principle

Impartiality is essential to the proper discharge of the judicial office. It applies not only to the decision itself but also to the process by which the decision is made.

Application

2.01 A judge shall perform his or her judicial duties without favour, bias or prejudice.

2.02 A judge shall ensure that his or her conduct, both in and out of court, maintains and enhances the confidence of the public, the legal profession and litigants in the impartiality of the judge and of the judiciary.

2.03 A judge shall, as far as is reasonable, so conduct himself or herself as to minimize the occasions on which it will be necessary for the judge to be disqualified from hearing or deciding cases.

2.04 A judge shall not knowingly, while a proceeding is before, or could come before, the judge, make any comment that might reasonably be expected to affect the outcome of such proceeding or impair the manifest fairness of the process, nor shall the judge make any comment in public or otherwise that might affect the fair trial of any person or issue.

2.05 A judge shall disqualify himself or herself from participating in any proceedings in which the judge is unable to decide the matter impartially or in which it may appear to a reasonable observer that the judge is unable to decide the matter impartially. Such proceedings include, but are not limited to, instances where:

(a) The judge has actual bias or prejudice concerning a party or personal knowledge of disputed evidentiary facts concerning the proceedings;

(b) The judge previously served as a lawyer or was a material witness in the matter in controversy; or

(c) The judge, or a member of the judge's family, has an economic interest in the outcome of the matter in controversy;

provided that disqualification of a judge shall not be required if no other tribunal can be constituted to deal with the case or, because of urgent circumstances, failure to act could lead to a serious miscarriage of justice.

Value 3
Integrity

Principle
Integrity is essential to the proper discharge of the judicial office.

Application
3.01 A judge shall ensure that his or her conduct is above reproach in the view of a reasonable observer.
3.02 The behaviour and conduct of a judge must reaffirm the people's faith in the integrity of the judiciary. Justice must not merely be done but must also be seen to be done.

Value 4
Propriety

Principle
Propriety, and the appearance of propriety, are essential to the performance of all of the activities of a judge.

Application
4.01 A judge shall avoid impropriety and the appearance of impropriety in all of the judge's activities.
4.02 As a subject of constant public scrutiny, a judge must accept personal restrictions that might be viewed as burdensome by the ordinary citizen and should do so freely and willingly. In particular, a judge shall conduct himself or herself in a way that is consistent with the dignity of the judicial office.
4.03 A judge shall, in his or her personal relations with individual members of the legal profession who practise regularly in the judge's court, avoid situations that might reasonably give rise to the suspicion or appearance of favouritism or partiality.
4.04 A judge shall not participate in the determination of a case in which any member of the judge's family represents a litigant or is associated in any manner with the case.
4.05 A judge shall not allow the use of the judge's residence by a member of the legal profession to receive clients or other members of the legal profession.

4.06 A judge, like any other citizen, is entitled to freedom of expression, belief, association and assembly, but, in exercising such rights, a judge shall always conduct himself or herself in such a manner as to preserve the dignity of the judicial office and the impartiality and independence of the judiciary.

4.07 A judge shall inform himself or herself about the judge's personal and fiduciary financial interests and shall make reasonable efforts to be informed about the financial interests of members of the judge's family.

4.08 A judge shall not allow the judge's family, social or other relationships improperly to influence the judge's judicial conduct and judgement as a judge.

4.09 A judge shall not use or lend the prestige of the judicial office to advance the private interests of the judge, a member of the judge's family or of anyone else, nor shall a judge convey or permit others to convey the impression that anyone is in a special position improperly to influence the judge in the performance of judicial duties.

4.10 Confidential information acquired by a judge in the judge's judicial capacity shall not be used or disclosed by the judge for any other purpose not related to the judge's judicial duties.

4.11 Subject to the proper performance of judicial duties, a judge may:

(a) Write, lecture, teach and participate in activities concerning the law, the legal system, the administration of justice or related matters;
(b) Appear at a public hearing before an official body concerned with matters relating to the law, the legal system, the administration of justice or related matters;
(c) Serve as a member of an official body, or other government commission, committee or advisory body, if such membership is not inconsistent with the perceived impartiality and political neutrality of a judge; or
(d) Engage in other activities if such activities do not detract from the dignity of the judicial office or otherwise interfere with the performance of judicial duties.

4.12 A judge shall not practise law while the holder of judicial office.

4.13 A judge may form or join associations of judges or participate in other organizations representing the interests of judges.

4.14 A judge and members of the judge's family shall neither ask for, nor accept, any gift, bequest, loan or favour in relation to anything done or to be done or omitted to be done by the judge in connection with the performance of judicial duties.

4.15 A judge shall not knowingly permit court staff or others subject to the judge's influence, direction or authority to ask for, or accept, any gift, bequest, loan or favour in relation to anything done or to be done or omitted to be done in connection with his or her duties or functions.

4.16 Subject to law and to any legal requirements of public disclosure, a judge may receive a token gift, award or benefit as appropriate to the occasion on which it is made provided that such gift, award or benefit might not reasonably be perceived as intended to influence the judge in the performance of judicial duties or otherwise give rise to an appearance of partiality.

Value 5
Equality

Principle
Ensuring equality of treatment to all before the courts is essential to the due performance of the judicial office.

Application
5.01 A judge shall be aware of, and understand, diversity in society and differences arising from various sources, including but not limited to race, colour, sex, religion, national origin, caste, disability, age, marital status, sexual orientation, social and economic status and other like causes ("irrelevant grounds").
5.02 A judge shall not, in the performance of judicial duties, by words or conduct, manifest bias or prejudice towards any person or group on irrelevant grounds.
5.03 A judge shall carry out judicial duties with appropriate consideration for all persons, such as the parties, witnesses, lawyers, court staff and judicial colleagues, without differentiation on any irrelevant ground, immaterial to the proper performance of such duties.
5.04 A judge shall not knowingly permit court staff or others subject to the judge's influence, direction or control to differentiate between persons concerned, in a matter before the judge, on any irrelevant ground.
5.05 A judge shall require lawyers in proceedings before the court to refrain from manifesting, by words or conduct, bias or prejudice based on irrelevant grounds, except such as are legally relevant to an issue in proceedings and may be the subject of legitimate advocacy.

Value 6
Competence and diligence

Principle
Competence and diligence are prerequisites to the due performance of judicial office.

Application
6.01 The judicial duties of a judge take precedence over all other activities.
6.02 A judge shall devote the judge's professional activity to judicial duties, which include not only the performance of judicial functions and responsibilities in court and the making of decisions, but also other tasks relevant to the judicial office or the court's operations.
6.03 A judge shall take reasonable steps to maintain and enhance the judge's knowledge, skills and personal qualities necessary for the proper performance of judicial duties, taking advantage for that purpose of the training and other facilities that should be made available, under judicial control, to judges.
6.04 A judge shall keep himself or herself informed about relevant developments of international law, including international conventions and other instruments establishing human rights norms.
6.05 A judge shall perform all judicial duties, including the delivery of reserved decisions, efficiently, fairly and with reasonable promptness.

6.06 A judge shall maintain order and decorum in all proceedings before the court and be patient, dignified and courteous in relation to litigants, jurors, witnesses, lawyers and others with whom the judge deals in an official capacity. The judge shall require similar conduct of legal representatives, court staff and others subject to the judge's influence, direction or control.

6.07 A judge shall not engage in conduct incompatible with the diligent discharge of judicial duties.

Implementation

By reason of the nature of judicial office, effective measures shall be adopted by national judiciaries to provide mechanisms to implement these principles if such mechanisms are not already in existence in their jurisdictions.

Definitions

In this statement of principles, unless the context otherwise permits or requires, the following meanings shall be attributed to the words used:

"Court staff" includes the personal staff of the judge, including law clerks;

"Judge" means any person exercising judicial power, however designated;

"Judge's family" includes a judge's spouse, son, daughter, son-in-law, daughter-in-law and any other close relative or person who is a companion or employee of the judge and who lives in the judge's household;

"Judge's spouse" includes a domestic partner of the judge or any other person of either sex in a close personal relationship with the judge.

APPENDIX IX

KIEV RECOMMENDATIONS ON JUDICIAL INDEPENDENCE

Organized by: Organization for Security and Co-operation in Europe (OSCE) – Office for Democratic Institutions and Human Rights and Max Planck Minerva Research group on Judicial Independence

Index

Annexes

1. Background

Judicial independence is an institutional requirement for all OSCE participating States. Only an independent judiciary can adjudicate cases in a just manner, respecting the rights of accused persons to a fair trial. Judicial independence is one of the hallmarks of a state that respects the principle of separation of powers, which is indispensable for a genuine democracy. The participating States most recently reaffirmed their commitment to judicial independence in the Helsinki Ministerial Council Decision no. 7/08 on *Further strengthening the rule of law in the OSCE area* (MC.DEC/7/08). The principle of judicial independence is at the forefront of the organization's rule of law-related commitments and has repeatedly been the focus of human dimension meetings, most recently the Human Dimension Seminar on Strengthening Judicial Independence and Public Access to Justice in May 2010.

In earlier documents, the participating States have acknowledged the significance of judicial independence for the full expression of the inherent dignity and of the equal and inalienable rights of all human beings (Copenhagen 1990); committed to respect the related international standards, and ensure that the independence of the judiciary is guaranteed and enshrined in the constitution or the law of the country and is respected in practice, paying particular attention to the Basic Principles on the

Independence of the Judiciary; and recognized the importance of associations of judges for the promotion of judicial independence (Moscow 1991). In the Charter for European Security participating States agreed to promote the development of independent judicial systems (Istanbul 1999).

Discussions at the 2010 Human Dimension Seminar on Strengthening Judicial Independence and Public Access to Justice, as well as the 2009 Human Dimension Seminar on Strengthening the Rule of Law in the OSCE Area confirmed that judicial councils and judicial administration more generally, selection and appointment of judges, as well as accountability including discipline and removal of judges are crucial aspects of judicial independence that deserve more in-depth examination and further discussion. Recommendations made at the seminars called on the OSCE, its institutions and field operations, to continue facilitating exchanges of practices and contacts between the judiciaries of participating States.

2. Introduction and Methodology

Balancing the independence of the judiciary with the need for democratic legitimacy in a society governed by the rule of law is a challenge for every participating State. The legacy of the Socialist legal tradition has shaped justice systems in a great number of OSCE participating States. After departure from the doctrine of "unity of state power", these States in the past two decades have implemented numerous reforms, both legislative and institutional, which were intended to foster separation of powers and judicial independence. The time is now ripe for a fresh look at these efforts, to assess their success in establishing truly independent judiciaries, as well as identify remaining challenges in strengthening them. Therefore, ODIHR and the Max Planck Institute for Comparative Public Law and International Law (MPI) have undertaken an assessment of the state of judicial independence across the OSCE region which provides the basis for developing an ODIHR strategy for this sector. The primary purpose of the project is to identify impediments and recognize good practices for the makeup of independent judiciaries in the participating States of the OSCE, and assist the States, with a predominant focus on Eastern Europe, South Caucasus and Central Asia, in adhering to their commitments.

For the assessment phase of the project, ODIHR designed a questionnaire on judicial independence and commissioned country reports from independent experts. The questionnaire benefitted from feedback by MPI and the Council of Europe Venice Commission and covers the most relevant aspects of judicial independence, as outlined in several international instruments. Special attention has been given, *inter alia*, to the administration of the judiciary including budget management, the role of judicial councils, selection and appointment of judges, tenure and promotion, remuneration, case assignment systems, disciplinary procedures, immunity, ethics and resources.

As second step in the assessment phase of the judicial independence project, the expert meeting in Kiev was intended to result in concrete recommendations to the participating States on how to further strengthen judicial independence in the region. The comparative analysis of independent expert reports in the first step had led to the identification of subtopics for the expert meeting, namely (1) Judicial Administration – judicial councils, judicial self-governing bodies and the role of court chairs; (2) Judicial

Selection – criteria and procedures; and (3) Accountability *versus* Independence in Adjudication. These subtopics were also subject to discussion at separate working sessions at the recent Human Dimension Seminar on Strengthening Judicial Independence and Public Access to Justice on 17–19 May 2010 in Warsaw.

The meeting was attended by 27 prominent scholars and senior practitioners from 19 participating States, in addition to experts from ODIHR, MPI and the Council of Europe including its Venice Commission. The OSCE field presences in Moldova, Ukraine and Skopje were also represented. The meeting aimed to serve as a platform for in-depth discussion of challenges in selected areas related to judicial independence, critical examination of the impact of past reforms, as well as identification of good practice examples from participating States.

3. Selected Findings and Recommendations

The meeting resulted in adoption of the "Kiev Recommendations on Judicial Independence in Eastern Europe, South Caucasus and Central Asia", a set of concrete and specific recommendations to the participating States for future reforms to strengthen judicial independence (Annex 1).

Regarding judicial administration, the experts concluded that the administration of courts and the judiciary shall enhance independent and impartial adjudication in line with due process rights and the rule of law. Judicial administration must never be used to influence adjudication as regards content of judicial decision-making. The process of judicial administration must be transparent. Concrete recommendations in relation to judicial councils included, *inter alia*, that an all-encompassing authority and autonomy of a single such body is undesirable. Instead, one option would be to establish different independent bodies competent for specific aspects of judicial administration without subjecting them to the control of a single institution or authority.

In particular, a separate expert commission should be established which is entrusted with the competence to conduct written and oral examinations in the process of judicial selection. In this case the competence of the judicial council should be restricted to verifying that the correct procedures have been followed. In order to prevent allegations of corporatism and guarantee a fair disciplinary procedure, judicial councils shall not be competent both to a) receive complaints and conduct disciplinary investigations and at the same time b) hear a case and make a decision on disciplinary measures. Disciplinary decisions shall be subject to appellate oversight by a competent court.

Regarding the composition of judicial councils, experts concluded that they should not be dominated by appellate court judges. It was recommended that where court chairs are appointed to the council, they must resign from their position as court chair. Prosecutors should be excluded where they do not belong to the same judicial corps as the judges. Neither the State President nor the Minister of Justice should preside over the council. The president of the judicial council should be elected from among its members. More specifically the expert meeting recommended that bodies deciding on cases of judicial discipline must not be controlled by the executive branch nor shall there be any political influence pertaining to discipline. Any kind of control by the executive branch over judicial councils or bodies entrusted with discipline is undesirable.

The expert meeting concluded that the role of court chairs should be limited to representative and court managerial functions. Court presidents must not interfere with the adjudication by other judges. Apart from their administrative functions, which require training in management capacities, they may only assume judicial functions which are equivalent to those exercised by other members of the court. Court presidents shall not be involved in judicial selection. Neither shall they have a say on remuneration, bonuses or privileges. The experts recommended that on a long term basis, bonuses and privileges should be abolished and salaries raised to an adequate level which satisfies the needs of judges for an appropriate standard of living and adequately reflect the responsibility of their profession. As long as bonuses and privileges exist, they should be awarded on the basis of predetermined criteria and a transparent procedure.

Administrative decisions which may affect substantive adjudication should not be within the exclusive competence of court presidents. Furthermore, it was recommended that court chairs should not have the power to either initiate or adopt a disciplinary measure. Regarding the appointment of court chairs, experts recommended as one option to have the judges of the particular court elect them. In case of executive appointment, the term should be short without possibility of renewal.

Regarding access to the judicial profession the expert meeting concluded that it should be open not only to young jurists with special training but also to jurists with significant experience in the legal profession (through mid-career entry into the judiciary). Where schools for judges are part of the selection procedure, they have to be independent from the executive power. Training programmes should focus on what is needed in the judicial service and compensate for any shortcomings of university education. They should include aspects of ethics, communication skills, dispute settlement, management skills and legal drafting skills.

The expert meeting concluded that the procedure and criteria for judicial selection must be clearly defined by law in order to ensure transparency in the selection process. The competition for a vacancy, as well as the terms and conditions, should be widely, publicly announced. If there are background checks, they should be handled with utmost care. The candidate has a right to be heard and should be granted a right to judicial review in case of refusal of the candidature on the basis of secret information. The decision to refuse a candidate on such grounds has to be reasoned.

Where the final appointment of a judge is with the State President, the expert group recommended that eventual discretionary powers related to the appointment of candidates should be limited to those nominated by the selection body. Refusal to appoint such a candidate may be based on procedural grounds only and must be reasoned. Experts recommended giving the selection body the power to overrule a presidential veto by qualified majority vote.

Experts also concluded that it would be desirable if the composition of the judiciary reflects the composition of the population as a whole. Underrepresented groups should be encouraged to acquire the necessary qualifications for being a judge.

With a view to balancing judges' accountability with their independence in adjudication, the expert meeting concluded that disciplinary responsibility of judges shall not extend to the content of their rulings or verdicts, including differences in legal interpretation among courts, or to examples of judicial mistakes. The bodies that adjudicate cases of judicial discipline may not also initiate them or contain as members persons who can initiate them. Judges facing these bodies shall enjoy procedural safeguards, including the rights to present a defence and to appeal to a competent court. Transparency shall be the rule for disciplinary hearings of judges. Such hearings shall be open, unless the judge who is accused requests that they be closed. The decisions regarding judicial discipline shall provide reasons.

Experts recommended that judges shall not be evaluated under any circumstances for the content of their decisions or verdicts (either directly or through the calculation of rates of reversal). How a judge decides a case must never serve as the basis for a sanction. While a judicial council may play a role in specifying the criteria and the procedure, professional evaluations should be conducted at the local level. Assessments shall be conducted mainly by other judges. Court presidents should not have the exclusive competence to evaluate judges.

The group also adopted a recommendation that hearings shall be recorded by electronic devices providing full reproduction, as well as accurate trial records, as evidence of the conduct of judges in the courtroom. To enhance the professional and public accountability of judges, decisions shall be published in databases and on websites in ways that make them truly accessible and free of charge. Decisions must be indexed according to subject matter, legal issues raised, and the names of the judges who wrote them. To facilitate public trust in the courts, authorities should encourage the access of journalists to the courts, and establish positions of press secretary or media officer. There shall be no barriers or obstacles to journalists attending trials, unless they are justifiable.

The expert meeting also concluded that the accusatory bias found in most countries of Eastern Europe, South Caucasus and Central Asia requires remedies. To diminish pressure on judges to avoid acquittals, there must be a change in the system of their professional evaluation where acquittals are now considered a black mark or failure. The number of acquittals should not be an indicator for the evaluation of judges. Furthermore, experts concluded that judges need to gain real discretion in reviewing requests for approval of pretrial detention.

4. Summary of the Discussions

Following the opening session with the Senior Project Officer, OSCE Project Co-ordinator in Ukraine, Rene Bebeau, the first plenary session began with short introductions presenting the research results regarding each of the three sub-topics of the meeting followed by a brief initial discussion. A representative of MPI presented on "Judicial Administration – judicial councils, judicial self-governing bodies and the role of court chairs"; two ODIHR Rule of Law staff talked about "Judicial selection – criteria and procedures" and introduced the sub-topic "Accountability *versus* Independence in Adjudication" respectively. The presentations were intended to prepare the ground for and at the same time focus the discussion in the working groups on the three sub-topics of judicial independence identified to be of continuing concern in the target region. They were also meant to inform all experts on the scope of discussions in the parallel sessions of the groups in order to enable cross-input from members of one working group to the discussion in another working group.

The largest amount of time was dedicated to the discussion and work in three groups. The groups were tasked to discuss remaining challenges regarding the specific aspect of judicial independence they were each dealing with, critically examine the impact of past reforms, as well as identify best practice examples from participating States. Experts were expected to identify concrete measures and practical tools to be recommended to the participating States for strengthening judicial independence in practice. Midway through the meeting, moderators gave a brief heads-up of the discussion in their respective working group to the plenary, in order to enable the above mentioned cross-input from all experts to each of the working groups. After another few hours of work in groups, moderators presented the final result of their respective group in the final plenary session.

Working Group 1 – Judicial Administration

Moderator: Prof. Giuseppe Di Federico

The moderator gave an introduction to the topic, describing examples of judicial councils in western countries, their competences and composition, which was followed by a general discussion on judicial councils and court chairs in Central and Eastern Europe, South Caucasus and Central Asia. Experts deplored executive interferences in the work of judicial councils which sometimes result in tensions with the administration. Examples were also given for inappropriate influence by court chairs, both directly on judges and through the council, even if they do not have a formal role in the council or should not be members according to the law. Consequently, the group discussed suggestions how to limit the concentration of power in judicial councils, as well as court chairs.

Following a discussion on the competences of judicial councils, it was agreed that they should not be given the full responsibility on disciplinary proceedings; namely the right to initiate disciplinary proceedings and the right to decide on disciplinary proceedings should not be in one hand, and while councils could have the right to initiate disciplinary proceedings the power to decide should be given to another body, *or vice versa*.

The experts also raised concerns with regard to the councils' role in judges' selection and called for limiting the concentration of competences. The group agreed that there should be special selection commissions, including lawyers and professors appointed by the council, to administer written and/or oral exams. While the judicial council should have the right to specify in detail the ways in which the candidates for the office of judge should be evaluated as well as the relevant criteria, the respective technical commissions should make the decision on who to appoint/recommend as final candidate(s). Judicial councils should only be in charge of controlling the regularity of proceedings.

Discussing the competence for judges' professional performance evaluation, experts raised reservations with respect to judicial councils' having a strong role in it. Various proposals were made as to what kind of body should conduct evaluations, e.g. that it should be a board or panel rather than an individual, at the local level rather than centralized, and that judge members should be elected by their fellow judges at the same court. Experts were critical of overly strong involvement of higher court judges in the evaluation. While some called for a role of court chairs in evaluation, others called for restricting it. Finally, it was agreed that they should not have the exclusive competence but otherwise be involved, since they have relevant information at their disposal concerning judges in their courts. It was also suggested to involve independent experts and lawyers in the process. The working group agreed that professional evaluation should be performed at the local level, that decisions should be taken by an independent body, and that the evaluation criteria should be due diligence, respect for the parties, and respect for the rules.

The working group then discussed judicial councils' budgetary competences. Various models suggested included affording an advisory role to the council, that it should give a reasoned proposal to the Parliament or as a minimum an opinion. While experts acknowledged the role of the executive, in particular the Ministry of Justice, in proposing the budget, they suggested that the councils should have more of a watch-dog function. Additionally, it was agreed that judicial councils should have a role in budgetary matters, and make requests to the government that financial needs of the judiciary are taken into account in Parliament.

Other issues of concern mentioned during the discussion included the problem that councils meet too rarely (and therewith giving room for other structures to fill gaps in judicial administration), their lack of crucial information, and the problem that members do not always serve on a full-time basis. Regarding the composition of councils, it was agreed that judicial representatives in the council should be elected by the judiciary.

Moreover the group touched upon the role of court chairs in judicial councils, which was a matter of concern for two reasons: Firstly, in many States the council has the competence to control court chairs. With court chairs sitting themselves on the council, it was deemed questionable that this control function can be assumed properly. Secondly, experts reported that in practice other judge members of the council feel intimidated by court chairs sitting on the council. Consequently, it was agreed that they should resign from their former function as court chair if elected to the council. Experts acknowledged that there are significant differences in the composition of councils in parliamentary systems and presidential systems. The group then discussed a proposal to exclude the Prosecutor's Office and Intelligence Service/law enforcement agencies from the councils. It was agreed that the Chief Prosecutor or a representative should be part of the council only if the prosecution belongs to the judiciary, but excluded if the prosecution belongs to executive, and that members of law enforcement agencies should generally be excluded. The group agreed that judicial councils should not be dominated by higher level judges, or by the executive and legislative branches of power. Experts did not come to a conclusion about whether Bar members should be included in the councils. However, they agreed that law professors should be involved.

The group also addressed the situation in countries where judicial councils in the strict sense do not exist. Experts described the competences and composition of qualification commissions or qualification *collegia*, and concluded that the measures agreed with regard to councils are also applicable in countries that have other bodies fulfilling partly the same or similar functions.

The working group then turned to discussing the appointment of court chairs and their role in administering the judiciary. It was concluded that their authority needs to be limited to representative functions and court management decisions, and that they should not be able to interfere with the judges' adjudication of cases. Experts further agreed that case assignment should not be the responsibility of court chairs. In this context experts suggested the introduction of a random system or establishment of an independent board made up of judges, which would assign cases following clear and objective criteria developed in advance.

Experts expressed concern regarding the role of court chairs in establishing or influencing the level of remuneration through promotion, awards, or bonuses. As long as bonuses exist, they should be based on predetermined clear criteria and a transparent procedure. More generally, the group agreed that court chairs must not misuse their competence to distribute facilities such as court rooms to exert influence.

With regard to disciplinary matters, experts concluded that court chairs should be entitled to file a complaint to the independent organ competent for the initiation of disciplinary proceedings as any other citizen, but that they should not be able to initiate proceedings.

Moreover the group discussed the appointment of court chairs. The experts concluded that they should be appointed for a fixed and limited term, and that reappointment should be possible only once. The working group agreed that vacancies should be published and all persons who have the necessary qualifications may submit an application. It was concluded that participating States may want to consider publishing lists of candidates. Experts suggested various options of who should appoint court chairs. The group agreed that they should be elected by their fellow judges. Another option would be to have court chairs appointed by the President, provided that the judicial council or qualification commission proposed the candidate according to its fair and transparent procedures. In case the President refuses to appoint the candidate, one option discussed and approved was the possibility that the advisory body (judicial council or qualification commission) could overrule a veto by the President and impose a rejected candidate by qualified majority vote. Furthermore it was concluded that the President should have to give reasons for rejecting a candidate.

Following a discussion on accountability of the council and transparency of its activities, the working group agreed that public access to its deliberations should be guaranteed, also in practice. Experts also recommended the publication of decisions of the judicial council on its website.

Working Group 2 – Judicial Selection: Criteria and Procedures

Moderator: Prof. Angelika Nußberger

The discussion began with comparing eligibility criteria in different jurisdictions. The moderator pointed out that they were largely similar and could be divided into positive ones, such as requirements of a certain educational level and professional experience, and negative ones or prohibitions – for example, the lack of a criminal record.

It was pointed out that knowledge of several languages or very well qualified court interpreters may be required in some countries, especially with ethnically diverse populations. In most countries the requirement is limited to the knowledge of the official state language(s). One expert addressed also the criterion of citizenship, pointing out that it presents a problem in his country where judicial candidates are prohibited from holding dual citizenship.

On the criterion of minimal age, the experts gave examples of different age requirements for judicial candidates, starting from 23. One expert suggested that this bar should not be set too high because in his country this would prevent young talented lawyers, often with high-quality western education, from pursuing judicial careers. Another expert retorted that in his country the age limit of 27 is criticized as being too low and that young judges may not have sufficient maturity and life experience to act independently. In this connection, other experts confirmed that the career judiciary model is being criticized in a number of transition countries. Its critics maintain that it does not create a sufficiently solid basis for an independent judiciary. The experts agreed that these criticisms have led to initiatives in some countries to modify their judicial recruitment systems to attract not only young candidates but also mid-career lawyers to become judges. They concluded that this should be regarded as a welcome development.

Legal degrees and the quality of legal education in the region were then discussed at some length. Several experts pointed out that many universities continue with highly theoretical legal education which does not provide future lawyers and judges with sufficient analytical skills. Some experts also expressed concerns about differences in the quality of education between public and private schools. Experts concluded that university curricula should give more attention to training analytical skills. To this end, universities should strive to incorporate in their studies such elements as case studies, law clinics, and moot courts. In countries where all judicial candidates graduate from judicial schools, it was emphasized that these should not only teach judges the necessary skills but also the prerequisite values and ethics for independent adjudication. One expert suggested that ODIHR should organize a human dimension event on legal education on the OSCE area.

One expert noted that in some countries there is a lack of clarity about the necessary educational qualifications for a judicial examination. This lack and the corresponding discretion authorities have in interpreting the legislative requirement may lead to discrimination against candidates from certain educational institutions.

The working group also discussed education in special schools for judges (magistrates). Several experts expressed concerns that access to such schools is insufficiently transparent and there is a perception that candidates are admitted on the basis of connections rather than merit. Experts agreed that access to judicial (magistrates) schools should not be a barrier to the judicial profession. It was suggested that a unified qualification examination for all judicial candidates regardless of their prior education may be a solution to this problem. One expert, however, noted that this approach may create disincentives for potential applicants to judicial schools.

Another participant challenged the judicial school model for selecting and educating future judges. In particular, he questioned the extent to which this model is capable of promoting openness and pluralism in the judiciary. He suggested that the judiciary should be open to different legal professions, especially lawyers (advocates) and academics. Several experts agreed and added that a special challenge for post-Soviet countries is to make the judicial career a "crown" of the legal profession, so that lawyers may become judges later in their career, and not the other way around. This may be achieved through creating different avenues of access to the judicial profession instead of monopolizing this access within judicial schools.

The discussion then moved to the procedure of selection and appointment. In this regard, experts first discussed a number of general principles that should be followed, including separation of powers, transparency, responsibility, and legitimacy. The working group then discussed the following key elements of the selection procedure.

First, competition for all judicial vacancies should be publicly announced. The vacancies should be widely published in public media. The vacancy announcements should clearly spell out the requirements for judicial candidates.

Second, an autonomous body in charge of selection should compile the list of applicants with basic information about them. This list should be publicly available; although one expert pointed out that the information to be disclosed should not breach the applicants' reasonable expectations of privacy. The working group agreed that the selecting body should be appointed for a short and limited term and include representatives from outside the judiciary, although judges should form a majority.

Third, rules for assessing candidates applied by the selecting body should exist and also be publicly available. These rules should provide for objective assessment of the applicants and guarantee proper evaluation of candidates from different backgrounds: graduates of judicial schools, as well as practicing lawyers and other legal professionals. The selecting body should make a final decision or recommend one candidate for appointment by the appointing authority (most commonly the president).

Finally, the working group discussed the involvement of political organs in the appointment of judges. It was debated whether the president should merely provide a stamp of approval or have an opportunity to reject appointment with a reasoned decision. The use of the legislature as appointing authority was questioned by the experts, who pointed out that the legislature takes a vote but cannot provide reasoning for its decision. The experts agreed that refusal to appoint may only be based on procedural grounds. One expert was of the opinion that the selecting body's decision should be binding and that the appointing authority should not have any power to veto the chosen candidate. All experts agreed that if the veto is applied by the appointing authority, the selecting body should re-examine its decision and have the option to override this veto by a qualified majority. This should be done within a short time-frame to avoid uncertainty for the candidates waiting for appointments.

Several experts raised concerns about the formal and informal vetting procedures and background checks which are carried out in some countries in relation to judicial candidates. It was suggested that the selecting body should request a standard check for a criminal record and any other disqualifying grounds from the police. The results from this check should be available to the applicant, who should be entitled to appeal them in court. No other background checks should be performed by any security services.

Representation of minorities in the judiciary was also discussed by the working group. Several experts suggested that it would be desirable if the composition of the judiciary reflected the composition of the population as a whole. However, many experts did not feel that recommending quotas for minorities may be an appropriate solution. Instead, all experts agreed that underrepresented groups should be encouraged to acquire the necessary qualifications for becoming judges. In particular, it was suggested that promotion of university legal education for minorities would help increase the number of judges who belong to minorities.

Working Group 3 – Accountability

Moderator: Prof. Peter Solomon

Regarding discipline, the group discussed at length whether it would be appropriate to come up with or recommend a detailed and specific definition of disciplinary offences.

Many experts pointed at broad and unclear provisions in their countries. They considered it necessary to reduce the scope of disciplinary laws, and thereby limit the discretion and subjectivity in their application. Some expressed hope that a more specific and detailed description of grounds for disciplinary proceedings would help prevent the abuse of disciplinary proceedings to get rid of unwanted judges. On the other hand, experts agreed that it was not appropriate in a number of legal cultures to define and enumerate the grounds for discipline in detail, because this may unduly limit the scope and exclude unforeseen circumstances that would merit disciplinary proceedings. The group therefore concluded that instead, the recommendations should define discipline more generally (serious violation, inexcusable, and bringing the judiciary into disrepute). It was also agreed to specify the elements that should not be handled in the framework of judges' discipline, namely all aspects related to the content of a judge's decision, divergence of opinion between judges at a lower and a higher court or alleged mistakes in applying the law, and criticism of the courts. In a number of the experts' countries, judges are influenced by the fear that their decision may be overturned. Some experts mentioned the fact that due to the absence of audio-recording of proceedings in many places, it was often impossible to prove or disprove charges or inappropriate behaviour of a judge during a hearing. As a consequence, a recommendation was phrased to call for complete recording of hearings.

The group then turned to discussing the composition and competences of bodies in charge of disciplinary proceedings. While it was acknowledged that the disciplinary competence lies with a judicial council in many countries, experts agreed that this practice bears many problems. Judicial councils are considered to be in charge first and foremost of judicial administration, and are often dominated by representatives of the executive, court chairs, and judges from higher instance courts. In the majority of countries discussed, a commission or board within the council has some competence over discipline, but often the council has to validate decisions of the commission, and the scope of this validation is not clear. Therefore, the group concluded that bodies dealing with discipline of judges should be separate and independent from the bodies in charge of judicial administration, and that it should be composed of at least 2/3 judges.

Discussing the role of court chairs in initiating discipline against judges, including for matters of work discipline, the group could not agree to exclude this possibility. Experts also raised the issue of *ex-parte* communications and related concerns for judicial independence, but the group did not conclude to craft a related recommendation. Moreover the working group talked about the fact that judges tend not to protest against interference, or bring it to public attention. In this regard, the group agreed that legal protection of judges needed to be enhanced. This part of the discussion resulted in recommendations in connection to judicial safeguards for judges during disciplinary proceedings. More specifically the group also agreed to recommend that as a rule, disciplinary hearings should be public.

Turning to the matter of holding judges accountable through a system of performance evaluation, the working group discussed different models and related concerns. Experts pointed out that performance evaluations can be a useful tool to hold judges accountable to professional and ethical standards, motivate them and stimulate their professional development. However where performance evaluation is in the hands of the respective court chairs alone, experts agreed that the individual judge's independence may be at risk. Another concern raised by experts from Eastern Europe is the use of statistical data or quantitative indicators to evaluate judges' performance. The group agreed that the quality of a judge's performance cannot be measured by counting the number of cases processed regardless of their complexity, or the number of judgments upheld at the higher instance. While it was acknowledged that statistics regarding case processing and reversal rate can be useful for purposes of judicial administration, management and budgeting, they should not be used to the detriment of the individual judge. The experts concluded that judges' performance evaluations should not relate to the so-called stability of judgment upon appeal, that they should be focused on skills and competencies, and that the evaluation procedure should contain clearly regulated criteria, be transparent and fair, with possibility of appeal by the relevant judge.

It was also agreed that retired judges could be involved in a body or panel that is performing the evaluations. The question whether public observers should be included was briefly discussed, without a conclusion. There were differences in opinion whether performance evaluations should influence promotion and ranking decisions. The group agreed however that "attestations", i.e. periodic exams that may lead to the dismissal of a judge with permanent tenure, are not appropriate. It was concluded that where such attestations are required, the system should be changed into a system of performance evaluations or a similar system instead. It was suggested that OSCE/ODIHR could assist in developing a set of criteria for evaluating judges.

On a more general note, the group discussed concerns related to criminal and disciplinary responsibility, as well as civil liability of judges for the content of their decisions. Consensus was reached that judges' wilful misapplication of the law or a gross inexcusable breach may be punishable. It was agreed however that those offences should be covered by disciplinary responsibility for serious professional misconduct or criminal responsibility for abusing a judge's position, and that special criminal or disciplinary offences regarding the content of the judge's decision are not necessary. Different interpretations of the law should never be a reason for dismissal of a judge.

Moreover, the working group addressed the issue of low rates of acquittal, an outcome expected of judges and for whose absence they are often held responsible. The experts reported that in some systems judges are held responsible for low acquittal rates directly because it is one criterion in their evaluations. In countries where this is not the case, experts explained how judges are held accountable for acquittal rates indirectly: acquittals have a high risk of being overturned upon appeal, and court chairs exercise pressure on judges to keep the number of acquittals low in order to avoid a high number of reversals of decisions taken at their courts. Consequently, the group formulated a recommendation to reduce the pressure on judges to avoid acquittals by, *inter alia*, reviewing the criteria for the evaluation of judges. Several experts expressed concern regarding the *prokurator's* power in some countries, and suggested that OSCE/ODIHR address this more generally.

The moderator then drew the group's attention to what he called "professional accountability". While bureaucratic accountability makes judges answerable to court chairs, higher court judges and bureaucratic structures and hence bears the risk of undue influence, professional accountability enables more appropriate control over judges. Under the so-called professional accountability, judges are mainly accountable to their peers, the wider legal community and the public. With this form of mild or benign pressure, judges do not worry about their careers but rather about their public reputation as a good judge and respect of the legal community. The group discussed what is necessary to foster professional accountability and elaborated a number of recommendations. Namely it was agreed that judges' specialized education should include training on what makes a good judge and how to reason a judgment. More specifically, experts suggested that OSCE/ODIHR may assist in developing such training curricula and hold a human dimension meeting on the topic of legal education. Furthermore the group concluded that publicity of hearings and transparency of decisions and media access are crucial for professional accountability because they enable scrutiny and critical discussion. In this context it was suggested that OSCE/ODIHR support participating States in making judgments available and searchable online and hence truly accessible to the public and legal and academic community.

The working group also addressed the significant role that judges' associations can play in upholding judges' professional accountability. In this regard experts concluded that OSCE/ODIHR could support the formation and activities of judges' associations, mainly through facilitating exchange of experiences within the OSCE region.

Finally, the group turned to discussing the phenomenon of higher courts' directives, resolutions or decisions that are afforded so-called precedential effect. It was acknowledged that a certain degree of uniformity of jurisprudence is desirable, and that the highest courts have a mandate in this regard. However the group agreed that such decisions may not be binding on judges of lower level courts.

5. Conclusion

During the final plenary session, the group of all experts had a discussion of the recommendations prepared in the three working groups and adopted them as the "Kiev Recommendations on Judicial Independence in Eastern Europe, South Caucasus and Central Asia" (Annex 1). To begin the next phase of the project, discussions with OSCE staff in field operations and independent experts will prepare the ground for pilot-projects in selected countries to begin implementing the recommendations.

Participating States are invited to review the ideas contained in the Kiev Recommendations, identify areas where their practice already corresponds to what is recommended, and share relevant information with ODIHR. ODIHR will accordingly consider facilitating the exchange of expertise and technical assistance for the benefit of participating States that express the interest to further strengthen the independence of their judiciaries by implementing some of the measures recommended in the Kiev Recommendations.

ANNEX 1

The Kiev Recommendations on Judicial Independence in Eastern Europe, South Caucasus and Central Asia

OSCE Office for Democratic Institutions and Human Rights

Max Planck Minerva Research Group on Judicial Independence

Judicial Administration, Selection and Accountability

Kiev, 23–25 June 2010

Judicial independence is an indispensable element of the right to due process, the rule of law and democracy. In an effort to support countries in Eastern Europe, South Caucasus and Central Asia in strengthening judicial independence in line with these principles, the OSCE Office for Democratic Institutions and Human Rights (ODIHR) together with the Max Planck Institute for Comparative Public Law and International Law (MPI), organized and hosted a regional expert meeting on Judicial Independence in Kiev. The meeting was attended by approximately 40 independent experts, among them prominent scholars and senior practitioners from 19 OSCE participating States, and from the Council of Europe and its Venice Commission.

Following an in-depth research of legal systems and practices regarding judicial independence, ODIHR and MPI selected three themes that are of particular relevance for judicial independence: (1) Judicial Administration with a focus on judicial councils, judicial self-governing bodies and the role of court chairs; (2) Judicial Selection – criteria and procedures; and (3) Accountability of Judges and Judicial Independence in Adjudication. The meeting concluded with the adoption of a – non-exhaustive – set of recommendations (enclosed "Kiev Recommendations on Judicial Independence in Eastern Europe, South Caucasus and Central Asia"). The purpose of these recommendations is to further strengthen judicial independence in the region within the three selected topical areas.

Participating States are invited to review the ideas contained in the Kiev Recommendations, identify areas where their practice already corresponds to what is recommended, and share relevant information with ODIHR. ODIHR will accordingly facilitate the exchange of expertise and provide technical assistance for the benefit of participating States that express the interest to further strengthen the independence of their judiciaries by implementing the measures contained in the Kiev Recommendations.

Part I – Judicial Administration

1. The administration of courts and the judiciary shall enhance independent and impartial adjudication in line with due process rights and the rule of law. Judicial administration must never be used to influence the content of judicial decision making. The process of judicial administration must be transparent.

Judicial Councils, Qualification Commissions and Self-governing Bodies

Division of Competences in Judicial Administration

2. Judicial Councils are bodies entrusted with specific tasks of judicial administration and independent competences in order to guarantee judicial independence. In order to avoid excessive concentration of power in one judicial body and perceptions of corporatism it is recommended to distinguish among and separate different competences, such as selection (*see paras 3-4, 8*), promotion and training of judges, discipline (*see paras 5, 9, 14, 25-26*), professional evaluation (*see paras 27-28*) and budget (*see para 6*). A good option is to establish different independent bodies competent for specific aspects of judicial administration without subjecting them to the control of a single institution or authority. The composition of these bodies should each reflect their particular task. Their work should be regulated by statutory law rather than executive decree.

Judicial Selection

3. Unless there is another independent body entrusted with this task, a separate expert commission should be established to conduct written and oral examinations in the process of judicial selection (*see also para 8*). In this case the competence of the Judicial Council should be restricted to verifying that the correct procedures have been followed and to either appoint the candidates selected by the commission or recommend them to the appointing authority. (*For the recruitment process see paras 21-23*).

4. Alternatively, Judicial Councils or Qualification Commissions or Qualification Collegia may be responsible directly for the selection and training of judges. In this case it is vital that these bodies are not under executive control and that they operate independently from regional governments (*for the composition see also para 8*).

Discipline

5. In order to prevent allegations of corporatism and guarantee a fair disciplinary procedure, Judicial Councils shall not be competent both to a) receive complaints and conduct disciplinary investigations and at the same time b) hear a case and make a decision on disciplinary measures. Disciplinary decisions shall be subject to appellate oversight by a competent court (*see also paras 9, 14, 25-26*).

Budgetary Advice

6. Without prejudice to existing responsibilities of the government for proposing the judicial budget and of parliament for adopting the budget, it would be advisable for a body representing the interests of the judiciary, such as a Judicial Council, to present to the government the budgetary needs of the justice system in order to facilitate

informed decision making. This body should also be heard by parliament in the deliberations on the budget. Judicial Councils may play a role also in the distribution of the budget within the judiciary.

Composition of Judicial Councils

7. Where a Judicial Council is established, its judge members shall be elected by their peers and represent the judiciary at large, including judges from first level courts. Judicial Councils shall not be dominated by appellate court judges. Where the chairperson of a court is appointed to the Council, he or she must resign from his or her position as court chairperson. Apart from a substantial number of judicial members elected by the judges, the Judicial Council should comprise law professors and preferably a member of the bar, to promote greater inclusiveness and transparency. Prosecutors should be excluded where prosecutors do not belong to the same judicial corps as the judges. Other representatives of the law enforcement agencies should also be barred from participation. Neither the State President nor the Minister of Justice should preside over the Council. The president of the Judicial Council should be elected by majority vote from among its members. The work of the Judicial Council shall not be dominated by representatives of the executive and legislative branch.

Membership of Bodies Deciding on Judicial Selection

8. Members of special commissions for judicial selection (*see para 3*) should be appointed by the Judicial Council from the ranks of the legal profession, including members of the judiciary. Where Judicial Councils, Qualification Commissions or Qualification Collegia are responsible directly for judicial selection (*see para 4*), the members should be appointed to fixed terms of office. Apart from a substantial number of judicial members in this selection body, the inclusion of other professional groups is desirable (law professors, advocates) and should be decided on the basis of the relevant legal culture and experience. Its composition shall ensure that political considerations do not prevail over the qualifications of a candidate for judicial office (*see para 21*).

Membership of Bodies Deciding on Discipline

9. Bodies competent to hear a disciplinary case and to take a decision on disciplinary measures (*see para 5, b*) shall not exclusively be composed of judges, but require representation including members from outside the judicial profession. Judicial members during their time of office shall not perform other functions relating to judges or the judicial community, such as administration, budgeting, or judicial selection. Bodies deciding on cases of judicial discipline must not be controlled by the executive branch nor shall there be any political influence pertaining to discipline. Any kind of control by the executive branch over Judicial Councils or bodies entrusted with discipline is to be avoided. (*See also paras 5, 25-26.*)

Transparency of Judicial Administration

10. The Judicial Council shall meet regularly so that it can fulfil its tasks. Public access to the deliberations of the Judicial Council and publication of its decisions shall be guaranteed in law and in practice.

The Role of Court Chairpersons

11. The role of court chairpersons should be strictly limited in the following sense: they may only assume judicial functions which are equivalent to those exercised by other members of the court. Court chairpersons must not interfere with the adjudication by other judges and shall not be involved in judicial selection. Neither shall they have a say on remuneration (*see para 13 for bonuses and privileges*). They may have representative and administrative functions, including the control over non-judicial staff. Administrative functions require training in management capacities. Court chairpersons must not misuse their competence to distribute court facilities to exercise influence on the judges.

Case Assignment
12. Administrative decisions which may affect substantive adjudication should not be within the exclusive competence of court chairpersons. One example is case assignment, which should be either random or on the basis of predetermined, clear and objective criteria determined by a board of judges of the court. Once adopted, a distribution mechanism may not be interfered with.

Individual Bonuses and Privileges
13. On a long term basis, bonuses and privileges should be abolished and salaries raised to an adequate level which satisfy the needs of judges for an appropriate standard of living and adequately reflect the responsibility of their profession. As long as bonuses and privileges exist, they should be awarded on the basis of predetermined criteria and a transparent procedure. Court chairs shall not have a say on bonuses or privileges.

Limited Role in Disciplining Judges
14. Court chairpersons may file a complaint to the body which is competent to receive complaints and conduct disciplinary investigations (*see para 5, a*). In order to ensure an independent and objective review of the complaint, court chairpersons should not have the power to either initiate or adopt a disciplinary measure.

Limited Term of Office
15. Court chairpersons should be appointed for a limited number of years with the option of only one renewal. In case of executive appointment, the term should be short without possibility of renewal.

Transparent and Independent Selection of Court Chairpersons
16. The selection of court chairpersons should be transparent. Vacancies for the post of court chairpersons shall be published. All judges with the necessary seniority/experience may apply. The body competent to select may interview the candidates. A good option is to have the judges of the particular court elect the court chairperson. In case of executive appointment, an advisory body - such as a Judicial Council or Qualification Commission (*see para 4*) - taking also into consideration views from the local bench, should be entitled to make a recommendation which the executive may only reject by reasoned decision. In this case the advisory body may recommend a different

candidate. Additionally, in order to protect against excessive executive influence, the advisory body should be able to override the executive veto by qualified majority vote.

Part II – Judicial Selection and Training

Diversity of Access to Judicial Profession

17. Access to the judicial profession should be given not only to young jurists with special training but also to jurists with significant experience working in the legal profession (that is, through mid-career entry into the judiciary). The degree to which experience gained in the relevant profession can qualify candidates for judicial posts must be carefully assessed.

Improvement of Legal Education

18. Access to the judicial profession should be limited to those candidates with a higher law degree. In the university curriculum more attention should be given to the training of analytical skills. Elements such as case studies, practical experience, law clinics and moot courts should be integrated. The same level of education should be guaranteed in State and private universities, including distant learning programmes. External evaluation of the university curricula may positively contribute to their improvement.

Improvement of Special Training of Judges

19. Where schools for judges are part of the selection procedures, they have to be independent from the executive power. Training programmes should focus on what is needed in the judicial service and complement university education. They should include aspects of ethics, communication skills, the ability to settle disputes, management skills and legal drafting skills. Where a Judicial Council exists, it may adopt recommendations for the legal education of judges. This includes the specification of relevant skills and advice on the continuing education of judges.

20. Special training as referred to in para 19 should also be provided for representatives of other legal professions joining the judiciary.

Recruitment Process

21. In order to ensure transparency in the selection process, the procedure and criteria for judicial selection must be clearly defined by law. The vacancy note, as well as the terms and conditions, should be publicly announced and widely disseminated. A list of all candidates applying (or at least a short list) should be publicly available. The selection body should be independent, representative and responsible towards the public (*see paras 3-4*). It should conduct an interview at least with the candidates who have reached the final round, provided that both the topic of the interview and its weight in the process of selection is predetermined.

22. If there are background checks, they should be handled with utmost care and strictly on the basis of the rule of law. The selecting authority can request a standard check for a criminal record and any other disqualifying grounds from the police. The

results from this check should be made available to the applicant, who should be entitled to appeal them in court. No other background checks should be performed by any security services. The decision to refuse a candidate based on background checks needs to be reasoned.

23. Where the final appointment of a judge is with the State President, the discretion to appoint should be limited to the candidates nominated by the selection body (e.g. Judicial Council, Qualification Commission or Expert Commission; *see paras 3-4*). Refusal to appoint such a candidate may be based on procedural grounds only and must be reasoned. In this case the selection body should re-examine its decision. One option would be to give the selection body the power to overrule a presidential veto by a qualified majority vote. All decisions have to be taken within short time limits as defined by law.

Representation of Minorities within the Judiciary

24. Generally it would be desirable that the composition of the judiciary reflects the composition of the population as a whole. In order to increase the representation of minorities in the judiciary, underrepresented groups should be encouraged to acquire the necessary qualifications for being a judge. Nobody must be excluded because they are a member of a certain minority group.

Part III – Accountability of Judges and Judicial Independence in Adjudication

Disciplinary Proceedings

25. Disciplinary proceedings against judges shall deal with alleged instances of professional misconduct that are gross and inexcusable and that also bring the judiciary into disrepute. Disciplinary responsibility of judges shall not extend to the content of their rulings or verdicts, including differences in legal interpretation among courts; or to examples of judicial mistakes; or to criticism of the courts.

Independent Body Deciding on Discipline

26. There shall be a special independent body (court, commission or council) to adjudicate cases of judicial discipline (*see para 9*). The bodies that adjudicate cases of judicial discipline may not also initiate them or have as members persons who can initiate them. These bodies shall provide the accused judge with procedural safeguards, including the right to present a defence and also the right to appeal to a competent court. Transparency shall be the rule for disciplinary hearings of judges. Such hearings shall be open, unless the judge who is accused requests that they be closed. In this case a court shall decide whether the request is justified. The decisions regarding judicial discipline shall provide reasons. Final decisions on disciplinary measures shall be published.

Professional Evaluation of Judges

27. Where professional evaluations of judges are performed, they must not be used to harm independent adjudication. The evaluation of judges' performance shall be primarily qualitative and focus upon their skills, including professional competence

(knowledge of law, ability to conduct trials, capacity to write reasoned decisions), personal competence (ability to cope with the work load, ability to decide, openness to new technologies), social competence (ability to mediate, respect for the parties) and, for possible promotion to an administrative position, competence to lead. These same skills should be cultivated in judicial training programmes, as well as on the job.

28. Judges shall not be evaluated under any circumstances for the content of their decisions or verdicts (either directly or through the calculation of rates of reversal). How a judge decides a case must never serve as the basis for a sanction. Statistics on the efficiency of court operations shall be used mainly for administrative purposes and serve as only one of the factors in the evaluation of judges. Evaluations of judges may be used to help judges identify aspects of their work on which they might want to improve and for purposes of possible promotion. Periodic exams for judges (attestations) that may lead to dismissal or other sanctions are not appropriate for judges with life tenure.

29. The criteria for professional evaluation should be clearly spelled out, transparent and uniform. Basic criteria should be provided for in the law. The precise criteria used in periodic evaluations shall be set out further in regulations, along with the timing and mechanisms of performing evaluations.

Independent Evaluations

30. While a Judicial Council may play a role in specifying the criteria and the procedure, professional evaluations should be conducted at the local level. Evaluations shall be conducted mainly by other judges. Court chairpersons should not have the exclusive competence to evaluate judges, but their role should be complemented by a group of judges from the same and other courts. That group should consider also the opinions of outsiders who regularly deal with the judge (such as lawyers) and law professors, with respect to the diligence, respect for the parties and rules of procedure by a judge.

31. Evaluations should include review of the judge's written decisions and observation of how he or she conducts trials. Evaluations shall be transparent. Judges should be heard and informed about the outcome of the evaluation, with opportunities for review on appeal.

Professional Accountability through Transparency

32. Transparency shall be the rule for trials. To provide evidence of the conduct of judges in the courtroom, as well as accurate trial records, hearings shall be recorded by electronic devices providing full reproduction. Written protocols and stenographic reports are insufficient. To enhance the professional and public accountability of judges, decisions shall be published in databases and on websites in ways that make them truly accessible and free of charge. Decisions must be indexed according to subject matter, legal issues raised, and the names of the judges who wrote them. Decisions of bodies deciding on discipline shall also be published *(see also para 26)*.

33. To facilitate public trust in the courts, authorities should encourage the access of journalists to the courts, and establish positions of press secretary or media officer. There shall be no barriers or obstacles to journalists attending trials.

Independent Criminal Adjudication
34. The accusatory bias of justice systems in most countries of Eastern Europe, South Caucasus and Central Asia requires remedies. Acquittals are still considered a black mark or failure. To diminish pressure on judges to avoid acquittals, a change in the system of their professional evaluation (and if appropriate, considering changes in the assessment of prosecutors and investigators as well) is strongly recommended. The number of acquittals should never be an indicator for the evaluation of judges. Judges need to gain real discretion in reviewing requests for approval of pre-trial detention. Appellate review of acquittals shall be limited to the most exceptional circumstances.

Internal Independence
35. The issuing by high courts of directives, explanations, or resolutions shall be discouraged, but as long as they exist, they must not be binding on lower court judges. Otherwise, they represent infringements of the individual independence of judges. In addition, exemplary decisions of high courts and decisions specifically designated as precedents by these courts shall have the status of recommendations and not be binding on lower court judges in other cases. They must not be used in order to restrict the freedom of lower courts in their decision-making and responsibility. Uniformity of interpretation of the law shall be encouraged through studies of judicial practice that also have no binding force.

ANNEX 2

Annotated Agenda

I. *Introduction*

Judicial independence is an institutional requirement for all OSCE participating States. Only an independent judiciary can adjudicate cases in a just manner, respecting the rights of accused persons to a fair trial. Judicial independence is one of the hallmarks of a state that respects the principle of separation of powers, which is indispensable for a genuine democracy. The participating States most recently reaffirmed their commitment to judicial independence in the Helsinki Ministerial Council Decision no. 7/08 on *Further strengthening the rule of law in the OSCE area* (MC.DEC/7/08). The principle of judicial independence is at the forefront of the organization's rule of law-related commitments and has repeatedly been the focus of human dimension meetings, most recently the Human Dimension Seminar on Strengthening the Rule of Law in the OSCE Area in 2009.

In earlier documents, the participating States have acknowledged the significance of judicial independence for the full expression of the inherent dignity and of the equal and inalienable rights of all human beings (Copenhagen 1990); committed to respect the related international standards, and ensure that the independence of the judiciary is guaranteed and enshrined in the constitution or the law of the country and is respected in practice, paying particular attention to the Basic Principles on the Independence of the Judiciary; and recognized the importance of associations of judges for the promotion of judicial independence (Moscow 1991). In the Charter for European Security participating States agreed to promote the development of independent judicial systems (Istanbul 1999).

Balancing the independence of the judiciary with the need for democratic legitimacy in a society governed by the rule of law is a challenge for every participating State. The legacy of the Socialist legal tradition has shaped justice systems in a great number of OSCE participating States. After departure from the doctrine of "unity of state power", these States in the past two decades have implemented numerous reforms, both legislative and institutional, which were intended to foster separation of powers and judicial independence. The time is now ripe for a fresh look at these efforts, to assess their success in establishing truly independent judiciaries, as well as identify remaining challenges in strengthening them. Therefore, ODIHR and the Max Planck Institute for Comparative Public Law and International Law (MPI) have undertaken an assessment of the state of judicial independence across the OSCE region which provides the basis for developing an ODIHR strategy for this sector. The primary purpose of the project is to identify impediments and recognize good practices for the makeup of independent judiciaries in the participating States of the OSCE, and assist the States, with a predominant focus on current and former members of the Commonwealth of Independent States (CIS), in adhering to their commitments. This approach is expected to result in practical and relevant recommendations to strengthen judicial independence.

For the research phase of the project, ODIHR designed a questionnaire on judicial independence for the experts. The questionnaire benefitted from feedback by MPI and the Council of Europe's Venice Commission and covers the most relevant aspects of judicial independence, as outlined in several international instruments. Special attention has been given, *inter alia*, to the administration of the judiciary including budget management, the role of judicial councils, selection and appointment of judges, tenure and promotion, remuneration, case assignment systems, disciplinary procedures, immunity, ethics and resources.

Discussions at the 2009 Human Dimension Seminar on Strengthening the Rule of Law in the OSCE Area confirmed that judicial councils and judicial administration more generally, selection and appointment of judges, as well as accountability including discipline and removal of judges are crucial aspects of judicial independence that deserve more in-depth examination and further discussion. A recommendation made at this Seminar called on the OSCE, its institutions and field operations to continue facilitating exchanges of practices and contacts between the judiciaries of participating States. **The expert meeting in Kiev therefore will concentrate on these aspects of judicial independence and will consider in detail judicial administration with a special focus on judicial councils and the role of court presidents, criteria and procedure for the selection of judges, and the question how to properly balance the accountability of judges while maintaining independence in adjudication. It is intended to provide recommendations for future reforms and for assistance by the OSCE in this field, particularly in Eastern Europe, the South Caucasus and Central Asia.**

II. *Aims*

In Helsinki in 2008, the Ministerial Council encouraged "participating States, with the assistance, where appropriate, of relevant OSCE executive structures in accordance with their mandates and within existing resources, to continue and to enhance their efforts to share information and best practices and to strengthen the rule of law, *inter alia* in the area of independence of the judiciary."

More specifically, in the Document of the Moscow Meeting of the Conference on the Human Dimension of the CSCE (Moscow 1991), participating States committed themselves, for the promotion of the independence of the judiciary, to

(20.2) - promote and facilitate dialogue, exchanges and co-operation among national associations and other groups interested in ensuring respect for the independence of the judiciary and the protection of lawyers;
(20.3) - co-operate among themselves through, inter alia, dialogue, contacts and exchanges in order to identify where problem areas exist concerning the protection of the independence of judges and legal practitioners and to develop ways and means to address and resolve such problems;
(20.4) - co-operate on an ongoing basis in such areas as the education and training of judges and legal practitioners, as well as the preparation and enactment of legislation intended to strengthen respect for their independence and the impartial operation of the public judicial service.

In line with these goals, the expert meeting in Kiev aims to serve as a platform for in-depth discussion of remaining challenges in selected areas related to judicial independence, critical examination of the impact of past reforms, as well as identification of best practice examples from participating States on the issues related to judicial independence. Discussions are expected to lead to the identification of concrete measures and practical tools to be recommended to ODIHR and the participating States for strengthening judicial independence in practice. The discussions will be structured in three parallel Working Groups as outlined in the Work Plan below.

III. *Organization*

The expert meeting is held at the Radisson Hotel in Kiev, from Wednesday 23 June 16:00h to Friday 25 June 14:00h. The three working group sessions are held in parallel.

The three parallel working groups are tasked to discuss remaining challenges in their specific area of judicial independence, critically examine the impact of past reforms, as well as identify best practice examples from participating States. The groups are expected to identify concrete measures and practical tools to be recommended to ODIHR and the participating States for strengthening judicial independence in practice. These measures and tools will be presented and discussed in the plenary session.

- Working Group I: Judicial Administration
  - 1. Judicial Councils and Judicial Self-governing Bodies and
  - 2. Role of Court Presidents

  Moderator: Prof. Giuseppe Di Federico

Judicial Councils and bodies of judicial self-governance are in many participating States tasked to protect the independence of the judiciary, and play a vital role in judicial administration. The composition of these bodies, their appointment, status and competencies differ from country to country. Risks which have to be mitigated in these systems of judicial administration are on the one hand undue influence over the judiciary and threats to internal independence and the danger of insufficient accountability and allegations of judicial corporatism on the other.

Judicial councils often share competencies for judicial administration with the executive. What should be the respective role of judicial councils and the executive in judicial administration? What is the role of judicial self-governance bodies, especially where judicial councils are primarily composed by members appointed by the executive and not considered part of the judiciary? In many participating States, judicial councils have the mandate to protect the independence of the judiciary. What are the powers and mechanisms necessary for this task? Are judicial councils willing and able to protect judges from improper influences in individual cases?

How are the members of judicial councils appointed and dismissed? In some countries judicial councils consist primarily of judges, while in other countries the three branches of power are represented equally, or the executive plays the strongest role. Should the composition of the judicial council or other bodies ensure a balance of the need for independence with the requirements of democratic accountability? If so, how?

Court presidents regularly play a crucial role in the administration of their respective courts. In some countries, court presidents are selected by the executive and have an important role in selecting judges, evaluating them for promotion purposes or before permanent appointment, and disciplining them. Sometimes, the assignment of cases to judges is entirely in their hands, *de facto* or even *de jure*. When does their influence jeopardize the independence of judges? What models of random case assignment can serve as best practices to prevent undue influence in case assignment?

Task: Discuss challenges and agree on main ones (5-6), achievements (3-5) and develop recommendations, propose a catalogue of tools and measures to strengthen judicial independence (5-10), either to be implemented by ODIHR with (all or selected) participating States, or only the latter.

- Working Group II: Judicial Selection (criteria and procedures)
  Moderator: Prof. Angelika Nußberger

A competent and independent judiciary requires merit-based selection and appointment procedures. Objective criteria should enable the selection of the most qualified candidates for the judicial profession. Subjective criteria which are in the hands of the selecting authority give room for arbitrary decisions, they bear the risk of undue executive influence to block politically unwanted candidates, and have the potential of undermining public trust in judicial independence. Which criteria guarantee a merit-based selection, while ensuring the identification of candidates with the appropriate character and values to maintain independence? How can a representative and pluralistic composition of the judiciary be ensured?

Written examinations and personal interviews are widely used to assess candidates' knowledge, skills and character. How are these components weighted to ensure the most effective testing of future judges? What elements should guarantee the fairness and transparency of evaluation systems for candidates and the public?

Executive authorities in many participating States are involved in the appointment of judges, even when the selection and nomination is left entirely to the judiciary. In most countries, the discretion of the appointing authority is limited. During the

Human Dimension Seminar 2009 it was suggested that executive and legislative branches of government should be limited to confirming the nominations made by an independent body. What is the role of executive and legislature in selecting and appointing judges? When does the involvement of executive authorities in the actual selection or their discretion in appointments become an obstacle for the actual or perceived independence of the judiciary?

Task: Discuss challenges and agree on main ones (5-6), achievements (3-5) and develop recommendations, propose a catalogue of tools and measures to strengthen judicial independence (5-10), either to be implemented by ODIHR with (all or selected) participating States, or only the latter.

- Working Group III: Accountability vs. Independence in Adjudication
  Moderator: Prof. Peter Solomon

Accountability of judges is often seen as a threat to their independence so that the need for judicial independence reduces the scope of holding judges accountable as compared to other public officials. However, to maintain professionalism and integrity and thus to ensure that the rule of law is upheld, judges should be held accountable for abusive conduct in disciplinary proceedings. Only a professional and ethical judiciary can win public trust, and be independent and strong enough to withstand attempts of undue influence. Therefore, it is necessary to find the right balance between independence and accountability of judges. There is a need to identify adequate means of accountability which ensure professionalism without jeopardizing substantive judicial independence.

For this purpose it is mandatory to first identify disciplinary and removal procedures and sanctions posing a threat to judicial independence and ask then for alternative means of accountability. While judges enjoy a certain degree of immunity from criminal prosecution in most participating States, there are specific offences related to adjudication of cases. Criminal and disciplinary offences in several participating States relate to "wrong application of the law" or similar, and are sometimes related to the reversal of the relevant judgments on appeal. When does criminal prosecution and the threat of regress compromise judicial independence inadequately? Which practices effectively balance accountability with the need for independence in adjudication?

Apart from disciplinary and criminal measures it is also necessary to consider other means of oversight relevant to judges' accountability, such as performance evaluations. In several participating States, the number of reversed judgments plays a role for evaluating judges' professional performance, and consequently for their career and financial status, sometimes even their tenure. Is this an adequate means to ensure professionalism? How can the need for accountability and independence be balanced in this regard? What is necessary to ensure that a skill based assessment of judges does not jeopardize substantive independence? How could managerial evaluations be introduced which do not compromise the rule of law?

Those participating States which do not provide for a career judiciary within a hierarchical structure have developed different means to prevent abuse of power and ensure efficiency such as specialized training for judges and a stronger role of the legal profession in ensuring professionalism. Which lessons can be learned from such countries which have put a greater emphasis on alternative means of accountability that focus on the transparency of judicial activities?

ANNEX 3

List of Participants

ABDURAKHMONOV Vatanzhon (Tajikistan)
ALARCON JIMENEZ Oscar (Council of Europe)
BODNAR Adam (Poland)
BOKHASHVILI Irene (Georgia)
DI FEDERICO Giuseppe (Italy)
DÜRR Schnutz (Council of Europe Venice Commission)
FLECK Zoltán (Hungary)
GRIBINCEA Vladislav (Moldova)
HRIPTIEVSCHI Nadejda (Moldova)
KACHKEEV Maksat (Kyrgyzstan)
KHVAN Leonid (Uzbekistan)
KIENER Regina (Switzerland)
KOLIUSHKO Ihor (Ukraine)
KONONOV Anatoly (Russian Federation)
KRÜSI Melanie (Switzerland)
KÜHN Zdeněk (Czech Republic)
KUYBIDA Roman (Ukraine)
LALIASHVILI Tamara (Georgia)
LIGI Timo (Estonia)
MALESHIN Dmitry (Russian Federation)
MÎTCU Dinu (OSCE Moldova)
MORSHCHAKOVA Tamara (Russian Federation)
MÜLLER Lydia F. (Max Planck Institute)
MURADJAN Grigor (Armenia)
NURUMOV Dmitry (ODIHR)
NUSSBERGER Angelika (Germany)
PETIT Denis (ODIHR)
ROMER Maria Teresa (Poland)
SCHMIDT Eva Katinka (ODIHR)
SEIBERT-FOHR Anja (Max Planck Institute)
SOLOMON Peter H., Jr. (Canada)
SULEYMENOVA Gulnara (Kazakhstan)
SYROYID Oksana (OSCE Ukraine)
TAMM Rita (OSCE Moldova)
TILNEY Lisa (OSCE Skopje)
TURENNE Sophie (United Kingdom)
VASHCHANKA Vasily (ODIHR)
VASHKEVICH Alexander (Belarus)
VOITYUK Iryna (Ukraine)
WEBER Carsten (ODIHR)

INDEX